EUROPEAN LABOUR LAW

EUROPEAN LABOUR LAW

Edited by
Teun JASPERS
Frans PENNINGS
Saskia PETERS

INTERSENTIA

Intersentia Ltd
8 Wellington Street | Cambridge
CB1 1HW | United Kingdom
Tel.: +44 1223 736 170
Email: mail@intersentia.co.uk
www.intersentia.com | www.intersentia.co.uk

Distribution for the UK and Ireland:
NBN International
Airport Business Centre, 10 Thornbury Road
Plymouth, PL6 7PP
United Kingdom
Tel.: +44 1752 202 301 | Fax: +44 1752 202 331
Email: orders@nbninternational.com

Distribution for Europe and all other countries:
Intersentia Publishing nv
Groenstraat 31
2640 Mortsel
Belgium
Tel.: +32 3 680 15 50 | Fax: +32 3 658 71 21
Email: mail@intersentia.be

Distribution for the USA and Canada:
Independent Publishers Group
Order Department
814 North Franklin Street
Chicago, IL 60610
USA
Tel.: +1 800 888 4741 (toll free) | Fax: +1 312 337 5985
Email: orders@ipgbook.com

European Labour Law

Cover image: Raymond Forbes LLC/Stocksy

ISBN 978-1-78068-704-9
D/2019/7849/102
NUR 825

British Library Cataloguing in Publication Data. A catalogue record for this book is available from the British Library.

PREFACE

Through time European labour law has acquired a significant place in both European law and national law systems. For persons working in a Member State other than where they live or where they worked before, or for service providers, it has a large impact. But it also has a large impact for the 'immobile' EU citizens, although this is less visible: e.g. in situations of discrimination on the basis of sex or age; in case of transfer of the enterprise in which they work, for their working time, and for health and safety.

European labour law is not always visible for those not familiar with it. This is due to the fact that considerable parts of this law have been implemented in national law. Yet, as national implementation law has to be interpreted in the light of the directive concerned, these EU instruments remain very relevant. Moreover, European labour law is influenced by other parts of European law and, for a good understanding of European labour law, the interaction between national and EU law needs thorough explanation. European labour law is also influenced by sources of international law, in particular principles derived from the instruments of the Council of Europe. We will discuss this in Chapter 1.

The Court of Justice has given specific attention to the development of some areas of social policy, in particular free movement of workers and equal treatment of men and women. In the latter case it transformed a provision from 'a market making vehicle to a vehicle with market correcting potential',[1] i.e. from a rule that was meant to prevent distortion of competition to a rule that was meant to improve the working and living conditions. 'The social policy cases, with their direct impact on individuals, presented the Court with the opportunity to develop important principles, such as the direct effect of directives and even general principles of law.'[2]

However, the Court has met more criticism when it has had to balance the interests of national labour law and the principles of the single market.[3] An example is the *Laval* judgment,[4] and also some cases on collective redundancies, e.g. the *Alemo-Herron* case (see further Chapter 6).[5] This history

1 Barnard (2011), p. 662.
2 Ibid., p. 662.
3 Ibid., p. 663.
4 ECJ 2007, C-341/05 (*Laval*).
5 ECJ 2013, C-426/11 (*Alemo Herron*).

of developing social policy, with its specific roles for Union legislature, Member States, Court of Justice and social partners is the story of this book.

European labour law has changed national labour law by increasing and improving the protection of workers, which differs from Member State to Member State, since it depends on the structure and contents of the domestic systems. It has had a significant impact on the position of workers, e.g. working time, health and safety, equal treatment on various grounds, including sex, sexual orientation, age, handicap, protection of social security rights of mobile persons and free movement of workers.

There are also tensions between European and national labour law, since it is a product of the interaction of several, sometimes contradicting interests. Freedom to exercise economic rights may limit the granting or exercising of social rights considerably. An example is the area of posting, where requiring service providers to pay cross-border posted workers equally to national workers was not required, since that would infringe the freedom of services too much. In line with this priority given to freedom of services, the Court of Justice also restricted the right to strike of trade unions to pursue equal wages for posted workers.

However, as said, European labour law is the result of the interaction of different views, interpretations, activities and interests, including those of the Member States, the EU Institutions and the social partners – and this means that it never remains static. Indeed, as we will see in Chapter 2, the views on the remuneration of posted workers have changed recently.

The objective of this book is to give a thorough insight in European labour law and its development, the tensions underlying it, and the impact on inter alia national labour legislation and case law of national courts.

In view of these different dimensions of European labour law, we felt that a cross-national approach was needed to do justice to them. For that reason, authors from different European countries were invited to contribute to this book by writing their own chapters, with an open eye for the various national perspectives including their own. This has the advantage that references to literature are not mainly to sources in one or more country, but show more diversity. We are aware that authors have to make a selection of national issues and sources, but we think that the present result shows more diversity than is often found in this type of handbook.

Involvement of so many authors, experts in their fields, inevitably goes with differences in approach and style. We think that this reflects the diversity of European labour law and might indeed be instructive for readers to get a grip on this dynamic field.

The book is structured as follows. After Chapter 1, in which an overview of the sources and instruments of European labour law is given, Chapter 2 goes on to look at on the free movement of workers and persons, an area that is within the exclusive competences of the EU legislature. It shows the interpretation of this area by the Court of Justice, which has given full room for free movement, but it also shows the reactions of the Member States. The chapter also discusses the interaction with the freedom to provide services, showing the large impact of the internal market freedoms on European labour law.

Chapter 3 deals with an area of law that is relevant beyond cross-border situations: equal treatment law. EU law has been highly influential in this area and the Court of Justice has contributed substantively to this. We will see that there can be important differences in the interpretation of the EU provisions, depending on which equal treatment ground is concerned.

Chapter 4 is also not limited to cross-border situations; it concerns the impact on flexible working relationships. Although this area of European labour law could also be discussed as a form of discrimination, we have chosen to devote a separate chapter to this subject. After all, the European rules on flexible work involve more than equal treatment alone. Another distinctive feature is that most of these rules are created by agreements of social partners. Therefore, we consider it a specific area with its own dynamics.

Chapter 5, on collective bargaining, concerns the interaction of two main actors – i.e. trade unions and employers' organisations – and the specific rights each of these organisations have and how they make use of them. Insight into this interaction and into the framework and political reality in which this takes place, is of extreme importance for the development of European labour law. A major element of this chapter is the possibility to conclude agreement at the EU level; these may be of several types, including agreements that can be implemented by EU instruments.

The restructuring of enterprises is discussed in Chapter 6. Here we see the conflict of economic rights and interests on the one hand and social rights and interests on the other. This area has a large impact on national legislation of the Member States. Sometimes it might even be overlooked that these rules are of European origin. However, for the interpretation of these rules and the understanding of possible developments, insight into the original is essential.

The participation of employees' organisations in decision making in enterprises is the subject of Chapter 7. These rights can to some extent reconcile economic and social interests; as we will see this works out quite differently, depending on the national context.

Chapter 8 deals with health and safety and working time. Health and safety is already an 'old' area where the social action programmes of the European Commission of the 1970s have been elaborated in numerous instruments. The chapter shows how EU legislation takes account of differences between national legislations and leaves Member States to find their own solutions, thus letting enforcement remain an uncertain issue. It also shows that at the EU level there can be very serious discussions on whether EU legislation in these fields is possible and desirable.

The last chapter, Chapter 9, makes a crosscutting analysis of how the actors interact and may interact in the various fields, within the legal and political EU framework. Building on the preceding chapters, it considers the room for (different) choices and explores possible scenarios for further developments. In this chapter in particular, the overarching approach of this book comes to the fore: to fathom European labour law and its development as a dynamic product and process of the interaction of myriad interests of various actors.

The book is meant for readers who want to get acquainted with the major topics of European labour law, but also for those who want to gain a further insight in the area. For this purpose we are glad that we were able to involve so many eminent experts, from a large number of Member States, to describe the topic of their chapter, but also to give their views and to theorise on the topic, and mention very interesting sources for further reading. We also benefitted from their views on chapters other than their own.

Our aim was for a handbook comprehensively dealing with all important areas of labour law, written from several perspectives by experts, but within a restricted number of pages. We hope that we have succeeded in our objectives. Comments for further developing these are very welcome.

Teun Jaspers
Frans Pennings
Saskia Peters

CONTENTS

LIST OF CASES: ALPHABETICAL

COURT OF JUSTICE

EFTA

ECTHR

LIST OF CASES: CHRONOLOGICAL

COURT OF JUSTICE

EFTA

ECTHR

LIST OF LEGISLATION

TREATIES

DIRECTIVES

REGULATIONS

OTHER DOCUMENTS (EU, EUROPEAN SOCIAL PARTNERS, OECD)

EU

DECISIONS

RECOMMENDATIONS

RESOLUTIONS OF THE COUNCIL

EUROPEAN COUNCIL

EUROPEAN COMMISSION

EUROPEAN PARLIAMENT

AGREEMENTS CONCLUDED BY EUROPEAN SOCIAL PARTNERS

OECD

LIST OF ABBREVIATIONS

AG	Advocate General
ArbVG	Arbeitsverfassungsgesetz
BGB	Bürgerliches Gesetzbuch
CEACR	Committee of Experts on the Application of Conventions and Recommendations
CEEP	European Centre of Employers and Enterprises providing Public Services
CESCR	Covenant on Economic, Social and Cultural Rights
CFA	Committee for the Freedom of Association
CFREU	Charter of Fundamental Rights of the European Union
CJEU	Court of Justice of the European Union (also 'ECJ')
COM	Proposals and other acts adopted in the framework of a legislative procedure or communications, recommendations, reports, white papers, green papers
CRPD	Convention on the Rights of Persons with Disabilities
EC	European Community; Treaty of the EC
ECHA	European Chemicals Agency
ECHR	European Convention for the Protection of Human Rights and Fundamental Freedoms
ECJ	European Court of Justice (also 'CJEU')
ECSR	European Committee of Social Rights
ECtHR	European Court of Human Rights
EEA	European Economic Area
EEC	European Economic Community; Treaty of Rome
EESC	European Economic and Social Committee
EFTA	European Free Trade Association
ESC	European Social Charter
ETUC	European Trade Union Confederation
ETUI	European Trade Union Institute
EU	European Union
EWC	European Works Council
FNV	Federatie Nederlandse Vakbeweging (Dutch trade union)

FRA	Fundamental Rights Agency
ICCPR	International Covenant on Civil and Political Rights
ICESCR	International Covenant on Economic, Social and Cultural Rights
ILO	International Labour Organization
NGO	Non-governmental organisation
OECD	Organisation for Economic Cooperation and Development
OJ	Official Journal
OMC	Open Method of Coordination
REACH	Regulation 1907/2006 on the Registration, Evaluation, Authorisation and Restriction of Chemicals
RESC	European Social Charter (Revised)
SCE	European Cooperative Society
SCOEL	Scientific Committee on Occupational Exposure Limits
SEC	Staff working documents of the EC prior to 2012 (now SWD)
SMEs	Small and Medium-sized Enterprises
SWD	Staff and joint staff working documents
TCA	Transnational Company Agreements
TEC	Treaty establishing the European Community
TEU	Treaty on European Union
TFEU	Treaty on the Functioning of the European Union
UEAPME	Union Européenne de l'Artisanat et des Petites et Moyennes Entreprises (European Association of Craft, Small and Medium-sized Enterprises)
UK	United Kingdom
UN	United Nations
UNESCO	United Nations Educational, Scientific and Cultural Organization
US	United States of America
WHO	World Health Organization

LIST OF CONTRIBUTORS

Edoardo Ales
Professor of labour and social security law at the University of Naples Parthenope.

Mark Bell
Regius Professor of laws, Trinity College Dublin.

Niklas Bruun
Professor Emeritus at Hanken School of Economics in Helsinki. He is also a Research Fellow at Stockholm University on the research project *An inclusive and sustainable Swedish labour law – the ways ahead*, funded by the Swedish Research Council.

Mijke Houwerzijl
Professor of labour law at Tilburg University and Professor of comparative and European labour law at the University of Groningen.

Teun Jaspers
Professor Emeritus of labour law and social security law at Utrecht University. He is also Senior Research Fellow on European and national labour law at the University of Amsterdam.

Sylvaine Laulom
Professor of private law at Université Lumière Lyon 2. She is also Advocate General at the Cour de Cassation (Chambre sociale).

Antonio Lo Faro
Professor of labour law and EU labour law at the University of Catania.

Pascale Lorber
Associate Professor, specialising in employment law at the University of Leicester Law School.

Ann Numhauser-Henning
Professor Emerita of private law at Lund University.

Frans Pennings
Professor of labour law and social security law at Utrecht University.

Saskia Peters
Professor of labour law at the University of Groningen.

Jan Popma
Senior Researcher in occupational health and safety at the Dutch Labour Inspectorate.

Sophie Robin-Olivier
Professor of European and comparative law at the Sorbonne School of Law (Université Paris 1 Panthéon-Sorbonne).

Herwig Verschueren
Professor of international and European social law at the University of Antwerp.

CHAPTER 1

AN INTRODUCTION TO EUROPEAN LABOUR LAW

Frans PENNINGS and Saskia PETERS

1.1. EUROPEAN LABOUR LAW: SIGNIFICANCE, SOURCES AND SCOPE

In the past decades the impact of international and European law on national labour law has grown significantly. One part of European labour law, i.e. EU labour law, is, by far, the main source of this external influence on the national law of EU Member States. Important examples are equal treatment of men and women, regulation of working time, consultation of workers, transfer of enterprises, health and safety and free movement.[1]

In the literature the term 'European labour law' is often used to refer to EU labour law. However, European labour law in the broad sense of the word also includes a second source: the instruments of the Council of Europe, i.e. the European Social Charter (ESC) and the European Convention for the Protection of Human Rights and Fundamental Freedoms (ECHR).

A third source, not of European labour law, but of international labour law, is the International Labour Organization (ILO). The ILO, established in 1919, has 185 Member States and is a tripartite organisation, consisting of representatives of employers' and workers' organisations and of Member States. The labour law created by the ILO can be found in, inter alia, more than 200 conventions, e.g. on freedom of association of trade unions and the right to collective bargaining.

1 See also Bobek (2017).

A fourth source of international labour law is the United Nations, which has adopted the International Covenant on Civil and Political Rights (ICCPR) and International Covenant on Economic, Social and Cultural Rights (ICESCR).

This book will mainly discuss the first source of international and European labour law, i.e. EU labour law, but where relevant it will refer to the latter three sources.

While EU labour law also covers social policy in the broad sense, this book will concentrate on the law that is relevant to employment relationships. Some chapters will, however, include broader European labour law topics. Social security will, for instance, be addressed in the chapters on free movement of workers (Chapter 2) and on equal treatment (Chapter 3).

1.2. THE EUROPEAN UNION AND DEVELOPMENT OF SOCIAL POLICY

1.2.1. INTRODUCTION

> The Union cannot be based exclusively on purely economic considerations. On the contrary, it must henceforth seek its roots in the fundamental human values common to all European countries. This is a necessary precondition if the people of Europe are to place their trust in the continuing task of European integration. We must prove to them that the Union provides a framework with which they can identify.[2]

This statement by the European Commission is an example of its numerous acknowledgements that a union has to be developed in which labour and social values must play an essential role. Such a statement was deemed essential, since the European Economic Community was – as its name already suggests – established as an economic community, in which there was very little (legislative) room for social policy measures. In the course of time, competences for social measures were introduced in the treaties and social programmes were launched.

EU social policy already has a considerable history, which will be outlined in the following section. Some provisions, e.g. on equal treatment of men and women, have been interpreted in a way that gives them a major impact, which can largely be attributed to the case law of the Court of Justice.[3] However, the values of EU social policy and labour law still struggle to be fully acknowledged in the (legal) practice in those cases where they clash with economic freedoms,

2 European Commission (2000), Communication on the preliminary draft Charter of Fundamental Rights.

3 See also Dehousse (1998).

such as the free movement of services. Where tensions between social and economic interests also exist at the national level, EU labour law faces particular difficulties in such clashes. This is, in part, because there are fewer competences in these areas at EU level and employees' organisations are less powerful at the EU level.

1.2.2. THE EEC TREATY OF 1957

The principal objective of European cooperation, elaborated in the Treaty establishing the European Economic Community of 1957 (EEC Treaty or Treaty of Rome), was an economic one, i.e. to establish a common market to further the economic progress of the – then six[4] – participating countries. Consequently, its key elements were, along with a customs union and common agricultural policy, the four so-called economic freedoms: the free movement of goods, workers, services and capital. It was assumed, according to the economic theory at that time, that economic progress and prosperity as the result of the creation of a common market would lead to increased social welfare.

The objective of one of the freedoms, the free movement of workers, was that workers would be able to move to areas where there was a need for them, without being confronted by national rules blocking their access to the labour market (e.g. by requiring work permits). This was not only in the interests of these workers, but also benefited employers, who could in this way more easily acquire the needed manpower. The freedom of movement of workers, laid down in Article 48 EEC, entailed an important social dimension: workers from other Member States must not be discriminated on the ground of nationality, and therefore must not be paid lower wages than national workers on the ground of nationality. This provision was intended to protect the social systems of the host States, which might otherwise be under pressure if employers could employ cheap workers from abroad (see also, on this 'social dumping' discussion, Chapter 2).

Another social policy measure that originated in the economic context of the Treaty was that on equal pay for men and women (Article 119 EEC). Some signatory countries (in particular France) were bound by ILO Convention 100 requiring equal pay for men and women, and they feared that countries not bound by the convention would be 'better off' by having cheaper (female) labour.[5] Therefore this article was included in the Treaty.

Such competition problems could also exist in other areas and for this reason France proposed powers for an assimilation of the entire labour and social

---

4 Belgium, France, Germany, Italy, Luxembourg and the Netherlands.

5 See also Barnard (2011), p. 643.

legislation of the Member States. Other countries, however, were opposed to this, since they preferred minimum public intervention in social policy areas. The result was the compromise laid down in Article 117 EEC. Article 117 provided:

> Member States hereby agree upon the necessity to promote improvement of the living and working conditions of labour so as to permit the equalisation of such conditions in an upward direction. They consider that such a development will result not only from the functioning of the Common Market which will favour the harmonisation of social systems, but also from the procedures provided for under this Treaty and from the approximation of legislative and administrative provisions.

This provision expressed the belief that the living and working conditions will be promoted because of the Common Market and the procedures of the Treaty, but did not give any powers for improvement of the living standards.[6]

1.2.3. THE INTRODUCTION OF SOCIAL POLICY MEASURES IN THE 1970s

In the 1970s, the European Heads of State and Government decided that Europe needed a social face. A strong reason was the economic recession in those years and the striking inequalities in levels of employment and prosperity which existed within the Community. Furthermore, it became acknowledged that economic developments and social progress did not always go hand in hand. Partly because of the development of the common market, companies began to work on a larger scale and also across borders. This made employees' organisations fear that employment was being moved to other European countries where wages and other conditions of employment were at a lower level.

During the 1972 Paris Summit, the European leaders emphasised that vigorous action in the social field is as important as the achievement of an Economic and Monetary Union.[7] Thereupon, the European Commission launched its *social action programmes* aimed at achieving 'full and better employment, the improvement of living and working conditions and increased involvement of management and labour in the economic and social decisions of the Community, and of workers in the life of undertakings'.[8] These action programmes were the prelude to Community labour law – mainly by means of directives – in the areas of, inter alia, equal treatment of men and women (in employment and social security), health and safety, collective redundancies, insolvency of the employer and transfer of undertakings.[9]

---

6 See also Barnard (2012a), p. 6.
7 Council (1974) (Resolution concerning a social action programme).
8 Ibid., p. 1.
9 For extensive discussion regarding these developments: Fuchs (2004a), pp. 155–76.

As a result, the 1970s became a period in which important progress was made in establishing binding European labour law legislation.

The social dimension was also developed by the case law of the Court of Justice, in particular the *Defrenne* judgments[10] on Article 119 EEC. As seen in Section 1.2.2, this article was introduced primarily for economic reasons. In the *Defrenne II* judgment the Court held that Article 119 EEC is not only based on an economic objective, but 'this provision forms part of the social objectives of the Community, which is not merely an economic union, but is at the same time intended, by common action, to ensure social progress and seek the constant improvement of the living and working conditions of their peoples'. The Court deduced from this double objective – economic and social – that the principle of equal pay forms part of the foundations of the Community.[11]

This double objective was also the basis for the Court to conclude that this provision (now Article 157 TFEU) has direct effect and can be invoked in horizontal relations (employee versus employer) before the national courts.[12] This case law made this provision much more effective than when it was left to the Member States only to enforce.

The *Defrenne* judgment clearly shows the ambition of the Court to realise the social objectives it discerned in the Treaty.

1.2.4. THE 1990s

Still, the willingness of Member States to adopt social policy instruments was rather limited, and since many of the Treaty provisions required unanimity, progress was very slow. Chapter 4, Section 4.1 mentions the fate of Commission proposals for flexible work directives. Only one proposal, based on a Treaty provision requiring qualified majority, was adopted; the other two – requiring unanimity – were blocked by the use of the veto in the Council.

During the drafting process of the Treaty of Maastricht (1992) it was proposed to introduce more powers for social policy instruments, but no consensus could be reached. In order to resolve this impasse, a Social Policy Protocol that refers to the Agreement on Social Policy was signed by 11 EU Member States, i.e. not including the United Kingdom. The agreement went back to the Joint Agreement of the Social Partners of 31 October 1991, which the EU social partners had elaborated: both texts were almost identical. The Agreement on Social Policy proposed a role for the social partners in the community legislative process and a major extension of competences on labour law, allowing for qualified

---

10 ECJ 1971, 80/70 (*Defrenne I*); ECJ 1976, 43/75 (*Defrenne II*); ECJ 1978, 149/77 (*Defrenne III*).

11 ECJ 1976, 43/75 (*Defrenne II*).

12 See on direct, vertical and horizontal effect of EU law, Section 1.4.4.2.

majority voting with respect to some of the new competences. Since the Protocol exempted the UK from this, the way was left free for making use of the new powers. The Protocol declared that social policy was to be developed, not as part of an economic policy, but as an end in itself.

Four labour law directives were thus made possible: the Directives on part-time work (97/81/EC) and parental leave (96/34/EC), which both resulted from the newly created role of the social partners (see Section 1.3.3.2(c)); burden of proof (97/80/EC); and the European Works Council (94/45/EC).

In 1997, with a Labour government in the United Kingdom, the powers mentioned in the agreement were made part of the Treaty of Amsterdam (1997) i.e. the Title on Social policy. This Title contains a specific mandate for the EU to conduct a social policy (Article 153 TFEU), in order to achieve the social objectives of Article 151. Article 153 TFEU indicates the areas in which the Union has specific power to regulate, including workers' health and safety, working conditions, social security, information and consultation of employees and equality between men and women.

A final element to be mentioned, which was introduced by the Treaty of Maastricht, is European citizenship. This was an important development, since it implied that the European Union was relevant not only for economically active persons (workers and self-employed), but also for other persons. Thus, economically non-active persons acquired the right to free movement and the ability to invoke the rights laid down in EU law. However, EU law allows more restrictions to be placed on exercising these rights for economically non-active persons than for workers and self-employed. Still, it shows once again that economic objectives are not the only objectives underlying the Union.

The Treaty of Maastricht also introduced a provision that reduced the possibilities for developing law in the social policy domain. This is the so-called 'subsidiarity principle', according to which the EU may make laws only if and in so far as the objectives of the proposed action cannot be sufficiently achieved by the Member States, but can, by reason of the scale or effects of the proposed action, be better achieved at Union level. This principle requires that each time when a proposal for a social policy measure is made, it must be demonstrated that the Member States cannot sufficiently achieve the objective. It reflected the growing reluctance of Member States to accept social policy measures made by the EU. One reason was that Member States increasingly began to experience the effects of competition from other Member States and from third countries (globalisation) and were afraid to lose competitive powers if they were bound too tightly by labour law.[13]

---

13 Currently Article 5(3) TFEU.

In order to have instruments for developing social policy in this period, an alternative instrument was developed: the Open Method of Coordination (OMC). This was initially developed for the European employment strategy (EES) and elaborated in the Title on Employment (now Title IX TFEU).[14] The European employment strategy did not aim at partially harmonising parts of national labour law through directives, but more broadly at improving the functioning of the labour markets of the Member States. Relevant for this strategy was that promoting employment became a 'matter of common concern' (see now Article 146(2) TFEU). This was not only a reaction to the high level of unemployment that existed in many Member States at the time, but also related to the fact that national social policy and the EU's economic policy had become closely connected. Gradually, Member States had less and less room for manoeuvre to pursue their employment policies, since within the Economic and Monetary Union (EMU) the economic and monetary policies had to be coordinated (Article 3(4) TFEU). The strategy focused, inter alia, on creating more and better-quality jobs, increasing labour participation (of older workers and women), promoting flexibility without compromising employment security ('flexicurity'), and encouraging lifelong learning.[15]

Initially, the strategy was pursued under the name Lisbon Strategy,[16] and was followed up by the EU 2020 strategy, launched in 2010.[17] The main objective is to create an economy with a high level of employment (aiming for 75% in 2020).

Although employment policy was now mentioned as a common concern, there were no competences in the Treaty to develop EU measures and it was not considered desirable or possible to create such competences for employment policies. Instead, the OMC was introduced. Basically, the European Commission requires Member States to make reports on their national situations, and subsequently gives guidelines to reach the objectives for employment policy. A following step is that the European Commission asks the Member States to report on the follow up of the guidelines. Although the OMC is a form of soft law, it has effects in practice, since Member States have to report on how they follow up the guidelines.

After the introduction of the OMC for employment, the OMC has also been used in other policy areas, including social inclusion, modernisation of social protection, pensions and healthcare. In contrast to OMC employment there is no legal basis for this procedure. Although the OMC may have practical

14 The Title on Employment was introduced by the Treaty of Amsterdam.

15 See e.g. European Commission (2005) (Integrated Guidelines for Growth and Jobs). Also the promotion of part-time work has to be mentioned, see Chapter 4 for criticism on how this is brought into practice.

16 European Council (2000) (Lisbon European Council 23 and 24 March 2000 – Presidency conclusions).

17 European Commission (2010) (Europe 2020).

results – although it is difficult to measure these – it is often criticised since it is difficult for stakeholders who are not directly involved to register what is actually happening and to influence these processes. In Section 1.3.4, further attention will be paid to the OMC.

1.2.5. THE DEVELOPMENTS IN THE AREA OF SOCIAL POLICY SINCE 2000

Some important developments have significantly influenced the development of the social face of the Union since the turn of the century.

One is the accession to the Union of a series of Member States that previously had a centrally planned economy. These Member States had to make large efforts in restructuring their economies and revising their systems to be fit for accession to the EU. One requirement was that the so-called *acquis communautaire* (i.e. accumulated legislation, legal acts, and case law of the EU) had to be adopted by these countries. But after they had joined the Union, they were, of course, entitled, as were the 'old' Member States, to vote in favour of new legislation, but also to reject it.

In general it can be said that the new Member States were (and still are) primarily focused on the development of their economies, of which cheap labour was often a major asset. As a result, they appeared reluctant to adopt EU measures that could lead to increases in labour costs.

An area where the differences between the new Member States and the older ones led to considerable tensions is that of posting of workers. Based on the free movement of services rules, companies can post their workers to do work in another Member State and initially it was unclear which part of the labour law of the host State they would have to respect. By paying only the wages due according to their own legislation, companies from new Member States could have a large competitive advantage compared to companies in the old Member States. This constitutes an important area where social and economic interests clash. To reach a compromise, the Posted Workers Directive was adopted in 1996 and this considerably restricted the possibilities for host States to impose their labour law.[18]

This directive is the background of the notorious *Laval* judgment[19] of the Court of Justice, which has led to many reactions and debates, since it considerably restricted the right to strike and allowed economic criteria to play a large role in this restriction (see further Chapter 5). As a result, the relationship between economic and social values in the EU became high on

18 Directive 96/71/EC (Posted Workers Directive).

19 ECJ 2007, C-341/05 (*Laval*).

the agenda and also led to pessimism on whether the EU's social face could be further developed.

However, the revision of the Posted Workers Directive in 2018 – requiring, under some conditions, equal pay for posted workers – shows that the development is not a linear and unambiguous one. See further Chapter 2.

Another important development was the economic crisis that started in 2008. This led to radical austerity measures, both from the EU and from Member States, to reduce inter alia labour costs. In some countries wages and other working conditions were severely reduced under large pressure to rescue the euro. Although these measures have never been laid down in European labour law rules, they are mentioned here, since they have led to considerable pessimism on the social dimension of the EU.

Finally, the Treaty of Lisbon (2009), the Treaty on European Union (TEU) and the Treaty on the Functioning of the European Union (TFEU), must be mentioned. Article 6 TEU provides that the Union recognises the rights, freedoms and principles set out in the Charter of Fundamental Rights of the European Union, which shall have the same legal value as the Treaties. Thus, it includes important fundamental rights, including social ones. However, this article also provides that the provisions of the Charter shall not extend in any way the competences of the Union as defined in the Treaties. The Charter can be a source for the further development of social measures, but the legal basis for these measures must be found elsewhere in the Treaty.[20]

Since there has been relatively few new social policy legislation since the turn of the century, and since the interventions to rescue the euro have led to serious doubts about the EU's social face, the European Commission launched a recommendation in 2017 on a *European pillar of social rights*.[21] To give it more importance, this recommendation was also proclaimed and signed by the Council of the EU, the European Parliament and the Commission in November 2017.[22] The Pillar expresses 20 principles and rights essential for fair and well-functioning labour markets and welfare systems. It is mainly a confirmation of principles and rights already present in the EU and in the international legal acquis, but some new principles have been added, which address new realities arising from societal, economic and technological developments. An example of this is the inclusion of the self-employed in the right (no. 12) to adequate social protection. This reflects the increasing number of workers in many Member States who are self-employed and whose socio-economic position is very similar to that of employees, but who often lack similar protection.

---

20 See regarding the impact of the Charter, De Vries, Bernitz & Weatherill (2015).

21 Commission Recommendation (EU) 2017/761 of 26 April 2017 on the European Pillar of Social Rights.

22 COM(2017)251 final (Social Pillar).

The ambition of the pillar is for the principles to be implemented by the Member States; for this purpose, in particular, the staff working document of the Commission that describes the actions that can be undertaken is relevant.[23] In a so-called 'social scoreboard' the actions of the Member States and their results will be registered.

Albeit the Pillar is also driven by economic considerations,[24] it may mean a renewed focus on the social dimension of the EU. 'Social Europe' is clearly again on the agenda of the Commission.[25] Examples are a proposal for a directive on work-life balance for parents and carers;[26] and for a directive on transparent and predictable working conditions (which will replace the Written Statement Directive 91/533/EEC),[27] and a Council Recommendation on access to social protection for all workers and self-employed (especially for those who, due to their employment status, are not sufficiently covered by social security schemes).[28]

1.2.6. THE GRADUAL RECOGNITION OF FUNDAMENTAL RIGHTS

As the previous section has shown, social policy has gradually – although not always smoothly – gained room in the European Union. Parallel with this, fundamental rights have also acquired a place within the legal order of the European Community and the European Union.[29]

1.2.6.1. Community Charter of the Fundamental Social Rights of Workers (1989)

A first milestone in the integration of fundamental rights in the EU legal order was the acceptance of the Community Charter of the Fundamental Social Rights

23 European Commission (2017) (Staff Working Document Accompanying the document establishing a European Pillar of Social Rights).

24 See e.g. Recital 11 and 13 of the Preamble. See for critical assessment De Becker & Schoukens (2017), p. 8. See for a highly critical assessment, Lörcher & Schömann (2016), albeit that their criticism relates to an earlier version of the Pillar. As a response to the effects of the euro crisis, the Pillar was primarily conceived for the euro area, but other Member States may join in the programme (Recital 13). See also Rasnača (2017).

25 See also European Commission (2017) (White Paper on the Future of Europe) and Commission (2017) (Reflection paper on the social dimension of Europe).

26 European Commission (2017) (Proposal for a Directive on work-life balance for parents and carers).

27 European Commission (2017) (Proposal for a Directive on transparent and predictable working conditions in the EU).

28 European Commission (2018) (Proposal for a Council Recommendation on access to social protection for workers and the self-employed).

29 See for instance De Búrca (2013), Amalfitano (2018).

of Workers in 1989 by 11 of the then 12 Member States. The Community Charter contains 12 'fundamental social rights of workers', e.g. in the areas of freedom of movement, freedom of association and collective bargaining, equal treatment for men and women, health protection and safety at the workplace, and information, consultation and participation for workers. The Charter was meant to serve for the 11 Member States 'as a reference point for taking fuller account in future of the social dimension in the development of the Community'.[30] Inspiration was drawn from the Conventions of the International Labour Organization (ILO) and the European Social Charter of the Council of Europe.

The Community Charter was only a political declaration, initially without any legal status, and it was not published in the *Official Journal*. Despite the lack of binding force, the Charter was an important basis for the further development of the social policy of the Union.[31] In the Maastricht Treaty a reference was made to the Charter (Article 136 EC); currently Article 151 TFEU does the same.

1.2.6.2. Charter of Fundamental Rights of the EU (Nice 2000)

The European Parliament, the Council and the Commission jointly proclaimed the Charter of Fundamental Rights of the European Union in Nice on 7 December 2000.[32] All fundamental rights protected in the Union were brought together in the Charter in order to underline the great importance of these rights for the Union and to strengthen the protection of these fundamental rights.[33] According to the preamble, the Charter also derives the content of fundamental rights from the case law of the Court of Justice, where it accepts fundamental rights laid down in international human rights treaties, the ECHR and the constitutional traditions of EU Member States. In this case law these fundamental rights are recognised as general principles of EU law, and thus they have become part of EU law.[34]

The Charter is primarily a confirmation of the already existing European value system, and does not create new rights. It is only a political statement (without formal legal status), although the Court of Justice sometimes refers to it in its case law. AG Tizzano referred to the Charter as a source for the

---

30 Conclusions of the Presidency European Council Strasbourg, 8 and 9 December 1989, section II G (SN 441/2/89).

31 See Barnard (2012a), p. 33; Watson (2009), No. 3.42–49; Fuchs (2004a), pp. 168–69. See also Bercusson (2006). The Court sometimes referred to the Charter in its case law, see e.g. ECJ 2004, C-3971/01 (*Pfeiffer*), §91 and ECJ 2001, 173/99 (*Bectu*), §39.

32 OJ 2000, C 364/1 (Community Charter of Fundamental Rights).

33 See the preamble to the Charter and European Commission (2000), (Communication on the Charter of Fundamental Rights of the European Union).

34 See extensively on these general principles, Amalfitano (2018).

interpretation of social rights in his conclusion to the *BECTU* case,[35] but it took until 2006 before the Court quoted the Charter for the first time.[36]

1.2.6.3. A European Constitution and the Charter of Fundamental Rights of the EU (Lisbon 2009)

A milestone for the incorporation of fundamental rights should have been the Treaty establishing a Constitution for Europe.[37] However, the proposal for such a constitution was not adopted after the French and Dutch citizens voted against it in national referenda. A European Constitution was apparently still a bridge too far.[38]

Despite this history, a kind of constitution was adopted five years later with the Treaty of Lisbon (2009). Although the Charter remained a separate declaration, the Treaty on European Union recognises the rights, freedoms and principles set out in the Charter and makes its provisions legally binding (Article 6(1) TEU).[39] However, a Protocol to the Treaties created a special position for Poland and the United Kingdom: the Court of Justice may not provide that national legislation or administrative practices in those countries are inconsistent with the fundamental rights, freedoms and principles recognised in the Charter; the same applies to Polish and British courts.[40]

Since the entry into force of the Lisbon Treaty in December 2009, there has been a marked increase in litigation involving the Charter.[41] The Charter not only leads to stronger social rights, but it also mentions economic rights that must be reconciled with social rights. This is mainly due to Article 16 of the Charter, which reads 'The freedom to conduct a business in accordance with Community law and national laws and practices is recognised'. As will be seen in Chapter 7, this provision has been used by the Court of Justice to interpret the provisions of the Transfers of Undertakings Directive and the Collective Redundancies Directive in a sense that provides less protection to workers.

---

35 AG Tizzano at ECJ 2001, 173/99 (*BECTU*), §28.

36 ECJ 2006, C-540/03 (*Parliament v. Council*); see Bercusson (2009), pp. 386–87.

37 OJ 2004, C-310/01. See Jacobs (2005).

38 See De Búrca (2008).

39 See Guðmundsdóttir (2015).

40 See Protocol No. 30 to the Treaties. However, this opt-out appears to be ineffective, since the Court ruled that Article 1(1) of the Protocol merely explains the scope of the Charter and does not intend to exempt Poland or the UK from the obligation to comply with the provisions of the Charter or to prevent a court of one of those Member States from ensuring compliance with those provisions (ECJ 2011, C-411/10 (*N.S./ Secretary of State*), §§117–20). In the Polish case, ECJ 2012, 325/11 (*Alder*) the Court applied the Charter to Poland without further ado.

41 See De Búrca (2013).

1.3. THE COMPETENCES OF THE EU LEGISLATURE

1.3.1. INTRODUCTION

In this section the powers of the EU legislature to adopt legislation will be discussed. This introduction presumes knowledge of the basics of EU law and will address mainly those elements relevant to making European labour legislation. This section will also address the special role for social partners in the process of making EU law (see Section 1.3.3.2). The legislative activities of the Union are not restricted to legislation in the sense of 'hard law', but include also 'soft law' measures, in particular the Open Method of Coordination (see Section 1.3.4). Section 1.4 will deal with enforcement of EU law and its effect on national legal orders.

1.3.2. THE LEGISLATIVE COMPETENCES

The competences of the bodies of the EU are found in the TEU and the TFEU, which both have the same legal force. The TEU concerns the constitutional law of the Union plus the common foreign and safety areas, and the TFEU contains chapters on material EU law, including Title X on Social Policy. These Treaties do not give general legislative powers (see Articles 4(1), 5(1) and (2) and Article 13(2) TFEU), but the Union can act only if certain specific conditions are fulfilled.

1.3.2.1. Conferral of Powers and Types of Powers

A preliminary question is whether the Union has any power at all to act in a particular area or whether the Member States have exclusive powers, i.e. the issue of conferral of powers. Article 5(2) TEU reads that 'the Union shall act only within the limits of the competences conferred upon it by the Member States in the Treaties to attain the objectives set out therein. Competences not conferred upon the Union in the Treaties remain with the Member States'. In other words, each legislative act of the Union must have a legal basis in one of the Treaties. This means that close reading of the provision concerned is essential: some treaty provisions mention social issues, e.g. Article 151 TFEU, but do not provide for powers. The necessary powers can be found in Article 153(2) TFEU, but only for minimum provisions in a specified number of areas.

Articles 2 to 6 TFEU distinguish three types of competences: exclusive, shared and supplementing.

When the Treaties confer on the Union an *exclusive* competence in a specific area, only the Union may legislate and adopt legally binding acts in that area. If such exclusive competence exists, Member States can legislate in that area only if so empowered by the Union or in order to implement Union acts (Article 2(1) TFEU). Only very few Treaty provisions give the Union exclusive competence.

Most competences are *shared ones*, meaning that both the Union and the Member States are empowered to undertake legislative activities (Article 2(2) TFEU). The areas of shared competences are listed in Article 4 TFEU, including the internal market and social policy. It is important, however, to keep in mind that once the Union has adopted a legislative act in an area, the shared competence becomes an exclusive one. In such a situation, Member States can only adopt binding acts if Union legislation requires or allows this. Union legislation often requires such further national legislation, as it often takes the form of directives that must be implemented. Moreover, this type of legislation can be supplemented since these directives require a form of minimum harmonisation only and thus leave it to the Member States to prescribe a higher level of social protection than mentioned in the directive (see also Section 1.3.3.1).

In some areas the Union's powers are solely to *co-ordinate, support and supplement* the acts of Member States, thus leaving the powers of the Member States unaffected. An example in social policy is Article 5(2) TFEU: 'The Union shall take measures to ensure coordination of the employment policies of the Member States, in particular by defining guidelines for these policies' (see Section 1.3.4).

1.3.2.2. Subsidiarity and Proportionality

When the Union has (shared) powers to make legislation, it must be investigated whether it is the most appropriate legislature. If that is not the case, the Union cannot use its powers to make legislation on the topic concerned. This follows from the so-called 'subsidiarity principle', laid down in Article 5(3) TEU, which is mentioned in Section 1.2.4. This subsidiarity principle can be called 'bottom up' or decentralised, since it presupposes that the powers are primarily with the Member States.[42] The Union is allowed to act only if this has advantages (given the scale or effects) compared to national activities. Such advantages can be expected in case of topics with transnational aspects that cannot be comprehensively regulated by Member States acting separately.

If the Union is competent to exercise its powers, the use of the powers must also satisfy the proportionality principle. This means that the content and form of Union action shall not exceed what is necessary to achieve the objectives of the Treaties (Article 5(4) TFEU). Whereas the subsidiarity principle is to be used to decide *whether* the Union can act, the proportionality principle is important

42 Barnard (2012a), p. 56.

to *delimit* the way the Union can act. A Protocol attached to the Treaty describes how the subsidiarity and proportionality principles must be applied.[43]

The Court of Justice has the power to decide whether institutions of the Union have applied the principles of subsidiarity and proportionality correctly.[44] However, the Court does not play an active role in this; so far it has never considered an EU legislative act void because of infringement of the subsidiarity principle. Also, the test to the proportionality principle is only applied marginally. The Court considered in a landmark case (*UK v. Council*) that the Union legislature (at the time, the Council) must be allowed a wide discretion, in areas which involve the legislature in making social policy choices and require it to carry out complex assessments.[45] 'Judicial review of the exercise of that discretion must therefore be limited to examining whether it has been vitiated by manifest error or misuse of powers, or whether the institution concerned has manifestly exceeded the limits of its discretion.'[46]

In addition, the Union institutions have their own procedures to consider whether the subsidiarity and proportionality principles have been followed correctly, laid down in Protocol No. 2.[47] The European Commission, which has the exclusive right to submit proposals for legislative acts to the Council and European Parliament, has to follow an extensive procedure to consider whether its activities remain within the limits of subsidiarity and proportionality and to account for this decision.[48] Member States are involved in this procedure according to the procedure laid down in the Protocol.[49] National parliaments can, if they disagree with the decision, draw the so-called 'yellow card'. This means that where reasoned opinions on the non-compliance of a proposal for a legislative act with the principle of subsidiarity represent at least one third of all the votes allocated to the national Parliaments, the Commission must review the proposal. It may decide to maintain, amend or withdraw the draft. Reasons must be given for this decision.[50]

This procedure was followed for the first time in 2012, when the Commission made a proposal for a 'Monti II regulation',[51] which envisaged regulation of

43 Protocol No. 2, OJ 2016, 202/208.

44 See inter alia ECJ 1996, C-84/94 (*UK v. Council*), §§46–67; ECJ (2002, C-491/01 (*British American Tobacco*); and ECJ 2015, C-508/13 (*Estonia v. European Parliament and Council*).

45 ECJ 1996, C-84/94 (*UK v. Counciol*), §58.

46 Ibid., §58. The case concerned the Working Time Directive; see also Section 1.3.3.2. The case shows also that the tensions that can exist between Member States and European Commission when initiatives are taken to develop social policy measures.

47 OJ 2012, C 326/206.

48 See Protocol No. 2, Articles 2–5.

49 Protocol No. 2, Articles 4, 6 and 7.

50 Protocol No. 2, Article 7(2). See on the procedure also Fromage & Kreilinger (2017).

51 European Commission (2012) (Proposal for a Regulation on the exercise of the right to take collective action within the context of the freedom of establishment and the freedom to provide services).

the right to strike in relation to the freedom of services and establishment. The proposal was heavily criticised by national parliaments, since it failed to demonstrate that there was an added-value of action at EU level, and since it was not properly justified and because of the choice of the legal basis. Finally, the Commission had to withdraw the proposal.

Another time the card was drawn concerned the proposal for revision of the Posted Workers Directive, against which 11 Member States drew the yellow card (see also Chapter 2, Section 2.3.5).[52] As Fromage and Kreilinger remark, this (third) yellow card procedure highlighted an East-West divide: 10 out of the 11 Member States whose parliamentary chambers issued reasoned opinions are in Central and Eastern Europe. The Commission responded to this yellow card by stating that the proposal was justified since 'an amendment to an existing Directive can only be achieved by adopting a new Directive'.[53] This argument met serious criticism; as Fromage and Kreilinger point out, admittedly a directive can only be amended by a directive, but this does not automatically mean that the objective set for the revision of the said directive can only be achieved by this means. The Member States that had drawn the yellow card, however, offered no more than this procedural argument. In addition, they mentioned a number of arguments on substantive issues, i.e. that the proposal 'restricted the opportunities and incentives for businesses to provide cross border services'.[54] It is not difficult to see that here the veil of a procedural rule was invoked for a substantive issue.

In response, the Commission declared that it had come, after an 'open political dialogue' with the national parliaments concerned, to the conclusion that its proposal did not infringe the subsidiarity principle.[55] Subsequently the legislative procedure was continued (see Chapter 2).[56]

The yellow cards change colour to orange when most of the national parliaments argue that a proposal infringes the subsidiarity principle. After such review, the Commission may decide to maintain, amend or withdraw the proposal. If it chooses to maintain the proposal, the Commission must, in a reasoned opinion, justify why it considers that the proposal complies with the principle of subsidiarity. This reasoned opinion, is submitted to the Union legislator, along with the reasoned opinions of the national Parliaments, for consideration in the procedure.

---

52 European Commission (2016) (Proposal for a directive amending Directive 96/71/EC). The third time concerned the European Public Prosecutors office, so most yellow card procedures concern social policy instruments. See also Fromage & Kreilinger (2017), p. 133.

53 European Commission (2016), (Proposal for a Directive amending Directive 96/71/EC), Explanatory Memorandum, point 2.2.

54 Fromage & Kreilinger (2017), p. 149.

55 <http://europa.eu/rapid/press-release_IP-16-2546_en.htm> accessed 05.06.2019.

56 Protocol No. 2, Article 7(3).

There is no 'red card' procedure for national parliaments in the sense that they can force the Commission to withdraw a proposal. However, since in case of an orange card the Council has the final say on the proposal, the majority in this body will most likely stop the procedure.

1.3.3. EU LABOUR LEGISLATION: FORM AND LEGAL BASIS

This section will discuss *hard law* on labour issues. Other, non-binding forms of regulation in labour law (*soft law*) will be discussed in Section 1.3.4.

1.3.3.1. EU Legislative Instruments for Labour Law

EU legislation on labour law is mainly laid down in a regulation or directive. Regulations and directives are adopted according to the ordinary legislative procedure; i.e. joint adoption by the European parliament and the Council, on a proposal of the Commission. Legal acts adopted by such legislative procedure constitute legislative acts, according to Article 289(3).

(a) Regulations and Directives

A Regulation has general application. It is binding in its entirety and directly applicable in all Member States (Article 288 TFEU). As a result, a regulation does not have to be transposed in national legislation.[57] A regulation is adopted if the applicable rules must be identical for all Member States. This is the case, in particular, for the economic freedoms, since these rules apply in cross-border situations and must therefore be the same, regardless of the Member State involved. Examples in labour law are Regulation 492/2011 on freedom of movement for workers and Regulation 883/2004 on the coordination of social security (Chapter 2).

In labour law, regulations are exceptional; for the major part of EU labour law the main principle is that Member States remain competent to design and organise their national system.

Article 288 TFEU provides that '[a] directive shall be binding, as to the result to be achieved, upon each Member State to which it is addressed, but shall leave to the national authorities the choice of form and methods'. This instrument is therefore appropriate to leave the national autonomy intact and therefore very suitable as an instrument for social policy. National systems have important differences, for instance in the relationship between statutory labour law and

[57] See ECJ 1973, 39/72 (*Commission/Italy*), §§20–25 on the (enforcement of) obligations for Member States to implement regulations.

the system of collective bargaining resulting in collective labour agreements. There are also differences in the contents of national labour law regulations: some countries have considerably more rules than others. For Member States sovereignty and autonomy in labour law are very important, and the directive is an instrument that both allows EU standards to be introduced and gives Member States the room to implement these in the ways that fit best in their systems.

Unlike regulations, directives must be transposed in national legislation. This means that, in principle, directives do not create directly applicable rights or duties for private persons or organisations, including enterprises. Directives have an implementation period (usually a couple of years) within which they must be implemented.

(b) Specific Characteristics of Labour Law Directives: Implementation by Social Partners

Maybe the most characteristic point of legislative procedures on labour law is that European labour law gives social partners (i.e. employers' and employees' organisations) – at European as well as at national, sectoral and undertaking level – an important role, which can be seen as contributing to flexibility. It also fits with the idea of subsidiarity.

The role of social partners is regulated, in the first place, by Article 153(3) TFEU, which provides that a Member State can leave it to 'management and labour' (a formal term for 'social partners') to introduce the necessary measures by agreement to transpose or implement a directive or decision. The Member State concerned has to take any necessary measure enabling it at any time to be in a position to guarantee the results imposed by that directive or that decision.[58] A 'necessary' measure may, for instance, be that a Member State declares an agreement implementing a directive generally binding or makes supplementary legislation to ensure access to court for those covered by the agreement. Countries may have quite varying ways to ensure that a collective labour agreement extends to all workers and employers. One such method is a national collective labour agreement, which is declared universally binding (e.g. in Belgium). An alternative is to make a special act covering all workers not falling within the scope of the collective labour agreement.

---

[58] E.g. ECJ 1988, 312/86 (*Commission v. France*): 'National legislation which, several years after the expiry of the period prescribed for the implementation of Directive 76/207, makes the two sides of industry responsible for removing certain instances of inequality without laying down any time-limit for compliance with that obligation does not adequately implement the directive.' The Court had already allowed Member States to make use of collective agreements before this was formally laid down in the Maastricht Treaty, see also Bercusson (2009), p. 455. For the Danish way of implementing EU law by means of collective agreements, see Nielsen (2002).

A second special role for social partners exists at the EU level – their agreements can under some conditions be implemented by means of a directive. This possibility will be discussed in the next section, under Article 155 TFEU.

1.3.3.2. Legal Basis

Since all EU legislation needs a legal basis in a specific provision of the Treaty, it is important to discuss the Treaty provisions based upon which labour legislation can be made. These are Article 153 TFEU, Article 157(3), Article 115 and Article 352 TFEU. All these legal bases mention which legislative procedure must be followed and which requirement is to be met for adoption of an instrument based on the article (qualified majority or unanimity in voting). In addition, they define the material scope of the legislative powers derived from the article concerned and what type of instrument can be adopted (e.g. directives, regulations).

(a) Article 153 TFEU

Article 153 TFEU gives a legal basis for adopting legislation on social policy issues, including labour law. This article was introduced in the Treaty in 1999 (Treaty of Amsterdam) and implied a simpler procedure for adopting labour legislation (see Section 1.2.4). Before this, labour legislation had to be based on Article 115 TFEU (internal market) or the 'catch all provision' of Article 352 TFEU; both articles require unanimity. Note that Article 151 TFEU provides that the Union and the Member States shall implement measures which take account of the diverse forms of national practices, in particular in the field of contractual relations, and the need to maintain the competitiveness of the Union economy. Thus, this provides for a restriction when adopting social policy instruments.

There is no general legislative competence to adopt social policy instruments; the competences are regulated by Article 153(2). This legislative power can be used 'with a view to achieving the objectives of Article 151' and includes workers' health and safety; working conditions; social security and social protection of workers; the information and consultation of workers; representation and collective defence of the interests of workers and employers, including co-determination; and the combating of social exclusion. The powers vary, depending on the area concerned.

According to Article 153(2) TFEU, directives can be adopted following the ordinary legislative procedure (Article 294 TFEU) by the European Council and European Parliament, after consulting the Economic and Social Committee and the Committee of the Regions, on the following areas:

- improvement in particular of the working environment to protect workers' health and safety;

- working conditions;
- the information and consultation of workers;
- the integration of persons excluded from the labour market; and
- equality between men and women regarding labour market opportunities and treatment at work.

Directives can also be adopted in four other areas, but only after a special procedure in which unanimity in Council voting is required. As part of this procedure the Committees that are mentioned when the ordinary procedure is followed are to be consulted, but the European Parliament does not have co-decision rights. The reason for the unanimity requirement is that these areas concern politically sensitive issues, in respect of which Member States wanted to maintain their veto right. These four areas are:

- social security and protection of workers;
- protection of workers where their employment contract is terminated;
- representation and collective defence of the interests of workers and employers, including co-determination; and
- conditions of employment for third-country nationals legally residing in Union territory.[59]

In addition, Article 153(4) TFEU provides that the directives shall not affect the right of Member States to define the fundamental principles of their social security systems and must not significantly affect the financial equilibrium thereof.

There are also two areas where, according to Article 151 TFEU, the Union shall support and complement the activities of the Member States, but where there are no powers to adopt legislative instruments. These are:

- the combating of social exclusion; and
- the modernisation of social protection system (without prejudice to the social security and social protection of workers, which was mentioned under the unanimity category).

Consequently, in these areas only the measures mentioned in Article 153(2)(a) TFEU can be taken, i.e. 'measures designed to encourage cooperation between Member States through initiatives aimed at improving knowledge, developing exchanges of information and best practices, promoting innovative approaches

59 The Council can decide (with unanimity) to render the ordinary legislative procedure applicable to the last three areas mentioned here, so for later proposals that procedure can be followed.

and evaluating experiences, excluding any harmonisation of the laws and regulations of the Member States'.

Such measures are often called *soft law* instruments and *best practices*; they are definitely not meant to harmonise national legislations by binding law, in the way that, for instance, directives do. The soft law instruments of Article 153(2)(a) are also possible in the areas where directives can be adopted; the legislature has the choice of the instrument that is politically feasible for the objective concerned.

Article 153(5) TFEU mentions explicitly in which areas of labour law the EU does not have any legislative powers at all: pay, the right of association, the right to strike or the right to impose lock outs. These areas are too sensitive for the EU to be allowed to adopt legislation. Moreover, these topics are specifically connected to the system of Member States, e.g. by the way they leave autonomy to the parties in the industrial relations systems, and the way the government approaches these issues. This area of law has great diversity in its regulations and varies much from country to country. Another important factor is also that the legal status of collective agreements and the dispute resolution systems may vary substantially.[60]

Despite this lack of legislative power in the areas mentioned in Article 153(5) TFEU, it cannot be said that the Union has not had any impact at all on these areas. The freedom to provide services and the freedom of establishment, for instance, have had, in their interpretation by the Court of Justice, serious influence on the right to strike. And the Posted Workers Directive, for instance, was the reason behind the introduction of a statutory minimum wage by some Member States (see Chapter 9).

Finally, other measures apart from legislative acts of the Union may have an impact on an excluded area. An example is that employment policy measures may have effects on wages (see Section 1.3.4).[61]

The directives based on Article 153(2) have two specific characteristics. One is that they can only impose minimum requirements (see Article 153(2)(b)). This implies that they only set a floor of rights; legislation of Member States can have more favourable provisions, as is often explicitly mentioned in the directive. The other characteristic is the requirement, mentioned in the same provision, that the interests of small and medium-sized undertakings should be considered: 'Such directives shall avoid imposing administrative, financial and legal constraints in a way which would hold back the creation and development of small and medium-sized undertakings.' This provision sometimes has the effect that directives can apply only to enterprises with a certain minimum number of workers.[62]

---

60 See also Davies (2012), pp. 31–32, who offers a different explanation.
61 Davies (2012), pp. 31–32.
62 See for instance Article 3 of the Consultation Directive 2002/14/EC.

Finally, it must be remarked that Article 157(3) TFEU, which is also part of Title X on Social Policy, provides a legal basis for measures to ensure the application of the principle of equal opportunities and equal treatment of men and women in matters of employment and occupation, including the principle of equal pay for equal work or work of equal value. For these objectives the European Parliament and the Council must act in accordance with the ordinary legislative procedure and to consult the Economic and Social Committee.

This Article exists alongside with Article 153(1)(i), which mentions 'equality between men and women regarding labour market opportunities and treatment at work'.[63]

(b) Article 155 TFEU: European Social Partners as 'Legislature'

A very special provision is that in the areas mentioned in Article 153 TFEU social partners can make agreements that can – under certain conditions – be implemented by EU directives. This possibility contributes to the so-called 'European social dialogue',[64] which the European Commission must support (Article 154(1) TFEU).

First, it is relevant to remark that Article 154(2–3) TFEU provides that the European Commission must consult management and labour (the social partners) on the possible direction of Union action before submitting proposals in the social policy field. If, after such consultation, the Commission believes that Union action is advisable, it also must consult the social partners on the content of the envisaged proposal. The social partners can give their opinion or recommendation, but they may also inform the European Commission that they want to start negotiations with each other on a topic falling under Article 153 TFEU. If these lead to agreements, they can be implemented by national social partners.

However, according to Article 155(2) TFEU, the agreement can also be implemented by a decision – i.e. a directive – of the Council after a joint request by the signatory parties. After such decision is taken, the agreement has the same force as a directive adopted by the Council.

Note that the Council has, in implementing the agreement, the same restrictions as if it were a proposal by the Commission. Thus, the conditions on the procedure, the requirements on the voting and the excluded areas are also relevant here. For example, an agreement of the social partners regarding pay or strikes cannot be implemented by Council decision.

---

63 Articles 153 and 157 have some differences. Article 153 only allows directives or cooperation promoting measures. Article 157(3) does not have this restriction, since it only mentions measures, that may include a regulation. Moreover, the restrictions of Article 153 do not apply to the measures based on Article 157.

64 On this term, see also Chapter 5, Section 5.2.

Since the Treaty does not define who are to be considered and consulted as social partners, the European Commission has developed criteria in the *Communication concerning the application of the Agreement on social policy.*[65] On the basis of these criteria, a list is made of organisations to be consulted and this list is continuously updated. Currently, 80 organisations are mentioned on the list.[66] These 80 organisations are to be *consulted*, but it is not required that all of them must be admitted to *negotiations*. Social partners decide themselves which organisations they want to negotiate with.

In this respect, there is an interesting Court of Justice judgment, in which employers' organisation Ueapme disputed its exclusion from negotiations on an agreement that was later implemented by a directive. It argued that the result of these negotiations should not be implemented.[67] In the judgment the Court considered that although Ueapme was on the list of representative organisations, there was no right based on the Treaty or communication to take part in any negotiations. The Court added, however, that Article 155 TFEU provides that the Commission must examine the representativity of the signatories to the agreement in question. This is the more important, the Court remarked, if the agreement is implemented as EU law, since in that case the regular procedures of the Treaty are not followed. A major difference is that the European Parliament is not involved in decision making. Therefore, the principle of democracy requires that the participation of the people be otherwise assured, in this instance through the parties that concluded the agreement. Therefore, when a degree of representativity is lacking, the Commission and the Council must refuse to implement the agreement at Community level. In the *Ueapme* case the request for annulment was not successful (see also Chapter 5).[68]

Directives that implement agreements of social partners contain, after several recitals, a very small number of provisions. For instance, in the Directive on fixed-term contracts, Article 1 mentions that the purpose of the directive is to put into effect the framework agreement on fixed-term contracts; Article 2 mentions the date before the agreement is to be implemented; and Article 3 provides when the directive enters into force.

Such directives contain an annex, which is the agreement of the social partners. The directive itself does not add anything to this agreement, apart from the obligation for Member States to bring into force the laws, regulations and administrative provisions necessary to comply with this directive, or ensure that management and labour have introduced the necessary measures by agreement.

---

65 COM(93)600, p. 22.

66 <http://ec.europa.eu/social/main.jsp?catId=329&langId=en> accessed 05.06.2019.

67 ECJ 1998, T-135/96 (*Ueapme*). The employers' organisation concerned was that of the small and medium enterprises (Ueapme) and the directive was Directive 96/34/EC.

68 ECJ 1998, T-135/96 (*Ueapme*). See also Veldman (2011).

After the directive has been adopted, it is treated as a regular directive and, as a result, interpretation issues on it (including the attached agreement) can be brought before the Court of Justice.

Agreements of European social partners that have been implemented by a directive are: the Directive on parental leave (96/34/EC), the Directive on part-time work (97/81/EC) and the Directive on fixed-term labour contracts (1999/70/EC).

Since the agreement is the result of negotiations, there is a risk that the outcome will be rather meagre, for instance if social partners do not have an interest to come to certain results. See Chapter 4, Section 4.2.1, which remarks that the Part-time Work Directive is generally described as a minimalistic, if not poor, piece of supranational social legislation.

As far as known, so far all joint requests of social partners to make such implementing directive have been granted.[69] However, in some cases, the social partners were not successful in making an agreement; an example is that of temporary agency work (see also Chapters 4 and 5). In such case the Commission can itself present a proposal for a directive.[70] The views of the social partners during the negotiations may still have an influence on such a proposal.

(c) Article 115 TFEU

Although Article 115 TFEU is not related directly to social policy objectives and subjects, it can serve as the legal basis for directives intended to harmonise parts of national labour law. Article 115 TFEU gives powers to the Council, acting unanimously in accordance with a special legislative procedure and after consulting the European Parliament and the Economic and Social Committee, 'to issue directives for the approximation of such laws, regulations or administrative provisions of the Member States as directly affect the establishment or functioning of the internal market'.

Since differences between national labour law can lead to distortion of competition on the internal market, Article 115 has been used as legal basis for adopting directives in the area of collective redundancies (Directive 98/59/EC), transfer of undertakings (Directive 98/59/EC), on the protection of employees in the event of the insolvency of their employer (Directive 2008/94/EC), information on the employment relationship (Directive 91/533/EEC) and equal pay for men and women (Directive 75/117/EEC). The first directives on equal pay, collective redundancies, transfer of

---

69 The Agreement on the protection of health and safety of hairdressers was not accepted for implementation by a Council Directive, see Chapter 8, Section 8.4.3.

70 Examples are Directive 2008/104 (Temporary work agencies) and Directive (94/15) (European works councils).

undertakings and insolvency have been adopted in the period before the legal basis for 'social' directives (Article 153) was introduced. However, the amended directives were also based on the article that served as the legal basis for the original directive. For some instruments, e.g. information on the employment relationship, Article 153 does not seem to give a legal basis and for that purpose Article 115 TFEU is still necessary.

(d) The 'Catch All' Provision of Article 352 TFEU

Finally, the 'catch all' provision of Art. 352 TFEU must be mentioned. This provision gives the Council the power to adopt the appropriate measures if action by the Union should prove necessary, within the framework of the policies defined in the Treaties, to attain one of the objectives set out in the Treaties, and the Treaties have not provided the necessary powers. In such a case the Council must act unanimously on a proposal from the Commission and first obtain the consent of the European Parliament.[71]

This provision has been used, in labour law, as a legal basis for the directives on equal treatment for men and women as regards access to employment, vocational training and promotion, and working conditions (Directive 76/207/EEC) and on the progressive implementation of the principle of equal treatment for men and women in matters of social security (Directive 79/7/EEC). At the time of adoption of these directives there was a specific legal basis for an instrument on equal pay for men and women, but not for equal treatment of men and women in a broader sense. Therefore Article 352 TFEU was used.

(e) The Relevance of the Correct Legal Basis

For the EU legislature it is of utmost importance to apply the correct legal basis for a legislative instrument and to remain within the powers mentioned in that legal basis. After all, the Union has only legislative powers if these are granted by a specific Treaty provision and these may be used only to realise the objectives mentioned in that provision (see also Article 5(2) TEU).

The choice of a legal basis can lead to disputes if a legislative instrument has more than one objective and thus could potentially be based on separate legal bases. If the relevant Treaty provisions require the same legislative procedures and have the same requirements for adopting the proposal (majority/unanimity), the possibility to choose between legal bases does not lead to principal problems.

---

71 Article 352(3) provides that the measures based on this Article shall not entail harmonisation of Member States' laws or regulations in cases where the Treaties exclude such harmonisation. An example of a specific exclusion of harmonisation exists in health care (Article 168(5) TFEU).

If, however, they describe different procedures, it becomes more problematic. This double legal basis is possible for labour law directives, since they may also have an impact on the internal market; consequently, both Article 153(2)/Article 157(3) and Article 115 TFEU may be used. Such choice can lead to political problems between the EU institutions and the Member States, in particular when one instrument requires unanimity and the other suffices with majority voting.

If a legislative act is (allegedly) based on the wrong legal basis, a Member State, the European Parliament, the European Council or the European Commission can ask the Court of Justice to review its legality (Article 263 TFEU). A legislative act can also be declared void in a preliminary procedure before the Court of Justice (Article 267 TFEU).[72] For the Court, the objective and the contents of, for instance, a directive are, in particular, relevant; these must be sufficiently in line with the legal basis.[73]

A well-known example is the judgment *United Kingdom/Council* on the Working Time Directive (Directive 93/104/EC, now Directive 2003/88/EC).[74] This directive gives provisions on minimum rest periods, maximum working time, night work and annual holidays.[75] This directive was based on Article 118A EC Treaty (now Article 153(1)(a) TFEU). Article 118A EC Treaty provided that Member States shall pay particular attention to encouraging improvements, especially in the working environment, as regards the health and safety of workers. For this purpose, the Council shall adopt, with a qualified majority, 'by means of directives, minimum requirements for gradual implementation, having regard to the conditions and technical rules obtaining in each of the Member States'. The UK was of the view that the EU should not interfere with working time at all since this matter – working time – was not covered by Article 118A. It addressed the Court of Justice with a request for nullification of the directive[76] arguing that Article 118A EC Treaty was an incorrect legal basis for the directive. The legal basis should have been Article 115 TFEU (the internal market) or Article 352 TFEU (rest provision).[77] The relevance of the proposed alternatives is evident; these both require unanimity voting in the Council and thus the UK would have a veto right. The UK added that Article 118A EC Treaty (now Article 153(1)(a) TFEU) only concerns physical health and safety of workers and not working time; the connection between working time and health and safety was,

72 An example of a judgment in which the Court declared a directive void because of the lack of a legal basis is ECJ 2000, C-376/98 (*Germany v. European Parliament and Council*).

73 See e.g. ECJ 1996, C-84/94 (*UK v. Council*) §25 and the case law mentioned.

74 Ibid.

75 On this directive, see Chapter 8.

76 Based on Articles 263–64 TFEU.

77 At the time, Articles 94 and 308 EC respectively.

in its view, too weak to justify Article 118A being the legal basis for this instrument.[78]

The Court of Justice, however, did not follow these arguments. There is nothing in the wording of Article 118a, the Court argued (§15), to indicate that the concepts of 'working environment', 'safety' and 'health' as used in that provision should, in the absence of other indications, be interpreted restrictively, and not as embracing all factors, physical or otherwise, capable of affecting the health and safety of the worker in the working environment, including in particular certain aspects of the organisation of working time. On the contrary, the Court added, the words 'especially in the working environment' militate in favour of a broad interpretation of the powers which Article 118a confers upon the Council for the protection of the health and safety of workers. Moreover, the Court concluded, such an interpretation of the words 'safety' and 'health' derives support in particular from the preamble to the Constitution of the World Health Organization, to which all the Member States belong. Health is there defined as a state of complete physical, mental and social well-being that does not consist only in the absence of illness or infirmity.

Where the principal aim of the measure in question is the protection of the health and safety of workers, Article 118a must be used, the Court added, albeit such a measure may have ancillary effects on the establishment and functioning of the internal market.[79] It follows that Article 118A EC was the correct legal basis for this directive and the directive was not to be nullified.

1.3.4. OTHER METHODS FOR REGULATING LABOUR LAW ISSUES: SOFT LAW, OMC

EU social policy can be regulated not only by means of legislation (*hard law*), but also, and this is increasingly the case, by forms of *soft law*. These can have many different varieties, including recommendations, conclusions and other non-binding measures encouraging Member States and other actors to voluntarily adopt a specific measure or policy.

A special form is the Open Method of Coordination (OMC),[80] already mentioned in Section 1.2.4. This method was introduced to implement the European employment strategy. The legal framework is Article 146 TFEU et seq, which mention the obligations for the Member States. Member States shall, through their employment policies, contribute to the achievement of the

---

78 ECJ 1996, C-84/94 (*UK v. Council*), §31.

79 Ibid., in particular §§15, 22 and 43.

80 The term was used for the first time in European Council (2000) (Lisbon European Council 23 and 24 March 2000 – Presidency conclusions), point 7. See also Ter Haar (2012) and (2013); Pennings (2011).

objectives referred to in Article 145 in a way consistent with the broad guidelines of the economic policies of the Member States and of the Community adopted pursuant to Article 121(2). These provisions, together with Article 147, constitute the legal basis for the OMC on employment policy. The Treaty itself does not use the term 'Open Method of Coordination'.

The OMC procedure is described in Article 148 TFEU. First, each year the European Council must consider the employment situation in the Community. Based on a joint annual report by the Council and the Commission, the Council adopts conclusions on this employment situation. Based on these conclusions, the Council, acting by a qualified majority on, inter alia, a proposal from the Commission, must, each year, draw up guidelines which the Member States must consider in their employment policies. Subsequently, each Member State must write an annual report on the principal measures taken to implement its employment policy in the light of these guidelines; these reports are sent to the Council and the Commission. The Council examines these reports – i.e. on the employment policies of the Member States – in the light of the employment guidelines.

The Council can, if it considers it appropriate in the light of that examination, make recommendations to Member States on a proposal from the Commission. Finally, based on the results of the reports, the Council and the Commission must make a joint annual report to the European Council on the employment situation in the Community and on the implementation of the guidelines for employment.

This method is also used for other areas of the Treaty, including social inclusion, health care and economic policy, but there is no legal basis for the OMC in these areas (this is sometimes called 'OMC light').

The OMC consists of the following ingredients:

- Guidelines are adopted specifying time schedules for reaching the specified objectives (what is to be reached?).[81]
- These define common methods of measurement, e.g. statistics, quantitative and qualitative indicators, benchmarks etc. (how can we measure whether the objectives are reached?).
- The area is periodically monitored, evaluated and *peer reviewed* (the Member States review each other) and exchange *good practices* (what can we learn from each other?).

According to the OMC, it is the Member States that must translate the policy objectives and guidelines to the national level. They must make national action plans and they must report to the European Commission. The 'OMC

[81] See Article 148(1) and (2) TFEU.

Employment' also has a role for the European Council (the heads of the governments), the Council and the Commission. The European Parliament is only consulted on the guidelines to be made; it has only a marginal role. Also, there is hardly any role for the Court of Justice in OMC procedures.

In contrast with regulations and directives, the OMC is not a static, but a dynamic instrument. This allows periodically adapting the objectives and guidelines to respond to, for instance, developments of the economy or society.[82]

Initially, it was feared that the OMC would not have much effect. However, the Council issued detailed and specific recommendations. These recommendations are to be taken into account for the next reports Member States must write. Thus, Member States must consider these recommendations when developing their policies.[83]

1.4. ENFORCEMENT AND REALISATION OF EU LABOUR LAW

1.4.1. INTRODUCTION

Enforcement of European labour law has several dimensions. One is that Member States may be unwilling to apply or implement part of EU law, since they may consider it undesirable, expensive, unpractical or unclear, or for other reasons.

A second dimension is that the national labour law systems and their enforcement systems differ from Member State to Member State.[84] Member States may enforce (parts of) their labour law through various bodies, e.g. the judiciary and public institutions, but also through social partners (see Section 1.3.3.1). As a result, there may be large differences in how European labour is implemented and enforced at the national level and this may cause difficulties for the enforcement of European labour law.[85]

A third dimension is that national actors (e.g. national agencies, employers, judges) are often unaware of European labour law rules. There is a natural tendency to look only at the national rules.

A fourth dimension is that some provisions result from a compromise after long discussions during drafting and can be rather vague. This may make

---

82 On the democratic deficits, see also Pennings (2011).

83 See also Ter Haar (2013) on the impact of the OMC.

84 Malmberg (2003); Bercusson (2009).

85 A historical example, mentioned in Bercusson (2009), p. 417: by 1988 Italy had failed to implement 278 of the total number of EC directives, including the directive on collective dismissals and the directive on transfers of undertakings.

it difficult to actually grant individuals the rights that are envisaged by the provision.

The infringement procedure (Section 1.4.3.1) is relevant in case a Member State has a different view on a particular provision. It can also be used to redress a situation where a national court has taken a (in the view of the Commission) wrong decision. The preliminary procedure (1.4.3.2) is used to ensure the uniform interpretation of EU law, and can thus be helpful to overcome the effects of the differences between national systems as regards implementation and enforcement. These instruments cannot overcome all perceived weaknesses in enforcement. To respond to these, the Court of Justice has developed particular doctrines (Section 1.4.4) that give, in particular, individual parties the possibility of invoking European labour law in national procedures, which is potentially a very important instrument for enforcement.

1.4.2. ADMINISTRATIVE ENFORCEMENT OF EUROPEAN LABOUR LAW

'The EU institutions do not possess the resources which can even begin to equate to the resources of national Ministries of Labour or labour inspectorates'.[86] However, in 2017 the European Labour Authority was announced by President Juncker in his 2017 State of the European Union address, in order to ensure that EU rules on labour mobility will be enforced in a fair, simple and effective way. The Authority should be up and running in 2019 and reach its full operational capacity by 2023. The Authority must facilitate access for individuals and employers to information on their rights and obligations as well as to relevant services; support cooperation between EU countries in the cross-border enforcement of relevant Union law, including facilitating joint inspections; and mediate and facilitate a solution in cases of cross-border disputes between national authorities or labour market disruptions.

As can be seen, the scope of its activities is restricted to cross-border problems and to support the actors. It has therefore a much more restricted role than national labour inspections.[87]

The absence of a 'real' labour inspectorate at EU level means that Member States have a major responsibility for enforcement of European labour law; if they do not do so satisfactorily, the Commission can start an infringement procedure.

86 Bercusson (2009), p. 417.

87 Bercusson (2009), p. 420 mentions the OMC as a form of administrative enforcement of European labour law. As seen in Section 1.3.4, this mechanism does not provide independent powers of enforcement and that 'means placing a great burden on this iterative pattern alone to achieve the desired results' (Bercusson (2009), p. 422).

1.4.3. PROCEDURES BEFORE THE COURT OF JUSTICE

1.4.3.1. The Infringement Procedure

In the view of the drafters of the EEC Treaty (1957), it was mainly the European Commission that, together with the Court, was responsible for the enforcement of European law. This is reflected in the task assigned to the Commission to oversee the application of Union law under the control of the Court of Justice (see now Article 17(1) TEU). The most powerful instrument is the infringement procedure that the Commission can initiate against a Member State (Article 258 TFEU).

This is useful, in particular, if a Member State deliberately does not obey EU law provisions. The infringement procedure starts with a letter of formal notice, by which the Commission allows the Member State to present its views regarding the breach observed. The Member State can then take measures to be in compliance with EU law and if the Commission is satisfied, the procedure stops. Certainly, in cases where the government was not aware of the non-observance – e.g. lower bodies or officials did not know the EU law rule concerned or did not dare to give EU law priority over a national provision that was not in line with it – this contributes to enforcement of European labour law.

If no reply to the letter of formal notice is received, or if the observations presented by the Member State in reply to that notice cannot be considered satisfactory, the Commission can move to the next stage of infringement procedure, which is the reasoned opinion; if necessary, the Commission will then refer the case to the Court of Justice.

It can happen that a national court gives a wrong interpretation of EU law (and omitted to ask the Court of Justice for an interpretation) and this may be a reason for the Commission to start an infringement procedure.[88] This may be a somewhat awkward situation for the Member State, since on the one hand it has to respect the separate roles of national court and government and on the other it has to defend its case in the infringement procedure.

The infringement procedure is certainly not a panacea, since the capacity of the Commission to start infringement procedures is limited. There may also be political reasons for the Commission not to start this procedure in all cases where EU law is not obeyed.

An additional dimension of enforcement, in practice very relevant, is that the European Commission (and European Parliament) receives many letters each year from individuals (and sometimes their advisers) complaining about

---

88 ECJ 2003, 311/01 (*Commission v. the Netherlands*).

ignorance of, or wrong application of, EU law. This may lead to an infringement procedure,[89] but the problem may also be solved by informal contact.

1.4.3.2. The Preliminary Procedure[90]

In one of its first judgments, *Costa/E.N.E.L.*,[91] the Italian Government complained that the national court did not restrict itself to asking the Court to interpret the Treaty, but also asked it to declare whether the Italian law in dispute was in conformity with the Treaty; because of this the request for the preliminary ruling was inadmissible.

The Court of Justice made it clear that as opposed to other international treaties, the Treaty instituting the EEC created its own order which was integrated with the national order of the Member States the moment when the Treaty came into force; as such, it is binding upon them. In fact, by creating a Community of unlimited duration, having its own institutions, its own personality and its own capacity in law, apart from having international standing and more particularly, real powers resulting from a limitation of competence or a transfer of powers from the States to the Community, the Member States, albeit within limited spheres, have restricted their sovereign rights and created a body of law applicable both to their nationals and to themselves. Thus, European law differs from international law in that it is part of the national legal order of all Member States, regardless of their system for implementing international law.

As a result, national courts can ask the Court of Justice whether national law is consistent with EU law and nationals may, in proceedings before national courts, rely directly on provisions of EU law if they have direct effect.[92] The primacy of EU law over national law applies to all national legal rules, including rules of constitutional law.[93] This interpretation has had a large impact, since it gives the room for national courts to challenge national rules considered inconsistent with EU law; if national law implementing EU labour law is not adequately enforced, EU law on remedies, procedures and sanctions may be invoked to achieve the effectiveness required by EU law. In this way the Court of Justice has engaged domestic courts deeply in the enforcement of EU law.[94]

---

89 After the national court had given its decision in the case mentioned in the previous note, the Commission started the procedure. See, for another procedure, ECJ 2016, C-308/14 (*Commission v. UK*), §21.

90 See also De La Mare & Donelly (2011).

91 ECJ 1964, 6/64 (*Costa v. E.N.E.L.*). For the development of the legal order the *Van Gend & Loos* judgment (ECJ 1963, 26/62) is also extremely important.

92 This is explicitly stated in Article 288(2) TFEU with regard to regulations.

93 ECJ 1976, 11/70 (*Internationale Handelsgesellschaft*), §3.

94 Bercusson (2009), p. 468.

According to Article 267 TFEU, national courts can or have to ask for a decision on interpretation of an EU law provision that is unclear. This is an important instrument to ensure a uniform interpretation of EU law. When it asks for a preliminary ruling, the national court suspends the procedure and waits for the judgment of the Court of Justice (which may take a considerable time). It is the national court that resolves the dispute with due regard for the Court's replies.

The referral of preliminary questions to the Court of Justice may be a possibility or an obligation of the national court. If appeal against the decision of the national court is possible under national law, the court *can* ask for a preliminary ruling. Courts against whose decisions no appeal can be lodged are, however, *obliged* to refer interpretation questions to the Court, unless the Court has already answered the question concerned (*acte éclairé*) or the answer to the question is so obvious as to leave no scope for any reasonable doubt (*acte clair*).[95] It is the sole responsibility for the national court before which the dispute has been brought to determine whether there is an *acte clair*.[96]

Formally, judgments of the Court are binding only on the court who has submitted the request for a preliminary ruling but, mainly because of the notion of the *acte éclairé*, judgments of the Court have a kind of *erga omnes* effect. In practice, they are of major legal importance for all national courts.

When the highest national court has decided that there are no questions which need to be answered by the Court of Justice, it is not possible for parties to address the Court of Justice to correct this. As discussed in Section 1.4.3.1, sometimes a party contacts the European Commission, and this may lead (in exceptional cases) to an infringement procedure.

An alternative route was opened by the European Court of Human Rights (ECtHR), according to which Article 6(1) of the ECHR (right to a fair trial) requires national courts (in final instance) to give reasons for any decision refusing to request a preliminary ruling from the Court of Justice.[97]

It is clear, however, that these possibilities do not really remedy the lack of legal protection of parties in such cases.

The national court is obliged to interpret national implementation law in conformity with the directive in question. This obligation only applies (completely) after the expiry of the time-limit for the transposition of the

---

95 ECJ 1982, 283/81 (*CILFIT*).

96 ECJ 2015, C-72/14 (*Van Dijk*), §§56–59. Even if a lower court has referred a question for a preliminary ruling still pending before the Court, the national court ruling at final instance may conclude that the case before it involves an *acte clair*. In that case, that court does not have to wait until the Court has given an answer to that question (see §§60–61). See Kornezov (2016).

97 ECtHR 2014 (*Dhahbi*), §§31–34.

directive; during that period, national courts have only a 'passive obligation'.[98] This applies irrespective of whether the provisions of national law were adopted before or after the directive in question entered into force.[99]

The interpretation given in a preliminary ruling to a provision of EU law applies in principle from the entry into force of that provision. Only exceptionally does the Court limit the retroactive effect of the interpretation it has given to a provision. In such cases, the Court refers to pressing considerations of legal certainty and respect for good faith expectations, which happens in practice when the judgment may have excessive financial consequences. It is precisely in labour law and equal treatment law that examples can be found, namely in the case of discrimination on grounds of nationality[100] and in particular in the case of equal treatment of male and female employees. An example is the *Defrenne II* judgment, mentioned previously, in which the Court ruled that (what is now) Article 157 TFEU on equal pay has direct horizontal effect. It considered, however, that as the general level at which pay would have been fixed cannot be known, important considerations of legal certainty make it impossible to reopen the question as regards the past and therefore this direct effect could not be invoked with regard to pay claims for periods prior to the date of the judgment.[101] Another example is the *Barber* judgment (1990), in which the Court ruled that private occupational pension schemes fall within the scope of (now) Article 157 TFEU, has a restriction on its retroactive effect.[102]

1.4.3.3. The Doctrine of Liability of the State

When a Member State has not correctly implemented a directive and an individual cannot rely on the rights granted by the directive (since it does not have vertical or horizontal effect), the individual may suffer damage because of that failure. In the famous *Francovich* judgment the Court created the possibility for the individual to claim compensation from the State in that situation.[103] In *Francovich*, Italy had not implemented the Directive on the protection of employees in the event of the insolvency of their employer (see Chapter 6),

98 They should refrain from an interpretation of national law which could seriously compromise the attainment of the result prescribed by that directive, ECJ 2006, C-212/04 (*Adeneler*), §§121–22.

99 ECJ 1990, C-106/89 (*Marleasing*), §8.

100 ECJ 1999, C-262/96 (*Sürül*), §§108–13. The pressing consideration of legal certainty here was that retroactive effect would seriously disrupt the financing of the social security systems of the Member States.

101 Except as regards those workers who had already brought legal proceedings or made an equivalent claim. See ECJ 1976, 43/75 (*Defrenne II*), §§74–75.

102 ECJ 1990, C-262/88 (*Barber*). See also ECJ 1993, C-109/91 (*Ten Oever*) regarding survivor's pensions provided for by an occupational pension scheme.

103 ECJ 1990, C-6/90 and 9/90 (*Francovich*).

and when his employer went bankrupt, Mr Francovich suffered damages as a result. Mr Francovich could not claim his unpaid wages, because Italy had not fulfilled its obligation to organise the prescribed institutional guarantee system. He claimed compensation of damages from the Italian State. Although this concerned a vertical relationship – an employee versus the State – the relevant directive provisions did not meet the technical requirements of being sufficiently precise and unconditional. Therefore, the provisions of the directive could not be invoked directly against the State and interpretation of Italian law in conformity with the directive was not possible either. The Court argued that the full effectiveness of EU rules would be impaired and the protection of the rights which they grant would be weakened if individuals were unable to obtain redress when their rights were infringed by a breach of EU law for which a Member State can be held responsible. The basis for this was, according to the Court, Article 5 EEC (now Article 4(3) TEU), requiring the Member States to take all appropriate measures to ensure fulfilment of their obligations under Community law. Among these is the obligation to nullify the unlawful consequences of a breach of Community law. From this it follows that Member States are obliged to make good loss and damage caused to individuals by breaches of Community law for which they can be held responsible.[104] As a result Mr Francovich could hold Italy liable for not taking the necessary implementing measures within the prescribed period. In *Francovich* and the subsequent *Brasserie du Pecheur* judgment[105] the Court made the right to financial compensation dependent on the fulfilment of three conditions:

- the breached directive provision is intended to confer rights on individuals and it is possible to identify the content of those rights based on the provision(s) of the directive;
- the breach must be sufficiently serious; and
- there is a direct causal link between the breach of the obligation resting on the State and the damage sustained by the injured parties.

Of these conditions the second is the most difficult, because Member States have a certain degree of discretion. Therefore, this condition is met only if the Member State has 'manifestly and gravely disregarded the limits on its discretion'.[106] In cases where Member States have little or no margin for discretion, a single infringement of EU law may suffice, for example, if a Member State has not taken any measures to transpose a directive into national law in time.[107]

104 Ibid.

105 ECJ 1996, 46/93 and 48/93 (*Brasserie du Pecheur*), §55.

106 Ibid.

107 ECJ 1996, C-178/94 et al. (*Dillenkofer*).

A Member State can be held liable regardless of the government body responsible for the violation, and this can include courts adjudicating at last instance.[108]

A national example of a *Francovich* claim can be found in the situation where, because of the application of Dutch law, long-term sick employees only accrued the right to paid annual leave during the first six months of sick leave; this provision was considered in breach of Article 7 of Directive 2003/88/EC. An interpretation of the Dutch provision in conformity with the directive was not possible, as that would have been *contra legem*. The employees concerned were successful in their '*Francovich* claims'.[109]

1.4.4. THE COURT'S INTERPRETATION OF EU LAW TO REALISE ITS OBJECTIVES

For European labour law the general enforcement instruments of EU law – discussed in the previous section – apply. In addition, the Court has developed some doctrines to make enforcement of European labour law more effective, although these doctrines may also be applied in other areas of EU law. The need for such doctrines appeared since some of the texts are vague and the result of a compromise. This may in particular lead to problems with enforcement where EU labour law confers rights on individuals, but the implementation in national law is not fully adequate.[110] In such judgments it can be seen that the Court tries to give full effect to the objectives of the EU law provisions concerned and that the Court acknowledges that it has a special role in this as interpreter of EU law.

1.4.4.1. Doctrine of Indirect Effect

Directives generally do not have direct effect; they always require national implementing measures, since they must be implemented in national law (Article 288 TFEU, see Section 1.3.3.1). However, a Member State can be negligent or unwilling to implement a directive correctly or in a timely manner. For that reason, it is important that the Court has ruled that in some cases a provision of a directive can have direct effect (see Section 1.4.4.2). As this is only possible in some cases and most labour law rules are laid down in directives, the doctrine of indirect effect, developed by the Court of Justice, is of great importance.

In the *Marleasing* case,[111] the Court ruled that a national court is required to interpret its national law 'as far as possible' in the light of the wording and

108 ECJ 2003, 224/01 (*Köbler*), §§33–34.
109 HR 18 September 2015, ECLI:NL:HR:2015:2723.
110 Bercusson (2009), p. 403.
111 ECJ 1990, C-106/89 (*Marleasing*), §8.

the purpose of a directive that is referred to.[112] It argued that by ensuring the full effectiveness of EU law national courts do not exceed their limits of the jurisdiction.[113]

However, a *contra legem* interpretation of national law is not required.[114] The national courts are required to do whatever lies within their jurisdiction, having regard to the whole body of rules of national law (instead of merely the law provisions at issue) to ensure that the EU instrument in question is fully effective.[115]

According to the Court, this obligation of EU law compliant interpretation also exists – in a more 'passive' way – during the period of transposing a directive in national law: the national courts must refrain from taking any measures which could seriously compromise the attainment of the result prescribed by it.[116]

This doctrine obliges national courts to interpret their national law not only in conformity with a directive, but also with other sources of EU law, in particular the Treaty itself.

1.4.4.2. Doctrine of Direct Effect[117]

EU law provisions can also have direct effect. This doctrine of direct effect is extremely important, since with such effect individuals can invoke the provision concerned directly and are not dependent on activities of the Member State to implement that provision.

Certainly not all EU law provisions have direct effect. To have direct effect, the provision must be *sufficiently clear and unconditional*, and not dependent on further implementing acts.[118]

The Court has – in respect of some *Treaty* provisions dealing with labour law – been generous in accepting direct effect, both vertically and horizontally. An example is Article 45(2) TFEU and its predecessor, although the text is, literally speaking, no more than a definition: 'Such freedom of movement shall entail the abolition of any discrimination based on nationality between workers of the Member States as regards employment, remuneration and other conditions of work and employment.'[119] Also, the exception – Member States are

112 Bercusson (2009), p. 476 calls this the 'horizontal indirect effect of directives'.

113 ECJ 2004, C-3971/01 (*Pfeiffer*), §114; ECJ 2010, C-555/07 (*Kücükdeveci*), §48.

114 ECJ 2006, C-212/04 (*Adeneler*), §110; ECJ 2008, C-68/06 (*Impact*), §100; and ECJ 2009, C-378/07 to C-380/07 (*Angelidaki*), §199, all labour law cases.

115 ECJ 2009, C-378/07 to C-380/07 (*Angelidaki*), §200; ECJ 2004, C-3971/01 (*Pfeiffer*), §115.

116 ECJ 2006, C-212/04 (*Adeneler*), §§121–22.

117 See for an elaborate discussion De Witte (2011) and, with regard to fundamental rights, Frantziou (2019).

118 ECJ 1964, 6/64 (*Costa/E.N.E.L.*).

119 ECJ 1974, 41/74 (*Van Duyn*), in particular §6.

allowed to limit this right for the protection of public policy, public security or public health – is not in itself a reason for denying direct effect.

Another example is Article 119 EEC, which rules that 'Each Member State shall in the course of the first stage ensure and subsequently maintain the application of the principle of equal remuneration for equal work as between men and women workers'. Member States appeared very reluctant to implement this principle, and extended the stage within which it had to be realised. Even though this text is vague, the Court gave it vertical and horizontal direct effect. As a result, employees can invoke it against the employer before a national court, which can have much more forceful results than if Member States are left room to ensure 'this principle'.[120]

Not all Treaty provisions have direct effect. An example of a provision that has no direct effect is Article 151 TFEU, that mentions objectives of EU social policy. According to the Court, this provision 'has essentially the nature of a programme'.[121] Therefore it cannot have direct effect. The programmatic nature does not imply, however, that the provision is deprived of any legal effect. The social policy objectives of Article 151 constitute an important aid for the interpretation of other provisions of the Treaty and of secondary EU legislation in the social field. However, implementing measures are necessary to achieve these objectives.[122]

Some examples of Treaty provisions that have direct effect have been given above; in addition, regulation provisions can have direct effect – also horizontally in some cases – if they satisfy the previously mentioned conditions that they are *sufficiently clear and unconditional*.

Directives generally do not have direct effect, since they always require national implementing measures (Article 288 TFEU, see Section 1.3.3.1). However, a Member State may have failed to implement a directive correctly or in a timely fashion and it will not always be possible to interpret national (labour) law in accordance with the directive (see Section 1.4.4.1). For that reason, it is important that the Court has ruled that in some cases a provision of a directive can have direct effect if the directive has not (yet) been implemented or has not been correctly implemented by a Member State at the end of the implementation period; and the directive provision is unconditional and sufficiently precise.[123]

120 See now Article 157 TFEU.

121 ECJ 1987, C-128/86 (*Zaera*), §§13–18.

122 ECJ 1987, C-128/86 (*Zaera*). For an example of the relevance of Article 151, see ECJ 1976, 43/75 (*Defrenne II*), §11.

123 See e.g. ECJ 1974, 41/74 (*Van Duyn*), §§11–15 and ECJ 1986, 152/84 (*Marshall*), §46.

It is important to note that this direct effect of directive provisions is relevant only for vertical relationships, i.e. between an individual and the State or its organs. For European labour law it is relevant that this direct effect exists not only if a State operates as a public organ, but also where it acts as an employer.[124] This may mean that public sector employees may claim rights mentioned in directives that are not available to private sector employees.[125] In its case law the Court uses a wide definition of 'State': it includes decentralised and semi-governmental authorities and private law bodies on which a Member State has conferred a task in the public interest.[126]

In the *Impact* judgment,[127] the Court considered that Clause 5 of the Framework agreement on fixed-term contracts, enumerating a series of abuse-prevention measures through which Member States are called to pose limits to the recourse to several successive fixed-term contracts, does not have direct effect. It 'does not contain any unconditional and sufficiently precise obligation capable of being relied upon, in the absence of transposing measures taken within the requisite period, by an individual before a national court'.[128] However, the equal treatment rule of this directive (Clause 4) is sufficiently clear and unconditional to have direct effect in vertical labour relationships.[129]

Direct effect of directives cannot be invoked in horizontal relationships between private parties, for instance an employee against his employer. The reason for this is that pursuant to Article 288 TFEU the binding nature of a directive exists only in relation to 'each Member State to which it is addressed'. This implies, according to the Court, that a directive cannot of itself impose obligations on individuals.[130]

It is interesting to note that the Court has in some cases helped individuals who were confronted with the fact that they could not invoke the directive due to the lack of horizontal effect. This was the case where the Court considered that a *fundamental right* (as a general principle of Union law or under the Charter) underlies the disputed provision of the directive. In the *Kücükdeveci* judgment, the Court considered that the principle of non-discrimination on ground of age is a general principle of EU law and that this principle underlies Directive 2000/78/EC.[131] This means, according to the Court, that this general

---

124 ECJ 1986, 152/84 (*Marshall*), §§46–49.

125 Bercusson (2009), p. 404.

126 ECJ 2012, C-282/10 (*Maribel Dominguez*), §39; ECJ 2017, C-413/15 (*Farrell/Whitty and others*).

127 ECJ 2008, C-268/06 (*Impact*).

128 See Chapter 4, Section 4.3.2.

129 See Chapter 4, Section 4.3.3.

130 ECJ 2012, C-282/10 (*Maribel Dominguez*), §39; ECJ 2017, C-413/15 (*Farrell/Whitty and others*).

131 ECJ 2010, C-555/07 (*Kücükdeveci*).

principle, 'as given expression in Directive 2000/78', must be the basis of the examination (instead of the directive provision concerned).[132] According to the Court, it is for the national court to ensure that individuals enjoy the legal protection of Community law and that those rules are fully effective, setting aside if need be any provision of national law which may conflict with that Union fundamental right. This implies that the provision of the directive concerned is given *de facto* a horizontal direct effect.[133] This can (thus) even mean that national law inconsistent with EU law has to be disapplied.[134]

Finally, it is apparent from recent case law of the Court of Justice that certain Charter provisions may also be directly relied on in disputes between employees and their employer in a field covered by EU law and therefore falling within the scope of the Charter.[135] The Court ruled in *Egenberger* that both Article 21 (non-discrimination, in this case on ground of religion) and Article 47 (the right to effective judicial protection) of the Charter are sufficient in themselves to confer on individuals a right which they may rely on as such in disputes between them in a field covered by EU law. Consequently, in the situation where it is impossible to interpret the disputed national provision in conformity with EU law, in order to guarantee the full effectiveness of these Charter provisions, the national court needs to disapply contrary provisions of national law.[136] This also applies to Article 31(2) of the Charter (right to paid annual leave).[137]

It remains to be seen which other Charter provisions are deemed to have horizontal direct effect in employment relationships. It is clear that Article 27 of the Charter (right of workers' participation) does *not* have this effect. In the *AMS* judgment the Court ruled that the employees could not invoke Article 27 directly, either by itself, or in conjunction with the provisions of Directive 2002/14 (as in *Kücükdeveci*), because that provision does not confer on individuals an individual right which they may invoke as such.[138] The latter – the

---

132 ECJ 2010, C-555/07 (*Kücükdeveci*), §27. See also the earlier *Mangold* judgment, ECJ 2005, C-144/04 (*Mangold*). This obligation of the national courts is based on the obligations arising from Article 288 TFEU in conjunction with Article 4(3) TEU which apply to all the authorities of Member States including, for matters within their jurisdiction, the courts, see e.g. ECJ 1984, 14/83 (*Von Colson and Kamann*).

133 ECJ 2010, C-555/07 (*Kücükdeveci*); ECJ 2005, C-144/04 (*Mangold*). See Barnard (2012a), p. 276/277.

134 ECJ 2010, C-555/07 (*Kücükdeveci*), §51.

135 ECJ 2018, C-570/16 (*Broßonn*), §85. According to the Court (see §87) Article 51 of the Charter does not preclude this possibility, since it does not address the question of horizontal direct effect.

136 ECJ 2018, C-414/16 (*Egenberger*), §§75, 78–79.

137 ECJ 2018, C-570/16 (*Broßonn*). This right is, as regards its very existence, both mandatory and unconditional in nature, and does not need to be given concrete expression by the provisions of EU or national law (§85).

138 ECJ 2014, C-176/12 (*AMS*), §47.

conferral of an individual right – seems to be the most important, though not clearly defined, criterion for deciding whether a Charter provision has horizontal effect.[139]

1.5. THE INTERPRETATION OF THE TERMS 'WORKER' AND 'EMPLOYEE' IN EU LAW

At various places in the Treaty and secondary EU law (directives and regulations) the terms 'worker' and 'employee' are used, in order to determine which persons are covered by that provision or instrument. The meaning of these terms in the various instruments will be explained in the subsequent chapters. However, since these analyses are related to each separate subject, here some general remarks on their interrelationship will be made, since the terms worker and employee – which are used interchangeably in EU law – do not have a common meaning.

As will be seen in Chapter 2, Section 2.2.4, the Court has developed a Community interpretation of the term worker in the free movement provisions (Article 45 TFEU and Regulation 492/2011). This is a broad interpretation: 'the essential feature of an employment relationship is that for a certain period of time a person performs services for and under the direction of another person in return for which he or she receives remuneration'.[140] This formula is also used in case law on the other provision of the Treaty containing a substantive social right, i.e. Article 157 TFEU on equal pay of men and women (Chapter 3, Section 3.4.1).[141]

An EU definition of worker was also given in respect of another type of Treaty provision, that on competition. In earlier case law,[142] the Court ruled that the EU competition rules do not extend to collective labour agreements made in order to improve the employment conditions of workers if they have been laid down in collective labour agreements made in negotiations between both sides of industry. In the *FNV Kiem* judgment,[143] the Court decided that persons who were considered self-employed in national law could be considered as workers, as long as they acted under the direction of their employer as regards, in particular, their freedom to choose the time, place and content of his work,

139 ECJ 2016, C-441/14 (*Dansk Industri*), §36, ECJ 2018, C-414/16 (*Egenberger*), §76 and ECJ 2018, C-570/16 (*Broßonn*), §85. See extensively on the horizontal effect of the Charter, Frantziou (2019), chap. 4.

140 ECJ 1986, 66/85 (*Lawrie-Blum*).

141 ECJ 2004, C-256/01 (*Allonby*).

142 ECJ 1999, C-67/96 (*Albany*), see Chapter 5.

143 ECJ 2014, C-413/13 (*FNV Kiem*), §36.

do not share in the employer's commercial risks, and, for the duration of that relationship, form an integral part of that employer's undertaking, thus forming an economic unit with that undertaking (see Chapters 5 and 9).

Directives with social provisions do not have the same definition, but show a large variety of approaches. One directive (Occupational Health and Safety Directive, Chapter 8) gives a definition of its own, others refer to national legislation for the meaning of the term worker or employee, and others give no such reference to national legislation.[144] This situation can give room to disparities of implementation in national law, although the Court has given a ruling that restricts the power of the Member States to exclude at their discretion certain categories from the benefit of the protection intended by the directive.[145]

Apart from legal uncertainty, an issue that is becoming more and more urgent is that several new types of working relationships are becoming more and more frequently used in the Member States, such as that of solo-entrepreneur, on call worker and platform worker, and it is not ensured that the protection of the directives extends to such workers who often have a position that is as economically dependent as that of workers.

As is pointed out by Risak and Dullinger (2018), although the broad definition in *Lawry-Blum* seems to give a broader protection than many national legislations and therefore is sometimes proposed as a possible solution to cover also the newer working relationships, the problem is that this definition still requires a supervisory relationship with another person and that is sometimes unclear or missing in those working relationships. The definition therefore includes all workers, no matter what their job may be, in the free movement provisions, but does not give protection to persons without a formal employer.[146] Solutions must therefore be found elsewhere, but where that may be is still unclear.[147]

---

144 Risak & Dullinger (2018), p. 23.

145 ECJ 2016, C-216/15 (*Betriebsrat der Ruhrlandklinik*).

146 Risak & Dullinger (2018), p. 18.

147 See, for an analysis and proposal, Risak & Dullinger (2018).

CHAPTER 2

FREE MOVEMENT OF (POSTED) WORKERS AND APPLICABLE LABOUR AND SOCIAL SECURITY LAW

Mijke Houwerzijl and Herwig Verschueren

2.1. INTRODUCTION

2.1.1. ESSENTIAL CORNERSTONE OF THE INTERNAL MARKET

Free cross-border labour mobility within the European Union is one of the most visible aspects of the European integration. Ever since the Rome Treaty of 1957 economic migration between the Member States has been one of the cornerstones of the process of economic integration through the internal market.[1] The original Article 48 EEC (now Article 45 TFEU) secured the freedom of movement for workers, which entails the right to move freely within the territory of the Member States for the purpose of employment, the right to stay and remain in the host Member State as well as the prohibition of any discrimination on grounds of nationality between the workers of the Member States in terms of employment, pay and working conditions.

Sixty years later, this Treaty provision is still essential to the European internal market. The right to move freely and to equal treatment were recently confirmed as being fundamental in Articles 15(3) and 21(2) of the Charter of Fundamental Rights of the EU. They have led to a process of Europeanisation of the labour markets of the different Member States. The free movement of workers is indeed 'a key element in the development of a genuine Union labour

1 To a certain extent, free labour mobility is a return to the past. Prior to the beginning of World War I in 1914, there were virtually no border controls or restrictions to labour mobility across Europe. From World War I on, crossing borders by foreigners began to be considered a security concern, and it was at this time that passports and visas were introduced in Europe.

market, allowing workers to move to areas where there are labour shortages or more employment opportunities, helping more people find posts which are better suited to their skills and overcoming bottlenecks in the labour market'.[2] Over the years, obstacles which hinder the mobility of EU workers have been considerably decreased in an effort to bring closer a single EU labour market, in the context of the EU 2020 targets of smart and inclusive growth.[3] Moreover, alternative ways to move have been developed, such as the so-called cross-border posting of workers and cross-border mobility of (posted) self-employed persons, covered by the freedom to provide services (Article 56 TFEU) and of establishment (Article 49 TFEU).

This chapter will address the various legal aspects of free labour mobility within the EU. Before doing so, it is apt to devote a few words to its societal impact and in particular to recent factual and political developments which have made free labour mobility within the EU a rather contested phenomenon.

2.1.2. FACTUAL AND POLITICAL DEVELOPMENT

Until the beginning of the twenty-first century, cross-border labour mobility within the EU used to consist of a comparatively small group of migrant workers, who made use of their right to free movement enshrined in Article 45 TFEU.[4] Facing the inflows of workers in recent years from new Member States (EU8[5] and EU2) into old Member States (EU15[6]), this image had to be revised. Despite the existence of transitional arrangements in most of the EU15,[7] demand factors, such as the demand for low-skilled and flexible labour, led to a steady increase of intra-EU labour mobility from new to old Member States.

---

2 Recital 2 of Directive 2014/54/EU (rights in the context of freedom of movement for workers).

3 Barslund, Busse & Schwarzwälder (2015), p. 2.

4 Due to a decline in economic motivations for movement, such as differences in wage levels, living standards and employment opportunities across EU Member States, the geographical mobility of EU citizens in the 1970s, 1980s and 1990s was lower than in the 1950s and 1960s. In 2002, only 600,000 people, or 0.4% of the total employed population, worked in a country other than their country of residence. However, cross-border commuting continued to grow. See *Report The Social Situation in the European Union 2002*, p. 23.

5 The EU8 States are the Czech Republic, Poland, Slovakia, Hungary, Estonia, Latvia, Lithuania and Slovenia; the EU2 States are Bulgaria and Romania. In 2013 Croatia joined the EU.

6 The EU15 are States that were EU members prior to 1 May 2004: Austria, Belgium, Denmark, Finland, France, Germany, Greece, Ireland, Italy, Luxembourg, the Netherlands, Portugal, Spain, Sweden and the United Kingdom.

7 Apart from Ireland, Sweden and the United Kingdom, all other EU15 States initially imposed transitional restrictions on the right to free movement of workers for citizens of the EU8. The citizens of the other two acceding States in May 2004 – Malta and Cyprus – were granted full free movement of workers because of the countries' small size and relative economic strength. For citizens of the EU2, transitional restrictions on the right to free movement of workers were imposed by all EU15 States, except Finland and Sweden.

Supply factors, such as the chance to improve living standards, were also strong drivers behind (the size of) this trend. The enlargement of the EU of 2004 was unprecedented in terms of the number of States and people joining the EU. The 12 Member States that joined the EU in 2004 and 2007 represented almost 21% of the EU27's population in 2007, some 103.3 million persons.[8] Compared with previous enlargements in the EU, there was also a larger gap than ever before in average wealth and minimum wage levels between new and old Member States.[9]

With regard to the freedom to provide services (Article 56 TFEU) and of establishment (Article 49 TFEU), no transitional arrangements were agreed upon in the Accession Treaties.[10] Therefore, cross-border mobility of self-employed persons and so-called posting of workers from new to old Member States seem to have been discovered as alternative ways to move to the desired destination.[11] After the Eastern enlargements in 2004 and 2007, the number of posted workers from acceding Member States to the old Member States grew considerably.[12] For example, following the most recent EU enlargement in 2013, 91% of Croatian posted workers went to the old Member States, mainly to Germany, Austria and Italy.[13] Notably, only a hard core of labour standards may apply mandatorily during the temporary posting in the host country.[14] Also, the posted worker stays insured under the social security schemes in the sending Member State.[15] It is reported that in certain sectors and Member States posted workers' wages can be up to 50% less than those of the locals, which undeniably distorts the smooth functioning of the single market. High demand

8 Eurostat, *Europe in figures: Eurostat Yearbook 2008*, p. 23.

9 At the accession date, the EU8 countries had attained only about one-third of average EU15 per capita income. Measured in euros, the ratio of the lowest minimum wage level (Bulgaria) to the highest minimum wage level (Luxembourg) was 1:13 in 2009. Measured in purchasing power this ratio dropped to 1:6. According to a press release of the European Commission in 2003, 'average GDP per head in the EU would fall by 13 per cent in EU25 or by 18 per cent in EU27' (see IP/03/265). Levels of unemployment also played a role; for instance, in some Polish regions the unemployment rate in 2004 was above 20% (Eurostat, *Regions: Statistical yearbook 2005* (Office for Official Publications of the European Communities, 2005), p. 68).

10 Austria and Germany, however, were entitled to impose transitional restrictions on EU8 nationals concerning the freedom to provide services in certain sectors because of the potential for serious labour market disturbances in sensitive sectors, such as construction and industrial cleaning.

11 Holland et al. (2011), pp. 33 and 34.

12 For example in Romania, the number of posted workers sent rose from 9,000 to 52,000 between 2007 and 2013. See De Wispelaere and Pacolet (2016).

13 Fihel et al. (2015), pp. 74–76.

14 Pursuant to Article 3 of the Posting of Workers Directive. For more details see Section 2.4.

15 Pursuant to Article 12 of Regulation 883/2004 (Coordination of social security Regulation). For more details, see Section 2.5, which deals with the issue of affiliation to a social security system in case of movement to another Member State. In principle, during the first 24 months of posting, the worker remains affiliated to the social security system of the Member State where the worker's employer normally carries out its activities.

for 'cheap labour' on the demand side, combined with abundant availability of workers willing to move on the supply side, seems to have encouraged the reliance on migration facilitators, ranging from bona fide temporary agencies and subcontractors to middlemen and gangmasters operating in the shadow economy. Clearly and despite their relatively low number, posted workers have become a symbol of 'social dumping', i.e. competition on labour costs across EU labour markets by 'regime competition'.[16]

The position of the United Kingdom in the controversies surrounding posting is a special one. Posting is a relatively unimportant phenomenon in the UK. In the UK, the discussions about the impact of increased migration and mobility from the new Member States focused on 'social welfare tourism'. The claim that played a role in the Brexit campaign was that the British social benefits system creates financial incentives to move to the UK rather than to France or Germany.[17] As was shown by the rise of populist parties in many Member States and which culminated in the UK with the referendum vote for Brexit, the factual increase in mobility of, in particular, 'low wage and flexible forms of labour' within the EU has tested and will continue to test solidarity and trust between Member States. While on the one hand stating firmly that 'freedom of movement is non-negotiable as long as one is Member of the EU or if Britain wants access to the single market',[18] the European Commission has also 'learnt from Britain's vote to leave the EU that many Europeans fear globalisation and want the EU to provide more social protection in the internal market'.[19] As one of the outcomes of this 'learning process', in 2016, the Commission launched a proposal to achieve a 'stronger framework for posting in the EU, contributing to a fairer and deeper Single Market'.[20] The aim was to make 'the free movement of people to be based on rules that are clear, fair for everybody and enforced on the ground'.[21]

---

16 Cremers, Dølvik & Bosch (2007), pp. 524–41. See on 'varieties of social dumping', Berntsen & Lillie (2015).

17 Gaffney (2014); Vandenbroucke (2016).

18 See speech Viviane Reding, cited by Kevin Doran, 'Commission warns Cameron: EU freedom of movement is non-negotiable', *Policy Review*, November 2013 <https://www.policyreview.co.uk/commission-warns-cameron-eu-freedom-of-movement-is-non-negotiable/> accessed 05.06.2019). More recently 'Donald Tusk: Freedom of movement is non-negotiable if Britain wants access to single market', *The Independent*, 5 July 2016 <www.independent.co.uk/news/uk/politics/donald-tusk-says-access-to-the-single-market-means-britain-must-accept-eu-four-freedoms-a7120191.html> accessed 05.06.2019.

19 EU Observer, 'Eastern EU states lose battle on workers' pay', Brussels, 20 July 2016 <https://euobserver.com/economic/134433> accessed 05.06.2019.

20 European Commission, *Revision of the Posting of workers directive-frequently asked questions*, 2016, Strasbourg <http://europa.eu/rapid/press-release_MEMO-16-467_en.htm> accessed 05.06.2019.

21 EU Observer, 'Eastern EU states lose battle on workers' pay', Brussels, 20 July 2016 <euobserver.com/economic/134433> accessed 05.06.2019.

2.1.3. OVERVIEW

Below, the various aspects of the legal framework for intra-EU labour mobility will be described and analysed. Each of the sections will analyse the applicable primary and secondary EU legislation and focus on the most relevant case law of the Court of Justice of the European Union on these matters. This case law is often a response to national measures breaching relevant EU law. Some sections will develop in more detail examples of such situations, and highlight a number of specific issues in some Member States (such as language requirements for accessing a job in Belgium). Where applicable, the sections will also examine some difficulties in the implementation and enforcement of the relevant provisions by referring to experiences in some Member States. The structure of the rest of this chapter is as follows.

Section 2.2 starts by discussing the rights of EU citizens to seek and take up employment in another Member State and for equal treatment with the workers of that State (material scope). These rights are laid down in Article 45 TFEU, and are further implemented in secondary law, more specifically in Regulation 1612/68,[22] which was replaced by Regulation 492/2011.[23] The examination of the material scope also includes the prohibition of obstacles to free movement and highlights the role of the recently adopted Directive 2014/54 on measures to facilitate the exercise of the rights on free movement for workers. Then, the focus switches to the personal scope of these provisions. Who is a 'worker' in the meaning of Article 45 TFEU and therefore may claim these rights? The final part of this section comments on the exceptions provided for in the Treaty provision on free movement for workers.

Section 2.3 deals with the specific status of workers temporarily posted by their employer established in one Member State to carry out work on behalf of this employer in another Member State. This situation is in the first place subject to the rules on the freedom to provide services across the border (Article 56 TFEU), which prohibit all restrictions to such freedom. A special directive on the posting of workers was adopted in 1996 to balance workers' protection, fair competition and the freedom to provide services.[24] In this section the employment rights of posted workers enshrined in the Posting of Workers Directive are examined, as well as the personal scope of this directive. Moreover, the sometimes unclear and controversial demarcation of a 'worker' within the meaning of Article 45 TFEU is discussed. Finally, the Posting of Workers Enforcement Directive,[25] and the Directive to revise the Posting of

22 Regulation 1612/68 (Freedom of movement within the Community).
23 Regulation 492/2011 (Freedom of movement for workers).
24 Directive 96/71/EC (Posting of Workers Directive).
25 Directive 2014/67/EU (Enforcement Directive).

Workers Directive are addressed.[26] The rights for migrant and posted workers in the framework of the free movement of workers and the freedom to provide services interact with the law applicable to the employment contract. The rules governing the determination of the applicable law were initially laid down in the Rome I Convention of 19 June 1980 (Rome I Convention),[27] which was replaced by the Rome I Regulation at the end of 2009.[28]

Section 2.4 analyses the meaning of these rules. They can lead to a situation in which labour performed in the territory of a Member State is not (or only partially) subject to the labour law of that Member State, but (also) to the labour law of another Member State.

In Section 2.5, an important element for guaranteeing the right to free movement for workers is addressed: the need to avoid a situation where workers would lose social security rights when looking for or accepting a job in another Member State. Such loss can be the consequence of the application of the Member State's social security systems and more specifically of their territorial scope and of waiting periods. Therefore the Union legislature set up an EU system of coordination of the national social security schemes. Until 1 May 2010 this coordination system was formalised by Regulation 1408/71[29] and Regulation 574/72,[30] and since then by Regulation 883/2004[31] and Regulation 987/2009.[32] This section provides an overview of the scope and general principles of the social security coordination system and analyses in more detail the rules on the determination of the applicable social security legislation in cross-border situations with special attention to the rules applicable to posted workers.

2.2. FREE MOVEMENT OF WORKERS

2.2.1. PROHIBITED DISCRIMINATION ON GROUNDS OF NATIONALITY AND OBSTACLES TO FREE MOVEMENT

2.2.1.1. Types of Barriers to Free Movement of Workers

EU citizens have the right to seek and take up employment in another Member State and for equal treatment compared to the workers of that State

26 Directive 2018/957 (Revised Posting of Workers Directive).

27 Rome Convention (Law applicable to contractual obligations).

28 Regulation 593/2008 (Law applicable to contractual obligations). This regulation applies to employment contracts concluded after 17 December 2009.

29 Regulation 1408/71 (Coordination Regulation).

30 Regulation 574/72 (Implementing Regulation of Regulation 1408/71).

31 Regulation 883/2004 (Coordination Regulation).

32 Regulation 987/2009 (Implementing Regulation of Regulation 883/2004).

(material scope). The equal treatment right is, in the first place, laid down in the directly[33] and horizontally[34] applicable Article 45 TFEU (primary law), and is further elaborated in secondary law, more specifically in Regulation 1612/68, which was replaced by Regulation 492/2011. Both for the applicability of Article 45 TFEU and of Regulation 492/2011, it is imperative that the facts are not limited to one Member State.

Three different (in principle) prohibited types of barriers to free movement of workers can be distinguished:

1. *Direct discrimination*: where a migrant worker is treated differently on the grounds of that worker's nationality, such as (a) through prescribing a special recruitment procedure for foreign nationals; (b) through limiting or restricting the advertising of vacancies in the press or any other medium; (c) through subjecting eligibility for employment to conditions of registration with employment offices or impeding recruitment of individual workers, where persons who do not reside in the territory of that State are concerned.[35] Only measures which expressly distinguish on grounds of nationality are considered directly discriminatory. As a rule, directly discriminating provisions can only be justified by invoking one of the Treaty derogations of public policy, public security, public health; or the public service exception (see Section 2.2.5). These limited grounds of exception to the non-discrimination rule apply also in the case of the non-discrimination provisions of the Regulations based on Article 45 (Regulation 492/2011).
2. *Indirect discrimination*: where an apparently neutral condition impacts disproportionately on migrant workers, for example a residence condition. Article 3(1)(b) Regulation 492/2011 explicitly prohibits provisions laid down by law, regulation or administrative action or administrative practices where, though applicable irrespective of nationality, their exclusive or principal aim or effect is to keep nationals of other Member States away from the employment offered or from social rights. The Court of Justice defined indirect discrimination very widely in the case *O'Flynn*, as any provision of national law 'intrinsically liable to affect migrant workers more than national workers and if there is a risk that it will place the former at a particular disadvantage'.[36] It is not necessary to show that an indirectly discriminatory provision actually has a detrimental effect on EU migrant workers. On the contrary, it suffices that the provision is

33 See inter alia ECJ 2004, C-138/02 (*Collins*) and ECJ 2014, C-507/12 (*Sant-Prix*).
34 ECJ 1995, C-415/93 (*Bosman*), §82 and ECJ 2010, C-325/08 (*Olympique Lyonnais*), §30.
35 Examples drawn from Article 3(2) Regulation 492/2011.
36 See ECJ 1996, C-237/94 (*O'Flynn*), §18.

liable to have such an effect. However, a provision that raises the suspicion of indirect discrimination is not always prohibited. Unlike the situation regarding directly discriminating provisions, justification of an indirectly discriminatory measure is not limited to express derogations, but can be justified by objective reasons unrelated to nationality. It is difficult to establish precisely when this is the case. However, in general the 'justification test' in the case law of the CJEU consists of the following three elements: (1) the measure at stake must have a legitimate aim; (2) the measure is appropriate to achieve that aim; (3) the measure does not go beyond what is necessary to achieve the legitimate objective pursued.

3. *Measures which 'hamper or render less attractive' the exercise of the right of free movement.* This concerns barriers to the free movement of workers which go beyond the mere prohibition of discrimination.[37] As the Court of Justice defined it in *Bosman*: 'Provisions which preclude or deter a national of a Member State from leaving his country of origin in order to exercise his right to freedom of movement constitute an obstacle to that freedom *even if they apply without regard to the nationality of the workers concerned*' (emphasis added).[38] In this case the Court had to assess whether rules laid down by sporting associations were in accordance with Article 45 TFEU. One of the rules at stake stipulated that a professional footballer who is a national of one Member State could not, on the expiry of his contract with a club, be employed by another club unless the latter club had paid to the former a transfer, training or development fee. The rules applied to all transfers regardless of whether the footballer moved clubs within the same Member State or between different Member States. The Court ruled that the transfer rules hindered market access for Bosman and therefore constituted an obstacle to freedom of movement for workers prohibited in principle by Article 45 TFEU. The crucial factor was the requirement to pay a transfer fee. This hindered Bosman from being able to obtain employment in another Member State. The Court followed similar lines of argumentation in two other sports cases.[39] Notably, in order to claim an obstacle it is sufficient to show that the rule might discourage the free movement of workers or might constitute a barrier to market access; no particular evidence is required. Nevertheless, in another case, *Graf*, the Court took the opportunity to limit its case law on non-discriminatory obstacles to free movement of workers to an extent. It ruled that not every rule which might potentially discourage movement is an obstacle caught by Article 45 TFEU. Rather, the rule needs to affect access to the employment

---

37 This approach was developed for other internal market freedoms as well, such as the freedoms of goods and services.

38 ECJ 1995, C-415/93 (*Bosman*).

39 ECJ 2000, C-176/96 (*Lehtonen*); ECJ 2010, C-325/08 (*Olympique Lyonnais*).

market in a way that is not too uncertain and indirect.[40] Hence, the provision at stake in that case was not deemed to form a restriction on the free movement of workers, because it did not substantially impede market access.

Notwithstanding the distinction in three types of barriers to free movement of workers explained above, it is often hard to identify, which of the elements plays the decisive role in judgments of the Court: notions of market access and discrimination are not always used clearly and in a consistent way. For instance, because the notion of 'a non-discriminatory obstacle' is broader than that of indirect discrimination, the distinction between the two notions is not always rigidly applied. In some cases, the reasoning of the Court is elusive and difficult to grasp.[41] Hence, what really seems to be important to the Court is whether the restrictive and/or discriminatory measure has an effect on intra-EU labour migration. If such an effect is found, the rule will have to be objectively justified.[42]

2.2.1.2. Horizontal Direct Effect

In *Walrave*, it became clear that according to the Court of Justice, the wording of Article 45 TFEU does not prevent the provisions being applied to associations which are governed by private law. It was argued that the cycling association in *Walrave* was assuming the same role as the state in its task of regulating working conditions. The principle of *effet utile* of Union law would be compromised if rules by private organisations fell outside these provisions. Union law must be applied in an equal manner and the fundamental free movement of workers cannot thus be dependent upon whether working conditions are regulated by law or by private agreements.[43] From a practical point of view, it has been submitted that the underlying reason for the Court of Justice to give horizontal effect to Article 45 and Article 56 TFEU was in

40 ECJ 2000, C-190/98 (*Graf*), §23. See also joined cases ECJ 2000, C-51/96 and 191/97 (*Deliège*). Once discrimination is established the '*Graf* doctrine' (effect of rule too remote and indirect) cannot be invoked: no matter how minimal the discrimination is, it always needs to be justified.

41 In ECJ 1995, C-415/93 (*Bosman*) another measure apart from the transfer rules was also at stake, namely the so-called '3 + 2 rule' enacted by the UEFA, under which football clubs in Belgium were only allowed to field a limited number of professional players were are nationals of other Member States. Here, the Court was not entirely clear as to whether 'pressing reasons of public interest' were considered as enshrined in Art. 45 TFEU or extraneous objective justifications in relation to the directly discriminatory 3+2 rule (§104). Moreover, the Court used both the tests on direct discrimination (§§104, 116–21) and restriction (§121), without a clear and consistent explanation.

42 Van Overmeiren et al. (2014), pp. 5 and 6.

43 ECJ 1974, C-36/74 (*Walrave*), §19 and ECJ 1995, C-415/93 (*Bosman*), §84.

the fact that 'much employment and provision of services takes place in the service sector. If these provisions would not be applied to private parties they would be deprived most of their practical meaning.'[44]

2.2.1.3. Language Requirements

For a number of jobs specific linguistic knowledge is required. Normally, such a requirement can be fulfilled more easily by native speakers, who are very often nationals of the Member State concerned. Therefore, such requirements may be seen as an indirect discrimination on grounds of nationality or as obstacles to the free movement for workers coming from another Member State. However, Article 3(1) final sentence of Regulation 492/2011 (as well as the same provision in Regulation 1612/68) permits such language requirements, provided they are required by reason of the nature of the post to be filled. This is explicitly confirmed by the Court of Justice in *Groener*.[45] In this case, a Dutch national was refused a permanent full post as a lecturer in art in Ireland because she could not prove sufficient knowledge of the Irish language. Despite the fact that her teaching was exclusively conducted in English, and therefore knowledge of Irish was not required for the performance of the duties which the teaching entails, the Court accepted this requirement provided that it was applied in a proportionate and non-discriminatory manner. The reason why the Court accepted such a requirement in this case was that the obligation imposed on lecturers in public vocational education schools to have a certain knowledge of the Irish language is one of the measures adopted by the Irish government to maintain and to promote the use of Irish as a means of expressing national identity and culture. The Court also recognised the importance of such a policy and the fact that teachers play an essential role in this through their participation in the daily life of the school. Considering those circumstances, the Court found that it is not unreasonable to require teachers to have some knowledge of the first national language even if this language is not the one in which the teaching is conducted.

In *Angonese*, the Court first of all answered (again) the essential question of whether what is now Article 45 TFEU can be invoked against private parties, in relation to certain administrative requirements on bilingualism laid down by a private bank in Bolzano, Cassa di Risparmio. Angonese was an Italian citizen but he had German as his mother tongue. Moreover he had studied in Austria between 1993 and 1997.[46] In 1997 Angonese responded to a notice in the local Italian newspaper in which he notified his intention to apply for a job at Cassa di Risparmio. In order to participate in the competition for the post at

44 See Quinn and McGowan (1987), p. 165.

45 ECJ 1989, C-379/87 (*Groener*).

46 ECJ 2000, C-281/98 (*Angonese*).

Cassa di Risparmio all applicants had to provide a certain certificate, the B-certificate (which was the only way that the applicants could prove their bilingualism in German and Italian). The certificate was issued by the public authorities after an examination which had to take place in Bolzano. According to the facts of the case, most citizens in the province of Bolzano had obtained this certificate. As Angonese could not provide this certificate, the Cassa di Risparmio sent him a letter informing him that he was not permitted to take part in the competition for the employment in the bank. In its judgment the Court pronounced in a decisive manner that Article 45 had horizontal direct effect, referring to its rulings in *Walrave* and *Bosman*.[47] Since working conditions in the different Member States are governed sometimes by provisions laid down by law or regulation and sometimes by agreements and other acts concluded or adopted by private persons, limiting application of the prohibition of discrimination based on nationality to acts of a public authority risks creating inequality in its application.[48] The Court also ruled that the fact that certain provisions of the Treaty are formally addressed to the Member States does not prevent rights from being conferred at the same time on any individual who has an interest in compliance with the obligations thus laid down.[49] Regarding the issue at stake, the Court of Justice found the requirement for the language certificate indirectly discriminatory and disproportionate: although demanding proof of a certain level of linguistic knowledge was deemed justified, the impossibility of showing this knowledge by any other means breached Article 45 TFEU.[50] More recently, the issue of language requirements in employment was brought back to the attention in a case regarding legislation in Flanders (which is a federated entity of Belgium). The legislation required all employers whose established place of business is located in Flanders to draft cross-border employment contracts exclusively in Dutch (the only official language in Flanders), failing which the contracts were to be declared null and void by the national courts of their own motion.[51] Only the Dutch version of the contract was considered authentic. The Court found this requirement as being capable of hindering or rendering less attractive the exercise of the right to free movement as workers by non-Dutch speaking EU nationals. Once again, however, the Court recognised that the objective of promoting and encouraging the use of Dutch, which is one of the official languages of Belgium, constitutes a legitimate interest which, in principle, justifies such a restriction. The Court referred in this respect to the fourth subparagraph of Article 3(3) TEU and Article 22 of the Charter of Fundamental Rights of the European Union, according to which the Union

47 See ECJ 1974, 36/74 (*Walrave*) and ECJ 1995, C-415/93 (*Bosman*), §83.

48 ECJ 1974, 36/74 (*Walrave*), §19 and ECJ 1995, C-415/93 (*Bosman*), §84.

49 Here, the Court referred to its judgment in the ECJ 1976, 43/75 (*Defrenne*), §31.

50 ECJ 2000, C-281/98 (*Angonese*), §44.

51 ECJ 2013, C-202/11 (*Las*).

must respect its rich cultural and linguistic diversity, as well as to Article 4(2) TEU, which says that the Union must also respect the national identity of its Member States. As far as the Court is concerned, this includes protection of the official language or languages of those States.[52] It also accepted that the objective of ensuring the protection of employees by enabling them to examine employment documents in their own language, as well as ensuring the efficacy of the checks and supervision of the employment inspectorate is an overriding reason in the general interest capable of justifying such restrictions. However, the Court stated that the requirement as laid down in the legislation of Flanders was not proportionate to those objectives, and more specifically the nullity of the employment contract as penalty for the breach of the obligation to draft this contract in Dutch was deemed to be disproportionate. The Court was of the opinion that parties to a cross-border employment contract do not necessarily have knowledge of the official language of the Member State concerned. In such a situation, the establishment of free and informed consent between the parties requires those parties to be able to draft their contract in a language other than the official language of that Member State. The Court suggested that it would be less prejudicial to the freedom of movement for workers if the legislation of a Member State would not only require the use of the official language of that Member State for cross-border employment contracts, but if it would also permit the drafting of an authentic version of such contracts in a language known to all parties concerned. This would not jeopardise the objectives pursued by that legislation.

Subsequent to this judgment the Flemish authorities adapted their legislation via the Decree of 14 March 2014. The new legislation confirms that an employment contract with an employer established in Flanders must be drafted in Dutch, but it also allows for a version in the official language of another EU Member State. The latter version will also be an authentic one. However, if the Dutch version differs from the version in the other language, the Dutch one takes precedence.[53]

2.2.2. EQUAL TREATMENT AS REGARDS EMPLOYMENT, WORKING CONDITIONS AND SOCIAL ADVANTAGES

2.2.2.1. Right to Equal Treatment Regarding Access to Employment

Articles 1–6 of Regulation 492/2011[54] provide that an EU citizen should have the same access to employment as a national of a Member State. By granting

[52] See also ECJ 2011, C-391/09 (*Runevič-Vardyn and Wardyn*).
[53] For more details, see Cuypers & Verschueren (2015), pp. 883–903.
[54] See Section 2.2.1 for an introduction to this regulation.

entitlement to EU nationals to access the labour markets of the other Member States these provisions are meant to be the main source (the 'cornerstone') of EU labour movement to another Member State. These provisions aim to remove any discrimination, whether direct or indirect. Moreover, as explained above, non-discriminatory measures which substantially impede access to employment also breach Article 45 TFEU, unless objectively justified.

2.2.2.2. *Right to Equal Treatment Regarding Terms and Conditions of Employment*

Pursuant to Article 7 of Regulation 492/2011, EU nationals who move as employees to another Member State are entitled to equal treatment with national workers as regards remuneration, dismissal, and other labour conditions in law, laid down in collective or individual agreement or any other collective regulation and, should they become unemployed, reinstatement or re-employment and access to training in vocational schools and retraining centres. This applies, however, only if it is to prepare the individual for a particular occupation and not simply for a person to improve their general knowledge.[55] Also, EU nationals are entitled to the same social and tax advantages as national workers (see Section 2.2.2.3). Equal treatment is also guaranteed regarding membership of trade unions (Article 8) and housing (Article 9) as well as regarding the migrant workers' children's access to education (Article 10 Regulation 492/2011, formerly Article 12 Regulation 1612/68). Workers moving under Article 45 TFEU will also be able to utilise the provisions on the aggregation and exportability of social security benefits under Regulation 883/2004 (see Section 2.5).

So, migrant and domestic workers must be treated equally in their access to the labour market, wages and other working and employment conditions. This primary principle of equal treatment and non-discrimination on grounds of nationality is however not only meant to entitle migrant workers to a decent employment protection but also to prevent unfair competition with domestic workers (often referred to as 'social dumping'). In 1974, the Court of Justice confirmed the double intention behind the equal treatment provision in the free movement of workers legislation.[56]

2.2.2.3. *Social Advantages*

Article 7(2) Regulation 492/2011 also prohibits discrimination on the ground of nationality for social and fiscal advantages (as did the same article of

---

55 ECJ 1988, 24/86 (*Blaizot*).

56 ECJ 1974, 67/73 (*French seamen*), §45.

Regulation 1612/68).[57] The notion of 'social advantage' is not further defined in these regulations. The Court of Justice held that this concept must not be interpreted restrictively and that these advantages are all those which, whether or not linked to an employment contract, are generally granted to national workers, primarily because of their objective status as workers or by virtue of the mere fact of their residence on the national territory.[58] It considered, inter alia, the following 'social advantages' to fall within this meaning: reduced public transport fares,[59] maintenance grants for students supported by a migrant worker,[60] social assistance,[61] funeral allowances,[62] pre-retirement benefits,[63] the tide-over allowance for young people seeking their first employment,[64] as well as social security benefits in general.[65] Conversely, the Court has accepted that an allowance granted to former prisoners of war and therefore paid as a quid pro quo for the service they rendered to their country, does not fall within the category of social advantages within the meaning of Article 7(2) of Regulation 1612/68 (now Regulation 492/2011).[66]

The social advantages in question may also be advantages granted to family members supported by the migrating worker, such as financial support for students[67] or housing assistance, even if the worker has left the host State.[68] It appears that the migrant worker's family are the indirect recipients of the equal treatment granted to the worker under Article 7(2) Regulation 492/2011. Since this constitutes a social advantage for the migrant worker, the worker's children may themselves rely on that provision in order to obtain directly such benefit.[69] In addition, the right to equal treatment for social advantages in the State where the migrant worker is employed benefits both migrant workers residing in the host State, and frontier workers (and their family members) employed in that State while residing in another Member State.[70]

57 This chapter does not deal with the Court's case law on the prohibition of discrimination regarding 'fiscal advantages'.

58 See inter alia ECJ 1979, 207/78 (*Even*) and ECJ 1985, 249/83 (*Hoeckx*).

59 ECJ 1975, 32/75 (*Cristini*).

60 See, inter alia, ECJ 1992, C-3/90 (*Bernini*); ECJ 1999, C-337/97 (*Meeusen*) and ECJ 2012, C-542/09 (*Commission v. Netherlands*), §34.

61 ECJ 1985, 249/83 (*Hoeckx*); ECJ 1987, 316/85 (*Lebon*) and ECJ 1986, 139/85 (*Kempf*).

62 ECJ 1996, C-237/94 (*O'Flynn*).

63 ECJ 1998, C-35/97 (*Commission v. France*).

64 ECJ 1996, C-278/94 (*Commission v. Belgium*).

65 ECJ 1993, C-310/91 (*Schmid*); ECJ 2001, C-43/99 (*Leclere*) and ECJ 2006, C-137/04 (*Rockler*).

66 ECJ 2004, C-386/02 (*Baldinger*).

67 ECJ 1987, 316/85 (*Lebon*); ECJ 1999, C-337/97 (*Meeusen*); ECJ 2012, C-542/09 (*Commission v. Netherlands*) and recently ECJ 2016, C-238/15 (*Brangaça Linares Verruga*), §39.

68 As in ECJ 2010, C-310/08 (*Ibrahim*).

69 ECJ 2013, C-20/12 (*Giersch*), §40; ECJ 2016, C-238/15 (*Brangaça Linares Verruga*), §40 and ECJ 2016, C-401/15 to C-403/15 (*Depesne and others*), §40.

70 ECJ 1997, C-57/96 (*Meints*), §50; ECJ 2013, C-20/12 (*Giersch*), §37 and ECJ 2016, C-238/15 (*Brangaça Linares Verruga*), §39.

It is clear that the Court of Justice has given considerable scope to the concept of social advantage by describing as such advantages that have no connection with a contract of employment. This scope comes from the fact that the Court considers as a social advantage any advantage that appears to be conducive to the mobility of workers within the Union or to the integration of EU workers in the host country.[71]

However, in more recent case law the Court of Justice seems to depart from the 'automatic' application of the equal treatment provisions concerning migrant workers' claims for social benefits. In *Geven*, the Court had to rule on the refusal of the competent German authorities to grant a child-raising allowance to a Dutch national who resided in the Netherlands and worked in Germany between 3 and 14 hours a week. The Court accepted the justification that the measure was intended to encourage the birth rate in Germany and that the benefit could be limited to migrant workers having a sufficient link with Germany. For the Court of Justice, the fact that a non-resident worker does not have a sufficiently substantial occupation in the Member State concerned may constitute a legitimate justification for refusing to grant the child-raising allowance.[72] More recently, as regards migrant workers as well as frontier workers, the Court confirmed that the fact that they have participated in the employment market of a Member State establishes, in principle, a sufficient link of integration with the society of that Member State, allowing them to benefit from the principle of equal treatment as regards social advantages. The link of integration arises from, inter alia, the fact that, through the taxes which workers pay in the host Member State by virtue of their employment, the migrant workers also contribute to the financing of the social policies of that State and should profit from them under the same conditions as national workers.[73] However, the Court also accepted that indirectly discriminatory national legislation restricting the grant to frontier workers of social advantages within the meaning of Article 7(2) Regulation 492/2011 where there is not a sufficient connection to the society in which they are pursuing their activities without residing there, may be objectively justified and proportionate to the objective pursued.[74] In the *Giersch* case, the Court of Justice suggested that Luxembourg could make the entitlement to a study loan or the non-reimbursement thereof

71 ECJ 1989, C-389/87 and C-390/87 (*Echternach and Moritz*), §35.

72 ECJ 2007, C-213/05 (*Geven*), §26. See also the reference to 'an occupation of more than minor extent' in ECJ 2007, C-212/05 (*Hartmann*), §35. For a critical comment, O'Leary (2008), pp. 167–93.

73 ECJ 2012, C-542/09 (*Commission v. Netherlands*), §§64–65; ECJ 2013, C-20/12 (*Giersch*), §63 and ECJ 2016, C-238/15 (*Brangaça Linares Verruga*), §§49–50.

74 See, to that effect, ECJ 2007, C-212/05 (*Hartmann*), §§30–35 and 37; ECJ 2007, C-213/05 (*Geven*), §26; ECJ 2013, C-20/12 (*Giersch*), §64 and ECJ 2016, C-238/15 (*Brangaça Linares Verruga*), §51.

subject to the condition that the student returns to that State after the studies. It also stated that in order to avoid the risk of 'study grant forum shopping', and in order to ensure that the frontier worker who is a taxpayer and who makes social security contributions in Luxembourg has a sufficient link with Luxembourg society, the financial aid could be made conditional on the frontier worker, i.e. the parent of the student who does not reside in Luxembourg, having worked in that Member State for a certain minimum period of time.[75]

These more recent rulings seem to indicate that migrant workers can no longer claim equal treatment for social advantages in all circumstances in the Member State where they work, in particular when they live in a different Member State (frontier workers). There should be a sufficient link with that Member State, and the nature of the benefit claimed should also be taken into account. In *Geven*, the right to a child-raising allowance was linked to the objective of encouraging the birth rate in the host Member State, and in *Giersch* the objective of the study grant was to raise the number of highly educated youngsters in Luxembourg, which would justify the exclusion of students not living in that State.

2.2.3. GUARANTEEING THE RIGHTS: THE 'FACILITATING' DIRECTIVE 2014/54

According to recital 6 of the Preamble of Regulation 492/2011: 'The right of freedom of movement, in order that it may be exercised, by objective standards, in freedom and dignity, requires that equality of treatment be ensured *in fact* and in law in respect of all matters relating to the actual pursuit of activities as employed persons' (emphasis added).

In order to effectively increase the adequate and effective application and enforcement of the rights of migrant workers and the members of their families, the EU legislature adopted Directive 2014/54 in 2014. This directive aims to ensure that Union workers and members of their family, as well as employers, public authorities, and other persons concerned, are better informed about free movement rights and responsibilities; to assist and protect Union workers and members of their family in the exercise of those rights; and to combat circumvention of those rules by public authorities and public and private employers. Pursuant to its Article 3, this directive obliges the Member States to guarantee real and effective judicial protection to migrant workers and the members of their family who have been subject to discrimination on the grounds of nationality, or to any unjustified restriction or obstacles to exercising their right to free movement.

[75] ECJ 2013, C-20/12 (*Giersch*), §§65–80 and ECJ 2016, C-238/15 (*Brangaça Linares Verruga*), §69.

In order to provide more effective levels of protection, associations and legal entities, including the social partners, should also be empowered to engage in proceedings, either on behalf of or in support of any alleged victim. In addition, Member States must designate one or more structures or bodies for the promotion, analysis, monitoring and support of the rights of Union workers and members of their family (Article 4). These bodies must be made competent, inter alia, to provide independent legal and/or other assistance to migrant workers; to conduct or commission independent surveys and analyses of the restrictions to the rights of migrant workers; to ensure publication of these reports and to make recommendations; as well as to publish relevant information on the application at national level of Union rules on the free movement of workers. The Member States must also provide, in more than one official EU language, information that is clear, free of charge, easily accessible, comprehensive and up-to-date on the rights of migrant workers (Article 6).

2.2.4. PERSONAL SCOPE OF THE FREE MOVEMENT OF WORKERS

2.2.4.1. EU Nationals in a Cross-Border Situation and their Family Members

The right to free movement as a worker depends on the worker possessing the nationality of a Member State.[76] On the basis of the Treaty establishing the European Economic Area,[77] the nationals of Norway, Iceland and Liechtenstein have the same rights as the nationals of the Member States. The same applies to the nationals of Switzerland, a country with which a separate agreement was concluded.[78] But other third country nationals cannot rely on the provisions concerning the free movement of workers to look for or take up employment in a Member State other than the one in which they reside or work.

However, members of the family of EU workers can indirectly benefit from certain rights stemming from EU free movement law, irrespective of their nationality.[79] First, they have the right to reside in the Member State in which

76 Article 1 Regulation 492/2011 explicitly refers to a 'national of a Member State'. See also as regards the personal scope of Article 45 TFEU, ECJ 1998, C-230/97 (*Awojemi*), §29. See also Article 3(1) of Directive 2004/38 (citizenship directive).

77 Agreement of 2 May 1992 on the European Economic Area, [1994] OJ L 1/ 3.

78 Agreement of 21 June 1999, [2002] OJ L 114/6.

79 Article 2(2) Directive 2004/38 defines who is to be considered as family member: the spouse; the partner with whom the Union citizen has contracted a registered partnership, on the basis of the legislation of a Member State, if the legislation of the host Member State treats registered partnerships as equivalent to marriage and in accordance with the conditions laid down in the relevant legislation of the host Member State; the direct descendants who are under the age of 21 or are dependants and those of the spouse or partner and the dependent

the EU migrant worker resides.[80] Next, they also have the right to take up employment or self-employment in that State.[81] In addition they can benefit from the right to equal treatment with nationals of the host State for all benefits within the scope of the Treaty.[82] The Court of Justice has also recognised their right to equal treatment for social advantages on the basis of Article 7 Regulation 492/2011.[83]

EU law on the free movement of workers only applies in situations with a cross-border element between Member States.[84] This covers the situation in which the worker moves physically to another Member State, but also the situation in which a workers lives in one Member State but works in another.[85] This means that the Treaty rules governing freedom of movement for persons – and the measures adopted to implement them – cannot be applied to activities which have no factor linking them with any of the situations governed by EU law and which are confined in all relevant respects within a single Member State.[86]

This may lead to what is called 'reverse discrimination', whereby EU law grants more rights to persons who can rely on EU law than to persons who find themselves in a purely internal situation and are, therefore, merely subject to the relevant domestic legislation. This can, for instance, have consequences for the right to family reunification, the conditions for which might be stricter in domestic law than in EU law. However, the Court emphasised that citizenship of the Union is not intended to extend the material scope of the Treaty to internal situations which have no link with EU law.[87]

Still, nationals of a Member State can in some circumstances invoke the right to free movement as workers against their own Member State when they are exercising or have exercised the right to free movement. Indeed, the home Member State is not permitted to create obstacles to the free movement by denying benefits or advantages because of the fact that the worker carries out

---

direct relatives in the ascending line and those of the spouse or partner. The Court of Justice confirmed that for the implementation of Regulation 492/2011 the concept of family member should be the same as the concept used in Directive 2004/38: ECJ 2016, C-401/15 to C-403/15 (*Depesne and others*).

80 Article 7(1)(d) Directive 2004/38.

81 Article 23 Directive 2004/38.

82 Article 24(1) Directive 2004/38.

83 See further on this case law, Section 2.2.2.

84 ECJ 1982, 35/82 and 36/82 (*Morson and Jhanjan*); ECJ 1997, C-64/96 and 65/96 (*Uekcer and Jacquet*) and ECJ 2008, C-212/06 (*Government of the French Community and Walloon Government*).

85 See for instance ECJ 2007, C-212/05 (*Hartmann*); ECJ 2007, C-213/05 (*Geven*) and ECJ 2014, C-457/12 (*S and G*).

86 ECJ 2008, C-212/06 (*Government of the French Community and Walloon Government*), §33.

87 ECJ 2008, C-212/06 (*Government of the French Community and Walloon Government*), §33; ECJ 2008, C-127/08 (*Metock*), §§76–77; ECJ 2010, C-245/09 (*Omalet*), §12 and ECJ 2011, C-434/09 (*McCarthy*), §45.

economic activities in another Member State.[88] Moreover, migrant workers who return to their State of origin after having worked in another Member State, can also rely on EU law *vis-à-vis* that own Member State, for instance in order to be joined by their spouse.[89]

2.2.4.2. Who is to be Considered as a 'Worker'?

In order to widely guarantee the right to free movement and to equal treatment, the Court of Justice has given a very broad interpretation to the concept of 'worker'. It is settled case law that within the meaning of Article 45 TFEU this concept has an autonomous meaning which is specific to EU law and must not be interpreted narrowly.[90] The main reason for the Court to adopt an autonomous meaning for the concept of 'worker' in EU law on the free movement of workers, is to prevent Member States from modifying the meaning of this concept and from eliminating at will the protection afforded by the Treaty to this category of persons.[91] Any person pursuing economic activities which are real and genuine, to the exclusion of activities on such a small scale as to be regarded as purely marginal and ancillary, must be regarded as a 'worker'.[92] The essential feature of an employment relationship is that, for a certain period, a person performs services for and under the direction of another person (subordination), in return for which that person receives remuneration.[93]

So the activity must be of an economic nature, which excludes purely marginal and ancillary activities or activities whose main purpose is not economic. The latter is for instance the case with regard to the composition of sport teams, in particular national teams, the formation of which is a matter of pure sporting interest and as such has nothing to do with an economic activity.[94]

The nature of the legal relationship between the employee and the employer, for instance public or private, is not decisive,[95] neither is the sector, for instance sports.[96] The origin of the funds from which the remuneration is paid or the limited amount of that remuneration also have no impact on a person's status as a 'worker'.[97] The fact that the income from employment is lower than the minimum required for subsistence does not prevent an employed person from

---

88 ECJ 1999, C-1895 (*Terhoeve*) and ECJ 2005, C-109/04 (*Kranemann*).

89 ECJ 1992, C-370/90 (*Singh*) and ECJ 2014, C-456/12 (*O and B*).

90 ECJ 1982, 53/81 (*Levin*) and ECJ 2013, C-46/12 (*L.N.*), §39.

91 ECJ 1964, 75/63 (*Hoekstra*).

92 ECJ 1982, 53/81 (*Levin*), §17 and ECJ 2013, C-46/12 (*L.N.*), §39.

93 ECJ 1986, 66/85 (*Lawrie-Blum*), §17 and ECJ 2014, C-270/13 (*Haralambidis*), §34.

94 ECJ 1974, 36/74 (*Walrave and Koch*), §8.

95 ECJ 2014, C-270/13 (*Haralambidis*), §40.

96 ECJ 1995, C-415/93 (*Bosman*) and ECJ 2010, C-325/08 (*Olympique Lyonnais*).

97 ECJ 1986, 66/85 (*Lawrie-Blum*), §21; ECJ 2013, C-46/12 (*L.N.*), §41 and ECJ 2015, C-316/13 (*Fenoll*), §34.

being regarded as a 'worker'.[98] Moreover, in the Court's view, the income can also consist of an indirect contribution, such as board and lodging.[99] Furthermore, regarding the duration of the activity pursued, the fact that the employment is of short duration does not exclude in itself this kind of employment from the scope of Article 45 TFEU.[100] In addition, the intention of the person involved had when that person entered a Member State, such as to follow a course of study, does not preclude that person from having the status of 'worker' within the meaning of Article 45 TFEU.[101]

Despite this abundant case law, it is not always easy to draw the line between 'work' that falls under these definitions and 'work' that does not.[102] The growing importance of non-standard work in the Member States as a result of the emergence of a-typical and hybrid working arrangements, has aggravated this issue.[103] How many hours a week does a person have to work for the employment to be considered as 'real and genuine' and not as 'purely marginal and ancillary'? In *Kempf*, the Court of Justice accepted 12 hours a week as sufficient; in *Megner and Scheffel* even 10 hours were accepted.[104] In *Genc*, the Court did not rule out that 5.5 hours a week may be considered as 'real and genuine', following an overall assessment of the employment relationship in question.[105] Students who work part-time,[106] trainees[107] or *au pairs*[108] could also be 'workers'. However, the low threshold that the Court applies may also include situations in which persons are very close to being economically inactive, as a result of which different rules on the right to reside and the right to equal treatment apply, leading to seemingly arbitrary outcomes.[109] Therefore, Member States may be tempted to apply a strict test and give a narrow interpretation to what is 'real and genuine' with a view to excluding certain migrants, such as part-time workers, from the 'worker' status and hence from the rights which this entails. By doing so, Member States also seek to protect themselves against claims to welfare benefits by migrant workers with limited participation in their economy, who try to obtain a sufficient level of income through these benefits.

---

98 ECJ 1982, 53/81 (*Levin*) and ECJ 1986, 139/85 (*Kempf*).

99 ECJ 1988, 196/87 (*Steymann*).

100 ECJ 1992, C-3/90 (*Bernini*), §16; ECJ 2003, C-413/01 (*Ninni-Orasche*), §25; ECJ 2005, C-109/04 (*Kranemann*), §13.

101 ECJ 2003, C-413/01 (*Ninni-Orasche*), §28 and ECJ 2013, C-46/12 (*L.N.*), §46.

102 See also O'Brien (2009), pp. 1107–41.

103 See on the growing importance of non-standard work in the Member States the different contributions in: Buelens & Pearson (2007) and Countouris (2007).

104 ECJ 1986, 139/85 (*Kempf*) and ECJ 1995, C-444/93 (*Megner & Scheffel*).

105 ECJ 2010, C-14/09 (*Genc*), §28.

106 ECJ 2013, C-46/12 (*L.N.*).

107 ECJ 1992, C-3/90 (*Bernini*), and ECJ 2005, C-109/04 (*Kranemann*).

108 ECJ 2008, C-294/06 (*Payir*).

109 Thym (2015), p. 43.

Questions were also raised concerning the nature of publicly subsidised work meant to promote the integration of the persons involved into society. Indeed, some Member States, e.g. Belgium, used the judgment in *Bettray*[110] as an argument (or pretext?) to exclude workers who were employed by public authorities in order to raise their chance of gaining access to the 'standard' labour market. Subsequently, because these persons were said to depend on social assistance, an expulsion measure was taken against them.[111] In *Bettray*, the Court refused to consider 'work merely as a means of rehabilitation and reintegration' as an economic activity since it was not 'employment under normal conditions'. Mr Bettray was a drug addict who was employed under the Dutch Social Employment Law. This law concerns employment with the purpose of enabling those persons, sooner or later, to recover their capacity to take up ordinary employment. This ruling could be understood because Mr Bettray's activities were 'merely' intended as a means of rehabilitation or reintegration and had very little or no economic value for the employer.[112] Indeed, later in *Birden* the Court held that its position in *Bettray* did not follow the general trend of the case law concerning the interpretation of the concept of 'worker' and that it could only be explained by the particular characteristics of that case.[113] In *Trojani* the Court added that Mr Bettray could not be qualified as a 'worker', because he was a person who was unable, by reason of circumstances related to his situation, to work under normal conditions.[114] The *Birden* case concerned a programme intended to provide paid employment, on a temporary basis, to recipients of social assistance in order to enable, in particular, unemployed persons with no entitlement to unemployment benefits to enter or re-enter the general labour market. For the Court, such a person must be regarded as a 'worker'. More recently, in its judgment of 26 March 2015 in *Fenoll* the Court explicitly confirmed that employment of severely disabled persons in a specialised centre for employment therapy could well be considered as not being purely marginal and ancillary and that such work could have some economic value, however limited it is.[115] Yet, the Court, in *Trojani* as well as in *Fenoll*, left it to the national courts to ascertain whether 'the services actually performed … are capable of being regarded as forming part of the normal labour market'. For that purpose, account may be taken of the

[110] ECJ 1989, C-344/87 (*Bettray*).

[111] Initially this was even confirmed by the Belgian judiciary, but subsequent to critical remarks of the European Commission both the competent authorities and the judiciary changed their position.

[112] Opinion of AG Geelhoed in ECJ 2004, C-456/02 (*Trojani*), §§33–34. See also Rogers, Scannell & Walsh (2012), p. 103.

[113] ECJ 1998, C-1/97 (*Birden*), §§30–31.

[114] ECJ 2004, C-456/02 (*Trojani*), §19.

[115] ECJ 2015, C-316/13 (*Fenoll*), §§38–40.

status and practices of the hostel, the content of the social reintegration programme, and the nature and details of performance of the services.[116]

Some new forms of labour and non-standard work could also run the risk of not being covered by the concept of 'worker'. This was illustrated by the *Raulin* case in 1992. In that case the Court had to decide on the question of whether a worker employed under a so-called 'on-call' contract (sometimes also called a 'zero-hours' contract) can be regarded as a worker. Such a contract is a means of recruiting workers in sectors where the volume of work is subject to seasonal or other variations. Under such a contract, no guarantee is given as to the hours to be worked and, often, the person involved works only a few days a week or a few hours a day. The employer is obliged to pay wages and grant social advantages only insofar as the worker has actually performed work. Such contracts normally mean that there is no obligation for employers to offer work, or for workers to accept it. The Court did not exclude that workers under such an 'on-call' contract could be regarded as migrant workers within the meaning of the Treaty. However, it also said that the national court may, when assessing the effective and genuine nature of the activity in question, take account of the irregular nature and limited duration of the services actually performed under a contract for occasional employment. The fact that the person concerned worked only a very limited number of hours in a labour relationship may be an indication that the activities exercised are purely marginal and ancillary.[117]

Remarkably, in its landmark ruling *Rush Portuguesa* of 1990, the Court established that Article 56 TFEU allows an EU-based service provider to move to another Member State with its own labour force, which the service provider brings from the State where they normally work, even if these workers do not have the right to move under Article 45 TFEU.[118] In later case law it was confirmed that the principle of freedom of movement for workers is not involved in the situation where posted workers return to their country of origin after the completion of their work without at any time having gained access to the labour market of the host Member State.[119] Thus the application of Article 45 TFEU as well as Regulation 1612/68 (now Regulation 492/2011) and of the prohibition of discrimination on grounds of nationality with regard to the pay and working conditions of Article 7 of these regulations was rendered inoperative. The European legislature (partially) filled in this gap by adopting the Posting of Workers Directive 96/71. In Section 2.3 the situation of the posted worker will be examined in more detail.

---

116 ECJ 2004, C-456/02 (*Trojani*), §24 and ECJ 2015, C-316/13 (*Fenoll*), §42.

117 ECJ 1992, C-357/89 (*Raulin*), §§11–14.

118 ECJ 1990, C-113/89 (*Rush Portuguesa*).

119 ECJ 1994, C-43/93 (*VanderElst*); ECJ 2001, C-49/98 et seq. (*Finalarte*); ECJ 2004, C-445/03 (*Commission v. Luxembourg*); ECJ 2006, C-244/04 (*Commission v. Germany*); ECJ 2006, C-168/04 (*Commission v. Austria*).

In contrast, jobseekers come within the scope of the EU provisions on the right of free movement for workers. Article 45(3) TFEU also entails a person's right to move to a Member State in order to seek employment there, as confirmed by the Court of Justice in *Antonissen* as early as 1991.[120] In this judgment the Court also held that after six months Member States may require proof that the person is continuing to seek employment and has genuine chances of being engaged.[121] This judgment was taken over in Directive 2004/38, which guarantees the right to reside as long as the first-time jobseekers produce evidence that 'they are continuing to seek employment and that they have a genuine chance of being engaged' (Article 14(4)(b)).

Moreover, in *Collins*, the Court not only held that nationals of a Member State seeking employment in another Member State fall within the scope of Article 39 EC (now Article 45 TFEU) on the right to free movement for workers and jobseekers, but also that, therefore, they have the right to equal treatment.[122] This right also applies to financial benefits intended to facilitate access to employment on the labour market of a Member State. The Court confirmed this approach in its subsequent case law.[123] However, this category of persons is excluded from the right to equal treatment for social assistance through Article 24(2) of Directive 2004/38.[124]

In certain circumstances EU citizens can retain, *vis-à-vis* the Member States in which the citizens concerned had previously exercised economic activities, their status as employee or self-employed person and the advantages linked to this status. This is confirmed in Article 7(3) Directive 2004/38, more specifically in the case where the Union citizen is temporarily unable to work as a result of illness or accident, or is in duly recorded involuntary unemployment or embarks on vocational training. In these circumstances the person concerned not only retains the right to reside in the host State, but also, on the basis of Article 24(1) of Directive 2004/38, can claim the same treatment as the nationals of this host country with regard to all kinds of social benefits, including study finance grants for persons undergoing vocational training. Their family members can also rely indirectly on that status of 'worker'.

Moreover, the Court has recently decided that the list in Article 7(3) of Directive 2004/38 containing the circumstances in which migrant workers who are no longer in an employment relationship may nevertheless continue

120 ECJ 1991, C-292/89 (*Antonissen*). See also Articles 1–6 of Regulation 492/2011.

121 ECJ 1991, C-292/89 (*Antonissen*), §21.

122 ECJ 2004, C-138/02 (*Collins*), §56. The Court came back from its previous case law in *Lebon*: ECJ 1987, C-318/85 (*Lebon*).

123 ECJ 2005, C-258/04 (*Ioannidis*); ECJ 2009, C-22/08 and C-23/08 (*Vatsouras and Koupatantze*), §§36–37 and ECJ 2012, C-367/11 (*Prete*), §25.

124 See on the concept of social assistance within the meaning of this provision: ECJ 2014, C-333/13 (*Dano*), §63 and ECJ 2015, C-67/14 (*Alimanovic*), §44.

to benefit from that status is not exhaustive. In *Saint-Prix*, the Court stated that a woman who gives up work or gives up seeking work because of the physical constraints of the late stages of pregnancy and the aftermath of childbirth retains the status of 'worker' within the meaning of Article 45 TFEU, provided she returns to work or finds a job within a reasonable period after the birth of the child.[125] The persons involved did not qualify for the retention of the status of worker under the circumstances covered by Article 7(3) of Directive 2004/38. This judgment is in line with the Court's previous case law, which stated that the concept of 'worker' must not be interpreted narrowly.

2.2.5 EXPRESS DEROGATIONS

2.2.5.1. General and Specific Derogations

Finally, Article 45 TFEU provides the Member States with so-called 'express powers' in order to prevent or restrict migrants from enjoying the right to free movement for workers in full. The express derogations laid down by the Treaty fall into two categories: general derogations (public policy, public security, and public health) laid down in Article 45(3) and a specific derogation (employment in the public service), laid down in Article 45(4). In accordance with the fundamental principle that exceptions to fundamental rights are to be narrowly construed, these limitations have been interpreted narrowly by the Court of Justice.[126]

2.2.5.2. The Public Service Exception

Article 45(4) TFEU makes a specific exception to the general right to free movement of workers for 'employment in the public service.' Potentially, this may affect many workers since the public sector accounts for around 20.3% (varying from 12% to 33.9%) of total employment in the Member States, including the fields of public health, education and research.[127]

---

125 ECJ 2014, C-507/12 (*Saint-Prix*).

126 ECJ 1977, 30/77 (*Bouchereau*); ECJ 1974, 152/73 (*Sotgiu*); ECJ 1980, 149/79 (*Commission v. Belgium*); ECJ 1986, 66/85 (*Lawrie Blum*).

127 There is strong fragmentation of the national public sectors: there are different levels of government (e.g. central government; regions; local authorities); different functions ascribed to the public administration and public enterprise; bodies which are formally separate from the state or the government, the so-called regulatory agencies; independent administrative authorities and executive agencies, as well as the traditional separation of ministries and government agencies according to policy specialisation. European Commission (2010), *Free movement of workers in the public sector*, SEC(2010)1609 final p. 3.

However, here again, the Court of Justice has stated that the meaning of the public service exception is determined by the Court, not by the Member States. A Member State cannot bring certain activities within the Treaty derogation simply by including them in the scope of the public service. The Court of Justice applies a functional concept and not an institutional concept which may be read from the wording of Article 45(4) TFEU. It ruled that the public service exception only covers restrictions of access to certain posts

> which involve direct or indirect participation in the exercise of powers conferred by public law and duties designed to safeguard the general interests of the State or of other public authorities. Such posts in fact presume on the part of those occupying them the existence of a special relationship of allegiance to the State and reciprocity of rights and duties which form the foundation of the bond of nationality.[128]

In subsequent case law, the Court has always confirmed this first interpretation and made it clear that the criteria are not alternative, but cumulative (exercising of powers conferred by public law *and* safeguarding general interests).[129] So, it is important to always bear in mind the purpose of the exception.

The definition of worker in the sense of Article 45 TFEU includes civil servants[130] and public sector employees with a work relationship under public law and public sector employees with a private law contract. As a matter of fact, the nature of the legal relationship between the employee and the employer is of no consequence in determining worker status.[131]

In 2001 the Court held that the exception of Article 45(4) TFEU cannot be applied to private security guards since they do not form part of the public service, whatever the duties of the employee.[132] However, in 2003 the Court gave an additional interpretation of the application of Article 45(4) TFEU to private sector posts to which the state assigns public authority functions. The judgments concern the posts of captain and chief mate on private sector ships flying the Member States' flags. According to the Court, a Member State may reserve those posts for its nationals only if the rights under powers conferred by public law

128 ECJ 1980, 149/79 (*Commission v. Belgium*).

129 From the *Sotgiu* judgment (ECJ 1974, 152/73) it could be concluded that in order to decide whether a nationality condition may be applied by a Member State for accessing employment in the public service, Article 45(4) TFEU needs to be applied in a post by post analysis, not to the public service considered as a whole.

130 ECJ 1994 C-71/93 (*Van Poucke*).

131 ECJ 1974, 152/73 (*Sotgiu*); these legal designations can be varied at the whim of national legislature and therefore cannot provide a criterion for interpretation appropriate to the requirements of Community law.

132 ECJ 2001, C-283/99 (*Commission v. Italy*).

on masters and chief mates are actually exercised on a regular basis and do not represent a very minor part of their activities.[133]

Clearly, the public service exception is of limited scope.[134] In a Communication of 2002, the Commission stated that the derogation in Article 45(4) TFEU as interpreted by the Court covers in particular specific functions of the state and similar bodies, carried out by the armed forces, the police and other forces for the maintenance of order, the judiciary, the tax authorities and the diplomatic corps. However, posts in these fields which do not fulfil the criteria, e.g. administrative tasks, technical consultation and maintenance, may not be restricted to nationals of the host Member State. Moreover, jobs such as postal or railway workers, plumbers, gardeners or electricians, teachers, nurses and civil researchers may not be reserved for nationals of the host Member State.[135]

It is crucial to note that Article 45(4) TFEU is not a requirement, but just a possibility to restrict some public service posts to nationals. Therefore, Member States are free to open up their public sectors at all levels as much as they wish in order to boost workers' mobility between Member States. Once a post is open to migrant workers (even if a Member State opens up a post which it could reserve to its nationals), no different treatment can be justified by invoking Article 45(4) TFEU.[136]

Notwithstanding this clear line in case law, in practice, according to a Commission report of 2010, there are still a number of issues surrounding employment in the public sector which may cause problems which do not occur in the same way in the private sector.[137] This includes tendencies in Member States to keep posts reserved for nationals through difficult recognition of foreign professional qualifications and of previous professional experience and seniority for access to posts and for determining working conditions; language requirements; inaccessible recruitment procedures; other issues like residence, status and coordination of social security schemes.[138]

Some Member States have tried to justify different treatment of non-nationals (such as taking only working periods with a national employer into account) by their intention to reward loyalty towards an employer. In *Köbler*, the Court of

133 ECJ 2003, C-405/01 (*Colegio de Oficiales de la Marina Mercante Española*) and ECJ 2003, C-47/02 (*Anker*).

134 ECJ 1974, 52/73 (*Sotgiu*); ECJ 1997, C-248/96 (*Grahame and Hollanders*); ECJ 2007, C-392/05 (*Alevizos*).

135 European Commission, *Free movement of workers – achieving the full benefits and potential* (COM(2002)694), p. 18 (<http://ec.europa.eu/social/main.jsp?catId=465&langId=en> accessed 05.06.2019), based on e.g. ECJ 1980, 149/79 (*Commission v. Belgium*).

136 ECJ 1974, 152/73 (*Sotgiu*), §4; ECJ 1986, C-307/84 (*Commission v. France*) §16; ECJ 1987, C-225/85, (*Commission v. Italy*), §§11–13; ECJ 2000, C-195/98 (*Österreichischer Gewerkschaftsbund*), §37.

137 SEC(2010)1609 final, *Free movement of workers in the public sector*, p. 3.

138 Ibid., p. 26 and p. 17.

Justice stated that 'it cannot be excluded that an objective of rewarding workers' loyalty to their employers ... constitutes a pressing public interest reason', which may lead to different treatment. However, the provisions judged so far are geared to mobility between different employers in the public sector of the Member States concerned rather than rewarding loyalty to one employer. For example, the provisions leading to entitlement to a 'special length-of-service' increment after 15 years of service at any Austrian university allow mobility of professors between the different universities without losing such increment.[139] The notion of loyalty used was therefore too broad to be accepted by the Court of Justice as a valid justification for different treatment.

2.2.6. THE RIGHT TO RESIDE

An essential element of the right to free movement for workers is the right to reside in the Member State where the worker is economically active. Article 45(3)(c) TFEU confirms that the right to free movement for workers entails the right to stay in a Member State for the purpose of employment. The right to reside is further laid down in detail in Directive 2004/38. In principle every EU citizen has a right to reside in another Member State for up to three months (Article 6). Article 7(1)(a) of this directive grants workers the right of residence for more than three months in the host Member State. The concept of 'worker' is not defined in this directive, but it is clear that the broad concept developed in the case law of the Court of Justice discussed above[140] should also be applied for the implementation of Directive 2004/38. So being a worker within the meaning of this concept is sufficient to obtain this right to reside in the host Member State.

Jobseekers also have the right to reside in the Member State which they have travelled to in order to find a job. Article 14(4) Directive 2004/38 provides that in no case expulsion measures may be taken against EU citizens (or their family members) if they entered the territory of the host State in order to seek employment. On the contrary, in that situation they retain the right to reside as long as they can provide evidence that they continue to seek employment and that they have a genuine chance of being employed.[141]

In addition, according to Article 7(3) Directive 2004/38 some categories of persons retain their status as a worker and the rights attached to it. This is the case when the EU citizen is temporarily unable to work as a result of illness or accident; when the EU citizen is in duly recorded involuntary unemployment

---

139 ECJ 2003, C-224/01 (*Köbler*), §§83–86.

140 See Section 2.2.4.

141 See already ECJ 1991, C-292/89 (*Antonissen*).

after having been employed for more than one year and has registered as a job-seeker with the relevant employment office; when the EU citizen is in duly recorded involuntary unemployment after completing a fixed-term employment contract of less than a year or after having become involuntarily unemployed during the first 12 months and has registered as a jobseeker with the relevant employment office;[142] or when the EU citizen embarks on vocational training.[143] This list is not limitative and other persons can also retain the status of 'worker' within the meaning of Article 45 TFEU, as was illustrated by the *Saint-Prix* case.[144]

Family members of the workers have the right to accompany or join them in the host State (Article 7(1)(d) Directive 2004/38). These family members are the spouse, the registered partner, children under 21 (or dependents of the worker or of the worker's spouse or partner) and the dependent parents (Article 2(2) Directive 2004/38). They also have the right to take up employment or self-employment in the host Member State (Article 23 Directive 2004/38). Article 12 guarantees, under certain conditions, the retention of the right of residence by these family members in the event of death or departure of the EU worker and Article 13 in the event of divorce, annulment of marriage or termination of registered partnership. On the basis of the case law of the Court of Justice these family members may also claim the right to reside in the Member State where the EU citizen worked before when they continue their education there,[145] or in the Member State where the worker resides while working in another Member State.[146]

Under this directive EU workers can also obtain the right of permanent residence, which gives the persons concerned an even better protection, more specifically against expulsion (see below). The usual way of acquiring this status is five years of legal residence in accordance with the provisions of Directive 2004/38 (Article 16).[147] But under some circumstances workers may enjoy this status before the completion of a period of five years of residence (Article 17). This is the case when, at the time they stop working, they have reached the

142 In this case, the status of worker shall be retained for no less than six months. The Court ruled that after this period of six months the former worker may still rely on (the above-mentioned) Article 14(4)(b) in order to retain the right to reside as a jobseeker in the host Member State: ECJ 2015, C-67/14 (*Alimanovic*).

143 Unless the person involved is involuntarily unemployed, the retention of the status of worker shall require the training to be related to the previous employment. This provision was inspired by the case law of the Court of Justice: see for instance ECJ 1988, 39/86 (*Lair*) and ECJ 2003, C-413/01 (*Ninni-Orache*).

144 See Section 2.2.4.

145 ECJ 2002, C-413/99 (*Baumbast*); ECJ 2010, C-310/08 (*Ibrahim*) and ECJ 2010, C-480/08 (*Teixeira*). According to this case law, the primary carers of these family members also maintain the right to reside.

146 ECJ 2014, C-457/12 (*S. and G.*).

147 ECJ 2011, C-424/10 and 425/10 (*Ziolkowski*).

retirement age or take early retirement provided that they have been working in the host Member State for at least the preceding 12 months and have resided there for more than three years. Workers can also acquire the right to permanent residence before the completion of the period of five years when they stop working as a result of permanent incapacity for work provided they have resided continuously in the host State for more than two years.

Expulsion measures may be taken against an EU migrant worker and the worker's family members under the strict conditions set out in Articles 27 to 33 of this directive. Such measures must be motivated on grounds of public policy, public security or public health.[148] However, these grounds may not be invoked for economic reasons, for instance if the person would be unemployed or if there is a high rate of unemployment in the host Member State.[149] In addition, the expulsion measures taken on these grounds must comply with the principle of proportionality and must be based exclusively on the personal conduct of the individual concerned, i.e. a type of conduct that represents a genuine, present and sufficiently serious threat affecting one or more of the fundamental interests of society. Moreover, before taking an expulsion decision on these grounds, the host Member State must take account of considerations such as the length of time the individual concerned has resided on its territory, the individual's age, state of health, family and economic situation, social and cultural integration into the host Member State and the extent of that person's links with the country of origin (Article 28(1)). Workers who have obtained the right of permanent residence may only be expelled for 'serious grounds of public policy or public security' (Article 28(1)).[150]

For the right to reside it remains of paramount importance for a person to be able to rely on the status of an economically active person, more specifically as a worker or as a member of the family of a worker. Indeed, for economically inactive EU citizens Article 14(1) states that they only have the right to three months' residence in the host Member State, as long as they do not become an unreasonable burden on the social assistance system of the host Member State. Moreover, the right of residence for more than three months and the retention of this right for economically inactive persons is conditional upon these citizens having sufficient resources for themselves and their family members so as not to become a burden on the social assistance system of the host Member State during their period of residence; they also have to have comprehensive sickness insurance in the host Member State (Article 7(1(b)) and Article 14(2)

148 This reflects Article 45(3) TFEU.

149 Guild, Peers & Tomkin (2014), p. 256.

150 For the implementation of these rules on expulsion see, inter alia, ECJ 2010, C-145/09 (*Tsakouridis*) and ECJ 2012, C-348/09 (*P.I.*).

Directive 2004/38).[151] However, Article 14(3) of this directive expressly provides that expulsion measures shall not be the automatic consequence of and EU citizen's recourse to the social assistance system of the host State.[152] It is only after five years of legal residence in the host Member State that a migrant EU citizen is granted the right to permanent residence that is no longer subject to any subsistence requirement (Article 16).

In addition, the Court of Justice found that economically inactive persons can only claim equal treatment with nationals of the host State in order to obtain social benefits if they have the right to reside there.[153] For economically inactive EU citizens this means that in the period before they have obtained a permanent right of residence, they may not become a burden on the social assistance system of the host State. Claiming social assistance, which would be considered as an unreasonable burden on the system of the host State, would jeopardise that person's right of residence in that State and therefore the entitlement to social benefits, including the social assistance benefit claimed.

The Court confirmed that those conditions are intended to prevent economically inactive EU citizens from becoming an unreasonable burden on the social assistance system of the host Member State[154] and that these provisions are based on the idea that the exercise of the right of residence for economically inactive persons can be subordinated to legitimate concerns of the Member States, such as the protection of their public finances.[155] However, it remains unclear when exactly the Member States could reach the conclusion that the burden put on their social assistance system by the EU citizen concerned is 'unreasonable' and what elements could play a role in this respect.[156]

Clearly, it continues to be important for an EU citizen's right of residence in a host Member State for that individual to be qualified either as an economically active person, more specifically as a worker, as a person who retains that status or as a member of the family of such a person.

---

151 See ECJ 2011, C-424/10 and C-425/10 (*Ziolkowski and Szeja*), §§39–41 and ECJ 2014, C-333/13 (*Dano*), §§70–73.

152 Recital 16 states on this point that 'the host Member State should examine whether it is a case of temporary difficulties and take into account the duration of residence, the personal circumstances and the amount of aid granted in order to consider whether the beneficiary has become an unreasonable burden on its social assistance system and to proceed to his expulsion'.

153 ECJ 2016, C-308/14 (*Commission v. United Kingdom*). For a comment on this judgment see Verschueren (2017).

154 ECJ 2011, C-424/10 and C-425/10 (*Ziolkowski and Szeja*), §40; ECJ 2014, C-333/13 (*Dano*), §74, and ECJ 2015, C-67/14 (*Alimanovic*), §50.

155 ECJ 2013, C-140/12 (*Brey*), §§54 and 72, and ECJ 2014, C-333/13 (*Dano*), §76.

156 Verschueren (2017), pp. 78–81.

2.3. POSTING OF WORKERS IN THE FRAMEWORK OF THE FREEDOM TO PROVIDE SERVICES

2.3.1. EVOLUTION AND LEGAL BASIS

2.3.1.1. Situation before the Adoption of the Posting of Workers Directive

As explained above, if EU nationals qualify as employees in the meaning of Article 45 TFEU, they may freely move to another Member State for work. Similarly, a company (legal person) or a self-employed person, qualifying as a service provider in the meaning of Article 56 TFEU, may freely provide services in another Member State, albeit on a temporary basis.[157] From the very beginning of the establishment of a 'common market', it was acknowledged that the law on the free provision of services may interfere with the law on the free movement of workers.[158] This was foreseen, in particular, in situations where an *employer* exercises the right to provide a cross-border service. Provision of services often involves employees who temporarily move across a border to carry out the tasks. Therefore, cross-border provision of services often means that the service provider may want to post employees temporarily to the Member State where the service is provided (the 'host Member State'). As early judgments of the Court of Justice in the cases *Manpower* and *Van der Vecht*[159] show, employee posting was already a phenomenon in the late 1960s and early 1970s. Traditionally, only 'key personnel' like managers, professionals and specialist technicians were posted, but due to a 'Europeanisation' of competition law and public procurement law, from the late 1980s onwards it became popular to post workers in the construction sector. The gradually increasing phenomenon of posting from 'low wage' Member States to 'higher wage' Member States in the 1990s, fuelled concerns about 'social dumping'.[160]

Originally, secondary legislation based on the freedom to provide services, used to include in a recital the following standard sentence, referring to the free movement of workers: 'Whereas the position of paid employees accompanying a person providing services or acting on his behalf will be governed by the provisions laid down in pursuance of Articles 48 and 49 of the Treaty (now Articles 45 and 46 TFEU).'[161] However, in its landmark judgment in the case

157 If companies or self-employed persons want to carry out services on a structural basis, they may use their freedom of establishment, enshrined in Article 49 TFEU.

158 See Vignes (1961), pp. 674 and 675; Everling (1963), pp. 72 and 73.

159 ECJ 1967, C-19/67 (*Van der Vecht*) and ECJ 1970, C-35/70 (*Manpower*).

160 See Köbele & Cremers (1994).

161 Cited from old Council Directive 64/429/EEC (now repealed) concerning the attainment of freedom of establishment and freedom to provide services in respect of activities of self-employed persons in manufacturing and processing industries falling within ISIC Major

Rush Portuguesa of 1990, briefly discussed above in Section 2.2.4, the Court of Justice ruled that the situation of employees travelling with their employer to another Member State in order to carry out works on a temporary basis would fall under the scope of free movement of services. The Court stated that 'an undertaking established in one Member State providing services in the construction and public works sector in another Member State may move with its own work-force which it brings from its own Member State for the duration of the work in question'.[162] This case postdated the accession of Portugal to the EU. Under the transitional provisions of the Accession Treaty with Portugal, the provisions of free movement of workers did not apply to the Portuguese staff (therefore they were seen as third-country nationals for whom work permits were required). Meanwhile, the other freedoms, among which was the free movement of services, could already be invoked by firms or persons from the new Member State. Rush Portuguesa, a Portuguese undertaking, had won a contract in France and carried out the work with its 58 Portuguese workers. After inspection of the building site, the French immigration authorities notified Rush Portuguesa of a decision to pay a (huge) fine for employing foreign workers in breach of the provisions of the French Labour Code. In proceedings for annulment of the decision of the French authorities, the undertaking argued that it was not the provisions of free movement of workers, but those of free movement of services that applied, and therefore its workers could not be hindered or prohibited from working in France. In answer to the preliminary questions of the referring judge, the Court of Justice decided not to apply the provisions of free movement of workers to posted workers, with the key argument that they would 'return to their country of origin after the completion of their work without at any time gaining access to the labour market of the host Member State'.[163]

Cleary, the context of the post-accession transition provisions played a major role in the *Rush Portuguesa* judgment. Under the transitional regime, the only way to bring the posted workers under the scope of EU law was to relocate them to the field of free movement of services. Hence, the revolutionary aspect of the ruling was that EU nationals from new Member States and third country nationals who did not (yet) have the right to freely move to another EU country to work without a work permit, acquired a right to movement derived from their EU-based employer, albeit a 'passive' one.[164] With regard to

---

Groups 23–40 (Industry and small craft industries). For an overview of the other Directives that contain this sentence, see Houwerzijl (2005), p. 35.

162 ECJ 1990, C-113/89 (*Rush Portuguesa*), §§17 and 19.

163 §15.

164 In this chapter, the position of third country national workers will not be dealt with in further detail.

the terms and conditions of employment of the posted worker, the Court stated that 'Community Law does not preclude Member States from extending their legislation, or collective labour agreements, to any person who is employed, even temporarily, within their territory, no matter in which country the employer is established'.[165] This consideration was apparently added to comfort France and possibly other host States that admission under the free movement of services would not lead to a massive influx of workers under the guise of service provision, nor create social dumping.[166] However, this consideration does not imply that posted workers have a *right* to equal treatment, only that Member States *may* extend domestic labour law provisions to them.[167]

The said considerations evolved in two – separate – lines of case law:

1. The first line of case law, building on §15 of *Rush Portuguesa*, concerns unjustified restrictions (administrative burdens) on the freedom of a service provider established in a Member State to post workers possessing the nationality of a non-Member State (third-country nationality) to another Member State. In this regard, the Court ruled that the authorities of the host State may not impose conditions relating to obtaining work permits, since posted workers who are 'lawfully and habitually'[168] employed by the service provider and only temporarily in the host country for the duration of the service are not deemed to enter the labour market of that State. A duty to notify the presence of a posted worker to the host State authorities was allowed, under certain conditions.[169] This line of case law was not influenced by the adoption and consequent implementation of the Posting

165 ECJ 1990, C-113/89 (*Rush Portuguesa*), §18, with reference to Joined Cases ECJ 1982, C-62/81 and C-63/81 (*Seco SA and Another v. EVI*) and confirmed subsequently, albeit amended with the crucial restriction to minimum wages, by ECJ 1994, C-43/93 (*Vander Elst*), ECJ 1996, C-272/94 (*Guiot*), ECJ 1999, C-369/96 and C-376/96 (*Arblade and Leloup*), ECJ 2001, C-165/98 (*Mazzoleni*), ECJ 2001, C-49/98 (*Finalarte*), ECJ 2002, C-164/99 (*Portugaia*).

166 See Gormley (1992), pp. 63 and 66.

167 See also Evju (2010), pp. 151 and 164.

168 ECJ 1994, C-43/93 (*Vander Elst*), §26. It must be observed that the Court did not couple the concept of 'lawful and habitual employment' of a non-Member State employee with a requirement of residence or employment for a certain period in the State of establishment of the service provider (ECJ 2006, C-244/04 (*Commission v. Germany*), §55; ECJ 2006, C-168/04 (*Commission v. Austria*), §51). The 12 months being imposed by Austria was considered disproportionate.

169 See ECJ 1994, C-43/93 (*Vander Elst*); ECJ 2006, C-244/04 (*Commission v. Germany*); ECJ 2004, C-445/03 (*Commission v. Luxemburg*); ECJ 2006, C-168/04 (*Commission v. Austria*). In ECJ 2014, C-91/13 (*Essent*) the Court made clear that all types of services are allowed, including a service consisting of the posting of employees within the meaning of Directive 96/71/EC, Article 1(3)(c). Therefore, the exclusion of workers of temporary agency firms, as stipulated in case ECJ 2011, C-307/09 (*Vicoplus*), referring back to §16 of *Rush Portuguesa*, only applies to workers in newly acceded Member States during the so-called transition period.

of Workers Directive, as the directive does not regulate access to the labour market of (third country national) posted workers but only coordinates which hard core of mandatory host State labour standards should be applicable to workers.

2. The second line of case law, building on §18 of *Rush Portuguesa*, concerns the wages and other working conditions of posted workers. Many aspects were touched on, but the main approach in these judgments starts with a comparison of labour law protection in the host State and that in the State where the posted worker allegedly is normally employed. If the protection is the same or 'in essence' the same, the labour standards of the latter State have priority. A precondition for the application of host State law is that it offers the posted worker a genuine and effective social advantage and that it does not disproportionally restrict the free movement of services.[170]

2.3.1.2. *Birth of the Posting of Workers Directive (PWD)*

In 1991, in the context of the Delors' project 'Europe 1992', an official proposal was launched for a Directive on the Posting of Workers, which gave rise to fierce debates in European Parliament and Council.[171] It was only after a six-year process of negotiations, deadlock and amended proposals that the Posted Workers Directive (Directive 96/71/EC, adopted on 16 December 1996) was finally adopted. The debates focused in particular on the extent to which Member States must be allowed, or should be required, to apply their mandatory wage provisions and other working conditions to workers posted to their territory. Another issue concerned the legal basis of the directive, which was found in the Treaty provisions establishing the freedom to provide services. This was legitimised by the argument that in order to promote a true single services market, a framework of rules for posted workers would have to be created in order to avoid unfair competition. The ruling in *Rush Portuguesa* paved the way for the said legal basis.[172] From a political point of view, the undoubted merit of

[170] See ECJ 2002, C-164/99 (*Portugaia*); ECJ 2001, C-165/98 (*Mazzoleni*); ECJ 2001, C-49/98 (*Finalarte*); ECJ 1999, C-369/96 and C-376/96 (*Arblade*); ECJ 1996, C-272/94 (*Guiot*). In all these rulings the facts of the case date from the period while the Posting of Workers Directive has not been adopted or was still subject to implementation and thus not (fully) applicable.

[171] See e.g. [1995] OJ 15, C 166/123.6.95, no. 4-464/204 and no. 4-464/206. The first documents on what would become the Posting of Workers Directive referred to the Community Charter for social fundamental rights of workers, see COM(89)568. See, for an extensive historical account, Houwerzijl (2005), p. 85. Also see Cremers, Dølvik & Bosch (2007), pp. 524–41; Evju (2010), p. 160. An overview of literature on the Posting of Workers Directive is provided by Kall & Lillie (2017).

[172] See Zahn (2017), p. 5. See also Houwerzijl (2005) and (2014). While Evju traces a much longer and more complex background to the Directive, he considers the decision in *Rush Portuguesa* a 'booster' for the Posting of Workers Directive (Evju (2010), p. 154).

grounding the Posted Posting of Workers Directive on the freedom to provide services is that it facilitated a qualified majority vote. Without this, the proposal for a Posting of Workers Directive would probably have become stranded.[173] Still, from a legal point of view, the disadvantage of the choice of (only) this legal base is that it suggests that the Posting of Workers Directive is purely intended to facilitate the cross-border provision of services. That it also serves to protect employees and to create a level playing field (and no unfair competition) is by no means evident from its legal base.

The Posting of Workers Directive aims to reconcile the exercise of companies' fundamental freedom to provide cross-border services under Article 56 TFEU (formerly Article 49 EC), on the one hand, with the need to ensure a climate of fair competition and respect for the rights of workers (recital 5).[174] In order to achieve these aims, it identifies which national mandatory rules of labour law in the host State must be guaranteed to posted workers (see Section 2.3.2).[175] The Posting of Workers Directive consists of nine provisions that can be divided into four categories:

- personal scope and definitions (Articles 1 and 2);[176]
- material scope: terms and conditions of employment for posted workers (Article 3);[177]
- measures to ensure information about and compliance with the directive (Articles 4, 5 and 6);[178] and
- 'organisational' and technical details (Articles 7, 8 and 9) that need no further explanation.

Notably, the position of posted workers is characterised by the fact that they maintain their employment relationship with their own employer, established

173 See regarding the political circumstances of the early 1990s (in which the British Conservative Government tried to veto almost everything that had to do with social policy), which influenced the political fate of the Posting of Workers Directive, (Biagi (1997), p. 175).

174 In the explanatory memorandum launching the proposal for a Posting of Workers Directive, the objectives were formulated as follows: 'To increase legal certainty, to ascertain in advance the working conditions applicable and to eradicate practices which may be both detrimental to a fair competition between undertakings and prejudicial to the interests of the workers concerned, a coordination of the law of the Member States is needed.' (COM(91)230, point 3).

175 According to the Preamble of the Posting of Workers Directive (recitals 7–11), the directive makes the optional character of Article 7 Rome I Convention (now Article 9 Rome I Regulation) obligatory, by defining those subjects of employment law in which the national mandatory rules must be seen as 'overriding mandatory provisions'.

176 See Section 2.3.3.

177 See Section 2.3.2.

178 These provisions were elaborated upon in the Enforcement Directive 2014/67. See Section 2.3.4.

in another Member State, during the posting in the host Member State. As a rule, the employment contracts of posted workers are governed by the law of their habitual country of work instead of that of the host country. This contractual perspective reveals an important aspect of the legal position of the posted worker: the employment contract of a posted worker is typically influenced by more than one legal system, as the employment contract is concluded in one Member State (home State) and the performance of the service takes place in another Member State (host State). The interface with private international law is discussed more in detail in Section 2.4.

2.3.2. THE MATERIAL SCOPE OF THE POSTING OF WORKERS DIRECTIVE

2.3.2.1. Hard Core of Host State Labour Standards

Pursuant to Article 3(1) Posting of Workers Directive, Member States are to ensure that undertakings falling within the scope of the directive guarantee workers posted to their territory a 'hard core' of host State labour standards. This concerns rules with a mandatory character, on the duration of the work, rest periods and holidays, minimum rates of pay, health, safety and hygiene at work, the conditions of hiring-out of workers, protective measures for pregnant women, for women who recently gave birth, for young people and children, and equality of treatment between men and women. Hence, Article 3 Posting of Workers Directive determines the nature of the labour standards that the Member States must apply, but does not cover the substance of these standards.

The 'hard core' labour standards must be laid down either by law and/or by collective agreements or arbitration awards which have been declared universally acceptable in the case of activities in the building work sector (referred to in the annex), while Member States are left the choice of imposing such rules laid down by collective agreements in the case of activities other than building work (according to Article 3(10), second indent). Article 3(8) allows Member States without a system for declaring collective agreements universally applicable to apply generally applicable agreements or agreements concluded by the most representative organisations, under the conditions mentioned therein. This provision was included in the directive inter alia to allay Denmark's fears that the directive would not be able to accommodate Denmark's autonomous system of standard setting.[179] Member States may also, in compliance with the Treaty,

179 See Ahlberg (2013), p. 302.

impose the application of terms and conditions of employment on matters other than those referred to in the directive in the case of public policy provisions (according to Article 3(10), first indent).[180] This was part of the delicate political compromise needed to get the directive adopted.

However, this material scope of the directive was subject to a strict interpretation by the Court of Justice in the triptych *Laval*, *Commission v. Luxemburg* and *Rüffert* cases.[181] In this case law it became clear that the directive imposes not only a 'floor', but also a 'ceiling' with regard to the application of host State law in the context of intra-EU provision of services.[182]

With regard to Article 3(10) first indent of the directive, allowing host Member States to add public policy provisions on other subjects than those explicitly listed in Article 3(1) Posting of Workers Directive, the Court choose a restrictive interpretation of this provision in *Commission v. Luxembourg*. Here, the margin of appreciation of Member States in defining what is to be understood under public policy was curbed. The Court pointed out that the concept of public policy, first, comes into play where a genuine and sufficiently serious threat affects one of the fundamental interests of society and, second, since it is a justification for a derogation from a fundamental principle of the Treaty, that it must be narrowly construed.[183]

In *Laval*, the main focus of the Court's judgment was whether the collective action in the form of a blockade by Swedish trade unions was compatible with the EU rules on the freedom to provide services (Article 56 TFEU). More specifically, the setting of Swedish minimum wages (and other work-related benefits) for posted workers of a Latvian firm by 'imposing' collective bargaining with Swedish trade unions was cast into doubt. The relevant collective agreement in this case provided for more favourable conditions than those envisaged by the directive. The Court, therefore, considered whether the collective action taken was justifiable in light of its objective, namely, to force a cross-border service provider to grant more favourable conditions to its workers than those prescribed by the directive.

In its ruling, the Court did not accept the method of implementation of the directive in Sweden, where the applicable rates of pay were negotiated on a case by case basis through the social partners without being supplemented by

180 See for further details the Communication of the Commission on the implementation of Directive 96/71/EC, COM(2003)458 final.

181 ECJ 2007, C-341/05 (*Laval*); ECJ 2008, C-346/06 (*Rüffert*); ECJ 2008, C-319/06 (*Commission v. Luxembourg*). These judgments, together with ECJ 2007, C-438/05 (*Viking*), gave rise to numerous conferences of scholars and policymakers and led to a 'tsunami' of (working) papers and articles in academic journals. See also many ETUC press releases and reports on the aftermath of this case law.

182 Barnard (2009a); Verschueren (2008).

183 ECJ 2008, C-319/06 (*Commission v. Luxembourg*), §50 and also ECJ 2000, C-355/98 (*Commission v. Belgium*), §28; ECJ 2007, C-465/05 (*Commission v. Italy*), §49.

legislation providing for universal applicability: it concluded that this leads to a climate of unfair competition between national and posting service providers.[184] The Court also deemed it problematic that Sweden had not explicitly based its implementation on Article 3(8) of the directive. According to the Court, the Swedish system made it 'excessively difficult in practice' for the posting undertaking 'to determine the obligations with which it is required to comply as regards minimum pay'.[185] Clearly, the Court put great weight on transparency, which entails that the employer should be able to discover in advance what its obligations are with respect to collective agreements (probably even before tendering for the contract). This rules out bargaining at company level, as is/was usual with regard to wages in Denmark and Sweden. Furthermore, the Court pointed out that the directive does not allow the host State to make the provision of services on its territory conditional on the observance of terms and conditions of employment which go beyond the mandatory rules for minimum protection, as laid down in Article 3(1).[186] The *Laval* judgment has been heavily criticised for its potential to limit trade unions' rights to take collective action[187] and for its failure to take into account the successful and flexible system of collective bargaining prevalent in Sweden.[188]

The *Rüffert* case concerned a German company which won a tender with the German state of Lower Saxony concerning construction work at a prison. According to the law on public procurement in Lower Saxony the contractor had to pay at least the remuneration prescribed by the collective agreement in the place where those services are performed. Such a 'social clause' was included in the contract with the German company. The German main contractor subcontracted work to a Polish service provider and the Polish workers were paid lower wages than prescribed by the relevant collective agreement. When Lower Saxony discovered that the German main contractor had not complied

184 ECJ 2007, C-341/05 (*Laval*), §§71 and 80–81.

185 ECJ 2007, C-341/05 (*Laval*), §110.

186 ECJ 2007, C-341/05 (*Laval*), §80.

187 Both in *Viking* and *Laval*, the Court balanced the fundamental social right to collective action and collective bargaining against the fundamental internal market freedoms of establishment and to provide services. The outcome in both judgments was that 'the fundamental social right at stake had to bend the knee to the freedoms of the internal market', Rocca (2012), pp. 28–29.

188 Malmberg & Sigeman (2008), Woolfson et al. (2014) argue the *Laval* judgment has re-defined the 'Swedish model' of industrial relations and diminished Swedish unions' capacity to defend local labour standards, especially in low-skill and low-wage occupations. After the amendments, the Swedish Posting of Workers Act stated that unions are subject to more restrictive regulations if they wish to take collective action with the aim of regulating posted workers' employment conditions (Rönnmar (2010b)). As a consequence, the position of Swedish unions in relation to posting companies has become weaker and the number of signed collective agreements with foreign construction companies has dropped dramatically (Seikel (2015)).

with the procurement contract in this respect, it annulled the contract and imposed financial penalties on the company.

In this public procurement case, the Court ruled that Lower Saxony could not prescribe the application of a regional collective agreement only covering a part of a given sector (public contracts).[189] According to the Court the wages were not fixed in accordance with one of the procedures provided for in the Posting of Workers Directive. The collective agreement mentioned in the Public Procurement Act in Lower Saxony was not universally applicable in accordance with Article 3(1) of the directive. Moreover, by referring to 'the actual wording' of Article 3(8), the Court made clear that recourse to non-extended collective agreements was only permitted if a Member State does not have a system for declaring collective agreements universally binding. If an 'erga omnes' system exists, but is not often used in practice, such as (traditionally) in Germany, recourse to agreements entered into by the most representative organisations and/or agreements that are generally applied was deemed problematic.

2.3.2.2. *Comparing 'Host' and 'Home' Labour Standards*

Another challenging issue concerns the comparison between 'host' and 'home' labour standards. The so-called 'favour principle' is stated in Article 3(7), first sentence, of the directive, as a guarantee that host labour standards only apply when working conditions in that Member State are better (more favourable) than in the 'home country' of the posted worker. In particular regarding minimum wages and paid holidays, *unconditional* application of host State law was deemed to infringe the free provision of services and the freedom of contract too much.[190] Hence, if the applicable law to the employment contract offers equivalent or even better protection, there is no need to set this aside. This seems to be the rationale behind Article 3(7), which is also supported by the early pre-of the directive case law of the Court on avoiding 'double burdens' for service providers in relation to their posted workers.[191] Nevertheless, it is easier to pay lip-service to the favour principle, than to operationalise it. For instance, how should the minimum rates of pay in the

---

189 Bruun, Jacobs & Schmidt (2010). In the more recent case ECJ 2015, C-115/14 (*RegioPost*), the applicable minimum wage was a result of regional German law, in which case it was not deemed problematic that it only applied to the public sector. *RegioPost* was generally welcomed because it reversed *Rüffert* on the basis of Article 26 Directive 2004/18. Still, as Novitz (2018) noted: 'this case law creates legal uncertainty concerning the interaction of the EU rules on the posting of workers, public procurement and fundamental internal market freedoms'. See also Pecinocsky (2016).

190 Health & safety rules were not addressed in the Explanatory Memorandum, nor the other items in the list included in Article 3(1). The character of health and safety rules makes it difficult to opt for a non-territorial application. Often the national rules do not apply to work performed outside the territory.

191 See Houwerzijl & Pennings (1999), pp. 91–112; Giesing (2003), p. 155.

host State be interpreted and how should this be compared with the level of wage actually paid by the service provider to the posted workers? While there is some case law on the latter issue,[192] the first issue remained for a long time unclear. In this respect, the last sentence of Article 3(1) stipulates that the concept of minimum rates of pay referred to in paragraph 1 (c) is defined by the national law and/or practice of the host State. Does this mean that Member States are entirely free to decide the way in which they define 'minimum rates of pay'?[193] Can the host State impose only a single (statutory or collectively agreed) minimum wage (flat rate),[194] or is it possible to apply a set of rules determining the minimum rate of pay in the individual case (wage structure/job ladder)?

The Court confirmed the latter interpretation in its judgment in the Finnish preliminary reference case *Sähköalojen ammattiliitto*.[195] Notably, the Court specifically pointed out that 'the minimum wage calculated by reference to the relevant collective agreements cannot be a matter of choice for an employer who posts employees with the sole aim of offering lower labour costs than those of local workers'.[196] Moreover, in this judgment the Court gave a broad interpretation of the freedom for host States to include in the minimum rates of pay specific allowances, such as a daily allowance intended to ensure the social protection of workers 'making up for the disadvantages' of their being posted 'as a result of the workers being removed from their usual environment', and a compensation for daily travelling time.[197] Regarding the coverage of the cost of accommodation (as obliged in the Finnish collective agreement) and meal vouchers (in accordance with the contract of employment between service provider and posted worker) the Court ruled that these should be regarded as compensation for expenses in line with Article 3(7), second sentence, which

192 ECJ 2005, C-341/02 (*Commission v. Germany*). Confirmed in ECJ 2013, C-522/12 (*Isbir*).

193 Apart from the guidance provided in Article 3(1)(c) regarding overtime charges (which are explicitly deemed to form part of the 'minimum rates of pay' to be applied to posted workers) and contributions to supplementary pension schemes (which are specifically excluded from the minimum rates of pay).

194 For a long time, this seems to have been the prevailing opinion in Germany, which was codified in the German implementation Act of the Posting of Workers Directive (*AEntG*) prior to its amendment in 2009. See for more detail about the German situation, Kullmann (2015), p. 80.

195 ECJ 2015, C-396/13 (*Sähköalojen ammattiliitto*), §43. Also, the Court clarified that host State rules may determine whether the calculation of the minimum wage must be carried out on an hourly or a piecework basis (§40) and that holiday pay constitutes part of the minimum wage (§§66–69).

196 ECJ 2015, C-396/13 (*Sähköalojen ammattiliitto*), §41. The Court also seemed to slightly restate the purpose of the directive as well as the objective of a nucleus of mandatory rules for minimum protection guaranteed to posted workers (§§28–30), emphasising the double aim of preventing unfair competition and ensuring the social protecting of the workers concerned.

197 ECJ 2015, C-396/13 (*Sähköalojen ammattiliitto*), §§48–52, 54–56.

does not permit such expenditure to be taken into account in the calculation of the workers' minimum wage. Consequently, the service provider cannot take these costs into account when comparing the actual wage paid with the prescribed level of minimum rates of pay in the host country.

Depending on the subject matter of their labour law entitlements, as defined in Article 3(1) of the directive, (genuine) posted workers belong both to the host and 'home' country. Regarding wages, working time, safety at work and other (minimum) labour standards which influence the day to day performance of the contract, the posted worker is guaranteed protection by the host country. Here, preference is given to the actual place of work instead of the habitual one. But what about the other side of the coin? When and why may the law applicable to the employment contract continue to be adhered to in the case of cross-border posting? As explained in the Explanatory Memorandum to the first draft of the directive, the designation and application of the mandatory rules to be observed by foreign service providers in the host State, had to be compatible with the temporary nature of the performance of work in the host country and consistent with the directive's stated aims and objectives. Regarding mandatory rules concerning the form, suspension, alteration and termination of the contract of employment and workers' rights on information, consultation and participation,[198] the idea is that the posted worker continues to 'belong' to the labour market on which that person habitually works.[199] However, this preference of the habitual over the actual place of work is by definition 'finite': the precondition is that the posting should remain an exceptional circumstance of *limited duration* within a contract habitually performed in another country. Therefore, the directive only covers workers who fulfil the definition of posted worker in Article 2 of the directive. And it is to this personal scope of the directive that this chapter now turns.

2.3.3. PERSONAL SCOPE OF THE POSTING OF WORKERS DIRECTIVE

In order to avoid stretching the scope of application of the directive (in interaction with the Rome I Regulation, see Section 4 to non-genuine situations of posting, the concepts of 'posting' and 'posted worker' are crucial.[200]

---

198 COM(91)230 final, p. 15, under point 25, third indent and p. 13 under point 19, third indent.

199 Indeed, in genuine cases of (short term) posting an overriding interest to apply host States' dismissal law is absent, since the labour market of the host country may be regarded as not being involved in such situations. In case of dismissal, a genuine posted worker (with a habitual country of work) will usually fall back on the labour market in the home country. Likewise, the host State has no (or only a limited interest) in regulating the co-determination rights within the foreign company.

200 Van Hoek & Houwerzijl (2012).

2.3.3.1. Concept of 'Posting'

With regard to the concept of 'posting', the directive covers three different types of posting which are described in Article 1(3): (a) posting to carry out service contracts in the context of transnational subcontracting; (b) transnational intra-company transfers and (c) transnational temporary agency work. For these three situations of posting covered by the directive, Article 1(3) states that there must be a link to a cross-border service provision that is temporary in nature. The requirement has two related aspects:

- The posting should be connected to provision (by the posted worker) of a cross-border service in the meaning of Article 56 TFEU (as defined in Article 1(1) of the directive).
- In two of the three situations of posting it seems to be required that there must be a service contract between the employer and a recipient established or active in the country where the service is performed. This requirement is mentioned in Article 1(3)(a) and (c), but does not seem to be a prerequisite in case of intra-company postings (Article 1(3)(b) of the directive).

In respect of the latter aspect, it is important to note that the provision of services is not the sole context in which posting (secondment) might take place. A worker may also be posted/seconded in the framework of a project for the account of the worker's own employer. This would include, for example, the activities of film crews, or employees who are sent abroad on business trips, or to attend seminars, or to perform harvesting activities.[201] As a result, instead of coming within the scope of the directive, this group of seconded workers will be covered by Article 45 TFEU in interaction with Article 8 (and 9) of Rome I (see Section 2.4). Apart from the fact that the directive does not cover all cross-border postings, it should be noted that it does not contain a full coordination of cross-border services either.[202] Moreover, it does not even fully coordinate all employment in this context.[203] Hence, the status of the employing company – as cross-border service provider – can and should be separated from the status of the worker – posted, migrant or otherwise.[204]

---

201 Interestingly, Article 4 of Directive 91/533 seems to encompass both groups of posting.

202 The coordination of cross-border services is regulated (inter alia) by the Services Directive. Labour law is specifically excluded from the fields coordinated by this directive; see preamble §§14 and 86–87 and Article 1(6) of Directive 2006/123.

203 For example, it would seem from the facts of the cases and ECJ 2011, C-384/10 (*Voogsgeerd*) and ECJ 2011, Case C-29/10 (*Koelzsch*) that neither Mr Voogsgeerd nor Mr Koelzsch were posted workers in the meaning of the directive – even though their employer was a cross-border service provider. See, for these judgments, Section 3.4.

204 Compare in the context of the transitional period and migration law ECJ 2011, C-307/09, 308/09 and C-309/09 (*Vicoplus and others*).

2.3.3.2. *Concept of 'Posted Worker'*

With regard to the concept of a 'posted worker', in Article 2(1) of the directive, the posted worker is defined as a worker 'who, for a limited period, carries out his work in the territory of a Member State other than the State in which he *normally* works' (emphasis added). This phrasing closely resembles Article 8(2) of the Rome I Regulation, although the directive uses the word 'normally', whereas the Rome I Regulation refers to a 'habitual' country of work. The interplay between the two concepts will be discussed in Section 2.4.

2.3.3.3. *What is Temporary?*

A controversial issue that was neither solved nor clarified by the directive, is the interpretation of 'a limited period' in Article 2(1). When approaching the temporary nature of the posting from an internal market perspective, it is remarkable that neither case law nor legislation based on Article 56 TFEU gives a practicable definition of 'temporary'. In *Rush Portuguesa*, the Court stated that a service provider 'may move with its own work-force which it brings from its own Member State for the duration of the work in question'.[205] Here, the temporary character of posting seems to be linked to the duration of the service abroad. So far, in this general case law on services *no limitation in time* to the temporariness of a service provision has been accepted.[206] As stated in *Gebhard*, the temporary nature of the activities has to be determined in the light, not only of the duration of the provision of the service, but also of its regularity, periodical nature or continuity.[207] In *Schnitzer*,[208] application of these criteria made the Court conclude that Article 56 TFEU includes services such as construction projects involving large building works which are provided over an extended period, up to several years. On the other hand, the Court held in *Trojani* that an activity carried out on a permanent basis or without any foreseeable limit would not be considered a service within the meaning of Article 56 TFEU.[209] Also, it was ruled that a construction company exclusively

205 ECJ 1990, C-113/89 (*Rush Portuguesa*), §§17 and 19.
206 ECJ 2006, C-514/03 (*Commission v. Spain*), §22.
207 ECJ 1995, C-55/94 (*Gebhard*), §27; ECJ 2003, C-131/01 (*Commission v. Italy*), §22.
208 ECJ 2003, C-215/01 (*Schnitzer*), §30.
209 As shown by the very wording of Article 56 TFEU, in contradistinction to the permanent nature of the activity carried out by an economic operator who is established in a Member State (observation of AG Lèger, Opinion in case *Gebhard*, §32). Notably, the distinction between Article 56 and Article 49 is in reality difficult to operationalise. In the words of A-G Léger in his Opinion to *Gebhard*: 'On the strictly legal level, this distinction is a tricky one, in so far as it is the upshot of a combination of criteria, closely depends on the factual circumstances in question and has never been precisely and systematically defined.'

focused on a different country than that of establishment cannot be considered a service provider by the Court.[210]

2.3.3.4. *Labour Market Access?*

In the case *Rush Portuguesa*, the Court made a distinction between migrant workers, who enter the labour market of the host State, and posted workers, who generally do not (see Section 2.3.1). The employer of a posted worker makes use of the free movement of services. The posted workers do not need to avail themselves of the free movement of workers, because according to the Court, they do not seek access to the labour market of the host Member State, but will instead immediately return to the State where they normally work once the service is carried out. This 'passive movement' (namely because the employer assigns the worker) may be illustrated by the fact that the posted worker has concluded an employment contract with the employer governed by the law of the habitual country of work. Another indicator of passive movement is the provision or reimbursement of travel, board and lodging costs by the employer.[211] Notably, in its judgment *Sähköalojen ammattiliitto*,[212] the Court brought the status of the posted worker (in this respect) closer to the traditional expatriate employee, by ruling that such special arrangements should be regarded as compensation for expenses in line with Article 3(7), second sentence of the directive.

The distinction based on labour market access is crucial if the posted workers do not enjoy free movement themselves, e.g. because they are covered by a transitional regime or because they are third-country nationals.[213] But the distinction between 'Article 45' mobility and 'Article 56' mobility also has an impact on the labour law protection of the workers involved. As discussed above, the directive intends to provide a significant but not a full level of host State protection for posted workers, who may be vulnerable given their situation (temporary employment in a foreign country, difficulty in obtaining proper representation, lack of knowledge of local laws, institutions and language). As Kilpatrick observes:[214] 'Socially, it is not difficult to imagine that long-stretches of life in a (typically more expensive) host State on a minimum skeleton of host State labour standards can seem exploitative to posted workers and host State inhabitants alike.'

210 This clearly follows from the judgment in ECJ 2000, C-404/98 (*Plum*), situated in the context of what is now Regulation 883/04.

211 This indicator is made explicit in Article 4(2)(d) of the Posting of Workers Enforcement Directive. See Section 2.3.4 and in more detail, Van Hoek & Houwerzijl (2012).

212 Elaborated in Section 2.3.2.

213 See Section 2.3.1.

214 Kilpatrick (2009), p. 27.

The differences in labour costs attached to both 'avenues' for worker mobility seem to be used more and more strategically by firms (as a business model) in order to gain this 'comparative advantage'. Labour law is but one of the points to be taken into consideration; social security and tax law being at least as important. Intermediaries in other Member States are used with the sole purpose of turning (temporary or seasonal) migration into posting. When, for example, a temporary work agency recruits Polish workers for jobs in Sweden, the actual circumstances may not change according to whether the agency is Polish or Swedish, but the legal situation does. Therefore, blurring regulatory concepts and criteria also generate ample opportunities for non-compliance, resulting in violation of labour law and other (fundamental) rights of migrant workers.[215]

2.3.4. ISSUES OF MONITORING AND ENFORCEMENT

2.3.4.1. Shortcomings

The European Commission has regularly monitored the implementation and enforcement of the Posting of Workers Directive to assess whether the aims of the directive were being met. A comprehensive monitoring exercise launched in 2006 by the European Commission led to the assessment that the directive's main shortcomings could be traced to a range of issues relating to its implementation, application and enforcement in practice.[216] This situation was caused by the virtual absence of administrative cooperation, unsatisfactory access to information, and cross-border enforcement problems; all of these were provided for in Articles 4 and 5 of the directive, which have proved inadequate in practice. The exercise in 2006 must be situated against the debate about the then draft Services Directive.[217] The Services Directive as adopted does not deal with labour law or the posting of workers within the EU, since these were deemed matters that were specifically to be dealt with in the Posting of Workers Directive and the Rome I Convention.[218] The controversies surrounding what was commonly referred to in the popular press as the 'Bolkestein directive' (i.e., the Services Directive), together with the EU's 2004 and 2007 enlargements, have played an important role in drawing attention to the limited impact of the Posting of Workers Directive.[219]

215 See for more detail, Houwerzijl (2014).

216 See the European Commission (2006) (*Guidance on the posting of workers*), followed by Communication (2007) (*Posting of workers in the framework of the provision of services*).

217 See for instance 14 February 2006 Commissioner Charlie McCreevy's Statement on the Services Directive at the European Parliament Plenary session of February 2006, SPEECH/06/84.

218 Directive 2006/123/EC (Services Directive).

219 See for an account of the 'integration fatigue' and '(single) market fatigue' in the old Member States in western Europe due to the enlargements and the unemployment and discrediting of financial capitalism in the credit crisis, Monti (2010).

Around 2011, studies had convincingly shown that there is, in practice, a huge lack of control, monitoring, and cooperation among Member States, and that enforcement of minimum terms and conditions of employment for posted workers is poor, e.g. on wages, working time, and costs of housing and transport.[220] Anecdotal evidence from media has been confirmed and elaborated upon by academic and policy research. Studies by Wagner and by Berntsen based on interviews with, for instance, foreign workers situated at the building sites of the European Central Bank in Germany and the 'Eemshaven' in the Netherlands, as well as in workplaces in the meat sector and the supermarket distribution centres, clearly show that the workers concerned often do not know their legal status.[221]

Hence, there is (reason for) clear concern about abuses of the freedoms granted by the EU internal market. Posting regulations are misused systematically and do create competition on wage levels and other labour costs in host State labour markets. Especially in the area of provision of manpower, the problem of combating illegal activities is encountered. However, these forms of abuse are not specific to posting (nor for provision of manpower). The illegal temporary work agencies may be established both in the country of recruitment (leading to posting) or in the county of work (leading to migration). Several reported cases of abuse have concerned migrant workers or even (bogus) self-employed.[222] These cases involve social dumping in its purest form – with no respect for either the protective system of the 'sending' country or that of the host country.

For trade unions and enforcement authorities it is difficult to trace and combat the situations mentioned above; the fluidity in the cross-border context, with firms often disappearing across borders or going bankrupt, complicates their efforts to enforce (and execute) local labour standards. Moreover, the employer-arranged migration context leads to isolation of migrants, as they often have limited knowledge of host State law and institutional structures. They are also often segregated spatially and socially from their host surroundings because they are housed near the place of work. And if trade unions and host State institutions succeed in reaching the workers, they experience enormous practical difficulties in establishing exactly which conditions (should) apply

220 See Van Hoek & Houwerzijl (2011/12); Cremers (2011).

221 Berntsen (2015) and Wagner (2015). They conducted micro-level research (based on interviews) regarding migrant/posted workers strategies and union strategies at two big building sites, in the supermarkets branch and in the meat sector in the Netherlands and Germany. See also, for the UK, Barnard & Ludlow (2016).

222 See Van Hoek and Houwerzijl (2011/12), pp. 50–60. The European Agency on Fundamental Rights called for 'zero tolerance for severe forms of labour exploitation', see its report FRA (2015).

to a specific individual employment relationship, because the rules are so complicated in cross-border situations.[223]

A different, more ambiguous, situation arises when the employment conditions do conform (more or less) to the standards of the home State, but not to those of the host State. As becomes apparent from several empirical studies, in such cases the workers may have no incentive to claim the extra rights awarded to them under the law of the host State. They often seem to be happy with the job opportunity and do not want to put that in danger by claiming host State entitlements.[224] As Berntsen puts it: 'the commodified employment context tends to disempower migrants, at the same time it enables them to live better lives then they would if they opted not to participate in this European market context'.[225] The harm of their passive attitude towards claiming their rights is (felt to be) done to third parties, and – more abstractly – to the social structure of the host State, rather than to one of the parties to the individual contract. In extreme cases the workers will even operate in cohort with the employer in order to evade the law of the host State.[226] In such cases the law of the host State will only be enforced if enforcement is entrusted to host State authorities or interested third parties (such as social funds or the unions in the host State).

2.3.4.2. Solutions Put Forward by the Enforcement Directive

In the field of free movement of workers, the EU legislature adopted Directive 2014/54 to enhance effective enforcement.[227] To remedy the monitoring and enforcement lacunae under the Posting of workers directive, a proposal for the 'Posting of Workers Enforcement Directive' was launched in 2012[228] and – after initial fierce resistance by 'sending countries'[229] – adopted on 15 May 2014. Its name acknowledges that the Posting of Workers

223 See Berntsen (2015), pp. 170–75; Kullmann (2015), pp. 211–25, 266–90; Wagner (2015), pp. 70–76.

224 See Van Hoek & Houwerzijl (2011), Section 4.5 on legal remedies.

225 Berntsen (2015), p. 171, a long quotation from a Polish scaffolder, 28 years old, shows that the sense of belonging to the 'home country' may also be lost: 'I don't see my future in Poland. I see my future where there is work, because without work ... you know how it is over there (in Poland), it is difficult to get a job', Berntsen (2015), p. 24.

226 In the country reports for the posting of workers study commissioned by the European Commission, this was specifically mentioned by the Estonian expert. See Van Hoek & Houwerzijl (2011).

227 See Section 2.2.3.

228 COM(2012)131, emphasis added. The proposal was adopted as Directive 2014/67/EU.

229 The controversial character may also be deduced from the large number of amendments (833) which were submitted for the draft report on the enforcement directive of the committee on employment of the EP (procedure file 2012/0061/COD).

Directive did not guarantee in practice any protection against abusive and exploitative practices. The Posting of Workers Enforcement Directive had to be implemented in the Member States by 18 June 2016.

The Posting of Workers Enforcement Directive focuses on those elements of the Posting of Workers Directive that were considered as problematic by stakeholders and that pertain to enforcement of compliance, improvement of legal certainty and strengthening administrative cooperation. The Posting of Workers Enforcement Directive's overall objective is to ensure that posted workers actually enjoy the minimum protection offered by the Posting of Workers Directive, whilst also facilitating the free provision of services. To achieve its aims, the Posting of Workers Enforcement Directive sets a common framework of measures and control mechanism. Its most important measures include the following:

- a non-exhaustive list of indicative factual elements to help competent authorities such as Labour Inspectorates in determining whether there is a genuine establishment of the posting company in the sending state (Article 4(2) of the directive) and in assessing whether posted workers are only temporarily carrying out their work in a Member State other than the one in which they normally work (Article 4(3) of the directive);
- a stricter framework for improving access to information in host Member States, relevant for the posting of workers (Article 5) to enhance legal certainty for service providers;
- a framework for enhancing administrative cooperation between authorities and other stakeholders across countries (Articles 6 and 7);
- a (non-limitative) list of justified and proportionate administrative requirements and control measures that might be applied by the Member States (Article 9);
- an obligation upon Member States to ensure effective mechanisms for posted workers to lodge complaints and institute juridical/administrative proceedings (also through trade unions) against their employers also in the Member State where they are posted (Article 11);
- a subcontracting liability arrangement for wages (Article 12). Regarding the construction sector this is phrased in mandatory wording, stipulating that posted construction workers can hold the contractor in a direct subcontractor relationship liable for any outstanding net remuneration corresponding to the minimum rates of pay, in addition to or in place of the employer. Nevertheless, Member States can escape the liability arrangement through implementation of 'equivalent measures' in a direct subcontracting relationship, to tackle fraud and abuse in situations when workers have difficulties in obtaining their rights (see Article 12(5)). On the other hand,

Member States are allowed to take more stringent liability measures, such as chain liability affecting all subcontractors in the chain.[230]

Clearly, the directive facilitates and stimulates enforcement in some respects, but asks for a real effort with budgetary implications and strong political will at the level of the host Member State. Ensuring that the rights of posted workers are adequately protected requires comprehensive cooperation – such as joint visits to work sites of posted workers, enhanced information exchange – of different national actors (depending on the national system these can be, for example, inspectorates, other state bodies or social partners). Moreover, although posting of workers falls under both sending and receiving country regulations, enforcers of the rights of posted workers (e.g. trade unions and labour inspectorates) do not have the competences to act beyond their own national jurisdictions. In order to more effectively monitor and enforce the rights of posted workers, cross-border cooperation seems crucial. Although cross-border cooperation has increased during the last decade, especially in relation to posting in the framework of the free movement of services, procedures are long and time-consuming and there are no proper sanctions available. Some enhancement may be expected from the directive where it links the inspectorates' information exchange to the so-called Internal Market Information System.

However, the reliability and compatibility of the information itself needs improvement as well. Stricter registration rules (like notification systems, dissuasive penalties for not following the rules, making service recipients co-responsible for registration) for service providers posting their workers have been introduced in several Member States in order to enhance the quality of data collection on postings and to facilitate monitoring and enforcing the rights of posted workers. The Belgian LIMOSA scheme was one of the first, and certainly the most well-known and advanced, notification system. Since 2007 all foreign undertakings have to notify their activities and posted workers through the LIMOSA system. All service providers who which to perform a temporary economic activity have to register online before they start the activity. At the same time, it is also a highly contested notification system, from the perspective that it limits the free provision of services too much. It has been subject of

230 The most well-known and far-reaching example of chain liability was established in Germany in 1995 for the construction sector and since then extended to several other sectors. The liability for wages and paid holiday contributions applies to the whole chain, so that each subcontractor up to the principal contractor might be held liable in the case of misconduct in these fields. In ECJ 2004, C-60/03 (*Wolff & Müller*) the Court ruled that the German chain liability system was in line with EU law. Its restrictive impact on the free movement of services was justified by the additional protection it provided to posted workers.

several procedures before the Court of Justice, with mixed outcomes.[231] More recently, LIMOSA has been acknowledged as a very interesting tool from the perspective of collecting statistical information. Its extensive information collection regarding posted workers is unique and provides currently the most accurate data source about postings. The advantages of the advanced LIMOSA database were highlighted by statistical research which made reliable estimates of the extent to which posting in the Belgian construction sector has resulted in displacement of local labour.[232]

2.3.5. 'TARGETED REVISION' OF THE POSTING OF WORKERS DIRECTIVE

The adoption of the Posting of Workers Enforcement Directive left a number of persisting problems largely unaffected. These were pinpointed in the impact assessment for the European Commission as well as in the different studies undertaken in its preparation.[233] In particular, the directive does not address the unequal labour standards of posted and local workers, nor the '*Laval* judgments', that were interpreted as setting a ceiling of protection (rather than a floor of rights) for posted workers. Combined with an ever growing number of (not always genuinely) posted workers being sent from new to old Member States, this led to waves of protest across old Member States against 'cheap labour' originating from new Member States.

Figures published by the European Commission indicate that between 2010 and 2014, the number of workers posted from one EU State to another increased by almost 49%. Moreover, 86% of workers are posted to the EU-15 Member States, with Germany, France and Belgium receiving the largest share. Poland, Germany and France accounted for the three largest senders of posted workers in 2014. Postings involve 0.7% of the total EU workforce but there are wide variations in different sectors. It is estimated that 42% of total postings occur in the construction sector but posting of workers is also important in the manufacturing industry (21.8%), and in other service sectors such as personal services (education, health and social work, 13.5%) and business services (administrative, professional, and financial services, 10.3%). It should be noted, however, that these statistics are far from perfect. The European Commission

---

231 Belgium had, for instance, to reduce the amount of information it collected initially because according to the Court of Justice the scheme restricted, without good justification, the free movement of services. See ECJ 2010, C-515/08 (*Dos Santos Palhota*); ECJ 2012, C-577/10 (*Commission v. Belgium*); ECJ 2014, C-315/13 (*De Clercq and others*).

232 De Wispelaere & Pacolet (2017).

233 See notably Van Hoek & Houwerzijl (2011), p. 12: Lhernould & Palli (2017); Pacolet & De Wispelaere (2016).

uses information provided by administrative forms (so-called 'A1-forms') issued by the social insurance authority of the posted workers' country of origin (see Section 2.5). But significant gaps arise between national and EU figures and there is a lack of precise data. Still, it is clear that the number of workers who are sent from one Member State – in which they supposedly normally work – to another for a limited period of time has increased sharply, whereas these so-called posted workers often earn substantially less than local workers for the same work. Moreover, concerns about posted workers being vulnerable to fraudulent activities such as undeclared work practices have also grown.[234]

Against this background, the European Commission launched, as part of a 'fair mobility package', a proposal for a targeted revision of the Posting of Workers Directive in March 2016.[235] According to the explanatory memorandum, the main aims for the revision are ensuring the smooth functioning of the single market and stopping 'unfair competition' on wage costs and working conditions, reflected in the mantra 'same pay for the same work in the same place'.

2.3.5.1. Diverging Interests between 'Host' and 'Sending' Member States

In the process which set the targeted revision process in motion, a letter of Ministers from seven countries from Northwest Europe, was very important. These Ministers pleaded a revision of the directive according to the principle of 'equal pay for equal work in the same place'. In their letter to the Commission, the representatives from (predominantly) host States made clear that they were worried about unfair competition: '... currently employers of posted workers may enjoy an unfair advantage vis-à-vis employers in the host country'.[236] However, they not only focused on equality of treatment between undertakings, but considered the position of the workers as well: 'In our view, fair competition is important to both cross-border workers and cross-border employers, as well as regular workers and employers in the host Member States.'[237] They signalled that, in some cases, services provided by posted workers have transformed into services of semi-permanent nature with a real and lasting presence on the domestic labour market. This viewpoint was, however, not shared by all Member States. In a letter of Ministers from nine countries, mainly from Middle and Eastern Europe, it was argued that it is too early to revise the directive, since the implementation period of the Posting of Workers Enforcement Directive had only finished in June 2016. These Ministers wanted to wait and see what

---

234 Impact assessment accompanying the proposal to amend the Posting of Workers Directive, SWD(2016)52 final, Strasbourg, 8 March 2016, pp. 6–7.

235 COM(2016)128 final of 8 March 2016.

236 Ibid., p. 4.

237 Ibid., p. 5.

the impact of the latter directive would be. Furthermore, they argued that 'the alignment of wages across Member States should come as a consequence of further economic development and not from the Union's legislative action'.[238] This is a nice way of saying that they feel their undertakings should be able to compete on wages until the difference in wage costs has decreased. Hence, the sending States stuck mainly to (their reading of) the services narrative, by expressing the concern 'that the principle of equal pay for equal work in the same place may be incompatible with the single market, as pay rate differences constitute one legitimate element of competitive advantage for service providers'.[239]

The initial responses to the proposed Directive by national parliaments again showed the diverging interests between Member States.[240] As of 10 May 2016, 14 Parliaments of 11 Member States (10 from Central and Eastern Europe, and Denmark) had made use of the Subsidiarity Control Mechanism to raise subsidiarity concerns and thereby triggered a 'yellow card'.[241] On 20 July 2016, the European Commission published a Communication which concluded that the proposed revision of the Posting of Workers Directive did not breach the subsidiarity principle.[242]

After fierce debates and considerable amendments to the Commission's proposal by Parliament and Council, the revised directive was finally adopted by majority vote on 28 June 2018. Two months later, the Hungarian and Polish governments decided to contest the revised directive before the Court of Justice. According to a Hungarian press release, this was because 'the extension of the principle of equal pay for equal work at the same workplace to the freedom of the provision of services does not, in actual fact, seek to protect posted workers; it forces them out of the labour markets of other Member States as a means of protectionism'.[243] In their official actions, Poland and Hungary seek annulment

---

238 Ibid., p. 5; European Commission (2016), *Communication from the Commission on the proposal for a Directive amending the Posting of Workers Directive*, COM(2016)505 final at 4.2.1.

239 Ibid., at 3.1.

240 Individual Member State opinions are available at: <http://ec.europa.eu/dgs/secretariat_general/relations/relations_other/npo/index_en.htm> accessed 05.06.2019.

241 See <http://www.euractiv.com/section/social-europe-jobs/news/national-parliaments-invoke-yellow-card-in-response-to-revised-posted-workers-directive> accessed 05.06.2019. This is only the third time that such a procedure has been triggered. Weber (14 May 2016), 'Third time's a charm? National Parliaments form bloc against posted workers directive', Leiden Law Blog, available at <http://leidenlawblog.nl/articles/third-times-a-charm-national-parliaments-form-bloc-against-posted-workers-d> accessed 05.06.2019.

242 Commission (2016) (Communication on directive amending the Posting of Workers Directive) at 4.2.1.

243 Press release October 5, 2018 12:09 PM. Available at <http://www.kormany.hu/en/prime-minister-s-office/news/hungarian-government-contested-amendment-of-posted-workers-directive-before-court-of-justice-of-european-union> accessed 05.06.2019.

of (at least) the provisions on the remuneration of posted workers,[244] since in their view these amendments to the directive infringe the freedom to provide services in an unjustified and disproportionate way by increasing the burden on service providers, with a view to eliminating their competitive advantage resulting from lower pay rates applicable in their country of establishment.[245] Poland and Hungary hope for a decision from the Court before they will have to implement the new Directive 2018/957, ultimately on 30 July 2020.

2.3.5.2. *Aims and Main Features of the Revised Directive*

What changes will the revised Directive bring? As its Preamble (e.g. recital 4), makes clear: 'More than 20 years after the adoption of the directive', it was time to reset 'the right balance between the need to promote the freedom to provide services and ensure a level playing field on the one hand and the need to protect the rights of posted workers on the other'. In recital 10, the need to ensure greater protection for workers is stressed, in order 'to safeguard the freedom to provide, in both the short and the long term, services on a fair basis, in particular by preventing abuse of the rights guaranteed by the Treaties'. According to its recital 16: 'In a truly integrated and competitive internal market, undertakings compete on the basis of factors such as productivity, efficiency, and the education and skill level of the labour force, as well as the quality of their goods and services and the degree of innovation thereof'.[246]

The revised directive is to amend the Posting of Workers Directive and to complement the Posting of Workers Enforcement Directive, rather than to replace these directives. The revised Posting of Workers Directive focuses on

244 Both ask for annulment of Article 1(2)(a) and Article 1(2)(b) Directive 2018/957. In addition, Hungary asks for annulment of Article 1(2)(c) and Article 3(3). The Hungarian Government claims that the contested directive was not adopted on the appropriate legal basis. Taking into account its purpose and its content, the EU legislature should, for the purpose of adopting the directive, have taken Article 153 TFEU as the legal basis or, at least, as the principal legal basis. This plea resonates the stance of the Social Committee of the European Parliament which had proposed to broaden the legal base of the Posting of Workers Directive with Article 153 TFEU, see Houwerzijl & Schrauwen (2018); Van Hoek (2018).

245 Pending cases, ECJ 2018, C-620/18 (*Hungary v. European Parliament and Council of the European Union*) and ECJ 2018, C-626/18 (*Republic of Poland v. European Parliament and Council of the European Union*).

246 Moreover, the principle of equal treatment, equal pay and the prohibition of any discrimination on grounds of nationality in EU law is emphasised (recital 6) and recital 3 refers expressly to Article 3 TEU, establishing that the Union is to promote social justice and protection and Article 9 TFEU, stating that the Union takes in defining and implementing its policies and activities, into account requirements linked to, for instance, the guarantee of adequate social protection.

three main areas: rules on temporary work agencies,[247] the remuneration of posted workers where it introduces the principle of equal pay for equal work, and rules applying to long-term posting.[248]

(a) Almost Full Equal Treatment in Case of Postings of Longer Duration

The revised directive enhances the protection of workers who are posted for a longer duration. It stipulates that 'where the effective duration of the posting exceeds twelve months', posted workers should be guaranteed 'all the applicable terms and conditions of employment which are laid down' in the host State (except for formalities and conditions for the conclusion and termination of contracts, non-competition clauses and supplementary pension schemes).[249] The reference period of 12 months may be extended to 18 months if the service provider submits a motivated notification. In such cases, for the obligation to ensure equal working conditions to arise, the duration of the posting must exceed 18 months. In contrast to the reasoning of the Court of Justice in *Rush Portuguesa*, the introduction of extended rights in relation to postings of longer duration as defined by a temporal criterion, implies a recognition that, after a certain defined period of time, posted workers do enter the labour market of the host State.[250]

(b) Extension of the 'Hard Core' of Applicable (Collectively Agreed) Labour Standards

The directive emphasises that the 'hard core' of labour standards that remain applicable for all workers posted less than one year should be guaranteed by the host State on the basis of equality of treatment. This amendment builds on the

247 The revised directive links the protection of posted agency workers to the 'equal treatment provision' of the Temporary Agency Work Directive 2008/104 (Article 5), stipulating equal treatment of temporary agency workers in the user company. In addition to the provisions of Article 5, Member States are entitled to require that posted temporary agency workers benefit from other terms and conditions that apply to temporary agency workers in the Member State where the work is carried out (see Article 1(2)(e) revised Posting of Workers Directive, amending Article 3(9) of the directive). Article 1(1)(c) of the revised directive adds to the protection of temp agency workers in specific situations.

248 The current Posting of Workers Directive does not define when a posting ceases to be 'temporary'.

249 Article 1(2)(b) of the revised directive, adding a paragraph 1a to Article 3 Posting of Workers Directive.

250 See recital 9: 'Posting is of a temporary nature and the posted worker usually returns to the country of origin after the completion of the work for which he has been posted. However, in view of the long duration of certain postings, and *in acknowledgment of the link between the labour market of the host country and the workers posted for such long periods*, it is necessary to provide that …' (emphasis added).

case law of the Court of Justice in *Sähköalojen ammattiliitto ry*. The minimum wage guarantee is deemed no longer enough to protect a level playing field, and is therefore replaced by a guarantee of equal remuneration, including all elements of remuneration that are mandatory in the host State (both in statutory law and in mandatory or generally binding collective labour agreements) and apply to both local and posted workers.[251] This means that employers have to apply all the rules of the host country in relation to pay/remuneration, as laid down by law or by universally applicable collective labour agreements, and not just the minimum rates of pay. Moreover, Article 3(8) of the Posting of Workers Directive is amended in a way that allows application of generally applicable agreements or agreements concluded by the most representative organisations not only in the absence of, but also 'in addition to' universally applicable ones.[252]

Constituent elements of remuneration include thirteenth month allowances, travel expenses, and compensation for work during public holidays or night work.[253] Conditions of workers' accommodation and allowances or reimbursements for travel, board and lodging cost for workers away from home for professional reasons, are added as matters belonging to the hard core of host labour standards.[254] Hence, there is still a ceiling of protection for posted workers, but at a higher level.

---

251 Articles 1(2)(a) of the revised directive, amending Article 3(1) of the Posting of Workers Directive. The explicit exclusion of supplementary occupational retirement pension schemes remains.

252 Article 1(2)(d) of the revised directive. In relation to what was discussed in Section 2.3.2, this solves problems as in Germany after the *Rüffert* judgment (C-346/06). However, problems as in Sweden and Denmark after the *Laval* judgment (C-341/05) seem not to be solved, although it remains to be seen whether Article 1(b)(1a) of the revised Posting of Workers Directive will make a difference in this respect. This clause stipulates that the directive does not affect inter alia the right to take collective action as well as the right to negotiate, to conclude and enforce collective agreements.

253 According to recital 18: when comparing the actual remuneration paid to a posted worker and the remuneration due in the host Member State, the gross amount of remuneration should be taken into account, rather than the individual constituent elements of remuneration which are rendered mandatory as provided for by this directive. Nevertheless, in order to ensure transparency and to assist the competent authorities and bodies in carrying out checks and controls it is necessary that the constituent elements of remuneration can be identified in enough detail. Unless the allowances specific to the posting concern expenditure actually incurred on account of the posting, such as expenditure on travel, board and lodging, they should be considered to be part of the remuneration and should be taken into account for the purposes of comparing the total gross amounts of remuneration.

254 The latter point shall apply exclusively to travel, board and lodging expenditure incurred by posted workers where they are required to travel to and from their regular place of work in the Member State to whose territory they are posted, or where they are temporarily sent by their employer from that regular place of work to another place of work. Regarding the compensation of travel, board and lodging costs incurred on account of the posting from the State of normal employment to the host State, Article 3(7) of the revised Directive clarifies the obligation for the employer to reimburse the posted worker these costs on top of the

(c) Strengthening of 'Transparency Requirements'

To foster legal certainty and law enforcement, Member States are obliged to publish 'without undue delay and in a transparent manner' information on the constituent elements of remuneration on their single official national website, next to the other information as referred to in Article 5 Posting of Workers Enforcement Directive, as well as information on the additional set of terms and conditions of employment applicable to postings exceeding 12 or, where applicable, 18 months. Each Member State should ensure that the information on the single official national website is accurate and is updated on a regular basis. Failure to comply with this obligation shall be taken into account when determining the fines applicable for infringement of the national provisions adopted pursuant to the (revised) directive, 'to the extent necessary to ensure the proportionality thereof'.[255]

(d) Other Measures, in Particular Regarding the Road Transport Sector

In the revised Posting of Workers Directive, some other surveillance and control measures are also further developed. In particular, it complements the Posting of Workers Enforcement Directive by establishing an obligation for the host State to create a sanctioning regime. Last but not least, the revised Posting of Workers Directive has specific implications for the road transport sector. The directive does not exclude specific branches of industry from its scope of application with the exception of the seagoing personnel of merchant navy undertakings (Article 1(2) Posting of Workers Directive). Nevertheless, comparative research commissioned by the European Commission revealed that the system of the Posting of Workers Directive is ill-fitted to deal with the kind of cross-border labour mobility characteristic for the international transport sector. At the time, with the most prominent exception of France,[256] the implementing statutes and regulations of the Member States did – implicitly – cover international transport, but did not contain any specific rules concerning this sector.

To tackle the complex set of problems in the road transport sector, the European Commission launched a comprehensive set of measures under the heading 'road mobility package' on 31 May 2017.[257] This package includes a

---

remuneration at the level of the host State, by stipulating that 'the employer shall, without prejudice to point (h) of the first subparagraph of paragraph 1, reimburse the posted worker for such expenditure in accordance with the national law and/or practice applicable to the employment relationship'.

255 Article 1(2)(a) of the revised directive.

256 See Van Hoek & Houwerzijl (2011/12).

257 *Mobility Package 'Europe on the Move' Occupation and Market Access*, COM(2017)281 – 1071/2009/EC; 1072/2009/EC; COM(2017)282 – 2006/1/EC.

proposal to amend a Directive concerning social legislation relating to road transport activities (Directive 2006/22), which is currently mainly concerned with (enforcing) driving and rest times. The proposal adds to this legal instrument specific rules and enforcement requirements, including whether host labour rules should apply to truck drivers on foreign trips and how many pick-ups and drop-offs drivers can do outside their home country. Therefore the proposal impacts on the relevance of the Posting of Workers Directive and the Posting of Workers Enforcement Directive in the road transport sector. Anticipating this pending proposal, Article 3(3) of the revised Posting of Workers Directive stipulates that it will only apply to the road transport sector from the date of application of a legislative act amending Directive 2006/22/EC. In this regard, recital 15 of the revised Posting of Workers Directive explains that, 'because of the highly mobile nature of work in international road transport, the implementation of this Directive [the revised Posting of Workers Directive] in that sector raises particular legal questions and difficulties, which are to be addressed, in the framework of the mobility package, through specific rules for road transport also reinforcing the combating of fraud and abuse'.[258]

Ultimately by 30 July 2023, the European Commission has to submit an evaluation report on the application and implementation of the revised Posting of Workers Directive to the European Parliament and the Council, which shall include an assessment of whether further measures to ensure a level playing field and protect workers are required, in particular in light of the developments concerning the envisaged amending of Directive 2006/22/EC.[259]

2.4. PRIVATE INTERNATIONAL LAW AND THE LAW APPLICABLE TO THE EMPLOYMENT CONTRACT

2.4.1. EVOLUTION AND LEGAL CONTEXT

An important impact on the labour standards of migrant workers (covered by Article 45 TFEU on the free movement of workers) and of posted workers (covered by Article 56 TFEU on the freedom of their employer to provide services), stems from private international law. Because of the private law character of the employment contract between employer and employee, parties enjoy the freedom of contract (party autonomy). In the international

[258] See in detail on this thorny issue Van Overbeeke (2018), Van Overbeeke (2017), Van Overbeeke (2016). Also Van Hoek (2018).

[259] As stipulated in Article 2(2)(b) of the revised Posting of Workers Directive.

context this principle translates into the right to freely choose the law applicable to their employment contract. This is one of the central subjects of private international law, which is the legal area made up of mechanisms to facilitate the settlement of international disputes.[260] It designates the rules concerning conflict of laws, and also includes the rules concerning the international jurisdiction of the courts and the recognition of foreign judgments.[261] Traditionally, each Member State has its own national rules of private international law. In 1980, the Member States signed the Convention on the Law Applicable to Contractual Obligations (the Rome I Convention).[262] The Rome I Convention came into effect as of 1991. Since the entry into force of the Treaty of Amsterdam, the European legislator is provided with near to full competences in the field of private international law.[263] This led to a 'Europeanisation of private international law', including the adoption of the Rome I Regulation (hereinafter 'Rome I') in 2008.[264] Contracts signed after 17 December 2009 must be interpreted according to the rules laid down in Rome I.

The uniform rules of Rome I apply to contractual obligations in any situation involving a choice between the laws of different countries (Article 1), i.e. in situations in which all the elements are not connected to the legal order of one and the same State. For instance, the parties to the contract may be of different nationality or domiciled in different States, or the contract may be made or performed in different countries or in a country different from that of the court hearing the case. In Rome I, Articles 8 and 9 contain the rules for international employment contracts. To further aligned interpretation (*Gleichlauf*) between the competent judge and the applicable law there is a close link between Rome I and the related instrument in matters of conflicts of jurisdiction, Brussels I*bis*.[265]

---

260 In contrast with private international law of contracts, the substantive law of contracts rules questions such as the validity, the conclusion and the performance of the contract.

261 However, not all Member States use the term private international law in such a broad sense. See COM(2002)654 final, 36. Practically speaking, where a court action is to be brought in an international dispute, the first question is which country's courts have international jurisdiction. Once this has been determined, this court will decide which law is applicable to the dispute. It is only when this court has given judgment that the problem of enforcement abroad will arise.

262 Convention on the Law Applicable to Contractual Obligations, OJ L 266/1 of 9 October 1980.

263 Article 61(c) in conjunction with Article 65(b) of the Treaty of Amsterdam, currently Article 81(1) and (2)(c) TFEU.

264 Regulation 593/2008 (Law applicable to contractual obligations).

265 Regulation 1215/2012 (on jurisdiction and the recognition and enforcement of judgments in civil and commercial matters).

2.4.2. ROME I: PROVISIONS ON APPLICABLE LABOUR LAW

Article 8 of the Rome I Regulation harmonises the conflict rules in Europe on the law applicable to individual contracts of employment. In principle, parties are free to choose the law applicable to their employment contract. Article 8(1) Rome I, however, limits the effect of a choice of law since such a choice by the parties cannot deprive the employee of the protection afforded to him by mandatory provisions of the law applicable in absence of this choice (the 'objectively applicable law'). According to the majority opinion in literature, this means that the law chosen by the parties applies to the contract in full, except when mandatory rules of the otherwise applicable law would provide the worker better protection.[266] Hence, the employee will always be protected by the law which offers the better protection; if the employer and employee agree on better employment conditions than enshrined in the law applicable in the absence of choice, Article 8(1) Rome I prioritises the chosen law. But, if the parties agree on worse employment conditions than enshrined in the objectively applicable law, the latter law prevails. This 'favourable principle' is meant to prevent employers from abusing their superior bargaining position.

Since the objectively applicable law acts as a 'floor', a minimum standard of protection, it is always relevant to ascertain the latter law, which can be done following the choice of law rules in Article 8(2)–8(4) Rome I. According to Article 8(2) Rome I, the employment contracts is governed in principle by the law of the country in which or, failing that, from which the employee habitually carries out his work in performance of the contract – i.e. the habitual place of work. The country where the work is habitually carried out shall not be deemed to have changed if the employee is temporarily employed (posted) in another country. By referring to the *habitual* place of work, rather than the *actual* place of work, this provision stabilises the law applying to the employment contract: during a temporary posting, the law of the home State remains applicable. Article 8(3) Rome I contains an alternative reference rule in case the country where the work is habitually carried out cannot be identified. In that case the contract shall be governed by the law of the country where the place of business through which the employee was engaged is situated. Under Article 8(4) Rome I both pre-established connecting factors – habitual place of work and engaging place of business – may be set aside where it appears from the circumstances as a whole that the contract is more closely connected with another country, in which case the law of that other country shall apply.

---

266 AG Trstenjak, Opinion to *Voogsgeerd*, §48; AG Wahl, Opinion to *Schlecker*, §24. The Court of Justice has not taken a clear position on this issue yet, see ECJ 2011, C-29/10 (*Koelzsch*), §35 and ECJ 2011, C-384/10 (*Voogsgeerd)*, §28.

2.4.2.1. *The Habitual Country of Work of the Employee*

Article 8(2) Rome I uses the habitual place of work as its primary connecting factor. Therefore, it is key to know how to interpret the concept 'habitual place of work'. However, up until 2008 the Court of Justice had no competence to interpret the existing choice of law instruments.[267] Therefore, the first case law on this concept was developed in the framework of Brussels I (on the jurisdiction of the Court). In a case on a sales representative working in different countries, the national court should try to determine in which place the employee has established the effective centre of the working activities.[268] When the employee carries out a large part of the work in the country in which the employee has established an office, that country is deemed to be the country *in or from which* the work is habitually performed. However, if a worker is sent to different locations to perform one and the same activity (a chef who cooks on oil rigs on the continental shelf, for example), no such effective centre of working activities can be determined, nor can any qualitative criterion be used to determine the 'essential' part of the performance. In that case, the relevant criterion for establishing an employee's habitual place of work is the place where the employee spends most of the working time engaged on the employer's business.[269] In principle the whole duration of the contract should be taken into account, unless there is a clear intention on the side of both parties to change the place of work, in which case only the most recent place of work will be relevant.[270]

Although the habitual place of work is clearly not a connecting factor that is easily applied to so-called 'peripatetic employees',[271] in the *Koelzsch* and *Voogsgeerd* cases the Court of Justice made clear that even in the case of a truck driver working in international transport (*Koelzsch*) or a sailor working on a seagoing vessel (*Voogsgeerd*) the national court should try to establish whether, based on the circumstances as a whole, the country can be identified where or from which the work is actually performed.[272] The Court justified this broad

---

267 The competence to interpret the predecessor of the Rome I Regulation, the Rome Convention, was established in a separate protocol which entered into force on 1 August 2004 (see ECJ 2011, C-29/10 (*Koelzsch*), §30. The Rome I Regulation only applies to contracts concluded as from 17 December 2009 (Corrigendum to Regulation (EC) No 593/2008 [2008] OJ L 177).

268 See ECJ 1997, C-383/95 (*Rutten*), §23.

269 See ECJ 1996, C-482/93 (*Weber*), §50.

270 See ECJ 1996, C-482/93 (*Weber*), §§52–54.

271 'Peripatetic' employees (such as airline pilots, international management consultants, sales staff and so on) are in Great Britain distinguished as a separate category, alongside 'expatriate' employees. Interestingly, AG Bot used the term in his Opinion of 11 June 2015 in the case *Tyco* (Case C-266/14) §32 and §36, where he considered that 'peripatetic workers may be defined as being workers who are not assigned a fixed or habitual place of work. Such workers are therefore required to work at different premises every day'.

272 See ECJ 2011, C-29/10 (*Koelzsch*), §§47–49.

interpretation by referring to the protective character of this provision.[273] When ascertaining the 'place where the employee habitually carries out his work' in case of international transport (including international shipping), the national courts must take account of all the factors which characterise the activity of the employee. These are, in particular, (i) the place from which the employee carries out the transport-related tasks; (ii) the place where the employee returns after the tasks, receives instructions concerning the tasks and organises the work; and (iii) the place where the employee's work tools are situated. Additionally, the court must determine the places where the transport is principally carried out, where the goods are unloaded and the place to which the employee returns after completion of the tasks.[274] Referring to *Koelzsch*, the Court observed in *Crewlink v. Ryanair* (a Brussels I case) that:

> That circumstantial method makes it possible not only to reflect the true nature of legal relationships, in that it must take account of all the factors which characterise the activity of the employee, but also to prevent a concept such as that of 'place where, or from which, the employee habitually performs his work' from being exploited or contributing to the achievement of circumvention strategies.[275]

2.4.2.2. The Place of Establishment of the Employer

In the *Koelzsch* and *Voogsgeerd* cases, the Court stressed the priority of the habitual place of work over the place of establishment of the employer.[276] Moreover, the Court emphasised that the reference to the place of business through which the employee was engaged in the Rome Convention is strictly secondary.[277] It is only when it is not possible to identify the country in or from which the work is habitually performed may recourse be had to the second connecting factor, the 'engaging place of business'.[278] By focusing on the effective performance of the contract of employment as the connecting factor

273 ECJ 2011, C-29/10 (*Koelzsch*), §42.

274 ECJ 2011, C-29/10 (*Koelzsch*), §§48–49 and ECJ 2011, C-384/10 (*Voogsgeerd*), §§38–39. Confirmed in joined Cases ECJ 2017, C-168/16 and C-169/16 (*Crewlink v. Ryanair*). At §64 in the latter case, Court ruled that the place where the aircraft aboard which the work is habitually performed are stationed must also be taken into account. The judgment clarified in particular the notion of 'home base', a term used in relevant EU civil aviation law. At §75, nationality of the aircraft is dismissed as being of no relevance at all.

275 See ECJ 2017, C-168/16 and C-169/16 (*Crewlink v. Ryanair*), §62.

276 This was innovative, as in many countries the employment contract of transport workers was deemed to be governed by the law of the place of establishment of their employer. For more details see Van Hoek & Houwerzijl (2016), 215–253.

277 See ECJ 2011, C-29/10 (*Koelzsch*), §§48–49 and ECJ 2011, C-384/10 (*Voogsgeerd*), §§34–35.

278 See ECJ 2011, C-384/10 (*Voogsgeerd*), §§32–35.

(which means priority of the habitual place of work over the engaging place of business of the employer), the Court prevented the law of a place with no real and relevant connection to the actual performance of the work being designated as the objectively applicable law.

Hence, in the case law of the Court, the place of work is deemed to be the primary connecting factor, with the place of engagement only filling a very subsidiary/ancillary role. Taking into account the very broad interpretation of the 'habitual place of work' in Article 8(2) Rome I, it may seem as if there are hardly any situations that will be covered by Article 8(3) Rome I – referring to the place of engagement.[279] Nevertheless, the Court did clarify this concept in the *Voogsgeerd* judgment. As the elements related to the performance of the contract are already taken into account in determining the habitual place of work, the assessment of the place of engagement has a more formal character and focuses on the recruitment procedure:

> the courts should take into consideration not those matters relating to the performance of the work but only those relating to the procedure for concluding the contract, such as the place of business which published the recruitment notice and that which carried out the recruitment interview, and it must endeavour to determine the real location of that place of business.[280]

Accordingly, this connecting factor does not establish a relevant link to the performance of work, but is linked to the very beginning of the employment contract. It serves to provide legal certainty in situations in which it would be impossible to provide a clear link to any particular jurisdiction.

2.4.2.3. *A Country More Closely Connected to the Contract*

The possibility to use the 'escape clause', currently regulated in Article 8(4) Rome I, was looked at in the *Schlecker* case.[281] The *Schlecker* case concerned a conflict between a German employee (Ms Boedeker) and her German employer (the Schlecker company), caused by the decision of the employer to terminate employment in the Netherlands and re-instate the employee in a different position in Germany. For the last 12 years (of a total of 27 years of service) the

---

279 However the provision may remain of or regain relevance for the emerging group of 'hypermobile' workers.

280 See ECJ 2011, C-384/10 (*Voogsgeerd*), §47. Furthermore, schematic interpretation of Article 8(3) Rome I requires the – subsidiary – factor laid down in that provision to be applied when it is impossible to situate the employment relationship in a Member State. Consequently, only a strict interpretation of that subsidiary factor can guarantee the complete foreseeability of the law applicable to the contract of employment.

281 ECJ 2013, C-64/12 (*Schlecker*).

employee had been employed as manager of the Dutch division of the employer, supervising its 300 local branches. There was no contestation as to the fact that the Netherlands was (had become) the habitual place of work.[282] Ms Boedeker lodged a complaint in a Dutch court against her employer's unilateral decision to change her place of work. She relied on the application of Dutch law, which in this case offered her better protection than German law. However, her employer Schlecker claimed that the contract was more closely related to Germany. Elements referring to Germany were inter alia the common nationality and place of domicile of both parties, the language and original currency of the contract, reference to provisions of German law in the contract and the fact that the employee was covered by German tax law, social security and additional pension schemes. Could the Court in this case ignore the connection based on the place of work in favour of German law?

In its judgment the Court considered that, whereas the habitual place of work does take priority over the engaging place of business, based on the protective character of the first connecting factor, no such hierarchy exists with regard to the escape clause referring to the closest connection. Hence, both connecting factors are put on the same footing in this regard. Although the national court must first determine the applicable law by reference to the pre-established connecting factors, it may disregard these connecting factors and apply the law of another country, 'even where an employee carries out the work in performance of the contract habitually, for a lengthy period and without interruption in the same country', where it is apparent from the circumstances as a whole that the employment contract is more closely connected with that country.[283] Furthermore, the Court stressed that the closer connection test cannot be performed by simply counting connecting factors: not all connecting factors carry the same weight. According to the Court

> among the significant factors suggestive of a connection with a particular country, account should be taken in particular of the country in which the employee pays taxes on the income from his activity and the country in which he is covered by a social security scheme and pension, sickness insurance and invalidity schemes. In addition, the national court must also take account of all the circumstances of the case, such as the parameters relating to salary determination and other working conditions.[284]

The content of the relevant laws is not decisive in this matter.

---

282 ECJ 2013, C-64/12 (*Schlecker*), §27.
283 ECJ 2013, C-64/12 (*Schlecker*), §§42, 35–36.
284 ECJ 2013, C-64/12 (*Schlecker*), §41.

Although it is too early to predict how extensive the Court's interpretation of Article 8(4) Rome I in future cases will be, it is beyond dispute that with *Schlecker*, the tax law and social security schemes applicable to the employee have gained importance. This furthers the alignment between applicable labour law and social security law. However, it may also open the door for possibilities to (mis)use *Schlecker*, especially in relation to a broad use of Article 16 of Regulation 883/04 on coordination of social security within the EU (see Section 2.5).[285]

2.4.3. INTERPLAY BETWEEN ROME I AND FREE MOVEMENT OF WORKERS

If Article 8 Rome I is applied to migrant, frontier and seasonal workers in the meaning of Article 45 TFEU in conjunction with Article 7 Regulation 492/2011 (see Section 2.2.2, in particular), the law objectively applicable in the absence of choice will almost always be the *lex loci laboris*, being the law of the country in which or from which the workers habitually carry out their work in performance of the contract. In terms of outcome, this means that in the absence of a choice of law, the labour law of the receiving Member State will apply in full. If a choice of law has been made, only the more favourable mandatory provisions of the receiving Member State's laws and collective agreements are applicable to the contracts. Hence, in a system with relatively few mandatory (statutory and collectively agreed) labour law standards, the equal treatment principle enshrined in Article 45 TFEU may suffer from the private international law rules.

However, Article 9(2) Rome I allows courts to apply domestic 'overriding mandatory' provisions (law of the forum), regardless of the (objectively) applicable law.[286] According to Article 9(1):

> Overriding mandatory provisions are provisions the respect for which is regarded as crucial by a country for safeguarding its public interests, such as its political, social or economic organisation, to such an extent that they are applicable to any situation falling within their scope, irrespective of the law otherwise applicable to the contract under this Regulation.

---

285 See Cornelissen (2016); Van Hoek & Houwerzijl (2016).

286 Moreover, Article 9(3) Rome I allows the courts to give effect to overriding mandatory provisions of the country of performance, in so far as those overriding mandatory provisions render the performance of the contract unlawful. This provision is not considered in this section. However, for a first ruling on this provision see ECJ 2016, C-135/15 (*Grigorios Nikiforidis*).

Many labour law rules have an overriding mandatory character, though the Member States traditionally draw the line between *lex causae*[287] rules and overriding mandatory provisions differently.[288] As a result, Article 9 Rome I facilitates labour law systems which rely (sometimes heavily) on overriding mandatory law.

2.4.4. INTERPLAY BETWEEN ROME I AND POSTING OF WORKERS DIRECTIVE

Regarding the posting of workers, it is important to note that the Posting of Workers Directive uses in essence the same technique as Article 9 Rome I (see Section 2.3.2) to achieve its aims. In Article 3, the directive identifies which national mandatory rules of the host State must apply to posted workers. In this manner a hard core of clearly defined terms and conditions of work and employment for minimum protection of workers (laid down in Article 3(1 a–g) is established, which must be complied with by the service provider in the host Member State. According to the Preamble of the directive (Recital 7–11), the directive thus makes the optional character of (now) Article 9 Rome I obligatory, by defining those subjects of labour law in which the national mandatory rules must be seen as 'overriding mandatory provisions'. Hence, the rules on mandatory protection laid down in the directive can – from a private international law perspective – be understood to form an application of Article 9 Rome I. Hence, the directive can and should not be read in isolation from Article 8 Rome I. From the perspective of the host state, the directive fills in the 'gap'[289] that Article 8 Rome I would create for the territorial application of labour law. As is well known, 'the directive, which was drafted in 1991, was partially intended to allay the fears of policymakers in high-wage economies that their markets would be flooded by increasing numbers of lower paid workers'.[290]

[287] *Lex causae* is the law or laws chosen by a forum court from among the relevant legal systems to arrive at its judgment.

[288] For a description of the different models of workers' protection in the Member States, see Van Hoek & Houwerzijl (2011) and (2012).

[289] As pointed out in Section 2.3, Article 8(2) stipulates that the country where the work is habitually carried out shall not be deemed to have changed if a worker is temporarily employed (i.e. posted) in another country.

[290] Kennett & Nesbitt (2000), pp. 399–406, at 400.

2.4.4.1. *Interplay Concerning the Material Scope of the Posting of Workers Directive*

Article 3(1) of the Posting of Workers Directive states that 'Member States shall ensure that, *whatever the law applicable to the employment relationship* [emphasis added], the undertakings referred to in Article 1(1) guarantee workers posted to their territory the terms and conditions of employment covering the following matters ...'. Thus, it is made clear that the law applying to the employment contract is regulated by private international law rules, but the directive superimposes – if necessary – the minimum protection of the law of the host State upon the protection already offered under the law applying to the contract by virtue of Article 8 Rome I.

An indication for the complementary character of the directive in relation to Article 8 Rome I may also be found in Article 3(7). Article 3(7), first sentence allows the *application* of better protection to posted workers than the minimum provided for by the directive.[291] In the *Laval* and *Rüffert* judgments (discussed in Section 2.3.3), the Court made it clear that this provision refers only to the more favourable terms and conditions of employment which those workers already enjoy pursuant to the law or collective agreements in the Member State of origin, or which have been agreed voluntarily by the employer.[292]

Nevertheless, if one reads the case law on the posting of workers in the context of the free provision of services from a lens of searching the applicable law to the contract between the parties involved, it seems as if the underlying assumption is that posted workers (always) ordinarily work in the country of establishment of their employer and therefore will be covered by the law of their (employer's) home State ('the country of origin'). This reading would however submit the posted worker to the laws of the country of establishment of the employer and disallow the application of more favourable provisions contained in the law applicable by virtue of Article 8 Rome I.[293] Admittedly, the reference to the 'country of origin' or 'home country' in the court's case law may cause confusion if the Member State where the employee is recruited or where the employee will habitually perform the work is not the same as the Member State

291 Recital 17 of the Posting of workers also refers to *application* of more favourable terms and conditions to posted workers. For the embodiment of the 'most favourable principle' in pre-Posting of Workers Directive case law, see Houwerzijl & Pennings (1999), p. 102.

292 See ECJ 2007 C-341/05 (*Laval*), §§79–81, 120 and ECJ 2008 C-346/06 (*Rüffert*), §§32–34. Compare Houwerzijl (2005), p. 161. See, also Evju (2009), p. 32: 'Initially it was clear from the wording of the proposed provision that it referred only to more favourable terms and conditions in a worker's home state (under the law applicable to the contract of employment) [D 2, Parliament, COM-93 – ctr WG 11 – Council 1994h]. There is no indication that the change of wording was intended to fundamentally depart from this.'

293 See e.g. Fornasier & Torga (2013), pp. 356–65, at 364.

where the employer is established. However, it seems more logical that 'country of origin' or 'home country' should be read to refer to the country whose law is objectively applicable in light of Article 8 Rome I. This will most often be the country in which the work is normally or habitually performed, rather than the country of establishment of the employer.[294] Support for this reading may also be found in Article 4(1) of Directive 91/533 which, under the heading 'expatriate employees', gives rules on information requirements in situations 'where the employee is required to work in one or more countries other than *the Member State whose law and/or practice governs the contract or employment relationship abroad*' (emphasis added).[295]

So far, the Court did not have to decide on the applicable law to the contract of a posted worker and this may explain why it never paid attention to the underlying contractual position of the parties. Until now, the case law has focused on establishing whether the application of host State law during the period of posting would (disproportionally) infringe the free provision of services. In this respect, as is common ground, the posting of workers in the context of the free provision of services opposes the interests of host State employers and workers to the interests of the company performing the cross-border service. But it also pitches the interests of high cost host States against those of low cost sending States.[296] This makes the topic highly controversial.

2.4.4.2. Interplay Concerning the Personal Scope of the Posting of Workers Directive

Concerning the definition of a 'posted worker', for a long time it was unclear whether there is a difference in meaning between the concept of 'habitual

294 See Van Hoek & Houwerzijl (2012), pp. 441–43.

295 Directive 91/533 was adopted a few months after the first draft was presented by the Commission for what has become the Posting of Workers Directive (see COM(91)230). The interrelationship between Directive 91/533 and the Posting of Workers Directive was emphasised during the implementation process of the latter directive. In the transposal stage, the Commission expressed its belief that compliance with the requirements laid down in Directive 91/533 (in particular Articles 2 and 4) should facilitate the implementation of the Posting of Workers Directive and in particular the process of comparing the home State's and host State's provisions on minimum wages and paid holidays (see *Report Working Party on the transposal of the Directive concerning the posting of workers, Brussels*: European Commission, Employment & Social Affairs, 1999, p. 13). The linkage between the two directives also has been at issue in the case law, see ECJ 1999, C-369/96 to C-376/96 (*Arblade*), §§61, 65, 67–68, 70, and ECJ 2008, C-319/06 (*Commission v. Luxembourg*), §§39–41. Directive 91/533/EEC requires that employers provide employees covered by the scope of the directive, in writing, the essential aspects of the contract or employment relationship, including, for posted workers the duration of the employment abroad, the benefits in cash or kind attendant on the employment abroad, etc. Directive 91/533 will be replaced by a new (strengthening) Directive 2019/1152 on Transparent and Predictable Working Conditions.

296 See Fornasier & Torga (2013), p. 358; Leczykiewicz (2015).

country of work' in Article 8(2) Rome I and the concept of the country where the posted worker 'normally works' in Article 2(2) Posting of Workers Directive; whereas the Rome I Regulation seems to focus on the habitual place of work *under the contract*, the concept of the Posting of Workers Directive may also be read in a purely literal way. In a literal reading, Article 2(1) of the directive would fit with the posting rule with regard to social security (see Section 2.5): here, previous insurance in the country of origin is required, not necessarily previous engagement with the posting undertaking.[297] However, a contextual reading would be more in line with the aims of the Posting of Workers Directive.

The difference between the two possible interpretations is important in the situation that workers are hired solely for the purpose of posting. In that case there will be no habitual place of work in the country of origin, at least not under the contract. So, according to the contextual interpretation of Article 2(1) of the directive, such a situation would not qualify as a genuine posting within the meaning of the directive. This approach is sometimes taken in national case law. For example in a Dutch case between Portuguese and English subsidiaries of the Atlanco Rimec group on the one hand and the Dutch parties to the collective labour agreement in the construction industry on the other hand. The 'posted' workers involved were, according to their employment contracts, explicitly and solely hired for a specific construction project in the Netherlands. Therefore, according to the Dutch court, their 'habitual' country of work under the contract was the Netherlands. As a consequence, Dutch law was deemed to be objectively applicable to the employment contracts of the workers pursuant to Article 8(2) Rome I.[298] The Posting of Workers Enforcement Directive seems to endorse this contextual approach: Article 4(3)(c) of this directive makes an explicit link between the concept of posting in the Posting of Workers Directive and the 'habitual country of work' under the Rome I Regulation.[299]

2.5. EU SOCIAL SECURITY COORDINATION

2.5.1. LEGAL CONTEXT

Under the terms of the EU Treaties, the Member States have retained the sovereign power to define their own social security systems. The starting point

297 See Article 12 Regulation 883/04 as implemented by Regulation 987/2009.

298 *Rechtbank Midden Nederland* 22 July 2015, ECLI:NL:RBMNE:2015:5393.

299 Albeit only as an indicative factor in the overall assessment of whether a posted worker temporarily carries out the work in a Member State other than the one in which the worker normally works.

of EU law and EU policy is indeed that the Member States are entirely free to organise their internal social protection systems as they see fit.

In the absence of harmonisation, it is for each Member State to determine the features of its own social security system, including which benefits are provided, the conditions for eligibility, how these benefits are calculated, the level of contributions to be paid by insured persons and the income to be taken into account when calculating social security contributions. However, when exercising their power in the field of social security, Member States must comply with EU law.[300] The most relevant area of EU law in this respect is the internal market law. In particular, the application of the Member States' social security legislation must not create unjustified obstacles to the exercise of the EU rights of free movement of persons and services.[301] In this context, the Treaty of Rome of 1957 already mandated in its Article 51 the EU legislator to adopt the necessary measures in the field of social security to provide freedom of movement for workers (now Article 48 TFEU). This Treaty provision refers to measures such as the aggregation, for the purpose of acquiring and retaining the right to benefits and of calculating the amount of benefits, of all periods taken into account under the laws of the various countries and the payment of benefits to persons residing in the territories of the Member States. In addition, the prohibition of discrimination on grounds of nationality as laid down in Articles 18 and 45 TFEU must also be respected by the Member States in their social security systems.

The European legislature has tried to attain these goals by adopting an elaborate social security coordination system. In 1958, it had already adopted Regulation 3 and 4 which were replaced by Regulation 1408/71 and Regulation 574/72 in 1971 and 1972. In their turn these regulations were applicable until 1 May 2010, when they were replaced by Regulation 883/2004 and Regulation 978/2009. The regulations have been subject to numerous judgments of the Court of Justice which applied and interpreted the provisions of these regulations in the light of the general objectives laid down in the Treaties. This case law forms an integral part of the EU coordination system.

It is not the intention of this coordination system to harmonise or approximate the systems of the Member States in any way. The purpose is to coordinate the social security systems of the Member States in such a manner as to eliminate any negative consequences for the migrating individual that may arise from differences between the various systems.[302] It does not affect

300 See inter alia ECJ 1998, C-158/96 (*Kohll*), §19; ECJ 2008, C-103/06 (*Derouin*), §25 and ECJ 2006, C-493/04 (*Piatkowski*), §33.

301 See e.g. ECJ 1994, C-165/91 (*Van Munster*), §27; ECJ 1995, C-443/93 (*Vougioukas*), §39 and more recently ECJ 2016, C-515/14 (*Commission v. Cyprus*), §38.

302 ECJ 2011, C-388/09 (*Da Silva Martins*), §70 and ECJ 2016, C-515/14 (*Commission v. Cyprus*), §34.

the material and formal differences between the social security regimes of the various Member States and therefore does not affect the divergent rights of the individuals working or residing in those States.[303] This implies, among other things, that (labour) migration between the Member States may give rise to more extensive or less extensive social protection depending on the system that is in place in the Member State where the individual concerned is working or residing.[304]

First and foremost, the coordination regime determines which Member State's social security legislation is applicable in a cross-border situation (Title II Regulation 883/2004). The underlying principles of the rules that determine the applicable legislation are the State-of-employment principle for economically active persons and the State-of-residence principle for economically inactive persons. Additionally, the coordination system is governed by the principle of equality of treatment for all persons and benefits covered by the Regulation with regard to the social security rights enshrined in the legislation of the Member State (Article 4 Regulation 883/2004). Furthermore, the coordination system contains rules with regard to the waiving of residence clauses in the allocation or preservation of social security benefits (Article 7 Regulation 883/2004). It also establishes a number of rules with regard to the aggregation of periods of insurance, employment and residence (e.g. Article 6). The purpose of this aggregation is to avoid that by dividing a person's insurance career between different Member States, that person would suffer a reduction in or loss of rights. Finally, a detailed system of collaboration was established between the social security institutions to facilitate the application of the regulation for insured persons who have ties with more than one Member State.

The EU social security coordination is a highly complex and technical piece of legislation, which is, inter alia, due to the complexity of and great diversity in the national social security systems and legislations which the regulations need to coordinate. This section will briefly analyse the scope of the EU regulations as well as the general principles underlying them. Subsequently, we will take a closer look at the rules for determining the applicable legislation. However, this chapter will not further discuss the specific chapters and provisions in the regulation regarding the different benefits covered by it. More details on the EU social security coordination can be found in other literature.[305]

---

303 See e.g. ECJ 1986, 41/84 (*Pinna*), §20; ECJ 1997, C-340/94 (*De Jaeck*), §18; ECJ 2006, C-493/04 (*Piatkowski*), §§19–20 and ECJ 2009, C-208/07 (*von Chamier-Glisczinski*), §84.

304 See, eg, ECJ 2002, C-393/99 and C-394/99 (*Hervein and others*), §50–51; ECJ 2006, C-493/04 (*Piatkowski*), §34 and ECJ 2009, C-208/07 (*von Chamier-Glisczinski*), §85.

305 Pennings (2015b) and Fuchs & Cornelissen (2015).

2.5.2. PERSONAL SCOPE

In principle, the EU social security coordination regulations are only applicable to nationals of an EU Member State, an EEA State[306] or Switzerland. They are also applicable to the members of the families and survivors of these persons.

In addition, Regulation 1231/2010[307] extends this personal scope to all third-country nationals as far as they are legally residing in a Member State and the situation of the person concerned is not in any way confined to a single Member State.[308]

Persons are only covered by the social security coordination in so far as they are or have been subject to the legislation of one or more Member States (Article 2). The question as to whether or not a person is covered by the legislation of a Member State depends on this legislation. Coverage may be based on mandatory or voluntary insurance (Bismarckian systems) or on residence in a Member State. In principle, it remains the prerogative of the Member States to decide which persons are covered by their systems, provided of course that they respect EU law. The definition of the personal scope is very wide, much wider than the initial coordination regulations of 1958 and 1971, that were limited to migrant workers. Now, the status under which a person is covered by the national legislation (workers, self-employed persons, or persons with another status) is irrelevant. As a result, almost all EU citizens and legally residing third-country nationals are nowadays covered by the EU social security regulations.[309]

Besides being covered by a national social security scheme, the person involved must also be in a cross-border situation. This means that a person in a purely internal situation which has no relation with another Member State does not fall under the personal scope of the EU social security regulations.[310] This can be the case if such a person is in a situation which only concerns a border between the regions of a Member State.[311] A cross-border situation

306 Norway, Iceland and Liechtenstein. Any reference hereinafter to an EU national also refers to nationals of these States as well as of Switzerland. References to an EU Member State also refer to these States.

307 Regulation 1231/2010 (nationals of third countries).

308 The personal scope of the former Regulations 1408/71 and 574/74 was extended to these third-country nationals by Regulation 895/2003. For more details see Cornelissen (2008). This extension does not apply to third-country nationals with regard to the United Kingdom and Denmark (Recitals 18 and 19 of Regulation 1231/2010) nor with regard to the EEA States and Switzerland (for the latter see: ECJ 2010, C-247/09 (*Xhymshiti*)). See for a recent interpretation of the condition to be legally residing in a Member State: ECJ 2019, C-477/17 (*Balandin*).

309 This was recently confirmed in ECJ 2019, C-322/17 (*Bogatu*).

310 ECJ 1992, C-153/91 (*Petit*).

311 ECJ 2008, C-212/06 (*Government of the French Community and Walloon Government*).

can take different forms, such as the person having the nationality of another Member State, the person's residence being outside a Member State, the person having worked in more than one Member State, or the person needing medical treatment during a stay in another Member State.[312]

2.5.3. MATERIAL SCOPE

The material scope of Regulation 883/2004 is defined in Article 3. It refers to all legislation concerning benefits in case of sickness, maternity and paternity, invalidity, old age and survivors, accidents at work and occupational diseases, unemployment and pre-retirement as well as benefits concerning death grants and family benefits. This is an exclusive list, but it applies to general as well as to special schemes, whether contributory or not. However, social and medical assistance schemes are excluded.[313] Still, benefits which have characteristics of both social security and social assistance are covered. Such benefits are called 'special non-contributory cash benefits', because they provide coverage against the risks listed in Article 3 while at the same time guaranteeing the persons concerned a minimum subsistence income in accordance with the economic and social situation in a Member State. They are subject to a special coordination regime laid down in Article 70 Regulation 883/2004, based on the person's residence.

The term 'legislation' is very broadly defined in Article 1(l) Regulation 883/2004. It includes all types of legislative, regulatory and administrative measures adopted by the Member States that have a direct or sufficiently relevant link with these branches of social security. The categorisation of the measure under national law (for instance as taxes and not as social security contributions) does not matter in this respect.[314] However, contractual provisions, such as occupational pensions agreed between employers and employees, are excluded.[315]

The Court of Justice has given a very extensive interpretation of this material scope. It is settled case law that a benefit may be regarded as a social security benefit if it is granted to the recipients without any individual and discretionary

---

312 Spiegel (2015), p. 75.

313 Nevertheless such schemes are considered as 'social advantages' within the meaning of Article 7(2) Regulation 492/2011. See Section 2.2.2. Also excluded are benefit schemes in relation to which a Member State assumes the liability for damages to persons (such as those for victims of war or terrorist attacks) and provisions in national legislation concerning ship owners' obligations.

314 ECJ 2000, C-34/98 (*Commission v. France*) and ECJ 2015, C-623/13 (*de Ruyter*).

315 Unless they serve to implement an insurance obligation arising from national legislation or unless a Member State has made a declaration to include such systems into the regulation.

assessment of personal needs, on the basis of a legally defined position and relates to one of the risks expressly listed in Article 3(1) Regulation 883/2004.[316] In addition, the precise nature of the benefit should not vary according to the particular features of each system of national law, but rests upon objective criteria defined in a context specific to EU law. The risk covered by each benefit must be taken into consideration.[317]

2.5.4. GENERAL PRINCIPLES

2.5.4.1. Equal Treatment

The principle of equal treatment, laid down in Article 4 Regulation 883/2004, or the prohibition of discrimination on ground of nationality guarantees that in social security matters nationals of a Member State are treated by any other Member State as if they are nationals of the latter State. This principle has always been interpreted broadly by the Court of Justice in social security matters. It applies to direct discrimination on grounds of nationality, which is nowadays rather rare in the field of social security,[318] as well as to indirect discrimination, meaning all forms of discrimination which, through the application of other distinguishing criteria, lead in fact to the same result.[319] However, the Court accepts such provisions, provided that they are appropriate for securing the attainment of a legitimate objective and do not go beyond what is necessary to attain that objective.[320] A clear example of such provisions are residence clauses. The Court repeatedly confirmed that a distinction based on residence is likely to operate mainly to the detriment of nationals of other Member States, as in the majority of cases non-residents are foreign nationals.[321]

In addition, EU law does not only prohibit discrimination on grounds of nationality regarding social security entitlements, but also all other measures capable of hindering or rendering less attractive the exercise by EU nationals of the right to free movement, even if they apply without regard to the nationality of the workers concerned. For instance, the Court condemned the legislation of a Member State which levied on a worker who had transferred his residence in the course of one year from one Member State to another in order to take up

316 ECJ 2011, C-388/09 (*da Silva Martins*), §38.

317 ECJ 2011, C-503/09 (*Stewart*), §§35–36.

318 For recent examples see: ECJ 2006, C-346/05 (*Chateignier*) (on Belgian unemployment benefits) and ECJ 2011, C-399/09 (*Landtová*) (on old age pensions in the Czech Republic).

319 See on these concepts Section 2.2.1.

320 ECJ 2008, C-228/07 (*Petersen*), §54; ECJ 2014, C-523/13 (*Larcher*), §83 and ECJ 2016, C-308/14 (*Commission v. United Kingdom*), §79.

321 See, inter alia, ECJ 1997, C-57/96 (*Meints*); ECJ 2008, C-228/07 (*Petersen*) and ECJ 2011, C-206/11 (*Commission v. Germany*).

employment there, higher social security contributions than those which would be payable, in similar circumstances, by a worker who had continued to reside throughout the year in the Member State in question.[322]

Such non-discriminatory obstacles to the free movement can be justified only if they are based on objective considerations of public interest, independent of the nationality of the persons concerned and proportionate to the legitimate objective of the national provisions.[323] This test is similar to the test that has to be applied for indirect discriminatory measures.

The principle of equal treatment is further developed in Article 5 Regulation 883/2004 on the equal treatment of benefits, income, facts or events. It makes sure that aspects of a person's situation which might be relevant for that person's social security rights, but which are linked to another Member State, should be taken into account. For instance, if under the legislation of a Member State entitlement to a benefit (such as a supplement to an old-age pension) depends on a person being already entitled to another social security benefit (in this case a basic old-age pension), the receipt of such a benefit acquired under the legislation of another Member State should be taken into account.

2.5.4.2. *Waiving Residence Clauses*

Regulation 833/2004 also contains a general rule on the waiving of residence clauses in the legislation of the Member States (Article 7). This is the so-called principle of the export of benefits. It waives the residence clauses in national legislation for the entitlement or acquisition of a benefit, as well as for the retention of already acquired rights. This holds first and foremost for benefits like old-age pensions or invalidity and long-term care benefits. It also applies to child benefits: the residence of a child in another Member State should not prevent a person from being entitled to child benefits for that child.[324]

There are, however, a number of exceptions to the export principle. One such exception is the special coordination regime that applies for the so-called special non-contributory benefits that lie between social security and social assistance. For these kinds of benefits, a State-of-residence-based coordination system is in place.[325] Another exception is unemployment benefits, which only need to be exported for a maximum of three months if the unemployment benefit recipient moves to another Member State in order to seek employment.[326] In other words, there is in effect a residence requirement for unemployment benefit entitlement.

322 ECJ 1999, C-18/95 (*Terhoeve*).
323 ECJ 2006, C-406/04 (*De Cuyper*), §40.
324 ECJ 2002, C-255/99 (*Humer*), §39.
325 Article 70 Regulation 883/2004. For more details see Pennings (2015b), pp. 65–77 and Verschueren (2009).
326 Article 64 Regulation 883/2004.

2.5.4.3. *Aggregation of Periods*

One of the essential measures to facilitate the free movement of persons within the EU is the aggregation of periods to which Article 48 TFEU explicitly refers. For entitlement to social security benefits sometimes the legislation of the Member States requires that the person concerned has completed certain periods. These periods can be periods of insurance, of residence or of employment. For instance, for entitlement to unemployment benefits, the legislation of Member States often requires that the unemployed person has previously worked or been insured for unemployment during a certain period of time. For entitlement to old-age pensions, too, very often the legislation of the Member States requires that the person involved has been insured for a certain period of time for this kind of benefit.

Such requirements become problematic for the exercise of the right to free movement if under the legislation of a Member State only periods fulfilled in that Member State are taken into consideration. Persons who have recently moved from one Member State to another would run the risk of having their claim for a social security benefit being denied by the latter Member State because they do not fulfil the necessary periods in that Member State. Let us take the example of the legislation of Member State A which submits entitlement to an unemployment benefit to a previous insurance period of a minimum of two years in that Member State. A person who had first worked for some years in Member State B before moving to work in Member State A, but became unemployed after only one year in Member State A, would not be entitled to an unemployment benefit in that Member State because that person had not fulfilled the required two years of insurance there. Such a situation would clearly be to the detriment of migrant workers and would constitute an obstacle to the free movement.

Therefore, the EU social security coordination contains a general principle, worded in Article 6 Regulation 883/2004, according to which a Member State whose legislation makes the acquisition, retention, duration or recovery of the right to benefits or the coverage by its legislation conditional upon the completion of periods of insurance, employment, self-employment or residence shall, to the extent necessary, take into account such periods completed under the legislation of any other Member State.

2.5.5. DETERMINATION OF THE APPLICABLE SOCIAL SECURITY LEGISLATION

One of the most important tasks of the coordination system is to determine the legislation applicable in cross-border situations. The relevant rules are contained in Title II of Regulation 883/2004 (Articles 11 to 16). This section will give an overview of the general principles underlying these rules and of the specific provisions thereof. Next, the specific rules applicable to posted workers will be analysed. From the outset, it must be emphasised that these rules of conflict differ from the rules of conflict applicable in labour law and that, in principle, they do not influence the latter. Consequently, it is possible that an employment contract may be subject to the legislation of Member State other than the State whose social security legislation is applicable to the employee and the employer involved.[327]

The rules of conflict of Regulation 883/2004 are intended, in the first place, to prevent the simultaneous application of several national legislative systems and the complications that might ensue from this. They also want to ensure that a person in a cross-border situation between Member States is not left without social security coverage because there is no legislation applicable to that person.[328]

The person in question shall be subject to the legislation to be determined in accordance with the relevant provisions of Regulation 883/2004.[329] These rules of conflict have a binding character, meaning that national affiliation conditions are overridden if their application is such as to deprive the conflict of law rule laid down in Regulation 883/2004 of all practical effect. For instance, the condition in the legislation of a Member State that a person is only insured for social security if that person resides in the territory of that Member State, will be overruled by the provision in Article 11(3)(a) Regulation 883/2004, which, in principle, obliges a Member State to insure all persons economically active in its territory, even if they reside in another Member State.

Another starting point of the conflict rules of Regulation 883/2004 is their exclusive effect or the single State principle. It means that the persons to whom that regulation applies are to be subject to the legislation of a single Member State only, which therefore excludes any possibility of an overlapping of the national legislation of several Member States with regard to one and the same period. This principle is intended to avoid double insurance and double contributions.

The basis of these rules of conflict is the territorial application of the social security law of the Member State where the work is carried out (the State-of-employment principle – *lex loci laboris*). It means that a person employed in the territory of one Member State shall be subject to the social security legislation of that State, even if that person resides in the territory of another Member State or if the employer is registered in another Member State.[330]

---

327 Cornelissen (2016).

328 ECJ 1998, C-275/96 (*Kuusijärvi*); ECJ 2000, C-202/97 (*Fitzwilliam*), §20 and ECJ 2013, C-548/11 (*Mulders*), §39.

329 ECJ 1986, 60/85 (*Luijten*), §14; ECJ 2015, C-623/13 (*de Ruyter*), §35 and ECJ 2016, C-269/15 (*Hoogstad*), §39.

330 Article 11 Regulation 883/2004.

The choice of this principle is inspired by the legal context in which the European social security coordination is applied: to ensure the free movement of workers and to preclude discrimination based on nationality by the Member State where the migrating worker is employed (Article 45(2) TFEU). The main reason for this State-of-employment principle is, indeed, to ensure equal treatment of all people working on the territory of a Member State, in accordance with the right to equal treatment for migrant workers. This prohibition holds not only for all conditions of employment and remuneration that apply in the State of employment, but also for social security provisions.[331] So, the State-of-employment principle is an expression of the premise that a migrating worker is entitled to the same rights in the State of employment as workers of that Member State.[332]

Nonetheless, the application of the State-of-employment principle does not imply that a migrant worker is invariably entitled to social security benefits provided in the State of employment. If a person resides in another Member State (e.g. frontier workers) then, for certain benefits (e.g. coverage of medical costs), that person shall be entitled first and foremost in accordance with the legislation of the State of residence (albeit at the expense of the State of employment).[333]

The provisions of Regulation 883/2004 contain a number of exceptions to the State-of employment principle. Civil servants, for instance, are subject to the social security of the Member State for which they work, even when they are working on the territory of another Member State (Article 11(3)b)). For seamen (Article 11(4)), for airline personnel (Article 11(5)) and in the case of simultaneous employment in more than one Member State (Article 13) there are special rules as well. For the latter category, the provisions of Article 13 refer to the State of residence, provided that substantial occupational activities are pursued in that country. In a number of other cases, it is the registered office or the place of business of the employing undertaking that determines to which country's social security legislation the person in question is subject.[334]

When workers are temporarily posted by their employers to pursue activities in another Member State on behalf of their employers, or when self-employed persons temporarily go to pursue their activities in another Member State, they remain, pursuant to Article 12 Regulation 883/2004, subject to the

331 See e.g. ECJ 1986, 41/84 (*Pinna*).

332 The relevance of the principle of equal treatment to the rules governing the determination of the applicable legislation was underlined by the Court of Justice in, among other judgments, ECJ 2006, C-493/04 (*Piatkowski*), §19; ECJ 2008, C-212/06 (*Government of the French Community and Walloon Government*), §48 and ECJ 2008, C-103/06 (*Derouin*), §20. See also recital 17 of the preamble to Regulation 883/2004. This was explicitly confirmed in ECJ 2018, C-527/16 (*Alpenrind*), §98.

333 See Article 17 of Regulation 883/2004. See also Cornelissen (2016), pp. 266 and 267.

334 For an application of this article see e.g. ECJ 2012, C-115/11 (*Format*).

social security legislation of the Member State in which they normally pursue their activities. This situation will be discussed in more detail in Section 2.5.6.

Finally, the implementation of the conflict rules in Article 11 to 15 Regulation 883/2004 do not always lead to appropriate results. Therefore Article 16 offers the possibility for the competent authorities of the Member States to provide by common agreement for exceptions to these rules. The only condition is that the exception is in the interest of the persons of categories of persons concerned.

2.5.6. SPECIFIC RULES APPLICABLE TO THE POSTED WORKERS[335]

The currently most disputed derogation from the State-of-employment principle concerns the rules applicable to the posting of workers from one Member State to another. Article 12 has 'special rules' for posting.[336] During 24 months at the most, a posted employee remains subject to the social security legislation of the Member State to which the employee was subject before the posting. Contrary to the provisions of the Posting of Workers Directive 96/71 this concerns the entire social security legislation of the Member State in question, and therefore the social security legislation of the host Member State does not apply for this period. As regards the employees, this provision specifies that the person concerned may not be sent to replace another posted worker.

Principally, the intention is to avoid that, as a result of a strict application of the State-of-employment principle, a short and temporary employment situation in a certain Member State would lead to an equally short and temporary change of the applicable social security law. Not only could this lead to administrative complications, but also to gaps in insurance cover that could work out badly for the person concerned. The application of the State-of-employment principle would then be an obstacle to the free movement of workers and service providers.[337]

Nonetheless, the Court of Justice explicitly regarded the posting provisions as an exception to the State-of-employment principle and held that they can only be applied if a number of conditions are met.[338] After all, this derogation

335 The provisions on posted self-employed persons (Article 12(2) Regulation 883/2004) will not be discussed in this chapter.

336 The provisions in Regulation 883/2004 do not differ substantially from those in the former Regulation 1408/71, more specifically Article 14. The case law of the Court of Justice on the posting provisions of the former regulation continue to be relevant as well.

337 ECJ 1970, C-35/70 (*Manpower*), §§10–12; ECJ 2000, C-202/97 (*Fitzwilliam*), §§28–31 and ECJ 2000, C-404/98 (*Plum*), §19.

338 ECJ 1970, C-35/70 (*Manpower*), §10; ECJ 2000, C-202/97 (*Fitzwilliam*), §§28 and 30 and ECJ 2000, C-404/98 (*Plum*), §14 and ECJ 2018, C-527/16 (*Alpenrind*), §95.

means that the worker concerned will not be able to invoke the right to equal treatment with the workers of the Member State where that person works. In addition, the application of the social security system of a Member State other than that where the activities are carried out could lead to competitive advantages for the sending company vis-à-vis the undertakings established in the host Member State, in particular when the former has to pay a lower level of social security contributions. The special rules with regard to posting in Regulation 883/2004 hover between the application of the State-of-employment principle as an expression of the principle of equal treatment and the removal of legal and administrative obstacles to the free movement of service providers. The balance between those two points of departure must be preserved by observance of a series of specific conditions to be met with a view to allowing exceptions to the State-of-employment principle as laid down by the EU legislator and interpreted by the Court of Justice.

Some of these conditions follow from the applicable provisions themselves, among which the provisions of Article 14 Regulation 987/2009. These can be summarised as follows. In the first place, there is the temporary character of posting. The duration to be expected may not exceed 24 months. This is quite a long period, the more so because from the European Commission's 'impact assessment' of the proposal for a change of the Posting Directive it is apparent that the average duration is only four months.[339] Replacement posting is not allowed.[340] Still, it is possible that the posted employee is recruited with a view to being posted to another Member State.[341] But before being posted the worker concerned must have been subject to the legislation of the State in which the employer is established.[342]

An additional condition is the continuation of an 'organic link' between the undertaking established in a Member State and the workers it has posted to the territory of another Member State.[343] The Court added that in order to ascertain the existence of such an organic link, the circumstances of

---

339 Document SWD(2016)52 final of 8 March 2016.

340 The Court recently specified that if a worker who is posted by an employer to carry out work in another Member State is replaced by another worker posted by another employer, the latter employee must be regarded as being 'sent to replace another person', within the meaning of Article 12(1) of Regulation 883/2004. As a consequence, that employee cannot benefit from the special rules laid down in that provision in order to remain subject to the legislation of the Member State in which that employee's employer normally carries out its activities. The fact that the employers of the two workers concerned have their registered offices in the same Member State or that they may have personal or organisational links is irrelevant in that respect: ECJ 2018, C-527/16 (*Alpenrind*), §100.

341 This is, among other things, important for posting by temporary employment agencies. See ECJ 2000, C-202/97 (*Fitzwilliam*).

342 See expressly Article 14(1) Regulation 987/2009. For a recent application see ECJ 2018, C-451/17 (*Walltopia*).

343 ECJ 2000, C-202/97 (*Fitzwilliam*), §24 and ECJ 2006, C-2/05 (*Herbosch Kiere*), §19.

employment must show that during the posting period the employee worked under the authority of that enterprise.[344]

Furthermore, the sending undertaking must be habitually active on the territory of the State where it has its seat.[345] In this respect Article 14(2) Regulation 987/2009 specifies that its activities must be substantial and go beyond purely internal management. With the requirement of significant activities in the sending State by the sending company the Court clearly wanted to avoid so-called 'letter box companies' using the posting provisions to escape the application of the social security legislation of the Member State where they usually carry out their activities. Indeed, by a fictitious construction they obviously would want to subject themselves to the (probably cheaper) social security legislation of another Member State.

2.5.7. CONTROL OF ABUSE AND FRAUD AND THE ROLE OF THE A1 CERTIFICATE

The A1 certificate (former E101 certificate) plays a key role in verifying whether or not the conditions for derogations of the State-of-employment principle are met. This is a document issued by the competent body of the sending State which proves that the persons concerned remain subject to the legislation of this Member State.[346] The body issuing the document is obliged to assess the relevant facts correctly and must guarantee the accuracy of the data that have been entered.[347]

In the same context it is also necessary to examine the legal significance of the A1 certificate issued by a competent body of a Member State. Is the delivery of such a declaration a sufficient condition to put into force a derogation of the State-of-employment principle? Can, if such a declaration has been issued by a Member State, the competent body of another Member State and, more specifically, of the Member State where the posted person temporarily carries out activities, still dispute that the abovementioned fundamental conditions have been met?

In its case law the Court stated that the principle that a worker or self-employed person can only be subject to the social security legislation of one Member State at a time prevents, during the validity period of the A1 certificate, this person from being subject to the regulations of a Member State other than

344 ECJ 2000, C-202/97 (*Fitzwilliam*), §24.

345 ECJ 2000, C-202/97 (*Fitzwilliam*), §§22, 23 and 43.

346 See Article 19 Regulation 987/2009.

347 This was expressly confirmed by the Court of Justice in ECJ 2000, C-202/97 (*Fitzwilliam*), §51; ECJ 2000, C-178/97 (*Banks*), §38 and ECJ 2012, C-115/11 (*Format*), §46.

the Member State that issued this certificate. This would oblige the person and employers concerned to pay social security contributions in two Member States at the same time, which would amount to an obstacle to the free movement of services. As long as the A1 certificate has not been withdrawn or declared invalid, the competent body of the receiving Member State must take into account that the workers concerned are already subject to the legislation of another State, meaning that it may not subject them to its own social security legislation.[348]

However, the Court of Justice added that in the case of a dispute between the competent bodies of the Member States about the question whether or not the certificate had been issued correctly, they have to contact each other. At the request of the body of the receiving State, the body of the sending State must re-examine whether or not the A1 certificate issued was correct and, if necessary, withdraw it. If they cannot reach an agreement, the Member States concerned can submit their dispute to the Administrative Commission.[349] If the Administrative Commission fails to reconcile the positions of the competent bodies, the receiving State has the right to bring a non-compliance case within the meaning of Article 227 EC Treaty (now Article 259 TFEU) before the Court of Justice. In this way the Court would have the possibility to examine the question regarding the applicable legislation and the accuracy of the data in the A1 certificate.[350]

Moreover, the Court also decided that the national courts of the receiving Member State cannot disregard an A1 certificate. It expressly stated that a judicial body of the receiving Member State is not authorised to verify the validity of an A1 certificate as regards the substantiation of the facts on the basis of which such a certificate has been issued, notably the existence of an organic link between the undertaking posting the employee and the posted worker.[351]

However, the effectiveness of these procedures largely depends on the *goodwill* of the bodies concerned. Meanwhile, this has led to much discontent on the part of a number of Member States, especially with regard to situations in which an A1 certificate validly issued was used to escape the application of the national security legislation in circumstances in which the conditions for a derogation of the State-of-employment principle were not complied with,

---

348 See recently ECJ 2015, C-72/14 and C-197/14 (*X and van Dijk*), §§40–42 and ECJ 2017, C-620/15 (*A-Rosa Flussschiff*), §38.

349 This Administrative Commission was established by Article 71 Regulation 883/2004 and consists of a government representative from each of the Member States. The duties of this Administrative Commission are listed in Article 72 Regulation 883/2004. See in this respect also Article 5 Regulation 987/2009 and Decision No. A1 of 12 June 2009 (establishment of a dialogue and conciliation procedure).

350 See for the procedures to be followed: ECJ 2000, C-202/97 (*Fitzwilliam*), §§57–59; ECJ 2000, C-178/97 (*Banks*), §§44–45; ECJ 2012, C-115/11 (*Format*), §47 and ECJ 2017, C-620/15 (*A-Rosa Flussschiff*), §§44–47.

351 ECJ 2006, C-2/05 (*Herbosch Kiere*) and ECJ 2017, C-620/15 (*A-Rosa Flussschiff*), §49.

especially in cases of posting. As a reaction to this, Belgium unilaterally took a number of measures such as the provisions of Articles 22 to 25 of the law of 27 December 2012.[352] These provisions are intended to fight abuse of law. According to Article 23 of this law, abuse of law occurs when, with regard to a worker or self-employed person, the provisions of the coordination regulations are applied to a situation in which the conditions laid down in the regulations are not observed, with the aim to avoid the Belgian social security legislation that should have been applied in that situation. This especially concerns the use of letter-box companies. As for social security, Article 24 provides that when the national courts, a public social security institution or a social inspector finds such abuse to have occurred, the worker or self-employed person concerned will be subjected to the Belgian social security legislation. The Belgian social security legislation will apply from the first day on which the conditions for its application are satisfied.

This measure runs counter to the above explained provisions of Regulation 883/2004 and Regulation 987/2009 as well as the case law of the Court of Justice, which do not permit unilateral actions by the Member States if an A1 certificate has been issued by the competent body of a Member State. The European Commission also held the view that this legislation constitutes a violation of the applicable Union law; it commenced an infringement procedure against Belgium and brought the case before the Court of Justice. In its judgment of 11 July 2018 the Court confirmed the Commission's position and declared the Belgian law contrary to EU law.[353]

However, in the meantime the Court of Justice also delivered an important judgment on the issue of combating abuse of, and fraud with, A1 certificates. In its judgment of 6 February 2018, the Court confirmed its previous case law on the validity of an E101 certificate (now A1 certificate), but added that this must not result in individuals being able to rely on EU law for abusive or fraudulent ends. The Court stated that the principle of prohibition of fraud and abuse of rights, is a general principle of EU law which individuals must comply with. The Court further added that findings of fraud are to be based on a consistent body of evidence that satisfies both an objective and a subjective factor. The objective factor consists in the fact that the conditions for obtaining and relying on an E101 certificate are not met. The subjective factor corresponds to the intention of the parties concerned to evade or circumvent the conditions for the issue of that certificate, with a view to obtaining the advantage attached to it. The Court recognised that the fraudulent procurement of an E101 certificate may thus result from a deliberate action, such as the misrepresentation of the real

---

352 *Belgian Official Journal*, 31 December 2012.

353 ECJ 2018, C-356/15 (*Commission v. Belgium*).

situation of the posted worker or of the undertaking posting that worker, or from a deliberate omission, such as the concealment of relevant information, with the intention of evading the conditions governing the posting provisions. If the institution of the Member State to which the workers have been posted puts before the institution that issued the E101 certificates concrete evidence that suggests that those certificates were obtained fraudulently, it is the duty of the latter institution, by virtue of the principle of sincere cooperation, to review, in the light of that evidence, the grounds for the issue of those certificates and, where appropriate, to withdraw them. However, if the latter institution fails to carry out such a review within a reasonable period of time, it must be possible for that evidence to be relied on in judicial proceedings, in order to satisfy the court of the Member State to which the workers have been posted that the certificates should be disregarded. The persons who are alleged, in such proceedings, to have used posted workers ostensibly covered by fraudulently obtained certificates must, however, be given the opportunity to rebut the evidence on which those proceedings are based before the national court decides, if appropriate, that the certificates should be disregarded and gives a ruling on the liability of those persons under the applicable national law.[354]

It is in this context, as well as that in December 2016, that the European Commission put up a number of proposals to make the receiving States' verification of the postings more efficient.[355] For instance, the Commission suggests to include in Article 5 Regulation 987/2009 that the documents (such as an A1 certificate) issued by the institution of a Member State are only valid if all sections indicated as compulsory are filled in on the form. Moreover, where the institution of a Member State has some doubts about the validity of a document or the accuracy of the facts on the basis of which it has been issued, the Commission proposes that if the Member State asks the issuing body for clarification or withdrawal of this document, the latter has to respond to this within 25 working days. If the inquiring body indicates that the matter is urgent, the other body must respond within two working days. If, moreover, it is clear that fraud is involved, the document must be corrected or withdrawn immediately and retroactively. In addition, the Commission proposes to include, explicitly, in Article 19 Regulation 987/2009 the obligation for the institutions of the Member States to make a proper assessment of the relevant facts and to guarantee that the information on the basis of which the certificates are issued is correct.

354 ECJ 2018, C-359/16 (*Altun*).

355 Proposal of 13 December 2016 to amend Regulation 883/2004 and Regulation 987/2009, COM(2016)815 final.

These changes are meant to offer the Member States the opportunity to obtain clarity, without delay, about the question to which Member State's legislation the posted worker or self-employed person concerned is subject in the case of disputes about, inter alia, the A1 certificate. Moreover, these adaptations will increase the pressure on Member States that want to issue or have issued an A1 certificate to actively examine whether all the conditions for posting have really been met. Whether or not this new text will effectively help to fight fraud in the case of posting will naturally depend on the willingness of all Member States to take this seriously.

2.6. FINAL REMARKS

In this chapter various legal aspects of intra-EU labour mobility, i.e. free movement of workers and posting of workers to carry out services across the EU have been discussed. Moreover, this chapter has examined the rules regarding the labour standards and social security systems that must be applied or should be guaranteed in situations of cross-border work.

Clearly, intra-EU labour mobility is not a static concept and the legal concepts and foundations upon which it is based will continue to evolve. In recent years, resonating the current mood against social dumping, several legislative initiatives have been taken to establish 'clear, fair and enforceable rules', in order to fight abuse and foster fair cross-border movement for work.[356] In order to guard and maintain 'one of the most cherished freedoms of our EU',[357] it is indeed important to reinforce intra-EU labour mobility as the human face of the EU, allowing workers to improve their living and working conditions and to gain social advancement while preventing (unfair) competition on social standards with local workers in the Member States.

---

356 Worth mentioning is the recently adopted Regulation (EU) 2019/1149 of the European Parliament and of the Council of 20 June 2019 establishing a European Labour Authority. The European Labour Authority is meant to stimulate cooperation of authorities, including joint inspections, across the legal areas of e.g. social security and labour law. Commissioner for Employment, Social Affairs, Skills and Labour Mobility Marianne Thyssen welcomed the agreement as follows: 'I have always said that we need clear, fair and enforceable rules on labour mobility. Today's agreement on the European Labour Authority is the cherry on the cake of a fair European labour market. It will serve the double mission of helping national authorities fight fraud and abuse and making mobility easy for citizens.' See <https://ec.europa.eu/social/main.jsp?langId=en&catId=89&newsId=9301&furtherNews=yes> accessed 05.06.2019.

357 As the European Commission likes to emphasise: more than 8 in 10 Europeans support the free movement of citizens and the possibility to live, work, study and do business anywhere in the EU. See leaflet *Social priorities under the Juncker Commission*, 29 January 2019.

CHAPTER 3
EQUAL TREATMENT

Mark BELL and Ann NUMHAUSER-HENNING

3.1. INTRODUCTION

3.1.1. THE FIRST STEPS FOR EQUAL TREATMENT IN EU LAW

Historically, many national systems of labour law did not include a specific body of rules on equal treatment of workers irrespective of personal characteristics such as gender, ethnicity or disability. A clear trajectory of labour law in the period since 1945 has been to create such provisions. In 1951, the International Labour Organisation adopted the Equal Remuneration Convention,[1] concerning equal pay for women and men, while in 1958 this was complemented by the Discrimination (Employment and Occupation) Convention.[2] From a national perspective, these norms had to be incorporated into a pre-existing body of labour law. In contrast, equal treatment has been one of the foundational elements of EU labour law, present from the outset of its development.

As is well-known, the European Economic Community (EEC) was initially focused on economic integration through the creation of a 'common market' between the six original Member States. The 1957 EEC Treaty did not anticipate a significant role for the Community in shaping national social policy. A striking exception to that picture was, however, the provision in Article 119 for equal pay between women and men. This was not included in the Treaty due to a principled commitment to advancing gender equality; rather it reflected a concern that, in

1 ILO Convention No. 100 (1951).
2 ILO Convention No. 111 (1958).

the absence of a shared obligation to ensure equal pay, some Member States could gain a competitive advantage through reliance on cheap female labour.[3] Although Article 119 EEC reflected a highly instrumental vision of the purpose of equal pay, it provided a foothold for the Community in the emerging field of anti-discrimination law. In the 1970s, a combination of judicial and legislative intervention led to the blossoming of EU law on gender equality in the workplace and social security.[4] In 1971, the Court of Justice issued its seminal decision in *Defrenne v. SABENA*,[5] recognising that the right to equal pay found in Article 119 EEC was capable of enforcement by individuals before their national courts due to the doctrine of direct effect. Another signal development of this period was the adoption in 1976 of legislation that prohibited discrimination on grounds of sex in employment and vocational training.[6]

3.1.2. WIDENING THE SCOPE OF EU ANTI-DISCRIMINATION LAW

After the headline advances of the 1970s, EU gender equality law entered a phase of gradual maturation. This often flowed through the case law of the Court of Justice, which proved an engine for growth and development of the law. During the 1990s, a debate grew on the absence of any corresponding measures on discrimination related to other personal characteristics. Most Member States already had some national legislation addressing discrimination based on ethnic origin, often because of the 1965 UN Convention on the Elimination of All Forms of Racial Discrimination. It was, however, less common to find legislation on other types of discrimination. The 1990s witnessed a trend towards enhancing existing legislative measures in relation to employment discrimination, but also their expansion to further protected characteristics, such as sexual orientation.[7] In 1997, the Member States agreed to amend the EC Treaty in order to create a new legal competence for the Union to adopt measures to combat discrimination on grounds of 'sex, racial or ethnic origin, religion or belief, disability, age or sexual orientation'.[8] In retrospect, it is significant that the new provision was not located alongside the other Treaty provisions on social policy; instead, it was placed amongst a series of cross-cutting provisions found at the outset of the EC Treaty. This reflected the possibility for anti-discrimination measures to extend beyond the scope of labour law and to be applied to other

---

3 Hoskyns (1996), p. 49.
4 See further, e.g. Hervey (2005), p. 307.
5 ECJ 1971, 80/70 (*Defrenne I*).
6 Directive 76/207 (Equal Treatment).
7 See Bell (2002), p. 181 Table 6.1.
8 *Ex* Article 13 EC, now Article 19 TFEU.

spheres of activity, such as service provision, education or housing. While the new generation of EU anti-discrimination legislation found its roots in labour law, it also was connected to broader policy on the protection of fundamental human rights. The new legal powers were swiftly deployed in 2000 to adopt two directives. First, the Racial Equality Directive,[9] which prohibits discrimination on grounds of racial or ethnic origin in employment, but also other fields, such as access to and supply of goods and services, social protection (including social security and healthcare), and education. In contrast, the Employment Equality Directive[10] prohibits discrimination on grounds of religion or belief, disability, age or sexual orientation. It is more easily viewed as a labour law instrument because its remit is mainly limited to employment and vocational training.

3.1.3. DEEPENING EU ANTI-DISCRIMINATION LAW

The directives of 2000 not only expanded the remit of anti-discrimination legislation, but also developed its substantive contents. For example, an express prohibition of harassment was introduced,[11] as well as new techniques for the enforcement of the legislation, such as the duty to create a body(s) for the promotion of equal treatment.[12] In turn, that prompted the revision and consolidation of earlier legislation via the 2006 'Recast' Gender Equality Directive,[13] the 2010 Equal Treatment in Self-Employment Directive,[14] as well as the 2004 extension of legislation on gender equality into the field of goods and services.[15] A summary of the principal legislation can be found in Table 3.1. This rapid period of legislative renewal stalled with the proposal in 2008 to extend the prohibition of discrimination to areas outside employment, in respect of the grounds of religion or belief, disability, age and sexual orientation.[16] This has not yet been adopted due to a lack of agreement in the Council. In a similar vein, a 2012 legislative proposal designed to enhance women's representation within company boardrooms has so far failed to find sufficient accord within the Council.[17] The latest initiative is the proposal for a new Directive on Work-Life Balance for Parents and Carers.[18]

---

9 Directive 2000/43 (Racial Equality).
10 Directive 2000/78 (Employment Equality).
11 Directive 2000/43, Article 2(3); Directive 2000/78, Article 2(3).
12 Directive 2000/43, Article 13.
13 Directive 2006/54 (Recast Gender Equality).
14 Directive 2010/41 (Equal Treatment in Self-Employment).
15 Directive 2004/113 (Gender Goods and Services).
16 European Commission (2008) (Proposal Equal Treatment).
17 European Commission (2012) (Proposal Gender Balance Non-Executive Directors).
18 European Commission (2017) (Proposal Work-life Balance). Directive 2019/1158 on work-life balance for parents and carers was adopted on 20 June 2019: [2019] OJ L 188/79.

Running parallel to the expansion of secondary legislation has been a strengthening of equal treatment provisions within the primary law instruments of the Union. This is discussed in more depth in the next section of this chapter, but the period since 2000 has witnessed the addition of further Treaty provisions relating to equal treatment; the adoption of the Charter of Fundamental Rights, which includes a chapter devoted to equality; and further elucidation by the Court of Justice of the rights that may be derived from the (unwritten) general principle of equal treatment found in EU law. These primary law sources apply to the full scope of EU law, but they have proven to be particularly influential within the field of labour law, which remains the most common source of discrimination litigation at the Court of Justice.

Table 3.1. Selected EU legislation on discrimination

Legislation	Discrimination Grounds	Material Scope
Recast Gender Equality Directive (2006/54)	Sex (including pregnancy, maternity leave, gender reassignment).	Employment, vocational training, occupational social security.
Equal Treatment in Self-Employment (2010/41)	Sex.[a]	Establishment of a business or company, self-employed activity.
Equal Treatment in Social Security (79/7)	Sex.[b]	Social security.
Gender Goods and Services (2004/113)	Sex (including pregnancy and maternity).[c]	Access to and supply of goods and services.
Racial Equality Directive (2000/43)	Racial or ethnic origin.	Employment, vocational training, social protection, social advantages, education, access to and supply of goods and services.
Employment Equality Directive (2000/78)	Religion or belief, disability, age, sexual orientation.	Employment, vocational training.

[a] There is no specific reference to the prohibition of less favourable treatment on grounds of pregnancy, maternity or gender reassignment, but this may be implied in the prohibition of sex discrimination.
[b] Including indirect sex discrimination by reference to 'marital or family status': Article 4(1). Case-law has recognised that this Directive also applies to discrimination on grounds of gender reassignment: ECJ 2006, C-423/04 (*Richards*).
[c] There is no specific reference to the prohibition of less favourable treatment on grounds of gender reassignment, but this may be implied in the prohibition of sex discrimination.

3.1.4. STRUCTURE OF THIS CHAPTER

After examining the fundamental sources of equal treatment law, this chapter turns to consider the concept of discrimination. It will look at: the grounds of discrimination; the prohibited forms of discrimination; justifications and exceptions to the prohibition; and the role for positive action. Thereafter, the chapter identifies the material scope of the prohibition of discrimination and presents the provisions relating to the enforcement of the legislation. It should be noted that there is also an extensive body of EU law addressing discrimination on grounds of nationality. In relation to EU citizens, this has developed as part of the law on the free movement of workers and persons, which is examined elsewhere in this book.[19] Discrimination in employment on grounds of non-EU nationality is also frequently prohibited by EU secondary legislation. Due to the constraints of space, these instruments are not examined in this chapter. They have evolved in a separate legal framework under the umbrella of legislation on immigration and asylum.[20] The same is to some extent true as regards flexible work and the non-discrimination clauses found in the directives regarding part-time work, fixed-term work and temporary agency work, respectively. They, too, are dealt with elsewhere in this book.[21]

3.2. FUNDAMENTAL SOURCES OF EQUAL TREATMENT LAW IN THE EU

Detailed legal requirements on equal treatment are to be found in legislation, namely the directives described above. These are the central influence on national legislation, which has been adopted or revised in response. Legislative acts are, however, subject to compliance with the primary law of the EU. Most obviously, this includes the provisions of the EU Treaties. For the most part, the Treaties do not include self-executing rights to equal treatment in the workplace, but a notable exception is Article 157 TFEU on the right of women and men to equal pay for work of equal value. This is examined in Section 3.3.2.6. Beyond the Treaties, there are two sources of primary law that warrant particular attention: the EU Charter of Fundamental Rights and the 'general principle' of equal treatment. In addition, the EU has ratified the UN Convention on the Rights of Persons with Disabilities (CRPD). This now imposes international law obligations on the Union to act in accordance with the Convention.

3.2.1. THE CHARTER OF FUNDAMENTAL RIGHTS OF THE EUROPEAN UNION

The Charter of Fundamental Rights was adopted in 2000, but it was only with the adoption of the Treaty of Lisbon in 2009 that it became legally binding.

---

19 See Chapter 2.

20 A comprehensive analysis of these Directives is provided by Dewhurst (2018).

21 See Chapter 4.

Article 6(1) TEU provides that the Charter 'shall have the same legal value as the Treaties'. Therefore, it is now part of the primary law of the EU. The Charter is particularly important for equal treatment law because it includes a chapter on 'equality'. This chapter includes provisions relating to specific equality issues (gender, disability, age, cultural, religious and linguistic diversity). It begins with two general provisions that apply to a wide range of forms of discrimination. Article 20 provides that 'everyone is equal before the law' and Article 21(1) states:

> Any discrimination based on any ground such as sex, race, colour, ethnic or social origin, genetic features, language, religion or belief, political or any other opinion, membership of a national minority, property, birth, disability, age or sexual orientation shall be prohibited.

An early example of how such rights could affect EU anti-discrimination legislation arose in the *Test-Achats* case.[22] This concerned the legality of an exception found within the EU Directive on gender equality in goods and services.[23] Specifically, it permitted sex to be taken into account as a factor in the calculation of premiums and benefits for insurance and related financial services, subject to requirements around the need for sound actuarial data. This permitted, for example, car insurance policies to be priced differently for women and men on the basis of statistics relating to the propensity to be involved in road traffic accidents. The Court held that this exception was incompatible with Articles 21 and 23[24] of the Charter. It held that women and men were in a comparable situation as regards insurance premiums and benefits, so a difference in treatment was contrary to the principle of equal treatment.[25] Moreover, the indefinite nature of the exception could not, in the Court's view, be justified.[26]

Test-Achats illustrated that the fundamental rights found in the Charter provide a minimum guarantee, from which neither the Union, nor (when applicable) its Member States, can deviate. Unsurprisingly, national courts are increasingly including questions about the meaning of the Charter when they make references to the Court about the interpretation of anti-discrimination legislation. Yet the Court has signalled that, where a case can be resolved through the interpretation of the relevant directive, it is not always necessary to go further and also consider the application of the Charter.[27]

22 ECJ 2011, C-236/09 (*Test-Achats*).
23 Directive 2004/113 (Gender Equality in Goods and Services).
24 'Equality between women and men must be ensured in all areas, including employment, work and pay ...'.
25 ECJ 2011, C-236/09 (*Test-Achats*), §30.
26 Ibid., §32.
27 E.g. ECJ 2016, C-395/15 (*Daouidi*), §67.

Although the Charter holds much potential for equal treatment law, its impact is constrained by the limitations on its scope. It always applies to the actions of the EU institutions, but, in respect of Member States, it only applies where they are 'implementing Union law'.[28] This phrase has given rise to a significant body of case law before the Court and considerable ambiguity still surrounds exactly when a situation falls within the scope of the Charter.[29] An example from equal treatment law will illustrate the difficulty of determining where this boundary lies.

In *Milkova*,[30] the case concerned a provision of Bulgarian law that required the consent of the Labour Inspectorate before employees with certain types of disability could be dismissed. This did not apply to those who were classified as civil servants (rather than employees). Ms. Milkova, who was a civil servant with a disability, challenged the absence of any requirement to seek authorisation from the Labour Inspectorate following her dismissal. On the face of it, the difference in treatment that she encountered was not one regulated by EU anti-discrimination legislation. It was between two categories of employment relationship: employees and civil servants. Moreover, no provision of EU legislation requires the involvement of the Labour Inspectorate in dismissals. Nevertheless, the Court took the view that the heightened protection offered by Bulgarian law was a form of positive action for disabled persons. The Employment Equality Directive permits, but does not require, Member States to authorise positive action within national law.[31] Even though this was a discretionary element of national law, the Court of Justice held that it was a discretion exercised in the framework of EU law and consequently the provisions of the Charter were applicable.[32] While it was for the national court to apply the law to the facts, the Court of Justice indicated that there did not appear to be sufficient grounds to distinguish employees from civil servants in this manner, and that this could be a breach of the principle of equal treatment in Articles 20 and 21 of the Charter.[33]

The case law of the Court of Justice on the Charter is at a relatively early stage in its evolution and there are many aspects of the equality rights found therein that have yet to be tested in litigation. Significantly, the Grand Chamber of the Court of Justice has recently held that Article 21 can be relied upon by individuals in legal proceedings in the same manner as directly effective provisions of the EU Treaties; this includes legal disputes between private parties.[34]

---

28 Article 51(1) CFREU.

29 Fontanelli (2014).

30 ECJ 2017, C-406/15 (*Milkova*).

31 Directive 2000/78 (Employment Equality), Article 7.

32 ECJ 2017, C-406/15 (*Milkova*), §53.

33 Ibid., §61.

34 ECJ 2018, C-414/16 (*Egenberger*), §77.

This underscores how the Charter has become a major source of law in the field of equal treatment.

3.2.2. THE GENERAL PRINCIPLE OF EQUAL TREATMENT IN EU LAW

One of the principal reasons for adopting the Charter was a desire to clarify the fundamental rights that were protected by EU law. The founding Treaties did not contain any catalogue of such rights, but the Court of Justice later recognised that respect for fundamental rights was a 'general principle' of EU law.[35] This formed part of a broader body of case law in which the Court held that there were 'general principles' of law implied within the Treaties and compliance with these must be ensured throughout the scope of EU law.[36] The contents of these general principles emerged gradually through the Court's case law, but equal treatment has been a core obligation. For example, in *Defrenne (III)*, the Court stated:

> … respect for fundamental personal human rights is one of the general principles of Community law, the observance of which it has a duty to ensure. There can be no doubt that the elimination of discrimination based on sex forms part of those fundamental rights.[37]

The Charter of Fundamental Rights provided a visible catalogue of fundamental rights, but it co-exists alongside the earlier doctrine of general principles.[38] This has proven significant, as the Court has occasionally turned to the general principle of equal treatment to provide a remedy for a litigant where this could not be obtained purely through the application of EU legislation.

Specifically, the Court has maintained that it is not possible for an individual to derive directly effective rights in relation to another private party from a directive (the notion of 'horizontal direct effect'). In the context of labour law, this means that workers will normally not be able to rely upon directly effective rights found in a directive in legal proceedings before national courts if their employer is not part of the State (or any emanation thereof). In several cases of age discrimination,[39] the Court was confronted with a situation where a private

35 ECJ 1970, 11/70 (*Internationale Handelsgesellschaft*), §4.

36 See further, Craig & De Búrca (2015), p. 111.

37 ECJ 1978, 149/77 (*Defrenne III*), §§26–27.

38 The general principle of respect for fundamental rights is now expressly recognised in Article 6(3) TEU.

39 ECJ 2005, C-144/04 (*Mangold*); ECJ 2010, C-555/07 (*Kücükdeveci*); ECJ 2016, C-441/14 (*Rasmussen*).

sector worker had encountered direct discrimination but the lack of horizontal direct effect meant that the Employment Equality Directive could not provide an immediate remedy.[40] Controversially, the Court turned instead to the general principle of equal treatment. Having found that this included non-discrimination on grounds of age, the Court held that the national court was obliged to disapply any national legislation that did not comply with the general principle.

The Court's recourse to the general principle of equal treatment as an alternative source of legal obligations has been debated within academic commentary and also amongst the Court's Advocates-General.[41] More recently, the Danish Supreme Court has also shown resistance to this approach following a preliminary ruling by the Court.[42] On the one hand, the Court has been sparing in its use of this novel interpretation of the law; the great majority of anti-discrimination cases are resolved without recourse to the case law on general principles. On the other hand, the Court has not retreated from this approach, notwithstanding the criticism that it has received. It remains, therefore, an alternative source of legal protection where the absence of horizontal direct effect might otherwise make it impossible for a worker to succeed in legal proceedings against a private sector employer.

3.2.3. UN CONVENTION ON THE RIGHTS OF PERSONS WITH DISABILITIES

In 2009, the EU decided to ratify the UN Convention on the Rights of Persons with Disabilities.[43] Whereas there are many international human rights treaties that have been ratified by individual EU Member States, this was the first time that the Union itself had become party to a human rights instrument. As such, the Union has assumed obligations in international law to respect the requirements of the UN Convention on the Rights of Persons with Disabilities. The Convention has been invoked before the Court and, as discussed further in Section 3.3.1.4, this has been influential in shaping the Court's case law on disability discrimination. Specifically, in 2013, the Court held that 'Directive 2000/78 must, as far as possible, be interpreted in a manner consistent with that Convention'.[44] In contrast, the Court has rejected the argument that the CRPD can be relied upon to create directly effective rights within EU law. In the *Z* case, the claimant argued that her inability to give birth to a child was due to

40 The alternative remedy would have been for the individual to have commenced legal proceedings against the State for failure to implement correctly the directive.

41 See further, Opinion of Advocate-General Sharpston 2008, C-427/06 (*Bartsch*), §§31–41.

42 See further, Rask Madsen et al. (2017).

43 Decision 2010/48/EC concerning the conclusion, by the European Community, of the UN Convention on the Rights of Persons with Disabilities.

44 ECJ 2013, C-335/11 and 337/11 *HK Danmark (Ring and Skouboe)* §32.

a physical impairment and that this amounted to a disability for the purposes of the Employment Equality Directive. The Court rejected this because, in its view, her impairment did not hinder her participation in professional life.[45] An alternative argument was that she was disabled for the purposes of the UN Convention on the Rights of Persons with Disabilities and that this could be relied upon even if the directive was not applicable to her situation. The Court held that:

> the provisions of that Convention are not, as regards their content, provisions that are unconditional and sufficiently precise ..., and that they therefore do not have direct effect in European Union law.[46]

This decision limits the capacity of the Convention to generate any 'free-standing' rights that go beyond the current state of EU law.[47]

3.3. THE CONCEPT OF DISCRIMINATION

This section considers the core meaning of discrimination according to EU law. It begins by examining the list of grounds protected by EU law, followed by a description of the forms of discrimination that are prohibited. It is also necessary to consider those situations where conduct that would normally constitute unlawful discrimination is otherwise permitted by EU law. Finally, this section concludes by examining the scope for positive action. Positive action is a mechanism for promoting equality, so it is not construed as an exception to the prohibition of discrimination. Nevertheless, litigation has challenged the boundary between lawful forms of positive action and unlawful discrimination.

3.3.1. GROUNDS OF DISCRIMINATION

An initial question for any legal framework on equal treatment is the approach taken to the list of protected grounds. Guarantees of equal treatment found in national constitutions or human rights instruments apply to a wide range of activities. They establish broad norms rather than the detailed rules that characterise legislation. Consequently, in such instruments, the list of protected grounds may be non-exhaustive. For example, Article 21 Charter of Fundamental

---

45 ECJ 2014, C-363/12 (*Z v. A Government Department*), §81.

46 Ibid., §90.

47 See further, Waddington (2015).

Rights refers to 'any ground such as'. Although Article 21 identifies 17 grounds upon which discrimination may occur, the door remains open to the Court of Justice to recognise further grounds in the future.

In contrast, anti-discrimination legislation tends to lay down more precise rules and it imposes obligations on both public and private actors, such as employers. Unlike constitutional equality guarantees, legislation constrains the possibility for certain types of conduct to be justified. As discussed in section 3.3.2.1, direct discrimination is normally not open to justification under EU equality legislation. The tighter regime found in legislation means that greater certainty is needed on which forms of discrimination fall within its net. Therefore, EU legislation applies to an exhaustive list of protected grounds. Indeed, the Court of Justice has held that the limited legal competence conferred on the Union by the Treaties means that the EU does not enjoy the power to enact legislation on grounds other than those mentioned in the Treaties.[48]

National legislation must, as a minimum, include the grounds found within EU legislation, but most Member States have chosen to go further and include additional grounds.[49] Some national laws have adopted a non-exhaustive list of grounds by including words like 'or any other ground'.[50] The 'closed list' of grounds found in EU legislation has the consequence that litigation tends to focus on the interpretation of those grounds and whether they can encompass related characteristics. This has been aided by the absence of definitions of these grounds within EU legislation. The remainder of this section looks at each of the grounds mentioned in Article 19 TFEU: sex, racial or ethnic origin, religion or belief, disability, age and sexual orientation.

3.3.1.1. Sex/Gender (Including Discrimination Related to Pregnancy/Maternity)

Sex – together with nationality – is thus a protected ground of discrimination already from the outset of the European Union (or as it was, the European Communities). The original Treaty ban on pay discrimination was in the 1970s followed by secondary legislation in the form of directives. Generally speaking, discrimination on the grounds of sex is understood as 'equal treatment between men and women'.[51] The growing acknowledgement of sex as a social construct in terms of gender has, over time, resulted in a somewhat more complex understanding of this ground.

48 For instance, the Union does not have the power under Article 19 TFEU to legislate on discrimination on grounds of obesity: ECJ 2014, C-354/13 (*Kaltoft*), §34.

49 For a complete list, see Chopin and Germaine (2016), pp. 12–14.

50 E.g. Cyprus, Estonia, Finland, Hungary, Latvia, Lithuania, Romania, Slovenia, Slovakia: ibid.

51 Compare Directive 2006/54 (Recast Gender Equality).

Recital 3 of the Preamble of the Recast Directive now states:

> … the scope of the principle of equal treatment of men and women cannot be confined to the prohibition of discrimination based on the fact that a person is of one or other sex. In view of its purpose and the nature of the rights which it seeks to safeguard, it also applies to discrimination arising from the gender reassignment of a person.

It was in the case *P v. S* that the Court found that the protection against discrimination on the grounds of sex also applied to a person in the process of gender reassignment.[52] The Court held that the dismissal of an employee following her decision to undergo gender reassignment surgery was contrary to, in this case, Directive 76/207 on Gender Equality:

> Such discrimination is based, essentially, if not exclusively, on the sex of the person concerned. Where a person is dismissed on the ground that he or she intends to undergo, or has undergone, gender reassignment, he or she is treated unfavourably by comparison with persons of the sex to which he or she was deemed to belong before undergoing gender reassignment.[53]

The Court's decision was later on followed up in relation to Directive 75/117 (Equal Pay) in *K.B.*[54] and Directive 79/7 (Social Security) in *Richards.*[55] In *K.B.*, the Court found that national legislation that did not permit a change in the registration of sex at birth (which was contrary to the European Convention on Human Rights (ECHR)), and which consequently made it impossible for a transsexual having undergone gender reassignment to fulfil the requirement of marriage in order to benefit from a survivor's pension, was contrary to Article 141 EC.[56] In *Richards*, the Court held that national legislation 'which denies a person who … has undergone gender-reassignment entitlement to a retirement pension on the ground that she has not reached the age of 65, when she would have been entitled to such a pension at the age of 60 had she been held to be a woman as a matter of national law' was in breach of Directive 79/7. The power of Member States to organise their social security systems did not alter this as 'Member States must comply with Community law when exercising that power',[57] nor did the derogation provided for by Article 7(1)(a) of the directive as this provision only related to the determination of different pensionable ages for men and for women.[58] In these cases, the comparator test, as indicated above,

52 ECJ 1996, C-13/94 (*P v. S and Cornwall County Council*).
53 Ibid., §21.
54 ECJ 2004, C-117/01 (*K.B.*).
55 ECJ 2006, C-423/04 (*Richards*). See also ECJ 2018, C-451/16 (*MB*).
56 Now Article 157 TFEU.
57 ECJ 2006, C-423/04 (*Richards*), §33.
58 Ibid., §38.

may appear somewhat more relaxed than is usually the case. Whereas in *P v S* the person having undergone reassignment was thus compared 'with persons of the sex to which he or she was deemed to belong before undergoing gender reassignment', in *K.B.* a comparison was made with 'other heterosexual couples', and in *Richards* with the gender she had undergone reassignment to, i.e. other women.

The principle of equality between men and women, according to Directive 76/207, already provided for the legitimacy of special protection for women's biological condition during pregnancy and maternity.[59] In the famous *Dekker* case,[60] the Court of Justice made it clear that unfavourable treatment of women on the grounds of pregnancy or maternity constitutes direct discrimination on the grounds of sex as 'it should be observed that only women can be refused employment on ground of pregnancy'.[61] The employer who refused to hire Patricia Dekker, whom the employer admittedly considered to be suitable for the job, based on the possible adverse consequences of employing a pregnant women, was found guilty of direct sex discrimination. Moreover, the fact that no man applied for the job was regarded as irrelevant, i.e. no comparator was required.

3.3.1.2. Racial or Ethnic Origin

The Preamble of the Racial Equality Directive indicates some of the debates that surround the meaning of 'racial or ethnic origin'.[62] Recital 6 states:

> The European Union rejects theories which attempt to determine the existence of separate human races. The use of the term 'racial origin' in this Directive does not imply an acceptance of such theories.

In the period following the Second World War, there were increasing challenges to the idea that humans could be categorised according to biologically distinct 'races'. This was discredited by research undertaken for UNESCO, summarised in the 1978 Declaration on Race and Racial Prejudice: 'all human beings belong to a single species and are descended from a common stock'.[63] This poses

---

59 Directive 76/207 (Gender Equality), Article 2(3).

60 ECJ 1990, C-177/88 (*Dekker*). This case law was later confirmed in ECJ 1990, C-179/88 (*Herz*); ECJ 1994, C-421/92 (*Habermann*); ECJ 1994, C-32/93 (*Webb*); and ECJ 1997, C-400/95 (*Larsson*).

61 ECJ 1990, C-177/88 (*Dekker*), §12.

62 For an extensive analysis of EU and national law on the meaning of 'racial or ethnic origin', see Farkas (2017).

63 Article 1, 20th General Conference of UNESCO, 27 November 1978. See further Bell (2008), p. 8.

a dilemma for anti-discrimination laws. On the one hand, there is a need to avoid reinforcing the false notion of human 'races'; on the other, discrimination continues to be motivated by perceived racial differences. In most EU Member States, anti-discrimination legislation includes 'race' as a prohibited ground of discrimination, but some States prefer to avoid this term.[64] For example, in Austria, federal anti-discrimination legislation only uses the term 'ethnic affiliation' given concerns about racial classifications.[65]

The inherent difficulties with the concept of 'race' may explain why contemporary case law places more weight on the meaning of ethnic origin. Ethnicity is frequently understood to be a socially constructed category founded on a combination of collectively experienced factors. In *CHEZ*,[66] the Court was asked whether 'ethnic origin' could be applied to a Roma community living in a particular neighbourhood in Bulgaria. Drawing upon the case law of the European Court of Human Rights (ECtHR), the Court stated:

> the concept of ethnicity, which has its origin in the idea of societal groups marked in particular by common nationality, religious faith, language, cultural and traditional origins and backgrounds, applies to the Roma community.[67]

In *Jyske Finans*,[68] the Court was confronted with a difference of treatment due to place of birth; those born outside Denmark had to provide additional proof of their identity when applying for a loan to purchase a car. The Court affirmed that the criteria for establishing ethnic origin that it identified in *CHEZ* are neither exhaustive, nor can they be applied in isolation from each other: 'ethnic origin cannot be determined on the basis of a single criterion, but, on the contrary, is based on a whole number of factors, some objective and others subjective'.[69] Place of birth could be one factor in identifying ethnic origin, but, as the sole criterion, it was not possible to presume that all persons born abroad were members of specific ethnic groups.[70]

The interpretation adopted in *Jyske Finans* might help to explain the difference between ethnic origin, religion and nationality. As mentioned in the introduction, discrimination on grounds of religion is prohibited by the Employment Equality Directive, which seems to imply that this is distinguished from the grounds of racial or ethnic origin found in the Racial Equality Directive. In a similar vein, the Racial Equality Directive expressly provides that it 'does not

64 E.g. Sweden and Finland; Chopin and Germaine (2016), p. 14.
65 Schindlauer (2016), p. 32.
66 ECJ 2015, C-83/14 (*CHEZ*). See further, Benedi Lahuerta (2016a).
67 Ibid., §46.
68 ECJ 2017, C-668/15 (*Jyske Finans*), §10.
69 Ibid., §19.
70 Ibid., §20.

cover difference of treatment based on nationality'.[71] Yet the definition of ethnic origin provided in *CHEZ* makes reference to both nationality and religious faith. After *Jyske Finans*, it seems that a group that is exclusively defined by a sole criterion, such as nationality or religion, will not constitute an ethnic group. At the same time, these factors can be part of the overall assessment of ethnicity.

Notwithstanding the above, it should be noted that the Court has not applied these boundary lines with excessive rigidity. In *Feryn*,[72] a company director made public statements that he did not hire 'immigrants' to be door-fitters because his customers did not want to grant them access to their private homes. Even though the language used was overtly connected to nationality, the Court recognised that such conduct constituted direct discrimination on grounds of racial or ethnic origin.[73]

3.3.1.3. Religion or Belief

The first cases involving discrimination on grounds of religion were decided by the Court of Justice in 2017. *Achbita* and *Bougnaoui* both concerned Muslim women who had been dismissed from their jobs because they wished to wear a headscarf at work due to their religion beliefs.[74] While it is obvious that Islam is a religion, the case did raise the question of whether the concept of religion includes the manifestation of a person's beliefs (such as wearing a particular garment). The Court of Justice stated that 'religion' should be interpreted consistently with Article 9 ECHR and Article 10 Charter of Fundamental Rights, both of which guarantee the freedom of religion.[75] The Court of Justice adopted the approach of the ECtHR that religion 'should be interpreted as covering both the *forum internum*, that is the fact of having a belief, and the *forum externum*, that is the manifestation of religious faith in public'.[76] This indicates that situations where individuals encounter limitations on how they can manifest their religious beliefs in the workplace may fall within the scope of the directive, even if this does not imply that such restrictions are always unlawful.[77]

Litigation at national level, and before the ECtHR, has probed the meaning of both 'religion' and 'belief'. In relation to 'religion', there may be dispute over less common and/or contemporary groups that claim the status of religion. It might seem even more difficult to place parameters on the category of 'belief'.[78]

---

71 Directive 2000/43, Article 3(2).
72 ECJ 2008, C-54/07 (*Feryn*).
73 Ibid., §25.
74 ECJ 2017, C-157/15 (*Achbita*); ECJ 2017, C-188/15 (*Bougnaoui*).
75 ECJ 2017, C-157/15 (*Achbita*), §§26–27; ECJ 2017, C-188/15 (*Bougnaoui*), §§28–29.
76 Ibid., §28.
77 See further Section 3.3.2.2.
78 See further Vickers (2016).

No Member State has sought to compile a comprehensive list of religions or beliefs protected by anti-discrimination legislation, but in some States there are official documents that provide guidance to national courts on the criteria to be applied.[79] The Commission has offered its interpretation of what is meant by 'belief':

> The concept of 'belief' should be read in the context of 'religion or belief'. It refers to a belief or a philosophical conviction (like those of atheists or agnostics, for example), which does not need to be of a religious nature, but it doesn't cover political opinion.[80]

This distinction between an opinion and a belief is also found in some national legislation and case law. Opinion might be regarded as views about narrow or specific issues. Belief is often associated with wider perspectives on how to pursue one's life or how society should be organised. In the Netherlands, this is captured by the use of the term *levensovertuiging* (philosophy of life).[81]

3.3.1.4. Disability

Experience with disability discrimination legislation shows a tendency for considerable litigation on the definition of disability. In part, this reflects the model of disability found in legislation and case law. A 'medical' model assumes that disability results from individual impairment. This has the consequence that establishing whether a claimant has a disability entails an analysis of the claimant's state of health and whether the impairment is sufficiently serious and/or long-term. In contrast, a 'social' model regards disability as caused by barriers that arise from the interaction between individual impairment and the surrounding environment (which includes physical infrastructure, the organisation of work and social attitudes).[82] This shifts the focus away from the medical circumstances of the individual and towards the social obstacles that have created disadvantage.

In *Chacón Navas*,[83] the Court held that the concept of disability had to be given 'an autonomous and uniform interpretation' throughout the EU.[84] The definition provided by the Court[85] was widely regarded as reflecting a medical

---

79 Chopin & Germaine (2016), p. 16.

80 European Commission (2014), *Annexes to the Joint Report on the application of the Racial Equality Directive and the Employment Equality Directive*, SWD(2014)5, p. 22.

81 Chopin & Germaine (2016), p. 16.

82 There is an extensive academic debate on what constitutes the social model of disability: see further, Shakespeare (2014), chap. 2.

83 ECJ 2006, C-13/05 (*Chacón Navas*).

84 Ibid., §42.

85 'A limitation which results in particular from physical, mental or psychological impairments and which hinders the participation of the person concerned in professional life', ibid., §43.

model of disability because it placed considerable emphasis on the individual's impairment.[86] As mentioned in Section 3.2.3, the EU subsequently ratified the UN Convention on the Rights of Persons with Disabilities. The Convention does not provide an exhaustive definition of disability, but its approach is more reflective of the social model.[87] This prompted the Court to adjust its definition of disability in *Ring and Skouboe Werge*, with the adoption of language that is similar (but not identical) to that found in the UN Convention on the Rights of Persons with Disabilities:

> ... the concept of 'disability' must be understood as referring to a limitation which results in particular from physical, mental or psychological impairments which in interaction with various barriers may hinder the full and effective participation of the persons concerned in professional life on an equal basis with other workers.
>
> In addition, it follows from the second paragraph of Article 1 of the UN Convention that the physical, mental or psychological impairments must be 'long-term'.[88]

Although the Court's *language* is now closer to the social model of disability, the case law continues to indicate that evidence of the individual's impairment remains central to the interpretation of disability.[89] For example, in *Kaltoft*, the question arose as to whether obesity could constitute a disability. Ultimately, the Court emphasised that the national court would have to examine whether Mr. Kaltoft's obesity gave rise to an impairment, such as 'reduced mobility or the onset, in that person, of medical conditions preventing him from carrying out his work or causing discomfort when carrying out his professional activity'.[90] This returned the spotlight to the degree of individual impairment and appeared to neglect the disabling role that environmental barriers may have played, such as social attitudes towards his obesity.[91]

The Court has recently had an opportunity to consider further the requirement that any impairment be 'long-term'. In *Daouidi*,[92] the claimant was dismissed from his job almost two months after a fall in the workplace where he dislocated his elbow. Six months later, Mr. Daouidi was still unable to work and the question arose as to whether his injury could be regarded as a disability.

---

86 E.g Waddington & Lawson (2009), p. 16.

87 Article 1 CRPD states: 'Persons with disabilities include those who have long-term physical, mental, intellectual or sensory impairments which in interaction with various barriers may hinder their full and effective participation in society on an equal basis with others'.

88 ECJ 2013, C-335/11 and 337/11 (*Ring and Skouboe*), §§38–39. This definition has been reiterated by the Court in subsequent case law: e.g. ECJ 2014, C-363/12 (*Z*), §77; ECJ 2014, C-354/13 (*Kaltoft*), §53.

89 Ferri & Lawson (2016), pp. 54–55.

90 ECJ 2014, C-354/13 (*Kaltoft*), §60.

91 See further, Waddington (2015).

92 ECJ 2016, C-395/15 (*Daouidi*).

The Court stated that this was ultimately a question of fact for the national court, taking into account any medical evidence. It held that:

> The evidence which makes it possible to find that a limitation is 'long-term' includes the fact that, at the time of the allegedly discriminatory act, the incapacity of the person concerned does not display a clearly defined prognosis as regards short-term progress or ... the fact that that incapacity is likely to be significantly prolonged before that person has recovered.[93]

While case law before the Court has gradually fleshed out the meaning of disability in the Employment Equality Directive, the approach found in national legislation varies considerably. Some Member States chose to include a specific definition of disability in their anti-discrimination legislation, but in others this is absent.[94] In the latter case, there is a risk that courts rely instead on existing definitions of disability found in other types of legislation, such as social security rules on the eligibility criteria for disability welfare benefits. Waddington and Lawson point out that the definition of disability in social security legislation tends to be narrower, because it is a threshold for the payment of a financial benefit.[95] If this is used in anti-discrimination legislation, it is likely to be more restrictive than the approach found in the UN Convention on the Rights of Persons with Disabilities and that endorsed by the Court.

3.3.1.5. Age

Age is one of the new discrimination grounds introduced by Article 13 (now Article 19 TFEU) in the Amsterdam Treaty and providing new competences in this area for EU institutions. Age is also included in Article 21(1) Charter of Fundamental Rights and now given a more specific expression in legislation by the Employment Equality Directive. In the famous *Mangold*[96] case, the Court also declared equal treatment on the grounds of age to be a general principle of Community law.

The Employment Equality Directive bans direct and indirect discrimination as well as harassment and instructions to discriminate on the grounds of age. The directive does not include any definition whatsoever of age and the prohibition of discrimination thus – unlike its US predecessor[97] – covers not only old age but any age. Nonetheless, the preamble can be said to reflect a special concern for older workers.[98]

---

93 Ibid., §56.
94 For an overview, see Waddington & Lawson (2009), pp. 18–24.
95 Ibid., p. 22.
96 ECJ 2005, C-144/04 *(Mangold)*.
97 The 1967 Age Discrimination in Employment Act (ADEA). See further Lester (2015).
98 See Recitals 6, 8 and 25.

A special characteristic of the age discrimination ban as compared to those of other grounds is its weak format – it opens up for the justification of direct discrimination.[99] Age as a ground of discrimination is special in that everyone has an age and that this age is constantly changing, as we grow older. Age is, however, also a traditional social stratifier as reflected in recital 25. Therefore, age discrimination has sometimes been regarded as more acceptable than other forms of discrimination.[100]

The weaker format is one of the reasons the Court was practically flooded by cases relating to the new age discrimination ban following the introduction of the Employment Equality Directive (at least in comparison to litigation on other grounds). At the heart of these cases lies Article 6(1), which permits the justification of differential treatment on the grounds of age, if 'objectively and reasonably justified by a legitimate aim, including legitimate employment policy, labour market, and vocational training objectives, and if the means of achieving that aim are appropriate and necessary'. Litigation has concerned both differential treatment on the grounds of young and old age. The cases *Kücükdeveci*[101] and *Hütter*[102] concerned detrimental working conditions for people under 25 years of age. The majority of cases have, however, concerned old age and most prominently rules on compulsory retirement and certain employment conditions such as redundancy compensation, etc., in relation to retirement. At the centre of these cases is scrutiny of the proportionality test applied by the Court and intergenerational conflict tends to come to the fore. This will be discussed in Section 3.3.3.

Age as a constant characteristic of all people, makes age a ground of particular interest when it comes to multiple and/or intersectional discrimination, an item dealt with in Section 3.6.

3.3.1.6. Sexual Orientation

Whereas the Court recognised in the mid-1990s that discrimination against transgender persons (in relation to gender reassignment) constituted sex discrimination, discrimination based on sexual orientation was deemed to fall outside the scope of these provisions.[103] Sexual orientation was, however, among the grounds covered by the new competences in Article 13 of the Amsterdam Treaty (now Article 19 TFEU) and is now regulated by the Employment Equality Directive.[104] The directive does not include a definition of sexual orientation, but

99 Article 6(1) Employment Equality Directive.
100 Meenan (2007) and O'Cinneide (2015).
101 ECJ 2010, C-555/07 (*Kücükdeveci*).
102 ECJ 2009, C-88/08 *(Hütter)*.
103 Compare ECJ 1998, C-249/96 (*Grant*).
104 On the way there, see Bell (2002), chap. 4.

the concept is known to refer to homosexuals (gays and lesbians) and bisexuals as well as heterosexuals, with an emphasis on the individual's capacity for profound emotional, affectionate and sexual attraction, and intimate and sexual relations.[105] 'Gender identity' – including not only gender reassignment situations but a broad variety of transgender persons not identifying themselves with the sex assigned at birth, or even any sex, and focused on the personal sense of the body and other expressions of gender[106] – is not the same as sexual orientation, and transgender persons may identify themselves as homosexual, bisexual or heterosexual. The issue of gender identity as a ground of discrimination will be discussed further at the end of this section.

With sexual orientation there is (still) a focus on direct discrimination and harassment and not so much on indirect discrimination and positive action. Only in exceptional cases is a person's sexual orientation regarded as relevant to working life. Instead, there is a significant human rights element to the prohibition of sexual orientation discrimination reflected in the Court's case law as well as the preceding/accompanying case law of the ECtHR. As in relation to other grounds, associated discrimination is also covered by the prohibition,[107] while the *Accept* case indicated that statements that discriminated on grounds of sexual orientation could be in breach of EU law (in that case regarding the possible recruitment of gay football players).[108]

Case law reflects a significant development of same-sex partnership rights.[109] In the case *Maruko*,[110] the Court regarded survivor's benefits related to occupation (and thus equalling 'pay') to be covered by the prohibition in Directive 2000/78, regardless of same-sex marriages not being allowed in the Member State in question (Germany) insofar as 'under national law, life partnership places persons of the same sex in a situation comparable to that of spouses so far as concerns that survivor's benefit'.[111] It is, however, ultimately left for the referring court to determine whether a surviving life partner is in a comparable situation (ibid.). Also *Römer*[112] concerned an occupational pension scheme in the form of a supplementary retirement pension for former employees and their survivors. Here it was the method of calculating the pension that favoured married recipients over those in a registered partnership. Also here, the Court found the benefit provisions to be covered by Directive 2000/78

105 Hammarberg (2011).
106 Compare the Yogyakarta Principles 2006 at <http://yogyakartaprinciples.org> accessed 05.06.2019.
107 See Section 3.3.1.7.
108 ECJ 2013, C-81/12 (*Accept*).
109 See further Bell (2002).
110 ECJ 2008, C-267/06 (*Maruko*).
111 Ibid., §73.
112 ECJ 2011, C-147/08 (*Römer*).

and that the relevant comparison was not 'whether national law generally and comprehensively treats registered life partnership as legally equivalent to marriage' (which it did not) but 'taking account of the purpose and the conditions for granting the benefit at issue'.[113] Direct discrimination was found to exist because under national law – creating a regime separate from marriage, the registered life partnership, which has been gradually made equivalent to that of marriage – the life partner is in a legal and factual situation comparable to that of a married person as regards the pension at issue, ultimately it being for the national court to assess this comparability.[114] In *Hay*,[115] the Court confirmed that the Employment Equality Directive precluded a collective agreement under which an employee, who concludes a civil solidarity pact with a person of the same sex is not allowed to obtain the same benefits as married persons where the national rules of the Member State do not allow persons of the same sex to marry, 'in so far as, in the light of the objective of and the conditions relating to the grant of those benefits, that employee is in a comparable situation to an employee who marries'. A recent case dealing with the payment of survivor's benefits to a same-sex civil partner is *Parris*.[116] In this case the Court sheds some further light on the meaning of recital 22 of Directive 2000/78, stating that Member States are 'free to provide or not provide for marriage for persons of the same sex, or an alternative form of legal recognition of their relationship, and, if they do so provide, to lay down the date from which such a marriage or alternative form is to have effect'.[117] It is only in the exercise of that competence that the Member States must comply with EU law and the principle on non-discrimination. The case concerned multiple grounds of discrimination (sexual orientation and age), but the Court held that it was not possible to find a breach of the directive on combined grounds unless there was a separate finding of discrimination on a single ground.[118] In summary, the case law indicates that the right to equal treatment for same-sex couples remains contingent upon a prior decision of the national legislature to create a legal framework for the recognition of such relationships.[119]

The concept of sexual orientation does not necessarily cover sexual behaviour,[120] although the demarcation line to sexual orientation proper can be hard to draw. This is where it becomes necessary to return to gender identity as a discrimination ground. Whereas gender reassignment thus is part and parcel

---

113 Ibid., §43.
114 Ibid., §52.
115 ECJ 2013, C-267/12 (*Hay*).
116 ECJ 2016, C-443/15 (*Parris*).
117 Ibid., §59.
118 Ibid., §80.
119 Bell (2012), pp. 139 and 141.
120 Compare the Commission's proposal for the Employment Equality Directive, COM(1999)565, 8.

of sex discrimination as a ground of discrimination, it remains ambiguous as to whether this prohibition can apply more broadly to gender identity discrimination.[121] It has been argued that the reference by the Court in *P v. S* to the need 'to respect the freedom and dignity' of the individual – and thus the human rights rationale of the ban – may lend itself to wider interpretation of the ban on sex discrimination.[122] As of yet, there are still important lacunae with respect to the protection of intersex and transgender people[123] and there is a quest for progress in the area of gender identity.[124] The coverage of national legislation differs. Whereas at least six Member States have included gender identity explicitly in comprehensive non-discrimination legislation, eight Member States treat discrimination on the grounds of gender identity or gender reassignment as a form of sex or gender discrimination.[125] Sweden has chosen a multiple ban; on the one hand, defining gender reassignment as sex discrimination, on the other hand, also prohibiting discrimination on the grounds of 'transgender identity and expression' covering a wider range of transgender persons.

3.3.1.7. *Discrimination by Association and/or Based on Assumption*

As discussed above, the directives are premised on the prohibition of discrimination on an exhaustive list of grounds. In 2008, the *Coleman* case posed the question of whether that prohibition extended to those who experienced discrimination due to being associated with one of those grounds. Specifically, the case concerned a woman who allegedly experienced discrimination and harassment in connection with her son's disability. The applicable national legislation prohibited discrimination against disabled persons, but she did not fall into this category. The Court held that the Employment Equality Directive 'applies not to a particular category of person but by reference to the grounds mentioned in Article 1'.[126] Discrimination and harassment experienced by a person who is the primary carer of a child with a disability was therefore unlawful because the treatment was on grounds of disability.[127]

The decision in *Coleman* was framed in broad terms that appeared applicable to any other ground of discrimination. This logic was subsequently confirmed

---

121 Gender identity is absent from the open list of non-discrimination grounds found in Article 21 CFREU.

122 Bell (2012), p. 138.

123 Tobler (2014).

124 See, for instance, the European Parliament's call on the Commission to adopt an EU Roadmap against homophobia and discrimination on grounds of sexual orientation and gender identity, adopted on 04.02.2014.

125 Hammarberg (2011), p. 42.

126 ECJ 2008, C-803/06 (*Coleman*), §50.

127 Ibid., §63.

by the Court in *CHEZ*. This case concerned discriminatory treatment in the provision of electricity meters to a neighbourhood that was predominantly inhabited by persons from the Roma community. The complaint was, however, brought by a non-Roma woman who ran a business in that district. The Court accepted that she could rely on the prohibition of either direct or indirect discrimination on grounds of ethnic origin:

> the fact remains that it is indeed Roma origin, in this instance that of most of the other inhabitants of the district in which she carries on her business, which constitutes the factor on the basis of which she considers that she has suffered less favourable treatment or a particular disadvantage.[128]

The combined effect of the decisions in *Coleman* and *CHEZ* is to establish firmly the principle that the directives will protect those who experience discrimination because of an association with a particular discrimination ground, even if they do not personally share the characteristic that has caused the discrimination.[129] There has been no case law before the Court on the related issue of discrimination due to a perception or assumption.[130] This can arise where, for example, an employee experiences harassment because her colleagues perceive that she is lesbian, even if this is not correct. Given that such treatment would be 'on grounds' of sexual orientation, then it would seem to follow from the existing case law that such discrimination is also contrary to the directives.

3.3.2. PROHIBITED FORMS OF DISCRIMINATION

This section concentrates on the forms of conduct that are prohibited in EU anti-discrimination legislation. In the 1976 Equal Treatment Directive, there was a simple text stating that 'there shall be no discrimination whatsoever on grounds of sex either directly or indirectly by reference in particular to marital or family status'.[131] Over time, Court case law provided elaboration on the meaning of 'direct' and 'indirect' discrimination, which was subsequently codified in the legislation. National experience (both within and beyond the EU Member States) led to the recognition of additional harms, such as 'harassment' or 'denial of reasonable accommodation'. Each of these concepts is considered

128 ECJ 2015, C-83/14 (*CHEZ*), §59.

129 However, in *Coleman*, the Court expressed the view that the duty of reasonable accommodation in Article 5 of the Employment Equality Directive could only apply to disabled people (§42).

130 Although the *Accept* case entailed discriminatory statements relating to the perceived sexual orientation of a professional footballer: ECJ 2013, C-81/12 (*Accept*).

131 Directive 76/207, Article 2(1).

further below. There is also analysis of the law on equal pay for women and men, as well as discrimination related to pregnancy, maternity and paternity. The longer history of EU gender equality legislation, as well as its interaction with other branches of labour law,[132] has allowed for the development of a specialised body of rules on these topics.

3.3.2.1. *Direct Discrimination*

There is a relatively consistent definition of direct discrimination across the EU Directives. For example, Article 2(1)(a) of the Recast Gender Equality Directive provides the following definition:

> Where one person is treated less favourably on grounds of sex than another is, has been or would be treated in a comparable situation.[133]

This definition places a test of comparison at the heart of establishing direct discrimination. As will be discussed further in Section 3.3.2.7, the Court does not require the application of a comparator test in cases of discrimination related to pregnancy or maternity (within the period of maternity leave protected by EU law).[134] For all other types of direct discrimination, the Court has generally maintained the need for comparison.[135] The strength of the concept of direct discrimination lies in the absence of any possibility to justify such conduct. So, for example, an employer cannot rely on the subjective preferences of clients or customers to justify not hiring Moroccans,[136] or dismissing a Muslim woman who wears the headscarf.[137] This is subject to two qualifications, both of which are examined in later sections of this chapter. First, direct discrimination on grounds of age is open to objective justification. Second, there are certain exceptions that may displace the prohibition of direct discrimination.

The role of the comparator test in establishing direct discrimination remains controversial. Fredman has argued that this tends to reinforce the norms and conduct of dominant groups who become the benchmark against which treatment is compared.[138] The comparator, whether real or hypothetical, is likely to have characteristics such as being white, abled-bodied or a man. The choice

---

132 Notably Directive 92/85 (Pregnant Workers).

133 See also Directive 2000/43, Article 2(2)(a); Directive 2000/78, Article 2(2)(a); Directive 2010/41, Article 3(a).

134 Directive 2006/54, Article 2(2)(c).

135 In some cases, the Court appears to place less weight on the identification of a comparator, e.g. case law relating to discrimination against transgender persons. See further, Bell (2012).

136 ECJ 2008, C-54/07 (*Feryn*).

137 ECJ 2017, C-188/15 (*Bougnaoui*); the situation is different if the employer has a policy of prohibiting all religious symbols in the workplace (see Section 3.3.2.2 on indirect discrimination).

138 Fredman (2011).

of comparator is often pivotal to the outcome of a case, but it is sometimes difficult to determine when a court will view two situations as comparable. The case law on equal treatment of same-sex couples discussed earlier in Section 3.3.1.6 provides an illustration of some of the difficulties encountered when applying the comparator test. Another example can be found in *Österreichischer Gewerkschaftsbund.*[139] Workers were entitled to a payment on the termination of their employment, but the level of this payment varied according to length of service. In calculating length of service, periods of parental leave were generally not taken into account, yet periods of leave for military service were included; however, 98% of people taking parental leave were women and compulsory military service exclusively concerned men. Nevertheless, the Court of Justice held that men taking military service were not in a comparable position to women taking parental leave. In its view, parental leave was a voluntary choice on the part of the worker, whereas in the relevant Member State military service was, at least initially, compulsory.

3.3.2.2. Indirect Discrimination

Indirect discrimination addresses rules or practices that apply in the same way to all persons, but that create disadvantage for particular groups. This was exemplified in a series of cases that concerned less favourable employment conditions for part-time workers compared to full-time workers.[140] There was no overt difference of treatment between women and men, both of whom could be part-time or full-time workers. In many Member States, the social reality is that part-time work is predominantly performed by women, so measures that privilege full-time work often constitute indirect discrimination on grounds of sex. The Court recognised this principle in its case law and this was subsequently codified in legislation.[141] The following definition is now found across the anti-discrimination directives:

> Where an apparently neutral provision, criterion or practice would put persons of one sex at a particular disadvantage compared with persons of the other sex, unless that provision, criterion or practice is objectively justified by a legitimate aim, and the means of achieving that aim are appropriate and necessary.[142]

This can be divided into two core elements: (i) evidence that the practice in question places a group of persons at a particular disadvantage; (ii) an assessment of whether that practice is objectively justified.

139 ECJ 2014, C-220/02 (*Österreichischer Gewerkschaftsbund*).
140 Ellis and Watson (2012), p. 148.
141 Directive 97/80, Article 2(2).
142 Directive 2006/54, Article 2(1)(b). See also Directive 2000/43, Article 2(2)(b); Directive 2000/78, Article 2(2)(b); Directive 2010/41, Article 3(b).

(a) 'Particular Disadvantage'

The case law on gender equality originally focused on numerical analysis as the primary method of identifying indirect discrimination. *Bilka-Kaufhaus* concerned the exclusion of part-time workers from an occupational pension scheme, which the Court recognised as potential indirect discrimination if it affected 'a far greater number of women than men'.[143] This approach was particularly apt when comparing the treatment of part-time and full-time workers because the statistical differences between the participation rates of women and men are often wide. Other cases, though, exposed the risk that indirect discrimination may become enmeshed in arguments over the most appropriate statistical comparison. For example, in *Seymour-Smith and Perez*,[144] British legislation limited protection from unfair dismissal to those employees who had completed two years of continuous service with their employer. If the focus was only on those employees who did not qualify for protection, then the gap between women and men was striking.[145] The Court, however, favoured a broader comparison between the proportion of male employees who could comply with the two-year requirement and the equivalent figure for female employees.[146] These figures were 77.4% of men and 68.9% of women, which the Court did not regard as a sufficient disparity to establish indirect discrimination.[147] In contrast, when the case returned to the UK House of Lords, it took the view that this gap did establish a prima facie case of indirect discrimination because it applied to the workforce as a whole and its effects extended over time.[148]

When the Union extended anti-discrimination legislation to cover grounds other than gender, it was evident that an approach founded on statistical comparison would not be appropriate. Gender disaggregated data on the labour market is (to some extent) collected by all national statistical agencies and individual employers will often be capable of assembling some data relating to male and female employees. Yet data collection practices are much weaker in relation to other characteristics (such as religion or sexual orientation). Consequently, the 2000 anti-discrimination directives adopted the threshold

---

143 ECJ 1986, 170/84 (*Bilka-Kaufhaus*), §31.

144 ECJ 1999, C-167/97 (*Seymour-Smith and Perez*).

145 In 1985, 31% of women did not qualify for unfair dismissal protection compared to 22.6% of men: *R v Secretary of State for Employment ex parte Seymour-Smith (no. 2)* [2000] 1 WLR 435, 443 (HL).

146 ECJ 1999, C-167/97 (*Seymour-Smith and Perez*), §59.

147 Ibid., §§63–64.

148 *R v Secretary of* State *for Employment ex parte Seymour-Smith (no. 2)* [2000] 1 WLR 435 (HL). The House of Lords held that the measure was, however, objectively justified by the goal of encouraging recruitment (pp. 450–51).

of 'particular disadvantage', which was also incorporated into gender equality legislation. Statistical data can be submitted as evidence of such disadvantage,[149] but it is not required. For example, in *Ring and Skouboe Werge*, the Court accepted that a provision of Danish law that permitted the dismissal of employees after 120 days of paid sick leave in a 12-month period placed employees with a disability at a particular disadvantage.[150] The Court was willing to accept, as a general proposition (and without statistical data), that an employee with a disability had an elevated risk of needing to take sick leave.

(b) 'Objective Justification'

Where it can be shown that a practice would put persons at a particular disadvantage (on grounds of sex, ethnic origin, etc.), then it is necessary to consider whether the respondent (e.g. the employer) can show that the practice is objectively justified. In the early case law on gender equality, the Court held that the measures taken by an employer had to 'correspond to a real need on the part of the undertaking'.[151] Where litigation challenged provisions of national legislation, the Court held that the measures contained therein must 'reflect a necessary aim of its social policy'.[152] States enjoyed a 'broad margin of discretion' in determining the goals of national social policy, but this had to be more than 'mere generalisations'.[153] Today, the statutory definition of indirect discrimination requires the identification of a 'legitimate aim'. It is often possible for the respondent to advance an objective that can be construed as legitimate. For example, the Court has accepted that wide goals, such as encouraging recruitment or promoting labour market flexibility, meet this requirement.[154]

Frequently, the key part of the objective justification test lies in the assessment of whether the measures adopted are both 'appropriate' and 'necessary' in pursuit of the identified aim(s). Necessity implies some analysis of whether alternative measures could have been taken that might have avoided, or mitigated, the discriminatory impact. In *CHEZ*, the Court added a further step to the test. It stated that, even if the measures taken were an appropriate and necessary way of pursuing the identified aim, 'the referring court will also have to determine whether the disadvantages caused

149 E.g. Directive 2000/43, Recital 15.

150 ECJ 2013, C-335/11 and 337/11 (*Ring and Skouboe Werge*), §76. Compare also ECJ 2018, C-270/16 (*Ruiz Conejero*).

151 ECJ 1984, 170/84 (*Bilka-Kaufhaus*), §36.

152 ECJ 1999, C-167/97 (*Seymour-Smith and Perez*), §69.

153 Ibid., §§74–76.

154 ECJ 2013, C-335/11 and 337/11 (*Ring and Skouboe Werge*), §82.

by the practice at issue are disproportionate to the aims pursued'.[155] While the framework for analysing objective justification is relatively clear, the degree of rigour with which it is applied seems to vary. Two examples provide a helpful contrast.

In *Ring and Skouboe Werge*, the Court accepted that permitting employers greater flexibility to dismiss workers after 120 days of paid sick leave could be an appropriate means of pursuing a flexible labour market and encouraging employers to recruit employees who have (potentially) a reduced work capacity. It required, however, the national court to examine whether the situation of workers with disabilities was sufficiently taken into account in the design of this general rule:

> In this respect, the risks run by disabled persons, who generally face greater difficulties than non-disabled persons in re-entering the labour market, and have specific needs in connection with the protection their condition requires, should not be overlooked.[156]

Nevertheless, in the *Skouboe Werge* case, the Danish Supreme Court ultimately concluded that the legislation was not disproportionate to the objectives that it pursued and consequently it was not incompatible with the Employment Equality Directive.[157]

In *Achbita*, the case concerned an employer's policy that prohibited the wearing of religious, political or philosophical signs in the workplace. Ms. Achbita was dismissed as she wished to wear a headscarf due to her religious beliefs. The national court had asked whether this constituted direct discrimination. The Court preferred to characterise this as (potential) indirect discrimination, on the basis that the evidence appeared to show that the employer applied this rule to all workers.[158] In *Achbita*, the Court appears more cautious in its application of the indirect discrimination test. In *Ring and Skouboe Werge*, the Court itself determined that the contested measures gave rise to particular disadvantage for disabled persons, but in *Achbita*, it said that this was a matter for the national court to determine.[159] The Court held that it was a legitimate aim for an employer to adopt a policy of neutrality in its dealings with customers, and prohibiting employees from wearing visible religious symbols was an appropriate means of pursuing this aim.[160] If the policy was limited to those employees who had

---

155 ECJ 2015, C-83/14 (*CHEZ*), §123.

156 ECJ 2013, C-335/11 and 337/11 (*Ring and Skouboe Werge*), §91.

157 See further: <https://www.equalitylaw.eu/downloads/2907-denmark-supreme-court-test-case-on-dismissal-because-of-disability-related-sickness-absence-pdf-83-kb> accessed 11.06.19.

158 ECJ 2017, C-157/15 (*Achbita*), §31.

159 Ibid., §34.

160 Ibid., §§37–41.

contact with customers, then it could be regarded as necessary. Ultimately, the Court accorded considerable discretion to the national court:

> it is for the referring court, having regard to all the material in the file, to take into account the interests involved in the case and to limit the restrictions on the freedoms concerned to what is strictly necessary.[161]

In summary, the concept of indirect discrimination has matured into an elaborate framework for scrutinising the discriminatory effects of measures that superficially appear neutral. It holds the potential to challenge structural causes of disadvantage that arise in areas such as workplace pay systems or national regulation of the labour market. Yet litigants face significant evidential hurdles in order to establish that the practice in question creates 'particular disadvantage'. Crucially, the impact of indirect discrimination depends heavily on the willingness of courts to apply the objective justification test with rigour.

3.3.2.3. Harassment

In a European perspective, harassment first caught our attention in relation to discrimination on the grounds of sex and then in the terms of sexual harassment.[162] As many as 55% of all women are estimated to have experienced sexual harassment of some kind during their life.[163] Nonetheless, it was not until the adoption of Directive 2002/73 (amending Directive 76/207 (Gender Equality)) that sexual harassment and harassment on the grounds of sex were explicitly recognised as forms of discrimination. Harassment on other grounds was, however, already recognised as discrimination in the 2000/43 and 2000/78 directives.

The following definition of harassment is now found across the anti-discrimination directives:

> Harassment shall be deemed to be a form of discrimination … when unwanted conduct … takes place with the purpose or effect of violating the dignity of a person and of creating an intimidating, hostile, degrading, humiliating or offensive environment. In this context, the concept of harassment may be defined in accordance with the national laws and practice of the Member State.

---

161 Ibid., §43.

162 The term sexual harassment was coined in the U.S. back in the 1960s, see Jones (1996), pp. 3–90. See also MacKinnon (1979). The origin was, however, discriminatory harassment of racial minorities and Title VII in the Civil Rights Act 1964.

163 FRA, *Violence against women: an EU-wide survey. Main results*, Luxembourg 2014, pp. 95–119.

In the Recast Gender Equality Directive there is also a definition of 'sexual harassment':

> Where any form of unwanted verbal, non-verbal or physical conduct of a sexual nature occurs, with the purpose or effect of violating the dignity of a person, in particular when creating an intimidating, hostile, degrading, humiliating or offensive environment.[164]

In Directive 2006/54, sexual harassment is declared to constitute discrimination on the grounds of sex for the purposes of that Directive (Recital 6)[165] and the omission of the concept of sexual harassment in both the Racial Equality Directive and the Employment Equality Directive has caused uncertainty regarding whether sexual harassment is related to discrimination on the grounds of sex only, or can apply to all protected grounds. Member States have chosen distinctive approaches in this regard. Whereas approximately 50% of the Member States expressly prohibit sexual harassment only in relation to sex discrimination, the remaining States, among them Sweden, recognise that sexual harassment can relate to any protected ground of discrimination.[166] It can also be argued, that in relation to prohibited grounds of discrimination other than sex, 'conduct of a sexual nature' can be regarded as included in the concept of unwanted conduct.[167]

The core elements of the ban on discriminatory harassment are thus (i) unwanted conduct, (ii) related to a protected ground and (iii) with the purpose or effect of violating dignity and of creating an offensive environment. (i) What is to be regarded as 'unwanted conduct' can be said to be in eyes of the beholder, i.e. the person claiming harassment discrimination. However, whereas some ways of conduct by nature may qualify as unwanted, in other cases the victim of perceived harassment may be required to make it clear to the perpetrator that the conduct is unwanted before discriminatory harassment can be deemed to exist. There is a recurring element to such cases. (ii) There must be a relationship between the alleged harassment and a protected ground, implying that normally the perpetrator (in case of individual harassment) should be aware of that the victim belongs to a certain group (or assume that the victim has such a characteristic). (iii) If there is a harassing effect this is enough for liability and this is also the case if there is a harassing intent.

Harassment discrimination thus recognises two types of harassment: harassment violating the dignity of an individual, and harassment creating an offensive environment. This differentiation has its background in early US case

---

164 Directive 2006/54, Article 2(1)(d). See also Directive 2004/113, Article 2(d).

165 Compare also Directive 2004/113, Article 4(3).

166 Numhauser-Henning and Laulom (2013), p. 15.

167 Clarke (2007), p. 98.

law developments. Initially, discrimination implied quid pro quo situations (in exchange for sexual favours the victim receives better treatment), but in the early 1980s hostile environment cases were also regarded as discrimination.[168] In the famous *Harris v. Forklift Systems*, the US Supreme Court stated that a claimant did not necessarily have to show economic or tangible discrimination, it was enough that the working environment was 'abusive'.[169]

At EU level there is hitherto but one case actually dealing with harassment. In *Coleman*,[170] the main issue was whether the Employment Equality Directive covered not only people who are themselves disabled but also a worker such as Ms. Coleman, who was differently treated on the basis of the disability of her child. One of the questions referred to the Court in this case was whether discrimination by association applied also to the ban on harassment (on discrimination by association, see further section 3.3.1.7). The Court answered this question in the affirmative where 'it is established that the unwanted conduct amounting to harassment which is suffered by an employee who is not himself disabled is related to the disability of his child'.[171] To establish the presence of harassment is thus, in the main, a task for the national court (the concept of harassment as such being open for definition in accordance with the national laws and practice of the Member States).[172] This may explain why alleged harassment only rarely reaches the Court.[173] In *Coleman*, the alleged harassment consisted of, among other things, abusive and insulting comments with reference both to the worker and her disabled child. Harassment cases – and mostly in the terms of sexual harassment – are somewhat more frequent at the national level of Member States.[174]

It is obvious from the *Coleman* case, that the provision of the shift in the burden of proof applies also in harassment cases so that:

> in the event that [the claimant] establishes facts from which it may be presumed that there has been harassment, the effective application of the principle of equal treatment then requires that the burden of proof should fall on the respondents, who must prove that there has been no harassment in the circumstances of the present case.[175]

---

168 *Bundy v. Jackson*, 641 F.2d 934 (D.C. Cir. 1981).
169 *Harris v Forklift Sys. Inc.*, 510 US 17 (1993), 14 S. Ct. 367 (1993).
170 ECJ 2008, C-803/06 (*Coleman*).
171 Ibid., §59.
172 Ibid., §60. Compare also the definition of harassment above.
173 Reference to the provisions on harassment has been made though in the cases ECJ 2013, C-81/12 (*Accept*) and ECJ 2015, C-83/14 (*CHEZ*), where the rules on harassment were referred to in the respective judgments.
174 Numhauser-Henning & Laulom (2013), p. 22.
175 ECJ 2008, C-803/06 (*Coleman*), §62.

Who then can be made responsible for a case of harassment? The prohibitions on discrimination in working life by nature are addressed to employers.[176] In relation to harassment these actors are explicitly approached in Recital 7 of Directive 2006/54: 'employers and those responsible for vocational training should be encouraged to take measures to combat all forms of discrimination on grounds of sex and, in particular, to take preventive measures against harassment and sexual harassment'.[177] However, at implementation level, where the prohibition on discriminatory harassment goes hand in hand with more general obligations in terms of bullying and health and safety, a broader notion of addressees is frequent. Broadening the scope can take on different forms. There may be a far-reaching liability for the person primary responsible for the workplace (i.e. the employer), but harassment can also be categorised in terms of a criminal misdemeanour or civil wrong in the law of tort, where the addressee can be any perpetrator or harasser, such as co-workers or clients.[178] Closely related to the issue of employers' responsibility for harassment is the duty on employers to investigate properly and remedy any situation of harassment which comes to their knowledge, which should it be neglected could lead to direct or indirect discrimination.[179]

Despite now explicitly stated to be – and de facto at Member State level formally implemented as – a form of discrimination, harassment is frequently perceived, regulated and analysed in terms of general bullying/mobbing and as a health and safety issue (e.g. in Belgium, France, Slovenia). This 'Dignity Harm Approach' tradition – as opposed to the US 'Discriminatory Approach', now adopted in EU legislation – is clearly reflected in the 'Framework Agreement on harassment and violence at work' entered into by the social partners at EU level in 2007.[180] In this context, sexual harassment is mentioned along with bullying and physical violence. This approach tends to make structural and individual oppression of the protected groups less visible. Harassing practices are not a mere reflection of 'bad manners' but reflect and reinforce societal hierarchies at the core of the problem that non-discrimination regulations are designed to combat. This is very well reflected in the *Me Too* movement,

176 Compare, however, ECJ 2013, C-81/12 (*Accept*) concerning statements from a person presenting himself and being perceived by public opinion as playing a leading role in a professional football club without necessarily representing the employer.

177 Compare also Article 26 in the Recast Gender Equality Directive on prevention.

178 Numhauser-Henning & Laulom (2013), p. 16.

179 In 1988, the US Supreme Court clarified that employers were strictly liable where sexual harassment had tangible employment consequences, such as dismissal, whereas in 'hostile environment' cases employers had a defence where they had acted reasonably to prevent harassment: see Clarke (2007), p. 81 and the cases *Brulington Industries Inc. v. Ellerth* 524 US 742 (1988) and *Faragher v City of Boca Raton* 524 US 775 (1998).

180 See European Commission, *Study on the implementation on the autonomous framework agreement on harassment and violence at work*, Brussels 2015.

an international movement against sexual harassment and assault. This spread virally in October 2017 as a hashtag on social media to help demonstrate the widespread prevalence of sexual assault and harassment, especially in the workplace. The movement took off in the film industry, in particular, when American actor Alyssa Milano encouraged women to tweet about these practices and thus give people a sense of the magnitude of the problem. It then spread rapidly to a multitude of – not least European – countries. In Sweden, for instance, the *Me Too* movement gave rise to a large number of professional groups coming forward with public accusations signed by thousands of women as of October 2017 onwards. In regard to sexual harassment, Member State implementation so far has resulted in a 'blurred approach' to harassment as a form of discrimination.[181]

3.3.2.4 *Instructions to Discriminate*

The 2000 Directives, and those adopted thereafter, expressly provide that discrimination includes an 'instruction to discriminate'.[182] To date, there has been no case law that examines this provision in detail. It is directed towards situations where one party instructs another to commit an action that constitutes discrimination under the directives. For example, this could arise in the employment relationship if a manager instructed entrance security staff not to permit persons from ethnic minority communities to enter a nightclub. Instructions could also find their source in third parties. In *Accept*, the Court considered public statements by a high-profile patron of a professional football club that the club would never hire a gay player. The Court held that these statements could be taken into account in establishing evidence of discrimination:

> a defendant employer cannot deny the existence of facts from which it may be inferred that it has a discriminatory recruitment policy merely by asserting that statements suggestive of the existence of a homophobic recruitment policy come from a person who, while claiming and appearing to play an important role in the management of that employer, is not legally capable of binding it in recruitment matters.[183]

The case did not focus on whether there was a breach of the prohibition of instructions to discriminate because it was directed towards the actions of the football club itself, rather than those of the patron. Importantly, it confirmed that legal proceedings to establish discrimination do not require the

---

181 Numhauser-Henning & Laulom (2013), p. 6.

182 Directive 2000/43, Article 2(4); Directive 2000/78, Article 2(4); Directive 2006/54, Article 2(2)(b); Directive 2010/41, Article 4(3).

183 ECJ 2013, C-81/12 (*Accept*), §49.

identification of an individual complainant who alleges to have been a victim of discrimination.[184] This is relevant to potential legal proceedings on instructions to discriminate where there may not be an identifiable victim.

In the absence of case law of the Court of Justice on the meaning of instructions to discriminate, some divergence within national legislation can be noted. In some States, national law requires a relationship of subordination or hierarchy between the person giving and the person receiving the instruction.[185] National law also differs on whether liability attaches only to the person giving the instruction or also the person who acts upon the instruction.[186]

3.3.2.5. Denial of Reasonable Accommodation

The Employment Equality Directive placed an obligation on employers to provide reasonable accommodation for workers with disabilities:

> employers shall take appropriate measures, where needed in a particular case, to enable a person with a disability to have access to, participate in, or advance in employment, or to undergo training, unless such measures would impose a disproportionate burden on the employer.[187]

The directive remains silent on how a breach of this duty should be categorised and whether a failure to provide reasonable accommodation is a form of unlawful discrimination. The UN Convention on the Rights of Persons with Disabilities explicitly provides that denial of reasonable accommodation is discrimination on grounds of disability.[188] In most Member States, it seems clear from legislation or case law that denial of reasonable accommodation is treated as discrimination, but there is divergence on whether this is regarded as a free-standing concept, or whether it is an aspect of direct or indirect discrimination.[189]

There are two key components to reasonable accommodation: (1) the provision of appropriate measures; and (2) an assessment of whether such measures would constitute a disproportionate burden for the employer. Case law before the Court has primarily focused on the first issue. In *Ring and Skouboe Werge*, the Court held that a transfer from full-time to part-time work could be an appropriate measure. Specifically, it held that both the directive and the UN Convention on the Rights of Persons with Disabilities 'envisage not only material but also organisational measures'.[190] Recital 20 of the Preamble to the

184 ECJ 2013, C-81/12 (*Accept*), §36; ECJ 2008, C-54/07 (*Feryn*), §§23–25.
185 E.g. Denmark, Sweden and Finland: Chopin & Germaine (2016), p. 53.
186 Ibid.
187 Directive 2000/78, Article 5.
188 Article 2.
189 Ferri & Lawson (2016), pp. 84–85.
190 ECJ 2013, C-335/11 and 337/11 (*Ring and Skouboe Werge*), §55.

directive provides a list of examples of 'appropriate measures' and this includes 'patterns of working time'. With regard to the assessment of disproportionate burden, the Court drew attention to Recital 21, which states that:

> account should be taken in particular of the financial and other costs entailed, the scale and financial resources of the organisation or undertaking and the possibility of obtaining public funding or any other assistance.

In relation to Ms. Ring, the Court pointed out that her employer had dismissed her because she was unable to continue working full-time, but the same company immediately sought to recruit a part-time worker in a similar role.[191] This may indicate that an accommodation could take the form of a transfer to another vacancy within the same organisation.

The cases of *Ring and Skouboe Werge* also contained an important recognition that if the employer fails to provide a reasonable accommodation and, as a consequence, the worker is compelled to remain on sick leave, then it will be contrary to the directive for the employer to dismiss the worker due to absence. The Court's view was that sick leave in these circumstances is 'attributable to the employer's failure to act, not to the worker's disability.'[192]

3.3.2.6. *Equal Pay between Women and Men*

The ban on unequal pay for women and men was in place from the outset in Article 119 of the Treaty of Rome. Since 1957, the ban has been made increasingly effective through both case law and legislation. Replacing the Equal Pay Directive 75/117, it is now regulated by the Recast Gender Equality Directive,[193] in the main consolidating case law developments. According to Article 4:

> For the same work or for work to which equal value is attributed, direct and indirect discrimination on grounds of sex with regard to all aspects and conditions of remuneration shall be eliminated.
>
> In particular where a job classification system is used for determining pay, it shall be based on the same criteria for both men and women and so drawn up as to exclude any discrimination on grounds of sex.

Significant and innovative developments have thus taken place in the case law of the Court. In the landmark case *Defrenne II*,[194] the Court found that Article 119

[191] Ibid., §62.
[192] Ibid., §66.
[193] Articles 1(b), 2(1)(e) and 14(c).
[194] ECJ 1976, 43/75 (*Defrenne II*).

in the Treaty was directly effective in both vertical (private person versus public authority) and horizontal (private person versus private person) relations.

Pay is now defined as follows in Article 157(2) TFEU:

> 'pay' means the ordinary basic or minimum wage or salary and any other consideration, whether in cash or in kind, which the worker receives directly or indirectly, in respect of his employment from his employer.[195]

This definition reflects important developments in case law having rendered a broad understanding to the concept of 'pay'. It thus includes fringe benefits (*Garland*),[196] sick-pay (*Rinner-Kühn*),[197] redundancy compensation (*Barber*),[198] bargained and unilateral bonuses (*Krüger*)[199] and special family benefits (*Alabaster* and *Hay*).[200] In *Barber*, the Court made in clear that 'pay' also includes occupational pensions as a form of deferred pay stemming from the employment relationship. This line of case law has been confirmed repeatedly in subsequent cases such as *Beune*,[201] and in *Niemi*[202] the Court made it clear that also statutory occupational pension schemes for a certain category of public officials must be regarded as pay in this sense. These developments are now clearly reflected in the provisions of the Recast Gender Equality Directive itself.[203]

Another important line of case law is related to differential pay and indirect sex discrimination. Over time, directly discriminatory pay scales referring to the sex of the employee have become less frequent. However, apparently neutral categorisations, such as in part-time and full-time employment, may also relate to sex. In *Bilka-Kaufhaus*,[204] a German department store company excluded part-time employees from its occupational pension scheme. As that exclusion affected a far greater number of women than men, the scheme was found to imply indirect sex discrimination, if the undertaking could not show 'that the exclusion (was) based on objectively justified factors unrelated to any discrimination on grounds of sex'. In *Jenkins*,[205] the Court had already stated that a difference in pay between full-time workers and part-time workers could amount to discrimination where it was shown that this was 'merely an indirect

195 See also Article 2(1)(e) the Recast Gender Equality Directive.
196 ECJ 1982, C-12/81 (*Garland*).
197 ECJ 1989, C-171/88 (*Rinner-Kühn*).
198 ECJ 1990, C-262/88 (*Barber*).
199 ECJ 1999, C-281/97 (*Krüger*).
200 ECJ 2004, C-147/02 (*Alabaster*) and ECJ 2013, C-267/12 (*Hay*).
201 ECJ 1994, C-7/93 (*Beune*).
202 ECJ 2002, C-351/00 (*Niemi*).
203 Articles 1(c), 2(1)(f) and 7.
204 ECJ 1986, 170/84 (*Bilka-Kaufhaus*).
205 ECJ 1981, C-96/80 (*Jenkins*).

way of reducing the pay of part-time workers on the ground that that group of workers is composed exclusively or predominantly of women'.[206]

In a case of alleged pay discrimination, the claimant must show detrimental treatment in relation to a relevant – though eventually hypothetical – comparator. The principle of equal pay is applicable to each pay element (*Barber*).[207] An important step towards the now consolidated principle of the shift in the burden of proof was taken in the cases *Danfoss*[208] and *Royal Copenhagen*.[209] In *Danfoss*, the Court found that 'where an undertaking applies a system of pay which is totally lacking in transparency, it is for the employer to prove that his practice in the matter of wages is not discriminatory', provided that a female worker had established that the average pay for women was less than that for men. In *Royal Copenhagen*, the Court spelled out the important elements to assess work of equal value: the nature of the work, the training requirements and the working conditions.[210] These elements are now addressed in Recital 9 of the Recast Gender Equality Directive.

In *Royal Copenhagen*, the Court stated that the fact that the elements of pay had been determined in a process of collective bargaining can be taken into account when assessing whether there are objective factors for existing pay differentials unrelated to any discrimination on the grounds of sex. In *Enderby*,[211] the Court also recognised that the state of the employment market, which may lead an employer to increase the pay of a particular job in order to attract candidates, may also constitute an objectively justified economic ground for pay differentials.[212] An employer does not have to provide special justification for recourse to the criterion of length of service in its pay practices.[213]

In the landmark cases *Lawrence*[214] and *Allonby*,[215] the Court declared that pay differentials must have a common source. Both cases concerned contracted-out services, where female former employees were re-engaged by a service-undertaking at considerably lower wages and put to work for their former employer. The comparison was made with male employees performing the same work or work of equal value in the latter's activities. The situation was deemed not to come under the scope of the equal pay provisions since 'the differences identified in the pay conditions of workers performing equal work or work of

206 See also e.g. ECJ 1991, C-184/89 (*Nimz*).
207 See also ECJ 2000, C-236/98 (*Jämställdhetsombudsmannen*).
208 ECJ 1989, 109/88 (*Danfoss*).
209 ECJ 1995, C-400/93 (*Royal Copenhagen*).
210 See also ECJ 2001, C-381/99 (*Brunnhofer*).
211 ECJ 1993, C-127/92 (*Enderby*).
212 Ibid., §26.
213 ECJ 1989, 109/88 (*Danfoss*), §25.
214 ECJ 2002, C-320/00 (*Lawrence*).
215 ECJ 2004, C-256/01 (*Allonby*).

equal value cannot be attributed to a single source, there is no body which is responsible for the inequality and which could restore equal treatment'.[216] Although not astonishing, this has shown to make it almost impossible to come to terms with gender pay discrimination in segregated labour markets. An important case is also *Wiener Gebietskrankenkasse*,[217] where the Court stated that it was not equal work (or work of equal value) when dealing with a situation 'where the same activities are performed over a considerable length of time by persons the basis of whose qualification to exercise their profession is different'.[218] The comparison concerned psychologists and doctors, respectively, employed as psychotherapists in seemingly identical activities.

Despite these developments and the fact that the principle of equal pay in principle is being fully reflected in the legislation of all Member States,[219] there is still today a significant gender pay gap in all Member States. The gender pay gap reflects the average difference in gross hourly earnings between women and men across the economy as a whole, and amounts to about 16% in the EU. Whereas direct pay discrimination is scarce these days, the persisting gender pay gap can be attributed to indirect discrimination and the effects of job classifications and pay-scales, making pay transparency a core concern.[220] First and foremost, however, the continued gender pay gap can be explained by the gender employment gap, labour market segregation, and problems relating to differences in work-life balance between women and men. Women's lower labour market participation, both in absolute terms, and in terms of marginalised part-time and precarious employment, together with a horizontally and vertically gender-segregated labour-market, make the gender pay gap an ongoing challenge. The European Pillar of Social Rights[221] addresses the issues of gender equality and work-life balance as core issues. It was accompanied by a proposal for a new Directive on Work-Life Balance for Parents and Carers,[222] representing a broad approach to women's underrepresentation in the labour market.[223] This proposal was recently adopted as Directive 2019/1158 implying among other things more flexible leave policies and presumably an increased sharing of care work between the sexes.

Labour market segregation thus remains a huge problem in relation to equal pay concerns. The requirement of 'one common source' for pay differentials in

---

216 ECJ 2002, C-320/00 (*Lawrence*), §18.

217 ECJ 1999, C-309/97 (*Wiener Gebietskrankenkasse*).

218 Ibid., §23.

219 Foubert et al. (2010) and Veldman and Timmer (2016).

220 Compare the European Commission Recommendation C(2014)1405 final. See also Veldman & Timmer (2016).

221 COM(2017)251 final.

222 COM(2017)253 final.

223 Compare also preamble 11 of the Recast Directive.

Allonby and *Lawrence* make pay differentials between sectors hard to tackle. It is a paradox that if trade unions manage to negotiate improvements in working conditions for those in part-time employment, this could attract more women with caring responsibilities to such roles, which may entrench gender inequalities in the labour market as a whole.[224]

3.3.2.7. *Pregnancy, Maternity and Paternity*

From an early point, there was space for special protection for pregnant women and motherhood within legislation on discrimination.[225] This is an area where the Court has made particularly strong contributions in the form of innovative interpretations and there is now comprehensive case law to justify this special heading.

In *Dekker*,[226] the Court thus made the ground-breaking decision that dismissal of a woman on grounds of pregnancy amounts to direct sex discrimination – regardless of intent and the absence of a male comparator. This, and other case law, is now consolidated in the Recast Directive 2006/54. Case law developments were also through the years accompanied by other legislative reforms such as the Pregnancy/Maternity Directive 92/85 and the Parental Leave Directive 2010/18 (replacing Directive 96/34). The Recast Directive thus prohibits any less favourable treatment of a woman related to pregnancy or maternity leave (Article 2(2)(c)), and it states that a woman on maternity leave shall be entitled, after the end of her period of maternity leave, to return to her job or to an equivalent post on terms and conditions which are no less favourable to her and also to benefit from any improvement in working conditions to which she would have been entitled during her absence (Article 15). According to this Directive, there is no obligation on Member States to recognise distinct rights to paternity and/or adoption leave, but, if they do recognise such rights, they must protect those employees against dismissal when exercising those rights, and ensure the same rights as those bestowed upon women returning from maternity leave.[227] Directive 92/85 was introduced with the aim of improving safety and health of pregnant workers and workers who have recently given birth or are breastfeeding and is thus (still) applicable alongside the Recast Directive.[228] Apart from protective rules on health and safety during pregnancy and in relation to night work, the Pregnancy Directive provides a right to maternity leave for 14 weeks in relation

224 See further Carlson (2007).
225 Directive 76/207, Article 2(3). Compare now preamble 24 of the Recast Directive.
226 ECJ 1990, C-177/88 (*Dekker*).
227 Article 16.
228 Recital 24 Recast Gender Equality Directive.

to confinement, including two weeks of compulsory leave.[229] It also contains an express rule on prohibition of dismissal during pregnancy and maternity leave 'save in exceptional cases not connected with their condition which are permitted under national legislation and/or practice'.[230] During maternity leave, there is a right to an 'adequate allowance', in principle amounting to sick-leave pay.[231] Directive 2010/18 – now repealed by Directive 2019/1158 – was based on a revised Framework Agreement. It provided a right for female and male workers to four months of parental leave on the grounds of the birth or adoption of a child in order to take care of that child, and, at least one of the four months should be provided on a non-transferable basis.[232] There was no right to remuneration during this leave, but the Agreement contained rules on employment rights and non-discrimination parallel to those of the Recast and Maternity/Pregnancy Directives.[233]

The Court's stand in *Dekker* – that unfavourable treatment on the grounds of pregnancy and maternity is equal to direct discrimination – is by now confirmed in extensive case law.[234] An important statement was, however, made in *Hertz*[235] – a judgment given on the very same day as the one in *Dekker.* During pregnancy and maternity leave, as accorded to a female employee pursuant to national law, a woman is protected against dismissal due to absence. However, 'in the case of an illness manifesting itself after the maternity leave, there is no reason to distinguish an illness attributable to pregnancy or confinement from any other illness'.[236] In *Larsson* this rule was confirmed: neither the Gender Equality Directive, nor Article 10 in the Pregnancy/Maternity Directive preclude a dismissal which is the result of absences due to an illness attributable to pregnancy or confinement, even where that illness arose during pregnancy and continued during and after maternity leave.[237] In *Webb*, however, the Court made it clear that a woman's absence during pregnancy and maternity leave cannot be taken into account for the computation of the period justifying her dismissal under national law due to absence.[238] When a woman, who as a commissioning mother has had a baby through a surrogacy arrangement, is denied the right to maternity leave, this does not amount to direct sex discrimination since she cannot 'be subject to less favourable treatment related to her pregnancy,

229 Article 8.
230 Article 10(1).
231 Articles 11(2)(b) and 11(3). Compare ECJ (1996, C-342/93) (*Gillespie*), where the Court declared that, whereas there is no right to full pay during maternity leave, the amount must not be set so low as to jeopardise the purpose of maternity leave.
232 Clause 2 Framework Agreement.
233 Ibid., Clauses 5 and 6.
234 Caracciolo di Torella and Masselot (2001).
235 ECJ 1990, C-179/88 (*Hertz*).
236 Ibid, §16.
237 ECJ 1997, C-400/95 (*Larsson*).
238 ECJ 1994, C-32/93 (*Webb*).

given that she has not been pregnant with that baby'.[239] Instead, the relevant comparator was found to be the commissioning father of such a baby, being treated in the same way as a commissioning mother. Article 10 in the Pregnancy/ Maternity Directive is interpreted as not extending to a female worker who is undergoing in vitro fertilisation treatment where, on the date of the dismissal, her ova had not yet been transferred into her uterus.[240] Such a dismissal, i.e. at an advanced stage of in vitro fertilisation treatment, can, however, amount to direct discrimination according to the Recast Gender Equality Directive.[241]

The fact that direct discrimination is in principle not justifiable has made these case law developments an effective tool when it comes to the gender employment gap and women's marginalisation on labour markets in the wake of the flexibilisation of work. In *Webb*, the Court stated that:

> Dismissal of a pregnant woman recruited for an indefinite period cannot be justified on grounds relating to her inability to fulfil a fundamental condition of her employment contract, even where the availability of the employee is necessarily, for the employer, a precondition for the proper performance of the employment contract, since the protection afforded by Community law to a pregnant woman cannot be dependent on whether her presence at work during maternity is essential to the proper functioning of the undertaking in which she is employed; any contrary interpretation would render ineffective the provisions of the directive.

This 'fundamentalist' view has been repeatedly confirmed. Whereas Mrs Webb was an employee recruited for an indefinite term, but with a view to replacing another employee during her maternity leave, something she could not do due to her own pregnancy, in *Habermann*[242] we dealt with a woman – likewise on a contract of unlimited duration – who due to her pregnancy (unknown to both her and the employer at the time of contracting) could not perform the necessary night work. Here, the Court reasoned that 'in the case of a contract without a fixed term, the prohibition on night-time work by pregnant women takes effect only for a limited period in relation to the total length of the contract'.[243] In *Mahlburg*, it was established that it was also directly discriminatory not to appoint a woman for a post for an indefinite period when it was clear from the beginning that her pregnancy prevented her from working in that post from the outset and for the duration of the pregnancy.[244] Nor was it permissible to dismiss an employee on the ground of pregnancy where she was recruited on a fixed-term contract, having failed to inform the employer of her pregnancy,

239 ECJ 2014, C-363/12 (*Z*), §57.
240 ECJ 2008, C-506/06 (*Mayr*).
241 Ibid., §50.
242 ECJ 1994, C-421/92 (*Habermann*).
243 Compare also ECJ 1998, C-394/96 (*Brown*).
244 ECJ 2000, C-207/98 (*Mahlburg*).

and because of her pregnancy she was unable to work during a substantial part of the term of the contract.[245] The fact that a woman has no duty to inform her employer about her pregnancy, despite this being a hindrance to her performing the job, was later also confirmed in *Busch*.[246] Whereas the termination of a fixed-term contract prior to its expiry in these cases has been seen as a dismissal contrary to Article 10 in the Pregnancy/Maternity Directive, this Article does not apply when the employee is denied the renewal of her fixed-term contract on those grounds. Instead, direct sex discrimination it dealt with directly under the Recast Directive.[247]

Protective measures in relation to pregnancy and motherhood as well as this fundamentalist view on pregnancy and maternity as unjustifiable direct discrimination have been argued to risk weakening women's position on the labour market.[248] No doubt, cultural stereotypes of motherhood, as well as more practical issues related to the lack of reconciliation between working life and family commitments (and the fact that men's share of unpaid work lags behind), are important explanations for the prevailing gender employment gap. The new Directive on Work-Life Balance for Parents and Carers,[249] adopted during the editing process of this book, reflects the insight that work-life balance is a key to gender equality. The Directive contains a right to 10 days of paternity leave and the right to four months of parental leave – whereof two months should be paid and provided on a non-transferable basis – accompanied by a non-discrimination ban regarding workers exercising their rights under the directive. It also introduces considerably more flexible leave policies.

As it is, Member States' rules on maternity/paternity/parental leave reflect the considerable differences and complexities there still are in those areas.[250] One conclusion is that there is a positive correlation between relatively long and generously paid periods of parental leave, a significant proportion of which must be taken by each parent if the full period is to be enjoyed, and good labour market outcomes for women, especially in addition to access to flexible working arrangements and reduced hours work.[251] A reflection from the Swedish experience: since 2006, legislation contains a prohibition on discrimination in relation to employees making use of their maternity/paternity/parental rights.[252] There is, however, a risk that such a ban in practice tends to 'replace' the prohibition of sex discrimination even when that is also applicable, with, possibly, detrimental effects on gender equality.

---

245 ECJ 2001, C-109/00 (*Tele-Danmark*).
246 ECJ 2003, C-320/01 (*Busch*).
247 ECJ 2001, C-438/99 (*Melgar*).
248 Compare the 'sameness/difference' debate within feminist legal theory, Williams (2010).
249 OJ 12.7.2019 L 188/79.
250 Compare Masselot et al. (2012), Palma-Ramalho et al. (2015) and McColgan (2015).
251 McColgan (2015), p. 10.
252 §16 in the (995:584) Act on Parental Leave.

3.3.3. JUSTIFICATION AND DISCRIMINATION ON GROUNDS OF AGE

The right to equal treatment on the grounds of age is a general principle of EU law,[253] included among the grounds listed in Article 21(1) of the Charter of Fundamental Rights and found in the Employment Equality Directive. Age is sometimes viewed as a less 'suspect'[254] ground than other grounds of discrimination. This is reflected in its 'weaker' format, providing for continued differential treatment on the grounds of age – not only when age is a genuine occupational requirement,[255] concerns a public interest[256] or relates to the armed forces[257] – but also as a justification of direct discrimination. This is sometimes ascribed to the 'double bind' behind the ban on age discrimination, relating not only to the individual human rights rationale common to all grounds of discrimination, but also to a collective interest rationale reflecting age as a traditional social stratifier and also demographic concerns with an ageing population.[258]

The possibility of justification of direct differential treatment on the grounds of age is regulated in Article 6(1) of the Employment Equality Directive:

> Member States may provide that differences in treatment on grounds of age shall not constitute discrimination, if, within the context of national law, they are objectively and reasonable justified by a legitimate aim, including legitimate employment policy, labour market and vocational training objectives, and if the means of achieving that aim are appropriate and necessary.

This scope is then exemplified in the second paragraph of Article 6(1) whereas Article 6(2) addresses the use of age criteria in occupational social security schemes.

The provision in Article 6(1) is at the heart of the Court's case law on age discrimination. There are three elements: assessing the aim and then whether the measures are appropriate and necessary to that aim. The latter can be seen as a proportionality test and the varying rigour of this test is the theme of much of the analyses of the Court's case law in this area.[259]

The majority of the existing case law has concerned old age and most prominently the continued acceptance of compulsory (mandatory) retirement.

---

253 ECJ 2005, C-144/04 *(Mangold)*.
254 On this concept see Gerards (2007).
255 Article 4 Employment Equality Directive.
256 Ibid., Article 2(5).
257 Ibid., Article 3(4).
258 Hendrickx (2012).
259 Schlachter (2011), Kilpatrick (2011), Tobler (2015) and Fudge (2017).

Here, the right of the individual to remain in employment is measured against the traditional trade-off in labour law between employment protection and wage-setting based on seniority on the one hand, and mandatory retirement on the other.[260] In these cases the Court is known to have applied quite a 'loose' proportionality test. The very first case was *Palacios de la Villa*,[261] where a Spanish worker was dismissed at the age of 65 in accordance with the collective agreement applicable. Here, the Court found a legitimate aim to be at hand even though national provisions did not expressly refer to an objective of the prescribed kind.[262] It was enough that 'other elements, taken from the general context of the measure concerned, enable the underlying aim of that law to be identified for the purposes of judicial review of its legitimacy'[263] and both the Member States and the social partners were said to have 'a broad discretion in their choice to pursue a particular aim ... (and) also in the definition of measures capable of achieving it'.[264] According to the Court the measure was both appropriate and necessary since:

> The relevant legislation is not based only on a specific age, but also takes account of the fact that the persons concerned are entitled to financial compensation by way of retirement pension ..., the level of which cannot be regarded as unreasonable.[265]

In *Palacios de la Villa* the Court made reference to the existence of a not 'unreasonable' pension. In later case-law it has become clear, however, that it is the pension system in place as such and not the individual pension that matters. In both *Rosenbladt*[266] and *Hörnfeldt*,[267] the claimants (due to earlier part-time work) had exceptionally low pensions, but that did not make compulsory retirement disproportionate in these cases. In *Hörnfeldt*, the Court summarised the reasons for its acceptance of compulsory retirement:

> The automatic termination of the employment contracts for employees who meet the conditions as regards age and contributions paid for the liquidation of their pension rights has, for a long time, been a feature of employment law in many Member States and is widely used in employment relationships. It is a mechanism which is based on the balance to be struck between political, economic, social, demographic and/or budgetary considerations.[268]

---

260 Lazear (1979).
261 ECJ 2007, C-411/05 (*Palacios de la Villa*).
262 Ibid., §54
263 Ibid., §57.
264 Ibid., §68.
265 Ibid., §73.
266 ECJ 2010, C-45/09 (*Rosenbladt*).
267 ECJ 2012, C-141/11 (*Hörnfeldt*).
268 Ibid., §28.

The Court assessing the appropriateness of the measure also referred to the avoidance of dismissal situations humiliating elderly workers as well as to intergenerational considerations concerning the access to labour markets.[269]

Despite the fact that the Court has accepted continued recourse to compulsory retirement, practices in this regard vary a lot among the Member States. Whereas the existence of compulsory retirement is still frequent among Member States as regard groups of civil servants, it is no longer the rule regarding labour markets in general.[270] In the UK one result of the abolishment of statutory compulsory retirement is an increased use of performance management; regular reviews, consultation and documentation designed to monitor employee performance and build a case for either voluntary retirement or a dismissal that will hold up against the UK unfair dismissal legislation.[271]

In cases concerning changes in retirement schemes for certain occupations, the Court has applied a somewhat stricter proportionality test. These cases have concerned Bulgarian university professors,[272] German dentists[273] and prosecutors.[274] A stricter proportionality test was also used in cases concerning certain employment conditions, such as redundancy pay, in relation to lay-offs. That a worker was eligible for an old-age pension from the employer was not a sufficient reason to deny him a severance allowance aimed at assisting workers in finding new employment at the age of 63.[275] It was deemed to go beyond what was necessary 'by not permitting payment of the severance allowance to workers who, although eligible for an old-age pension from their employer, nonetheless wish to waive their right to such a pension temporarily in order to continue with their career' and thus 'unduly prejudices the legitimate interests' of these workers.[276] In *Odar*,[277] however, a reduced redundancy payment related to the date of a right to early retirement was deemed appropriate, whereas in *Toftgaard*,[278] again, the denial of certain benefits even after the age of 65 was regarded as going beyond what was necessary. The conclusion is, that in regard to working conditions such as redundancy and availability pay, the Court does apply a strict proportionality test also in relation to workers 65 years or older, scrutinising the effects for the individual employee (despite, as in *Tekniq*,[279]

---

269 Ibid., §34. See also ECJ 2007, C-411/05 (*Palacios de la Villa*), §72 and ECJ 2010, C-45/09 (*Rosenbladt*), §51.

270 O'Dempsey and Beale (2011).

271 Barnard and Deakin (2015). Regarding the interrelations between compulsory retirement and employment protection regulation, see further Numhauser-Henning (2015).

272 ECJ 2010, C-250/09 and 268/09 (*Georgiev*).

273 ECJ 2010, C-341/08 (*Petersen*).

274 ECJ 2011, C-159/10 and 160/10 (*Fuchs and Köhler*).

275 ECJ 2010, C-499/08 (*Ole Andersen*).

276 Ibid., §47.

277 ECJ 2011, C-152/11 (*Odar*).

278 ECJ 2013, C-546/11 (*Toftgaard*).

279 ECJ 2015, C-515/13 (*Tekniq*).

accepting differential treatment of workers in terms of the right to a state pension, when these effects are limited).

The continued acceptance of compulsory retirement can be seen as a defence of traditional employment protection in times of continued flexibilisation of work.[280] It turns out that fixed-term work is frequently an alternative to continued open-ended employment beyond retirement age. In *Georgiev*, the Court assessed a system of successive fixed-term contracts 'post-65' as part of the proportionality test regarding the rule on compulsory retirement. It is clear from this judgment, however, that imposing that type of employment contract and preventing continued working under contracts of indefinite duration makes those affected 'more precarious' than younger employees and itself has to be justified under Article 6.1 of the directive.[281] In *Mangold*, the Court examined a German rule which allowed the employers to conclude fixed-term contracts of employment with workers who had reached the age of 52 with the objective 'to promote the integration of unemployed older workers' to be disproportionate and in breach of the general principle of equal treatment on the grounds of age.

When a case has concerned employment conditions detrimental to employees of younger ages, the Court has also applied a strict proportionality test. A rule on not taking into account the period of employment completed before the age of 25 in calculating notice periods was regarded as inappropriate after meticulous scrutiny 'since it applies to all employees who joined the undertaking before the age of 25, whatever their age at the time of dismissal'.[282] In *Hütter*,[283] a rule disregarding working experience acquired before the age of 18 for the purpose of grading within the scale of public service was deemed to be discriminatory in much the same way. A strict proportionality test was also used when assessing certain recruitment ages. Whereas an age limit of 30 years for firefighters was found acceptable as a genuine occupational requirement in *Wolf*,[284] the same age limit in relation to the recruitment of local police officers was deemed to be disproportionate in *Vital Pérez*.[285] On these cases see further Section 3.3.4.1.

Finally, one line of cases before the Court has concerned wage-setting based on seniority – an aspect of the traditional role of age in labour law. These practices tend to work to the detriment of active ageing as they become very expensive when employees grow older. Despite being 'part and parcel' of the logic behind

280 See further Chapter 4 and Numhauser-Henning (2015).
281 Ibid., §§33–35.
282 ECJ 2010, C-555/07 (*Kücükdeveci*), §40.
283 ECJ 2009, C-88/08 (*Hütter*).
284 ECJ 2010, C-229/08 (*Wolf*).
285 ECJ 2014, C-416/13 (*Vital Pérez*).

the acceptance of compulsory retirement,[286] the Court in *Hennigs*[287] declared that a collective agreement, where the basic pay was determined on appointment according to the employee's age, was impermissible under Article 6.1 of the Employment Equality Directive. There is, however, a broad scope for the social partners to provide a transitional way out of these practices.[288]

3.3.4. EXCEPTIONS TO THE PROHIBITION OF DISCRIMINATION

3.3.4.1. Occupational Requirements

As discussed earlier, one of the main differences between direct and indirect discrimination is that there is no possibility to offer objective justification for conduct that is directly discriminatory (unless it is on grounds of age). Nevertheless, there is an acceptance that, in exceptional situations, characteristics related to the discrimination grounds may be taken into account. Common examples relate to privacy and dignity considerations; it may be appropriate to ensure that intimate body searches are performed by security personnel sharing the same gender as the person being searched. Acting and modelling are occupations where reasons of authenticity may demand that the individual has a particular gender or ethnic origin. Yet there is a risk that such exceptions reinforce stereotypical social conventions. Exceptions for occupational requirements are phrased in the following terms:

> Member States may provide, as regards access to employment including the training leading thereto, that a difference of treatment which is based on a characteristic related to sex shall not constitute discrimination where, by reason of the nature of the particular occupational activities concerned or of the context in which they are carried out, such a characteristic constitutes a genuine and determining occupational requirement, provided that its objective is legitimate and the requirement is proportionate.[289]

In *Bougnaoui*, the Court clarified that genuine occupational requirements must relate to objective requirements. The case concerned a Muslim woman who was dismissed by her employer for refusing to remove her headscarf at work.

---

286 See further Numhauser-Henning (2015).

287 ECJ 2011, C-297/10 and 298/10 (*Hennigs*).

288 See also ECJ 2015, C-501/12 (*Specht*) and ECJ 2015, C-20/13 (*Unland*). Cf. also ECJ 2013, C-476/11 (*HK Danmark*), where age-related retirement contributions – increasing with age – were considered legitimate under Article 6(1) of the directive.

289 Directive 2006/54, Article 14(2); Directive 2000/43, Article 4; Directive 2000/78, Article 4.

The employer's actions were prompted by a complaint from a client of the company who did not want services to be provided by a woman wearing a headscarf. The Court rejected the idea that genuine occupational requirements included 'subjective considerations, such as the willingness of the employer to take account of the particular wishes of the customer'.[290] The headscarf in no way interfered with her ability to perform her job as an IT design engineer.

The Court has accepted that physical capability is an objective requirement for certain jobs and that, in limited circumstances, age is a genuine occupational requirement. In *Wolf*, the complainant challenged a maximum recruitment age for the fire service of 30. The Court accepted that those working in the fire service needed 'especially high physical capacities'.[291] The Court noted evidence that indicated that physical capacity began to decline between the ages of 45 and 50,[292] and accepted that it was justified for the fire service to impose a maximum age for recruitment. This served the objective of promoting a balanced age profile amongst existing staff and ensuring that recruits had the potential for sufficient length of service to justify the initial investment in training costs.[293] In *Salaberria Sorondo* the Court accepted a maximum recruitment age of 35 for police officers in general.[294] In contrast, in *Vital Pérez*, the Court rejected a maximum recruitment age of 30 for local police officers.[295] It found that the duties of local police officers were different in nature to those of the fire service and the demands of physical fitness were lower.[296] In such circumstances, a physical fitness test during recruitment was a sufficient means of ensuring the capacity of new police officers and the maximum recruitment age was disproportionate.[297]

The decision in *Wolf* indicates that the genuine occupational requirement exception is an instance where the law permits an assessment of individual merit to be supplanted by a generalisation or stereotype. There can be no doubt that certain individuals over the age of 30 possess the fitness needed to work in the fire service and some will retain this high level of capability for a longer period than average. Fundamentally, these are exceptional cases where the Court is permitting broader operational requirements to take priority. Over time, case law has indicated that it is often in the sphere of emergency and security services where the Court is willing to permit a departure from the norms of

290 ECJ 2017, C-188/15 (*Bougnaoui*), §40.
291 ECJ 2010, C-229/08 (*Wolf*), §40.
292 Ibid., §41.
293 Ibid., §43.
294 ECJ 2015, Case C-258/15 (*Salaberria Sorondo*).
295 ECJ 2014, C-416/13 (*Vital Pérez*).
296 Ibid., §54.
297 Ibid., §§55–57.

anti-discrimination law.[298] For example, in *Sirdar*,[299] women were excluded from an elite military unit in the British Army. This unit was the first line of attack in military operations and all members were required to serve as 'front-line commandos'.[300] The Court held that it was within the discretion of Member States to determine that such a unit should remain exclusively male.[301]

Article 4(2) of the Employment Equality Directive provides an additional exception relating to occupational requirements in 'churches and other public or private organisations the ethos of which is based on religion or belief'. This permits such organisations to justify differences of treatment based on a person's religion or belief. For example, it might allow a school with a Catholic ethos to impose a religious requirement relating to those positions that entail teaching religion or other involvement in the practise of religion, such as leading prayer. The exception is lengthy and complex, with many qualifications. It does not justify 'discrimination on another ground' (such as gender or sexual orientation), but employees can be required to 'act in good faith and with loyalty to the organisation's ethos'. In *Egenberger*, the Grand Chamber of the Court provided quite detailed guidance on how this exception is to be applied. In particular, the Court rejected the possibility for national law to defer entirely to the self-perception of the organisation in relation to which posts demanded the worker to hold a particular religious belief; national courts must provide 'effective judicial review' of situations when this is invoked.[302]

The Grand Chamber expanded further on the application of Article 4(2) in *IR v JQ*.[303] This case concerned the dismissal of a Catholic doctor following his divorce and remarriage. He was working in a private hospital that was primarily a non-profit organisation; it was established to carry out the work of a Catholic charitable confederation.[304] As a Catholic employee with managerial responsibilities, he was subject to heightened obligations in relation to acting with loyalty to 'principles of Catholic doctrinal and moral teaching'.[305] In contrast, it appeared that a non-Catholic employee would not have been dismissed in the same circumstances. The Court held that the requirements relating to marriage imposed by his employer did not fall within the concept of a 'genuine requirement of that occupational activity' for the purposes of Article 4(2). This finding was based upon the nature of the duties (provision of care and management of a medical department) and the fact that similar

298 E.g ECJ 1986, C-222/84 (*Johnson*).
299 ECJ 1999, C-273/97 (*Sirdar*).
300 Ibid., §30.
301 Ibid., §31.
302 ECJ 2018, C-414/16 (*Egenberger*), §55.
303 ECJ 2018, C-68/17 (*IR v. JQ*).
304 ECJ 2018, C-68/17 (*IR v. JQ*), §23.
305 Opinion of AG Wathelet, C-68/17 (*IR v. JQ*), §§21–22.

positions were entrusted by the same organisation to non-Catholic employees who were not subject to the obligation to act in good faith and with loyalty to the hospital's ethos.[306]

Taken together, the decisions in *Egenberger* and *IR v JQ* indicate that the Court has set a demanding standard in order for an employer to rely successfully upon the exception in Article 4(2).

3.3.4.2. *Article 2(5) Directive 2000/78*

In the Employment Equality Directive, there is a further exception that applies to any form of prohibited conduct. Article 2(5) states:

> This Directive shall be without prejudice to measures laid down by national law which, in a democratic society, are necessary for public security, for the maintenance of public order and the prevention of criminal offences, for the protection of health and for the protection of the rights and freedoms of others.

This was added to the directive at a late stage in the negotiations leading to its adoption and it is not immediately apparent why it was required, especially given the absence of any comparable provision in the Racial Equality and Gender Equality Directives. It echoes language found within the ECHR, such as Article 9(2) on justifications for imposing limitations on the freedom to manifest one's religion or beliefs.[307] A benevolent interpretation of Article 2(5) is that it seeks to strike a balance with other fundamental rights that may come into conflict with the non-discrimination rights protected in the directive. For example, the prohibition of discrimination on grounds of belief could come into conflict with the freedom of a trade union to exclude from membership those with certain political beliefs.[308] Today, fundamental rights are explicitly protected in the primary law of the EU by virtue of the Charter of Fundamental Rights, so this rationale for Article 2(5) is less sustainable.

Article 2(5) has been invoked in a number of cases on age discrimination.[309] In *Petersen*,[310] it was argued that a mandatory retirement age of 68 for dentists was justified by the 'protection of health' in Article 2(5). The Court noted that such dentists could continue to exercise their profession, but only outside the framework of the statutory health insurance system in Germany. It rejected, therefore, the contention that mandatory retirement was necessary due to

---

306 ECJ 2018, C-68/17 (*IR v. JQ*), §§58–59.

307 See also Articles 8(2), 10(2), 11(2) ECHR.

308 E.g. ECtHR 2007, application no. 11002/05. However, as discussed in Section 3.3.1.3, the ground of 'belief' may not cover political opinions.

309 E.g ECJ 2011, C-447/09 (*Prigge*); ECJ 2017, C-190/16 (*Fries*).

310 ECJ 2010, C-341/08 (*Petersen*).

concerns about the competency of the dentists; if this was the objective, then such dentists should have been prohibited from any continued activity.[311] The Court did accept that if the objective of the measure was 'to preserve the financial balance of the public healthcare system', then this could be a justification under Article 2(5).[312]

3.3.5. POSITIVE ACTION

Equality between men and women is a fundamental principle of Community law under Article 2 and Article 3(2) TEU. Those Treaty provisions proclaim equality between men and women as a 'task' and an 'aim' of the Community and impose a positive obligation to promote it in all its activities (mainstreaming). This reinforced protection is also reflected in the fact that sex is not only among the grounds listed in Article 21 Charter of Fundamental Rights but also has a special provision in its Article 23, enshrining the right to equal treatment of men and women in all areas.[313]

Positive action was an element of Community law already from the outset. It is now regulated in Article 157(4) TFEU as well as in Article 23 Charter of Fundamental Rights, in relation to sex, and in secondary legislation, with a broader coverage, such as Article 3 of the Recast Gender Equality Directive, Article 5 of the Racial Equality Directive, Article 7 of the Employment Equality Directive and Article 6 of Directive 2004/113. Article 157(4) TFEU reads:

> With a view to ensuring full equality in practice between men and women in working life, the principle of equal treatment shall not prevent any Member State from maintaining or adopting measures providing for specific advantages in order to make it easier for the underrepresented sex to pursue a vocational activity or to prevent or compensate for disadvantages in professional careers.

Article 23 Charter of Fundamental Rights has a somewhat more restrictive air to it, stating that the principle of equal treatment shall 'not prevent' the maintenance or adoption of measures providing for specific advantages in favour of the under-represented sex, implying a derogative character to positive action. The Recast Gender Equality Directive permits positive action in line with Article 157(4) TFEU, whereas the Racial Equality Directive and the Employment Equality Directive use a slightly different wording, leaving out a reference to measures 'providing for specific advantages'.

---

311 Ibid., §61.
312 Ibid., §63.
313 Compare Recitals 2 and 5 of the Recast Gender Equality Directive.

Despite a scope for positive action being in place for a long time, the meaning is far from clear. It can be said that positive action creates a bridge between formal and substantive equality as its purpose is to 'ensure full equality' as is reflected in Recital 22 of the Recast Gender Equality Directive. The limits of positive action are sometimes unclear in relation to legal concepts such as indirect discrimination and reasonable accommodation, as well as active measures in a broader sense.[314] Related concepts are also 'affirmative action' and 'reverse discrimination'.[315] It has been argued that, due to the demands of the case law on positive action, and for other reasons, in an EU setting positive action should be given a distinct understanding, which does not embrace all related phenomena.[316] In principle, this leads to lawful positive action in terms of preferential treatment as opposed to unlawful discrimination.[317] There is no express requirement for positive action measures to be temporary in EU law, but it is inherent to the provision that 'once a positive action measure has achieved its aim, and the situation of social or economic disadvantage or the consequences of past or present discrimination or disadvantage have been eliminated, the measure should be discontinued'.[318]

There is thus by now a quite extensive and well-established body of case law on positive action stemming from the Court to illustrate the scope of this concept. This case law has been summarised so that 'first, positive action must be proportionate in order to be permissible' and, 'secondly, ... lawful positive action does not extend to measures that automatically and unconditionally provide preferential treatment between equally qualified women and men at the point of selection for employment'.[319]

Positive action first became an issue in *Commission v. France*.[320] Here the Court stated that the exception provided for in (the then) Article 2(4) of the Gender Equality Directive 76/207 was 'specifically and exclusively designed to allow measures which, although discriminatory in appearance, are in fact intended to eliminate or reduce actual instances of inequality which may exist in the reality of social life'. The Court continued, 'a generalized preservation of special rights for women in collective agreements' does not correspond to the situation envisaged in that provision.[321] A provision in the French Labour Code, leaving in place contracts of employment and collective agreements already granting special rights to women, was not sufficiently precise and thus disproportionate.

---

314 Waddington and Bell (2011).
315 Affirmative action relates first and foremost to US practices, Bacchi (2004).
316 Waddington and Bell (2011), p. 1519.
317 Ibid., p. 1508.
318 Ibid., p. 1513.
319 Ibid., p. 1506.
320 ECJ 1988, C-312/86 (*Commission v. France*).
321 Ibid., §15.

A few years later came the famous judgment in *Kalanke*,[322] the first in a chain of cases dealing with preferential appointment of women as the under-represented sex. Here, according to a German rule, 'women who have the same qualifications as men applying for the same post are to be given priority in sectors where they are under-represented'. The Court made it clear that such national rules, which 'automatically give priority to women in sectors where they are underrepresented', went beyond what was permissible positive action under the Gender Equality Directive 76/207. Moreover, the Court said that 'such a system substitutes for equality of opportunity ... the result which is only to be arrived at by providing such equality of opportunity' as envisaged in Article 2(4).[323] This judgment became the starting point of a heated debate on quota systems as a way forward within European case law.[324]

Two years later, the Court mitigated somewhat the perceived consequences of the *Kalanke* case. In *Marschall*,[325] a parallel German scheme which contained 'a saving clause' 'to the effect that women are not to be given priority if reasons specific to an individual male candidate tilt the balance in his favour'[326] was found to be within the scope of permitted positive action. To justify the nevertheless preferential effects of such a scheme, the Court referred to the fact that 'such a rule may counteract the prejudicial effects on female candidates of the attitudes and behaviour' described elsewhere in the judgment and 'thus reduce actual instances of inequality which may exist in the real world'.[327] These realities are described by the Court:

> It appears that even where male and female candidates are equally qualified, male candidates tend to be promoted in preference to female candidates particularly because of prejudices and stereotypes concerning the role and capacities of women in working life and the fear, for example, that women will interrupt their careers more frequently, that owing to household and family duties they will be less flexible in their working hours, or that they will be absent from work more frequently because of pregnancy, childbirth and breastfeeding.[328]

The importance of a saving clause was later confirmed in *Badeck*,[329] where the Court itself summarised the scope for measures intended to give priority

322 ECJ 1995, C-450/93 (*Kalanke*).
323 Ibid., 23.
324 Blanpain and Numhauser-Henning (2006).
325 ECJ 1997, C-409/95 (*Marschall*).
326 Ibid., §24.
327 Ibid., §31.
328 Ibid., §29.
329 ECJ 2000, C-158/97 (*Badeck*).

in promotion to women in sectors where they are under-represented. Such measures must be regarded as compatible with Community law if:

- they do not automatically and unconditionally give priority to women when women and men are equally qualified, and
- the candidates are the subject of an objective assessment which takes account of the specific personal situations of all candidates.[330]

Up to this point, the case law had concerned situations where priority was given to the under-represented sex when men and women were equally qualified.[331] In *Abrahamsson*,[332] the Court dealt with a different situation. In Swedish law, women applicants for professorships, belonging to the under-represented sex and possessing only sufficient qualifications for the post, had to be chosen in preference to a candidate of the opposite sex who would otherwise have been appointed. The Court found this regulation 'on any view, to be disproportionate to the aim pursued'.[333]

No doubt, this case law confirms that there is a scope for positive action in Community law. Still, following the cases of *Kalanke, Marschall, Badeck* and *Abrahamsson*, the impression is that positive action – given its voluntary character – has been given a modest role in the practices of the Member States.[334] This is certainly true with regard to Sweden. As reflected in *Abrahamsson*, in Sweden the long-held view was that positive action only took place when a less qualified candidate of the under-represented sex was given priority in an appointment. Now, legislation has adjusted to the rulings of the Court; positive action also entails providing priority when candidates are equally qualified. In practice, nowadays positive action only occasionally occurs, when it is applied in the public sector for candidates possessing equivalent or substantially equivalent merits – as accepted by the Court in *Abrahamsson*. At EU level, the issue of quota systems was introduced again with the 2012 proposal designed to enhance women's representation within company boardrooms; a proposal that has so far failed to find sufficient support within the Council.[335]

Later, in *Lommers*,[336] the Court confirmed the importance of a 'saving clause', accepting a scheme where a limited number of subsidised nursery places, at a

330 Ibid., §23.

331 I.e. a 'tie-break preference' situation, as compared to those where 'strong preference' apply. Regarding these concepts as well as strict and flexible quotas, see further Selanec and Senden (2011), pp. 4–6.

332 ECJ 2000, C-407/98 (*Abrahamsson*).

333 Ibid., §55.

334 Selanec & Senden (2011).

335 COM(2012)614. Norway – an EEA country – introduced a statutory system requiring 40% women on the boards of commercial companies in 2006: Selanec & Senden (2011).

336 ECJ 2002, C-476/99 (*Lommers*).

Ministry where women were extensively under-represented, were reserved for the children of female officials alone, but 'only in so far, as the said exception in favour of male officials is constructed as allowing those of them who take care of their children by themselves to have access'.[337] In *Briheche*,[338] there was a generally applicable age limit for obtaining access to public sector employment, but an exemption applied to widows who had not remarried and who were obliged to work. To exclude widowers who had not remarried and who found themselves in the same situation was found to be disproportionate, no saving clause being in place. In *Griesmar*[339] too, a measure giving preferential treatment to women and not containing a saving clause for men in a parallel situation, was considered to infringe Community law, in this case the Agreement on Social Policy's rule on positive action and the equal pay principle. The measure at stake regarded a French occupational pension scheme, giving certain service credits for children to female civil servants but not so for male civil servants 'who are able to prove that they assumed the task of bringing up their children'.

Schnorbus[340] involved a different setting. Ms Schnorbus, a German citizen, having passed the first state examination in law, applied for practical legal training which would be necessary in order to later obtain a post in the judicial service or in the higher civil service. Her application was rejected, and subject to a 12-month delay, since preference was given to applicants who had completed compulsory military or civilian service. Despite such service only applied to men, the Court found this to be a case of indirect discrimination.[341] The preferential treatment was, however, justified since it was seen to be 'objective in nature and prompted solely by the desire to counterbalance to some extent the effects of' such services.[342]

Positive action is thus also provided for outside the area of sex discrimination with the difference that here the permissive rules are found only in secondary legislation. The asymmetrical character of the prohibition of discrimination on grounds of disability in relation to positive action can be said to be reflected in Article 26 Charter of Fundamental Rights, as well as in Article 7(2) the Employment Equality Directive. Unlike the situation regarding discrimination on the grounds of sex, positive action measures in

---

337 Ibid., §50.

338 ECJ 2004, C-319/03 (*Briheche*).

339 ECJ 2001, C-466/99 (*Griesmar*).

340 ECJ 2000, C-79/99 (*Schnorbus*).

341 Ibid., §39.

342 Ibid., §44. Compare also ECJ 2004, C-220/02 (*Österreich*), where taking leave for military service into account for calculating a termination payment, but not so time of parental leave, was found to be compatible with the Gender Equal Treatment Directive since 'parental leave is taken voluntarily', whereas national military service 'corresponds to a civic obligation' (§§60–61). See also ECJ 2003, C-186/01 (*Dory*).

relation to other grounds of discrimination have yet not really been tested in litigation before the Court. It is true that *Milkova*[343] concerned disability and positive action. Here, the Court regarded a provision of Bulgarian law, requiring the consent of the Labour Inspectorate before employees with certain types of disability could be dismissed, to be a form of positive action for disabled persons in accordance with Article 7(2) of the Employment Equality Directive as compared to employees without a disability. The core issue was, however, whether the fact that this law was not applied to private and public disabled employees alike amounted to an infringement of the equal treatment principle in Articles 20 and 21 Charter of Fundamental Rights. It was thus not the permissibility of the positive action measures per se that was at stake. At domestic level, some case law in this field exists and there is also permissive legislation in place in many Member States regarding disability, and sometimes also ethnicity.[344]

Finally, in much of the case law described above, the Court has implied that the provision on positive action is to be seen as a derogation from the principle of equal treatment and therefore to be interpreted restrictively.[345] As Treaty rules have developed,[346] for example, in relation to mainstreaming and a positive duty to promote equality more generally, the correctness of this view has been called into question.[347] Positive duties in a more general meaning have been seen as an evolution of mainstreaming and emphasise the need for equality to be pursued in a systematic fashion across all activities.[348] The UK, Sweden and Finland are examples of Member States using legally enforceable duties to promote equality, such as formal plans and/or procedures in combination with assessment mechanisms to analyse their effects. There are also elements of such positive duties in EU law and policy; for instance, the European Commission's Recommendation on Pay Transparency.[349] No doubt such positive duties may encourage Member States to engage in positive action.

3.4. MATERIAL SCOPE

EU anti-discrimination legislation applies to almost any activity that is normally understood to lie within the domain of 'labour law'. It begins from activities that precede the creation of an employment relationship, such as vocational

343 ECJ 2017, C-406/15 (*Milkova*), also discussed in Section 3.2.1.
344 For an overview, see Chopin & Germaine (2016), pp. 81–82.
345 Compare, for instance, ECJ 1995, C-450/93 (*Kalanke*).
346 Compare Articles 8 and 10 TFEU, as well as Article 23(1) CFREU.
347 Fredman (2009).
348 Waddington & Bell (2011), p. 1520.
349 C(2014)1405 final.

training and work experience,[350] and selection criteria and the recruitment process.[351] During the life of the employment relationship, it applies to employment and working conditions, including pay and dismissals.[352] The conditions for promotion are also expressly covered.[353] Significantly, the prohibition of discrimination can also reach into activities that occur after the end of the employment relationship. The most prominent example is occupational pensions, which are a form of deferred remuneration (see further below).

The directives are also addressed to the activities of key actors within the labour market and not only employers. Discrimination is prohibited in 'membership of and involvement in an organisation of workers or employers, or any organisation whose members carry on a particular profession, including the benefits provided for by such organisations'.[354] This section will not provide a comprehensive analysis of every area where the directives apply, but it will examine in more detail several topics of particular importance within labour law.

3.4.1. EMPLOYMENT AND SELF-EMPLOYMENT

There is no definition of 'employment' within the directives, but the Court of Justice has consistently interpreted this in a broad fashion. The wide definition of 'worker' found in the law on free movement[355] has been applied when interpreting the scope of anti-discrimination legislation.[356] A good illustration is the case of *Allonby*.[357] This concerned an equal pay claim brought by a lecturer who was employed via a temporary work agency. The latter emphasised that it applied a condition that all lecturers registering with the agency did so as self-employed persons.[358] There was no definition of 'worker' in former Article 141 EC (now Article 157 TFEU) and the Court accepted that it was not intended to 'include independent providers of services who are not in a relationship of

350 Directive 2000/43, Article 3(1)(b); Directive 2000/78, Article 3(1)(b); Directive 2006/54, Article 14(1)(b).

351 Directive 2000/43, Article 3(1)(a); Directive 2000/78, Article 3(1)(a); Directive 2006/54, Article 14(1)(a).

352 Directive 2000/43, Article 3(1)(c); Directive 2000/78, Article 3(1)(c); Directive 2006/54, Article 14(1)(c).

353 Directive 2000/43, Article 3(1)(a); Directive 2000/78, Article 3(1)(a); Directive 2006/54, Article 14(1)(a).

354 Directive 2000/43, Article 3(1)(d); Directive 2000/78, Article 3(1)(d); Directive 2006/54, Article 14(1)(d).

355 See further Chapter 2.

356 See further, Countouris (2007), pp. 179–185.

357 ECJ 2004, C-256/01 (*Allonby*).

358 Ibid., §31.

subordination with the person who receives the services'.[359] Nevertheless, it reiterated that a worker was 'a person who, for a certain period of time, performs services for and under the direction of another person in return for which he receives remuneration'.[360] The label applied to the relationship by national law does not determine whether a person falls within the EU law concept of 'worker'.[361]

In a similar vein, in *Danosa*,[362] the Court was willing to adopt a wide interpretation of worker in order to provide protection from pregnancy discrimination for the sole member of a Board of Directors of a limited liability company. The Court felt that the core elements of its concept of worker were present: remuneration for services performed and the carrying out of services under direction or control. In relation to the latter, the fact that the shareholders could dismiss Ms. Danosa was taken, in itself, to provide evidence that she was working under the control of another body.[363]

The Court's willingness to apply anti-discrimination law in the grey zone between employment and self-employment is facilitated by Directive 2010/41, which prohibits sex discrimination in 'the establishment, equipment or extension of a business or the launching or extension of any other form of self-employed activity'.[364] While this Directive is devoted to equal treatment of women and men in self-employment, the Racial Equality and Employment Equality Directives also state that they apply to the 'conditions for access to employment, to self-employment or to occupation'.[365]

3.4.2. THE DEFINITION OF PAY

Article 119 EEC defined 'pay' in the following terms: 'the ordinary basic or minimum wage or salary and any other consideration, whether in cash or in kind, which the worker receives directly or indirectly, in respect of his employment, from his employer'.[366] An extensive body of case-law has accumulated on the meaning of pay.[367] Critically, the Court took the view that payments that occur

359 Ibid., §68.
360 Ibid., §67. While Ms. Allonby's claim was not defeated by her classification as self-employed in national law, the Court held that she could not compare herself to the directly employed lecturers in an equal pay claim against the College, because there must be a single source for the pay of the workers who are being compared.
361 Ibid., §71.
362 ECJ 2010, C-232/09 (*Danosa*).
363 Ibid., §51.
364 Directive 2010/41, Article 4(1).
365 Directive 2000/43, Article 3(1)(a); Directive 2000/78, Article 3(1)(a). This text is also found in Directive 2006/54, Article 14(1)(a).
366 This text is now found in Article 157(2) TFEU.
367 See inter alia Ellis & Watson (2012), chap. 5.

after the end of the employment relationship, but to which entitlement arises because of employment, fall within the concept of (deferred) pay. For example, in *Seymour-Smith and Perez*, compensation where an employee had been unfairly dismissed fell within the definition of pay.[368]

The idea of deferred pay has had the greatest consequences in the sphere of occupational pensions. In 1990, in *Barber*,[369] the Court held that former Article 119 EEC could be applied to an occupational pension scheme, even where this took the form of a substitute for a statutory pension scheme (the notion of 'contracted-out' pensions). While accepting that such pensions replaced a state scheme, the Court placed weight on the fact that they arose by virtue of the employment relationship and reflected the financial contributions of the employer and the worker.[370] The decision had major ramifications. Existing EU legislation on occupational social security schemes permitted different retirement ages for men and women, but this was now overridden by the direct effect of Article 119 EEC.[371] Further litigation sought to clarify how the principle of equal treatment applied to such pensions. For example, in *Coloroll*,[372] the Court held that a survivor's pension arising under an occupational scheme was also within the scope of 'pay'.

The settled case-law of the Court on the meaning of pay in Article 157 TFEU has now been extended to the interpretation of the Employment Equality Directive. In *Maruko*, the dispute concerned the entitlement of a same-sex partner to a survivor's pension. The pension scheme applied to theatre workers, but it was made compulsory by statute and it was possible for the members to make voluntary contributions even during periods when they were not in employment. The Court applied its case-law on gender equality citing the need to consider 'if the pension concerns only a particular category of workers, if it is directly related to the period of service completed and if its amount is calculated by reference to the last salary'.[373] In this case, the scheme had sufficient characteristics to mean that it should be regarded as 'pay' for the purposes of the directive.

Although it is now well-established that retirement income from an occupational pension scheme falls within the scope of EU anti-discrimination law, there are boundaries to the concept of pay. The case of *C*[374] concerned a claim that a supplementary tax levied solely on income from retirement

368 ECJ 1999, C-167/97 (*Seymour-Smith and Perez*), §§27–28.
369 ECJ 1990, C-262/88 (*Barber*).
370 Ibid., §§25–27.
371 See further, Masselot & McLellan (2018).
372 ECJ 1994, C-200/91 (*Coloroll*).
373 ECJ 2008, C-267/06 (*Maruko*), §§48.
374 ECJ 2016, C-122/15 (*C*).

pensions constituted age discrimination falling within the scope of the Employment Equality Directive. The Court held that this was not covered because 'such taxation is external to the employment relationship' and lacked any link to the contract of employment.[375]

3.4.3. LIMITATIONS TO THE SCOPE OF THE PROHIBITION OF DISCRIMINATION

As mentioned in the introduction, each of the main anti-discrimination Directives has a different material scope. While those on the grounds of sex and racial or ethnic origin apply to some areas outside the field of employment, the Employment Equality Directive does not. Given that this book is focused on labour law, the scope of the law in areas outside employment is not discussed further. It should be noted that there are also several provisions within the directives that exclude activities that otherwise fall within the scope of employment. In the Employment Equality Directive, Member States are given the option of not applying the provisions relating to disability and age to the armed forces.[376] It appears that eight Member States have availed of that option, while others have maintained in force age and capability requirements.[377]

Both the Racial Equality and the Employment Equality Directives contain a provision stating that they do not apply to differences of treatment based on nationality, as well as treatment arising from the legal status of third country nationals.[378] On the one hand, this exclusion adds little to what is already implicit elsewhere; nationality is not a protected ground in either directive and the material scope of the directives does not extend into immigration law matters. On the other hand, it is possible to anticipate scenarios where the implementation of immigration control requirements in the workplace gives rise to claims of discrimination on grounds of racial or ethnic origin. Employers have legal duties to ensure that they do not employ non-EU nationals who lack authorisation to work. As discussed in Section 3.3.1.2, the *Jyske Finans* case posed the question of whether heightened identity checks for those who were born abroad constituted discrimination on grounds of ethnic origin.[379] The nationality/immigration exclusion in both Directives appears designed to reinforce the difficulty of challenging such measures.

---

375 Ibid., §25.

376 Directive 2000/78, Article 3(4).

377 Chopin and Germaine (2016), p. 69.

378 Directive 2000/43, Article 3(2); Directive 2000/78, Article 3(2).

379 ECJ 2017, C-668/15 (*Jyske Finans*). The case concerned access to a loan to finance a car purchase.

3.5. ENFORCING EQUAL TREATMENT

In general, the mechanism through which EU law is enforced is a matter left to the autonomy of each Member State, reflecting the diversity of national legal systems. In keeping with this outlook, the 1976 Equal Treatment Directive simply referred to the need for Member States to introduce 'such measures as are necessary' to permit individuals to enforce its provisions.[380] While the Court of Justice respects national procedural autonomy, this is qualified by obligations to ensure that the measures taken for the enforcement of EU law are (i) effective and (ii) equivalent to the mechanisms that apply to the enforcement of similar rights found in national law. A considerable volume of gender equality litigation has concerned situations where the procedures and/or remedies for the enforcement of the right to equal treatment fell short of these principles. A good illustration is the *Marshall* case,[381] which concerned the remedies available for a discriminatory dismissal. The Court emphasised that the measures found in national law must 'guarantee real and effective judicial protection and have a real deterrent effect on the employer'.[382] This meant that national law could not impose an upper limit on the amount of compensation in a case of sex discrimination; it 'must enable the loss and damage actually sustained as a result of the discriminatory dismissal to be made good in full'.[383]

A greater appreciation of the barriers encountered by individuals when trying to enforce equal treatment rights meant that the directives adopted since 2000 contain more detailed requirements. In the Gender Equality and Racial Equality Directives, there is also recognition of the need to go beyond individual litigation as the sole enforcement mechanism. These directives placed a new obligation on Member States to establish bodies for the promotion of equal treatment. This section begins by examining measures relating to individual enforcement and then considers the role of equality bodies.

3.5.1. INDIVIDUAL ENFORCEMENT

The seminal case of *Defrenne v. SABENA* is a powerful reminder of the capacity of individual cases to stimulate wider legal (and social) reform. Indeed, anti-discrimination legislation has often been characterised by this image of the intrepid individual seeking to enforce her rights before the courts. Unsurprisingly, each of the directives requires Member States to establish a

380 Directive 76/207, Article 6.
381 ECJ 1993, C-271/91 (*Marshall II*).
382 Ibid., §24.
383 Ibid., §26.

procedure through which individuals can raise complaints about a breach of the directives' provisions. The Racial Equality and Employment Equality Directives refer to 'judicial and/or administrative procedures',[384] but the Recast Gender Equality Directive requires access to a 'judicial' procedure.[385] Chopin and Germaine report that 'in no state are discrimination disputes resolved purely in the courts'.[386] States have created a variety of alternative mechanisms through which discrimination complaints can be examined. In some States, bodies that specialise in hearing other types of labour law dispute have been used. For example, in Ireland, discrimination complaints will normally be heard initially by an adjudicator of the Workplace Relations Commission.[387] Other States have chosen to create specialised forms of adjudication that are limited to discrimination complaints, or that fall within a broader category of 'rights' enforcement. For example, there is a Discrimination Tribunal in Finland.[388] In Austria, the Equal Treatment Commission can deliver opinions on complaints, as can the Institute for Human Rights in the Netherlands.[389] Both of the latter bodies deliver non-binding opinions, but it remains possible to initiate legal proceedings before the courts.

Pursuing a discrimination complaint is often difficult and individuals can be deterred by the emotional and financial costs that this may entail. The directives include a provision that requires Member States to ensure that 'associations, organisations or other legal entities ... may engage, either or behalf or in support of the complainant, with his/her approval, in any judicial and/or administrative procedure ....'[390] The exact modalities through which organisations can be involved in assisting individuals depends upon the national legal system. This entails questions such as: which organisations enjoy legal standing? Can they start legal proceedings in their own name or are they limited to providing legal advice/representation in support of the individual? In relation to workplace disputes, it is normal that workers' organisations play an important role. For instance, in France, representative trade unions can act on behalf or in support of individuals, while in Sweden trade unions have legal standing if one of their members is involved.[391]

Individuals can be deterred from bringing a complaint because of the potential consequences that it may have on the relationship with their employer.

---

384 Directive 2000/43, Article 7(1); Directive 2000/78, Article 9(1). See also Directive 2010/41, Article 9(1).

385 Directive 2006/54, Article 17(1).

386 Chopin & Germaine (2016), p. 78.

387 Workplace Relations Act 2015.

388 Chopin & Germaine (2016), p. 79.

389 Ibid., p. 80.

390 Directive 2000/43, Article 7(2); Directive 2000/78, Article 9(2); Directive 2006/54, Article 17(2); Directive 2010/41, Article 9(2).

391 Chopin & Germaine (2016), p. 83.

For example, in *Coote*,[392] the individual had settled a complaint of pregnancy discrimination with her former employer. She claimed that she had difficulty in finding future employment because this employer later refused to provide a reference for her to a temporary work agency. The Court held that effective judicial protection meant that Member States had to introduce measures to protect workers from retaliatory conduct after the end of the employment relationship.[393] The directives now contain provisions prohibiting victimisation, which is defined as 'dismissal or other adverse treatment by the employer as a reaction to a complaint within the undertaking or to any legal proceedings aimed at enforcing compliance with the principle of equal treatment'.[394] Victimisation can affect others who may be acting in support of the individual, such as co-workers who are witnesses. The language used in the directives seems broad enough to encompass any employee who is subject to dismissal or adverse treatment, but it is helpful that the Recast Gender Equality Directive makes explicit reference to protecting employees' representatives from victimisation.

Another factor that may influence the willingness of individuals to undertake legal proceedings is the remedies available. It would be reductive to assume that individuals are only motivated by the prospect of financial compensation, but it is also true that the absence of any effective remedy is likely to deter litigants. As described earlier, the Court had already established through case-law that remedies have to be effective. This is now an explicit requirement in the directives, which state that sanctions must be 'effective, proportionate and dissuasive'.[395] The Recast Gender Equality Directive goes a step further by specifying (in accordance with *Marshall II*) that there must be no upper limit on compensation.[396] In *Feryn* and *Accept*, there was no identifiable individual victim, but the Court emphasised that there must still be a sanction. This could include publicity for the finding of unlawful discrimination; award of legal costs against the respondent; an injunction; or damages to the party bringing the proceedings.[397] It is not compatible with the directive if the only remedy available is a warning to the respondent.[398]

---

392 ECJ 1998, C-185/97 (*Coote*).

393 Ibid., §28.

394 Directive 2006/54, Article 24. See also, Directive 2000/43, Article 9; Directive 2000/78, Article 11.

395 Directive 2000/43, Article 15; Directive 2000/78, Article 17; Directive 2006/54, Article 25. See also Directive 2010/41, Article 10.

396 Directive 2006/54, Article 18. This rule does not apply if the only damage caused to a job applicant is 'the refusal to take his/her job application into consideration', i.e. situations where, even in the absence of discrimination, the applicant would not have been selected for the vacancy.

397 ECJ 2008, C-54/07 (*Feryn*), §39.

398 ECJ 2013, C-81/12 (*Accept*), §73.

3.5.2. SHIFTING THE BURDEN OF PROOF

When pursuing a complaint of discrimination, a common difficulty is obtaining sufficient evidence. Take the situation where a woman applies for promotion, but she is not selected. The evidence pertaining to the reasons for the rejection of her application will typically lie in the hands of the employer. Where discrimination has affected the promotion process, the employer is unlikely to disclose that voluntarily to the employee. Indeed, in some situations, the preference for a male candidate might reflect a completely unconscious bias by the employer.

In the context of the case law on equal pay, the Court developed the concept of shifting the burden of proof.[399] If a pay system lacked transparency, but there was evidence of a disparity in the pay awarded to male and female workers, then the burden of proof shifted to the employer to establish a non-discriminatory reason for the pay inequality.[400] This principle was codified in legislation via the 1997 Burden of Proof Directive. The Directives now adopt the following definition:

> when persons who consider themselves wronged because the principle of equal treatment has not been applied to them establish, before a court or other competent authority, facts from which it may be presumed that there has been direct or indirect discrimination, it shall be for the respondent to prove that there has been no breach of the principle of equal treatment.[401]

This does not mean that the burden of proof shifts upon a mere allegation of discrimination. The claimant must identify evidence from which a presumption of discrimination could arise.

In *Meister*,[402] the claimant was an older woman of Russian nationality. She had applied on two occasions for a vacancy as a 'software developer', but without being called to interview. She brought legal proceedings alleging discrimination on grounds of sex, age and ethnic origin, but she also sought access to information on whether the vacancy had been filled, and, if so, the details of the person appointed. The Court held that there was no specific requirement to provide such information to her under the directives, but 'a defendant's refusal to grant any access to information may be one of the factors to take into account in the context of establishing facts from which it may be presumed that there has been direct or indirect discrimination'.[403] Ultimately, the

399 See further, Ellis & Watson (2012), p. 157.

400 E.g. ECJ 1989, C-109/88 (*Danfoss*).

401 Directive 2006/54, Article 19(1); Directive 2000/43, Article 8(1); Directive 2000/78, Article 10(1).

402 ECJ 2012, C-415/10 (*Meister*).

403 Ibid., §47.

determination of whether the claimant has amassed sufficient evidence to tip the scales towards the respondent is a question of fact that can only be resolved by a national court.

3.5.3. BODIES FOR THE PROMOTION OF EQUAL TREATMENT

The directives are premised on an enforcement model that relies heavily on individuals bringing complaints to assert their rights. Yet individuals confront many obstacles in practice. These include: having sufficient knowledge of their rights and the procedures for their enforcement; having the financial resources needed to pursue a complaint (especially if legal representation is required); and dealing with the emotional costs that are often associated with being involved in a dispute or litigation, such as stress and anxiety. The Racial Equality Directive marked a shift in the EU's approach to enforcement because it was not confined to the individual complaint model. Instead, there was a new duty on Member States to 'designate a body or bodies for the promotion of equal treatment'.[404] This could be an autonomous organisation or it could be part of existing national agencies for 'the defence of human rights or the safeguard of individuals' rights'.[405] The equality body aids the individual complaint model because one of its responsibilities must be 'providing independent assistance to victims of discrimination in pursuing their complaints about discrimination'.[406] Its remit must extend beyond this function and include 'conducting independent surveys concerning discrimination; publishing independent reports and making recommendations on any issue relating to such discrimination'.[407]

The Employment Equality Directive did not include any obligation on Member States to create an equality body. There is no obvious rationale for this gap other than the political will of the Member States to take stronger measures against racial discrimination. The Recast Gender Equality Directive included a duty to create an equality body, including a specific function of 'exchanging available information with corresponding European bodies'.[408] This takes place principally through Equinet, the European Network of Equality Bodies, whose activities cover all discrimination grounds.[409] Even if EU law only obliges

---

404 Directive 2000/43, Article 13(1).
405 Ibid.
406 Ibid., Article 13(2).
407 Ibid.
408 Directive 2006/54, Article 20(2)(d).
409 <http://www.equineteurope.org> accessed 06.05.2019.

Member States to designate bodies in respect of sex and racial or ethnic origin, over time almost all have chosen to establish one or more organisations with responsibility for all the discrimination grounds found in the EU Directives.[410] In 2018, a Commission Recommendation called for all Member States to consider designating an equality body to cover discrimination falling within the scope of the Employment Equality Directive.[411]

EU law provides flexibility for Member States on how they organise equality bodies and there is considerable diversity in national practice. This is reflected both in different institutional structures and in different mandates. In terms of institutional structure, some States have chosen to locate equality bodies within organisations that are broadly concerned with the protection of individual rights. These may have a remit that extends beyond discrimination issues (e.g. France (Defender of Rights)) or they may be specialised (e.g. Finland (Non-Discrimination Ombudsman), Sweden (Equality Ombudsman)).[412] Similarly, in some States, national human rights institutions have a mandate for dealing with discrimination, such as Denmark (Institute for Human Rights).[413] Notably, several States originally had separate equality bodies, but later combined these with human rights institutions (Ireland, the Netherlands, the UK).[414] Some States continue to have bodies that are dedicated only to the promotion of equal treatment, such as Hungary (Equal Treatment Authority) and Slovenia (Advocate of the Principle of Equality).[415]

The directives impose minimum obligations in terms of the mandates of these bodies, although some States have chosen to split these functions over more than one organisation. A significant difference in national practice is whether national equality bodies have a quasi-judicial function. The directives require the bodies to be able to make 'recommendations on any issue relating to such discrimination', but it is not clear that this creates an obligation for the equality body to be able to evaluate individual complaints. The Commission Recommendation on equality bodies suggests that this can be part of the function of providing independent assistance to victims: 'Member States should also take into consideration that assistance to victims can include issuing recommendations or, where so authorised under national law, legally binding decisions in individual or collective cases of discrimination'.[416]

410 Portugal and Spain remain exceptions to this trend: Chopin & Germaine (2016), p. 107.

411 Commission Recommendation (EU) 2018/951 on standards for equality bodies [2018] OJ L167/28.

412 Chopin & Germaine (2016), pp. 105–107.

413 Ibid.

414 Ibid.

415 Ibid.

416 Recommendation 2018/951, para. 1.1.2.

In 2015, 11 Member States were identified as having equality bodies with quasi-judicial functions, of which nine issued binding decisions.[417] Significantly, in *Belov*,[418] the Court held that the Bulgarian Commission for Protection Against Discrimination was not a 'court or tribunal' for the purposes of Article 267 TFEU and hence it rejected a request for a preliminary ruling on the interpretation of the Racial Equality Directive. The Court took the view that the Bulgarian Commission took administrative decisions, rather than decisions of a judicial nature.[419] In reaching this conclusion, it attached weight to the fact that the Bulgarian Commission could have initiated legal proceedings in its own name or joined as a party to such proceedings. In addition, the Commission became a defendant if its decisions were appealed to the courts.[420] In contrast, the Court has been willing to accept requests for preliminary rulings from other equality bodies that had a purely adjudicatory function.[421]

It is difficult to make an overall assessment of the impact of equality bodies given their diversity. De Witte observed that 'national political actors were able to re-contextualize the innovative European ideas by wrapping them in layers of existing national practices and adapting them to domestic political preferences'.[422] From a legal perspective, it is noteworthy that some equality bodies have been instrumental in bringing flagship cases before the Court. For example, the Belgian equality body initiated the legal proceedings in *Feryn*[423] and it provided legal support to the complainant in *Achbita*.[424]

3.6. CONCLUSIONS

If Article 119 EEC represented the seed of EU anti-discrimination law, it would be fair to observe that a relatively mature tree is found in its place today. This enjoys strong roots in the primary law of the Union, including the Treaties, the Charter and the general principles of EU law. The branches of this tree can be found in the body of legislation. This development has been uneven. In retrospect, the periods 1975–1979 and 2000–2006 were particularly critical in the evolution of the legislation, notwithstanding

417 Chopin & Germaine (2016), p. 112. One of these was the Irish Equality Tribunal, which has since been replaced by the Workplace Relations Commission, which has jurisdiction to adjudicate on a range of employment law disputes.

418 ECJ 2013, C-394/11 (*Belov v. CHEZ*).

419 Ibid., §51.

420 Ibid., §§47–49.

421 E.g. the former Irish Equality Tribunal: ECJ 2014 (*Z*).

422 De Witte (2012), p. 69.

423 ECJ 2008, C-54/07 (*Feryn*).

424 ECJ 2017, C-157/15 (*Achbita*).

significant instruments being adopted at other points. In fallow times, when little dynamism comes from the EU's legislative institutions, the Court has often provided the source for momentum. It made landmark decisions that transformed the understanding of the legal provisions and rippled through national legal systems afterwards. Recognising the directly effective nature of Article 119 EEC in *Defrenne v. SABENA* remains a seminal moment in EU law, but it is also possible to point to vanguard decisions, such as extending gender equality law to include discrimination related to gender reassignment in *P v. S* (1996), or the concept of discrimination by association in *Coleman* (2008). Other remarkable cases are *Dekker*, making differential treatment on the grounds of pregnancy direct sex discrimination, and *Feryn*, accepting discrimination to be at hand even where there is no identifiable victim. In every period, these breakthroughs have been accompanied by decisions that reflect caution, such as rejecting the proposition that gender equality law prohibited discrimination related to sexual orientation,[425] or the contemporary case law on mandatory retirement. Yet, across the years, the overall contribution of the Court has been progressive.

The dynamism of anti-discrimination law is, in part, driven by change in society and social values. Writing in 2016, Benedi Lahuerta identified two areas where pressure for reform has emerged.[426] First, discrimination related to gender identity. As mentioned in Section 3.3.1.6, there continues to be ambiguity in relation to how the law applies to those individuals whose gender identity or expression does not conform to the norms associated with the gender that they were assigned at birth. While the law protects individuals in relation to gender reassignment, many transgender people do not undergo the medical intervention that the term 'reassignment' evokes. Moreover, there is an emerging movement seeking the protection of intersex persons from discrimination related to sex characteristics.

Second, Benedi Lahuerta draws attention to the social pressure for employers to accommodate the manifestation of religious beliefs. In relation to the latter, the *Achbita* decision indicated that the Court is not currently minded to require employers to adapt the workplace to reflect religious diversity. Other jurisdictions, such as the US and Canada, have – in different ways – applied the concept of reasonable accommodation as a mechanism for striking a balance between the individual, the employer, and the rights of others.[427] In its current state, EU anti-discrimination law does not appear readily equipped to confront this social reality, the significance of which is likely to increase in time with the effects of demographic change and migration.

---

425 ECJ 1998, C-249/96 (*Grant*).

426 Benedi Lahuerta (2016b).

427 See Alidadi (2017), p. 69.

Looking back, a pivotal moment in EU anti-discrimination law was its opening to a wider range of personal characteristics in both the Treaties (1999) and the legislation (2000). This leap transformed the legal framework at both supranational and domestic levels. All Member States were required to undertake a substantial reform of their domestic legislation. The process of EU enlargement in the subsequent period exported anti-discrimination law to central and eastern Europe, as well as to those States that aspire to future membership of the Union. It is notable, however, that the framework remains characterised by a compartmental vision of identity. In the intervening period, academic scholarship has drawn attention to intersectionality.[428] Discrimination and inequality are often experienced through a combination of characteristics, such as women from ethnic minority communities. This is distinct from the experience of women or ethnic minorities, but is not merely the sum of gender and ethnic inequality. Taking a comprehensive response to intersectionality is hindered by the way in which the current legislative architecture differentiates between racial or ethnic origin; gender; and the other protected grounds. This is most pronounced in relation to areas outside employment, where there remains no legislation on discrimination on grounds of religion or belief, disability, age and sexual orientation. Even within the sphere of employment, the law grapples with claims that intertwine several discrimination grounds. The resistance on the part of the Court to a conjoined case of age and sexual orientation discrimination in *Parris*[429] is remarkable for the lack of social imagination that it belies. The Court appeared to close its eyes to the possibility that the history of legal exclusion of same-sex relationships means that the situation of an older gay couple may be distinct.

In conclusion, the maturity of EU anti-discrimination law should not be read as implying less need for the law to remain open to change in society or to continue to interrogate its own coherence and effectiveness. The history of this area of law shows an interplay between innovation through the courts and the legislature. During the past decade, the chill wind of the economic crisis meant that legislative reform met considerable political resistance. There are now signs that the political context is shifting towards a fresh interest in the social dimension of European integration, most notably through the flagship initiative of the European Pillar of Social Rights. This could provide an opening for a renewed legislative programme to address some of the ongoing challenges discussed in this chapter, including the work-life balance agenda in pursuit of elusive gender equality.

428 E.g. Schiek & Chege (2009); Atrey (2017).
429 ECJ 2016, C-443/15 (*Parris*).

CHAPTER 4
ATYPICAL FORMS OF EMPLOYMENT

Sophie ROBIN-OLIVIER and Antonio LO FARO

4.1. THE FAILURE TO REGULATE ATYPICAL WORK AND THE RECOURSE TO SOCIAL DIALOGUE IN THE 1990s

4.1.1. THE ORIGIN OF THE DIRECTIVES

The adjective 'atypical' may have many different meanings, as will be seen in this chapter. In any case, the story of the EU regulatory action on atypical work is a long and intricate one. After a couple of failed attempts in the early 1980s,[1] the European Community declared firmly that all 'forms of employment other than open-ended contracts' (as Article 7 of the Community Charter of Fundamental Social Rights of Workers defined them) should have be given the same legislative attention as 'standard' work. This declaration was part of what at that time was called the 'social dimension' of the integration process.

In its subsequent Communication drafting an action programme for the implementation of the 1989 Charter,[2] the Commission stressed again the need to have a European legislation on 'contracts and employment relationships other than full-time open-ended contracts', and announced its intention to present 'a single proposal for a Directive' aimed at correcting the 'quite anarchical manner' in which atypical work contracts were more and more being used.

The Commission, however, did not keep its promises nor did it stick to its goals, since it did not present a 'single' proposal, but rather three different proposals – for respectively fixed term work, part-time work and temporary agency work – founded on three different EEC Treaty legal bases.[3] Only the

1 European Commission (1981) (Proposal on part-time work); European Commission (1982) (Proposal on temporary work); European Commission (1984) (Proposal on temporary work and fixed-term work).

2 European Commission (1989) (Communication – Charter of Social Rights for Workers).

3 European Commission (1990a) (Proposal on working conditions, based on Article 100 of the Treaty); European Commission (1990b) (Proposal on distortion of competition, based on Article 100A); European Commission (1990c) (Proposal on safety and health at work of temporary workers, based on Article 118A).

proposal based on a Treaty provision requiring qualified majority was actually transformed into a directive;[4] the accomplishment of the other two proposals, which would require unanimity, was hindered by the national veto of some Member States that in those years produced the well-known stalemate of supranational social legislation. The crisis of the legislative harmonisation model remained in the social as well in other fields of European integration.

Moreover, the very same heading of the 1990 Commission proposals, referring both to improvement of working conditions of atypical workers, and to the need to avoid 'distortions of competition which could be caused by differences in the social costs resulting in particular from differences in the national rules governing these employment relationships',[5] showed that it was still not clear whether the rationale underlying the Community action on the issue was a 'market-making' or rather a 'market-correcting' one.

In the mid-1990s, after years of decisional impasse, the Commission finally acknowledged that incomplete 'decisional supranationalism' in the European integration process was not only a celebrated academic theory,[6] but rather a serious and actual threat to the progress of European social legislation. In its 1996 Report on the implementation of the Charter of Fundamental Social Rights, the Commission had to admit that reaching unanimous consensus on its atypical work proposals 'could no longer be expected in the near future',[7] and in order to overcome the crisis of supranational regulatory mechanisms it would have recourse to the social dialogue regulatory capacities, as they had been regulated by the Maastricht Agreement on Social Policy.

The new regulatory path followed by the Commission and the social partners was indeed successful, albeit partially. Following the consultation and negotiation model regulated by the Agreement on Social Policy, now incorporated in Articles 154–155 TFEU, the European Social partners concluded two cross-industry agreements on part-time and on fixed-term work: the first, signed on 6 June 1997, was implemented through Directive 97/81/EC (see Section 4.2); the second, signed on 18 March 1999, was implemented through Directive 1999/70/EC (see Section 4.3).[8] As far as temporary agency work was concerned, however, the social partners, albeit intensively pressed by the Commission since 1995, were unable to come to an agreement and in 2001 their negotiations finally failed. This gave the legislative initiative back to the Commission, which finally

4 Directive 91/383/EEC (safety and health of fixed-term and temporary agency workers), adopted on the basis of the qualified majority system provided by Article 118 EEC. The directive has been subsequently amended by Directive 2007/30/EC.

5 Memorandum on the proposals for directives concerning certain employment relationships, 1990, p. 5.

6 Weiler (1981).

7 Fourth Report on the Application of the Charter of the Fundamental Social Rights, 1996, p. 10.

8 See also Chapter 5.

succeeded in putting forward a proposal which was accepted by the Council, Directive 2008/104/EC/EC (see Section 4.4).

4.1.2. THE NATURE OF THE DIRECTIVES

Although connected by the common 'origin' which has just been described, the three directives differ in some respects. As a very general remark, which will be elaborated later in this chapter, it can be noted here that only the Temporary Work Directive contains specific provisions dealing with remedial measures to be applied if it is violated, whereas no such rules are provided in the Part-time and the Fixed-term Work Directives. This is basically due to the different periods in which the three directives were adopted: only the most recent – the 2008 Temporary Work Directive – can be counted among the 'second generation' directives paying due attention not only to the conferral of substantive rights, but also to the procedural measures facilitating their exercise and to the sanctions available in the case of infringements.

The three 'atypical work' directives also differ in another aspect; only the first two directives refer to the comparable worker as an essential part of the equality test, whereas the Temporary Work Directive does not.

All directives have the character of requiring minimal protection in common. Derogation *in melius* by national legislations and/or collective bargaining is possible: this possibility, especially with regard to the Fixed-term Work Directive, has brought about a number of interpretation questions related to the so-called 'non-regression' clauses.

4.2. PART-TIME WORK

4.2.1. THE POLICY DIMENSION

4.2.1.1. Part-Time Work as an Instrument of Employment Policies

When analysing the character of Community policies towards atypical work, a statement can be made, distinguishing between fixed-term work on the one hand and part-time work on the other. Whereas the regulation of the former has been basically perceived as a means to prevent an abuse of the contract, the regulation of the latter has been rather intended as a way to 'facilitate access to part-time work' and to remove 'obstacles of a legal or administrative nature which may limit the opportunities for part-time work'.[9]

---

9 See, respectively, Clause 1(b) and Clause 5(1)(a) of Directive 97/81/EC.

This difference is rooted in the traditional representation – always encompassed by the Community – of part-time work an instrument of employment policies capable of reducing unemployment rates (as the then much celebrated 'Dutch miracle' was supposed to demonstrate[10]), while at the same time allowing workers to 'prepare for retirement, reconcile professional and family life, and take up education and training opportunities to improve their skills and career opportunities'.[11]

It is not surprising, hence, that part-time work has been considered as a key issue of the European employment policies developed in the late 1990s within the framework of the Open Method of Coordination, introduced by the Maastricht Treaty, as it is demonstrated by the 'recurring mentioning of part-time work in at least three pillars of the Employment Guidelines'.[12] And it is accordingly consistent with such a policy stance that the directive has elevated the reach of employment policy goals among the goals to be pursued through the development of part-time work: it was one of the first occasions in which 'employment promotion objectives became firmly ensconced within the text of a social policy measure'.[13]

It is worth-noting, however, that – at least in its declared intentions – the promotion of part-time work cherished within the context of the EU employment policies is not unconditional. An analysis of the many EU documents released at the beginning of the new century within the frame of the so-called Lisbon Strategy reveals that a sheer quantitative increase of part-time work ratio,[14] achieved by measures aimed at increasing flexibility on the demand side, is not the only possible description of what an EU occupational policy was supposed to achieve.[15] Rather than on the reduction of unemployment rates, indeed, both the Lisbon Strategy and the Europe 2020 agenda focus on the target of increasing the employment rate of the population, to at least 75% by 2020. The shifting of the focus from a reduction of unemployment to an increase in the employment rate is not trivial. It means that efforts should be addressed to increase labour market participation rates, with special regard to the groups of workers who risk remaining inactive on the labour market: the elderly and women, according to statistical data. If the policy goal is to attract inactive people to the labour market, a series of activation measures have to be taken: addressing part-time work clearly being one of them, as the very same EU institutions have declared

10 See Visser & Hemerijck (1997) and Visser et al. (2004).

11 General Consideration no. 5 of the Framework agreement on part-time work.

12 Sciarra (2004).

13 Kilpatrick & Freedland (2004).

14 According to figures published by Eurostat the average percentage of part-time workers in the EU has increased overtime and has ended up to 19% in 2016. Between the Member States it varies from around 2% (Bulgaria) to 46% (Netherlands); cf. Eurostat, 2.4.2.-r2159-2016-08-11 (prod), The indicator 'part-time employment' represents employees who work part-time as a percentage of total employment.

15 Lo Faro (2004).

on many occasions, for instance as concerns the removal of barriers to female participation in the labour market,[16] and with regard to the integration in the labour market of young people and the elderly.[17]

4.2.1.2. Consequences on the Regulation of Part-Time Contracts

When referred to the regulation of the individual employment relationships, such policy objectives have, or should have, consequences in terms of the legislative regulation of part-time contracts: if part-time work is to be promoted in its role of 'activating' tool, it follows that legislative support should be addressed to make part-time work a 'good' or 'quality' job; i.e. as a contract whose flexibility is protected on the supply-side of the workforce, and not only as an instrument able to increment demand-side flexibility: 'quality in work is important for increasing participation at all ages and over time';[18] 'the quality of the jobs on offer has an influence on the decision to enter the labour market but also to stay in a job or on the labour market'.[19]

What has been described so far refers, however, to the declared policy objectives of part-time work within the EU. The analysis of the Part-time Work Directive adopted in 1997 reveals that a certain disproportion exists between those policy objectives and the actual way in which part-time work has been regulated at the European level. With the exception of the non-discrimination principle, whose effective implementation is to be credited to the Court of Justice's case law rather than to the directive, the Part-time Work Directive is generally described as a minimalistic, if not poor, piece of supranational social legislation, as the following discussion will demonstrate.

4.2.2. THE PROMOTION OF VOLUNTARY PART-TIME WORK

In a clear effort to preserve and boost the supply-side flexibility of the employment contract, Clause 1(b) of the Framework Agreement states that its

---

16 'Barriers to female participation in the labour market include lack of adequate work-life balance policies ... Flexible working arrangements can also help facilitate work-life balance', European Commission (2016) (consultation on a European Pillar of Social Rights).

17 Reference is made to the so-called 'old-age part-time work', which 'in some countries ... was designed to promote a gradual exit from work to retirement, thereby prolonging the employment career whilst also facilitating the integration of younger people into work', *Combining the Entry of Young People in the Labour Market with the Retention of older workers*, Directorate-General for Internal policies, 2013. On these issues see Kullmann & Rocca (2017).

18 *Jobs, Jobs, Jobs. Creating more employment in Europe*, Report of the Employment Taskforce chaired by Wim Kok, 2003.

19 European Commission (2003), *Communication on the future of the European Employment Strategy (EES)*, COM(2003)6 final.

purpose is 'to facilitate the development of part-time work *on a voluntary basis* (emphasis added)'. If intended as a programmatic norm, such provision has a crucial role, insofar as it represents the legislative translation of the EU policy statements described in the previous section. If intended as a way to actually modify a reality where '9.5 million part-time workers in the EU would prefer to work more',[20] however, it has not completely succeeded so far.

4.2.2.1. The (Non-Existent) Right to Part-Time Work

The main reason lying behind the quite ineffective provision regarding the voluntary character of part-time work is likely to be found in the fact that the Agreement does not take any position on one of the issues which could probably have contributed to the effective accomplishment of its purpose: i.e. the existence of a subjective right to part-time work, both at the beginning and in the course of the employment relationship. As it is confirmed by the lively discussions that occurred in many Member States,[21] a fully-fledged recognition of the right to part-time work would require the legislative regulation of part-time work to be orientated towards the supply-side flexibility of that contract, thus coupling legislation with the 'activating' function that such a contract is supposed to have according to the European policy guidelines, as described above. However, part-time work is an issue which also brings about strong constraints on demand-side flexibility, and this explains the tough opposition to the recognition of a worker's right to part-time work encountered in many Member States. In fact, a subjective right to part-time work is recognised in only few Member States: Germany, the Netherlands, France and Italy, albeit with some limitations specifically regarding the private sector. Up to now, the Court of Justice has not been called to decide whether or not the 'voluntary' character of part-time work enshrined in the directive entails the existence of a right to part-time work.

4.2.2.2. The Transition from Part-Time Work to Full-Time Work and Vice-Versa

The Agreement provisions which give effect to the voluntary principle are contained in Clause 5. According to Clause 5(2), the worker's refusal to change the nature of the relationship from full-time work to part-time work (and vice versa) cannot be a valid reason for dismissal *per se*, although it could constitute a valid reason for termination of the employment relationship to the

---

20 According to the Eurostat press release of 23 May 2017 (<https://ec.europa.eu/eurostat/web/products-eurostat-news/-/DDN-20170523-1> accessed 05.06.2019). Given that the number of part-time workers is 45.3 million in the EU, the ratio of involuntary part-timers is 20.9% of all part-time workers.

21 See e.g. for the German case, Fuchs (2004b), and for the Dutch, Visser et al. (2004).

extent that such refusal gives rise to operational difficulties for the employer. It is clear that the provision at stake does not really protect the position of workers willing to change their working time arrangements according to their own personal life choices. Clause 5(3) guarantees only that the employer should 'give consideration' 'as far as possible' to their request to transfer from full-time to part-time work that becomes available in the establishment. The same applies in the case of a worker's request to transfer from part-time to full-time work or for an increase in working hours. Again, the 'soft' language used by the Agreement does not really allow one to conclude that – despite the policy rhetoric of *temps choisi* – individual options regarding working time have been taken seriously by the directive.

In the only case in which the Court of Justice has been called to evaluate a national legislation clearly limiting individual choices related to part-time work, it considered that Clause 5 of the Agreement

> does not require the Member States to adopt rules making the conversion of a worker's part-time employment relationship to a full-time employment relationship subject to the worker's consent. That provision seeks merely to exclude the refusal of a worker, as regards such a conversion of his employment relationship, from being the only reason for the termination of his employment in the absence of other objective reasons. It follows that Clause 5(2) of the Framework Agreement does not preclude legislation which allows an employer to order, for such reasons, the conversion of a part-time employment relationship into a full-time employment relationship without the consent of the worker concerned.[22]

Although consistent with the text of the Clause, the interpretation given by the Court missed an occasion to take the principle of voluntary part-time work seriously. In explaining the reasons of its decision, the Court demonstrated a complete lack of awareness of the work-life balance dynamics often underlying 'voluntary' part-time work: according to the 'materialistic' vision of the Court of Justice, a situation in which a part-time worker is obliged to become a full-timer, and the opposite situation in which a worker has a full-time relationship converted into a part-time one contrary to the wishes of that worker, 'cannot be regarded as comparable because the reduction of working time does not involve the same consequences as an increase, in particular, as regards the worker's remuneration, which constitutes consideration for the work carried out'.[23] According to the Court, apparently, the simple fact of earning a higher salary as a consequence of working full-time is a sufficient reason to exclude the worker's right to transform the contract into a part-time one; a conclusion which could

22 ECJ 2014, C-221/13 (*Mascellani*), §§23–24.
23 Ibid., §27.

not be farther from how part-time work is presented in the EU employment policy documents.

4.2.2.3. *Measures to Facilitate Part-Time Work*

The proclaimed purpose of promoting part-time work (Clause 1 (b)) is supported by some 'facilitation measures', addressed at increasing *de facto* – but not *de jure* – the worker's actual capacity to enter into a part-time contract during the course of the employment relationship.

A first group of provisions refers to a series of commitments which employers are required – 'as far as possible' – to 'give consideration to' (Clause 5(3)). Namely: to provide in due time information on the availability of part-time and full-time positions in the establishment; to adopt measures to facilitate access to part-time work at all levels of the professional scale, including skilled and managerial positions; and where appropriate, to facilitate access by part-time workers to vocational training aimed at enhancing their career opportunities; and to provide workers' representatives with the relevant information.[24] As the text of Clause 5(3) reveals, these are, however, nothing more than 'recommendations': it would be really hard to find any sort of remedies available against an employer which did not 'give consideration' to such commitments because it deemed it 'not possible'.

The second group of facilitation measures is addressed to Member States and social partners, and refers to their obligation to identify and remove all the obstacles of a legal or administrative nature, which may limit the opportunities for part-time work.[25] The normative content of this provision is certainly more binding than the 'soft' recommendations contained in the previous group of provisions, and it is therefore not surprising that it is only this provision which has been object of a preliminary ruling of the Court of Justice. In the *Michaeler* case,[26] the Court held that the Italian law requiring undertakings to send to the competent public authorities a copy of every part-time employment contract concluded, must be considered as an administrative obstacle likely to limit the opportunities for part-time work within the meaning of Clause 5(1)(a) of the Agreement, especially when observing that no such obligation exists for full-time contracts. 'Because of the costs and the associated penalties', the Court stated, 'the obligation to notify the authorities of part-time contracts risks particularly affecting small and medium-sized undertakings which, not having the same resources as larger undertakings, may consequently be inclined to

[24] Clause 5(3)(c), (d), (e), respectively.

[25] Clause 5(1)(a) and (b).

[26] ECJ 2008, Cases C-55/07 and C-56/07 (*Michaeler et al.*).

avoid that form of organisation of work, namely part-time work, which it is the aim of Directive 97/81 to promote'.[27]

However, by linking Clause 5(1) with the general principle of non-discrimination provision of Clause 4 of the Agreement, the Court stated that this provision does not preclude national legislation which obliges employers to retain and make public the working time arrangements of part-time workers to the extent that such an obligation exists for full-time workers too, 'or, if there is such a difference in treatment, it is established that it is justified on objective grounds and does not go beyond what is necessary to attain the objectives thus pursued'.[28]

4.2.2.4. Non-Discrimination in Part-Time Work: A Goal or a Means?

It is crucial to recall here that the principle of non-discrimination in employment conditions is one of the – if not 'the' – milestones of European labour law. Starting from the original two principles related to gender and nationality contained in the founding Treaty, a sort of basic bipartition could be framed. On the one side is the right not to be discriminated against as an expression of a fundamental principle which is protected *per se;* in the case of gender discrimination, it is an expression of the general principle of equality. On the other side is the right not to be discriminated against, which is protected in its function as a tool able to attain different goals; e.g. in the case of workers exercising their freedom of movement, the goal of creating an internal market based on the four economic freedoms.

When analysing the way in which the non-discrimination principle has been conceived and framed within the Part-time Work Directive, one could come to the conclusion that what we face is a principle belonging to the second category: i.e. a non-discrimination principle with the main objective of reaching a goal other than merely equal treatment. In this case, the goal is the promotion of part-time work, and the prohibition of discriminating against part-time workers is the means functional to achieve that goal.

Although not universally shared, this interpretation of the non-discrimination principle in the EU regulation of part-time work is not only based on doctrinal opinions, but also rather explicitly supported in judgments of the Court of Justice. In one of the many cases based on Clause 4 of the Framework Agreement, the Court stressed that the purpose of the Agreement is twofold: 'first, to promote part-time work by improving the quality of such work and, second, to eliminate discrimination between part-time workers and full-time workers'. When discrimination occurs, the Court added, both objectives of

---

27 Idem §27.

28 ECJ 2011, C-349/11 (*Auditeur du travail v. Yangwei SPRL*) and in a similar way ECJ 2011, C-151/10 (*Dai Cugini NV*).

the directive are endangered, to the extent that discriminations 'tend to make part-time work less attractive for that category of workers; in other words, they are discouraged from pursuing their occupational activity on such a basis ... Such effects clearly run counter to the objective of the Framework Agreement, *which is to facilitate the development of part-time work*'.[29]

4.2.3. THE RIGHT NOT TO BE DISCRIMINATED AGAINST IN THE CASE LAW OF THE COURT OF JUSTICE

4.2.3.1. The Part-Time Work Directive and Beyond

As it is often the case in European labour legislation, the key provision of the Part-time Work Directive can only be fully understood through an analysis of the case law of the Court of Justice: 'Part-time workers shall not be treated in a less favourable manner than comparable full-time workers solely because they work part time unless different treatment is justified on objective grounds'.[30]

What is peculiar to the situation of part-time work is the fact that the most significant judicial interpretations of the non-discrimination principle have been based on normative grounds other than those of the Part-time Work Directive. To be more precise, the judicial implementation of the 'other' (and preceding) non-discrimination principles contained in the Treaty and in other 'general' directives has been able to compensate the limits of the directive, the most critical of which is its narrow scope.

The Preamble to the directive is resolute in declaring that the Agreement only 'relates to employment conditions of part-time workers, recognising that matters concerning statutory social security are for decision by the Member States'. The exclusion of social security from the scope of the directive is, of course, a serious flaw, hampering ability to secure part-time workers effective equal treatment, since most of the negative effects of part-time work are to be found precisely in the social security sphere, rather than in that of employment conditions. However, this problem has been partly solved by the case law of the Court of Justice, which – well before the adoption of Directive 97/81 – had already developed its indirect discrimination doctrine in cases related to part-time work and its different distribution across men and women.[31]

---

29 ECJ 2008, C-395/08 and 396/08 (*INPS v. Bruno et al.*), §§77–80.

30 Clause 4(1).

31 Starting from ECJ 1981, C-96/80 (*Jenkins*), and also in other well-known cases such as ECJ 1986, 170/84 (*Bilka*); ECJ 1989, C-171/88 (*Rinner-Kühn*); ECJ 1990, C-33/89 (*Kowalska*); ECJ 1991, C-184/89 (*Nimz*); and ECJ 1992, C-360/90 (*Bötel*).

Even after the adoption of the directive, and taking into account its limited material scope, however, the Court has continued to 'complement' Clause 4 of the Agreement with other normative grounds every time it has been asked to evaluate discrimination of part-time workers affecting their social security entitlements. This has happened in vertical part-time cases[32] in which the Court had to consider statutory provisions which f work excluded days not worked from the contribution history, thus reducing the amount of unemployment benefit payable. On those occasions, the Court stated that such discriminatory effect is precluded not by the Part-time work directive, but rather by Directive 79/7/EEC on the progressive implementation of the principle of equal treatment for men and women in matters of social security once it is 'established that the majority of vertical part-time workers are women who are adversely affected by such legislation'.[33] In other cases, still more clearly, the Court considered that the German legislation providing that part-time work may be authorised for public servants only if they have worked full-time for at least three of the five previous years, is to be considered as discriminatory on the basis of Directive 76/207/EEC[34] on equal treatment for men and women. It declared that 'Having regard to the fact that the scheme at issue in the main proceedings lays down rules concerning working conditions within the meaning of Article 5(1) of Directive 76/207, there is, in the circumstances, no need to consider whether Directive 97/81 is applicable to the case'.[35]

4.2.3.2. *The Mitigation of the Non-Discrimination Principle: Objective Reasons and Pro-Rata Temporis*

Notwithstanding the Court's assertions that 'Clause 4 of the Framework Agreement must be interpreted as articulating a principle of European Union social law which cannot be interpreted restrictively',[36] it is quite widely believed that the non-discrimination provision contained in Directive 97/81/EC gives rise to a weak or 'diluted'[37] version of the equality principle.

---

32 Part-time work is called 'vertical' when the person performing it concentrates the working hours on certain working days of the week, and 'horizontal' when the person performing it works part-time on every working day of the week.

33 ECJ 2017, C-98/15 (*María Begoña Espadas Recio*). Similarly, in a case regarding a discrimination flowing from a Spanish law requiring 'a proportionally greater contribution period from part-time workers, the vast majority of whom are women, than from full-time workers for the former to qualify for a contributory retirement pension', the Court based its decision on Directive 79/7/EEC, even though the national referring judge had invited it to answer on Clause 4 of the Part-time Directive (ECJ 2012, C-385/11 *Isabel Elbal Moreno*).

34 Now embodied in Directive 2006/54/EC.

35 ECJ 2003, C-77/02 (*Steinicke*), §52.

36 ECJ 2008, C-395/08 and 396/08 (*INPS v. Bruno et al.*), §32.

37 Fredman (2006). See also Jeffery (1998). Also before its formal adoption, the directive had been criticised by the European Parliament, which had noted that 'the actual substance of the

In addition to the limited material scope of the directive, this opinion can be based on multiple grounds: in the first place, it is noted that the non-discrimination principle might be circumvented when a 'different treatment can be justified on objective grounds' (Clause 4(1)); in the second place the uncertain application of the principle of pro-rata temporis might be pointed out; and finally one can point at the exclusion of 'part-time workers who work on a casual basis' (Clause 2(2)) and the notion of 'full-time comparable worker' (Clause 3(2)), which was used by the Court of Justice to frame one of its most criticised judgments.[38]

As the first reason – the ample room for justifications – is concerned, it cannot be disregarded that the possibility to treat part-timers differently if there is an 'objective ground' is not further specified by the Agreement, thus potentially leaving room for all kinds of abuse. This is particularly detrimental to the effectiveness of the non-discrimination principle to the extent that what is at stake in the case of Clause 4 of the Part-time Work Directive is a *direct* discrimination prohibition;[39] i.e. a provision protecting workers as part-timers, and not – as was the case in the Court's case law in the 1980s and 1990s – as women working part-time. This has some consequences on the level of justifications. As it is well-known, direct discrimination differs from indirect discrimination precisely in the working of justification grounds: direct discrimination is justifiable only when one of the specific and explicit grounds provided by the legislation exists; whereas indirect discrimination could also be justified by reasons not accurately indicated by law and/or indicated through the evocation of the necessity/proportionality criterion.[40] In the case of Clause 4, however, direct discrimination against part-timers is considered to be justifiable insofar as a generic and indefinite objective reason exists;[41] and even the necessity/proportionality test is not explicitly required, although one could argue that the same kind of jurisprudential limits developed in other fields of EU law apply here. In order to be capable of limiting the right of part-time workers not to be (directly) discriminated against, therefore, the 'objective ground' mentioned in Clause 4 of Directive 97/81 has to pursue a

agreement, once the declaratory elements have been removed, does not always do justice to its stated purpose, since the agreement does not eliminate discrimination against part-time workers and does not contribute to making part-time work more attractive', Resolution of the European Parliament on Part-time Work Directive, 1997.

38 ECJ 2004, C-313/02 (*Wippel*).

39 What Clause 4(1) guarantees, indeed, is the right 'not (to) be treated in a less favourable manner than comparable full-time workers *solely* because they work part time' (emphasis added).

40 See e.g. Article 2(1)(b) Equal Treatment Directive 2006/54/EC, according to which indirect discrimination might be allowed if it is 'objectively justified by a legitimate aim, and the means of achieving that aim are appropriate and necessary'. See also Chapter 3.

41 The fact that the Part-time Work Directive allows the possibility to justify a direct discrimination is defined as 'unusual in the non-discrimination field' by Rönnmar (2011a).

legitimate aim and must not go beyond what is appropriate and necessary in order to attain the objective pursued.[42]

The uncertainties and the 'timidity' of Clause 4 also affect another keystone of the direct discrimination's legal architecture, i.e. the identification of the *comparator*. Both in the Part-time and in the Fixed-term Work Directives, the possibility to enforce the right of non-standard workers not to be discriminated against implies a standard work comparator to be identified by 'standard comparable workers', meaning workers engaged in the same establishment and in the same or similar occupation.[43] The choice to make the equality claim depending on the actual identification of a comparable worker has been heavily criticised by the doctrine[44] and – *pour cause* – withdrawn when the Temporary Agency Work Directive was subsequently adopted. There is no doubt, indeed, that in many cases it could operate as a severe hindrance to the full effectiveness of non-discrimination legislation, as it is clear, for instance, in the case of 'part-time only' workplaces where no full-time comparable worker can be identified.[45]

The problematical nature of the comparable worker technique has become clear in the much debated *Wippel* case,[46] where the Court was requested to decide on the disadvantageous treatment of workers 'on demand', who had a contract on the basis of which working hours were determined on a case-by-case basis, with the workers concerned having the choice to accept or refuse the work offered. In that case the Court denied any kind of protection by declaring that Clause 4 could not be applied insofar as there was no 'comparable worker', since a 'normal' full-time employment relationship 'differs, as to subject-matter and basis, from that of a worker such as Mrs Wippel'.[47] Moreover, the Court also excluded the possibility that the remedies of indirect discrimination on the base of sex could apply in that case since, again, the situation of workers on demand could neither be compared to full-time nor to part-time workers. Such conclusions – however they could be evaluated on the 'doctrinal' level[48] – corroborated the fears of those who had noticed, well before *Wippel*, that in some Member States the question related to the identification of the 'comparable worker' risked ending up in justifying disadvantageous treatment of part-timers.[49]

42 On the principle of proportionality, see Ellis (1999) and Davidov (2013).
43 Clause 3(2) of both directives; in the Part-time Work Directive only, the further requirement to be engaged in 'same type of employment contract or relationship' is provided.
44 Bell (2011).
45 As stressed by Kountouris (2016).
46 See *supra* note 39.
47 ECJ 2004, C-313/02 (*Wippel*), §61.
48 According to Schiek, Waddington & Bell (2007), the Court's reasoning is 'with all respect to the learned jurists at the CJEU, erroneous' since 'introducing the category of comparability into the indirect discrimination test … is dogmatically unsound'.
49 With regard to the UK, see McColgan (2000).

The case of Mrs Wippel also highlights another possible flaw of the Part-time Work Directive, i.e. dealing with the notion of 'part-time worker' contained in Clause 3(1), and to the notion of 'casual part-time worker' contained in Clause 2(2). Even if the *Wippel* case was not decided on those bases, it is indeed possible to argue that 'extreme' working time arrangements implying reduced or casual working hours – as, for instance, the ever-increasing number of zero-hours contracts[50] – could escape the application of the directive to the extent that they could not fall within the notion of part-time work incorporated into it.[51] Member States are also free to exclude such kind of contracts from the application of the directive by making use of the possibility to 'exclude wholly or partly from the terms of this Agreement part-time workers who work on a casual basis' (Clause 2(2)).

Finally, also the principle of pro-rata temporis, allowed 'where appropriate' by Clause 4(2) of the Agreement, opens the way – reasonable as it may be in certain cases – to wide margins of interpretation as to the obligation to secure part-timers with employment conditions effectively equal to those of full-timers. Within this perspective framework the Court of Justice considered that the pro-rata temporis principle may justify: a reduction of child allowances for part-time workers;[52] a diminution of paid annual leave, even if 'that principle cannot be applied ex post to a right to annual leave accumulated during a period of full-time work';[53] a reduction of pension entitlements to the extent that such reduction is strictly proportionate – and not greater – to effective working time.[54]

However, more recently the Court held that the principle of pro-rata temporis cannot be evoked to justify disadvantageous treatment concerning pensions of vertical-cyclical part-time workers. The Court stated on that occasion that the Italian legislation disregarding periods not worked within a vertical part-time relationship from the calculation of the period of service required to qualify for a retirement pension, is contrary to the non-discrimination principle provided by the directive to the extent that it 'amounts to a difference in treatment based solely on the fact of part-time work'. The principle of pro-rata temporis cannot justify such unequal treatment, because it 'is not applicable for the purpose of determining the date required to acquire pensions rights, since that depends solely on the worker's length of service … The length of service is, in fact, the actual duration of the employment relationship and not the amount of time worked during that period'. It follows, the Court concluded, that 'the length of the period of service taken into account for the purpose of

50 On which see, as concerns the UK case, Kenner (2017).

51 According to Clause 3(1), 'The term "part-time worker" refers to an employee whose normal hours of work, calculated on a weekly basis or on average over a period of employment of up to one year, are less than the normal hours of work of a comparable full-time worker'.

52 ECJ 2014, C-476/12 (*Österreichischer Gewerkschaftsbund*).

53 ECJ 2010, C-486/08 (*Zentralbetriebsrat der Landeskrankenhäuser Tirols*), §33.

54 ECJ 2003, C-4/02 and C-5/02 (*Hilde Schönheit*), §§90–91.

determining the date on which a worker becomes entitled to a pension should be calculated for a part-time worker as if he had held a full-time post, periods not worked being taken into account in their entirety'.[55]

4.3. FIXED-TERM WORK

4.3.1. FIXED-TERM WORK: FLEXIBLE OR 'PRECARIOUS'?

Fixed-term Directive 1999/70/EC undoubtedly presents specific features that are different from the other two flexible work directives. Unlike part-time and temporary agency work, fixed-term contracts have never been perceived by the EU as something to be unconditionally encouraged and promoted with a view to reaching the objective of a more flexible labour market.

Contrary to the rhetoric of flexicurity, which dates back to 1994 Essen Summit and to the 1997 Green Paper on the 'New organisation of work',[56] the Framework agreement concluded on 18 March 1999 and implemented through Directive 1999/70/EC re-affirmed that 'contracts of an indefinite duration are, and will continue to be, the general form of employment relationship', to the extent that they 'contribute to the quality of life of the workers concerned and improve performance'.[57] As a consequence, they are far from being 'facilitated' (as is the case with part-time contracts) or 'developed' (as is provided for temporary agency work contracts), but are, rather, represented by the social partners and the European legislature as the object of a regulation aimed at preventing abuse being made of them.[58]

This different policy in the EU regulation of fixed-term work as compared to the other flexible contractual arrangements has possibly been amplified over the years, as both the Commission and the Court have progressively built on the idea that fixed-term work has less to do with the 'positive' notion of flexibility than with the 'negative' concept of *precariousness*. In its most recent documents related to the post-crisis developments, the Commission was unusually firm in fostering an agenda of employment stability which openly challenges the labour market policy options it had wholeheartedly promoted in the 1990s and 2000s:

> Stable and predictable work relationships and in particular more permanent types of contracts induce employers and employees to invest more in skills and life-long learning. They allow individuals to plan for their future by providing sustainable prospects of career and earnings progression ... The more general move towards

55 ECJ 2008, C-395/08 and 396/08 (*INPS v. Bruno et al.*).
56 COM(97)128 final.
57 The statement is repeated twice: in the Preamble and in the General considerations no. 6.
58 Clause 1(b) of the Agreement.

> more flexible labour markets should facilitate employment creation but should also enable transitions towards more permanent contracts. It should not result in more precarious jobs.[59]

And also within the Court's case law, although with some uncertainties and contradictions, the approach to fixed-term work as a contractual arrangement to be 'handled with care' and sensibly restricted[60] has become more clear over the years, as it has been asserted that 'the legislative action of the European Union in the area of employment law is based on the fundamental premise that contracts of indefinite duration are the general form of employment relationship'.[61] In such a perspective, 'a certain reservation' of the social partners themselves toward fixed-term work has also been stressed, which is clearly 'contrary to the perspective which prevailed in the Framework Agreement on Part-time work, which tended to favour this latter form of employment'.[62] It can be concluded that, despite its chronological connection with the triumph of the flexible labour market's narratives in the European Union, the text of the 1999/70/EC Directive fostered a judicial interpretation which is by now oriented towards overtly proclaiming that 'the use of fixed-term contracts as opposed to contracts of indefinite duration is therefore *exceptional*' (emphasis added).[63]

4.3.2. THE ABUSE-PREVENTION MEASURES

It is precisely because 'the benefit of stable employment is viewed as a major element in the protection of workers', that the Framework Agreement regards fixed-term contracts 'as a potential source of abuse to the disadvantage of workers',[64] and thus lays down a number of protective provisions designed to prevent the status of employees from being insecure.

As a matter of fact, the directive's aversion is not directed against fixed-term work as such, but rather (and only) towards the *abuse* of it and in particular to the consecutive use of fixed-term contracts. This very specific focus has been

---

59 Communication, *Strengthening the recovery and fostering convergence* 2015, p. 11.

60 Recent figures reported by Koukiadaki and Katsaroumpas (2017), pp. 45–46, show an increase of workers on a fixed term contract in the last 10 years in particular among young people. The percentage of fixed-term workers among employees having from 15 to 24 years is 43.8%, whereas among the working population between 25 and 54 years old is 12.1%, and for older people aged 55 to 64 only 6.7%. The differences between countries are however remarkable; see Eurostat, 2017 (last update: 14.03.2018). In some countries such as the Netherlands, nevertheless, fixed-term contracts are not seen as precarious.

61 Opinion of the Advocate-General Szpunar in ECJ 2015, C-533/13 (*AKT*), §111.

62 Opinion of the Advocate-General Jääskinen in ECJ 2011, C-313/10 (*Sylvia Jansen*), §57.

63 ECJ 2011, C-109/09 (*Deutsche Lufthansa AG*), §30.

64 Both the quotations are taken from the seminal judgment ECJ 2006, C-212/04 (*Adeneler*), §§62–63. Recently confirmed in ECJ 2018, C-46/17 (*Hubertus*), §§39–41.

accused by some authors of containing 'a certain level of ambiguity',[65] to the extent that it risks restricting the alleged intention to limit recourse to fixed-term work to exceptional cases. In particular, since the directive explicitly considers that abuse of fixed-term work can occur only in the case of a series of 'successive fixed-term employment contracts' (Clause 5 of the Agreement), it can be concluded that the directive does not limit in any way 'the parties' first entry into a fixed-term employment contract', as Rönnmar has observed.[66] Within this perspective, the actual judicial application of Directive 1999/70/EC has indeed confirmed over the time the critical remarks of those who, right before its adoption, had revealed its 'normalising' effect on fixed-term work.[67] In several occasions, in fact, the Court clarified that what the directive prevents is only *one* kind of abuse – that deriving from a succession of different fixed-term contracts – whereas, on the contrary, 'it has no application in the case of a worker engaged for a single fixed-term contract'.[68]

Having thus excluded 'spot' fixed-term contracts from the scope of the directive, Clause 5 of the Framework agreement enumerates a series of abuse-prevention measures through which Member States are called upon to impose limits to the recourse to several successive fixed-term contracts: (a) fixing the objective reasons justifying the renewal of such contracts or relationships; (b) determining the maximum total duration of successive fixed-term employment contracts; (c) or limiting the number of renewals of such contracts. Member States must adopt at least one of these methods where no equivalent measures already exist.

As it is clear from the same regulatory technique adopted – which quite unusually leaves Member States the possibility to choose which of the three measures they deem most appropriate – Clause 5 of the Agreement is not framed so as to allow it to have a (vertical) direct effect, since, as the Court has made clear, it 'does not contain any unconditional and sufficiently precise obligation capable of being relied upon, in the absence of transposing measures taken within the requisite period, by an individual before a national court'.[69]

65 Numhauser-Henning (2002), p. 433.

66 Rönnmar (2011a), p. 60.

67 Murray (1999). In 2008 the ETUC pointed to the case law of the Court stressing that 'fixed term contracts can only be accepted as a way to respond to specific and temporary needs of both employers and workers, not to create second class workers who would for long periods of time be denied the benefit of stable employment'.

68 In his Opinion in the *Mangold* case AG Tizzano mentions this principle for the first time (ECJ 2005, C-144/04 (*Mangold*), §§39–40). The principle has been subsequently proclaimed by the Court itself in ECJ 2009, C-378/07 to C-380/07 (*Angelidaki*), where it is clearly stated that 'clause 5(1)(a) does not apply to the first or single use of a fixed-term employment contract or relationship' (§90); and repeated in ECJ 2009, C-162/08 to C-164/08 (*Lagoudakis*); ECJ 2010, C-20/10 (*Vino*), §1; and ECJ 2014, C-362/13, C-363/13 and C-407/13 (*Fiamingo*), §57.

69 ECJ 2008, C-268/06) (*Impact*), §§73 and 79.

The directive's provision to 'assign to the Member States the general objective of preventing such abuse, while leaving to them the choice as to how to achieve this',[70] has raised major hermeneutical questions with regard to the notion of 'objective reasons' justifying the renewal (not the first conclusion) of fixed-term contracts. In the *Adeneler* case, regarding a Greek legislation authorising unlimited renewal of fixed-term contracts when statutory or secondary legislation so provided, the Court stated that a national provision merely authorising renewal of fixed-term contracts in a general and abstract manner does not match the concept of 'objective reasons' and it is therefore irreconcilable with the purpose of the Agreement and the requirement that it must have practical effect. On the contrary, in order for successive contracts to be objectively justified, Clause 5(1)(a) requires that reference must be made to

> precise and concrete circumstances characterising a given activity ... which may result, in particular, from the specific nature of the tasks for the performance of which such contracts have been concluded and from the inherent characteristics of those tasks or, as the case may be, from pursuit of a legitimate social-policy objective of a Member State.[71]

However, in the much debated *Kücük* case, regarding an employee who had worked for a period of 10 years on the basis of 13 fixed-term successive contracts, the Court did not exclude the possibility that such a series of successive contracts could – in principle – meet the requirement of 'objective reasons', even if it is ascertained that temporary replacements occur on a recurring, or even permanent, basis and that those replacements may also be covered by the hiring of employees under employment contracts of indefinite duration.[72] Even though in this judgment the Court left Member States a quite large margin of appreciation – by allowing national courts to verify whether the specific circumstances of the case, including the number and cumulative duration of the fixed-term contracts concluded in the past with the same employer, might substantiate an abuse – the *Kücük* decision has certainly marked a demurral in the restrictive attitude of the Court towards fixed-term contracts,[73] which nevertheless did not prevent national courts from continuing to consider as abusive 'extreme' cases of successive fixed-term contracts non-justified by objective reasons.[74]

It must also be added that, in its most recent judgments – essentially referring to the lengthy fixed-term relationships typically occurring in public employment – the Court has made clear that the use of successive fixed-term

---

70 ECJ 2015, C-238/14 (*Commission v. Luxembourg*).
71 ECJ 2006, C-212/04 (*Adeneler*), §§66–75.
72 ECJ 2012, C-586/10 (*Kücük*).
73 See the critical remarks by Robin-Oliver & Remy (2012) and Aimo (2016).
74 This is indeed what happened in Germany in the national follow-up of the *Kücük* case.

contracts to cover permanent needs is not justified for the purposes of Clause 5(1)(a) of the Framework Agreement. In order for Clause 5(1)(a) of the Framework Agreement to be complied with, it must therefore be specifically verified that the renewal of successive fixed-term employment contracts or relationships is intended to cover temporary needs and that a national provision allowing an unlimited renewal of fixed-term employment is not, in fact, being used to meet fixed and permanent staffing needs of the employer. These principles have been affirmed in cases concerning precarious workers in Italian public schools,[75] Spanish fixed-term workers hired in order to ensure the permanent and continuous operation of the healthcare institutions,[76] and Romanian fixed-term workers employed by the Veterinary public services, where the Court specified that neither budgetary considerations nor the allegation that fixed-term contracts have been concluded pending completion of competition procedures for recruiting permanent staff, can be considered as such as objective reasons justifying renewals according to Clause 5(1)(a).[77] In such occasions, however, the Court confirmed, as in the *Kücük* case, that national courts maintain ample discretion as to the specific circumstances to be taken into account when assessing whether there exists an objective ground for an unlimited renewal of fixed-term employment.

Despite some authors proposing a different interpretation,[78] the Court has, however, resolutely made clear that it is not possible to draw from the directive a general principle according to which any renewal of successive fixed-term employment must *always* be justified by objective reasons. The requirement to have an objective justification only applies where a Member State has not chosen to apply one of the other two measures contained in Clause 5(1) of the Agreement. According to the Court, a Member State, indeed, might

> legitimately choose not to adopt the measure referred to in Clause 5(1)(a), which requires the renewal of successive fixed-term contracts to be justified by objective reasons. It may, on the contrary, prefer to adopt one or both of the measures referred to in Clause 5(1)(b) and (c) which deal, respectively, with the maximum total duration of those successive fixed-term contracts and the number of renewals of such contracts.[79]

The argument put forward by the Commission, that the requirement of objective reasons is an immanent feature of the EU regulation of fixed-term work, has been explicitly discharged by the Court on the basis of a double statement: first, because the Commission's position 'introduces a hierarchy between the various

75 ECJ 2014, C-22/13, C-61/13 to C-63/13 and C-418/13 (*Mascolo et al.*), §§100–103.
76 ECJ 2016, C-16/15 (*Pérez López*), §56.
77 ECJ 2016, C-614/15 (*Popescu*), §69.
78 Bercusson & Bruun (1999).
79 ECJ 2014, C-362/13, C-363/13 and C-407/13 (*Fiamingo*), §61.

measures referred to in Clause 5(1) of the Framework Agreement, whereas the terms of that provision themselves unequivocally show that the various measures envisaged are intended to be equivalent'. And, second, because 'the interpretation proposed by the Commission would have the effect of rendering meaningless the choice of means allowed by Clause 5(1) of the Framework agreement'.[80] Should an objective reason always be required to renew a fixed-term contract, workers would, as a matter of fact, always be allowed to claim that their contract was unlawful, even where the renewals did not violate the limits relating to the maximum total duration and/or the maximum number of renewals.

As a result of that assumption, some Member States introduced statutory rules allowing 'free' fixed-term contracts, not justified by any reason, in so far as a maximum length period is respected, as, for instance, in Italy since 2014 and in the Netherlands since 1999. Other Member States have chosen to adopt the third abuse-prevention measure envisaged by Clause 5, thus limiting not the length but rather the number of successive fixed-term contracts. This has led to an extreme degree of variation across different Member States, further augmented after the completion of the enlargement process.[81]

4.3.3. THE EQUAL TREATMENT RULES

Alongside the abuse-prevention purpose proclaimed by Clause 1(a), the Framework Agreement also aims at improving the quality of fixed-term work by ensuring the application of the principle of non-discrimination (Clause 1(b)). In the same way as in the Part-time Work Directive, therefore, non-discrimination is qualified as an element ensuring the quality of work, even if, in contrast to what happens for part-time work, quality of work is here understood not as a means to promote voluntary fixed-term employment, but rather as an end in itself.

Shortly before the final date laid down for transposition of the directive in the Member States (10 July 2001), the Court of Justice declared in a case concerning working time and annual leave that rights conferred by EU law must also be recognised in the case of short-term employment contracts.[82] However, it is certainly on the basis of Clause 4 of the Agreement that the Court has had the possibility to develop wide-ranging case law implementing the principle of non-discrimination in fixed-term work.

The only limit the Court could not overcome relates to the limited material scope of the Agreement, which – as in the case of the Part-time Work

80 Both quotations are taken from ECJ 2008, C-268/06 (*Impact*), §§76–77.

81 See Sargeant (2007).

82 ECJ 2001, 173/99 (*Bectu*).

Directive – does not cover matters relating to statutory social security. Unlike the case of part-time work, this exclusion has not been repaired through the general tools related to the indirect discrimination model that applies, inter alia, in the case of discrimination on basis of gender (see Section 4.2.3) and age. The possibility of applying indirect discrimination remedies to fixed-term workers too has been suggested by some authors, building on the argument that according to statistical data the majority of fixed-term workers are young persons and women.[83] However, until now the Court has not demonstrated any real willingness to take seriously 'the disparate impact of precariousness on certain groups in the labour market, such as women and younger or older workers'.[84]

According to Clause 4(1) of the Agreement, the right of fixed-term workers not to be discriminated against relates to 'employment conditions'. The non-discrimination clause allows an exception if the different treatment is justified on 'objective grounds'. These notions have been extensively scrutinised by the Court in almost 60 cases in which it has been asked to decide upon issues related to fixed-term work.[85] With the debatable exception of the *Mangold* case,[86] the Court never refused to enter into the interpretation of the anti-discrimination clause by declaring firmly that 'notwithstanding the absence of a Community definition of the social-law terms included in those provisions'[87] it is sufficiently unconditional and precise for an individual to be able to rely upon it before a national court.[88] It must be noted, however, that in all the cases where the direct effect of Clause 4 was recognised, the employer was indeed a public administration, thus making clear that what the Court affirmed in those cases is (only) a *vertical* direct effect. However, the Court gave an extensive interpretation of the notion of 'public' employer by including also bodies which, whatever their legal form, have been made responsible, subject to the control of that public authority, for providing a service in the public interest and, for that purpose, enjoy exceptional powers as compared with the rules applicable to relations between private individuals.[89]

83 See Aimo (2016) and, more recently Koukiadaki & Katsaroumpas (2017), p. 45.

84 Bell (2016). An interesting conceptual analysis of direct versus indirect discrimination concepts in EU atypical work directives has been carried out by Pettersson (2015).

85 See the study of De la Porte & Emmenegger (2016). They analysed the Court's cases on the various issues as covered by the Agreement, in particular those (17) in which 'fixed time' was the central issue.

86 ECJ 2005, C-144/04 (*Mangold*).

87 ECJ 2008, C-268/06 (*Impact*), §61.

88 Ibid., §65.

89 Case law since ECJ 1986, 152/84 (*Marshall*) and ECJ 1990, C-188/89 (*Foster v. British Gas*). Explicitly confirmed in ECJ 2013, C-361/12 (*Carratù*), with regard to the Italian post company (Poste Italiane) as it is wholly owned by the Italian State through its sole shareholder, the Minister for Economy and Finances.

By building on the repeated assumption that the 'principle of equal treatment and non-discrimination is one of the general principles of Community law',[90] the Court has interpreted extensively the notion of 'employment conditions', reaching results which were far from being taken for granted. In the seminal *Del Cerro Alonso* case, indeed, the Court was faced with the issue of deciding whether or not pay could be considered as falling within the concept of employment conditions provided by Clause 4. Despite the negative Opinion of the Advocate General (and of several Member States), relying on the exclusion of pay from the sphere of EU competencies in Article 153(5) TFEU, the Court held that a restrictive interpretation of a general principle of EU law was not possible, and that 'the "pay" exception cannot, however, be extended to any question involving any sort of link with pay; otherwise some of the areas referred to in Article 137(1) EC [now: Article 153(1) TFEU] would be deprived of much of their substance'.[91] Consequently, by relying on a teleological method of interpretation, the Court concluded that 'the concept of "employment conditions" should be interpreted as meaning that it can act as a basis for a claim which seeks to grant to a fixed-term worker of a length-of-service allowance which is reserved under national law solely to permanent staff'.[92] The same wide notion of pay, drawn from Court's case law on equal treatment between men and women in the 1980s based on (then) Article 119 EEC (now Article 157 TFEU), was also evoked to cover pensions rights of fixed-term workers depending on the employment relationship, with the exclusion of those deriving from a statutory scheme, in the *Impact* case.[93]

The *Del Cerro Alonso* and *Impact* cases were only the first of a series of subsequent judgments through which the non-discrimination clause has been interpreted so as to expand its scope beyond its *prima facie* limits. When reading the text of Clause 4, for instance, it would be plausible to argue, at first sight, that it could not be used to tackle discrimination regarding two permanent workers, since the text of the clause is clear in providing that 'fixed-term workers shall not be treated in a less favourable manner than comparable permanent workers'. In the *Rosado Santana* case, however, the claim was brought precisely by a *permanent* worker who claimed to have been discriminated against because in assigning promotions the employer took account only of seniority periods accrued as a permanent civil servant and not also of the prior periods of service accumulated as fixed-term worker. Whereas in

90 ECJ 2005, C-144/04 (*Mangold*), §75 and particularly as for fixed-time contracts ECJ 2007, C-307/05 (*Del Cerro Alonso*), §27. Also ECJ 2010, C-444/09 and C-456/09 (*Gavieiro Gavieiro*), §41.

91 ECJ 2007, C-307/05 (*Del Cerro Alonso*), §41.

92 ECJ 2007, C-307/05 (*Del Cerro Alonso*), §48.

93 ECJ 2008, C-268/06 (*Impact*), §§131–32.

Del Cerro Alonso the Court had to cope with a divergent Opinion of the Advocate General, in *Rosado Santana* the Court had to deal with an opposite view of the Commission (and of the Spanish government) who both argued that the wording of Clause 4 could not but exclude its application to a discrimination between two permanent workers.[94] Should the Court have adopted the same evasive approach as in *Wippel* (see Section 4.2.3.2), it would have stuck to the text of the clause and discharged the claim. However, by adopting a purposive approach committed to give full effectiveness to the objective of Clause 4, the Court held that the discrimination suffered by a *permanent* worker is relevant to the directive insofar as it is rooted on periods of service completed by the same worker in his previous fixed-term career; Clause 4(4) of the Framework Agreement does not cease to be applicable to a fixed-term worker who has become a permanent worker.[95]

The same attitude was demonstrated by the Court in cases where it recognised that fixed-term workers are entitled to the same increments related to periods of service which the Spanish national legislation reserved to permanent workers;[96] or where it declared that Clause 4 precludes a national legislation excluding workers employed for a period not exceeding six months from the application of certain provisions regarding remuneration, entitlement to leave, additional payments and overtime supplements;[97] or where it affirmed that it is contrary to the directive to exclude fixed-term teachers from certain professional education benefits,[98] or to exclude non-permanent members of staff from the right to receive a three-yearly length-of-service increment granted to career civil servants.[99]

In a more recent series of cases, nevertheless, the Court adopted a more restrained approach. The issues at stake referred, again, to the Spanish legislation, according to which compensation to be paid in the event of the termination of employment contracts appears to be governed by a wide range of unequal treatments: the compensation amounts to 20 days of salary for permanent workers; 12 days of salary for fixed-term workers; and nothing at all for fixed-term workers employed under a temporary replacement contract. While declaring that the discrimination between fixed-term and permanent workers could not be compatible with EU law, the Court refused to pronounce about the 'internal' discrimination between different kinds of fixed-term workers,

---

94 A quite similar, if not identical, principle was followed by the Court in ECJ 2012, C-302/11 to C-305/11 (*Valenza*), regarding the applicability of Clause 4 to workers of the Italian antitrust authority who, once they became permanent employees, were not allowed to take into account periods of service accrued in previous fixed-term contracts.

95 ECJ 2011, C-177/10 (*Rosado Santana*), §§42–43.

96 ECJ 2010, C-444/09 and C-456/09 (*Gavieiro Gavieiro*).

97 ECJ 2010, C-486/08 (*Zentralbetriebsrat der Landeskrankenhäuser Tirols*), §33.

98 ECJ 2012, C-556/11 (*Lorenzo Martinez*).

99 ECJ 2015, C-177/14 (*Regojo Dans*).

by affirming that differences in treatment between specific categories of fixed-term staff are not covered by the principle of non-discrimination established by that framework agreement.[100] Without entering into the merit of the decision, it is, however, worth noting that such conclusions contradict what the Court declared in previous cases, when it admitted that Clause 4 could be applied to discrimination between two permanent workers.[101] It is quite hard to explain why the very same provision, referred to discrimination between a fixed-term and a permanent worker, could be extensively interpreted so as to cover discrimination between two permanent workers, and at the same time be restrictively interpreted so as to exclude discrimination between two fixed-term workers. It might be wondered, in this regard, whether a stronger integration of the general EU equality law provisions into the judicial implementation of atypical work directives[102] could be used as a means to overcome the shortcomings flowing from such a strict definition of the comparator, as maintained by those who note that 'the equality directives impose a more rigorous standard of protection than that found in the legislation on atypical work'.[103]

4.3.4. THE PERSONAL SCOPE

Although usually placed at the beginning of an analysis of a given legislation, the issue of the personal scope of the 1999/70/EC Directive – defined in Clause 2 of the Agreement – can be better dealt with at this point of the chapter because of its clear connection with the issue of equal treatment.

Beyond the possible limitations to the goal of an effective protection deriving from the judicial uncertainties described at the end of the previous Section, the purpose of 'improving the quality of fixed-term work by ensuring the application of the principle of non-discrimination' could indeed be jeopardised by reducing the personal scope of the legislation. In this regard, however, the case law of the Court of Justice has contributed to remove any possible limitations not explicitly provided by the same Agreement, which only excludes initial vocational training relationships and apprenticeship schemes (Clause 2(2)(a)), and contracts concluded within the framework of specific public or publicly-supported training, integration and vocational retraining programmes (Clause 2(2)(b)).

The most significant portion of such an expanding 'policy' has been certainly reserved by the Court of Justice to the sector of public employment.

100 ECJ 2016, C-596/14 (*De Diego Porras*), §38. The same in ECJ 2016, C-16/15 (*Pérez López*), §66, and in ECJ 2010, C-20/10 (*Vino*), §57, relating to the Italian legislation in the postal sector.

101 ECJ 2011, C-177/10 (*Rosado Santana*) and ECJ 2012, C-302/11 to C-305/11 (*Valenza*).

102 As advocated by Koukiadaki & Katsaroumpas (2017).

103 Bell (2016).

As it is demonstrated by what has been written in the above, a major part of the cases dealt with by the Luxembourg court with regard to fixed-term work, relates to the cases of (Italian and Spanish) fixed-term workers employed by public administrations and/or authorities. This is far from surprising, if one considers that most of these cases originate from legislations introduced in the twenty-first century as a consequence of the severe budgetary constraints induced by the economic crisis. In such a scenario, excluding public employment from the scope of the directive would mean removing the majority of fixed-term workers from the sphere of application of the directive.

The public nature of the employer characterising the major part of the EU litigation on fixed-term work[104] has raised a series of quite intricate problems relating to the remedies applicable in case the contract is considered unlawful (or abusive) within the meaning of Clause 5. Such issues will be dealt with in the following Sections (see Section 4.3.6). What is worth mentioning now, with regard to the personal scope limitations, is that the Court did not demonstrate a similar sensitivity with regard to another kind of 'precarious' work whose *ratio* is equally capable of being traced back to the same 'crisis legislation' introduced in many countries at the turn of the 2010s. Once more, it is a Spanish case which clearly demonstrates how a strict interpretation of the personal scope of the directive could exclude from any protection workers who, although they do not formally qualify fixed-term workers, are certainly to be considered as in employment which is 'precarious'.

Called to decide about the *Contracto de trabajo indefinido de apoyo a los emprendedores* – an employment contract of indefinite duration which can, however, be terminated at will by the employer after one year – the Court refused its jurisdiction on the case.[105] It did not want to admit that an open-ended contract with a 'termination at will clause' is, substantially, though not formally, indeed very close to a fixed-term contract.

4.3.5. THE NON-REGRESSION CLAUSE

As a 'geographical' and 'chronological' analysis of the Court's case law demonstrates, many of the cases in which the Court has been called to appraise national systems characterised by a high precariousness ratio of fixed-term work regulations, refer to legislation introduced in the twenty-first century in 'southern European countries with corporatist-conservative welfare states (Germany, Spain, Italy, Greece, Austria and France) where … the increasing of

104 On which topic, see Mazuyer (2014).

105 ECJ 2015, C-117/14 (*Poclava*). A quite different approach to similar matters was adopted by the Court in the subsequent case ECJ 2014, C-86/14 (*Medialdea*), dealt with under the heading of sanctions and remedies.

employment rates by means of labour market deregulation has been high on domestic political agendas'.[106] The decrease in the level of employment protection for fixed-term workers, in other terms, has been enacted by several Member States *after* Directive 1999/70/EC was adopted, in many cases by a reform of previous and more protecting regulations. This explains why the Agreement's non-regression clause (Clause 8(3)) has gained such a substantial role, certainly more significant than the one usually reserved to non-regression clauses in EU social law.[107]

In a series of cases brought before the Court, the question was whether national pejorative legislation of fixed-term work regulation introduced by Member States in the twenty-first century could be qualified as implementation measures of the 1999 Directive; and whether, consequently, the national legislator had to respect the non-regression clause, which thus produces what has been called the 'standstill effect' for national regimes of atypical work. Should the Court have answered in the positive, a major part of the national deregulatory reforms would have found an obstacle in EU law. The position of the Court in this regard has, however, been rather ambiguous.[108]

On the one hand, the Court seemed to take the non-regression clause quite seriously. At the first occasion it had to deal with it – in the *Mangold* case – the Court did not limit itself to affirming that the implementation of the directive cannot be an occasion for Member States to reduce protections previously granted in the domestic legal order. The Court added that

> The term 'implementation', used without any further precision in Clause 8(3) of the Framework Agreement, does not refer only to the original transposition of Directive 1999/70 … but must also cover all domestic measures intended to ensure that the objective pursued by the directive may be attained, including those which, after transposition in the strict sense, add to or amend domestic rules previously adopted.

On the other hand, however, the Court curtailed the far-reaching implications that its affirmations could have had, by adding that reducing the level of protection previously assured to fixed-term workers contracts (i) 'is not prohibited as such by the Framework Agreement where it is in no way connected to the implementation of that agreement'.[109] Moreover, (ii) on another occasion the Court made clear, that in order to be caught by the non-regression clause, the national legislation must first be connected to the 'implementation' of the Framework Agreement and, second, be framed so as not to worsen a single

[106] De la Porte & Emmenegger (2016), p. 15.
[107] See Corazza (2011).
[108] For a review see Sciarra (2008).
[109] All the quotations are taken from ECJ 2005, C-144/04 (*Mangold*), §§50–52.

profile of the fixed-term legislation, but rather 'the general level of protection afforded to fixed-term workers'[110]

This double caveat has been sufficient to bring the Court to exclude a violation of the non-regression clause in all the cases in which it had the occasion to decide on this point.

First, as concerns the assumption that national legislation submitted to the non-regression clause must be directly linked with the implementation of the directive, the relevant cases are *Mangold* and *Vino.* In *Mangold,* the German legislation on fixed-term work was deemed not to be covered by Clause 8(3) of the Agreement to the extent that it was justified 'not by the need to put the Framework Agreement into effect but by the need to encourage the employment of older persons in Germany'. And similarly, in *Vino*, the Court stated that modification *in pejus* of the legislative rules affecting fixed-term workers of the Italian postal services was not linked to the implementation of the Fixed-term Work Directive, and therefore not covered by the non-regression clause, but, rather, motivated by the objective to improve efficiency in that sector, namely by reducing the spending of public financial resources. It was irrelevant, the Court added, whether the purpose pursued by the regressive legislation was more or less worthy of protection than that pursued by the directive: it sufficed that it was different.[111]

Second, concerning the assumption that national legislation submitted to a non-regression clause must have an overall effect on the general level of protection, the relevant cases are *Angelidaki* and *Sorge.* In the *Angelidaki* judgment – containing the most extensive judicial interpretation of non-regression clauses – the Court stated that the reduction of protection regarding fixed-term workers in the Greek public sector, introduced by a law of 2004, could not in principle be considered contrary to the non-regression clause because it could not be deemed to lower the 'general level' of protection: first, because that legislation only related to a certain category of workers (i.e. public employees); and, second, because the reduction of the level of protection in one aspect of the fixed-term work legislation was counterbalanced by improvement in the level of protection as far as other aspects of that regulation were concerned.[112] In the *Sorge* case, which also referred to fixed-term work in Italian postal service, the violation of the non-regression clause was excluded by stressing that the modification *in pejus* of previous national legislation introduced in 2001 did not affect all fixed-term workers but only those which had concluded a contract to replace another employee:

> In so far as the latter workers do not represent a significant proportion of workers employed for a fixed term in the Member State concerned, which it is for the national

[110] ECJ 2009, C-378/07 to C-380/07 (*Angelidaki*), §126.
[111] ECJ 2010, C-20/10 (*Vino*), §§41–45.
[112] See ECJ 2009, C-378/07 to C-380/07 (*Angelidaki*), §§108–146.

court to ascertain, the reduction in the protection afforded to that limited category of workers is not, in itself, likely to have an effect overall on the level of protection applicable under the domestic legal order'.[113]

As has been duly commented, building a legal concept (the non-regression clause) upon sheer quantitative factors (the numbers of workers affected) is far from satisfactory,[114] up to the point that it has induced some authors to qualify the non-regression clause in the atypical work directives as nothing more than a 'fig leaf'.[115]

4.3.6. SANCTIONS AND REMEDIES: A NEVER-ENDING STORY?

Since the rise of the national labour law systems in the twentieth century, it is part of a European social law tradition that the typical remedy provided by legislation in the case of unlawful fixed-term contracts is constituted by the judicial requalification of such contracts into an open-ended employment relationship. The full achievement of such an outcome is, however, sometimes precluded by an opposing principle, also enshrined into the legal tradition of a number of Member States (Spain, Greece, Italy, France; Germany and Belgium in some respect), by virtue of which permanent access to public employment is made dependent on public competition. When combined, these two premises generate a situation, quite common in several Member States, according to which in the private sector unlawful fixed-term contracts are judicially transformed into contracts of indefinite duration, but the same result does not occur in public employment, where in the absence of more effective remedies affecting the transformation of the contract, usually only monetary compensation is recognised.

This heritage in several national legal systems has been severely challenged by the adoption of the EU regulation of fixed-term contracts. Even if Directive 1999/70/EC, like the Part-time Work Directive and, unlike the Temporary Work Directive, does not contain any clear rule about the kind of remedy to be applied in the case of an unlawful series of contracts, it is, however, undoubted that the principle of effective judicial protection as built by the Court over the years,[116] and now also recognised by the Treaty on European Union,[117] obliges Member States to adapt their own procedural legal system to provide remedies which must be sufficient to ensure effective legal protection in the fields covered by Union law.

---

113 ECJ 2010, C-98/09 (*Sorge*), §44.
114 Corazza (2011).
115 Peers (2010).
116 See Malmberg (2003).
117 Article 19(1).

The case-law analysis developed in the previous paragraphs has already made clear that most of the claims brought to the Court of Justice with regard to Directive 1999/70/EC are indeed 'public employment' cases, and that they refer in particular to countries such as Spain, Greece and Italy where the remedy consisting in requalifying the unlawful fixed-term contracts into an open-ended employment relationship is precluded by the principle of access to public employment through a public contest. This explains why all the Court's decisions relating to sanctions and remedies of the Fixed-term Work Directive have been dictated on the occasion of preliminary procedures raised by Spanish, Italian and Greek jurisdictions.

Within such a rich, long-lasting and still open judicial saga, it is possible to point out two basic questions. The first is whether or not judicial requalification of unlawful fixed-term contracts into contracts of indefinite duration is the only possible way to give full effectiveness to the rights provided for by the directive. The second, which presupposes that the previous question is answered in the negative, relates to the kind and the measure of the alternative remedies which Member states should provide in case no requalification of the contract applies.

Concerning the first question, being aware of the fact that remedies for unlawful fixed-term contracts have been quite diverse across the different Member States,[118] the Court decided not to give a decisive value to the (quite soft) Agreement clause providing that 'Member States after consultation with the social partners and/or the social partners shall, where appropriate, determine under what conditions fixed-term employment contracts or relationships shall be deemed to be contracts or relationships of indefinite duration'.[119] To the contrary, since the first occasions when it has had to deal with this issue the Court has made clear that the Agreement does not impose a general obligation to provide for the conversion of unlawful fixed-term contracts into contracts of indefinite duration.[120] On the contrary, the 'margin of discretion' which the directive leaves to Member States has induced the Court to state that 'clause 5 of the framework agreement does not preclude, as such, a Member State from treating misuse of successive fixed-term employment contracts or relationships differently according to whether those contracts or relationships were entered into with a private-sector or public-sector employer',[121] thus admitting that in certain cases monetary compensation could be an adequate sanction.

On other occasions, the Court has, however, clarified that if a Member State decides that the remedy for abuse of successive fixed-term contracts should

118 See European Commission (2006), *Report on the implementation of the Council Directive 1999/70/EC*, SEC(2006)1074 final.

119 Clause 5(2)(b).

120 ECJ 2006, C-212/04 (*Adeneler*), §91.

121 ECJ 2006, C-53/04 (*Marrosu and Sardino*), §§47–48. The same principle has been then applied in ECJ 2006, C-180/04 (*Vassallo*), §33; ECJ 2008, C-364/07 (*Vassilakis*), §§121–122; ECJ 2010, C-3/10 (*Affatato*), §§38–40.

be a requalification of these contracts into a contract of indefinite duration, such remedy must be 'real and effective'. In another Spanish case, the Court was confronted with quite peculiar legislation providing that the remedy for abusive fixed-term contracts might be, in some cases, their transformation into a somewhat contradictory 'non-permanent contract of indefinite duration' (*Relación laboral por tiempo indefinido no fijo*), i.e. an open-ended contract which can, however, be terminated unilaterally by the employer following budgetary consideration and/or the filling of the same post through a public competition. On that occasion the Court stated that such transformation cannot be considered a real and effective remedy, since the possibility for the employer to freely and unilaterally terminate an indefinite contract puts the worker in a situation basically identical to the one of a fixed-term worker.[122] In other terms, though apparently providing a remedy, the Spanish legislation at stake did not provide one. As confirmed in a subsequent case, the Spanish 'remedy' consisting in the conclusion of a 'non-permanent contract of indefinite duration' cannot be considered an effective measure to 'prevent and, where appropriate, penalise the misuse of successive fixed-term employment contracts'[123] concluded with a public administration.

Once it has been assumed that the requalification into an indefinite duration contract cannot be considered the sole and only possible remedy in the case of misuse of successive fixed-term contracts, the second question remains: what alternative sanctions could a Member State impose in order to make the directive fully effective?

By applying the general EU principle of effective judicial protection, the Court has reiterated in several occasions that, without prejudice to their national procedural autonomy, Member States must adopt sanctions 'that are not only proportionate, but also sufficiently effective and a sufficient deterrent to ensure that the measures taken pursuant to the framework agreement are fully effective'.[124] Such measures should be coherent with the well-known principles of equivalence and effectiveness, and should therefore be not less favourable than those governing similar domestic situations, or be framed so as to render impossible in practice or excessively difficult the exercise of rights conferred by EU law.[125] Those assumptions have been used in a series of cases to evaluate whether monetary compensation provided in the case of unlawful fixed-term contracts did in fact comply with the principles of equivalence and effectiveness. In the majority of cases, this has happened with regard to procedures raised by

---

122 ECJ 2014, C-86/14 (*Medialdea*), §50.

123 ECJ 2016, C-184/15 (*Martínez Andrés*), §47.

124 According to the settled case law of the Court, repeated from ECJ 2006, C-212/04 (*Adeneler*), §94 to ECJ 2016, C-184/15 (*Martínez Andrés*), §36 ff.

125 On the general principles of effective judicial protection of EU law, see Lenaerts, Maselis & Gutman (2014).

Italian judges. However, in the decade separating the first pronouncement from the last preliminary procedure,[126] the dialogue between the Court of Justice and the Italian Corte di Cassazione has not yet found a final accommodation.

After the 'invitation', dating back to 2006,[127] to the national authorities to find – in the absence of requalification to indefinite duration contracts – other equivalent (monetary) sanctions capable to adequately penalise the misuse of successive fixed-term employment contracts, Italian judges began to award various and heterogeneous levels of compensation, varying from six months of salary, to 15 months of salary, to the recognition of monetary sums corresponding to the damage suffered by fixed-term workers for the loss of an open-ended employment contract. Such a fragmented scenario was brought to the attention of the Court in the *Papalia* case, where the question related to the limits and conditions the Corte di Cassazione required for the fixed-term worker to obtain compensation. According to the Corte di Cassazione, before obtaining compensation workers must prove the damage they suffered; something which in most cases might be very difficult to achieve, since the worker has to prove the loss of better employment opportunities as a direct consequence of having been employed under an unlawful fixed-term contract. Such procedural obstacles have been evaluated by the Court of Justice in the light of the general principle of effectiveness, whose concrete application to the fixed-term work issues has induced the Court to declare that the 1999/70/EC Directive precludes national remedial measures which, in the event of misuse by a public employer of successive fixed-term contracts, only recognise the right of the worker to obtain compensation for damages 'where the right to that compensation is subject to the obligation on that worker to prove that he was forced to forego better work opportunities, although the effect of that obligation is to render impossible in practice or excessively difficult the exercise by that worker of rights conferred by EU law'.[128]

The last episode of the 'effective remedy' saga is related to the way that the Grand Chamber of the Italian Corte di Cassazione has reacted to the *Papalia* judgment.

By accepting the conclusions of the CJEU in *Papalia*, the Italian Corte di Cassazione admitted in 2016 that compensation for an unlawful fixed-term contract cannot be entirely conditioned by the burden for the worker to prove the actual damage suffered, consequently affirming that a lump sum amounting from 2.5 to 12 monthly salary payments is to be recognised to the worker without any probationary limit being imposed. According to the remitting judge in the *Santoro* case, however, this cannot yet be considered as an adequate

[126] From ECJ 2006, C-53/04 (*Marrosu and Sardino*) to ECJ 2018, C-496/16 (*Santoro*).

[127] ECJ 2006, C-53/04 (*Marrosu and Sardino*).

[128] ECJ 2013, C-50/13 (*Papalia*), §34.

and decisive answer to the long-lasting question related to the identification of effective alternative remedies since such a lump sum is too low, and it cannot be considered as a real deterrent for the misuse of fixed-term work by public administrations. Although the Advocate-General admitted that putting a ceiling to the monetary compensation could end up in insufficient penalisation of long-lasting abuses,[129] the Court's decision was indeed quite 'timid'. It merely reflected what in the last years has become a recurring argument: while reaffirming the principle of effectiveness, the Court has left to the national court the task to verify whether domestic remedies are framed so as to comply with it.

4.4. THE DIRECTIVE ON TEMPORARY AGENCY WORK

Temporary agency work is particularly atypical: not only because workers' contracts are often 'non-standard', but also because work relations imply three parties: a temporary work agency, a 'user' company and a (temporary agency) worker. According to Directive 2008/104/EC,[130] temporary work concerns 'workers with a contract of employment or employment relationship with a temporary-work agency who are assigned to user undertakings to work temporarily under their supervision and direction'.[131]

What made the adoption of the directive particularly difficult is that there were 'considerable differences in the use of temporary agency work and in the legal situation, status and working conditions of temporary agency workers within the European Union'.[132] In France, for instance, the activity of temporary work agencies was strictly regulated (and had been since 1972), and the same went for the use of temporary work and for the working conditions of temporary workers. In the Netherlands, from 1970 temporary work agencies had needed a special licence, until the 1990s when the licence obligation was banned.[133] In Germany the activity of temporary work agencies was also regulated, in 1972, in line with the French and Dutch regulations, but, as in the Netherlands, the law had become considerably less restrictive in recent times. When compared

129 The 'lack of proportion between the potential extent of the abuse, which may have had consequences over a number of years, and the lump sum compensation, which cannot exceed twelve monthly salary payments, is likely to weaken the deterrent effect of the penalties', Opinion of the Advocate General Szpunar in ECJ 2018, C-496/16 (*Santoro*).

130 Directive 2008/104/EC (Temporary Agency Work). The directive had to be implemented by 05.12.2011.

131 Article 1(1) Directive 2008/104/EC.

132 Recital 10 of Directive 2008/104/EC. For a comparative approach, see Sartori (2016) and the literature mentioned.

133 In 1965, Dutch law on Temporary Work was regulated in an Act (TAW Act). Temporary work agencies need a special licence since 1970. In the 1990s the licence obligation was banned. Some equal treatment provisions were adopted in a new legislation. In 1998 and 1999 two new acts were adopted, regulating the TAW relationship.

to these continental forms of regulation, the UK system lies at a distance: although the activity of temporary work agencies was also regulated in the 1970s (Employment Agencies Act 1973), no authorisation is required for temporary work agencies (except in certain sectors, since 2004) and the law has never guaranteed extensive protection to temporary agency workers. These differences both justified the competence of the European Union (in order 'to establish a harmonised Community-level framework for protection for temporary agency workers'[134]) and limited the scope of EU regulation (it imposed compromises, and resulted in a large margin of discretion being left to Member States).

4.4.1. PERSONAL SCOPE: WORKERS PROTECTED UNDER DIRECTIVE 2008/104/EC

As the other directives on atypical work, Directive 2008/104/EC formally relies on national legislations to define the notion of the employment contract or employment relationship. Article 3(1)(a) of Directive 2008/104/EC provides that 'worker' means 'any person who, in the Member State concerned, is protected as a worker under national employment law'. National law is supposed to define the notions of 'contract of employment, employment relationship or worker'.[135] However, the text of Directive 2008/104/EC (Article 3(2)) explicitly prohibits national law from excluding from the scope of the directive workers, contracts of employment or employment relationships 'solely because they relate to part-time workers, fixed-term contract workers or persons with a contract of employment or employment relationship with a temporary-work agency'.

Thus, a large margin of discretion, if not full discretion, seems to be granted to Member States regarding the notion of worker. This should have prevented the emergence of an autonomous definition, for European purposes. However, the Court of Justice has not strictly followed this line in the domain of atypical work (and not only for temporary agency workers). Rather, it has made clear that the scope of application of all directives relative to atypical work, which depends on the definition of employment contracts or relationships, cannot be totally left to the Member States. In the domain of temporary work, in particular, the Court of Justice decided that to limit the concept of 'worker' to persons falling within the scope of that concept under national law, and in particular, to those who have a contract of employment with the temporary-work agency, would jeopardise the attainment of the objectives of the directive. According to the Court, such a restrictive approach would undermine the effectiveness of the directive by

134 Recital 23 of Directive 2008/104/EC.

135 Article 3(2).

'inordinately and unjustifiably' limiting its scope of application.[136] The Court considered that 'neither the legal characterization, under national law, of the relationship between the person in question and the temporary work agency, nor the nature of their legal relationships, nor the form of that relationship' were decisive for the purposes of characterising that person as a 'worker'.[137] Thus, a nurse, who worked for an association of which she was a member (the German Red Cross), and who did not have the status of worker under national law, since she did not have a contract of employment with the association, could not be excluded from the concept of 'worker'.[138] According to the Court, that conclusion cannot be called into question by the fact that, under Article 3(2) of directive 2008/104/EC, the directive is to be 'without prejudice to national law as regards the definition of worker'. That provision only means that EU legislation intends to preserve the power of the Member States to determine the persons falling within the scope of the concept of 'worker' under national law and who must be protected under their domestic legislation.[139] Thus, Article 3(2) of the directive is not considered a waiver on the part of the EU legislature of its power to determine the scope of that concept for the purposes of Directive 2008/104/EC. According to the Court, the EU legislature does not leave it to the Member States to define that concept of worker unilaterally. On the contrary, it specified the contours of the notion of worker in Article 3(1)(a), and the definition of 'temporary agency worker' in Article 3(1)(c) of the directive.[140] According to Article 3(1)(a), the concept of 'worker' covers any person who carries out work and who is protected on that basis in the Member State concerned: two criteria which do not remain within the power of national law.[141] The solution reached by the Court is a compromise: EU law has (according to the letter of the directive) no exclusive competence to define the notion of worker but, in order to ensure the effectiveness of the directive, national authorities (courts, in particular) are required to take into account a series of principles and criteria to decide on the existence of a work relationship.

However, the scope of Directive 2008/104/EC is limited by the definition of temporary agency worker as a 'worker with a contract of employment or an employment relationship with a temporary-work agency with a view to being assigned to a user undertaking to work temporarily under its supervision and direction'.[142] As a result, in some Member States, like the UK, where the law does not prohibit open-ended assignments of workers to user

136 ECJ 2016, C-216/15 (*Betriebsrat der Ruhrlandklinik*).
137 Ibid., §29.
138 Ibid.
139 Ibid., §31.
140 Ibid., §32.
141 Ibid., §§25–43.
142 Article 1(1).

undertakings, workers may, for that reason, fall outside the field of application of the directive.[143] In France, in comparison, assignments can only be for a limited period, and, as a result, they are always covered by the directive in this respect.

4.4.2. A WEAK EQUAL TREATMENT RULE

According to Article 5(1) of Directive 2008/104/EC, the principle of equal treatment only applies to 'basic working and employment conditions'. The basic conditions are defined as 'working and employment conditions laid down by legislation, regulations, administrative provisions, collective agreements and/or other binding general provisions in force in the user undertaking relating to: the duration of working time, overtime, breaks, rest periods, night work, holidays and public holidays and pay'.[144] They also include 'protection of pregnant women and nursing mothers and protection of children and young people',[145] and equal treatment for men and women and any action to combat any discrimination based on sex, race or ethnic origin, religion, beliefs, disabilities, age or sexual orientation.[146] All in all, the scope of equal treatment is indeed limited, an option which is even more striking when compared to the larger scope of the principle of equal treatment in the two other directives on atypical work. However, in contrast to equal treatment rules in the two other directives on atypical work, the directive does not explicitly allow justification of differences based on 'objective grounds'. Thus, the limited scope of application of the equal treatment rule is counterbalanced by a stricter obligation to guarantee equal treatment (since departure from the equality principle should only be possible if situations are not comparable, see below).

Article 6(4) of the directive also requires access to other benefits that an employer offers to workers employed directly by the undertaking under the same conditions, unless the difference in treatment is justified by objective reasons. This will cover amenities or collective facilities in the user undertaking, in particular any staff canteen, child-care facilities and transport services. It has to be noted that this provision differs from Article 5(1) since it explicitly includes the possibility of justifying differences based on objective reasons. Although it is not easy to interpret the difference between these two provisions, the inclusion of possible justification of different treatment by objective reasons in Article 6(4) may be considered to be an indication that Article 5(1) does not implicitly include this possibility. But even if departure from equal treatment for

143 For an example, see UK judgment in *Moran v. Ideal Cleaning Services Ltd* (2014) 2 *CMLR* 37, (2014) IRLR 172 (EAT) cited by Kountouris (2016), p. 255.

144 Article 3(1)(i) and (ii).

145 Article 5(1)(a).

146 Article 5 (1)(b).

objective reasons is not allowed when basic working conditions are concerned, the directive allows, nonetheless, important derogations.

First, Member States, in consultation with social partners, can exclude temporary agency workers who are permanently employed by the agency and who receive remuneration between assignments from the benefit of the equal treatment principle (in respect of pay).[147] During the period between assignments, the directive does not regulate temporary workers' remuneration: depending on national laws, this can be very limited. As a result, this derogation can easily be exploited to exclude workers from the most important source of protection granted by the directive (the equal treatment rule), which can also be seen as a means to avoid abuses. This option is all the more detrimental to workers when national law offers little protection in the case of unilateral termination of open-ended employment contracts by employers, including temporary-work agencies. When termination of standard employment contracts is made very easy for employers (for instance, when no just cause is required, which is the case in the UK and Ireland, where there is a qualifying period of continuous service, e.g. two years in the UK and 12 months in Ireland, required before unfair dismissal can be claimed), temporary-work agencies have no problem hiring 'permanent' workers, who will not benefit from the equal treatment rule, but can be dismissed after a few assignments, or even after the first one. In the UK, the situation worsened for temporary workers when access to the employment tribunal became more expensive in 2013.

In addition, the directive also allows Member States, after consulting social partners, to give them the option of concluding collective agreements which, while respecting 'the overall protection of temporary agency workers', establish arrangements concerning the working and employment conditions of temporary agency workers which may not respect the equal treatment principle of Article 5(1).[148] When national law does not include a system for declaring collective agreements universally applicable or for extending their provisions to all similar undertakings in a certain sector or geographical area, Member States are also allowed, after consulting the social partners at national level and on the basis of an agreement concluded by them, to establish arrangements concerning the basic working and employment conditions which derogate from the principle of equal treatment, provided that 'an adequate level of protection is provided for temporary agency workers'.[149] Such arrangements may include a qualifying period for equal treatment.[150] In particular, the provisions allowing derogation through specific arrangements make it possible, if social partners agree, to exclude some agency workers – casual workers, in particular – from

---

147 Article 5(2).
148 Article 5(3).
149 Article 5(4).
150 Ibid.

the benefit of equal treatment. This option could have important consequences in the 'new economy', where very short contracts for very limited remuneration tend to develop. To be sure, the directive makes it clear that these arrangements must be in conformity with Community legislation and must be sufficiently precise and accessible to allow the sectors and firms concerned to identify and comply with their obligations. But this does seem neither very precise, nor very protective.

In France, this possibility to derogate from the equal treatment rule was not used. Although this may only seem to respect the non-regression provision of the directive (Article 9(2)), the very flexible conception of non-regression in the case law of the Court of Justice would probably not oppose an evolution of French law in this field. In contrast, in Germany social partners were allowed to negotiate derogations from the equal treatment rule. This possibility initially led in certain sectors to very low wages for temporary workers. Consequently, a statute was adopted in 2011 granting temporary workers a minimum wage (if agreed on by social partners and included in a collective agreement, the minimum wage had to be extended by the minister of labour to temporary workers). In the Netherlands, similarly, since 1999 equal treatment applies unless temporary workers are covered by a collective agreement determining the remuneration of temporary workers. If temporary workers are not covered by a specific agreement, they benefit from the collective agreement binding at the user company, which can also include derogations from the equal treatment rule. However, just as in Germany, the law has evolved to limit the wage gap: a collective agreement concluded in 2012 (which does not cover all temporary workers, but still more than 60% of them) requires equal remunerations with permanent workers of the user undertaking; from 2015 this applies from the first day of the assignment (in addition to ensuring a gradual protection of temporary workers).

In the UK, a statute adopted in 2010 granted temporary workers equal treatment with comparable 'permanent' workers of the user. The implementation of EU law increased the protection of temporary workers in this respect. However, equal treatment only applies after a 'qualifying period' of 12 weeks (in the same position, at the same company). Although this is allowed by Article 5(4) of the directive, such a solution excludes a large proportion of temporary workers.

4.4.3. PROTECTION AGAINST ABUSES AND THE APPLICATION OF FREE PROVISION OF SERVICES TO TEMPORARY AGENCY WORK

Abuse of temporary work is not central to Directive 2008/104/EC, which is an important difference from the framework agreement on fixed-term contracts

(Directive 1999/70/EC). Article 5(5) of Directive 2008/104/EC reads as follows: 'Member States shall take appropriate measures, in accordance with national law and/or practice, with a view to preventing misuse in the application of this Article and, in particular, to preventing successive assignments designed to circumvent the provisions of this Directive'. This provision is vague, and cannot be considered unconditional: it would be hard to argue that it creates, as Clause 5 of the Framework Agreement on Fixed-term Work does, clear obligations on Member States and employers.

The attempt to extend the provisions against abuses of Directive 1999/70/EC (Framework Agreement on Fixed-term Work) to temporary agency work failed. When it was argued, in a case related to the Framework Agreement,[151] that the Agreement could apply to temporary agency workers, on the basis of an extensive interpretation of its personal scope of application, the Court disagreed with this argument, considering that according to Clause 3 of the Agreement,[152] to which the Court referred explicitly: 'it is clear that the exclusion in the preamble of temporary agency work is expressly laid down in Clause 3(1) of the Framework Agreement, under which only the employment relationship Directive 1999/70/EC concluded "directly" with the employer comes within the scope of that framework agreement'.[153]

However, Directive 2008/104/EC does not bar, but rather encourages national laws, through its Article 5(5), to include measures against abusive use of temporary work. However, the directive is not without ambiguity in this respect. Indeed, Article 4(1) and (2) require Member States to 'review any restrictions or prohibitions on the use of temporary agency work' by 5 December 2011. Its aim is to verify whether they were justified 'on the grounds of general interest relating in particular to the protection of temporary agency workers, the requirements of health and safety at work or the need to ensure that the labour market functions properly and abuses are prevented'. Restrictions imposed on the use of temporary agency work differ from Member State to Member State. In more liberalised countries, such as the Netherlands and the UK, few restrictions apply. In other countries, strict conditions continue to apply, namely, on the reasons for 'hiring' temporary agency workers, on the duration of employment at the user firm, or on the proportion of temporary workers at the user firm. In a number of Member States, some limitations have been lifted in recent years.[154] In others, limitations have been imposed by collective agreements, usually on sectoral level. This practice was contested in the *AKT* case.[155] In that

151 ECJ 2013, C-290/12 (*Della Rocca*).

152 Clause 3(1) of the Agreement on Fixed-term Employment.

153 Cf. ECJ 2013, C-290/12 (*Della Rocca*), §§36–40. The Court explicitly refers to §4 of the Preamble of the Framework Agreement.

154 Cf. Sartori (2016), pp. 117–123.

155 ECJ 2015, C-533/13 (*AKT*).

case, Articles 4 and 5 of Directive 2008/104/EC were invoked to challenge a collective agreement limiting the possibility of making use of temporary agency workers. In its decision, the Court of Justice considered that these provisions do not prevent collective agreements from fixing conditions to avoid 'abuses'. This solution is in line with the letter of Article 4(1) of the directive, which not only requires that restrictions on the use of temporary agency work are justified, but also states that national law aiming at preventing abuses should not be called into question on the basis of the directive.

The solution in the *AKT* case seems to leave it to Member States to design, according to their general interest, the rules applying to the use of temporary agency work. However, the Advocate-General raised a question as to the compatibility of this practice with European competition law and free provision of services. He also mentioned that such a restriction to temporary work could be considered an obstacle to free provision of services even when it involves persons within the same Member State.[156] In his opinion, such a clause 'is manifestly capable of producing cross-border effects relevant for the purposes of Article 56 TFEU', in particular, since it could impede the company's access to services provided by temporary work undertakings established in other Member States. If followed by the Court of Justice, this reasoning could weaken national regulations restricting the use of temporary work. A case decided in 2011 pointed to this consequence. In that case, the Court considered that the Belgian legislation requiring that temporary work agencies limit their activity exclusively to the posting of workers, and be incorporated under a particular legal form, violated Article 56 TFEU.[157] In that particular case, no reason was brought forward by the Belgian government to justify the restriction to free provision of services. In other instances, national regulations or collective agreements could probably bring forward legitimate objectives of general interest. The major difficulty, as ever, would be for these regulations to pass the proportionality test, which outcome is always uncertain.

4.4.4. IDENTIFYING THE EMPLOYER AND EMPLOYER'S LIABILITY IN TEMPORARY AGENCY WORK

Although one of the major achievements of the directive is the recognition of temporary-work agencies as employers,[158] the distribution of responsibilities between the temporary-work agency and the 'user undertaking',[159] except for health and safety (regulated by Directive 91/383/EEC), remains uncertain,

156 Ibid. AG Szpunar in 2015, C-533/13 (*AKT*), §§105 and 145/146.
157 ECJ 2011, C-397/10 (*Commission v. Belgium*).
158 Article 2.
159 Defined in Article 3(1)(d).

under Directive 2008/104/EC. As a result, variations from State to State are barely limited, let alone excluded.

Regarding liability for the protection of workers' health and safety, Directive 91/383/EEC concerning safety and health at work of temporary workers, which explicitly applies to 'temporary employment relationships between a temporary employment business which is the employer and the worker',[160] includes provisions on the respective responsibilities of the agency and the user: in addition to the responsibility of the agency that may result from national legislation, the user undertaking is, under the directive, responsible during the assignment for the conditions governing the performance of the work.[161]

Beyond health and safety, the recognition at the EU level of a rule under which the agency and the user are jointly responsible for labour and employment law rules applying to temporary agency workers, would be a more favourable solution for workers.[162]

4.5. 'OTHER' FLEXIBLE ARRANGEMENTS

The decline of standard employment contracts around the world has been considered the cause and effect of major transformations in labour law, and a very serious threat to labour market regulation calling in question the protection of workers.[163] Unstable employment relationships have increased, undoubtedly, and they undermine the regulatory regimes that seek to regulate labour markets and employment relationships in the last decades.

As a result, regulating 'atypical employment', also called 'flexible working arrangements',[164] 'non-standard', contingent or 'precarious' contracts has become essential to ensure workers' protection. The need for regulation appeared even more necessary with recent evolutions, including 'digitalisation' of economic activities. But atypical employment and its regulation have a long history, well-illustrated by the development of EU legislation.[165] Among the many different types of 'unstable' relationships, only some 'atypical' contracts were submitted to EU legislation, as this Chapter illustrates: part-time work, fixed-term work and temporary agency work.

---

160 Directive of 25 June 1991 (safety and health at work of workers with a fixed-duration employment relationship or a temporary employment relationship), Article 1(2).

161 Article 7.

162 Chacartegui (2013), p. 213.

163 Stone and Arthurs (2013), p. 1.

164 Council Resolution of 22 February 1999 on the 1999 Employment Guidelines.

165 See above. For a recent analysis of the three instruments, see in particular: Kountouris (2016), pp. 246–266.

This segmented legislation could well be out of date in a new era of 'flexibilisation' of employment relations, encouraged by 'digitalisation'. The increase of very short work contracts, and/or employment for very few hours, the development of self-employment and the 'flexibilisation' of standard employment contracts themselves (through various versions of 'employment at will') have made European regulation of atypical work largely obsolescent. No EU instrument addresses directly the more and more frequent combination of self-employment, very short period of work, and low remuneration, and the consequences these have on the social security of these 'workers'. As a result, it is mostly for national laws and courts to decide, in labour relation conflicts, whether the contracts involved are employment contracts submitted to labour law.

Until recently, it was difficult to imagine that new social policies protecting precarious workers would be envisaged. Rather, flexible contracts were given impetus in the framework of the Economic and Monetary Union. To give just one example, countries facing bailouts were required to adopt 'measures to amend their part-time and temporary work regulation, in order to ensure more flexible labour market'.[166] This pressure towards more flexibilisation is difficult to reconcile with the direction previously taken by the case law of the Court of Justice in the field of atypical work: extensive interpretation of the directives in favour of worker protection.

In recent times, the Court has sometimes shifted towards a more restrictive interpretation of the Framework Agreement on Fixed-term Work.[167] Whether the context of the financial crisis and consecutive labour law reforms in Member States explain these decisions is difficult to say. Continuing on a rather restrictive line, in the *Poclava* case,[168] the Court refused to adopt a more radically inclusive approach concerning the field of application of atypical work directives that would have taken into account new forms of flexibilisations of work relations.

The recent initiative of the Commission that led to the proclamation, by the Commission, the Council and the Parliament of a 'European Pillar of Social Rights' may have opened a new era.[169] Within the framework of the Pillar of Social Rights, the Commission launched, namely, a revision of the 'written statement Directive'[170] in order to widen its personal scope of application and better protect all categories of workers, through information at the beginning

---

166 See e.g. in the case of Greece: European Commission, *The Economic Adjustment Program for Greece*, May 2010, Occasional Papers 61, p. 22.

167 ECJ 2012, C-586/10 (*Kücük*) and ECJ 2014, C-190/13 (*Márquez Samohano*) with more recent cases, reconnecting with the main thread of the case law: ECJ 2016, C-184/15 (*Martínez Andrés*) and ECJ 2016, C-16/15 (*Perez Lopez*).

168 ECJ 2015, C-117/14 (*Poclava*), by denying its jurisdiction on the claim lodged.

169 For the European Pillar of Social Rights, see also Chapter 1.

170 Directive 91/533/EEC (Information of Workers), p. 32.

of the work relationship (and not within two months as the directive currently requires). The proposal was adopted by the Council on 13 June, 2019. It indicates that the personal scope of the directive should be in line with the parameters set out by the Court of Justice to identify an employment relationship:[171] as a result, the directive could apply to every type of person performing services for and under the direction of another person in return for remuneration, including domestic workers, temporary agency workers, on-demand workers, intermittent workers, voucher-based workers and platform workers. The new directive on 'transparent and predictable working conditions' also removes of the exclusion of persons working less than eight hours a week or whose employment relationship lasts less than one month or is of a casual and/or specific nature, in view of the growth in short contracts and short working hours provisions (this exclusion was based on Article 1(2) of Directive 91/533): the new text applies to all individuals working more than 3 hours per week over four weeks (i.e. over 12 hours per month).[172]

In addition to regulating information for workers, substantial rights were added. New minimum rights aimed at reducing precariousness in employment were created, among which: a right to predictability of work (Article 10), a right to request another form of employment and receive a reply in writing (Article 12), and a right to a maximum duration of probation period (Article 8), a right to parallel employment (Article 9). The list, obviously, is not long, but considering the strong opposition of employers' organisations, that was probably the only option that the Commission found realistic. Last, but not least, the new directive on 'transparent and predictable working conditions' includes provisions to avoid abuses of 'on-demand' contracts, which are very similar to the provisions on abuses of fixed-term contracts (see above). Member states are required, when they allow 'on-demand' contracts, to take measures to prevent abuses: they can choose to introduce either 'limitations to the use and duration of on-demand or similar employment contracts' or 'rebuttable presumption of the existence of an employment contract with a minimum amount of paid hours based on the average hours worked during a given period' or 'other equivalent measures that ensure effective prevention of abusive practices' (Article 11).

Other legislative innovations could take place in the framework of the European Pillar of social rights. A right to conversion into more secure contracts after a succession of fixed-term contracts could be created,[173] portability of precarious workers' rights could be generalised or at least extended;[174]

[171] Article 1(2).

[172] Article 1(3).

[173] On this solution, and the requirement that it extends to public sector employees, see ECJ 2016, C-184/15 (*Martínez Andrés*) and ECJ 2016, C-16/15 (*Perez Lopez*).

[174] On portability, albeit for one specific right only, see ECJ 2015, C-65/14 (*Rosselle*).

compensation for precarious work by a special allowance to be paid upon termination of the contract could be envisaged. The case law on the notion of worker and employment contract could be clarified and rationalised through codification. To achieve this objective, a new 'horizontal' Directive specifically addressing and regulating the personal scope of application of the three directives could be adopted.[175]

Mobilising the Charter of fundamental rights is also a possible path for strengthening the rights of precarious workers. To be sure, it recently became clear that the Charter was a slippery slope for social policies, when it serves, on the basis of the right to free enterprise, to call in question national labour law.[176] However, the force recently given to the right to free enterprise does not mean that social rights in the Charter cannot be granted legal force by courts.[177] In particular, the right to fair and just working conditions (Article 31) or to equal treatment and non-discrimination (Articles 20 and 21) can serve the extension of the scope of application of the directives on atypical work.[178] They could, in particular, allow the inclusion of 'casual work' (mini jobs or zero hours contracts) in the scope of application of the agreement on part-time work, possibly through the annulment of the explicit clause excluding their protection.[179] Although the effect of this undefined exclusion was limited by the Court of Justice,[180] it seems, indeed, particularly inappropriate in the context of extreme unstable forms of employment that the new economy creates. To deal with other flexible contracts, not explicitly included in the scope of application of the directives on atypical work, an extensive interpretation of the contracts concerned could also be derived from the Charter (Article 31). Article 30 (right to protection against unjustified dismissal) could also be referred to, in cases in which flexibility is derived from 'at will' termination,[181] but that would require the Court to consider more extensively the field of application of EU law (and therefore, of the Charter of fundamental rights).

175 On this idea, see Kountouris (2016), p. 265.

176 Cf. namely ECJ 2016, C-201/15 (*Aget Iraklis*).

177 Direct effect of Article 31 of the Charter was recognised in a series of recent cases: ECJ 2018, C-684/16 and C-569/16 (*Max Planck*; *Bauer & Willmeroth*).

178 On equal treatment: see ECJ 2010, C-232/09 (*Danosa*).

179 Under Clause 2(2) of the agreement on part-time work, 'Member States, after consultation with the social partners in accordance with national law, collective agreements or practice, and/or the social partners at the appropriate level in conformity with national industrial relations practice may, for objective reasons, exclude wholly or partly from the terms of this Agreement part-time workers who work on a casual basis'.

180 ECJ 2004, C-313/02 (*Wippel*).

181 ECJ 2015, C-117/14 (*Poclava*).

CHAPTER 5

COLLECTIVE BARGAINING IN EU LAW

Teun JASPERS*

* With the collaboration of Eva Kocher, Europa-Universität Viadrina, Frankfurt (Oder).

5.1. INTRODUCTION

Since the end of the nineteenth century collective bargaining by social partners on labour issues has become common in Europe.[1] It started at the national level with the advent of trade unions and employers' organisations. The system of collective bargaining has developed separately within each country, with the result that it actually differs from country to country. By consequence it has taken different forms and is institutionalised in various ways. History, differing social and economic developments, and institutional structures and culture play an important role. The effects can be seen in particular when collective bargaining takes place at a multinational or transnational level. In addition, collective bargaining is subject to different legal regulations on aspects such as the bargaining process, who takes part in the collective bargaining process, and the binding effects of collective agreements. The law on this differs from country to country.[2] Lastly, institutional systems also vary in the forms and degree to which social partners are involved in public policy making. In some countries there is regular and institutionalised participation,[3] whereas in

1 This is so not only in Europe: it has become a generally recognised right and was laid down in the Constitution of the International Labour Organization in 1919. Cf. Servais (2009), p. 21 ff.
2 Cf. Glassner (2012), pp. 84–99; also Jaspers (2012b), pp. 246–52; and Rodríguez (2011).
3 In Europe examples are Belgium, the Netherlands, Austria and Slovenia.

others such participation is barely developed or practised.[4] In addition to the more traditional employees' representative organisations, the trade unions, in some countries another employees' representing body, the works council, takes part in a kind of collective bargaining.[5]

At transnational European level the social dialogue was introduced in the middle of the 1980s.[6] Social partners themselves developed forms of social dialogue. 'Val Duchesse' is a boundary stone. In the castle of Val Duchesse, Delors, the then president of the European Commission, initiated the involvement of social partners at the EU level.[7] It was the go-ahead for a development that granted social partners an increasingly important role with regard to the rules and regulations in the social sphere. In the European Union the role of the social partners was constitutionalised in the Single European Act.[8] Ever since, consultation of the social partners has been a regular feature of the legislative process when the European Commission considers regulatory measures in the social sphere. By being able to conclude (collective) agreements at their own initiative, the role of the social partners has become even more relevant. This could be in matters at EU level or at the level of a sector.[9] The legislative competence which Articles 154 and 155 TFEU grant to the social partners, meaning that they can formulate (legally) binding regulations, raises the question as to the conditions under which they can do this, especially with regard to the issue of representativeness).[10]

A more recent development in collective bargaining is that so-called transnational company agreements (TCAs) are being concluded at the level of multinationals, and these apply to both the multinational undertaking and its units. As this issue has become increasingly important over the past years it will be discussed in further detail in Section 5.2.3.

For a long time the right to collective bargaining was not a subject dealt with by EU legislation. In the European treaties it was expressly excluded from the legislative competence of the EEC (and later EC) and, according to

4 In countries like France and Italy tripartite bargaining at national public level takes place on an informal and ad hoc basis.

5 See Chapter 7 on this matter. In the field of health and safety at work, employees' representative bodies operate in a similar way; see Chapter 8.

6 See regarding the history of the developments of the European social dialogue: Bercusson (2009), p. 521 ff; and Welz (2008), pp. 244–88.

7 See Welz (2008), pp. 247–51. As early as 1973 Lyon-Caen advocated in a report to the European Commission that collective bargaining must be in the heart of a system of European industrial relations (Lyon-Caen (1972), p. 11).

8 Article 118 B SEA; later included in the Treaty of Amsterdam of 1999 in Article 138, now Article 154 TFEU.

9 At both levels the social partners have established rules and regulations.

10 In the *UEAMPE* case the Court of Justice gave a few guidelines (ECJ 1998, T-135/96, *UEAPME*, ECLI:EU:T:1998:128). Later the European Commission issued some guidelines. Section 5.3.2 will look into this subject.

Article 153(5) TFEU, which still excludes the right of association, the right to strike and lock-out from the EU's legislative competence, this is still the case.[11] By implication the right to collective bargaining, which is so closely linked to the right of association and the right to strike, is also excluded from the legislative powers on the basis of Article 153(5). Because the EU and its predecessors, the EEC and EC, lack competence they have deliberately abstained from interfering in any way in the national regulations on collective bargaining between social partners, on collective (labour) agreements and their binding effect in national law. These were and are still the terrains of the national legislators.

With the adoption of the EU Charter of Fundamental Rights, the right of association and its correlated rights are recognised as fundamental rights in the EU. Article 12 guarantees the right to freedom of assembly and freedom of association, including the right to form and join trade unions. Article 28 explicitly adds the right to collective bargaining, the right to conclude collective agreements, and the right to take collective action. These rights are guaranteed as fundamental rights and therefore must be respected by the Member States. However, since they do not have absolute validity, the exercise of these rights is subject to certain restrictions, as has been made clear by the Court of Justice in a number of judgments.[12] This is especially the case with regard to the right to take collective action. In Section 5.3.1.5 this will be discussed in detail.

Nevertheless, in spite of all the differences, all European legal systems have converged in one aspect: almost everywhere in Europe social dialogue in one form or another constitutes a central element of social policy, and this has become more and more important in EU labour law. First, there have been important developments in the harmonisation of the Member States' collective labour law, in particular in the field of workers' participation, information and consultation of employees.[13] And, second, collective bargaining and social dialogue on the EU level have been developed significantly, particularly since the Maastricht Treaty of 1992, discussed in Section 5.2.

The first subject of Section 5.2 is collective bargaining at European level. Subsequently, it will discuss the European social dialogue as laid down in Articles 154 and 155 TFEU, the procedures to be followed and the way the agreements can and will be implemented. It will also examine whether they have or can obtain (legally) binding effect. Finally, Section 5.2 will look at the phenomenon of transnational company agreements: how can they be concluded; can they obtain binding effect and, if so, under what conditions?

---

11 As also did its predecessor: Article 137(5) TEC.

12 See about this sensitive issue Section 5.3.1.5(c).

13 See Chapter 7 in general. It also can be demonstrated by examples dealt with in Chapter 6 (collective redundancies and transfer of enterprise) and Chapter 8 (health and safety at work).

Section 5.3 will focus on trade union rights in EU law. After a historical overview of the developments regarding collective bargaining and collective action it will examine the content of these rights. This is based partly on EU law, but even more on other international law instruments such as ILO Conventions and, in particular, the European Convention on Human Rights (ECHR) since recently the European Court of Human Rights has been taking some pioneering decisions. Finally, the European Social Charter of the Council of Europe also has had a certain influence on the interpretation and application of the right to take collective action. This concerns, in particular, the question as to what extent this right can be restricted. A special aspect in this context is whether any, and if so, how much, importance should be given to elementary principles of EU law with a view to the possible limitation of this fundamental workers' right.

5.2. COLLECTIVE BARGAINING AT EUROPEAN LEVEL

5.2.1. INTRODUCTION

In order to understand the developments in the European Union on the establishment and the meaning of the social dialogue a distinction has to be made between the, generally speaking, two forms and structures of social dialogue that have been developed in the EC/EU (namely co-lawmaking and information and consultation of workers).

Social dialogue started by the promotion of a dialogue between employers and their associations on the one side and trade unions on the other on European level with the purpose of co-lawmaking.[14] From there, it moved to sectoral and intersectoral levels regulating matters that are important and suitable for these levels. And, finally, it has led to collective bargaining on multi-enterprise level creating rules of a cross-border character to be applied on (multi-)company level. What these forms have in common is that workers organisations are taking part in lawmaking on matters that affect their members as workers. This assumes that organisations of employers and employees are very well – or on some issues even better – able and capable to regulate matters that have a great impact on the relationships between the employer and the employees and on the conditions under which the work has to be performed. It is also assumed that the rules established by social dialogue will be better accepted and fit better to the needs and wishes of both parties.

Also 'information and consultation of employees' by the employer can be considered as part of the social dialogue. This kind of dialogue takes place at enterprise level and is meant as a means for representatives of the employees of

14 Cf. Welz (2008), p. 243 ff. mentions the Val Duchesse process as the start of it.

the enterprise to influence decisions and practices of the employer on matters that directly affect employees. In a number of EU directives, representatives of employees are involved in business matters, be it in the capacity of trade union or in bodies elected by employees, usually works councils. Not only in practice, but also in EU law, the distinction between these two forms is not always clearly made. It is common for collective bargaining to be in the hands of trade unions, whereas works councils are involved in information and consultation on business matters. In recent years, it can be seen that also works councils operate as bargaining units, sometimes taking the place of trade unions. This situation varies from Member State to Member State. In some Member States, such as Germany, France, Austria, Belgium and the Netherlands, works councils at enterprise level are well developed,[15] whereas in other Member States that is not the case or this form of workers' participation is even absent. In Member States where works councils do not play an important role, it is mainly trade unions that deal with matters related to employment and employment conditions on enterprise level.[16] In a third group of Member States collective bargaining has, regardless of its form, barely been developed. Consequently, the system of collective bargaining or even workers' involvement is almost non-existent. Rules with binding hard law effect do not exist either.[17]

It has to be noted here that the social partners have been assigned a special position in regard to their competence to draw up rules to which binding effect can be granted. This position is exceptional in comparison with other private organisations. The EU Treaty itself confers this position explicitly by assigning in Article 155 TFEU authority to conclude agreements that can with a binding effect.[18] The role and power of the European Council in this specific procedure have been limited by purpose. It cannot change or amend the content of the agreement concluded, it only can reject the proposed agreement by refusing to adopt the agreement by a Council directive. The role of the European Parliament is even more limited, since it is excluded from the legislating process. In this respect the question may arise whether this system of collective bargaining by social partners on EU level resulting in binding regulations can be considered as sufficiently legitimate.[19] On the other hand, it can be noted that the EU is 'embracing' dialogues as a means of regulating issues relevant for the EU and the Member States. Apart from the social dialogue, the EU supports dialogues with societal organisations in other policy areas, notably NGOs aiming at increasing

---

15 In the Member States mentioned the trade unions' structure is also well developed.

16 Think of Denmark, Sweden and the UK – countries with a strong trade union tradition.

17 That is the case in a number of new Member States. Since the accession of these countries to the EU, the situation is changing. See on the developments in four Member States of this group, Palinkas (2016).

18 See on this issue Section 5.2.2.4.

19 See also Veldman (2011).

the involvement of citizens in EU policy in order to increase the participation in decision-making on EU level.[20]

5.2.2. INSTITUTIONS AND PROCEDURES OF SOCIAL DIALOGUE AT THE EU LEVEL

5.2.2.1. Introduction

Since the presidency of Jacques Delors, social dialogue has been recognised as an important feature of the European Social Model.[21] The European Treaties have assigned social partners on European Community/Union level a function and role in its institutional structure since the 1990s.[22] Article 3 of the Social Agreement of 1991 assigned the European Commission the task of 'promoting the consultation of management and labour at Community level and shall take any relevant measure to facilitate their dialogue'. It went further by involving social partners in the legislative process by giving social partners the opportunity to be consulted on community action in the social policy field (Article 3(2-4)). It even provided social partners the possibility to conclude, if they wish to do so, agreements that could have binding effect when adopted by the Council (Article 4).[23]

The current Treaty on this issue (TFEU) has taken over the approach and structure developed in 1991. Article 152 TFEU reads: 'The Union recognises and promotes the role of the social partners at its level, taking into account the diversity of national systems. It shall facilitate dialogue between the social partners, respecting their autonomy'. Compared to the Social Agreement, this made two additions. First, it considers explicitly the diversity of the social dialogue systems of the Member States. By that, it refers to the different systems of the institutional organisation of both sides of industry: employers and workers. Second, by respecting the autonomy of social partners it neither interferes in the way the organisations on EU level are organised and operate, nor in the way that they are composed and internally structured.

An exemption to abstain from interference has been made regarding to the issue of 'proper' representation of either employers or workers. It started with a

---

20 See European Commission, COM(2002)277 final, introducing general principles and minimum standards for consultation of interested parties. The communications refer to consumer organisations, environmental organisations, human rights organisations, educational and training organisations; ibid. p. 6.

21 Biagi (2001).

22 See Falkner (1996).

23 These articles have been inserted in the Treaty of Maastricht: Articles 118A and 118B TEU. Cf. Bercusson (2009), p. 141 ff.

case before the Court of Justice. In 1998 the Court was called to decide a case in which one of the employers' associations challenged the system because 'proper' representation was not ensured as they were being excluded from the bargaining process and the conclusion of a collective framework agreement on EU level (the *UEAPME* case).[24] The Court developed some representativeness requirements for being recognised and accepted as a party at the negotiations table, resulting in binding rules of EU law. A few years later the Commission drew up some guidelines on this issue (see Section 5.2.2.2).

The Treaty fails to give a clear definition of what is understood by employers' and workers' organisations. It calls them 'the organisations representing both sides of industry' and sometimes 'management and labour'. On the labour side it is and has to be an organisation of workers, but it is left to the Member States to determine which ones qualify as such. However, before they are invited by the Commission to take part in the collective bargaining at EU level – based on Articles 154 TFEU – the Commission considers whether the organisations at central level and at sectoral level are 'properly' representative. The Commission and Council check the representativeness of the organisations before proposing a directive to be adopted transposing the agreement into EU law.[25]

In social dialogue as a co-lawmaking instrument two forms can be distinguished:[26]

1. A bilateral, two-way dialogue between the European employers' and trade union organisations. Within this, another two forms exist:
   a. agreements between social partners related to co-law-making procedures based on the TFEU and initiated by the Commission;
   b. agreements initiated and concluded between social partners themselves without interference of the Commission. These agreements: (i) can be transposed into EU law according to normal EU law procedure, i.e. by Council directive; (ii) are autonomous agreements between employers and trade unions, based on negotiations on company level. They lack EU law status and are called transnational company agreements (TCAs). Their legal effect, if any, needs another contractual basis.[27] This type of agreement does not necessarily have a (binding) legal form; they may be characterised as, for example,

---

24 ECJ 1998, T-135/96 (*Ueapme*). See Section 5.2.2.2.

25 The European Commission has drawn up a list. See Annex 2 to COM (1993)600 final and Annex 1 to COM (98)322 final. The most recent list was published in July 2017 <ec.europa.eu/social/BlobServlet?docId=2154&langId=en> accessed 05.06.2019.

26 See e.g. Communication from the Commission, *The European social dialogue, a force for innovation and change*, COM(2002)341 final. The Commission issued on 26 June 2002 a proposal to establish a Tripartite Social Summit for Growth and Employment.

27 That may depend on the rules of private international law. Cf. Van Hoek & Hendrickx (2009).

'joint texts', 'guidelines' or 'codes of conduct'.[28] Often, enforcement of these 'agreements' is not ensured.

2. Tripartite, three-way dialogue involving the public authorities; on the European level, it is mainly the European Commission which will actively be involved.[29] This will not lead to agreements, but can be seen as a dialogue between social partners and the Commission on social policy issues.

Social dialogue between social partners is considered as a specific feature in the 'world of work'. It is promoted as a means to better governance.[30] Working conditions, definition of wage standards, continuing training, particularly in new technologies, organisation of work and working time to reconcile flexibility and security are considered as topics that can be left to social partners to regulate. It is assumed that they are in a better position to regulate matters in a way that they are better adapted to specific situations.[31]

It is the task of the Commission (Article 154(1) TFEU) to promote consultation of management and labour at EU level and to take any relevant measure to facilitate their dialogue. In order to fulfil its task, the Commission may, for example, finance meetings or translations at and beyond meetings.[32]

It also has to be mentioned that the European Union has to maintain neutrality in the promotion of bilateral social dialogue, which is mainly an instrument for the social partners themselves. That is the meaning of Article 154(1) TFEU emphasising that 'balanced support for the parties' has to be ensured. Neutrality and a balanced support are two sides of the same coin: the Commission may not use its means in order to seek a compensation of power imbalances between social partners or aim at an equilibrium. It has to accept existing different representativity of social partners and may not interfere in order to establish – in its view – a better balance of power.

The Commission has, over time and in cooperation with social partners, developed different institutional forms for the social dialogue. It has started at *cross-industry* level, but over time the sectoral level has gained importance. Social partners seem more inclined to make arrangements at sectoral level. In particular they feel that concrete issues better could be regulated at that level, since some issues are common to the sector and have a common cross-border nature. Since 1998 the Commission has promoted this form of collective negotiations at sectoral level. It considers this form as 'a key issue'.[33]

---

28 That does not imply per se that they are not effective.

29 Both forms are quite common in the Member States. On State level the aim is to discuss and elaborate a national social policy supported by the nationally organised social partners.

30 European Commission (2001), *European Governance A White Paper*, p. 14.

31 European Commission COM(2002)341 final, p. 7.

32 See also *Commission Communication on Adapting and promoting the Social Dialogue at Community level*, COM(1998)322, p. 22.

33 COM(1998)322, pp. 9 and 10.

To support this development the Commission has established Sectoral Social Dialogue Committees (SSDCs). The sectoral level is seen as the proper level for discussing on issues linked to employment, working conditions, vocational training, industrial change, the knowledge society, demographic patterns, enlargement and globalisation.[34]

5.2.2.2. Parties: Social Partners

The TFEU consistently names 'management' and 'labour' as the parties that will be consulted in the legislative process on social policy matters. In many Member States, the term 'social partners' is more common. Parties to collective bargaining on EU level are, in the first place, the European employers' associations and the European trade unions. Next to them, European Works Councils also act in a bargaining capacity. They are focused on bargaining with management, alone or together with the European trade unions, on matters related to business matters.[35] In the third place, national social partners can be granted a role when collective (framework) agreements on EU level have to be implemented in national law.

In the law-making process, three stages can be distinguished:

- consultation (Article 154(2/3) TFEU);
- negotiation between the social partners (Article 154(4) TFEU, Article 155(1) TFEU);
- agreement (Article 155(1) TFEU).

Participation in the legislative process is restricted to social partners. The Treaty itself does not define which parties will be or have to be accepted as taking part in the consultation procedures, or in negotiations. Articles 154 and 155 TFEU are silent as to which representative parties of management and labour are covered. It is unclear whether the parties that have access to the various procedures have to meet requirements depending on the type or phase of 'social dialogue procedure'. Initially, the Commission took the stand that it is up to the social partners themselves to determine who has access to the negotiation table, as the Commission wished to respect the autonomy of the unions.

---

34 COM(2002)341, p. 16. In 2003, 27 Sectoral Social Dialogue Committees had been established and were active. In 2015, 43 Sectoral Social Dialogue Committees were in operation varying from agriculture, banking, civil aviation, construction, the chemical industry, education, hospitals and healthcare, hotels and restaurants, to telecommunication and transport; cf. European Commission (2015), *A New Start for Social Dialogue*. See also Even (2008), p. 115, and García-Muñoz Alhambra (2017). The most recent is the adoption by the Council of an Agreement in the sector of seafarers aiming at improving the employment conditions of seafarers (Directive 2009/13/EC).

35 Restricted mainly to multi- or transnational level. See in more detail Chapter 7.

In the mid-1990s the problem of proper representation of social partners in an Article 154(2) TFEU procedure arose. In a document published in 1993,[36] the Commission set out a number of criteria in order to identify the organisations that are in the Commission's view entitled to be consulted during the initial stage of the social dialogue (based on Article 154(2/3) TFEU). An important, if not decisive criterion is 'representativity'.

In 1993 the Commission proposed three requirements to be fulfilled in order to identify which organisations of employers and of employees can qualify as parties acting in the legislative process by bargaining: the organisations must:

- be cross-industry or relate to specific sectors or categories and be organised at European level;
- themselves be an integral and recognised part of Member States' social partner structures and have the capacity to negotiate agreements, and be representative of all Member States, as far as possible;[37] and
- have adequate structures to ensure their effective participation in the consultation process.[38]

These are the criteria used[39] and applied by the Commission when making the list of 'representative' European organisations on both sides. It regularly assesses the representativeness of social partners participating in the European social dialogue with the help of external studies.[40] Currently on the employees' side, three organisations (the European Trade Union Confederation (ETUC), Confédération Européenne des Cadres (CEC), European Managers) and the Council of European Professional and Managerial Staff (EUROCADRES) are 'recognised' as representative organisations. They cooperate intensively, keeping their autonomy and acknowledge the key role of ETUC. On the employers' side there are two main organisations: the association representing the private sector (BusinessEurope[41]) and the association active in the public field (CEEP).

---

36 COM(93)600 final.

37 By this is meant that the organisations of employers and employees operating as bargaining actors are recognised as such in all or at least several Member States, and not only in just a few States. E.g. Even (2008), p. 136 ff; Franssen (1998), p. 1299 ff.

38 COM(93)600 final, §24, repeated in COM(1998)322, §24. The third criterion refers to the existence of contact bureaus with adequate resources in Brussels.

39 A fourth criterion was proposed: the bargaining parties have a mandate from their members, i.e. the national organisations. The Commission refused to include this criterion.

40 See Annex 2 to COM(1993)600 final and Annex 1 to COM(98)322 final.

41 In 1998 the association representing the SMEs (UEAPME) concluded a cooperation agreement with UNICE (since 2007 BUSINESSEUROPE) recognising UNICE as the sole European organisation representing cross-industry businesses of all sizes. Cf. Even (2008), p. 65 ff.

On the sectoral level a number of organisations of employers (26) and of employees (15) are recognised by the Commission as representative.[42]

The issue of being consulted according to Article 154(2)[43] has never been challenged before the Court. Consequently, the right to be consulted by the Commission on one of the social policy issues according to Articles 153 and 154 (1 and 2) is clarified by the Commission's list. The listed representative European organisations on the employers' and on employees' side have always been called by the Commission for consultation.

A specific problem – not only in legal terms but also from a practical point of view – is which EU institution has the competence to decide which employers' or workers' organisation is representative taking into account the autonomy of these organisations as also recognised by the EU. In practice the Commission does so, by sending the invitation for consultation.[44] From a theoretical as well from a practical point of view, when establishing binding (EU) law rules, parties need a democratic legitimisation for doing so. Representativity of the bargaining parties is the common instrument. Although the Commission in practice decides whether this is the case, it has to be assessed and checked by the European Council when transposing an agreement between the social partners into EU law (by means of a directive). If the Council is of the opinion that a party is lacking sufficient respresentativity[45] it can refuse the transposition. The decision of the Council whether it accepts the representativity of the parties on both sides or not can be challenged before the Court of Justice.

In the *UEAPME* case, the Court was asked to decide on the representativity of parties that concluded an agreement. In 1998, in the first consultation round the European Employers Association representing small and medium-sized enterprises (UEAPME) was consulted according to the procedure of Article 154(2) and (3) TFEU. In the second stage of the procedure (in line with Article 154(4) TFEU) the UEAPME did not participate. It claimed that its exclusion from collective bargaining, or the fact that it was not involved in this, was unjustified. The remaining parties concluded an agreement on parental leave that was offered to the European Council to be implemented by an EU directive.[46] The Council adopted the agreement by Directive 96/34 after which the framework agreement acquired legally binding effect. The Council simply stated that the Commission proposed to adopt the agreement by a directive, 'taking into account the representative status of the signatory parties, their

---

42 The most recent list was published in July 2017 <ec.europa.eu/social/BlobServlet?docId=2154&langId=en> accessed 05.06.2019.

43 Formerly Article 3(2) of the Agreement on Social Policy of 2 February 1992, now Article 138(2) TEC.

44 Based on Article 154(2) TFEU.

45 A notion developed by the Court in ECJ 1998, T-135/96 (*UEAPME*).

46 Directive 96/34/EC, revised by Directive 2010/18/EU.

mandate and the legality of the clauses of the framework agreement'.[47] The UEAPME lodged a claim at the European Court of First Instance for annulment of Directive 96/34 and claimed that since European law[48] demanded that any representative organisation should be consulted by the Commission in the first stage, such organisation has a right to take part in the negotiation process – the second stage.[49] The UEAPME argued that it should have been admitted to the bargaining table because it represents in particular the interests of the group of small and medium-sized enterprises (SMEs) and it doubted that their interests were properly represented by the colleague employers' associations.[50]

The Court made a distinction between the obligation to call all organisations for consultation in Article 154(2) and (4) TFEU procedures and the right of all organisations to sit at the bargaining table. The Court interpreted Article 154 as requiring the Commission to invite all representative organisations that meet the criteria of the Communications on this issue to give their opinion in accordance to Article 154(2) and (3) TFEU. On the other hand, neither Article 154(4) nor Article 155 identifies expressly the organisations for the purpose of negotiations. Article 154(2) and (3) does not lead necessarily to the conclusion that organisations can legally claim to take part in negotiations. As the Court states:

> The negotiation stage, which may come into being during the consultation stage initiated by the Commission, depends exclusively on the initiative of those representatives of management and labour who wish to launch such negotiations. The representatives of management and labour concerned in the negotiation stage are therefore those who have demonstrated their mutual willingness to initiate the process provided for in Article 4 of the Agreement and to follow it through to its conclusion.[51]

By this decision the Court 'embraced' the principle of freedom of contract.

It also went into the argument of the UEAPME that the employers' organisations that are signatories to the (framework) agreement do not represent the specific interests of the SMEs, at least not properly. UEAPME argued that the framework agreement was too rigid because it did not give enough room for postponing the granting of the parental leave due to the specific circumstances of a SME concerned. Based on these grounds UEAPME claimed that since

47 §13 of the preamble to Directive 96/34/EC.

48 At that time Articles 3 and 4 of the Agreement on Social Policy of 2 February 1992, now Articles 154 and 155 TFEU.

49 ECJ 1998, T-135/96 (*UEAPME*).

50 The subject was quite relevant for SMEs, since parental leave is assigned to both parent workers and SMEs felt this as a burden, in particular when it is (partly) paid leave. See on parental leave, Chapter 3.

51 ECJ 1998, T-135/96 (*UEAPME*), §75.

the Commission, as well as the Court, did not properly exercise their task, the regulation was invalid.

The Court, referring to the principle of democracy, stated that since the European Parliament had no part in this legislative procedure and therefore the democratic control by the Parliament was absent, it was the task of the Commission and the Council to examine the democratic quality of the regulation established by checking the representativity of the signatory parties ensuring the persons affected have been heard and their interests have been taken into account.[52] Therefore Commission and Council 'are under a duty to verify that the signatories to the agreement are truly representative'. In order to establish the compliance with this requirement the Court introduced the concept of *sufficiently and collectively representative*.[53] In the opinion of the Court, the Commission and the Council had done this in the case at hand. Moreover, the content of the framework agreement, in the view of the Court, did effectively take in account the specific interests of SMEs.[54] In conclusion the Court decided that the signatory parties had been representing the interests of SMEs 'sufficiently' with respect to the substantive scope of the framework agreement.[55]

In conclusion it can be stated that Article 154 guarantees that organisations of employers and of employees are entitled to be consulted on intended legislation on social matters when they meet the representativity requirements. However, that does not mean per se that they can claim a seat at the negotiating table.

It can be deducted from the *UEAPME* decision that it may be possible to claim access to collective bargaining if the organisation concerned represents the specific interests of a group of employers or employees that are not represented – sufficiently – by the negotiating parties. It is obvious that, in the case of a sectoral agreement, for the representativity criterion only representation in the relevant sector(s) is relevant.[56]

In the present situation, the employers' association, BusinessEurope (formerly Union of Industrial and Employers' Confederations of Europe (UNICE)), can be considered as qualifying as a representative party on basis of its cross-industry character and the general nature of its mandate. It represents undertakings of all sizes in the private sector, including associations of SMEs. According to the decision of the Court in the *UEAPME* case if

---

52 ECJ 1998, T-135/96 (*UEAPME*), §88.

53 ECJ 1998, T-135/96 (*UEAPME*), §§89 and 90.

54 The Court referred to the disputed provision (Clause 2.3(e) and (f)) that authorises the employer to make special arrangements to meet the operational and organisational requirements of small undertakings. ECJ 1998, T-135/96 (*UEAPME*), §107.

55 ECJ 1998, T-135/96 (*UEAPME*), §§91and 110. The decision of the Court has been criticised in the literature. See Bercusson (1999); Betten (1998); and Keller & Sörries (1999).

56 The Commission has listed quite a number of organisations on the employers' side as well as the workers' side (although a smaller number) that are assumed to be 'representative'. See SEC(2010)964 final, Annex 1.

'underrepresentation' on one of the sides is at stake, for instance one particular category of undertakings does not take part or is not a signatory party and is directly affected by (the content of) the agreement, that organisation would have been wholly without representation.[57] The consequence could be the annulment of the directive that implements the agreement concerned by which the binding effect has been refused fully. Another outcome could be that the agreement (and consequently the directive) will not cover that organisation (and the employees employed by the employers belonging to that group).

A second question decided by the Court is the acknowledgment of a wide prerogative to the negotiating partners as to how specific interests can be integrated in the policy of an employers' or employees' organisation: the signatory parties to the agreement will, apart from the core and general interests of the enterprises they represent, also have to keep specific interests in mind in order to be able to represent these interests as well. For example, the (framework) agreement should clarify if and how specific interests such as those of SMEs have been considered at the event of conclusion of the agreement.[58]

It has to be taken in mind that the internal structure of the employers' and workers' organisations may influence whether an Article 155 agreement that can be transposed into EU law will be made. In the ETUC a majority of members – affiliated national trade unions – is sufficient, whereas BusinessEurope requires unanimity. So one vetoing member organisation can block the establishment of an agreement.[59]

5.2.2.3. Procedures and Outcomes of Social Dialogue

Title X of the TFEU provides in Articles 154 and 155 two modalities of social dialogue at EU level. The first starts on the initiative of the European Commission by inviting the European social parties for consultation on a subject that the Commission intends to regulate on EU level. It can – although this is not necessary – be followed by negotiations by social partners resulting in an agreement by them (Article 154(4)). The other route is Article 155(1), by which social partners on their own initiative can start negotiations that can end up in 'contractual relations' including agreements.

---

57 ECJ 1998, T-135/96 (*UEAPME*), §100. For other questions as to the representativity of UNICE (now BusinessEurope) and the possible consequences see Lapeyre (2017), p. 160 ff. (also referring to the former EuroPMI and Eurocommerce).

58 Cf. ECJ 1998, T-135/96 (*UEAPME*), §107. The relevant provision (Clause 2.3(e) and (f)) authorises the employer to make special arrangements to meet the operational and organisational requirements of small undertakings.

59 The Constitution of the organisations can be decisive on this point. Cf. Bercusson (1999), p. 161; and Keller & Sörries (1999), p. 114 ff.

The outcomes of the negotiations of social partners can gain EU law status by a decision of the European Council, usually a directive. Article 154 agreements are restricted to subjects mentioned in Article 153 TFEU whereas the second category (Article 155 agreements) can also cover subjects outside the scope of Article 153. In this respect the question arises whether the route of granting EU law status to framework agreements is open only for agreements on issues mentioned in Article 153 TFEU. Article 155(2) TFEU seems to stipulate this. Consequently, it would not be possible for the parties to an agreement on a subject not listed in Article 153 to present the agreement to the Council requesting that it should be adopted and transposed into European law. The competence to grant European law status to agreements on such subjects fails. So, the only way of implementing such agreements is the way prescribed as the first alternative in Article 155(2): in accordance with the procedures and practices specific to management and labour and the Member States.[60]

It has to be noted that the third form of collective bargaining leading to transnational company agreements is not regulated in EU law. Usually, this route is called autonomous bargaining and autonomous agreements (see Section 5.2.3).

(a) Consultation of Social Partners by the Commission (Article 154(2) and (3) TFEU)

What can be described as the main route of consultation is the procedure of Article 154(2) and (3) TFEU. It guarantees the possibility for social partners to give their opinions to the Commission when it is considering and preparing a proposal for legislation in the social field. Their opinions have to be taken into account by the Commission but they are not binding on the Commission. This route is considered as a helpful means to formulate policies appropriate to the problems dealt with, in form as well as in substance.[61]

The mandatory involvement of societal organisations is a specific feature of the field of EU social policy measures. Consultation of social partners ('management and labour') on matters listed in Article 153(1) TFEU takes place in two steps, starting at a very early stage of the law-making process. Even before the Commission draws up a proposal, management and labour have to be given the opportunity to give their opinion 'on the possible direction of Union action' (Article 154(2) TFEU). In this first stage, the Commission and social partners discuss if, and what, Union action should be taken.

If 'after such consultation, the Commission considers Union action advisable', management and labour are to be consulted a second time, this

60 Looking at the list of agreements mentioned in the report *European Sectoral Social Dialogue* (2010) it appears that it only concerns matters as listed in Article 153 TFEU.

61 Cf. Communication from the Commission – *The European social dialogue, a force for innovation and change*, COM (2002)341 final, p. 8.

time on the content of the envisaged proposal (Article 153(3) TFEU). In this context, the social partners are asked to put forward an opinion or a recommendation on the Commission's proposal.

Usually, this will be the end of the consultation process with social partners in accordance with the Article 154 route. The next step in the law-making procedure will be the joint adoption of a legislative measure by the European Parliament and the Council.[62] There is another step to be taken before submitting the proposal to the European Parliament and the Council. The Commission has to consult two Committees: the Economic and Social Committee and the Committee of the Regions (Article 153 (2) TFEU). Both are asked to give their opinion on the proposal.

If the social partners wish so they can start negotiations aiming at reaching an agreement between them. They have a nine-month period to succeed (Article 154(4) TFEU). Extension of that period is possible by proposal of social partners and with the consent of the Commission.

If social partners reach an agreement on an Article 153 TFEU subject, they have to put a joint request for the agreement to be given EU law status via the Commission. The Commission has to offer to the Council a proposal for the adoption of a directive by which the agreement will receive binding effect.

In this respect the question is raised whether the Commission or the Council has the right to amend the agreement concluded by social partners in order to bring it in line with the view of the Commission and/or Council. This question is part of the rules of implementation of agreements between social partners into binding EU law (see Section 5.2.2.4(a)).

(b) Social Partners' Agreements at EU Level (Article 155 TFEU)

Article 155(1) TFEU provides for a procedure of collective negotiations between social partners resulting in contractual relations which could take the form of agreements, but also of other arrangements. This procedure can be used in the situations mentioned in Article 154(4) TFEU, as well as in situations in which social partners want to conclude agreements.[63] In both cases the agreement can be granted EU law status if the agreement is adopted by a Council decision, usually by a directive. Bargaining can take place on cross-industry level as well as on sectoral level. They are called 'framework' agreements because – in analogy to the Framework Directives on Safety and Health at Work (89/381/EEC) and on Equal Treatment in Employment and

---

62 In accordance with Articles 289 and 294 TFEU. From Article 153 TFEU, it can be derived that, except on the issues mentioned in §1(c), (d), (f) and (g), the Council can decide with a qualified majority. On the issues mentioned a unanimous Council decision is needed.

63 In the literature the negotiations as well as the agreements are called 'autonomous', because they were initiated by the parties themselves without interference by the Commission.

Occupation (2000/78/EC) – they are intended to provide general principles rather than a comprehensive regulation in the respective field.

Well-known examples of the first category are the cross-industry agreements:

- the European Framework Agreement on parental leave of 14 December 1995 (implemented by Directive 96/34/EC), revised by the Framework Agreement of 18 June 2009 (implemented by Directive 2010/18/EU);
- the European Framework Agreement on part-time work of 6 June 1997 (implemented by Directive 97/81/EC);
- the European Framework Agreement on fixed-term work of 18 March 1999 (implemented by Directive 1999/70/EC).[64]

At the end of the 1990s the momentum of cross-industry social dialogue seemed to have come to an end. National employers' organisations started to oppose the transfer of negotiating and legislating power to European level. In 1994, it proved impossible to have an agreement on European Works Councils. In 1998 UNICE (now BusinessEurope) refused to enter into negotiations on harmonising measures to regulate information and consultation of workers in national companies. In September 1999, 21 European employers raised their concerns about European social policy and social dialogue and, since then, there have been no more cross-industry agreements resulting in binding European law.[65]

Social partner negotiations on temporary agency work broke down in 2001; the respective Directive 2008/104/EC is no longer the result of a collective agreement. Apart from the revision of the Framework Agreement on Parental Leave in 2010, the partial revision of the European Works Council Directive in 2009 has so far been the last substantial result of this form of social dialogue. Even 'tripartite' negotiations on the revision of the Working Time Directive, i.e. negotiations not intended for agreement purposes but for the Commission's consultation, have repeatedly failed.[66]

As a consequence in the 2000s other forms of social dialogue have been developed and used to be characterised as 'soft forms' of law making, which have a much weaker legal effect than the framework agreements implemented on the basis of the Article 154 procedure.

Since the beginning of the twenty-first century other agreements have been concluded on cross-industry level without EU law status, since the social partners deliberately did not present them to Commission and Council for adoption. Implementation of these agreements has to be realised by the

---

64 See for the first directive Chapter 3 and for the second and third directives Chapter 4.

65 Cf. Degryse & Tilly (2013), p. 102.

66 See on successes and failures Welz (2008), pp. 379–481; and Degryse & Tilly (2013), pp. 100–06.

national law procedures of Member States (see hereafter Section 5.2.2.4(b)). Examples are:

- Framework Agreement on Telework of 16 July 2002;
- Framework Agreement on Work-Related Stress of 8 October 2004;
- Framework Agreement on Harassment and Violence at Work of 26 April 2007;
- European Framework Agreement on inclusive labour markets of 25 March 2010.

The establishment of these agreements in Article 154 TFEU procedure, but they ended up as 'autonomous' or 'voluntary' agreements between European social partners because they explicitly opted for an implementation in accordance with procedures and practices specific to management and labour.[67]

Parties to the cross-industry level agreements listed above are the European social partners on EU level: BusinessEurope, UEAPME (in combination with BusinessEurope) and CEEP on the employers' side and the ETUC and affiliated organisations on the workers' side.

In accordance with the task imposed on the European Commission in Article 154(1) TFEU to promote and facilitate social dialogue, a structure of negotiating has been set up by the Commission on sectoral level. It started in 1998 by creating European sectoral social dialogue committees.[68] The aim was to create 'an arena for trust-building, information sharing, discussion, consultation, negotiation and joint actions'. They evolved to negotiating bodies that produced several kinds of commitments by sectoral social partners. By 2010, in 39 sectors Social Dialogue Committees had been established and become active.[69] The composition of the Social Dialogue Committees is more diverse in numbers and fields of activity[70] due to the variety of interests that sectoral employers' organisations represent. The representation of employers differs significantly across the various sectors, ranging from one recognised employers' organisation in most sectors (e.g. commerce, construction, chemical industry, hospitals, etc.) to three or more employers' organisations in other sectors (civil aviation, extractive industries, audiovisual services, banking or insurance). On sectoral level, small and medium sized enterprises and large companies are all represented.

On the employees' side, sectoral trade union organisations at European level are operating in close cooperation with the ETUC. There is also more

67 See Welz (2008), pp. 408–432; see also Section 5.2.2.4(b).

68 Commission decision of 20 May 1998 (98/500/EC) on the establishment of Sectoral Dialogue Committees promoting the Dialogue between the social partners at European level.

69 European Commission, *European Sectoral Social Dialogue. Recent developments* (2010), pp. 11 and 92.

70 In the annex to European Commission SEC(2010) 964, pp. 21–22 the organisations on both sides are listed.

cooperation with European Work Councils on issues in which the European works councils are involved.

This type of agreement has also been concluded on the sectoral level. The most important examples are:[71]

- Agreement on training in agriculture (2002);
- Agreement on exposure to risk in agriculture (2005);
- Agreement on crystalline silica (2006);
- Agreement on hairdressing certificates (2009).

They entail an interesting mixture of 'programmatic', intentional provisions and concrete individualised rights.

Next to these agreements the committees have adopted arrangements ('joint texts') of various kinds, such as guidelines, codes of conduct or frameworks of action that disseminate good practices and promote voluntary standards within the sector.[72] They may also take the form of negotiated agreements to be implemented either in accordance with national procedures and practices[73] or by Council directive.[74]

An instrument of a soft law nature that has become more frequently used, is the 'framework of actions', a form of 'open method of coordination within the social dialogue'.[75] Illustrative examples of this kind of actions, all cross-industry, are:

- framework of actions on the lifelong development of competencies and qualifications (2002);
- framework of action on gender equality (2005);
- framework of actions on youth employment (2013).[76]

---

71 Most of them concerned health and safety issues. In agriculture the subject matter was work-related musculoskeletal disorders (MSD).

72 In the report of the European Commission (2010), *European Sectoral Social Dialogue*, SEC(2010)964 final, they are listed sector-wise. These texts have a non-binding nature according to European law.

73 Examples are: Agreement on Workers Health Protection through the Good Handling and Use of Crystalline Silica and Products containing it (2006/C 279/02), signed by 18 social partners and industry organisations from 14 sectors; Agreement of the social partners in personal services on the implementation of the European hairdressing certificates (2009).

74 These agreements can be and mainly are based on Article 155 TFEU. Such as Council Directive 2010/32/EU; Council Directive 2005/47/EC; Council Directive 2000/79/EC. See Clauwaert (2012), p. 132 ff. Framework agreements on working time in the railway sector (2004); Maritime labour conventions (2008); Framework agreement on prevention from sharp injuries in the hospital and healthcare sector (2009); European agreement on the organisation of working time of seafarers (1998).

75 Degryse and Tilly (2013), pp. 103–06. For an analysis of the 'open method of coordination', see Ter Haar (2012). See also Chapter 1, Section 1.3.4.

76 See previous footnote.

5.2.2.4. *Implementation of Agreements between Social Partners*

In order to make their agreement effective, the social partners may rely upon procedures provided by the Treaty. According to Article 155(2) TFEU, the social partners can choose between two ways of implementing collective agreements on EU level. The most important and most effective way is implementation by a Council decision at the joint request of the signatory parties. But the parties can also agree on implementation 'in accordance with the procedures and practices specific to management and labour and the Member States' (Article 155(2) TFEU).[77] A final possibility is implementation by national legislation, but that rarely happens.[78]

(a) Implementation by Council Decision

Implementation of agreements by social partners by Council decision according to the second alternative of Article 155(2) TFEU whether they are either of a cross-industry or of a sectoral nature can be called the 'royal way' in EU terms. The result of starting the negotiating procedure by social partners – in accordance with Article 154(4) TFEU – is a temporary suspension of the legislative process at EU level.[79] Although respecting the rights of the autonomous parties in this process, the Commission reserves its possibility to monitor the agreement as well as to assess the extent to which the agreement has contributed to the achievement of the Community's objectives. If in the view of the Commission the agreement does not satisfy these requirements, it may itself put forward a proposal for a legislative act. The consultation phase is ended then.

In this procedure the role of the European Parliament is marginal. According to Article 155(2) TFEU it only has to be informed. It lacks the power to influence the content of the agreement and the directive implementing the agreement.

The procedure of implementing a social partners' agreement into binding EU law starts by the signatory parties of the collective agreement making a joint request to the Commission. Subsequently, the Commission takes the lead and assesses of the possibility of proposing a Council decision. By virtue of a Council decision the agreement will have so-called 'direct effect' and is therefore to be implemented and applied in all Member States.

---

77 In the literature this is called 'autonomous' implementation, which means without interference by a Member State.

78 An example is the Framework Agreement on Telework. The European Commission regularly publishes reports on the implementation of framework agreements. See inter alia European Commission, *Study on the implementation of the autonomous framework agreement on harassment and violence at work. Final report* (2015).

79 Communication 2004(557) §4.4.

According to Articles 153 and 154 TFEU, for the implementation of the agreement a number of requirements has to be fulfilled.[80] Apart from the assertion by the Commission that the matter is covered by Article 153(1) TFEU the following requirements have to be met:

- The Commission has to assess and verifies the legality of all clauses in the agreements in relation to European Union law as well as the conformity of the negotiation processes with Article 155(1) TFEU. One of the issues here to check is the representativeness of the signatory parties[81] and the existence of their mandate from the national affiliates to negotiate and conclude the agreement.[82]
- The Council has no other choice to accept or to reject the Commission's proposal of adopting and implementing the agreement. Neither the Commission nor the Council may amend or alter the text of the agreement in any way.[83] The Council may implement or refuse to implement the agreement; it may not change its content in the course of the procedure. This is due to the fact that the social dialogue, in these cases, is a functional equivalent for the Parliament's participation, i.e. the central democratic element in the procedure.[84]
- Application of the subsidiarity principle. The assessment of whether this principle has been respected will take place by the Commission before it presents its proposal to the Council. If the Council wants to, it can still assess whether the agreement respects that principle.[85] It can be noted that where the social partners' agreement was negotiated in the context of the Commission's consultation procedure (Article 154 TFEU) it can be assumed that the question of appropriateness of supporting and complementing the activities of the Member States has already been answered by the Commission.[86] In other cases, i.e. in the case of social partners' negotiations having been started autonomously, the Commission will have to make up for this assessment in the course of determining whether to propose a Council decision, provided it is an Article 153 TFEU matter.

---

80 This procedure is laid down in points 38 to 42 of the 1993 Communication (COM(93)600), and the 1998 Communication COM(98)322 §5.4.2., pp. 19–20. Cf. Even (2008), p. 159 ff.; Bercusson (1999), p. 156 ff.

81 Based on the Communication of 1993 COM(93)600 final and ECJ 1998 T-135/96 (*UEAPME*) §§84–85.

82 See e.g. COM(1999)203.

83 See COM(2014)452, §2.2.

84 Weiss (2008), p. 961. A more practical reason might be that interfering in the substance can jeopardise further negotiations in the future.

85 See about this principle, Chapter 1, Section 1.2.4.

86 This procedure is based on Article 153 TFEU. The question has been assessed in the earlier stage of starting the consultation procedure.

- Finally, the Commission has to check, in conformity with Article 153(2(b)) TFEU, whether the interests of the SMEs are taken into account. It is also required that only 'minimum requirements for gradual implementation, having regard to the conditions and technical rules obtaining in each of the Member States' are allowed (Article 153(2(b)) TFEU).[87]

Should Commission and Council find fault with the social partner agreement and wish to adopt a somewhat modified legislative measure, the Commission would have to start the legislating procedure anew from the beginning (Article 154(1) TFEU).

The Council decides with the majority prescribed in Article 153 TFEU. In some matters only the Council shall act unanimously 'where the agreement in question contains one or more provisions relating to one of the areas for which unanimity is required pursuant to Article 153(2)'.

By transferring this type of agreement by Council directive they become effective and gain EU law status. The actual effect depends on the content of the agreement. The agreements adopted so far partly contain concrete rights which can be invoked by the parties covered and/or individual employers or employees.[88] The majority of the provisions in the agreements, however, are of a more programmatic or intentional character, such as obligations to provide for training or safe and healthy working conditions or informing employees.[89]

(b) Agreements Implemented Autonomously

The other route to transfer collective agreements into law is provided for in Article 155(2) TFEU by making use of the procedures and practices specific to management and labour and the Member States. For EU-wide binding effect the Treaty does not give a procedure. Implementation of an agreement concluded by European social partners, whether cross-industry or sector wise, should be done by procedures accepted by social partners on Member State level. Although since the 2000s the employers' side (BusinessEurope) has shown an increasing reservation towards negotiated legislation, some agreements have been reached, on a cross-industry level as well as on sectoral levels.[90] To have these agreements applied in the various Member States national procedures have to be used implementing the agreements. Where they contain concrete legal obligations

[87] See as an example of applying this requirement: general consideration 18 of Directive 97/81/EC.
[88] Among them the right to, or the obligation of the employer to provide, equal treatment of teleworkers compared to the employees at the employer's premises in the telework agreement.
[89] See for instance the Telework agreement and the Agreement on work-related stress. As a consequence they do not confer 'individual' rights that can be enforced in court.
[90] See Section 5.3.1.3(b).

to be complied with, the – legal – question arises whether the agreement is binding on the parties in the countries concerned and furthermore whether it is binding on employees when a provision of the agreement confers individual rights. Since these agreements have a transnational nature and content, private international law plays an important, decisive role to answer this question.[91]

The route of implementation of these 'autonomous' collective – framework – agreements is not by Council decision but by a specific one: 'in accordance with the procedures and practices specific to management and labour and the Member States' (Article 155(2) TFEU). It has to be kept in mind that since these agreements are not restricted to the subjects for which the TFEU provides legislative competence (Article 153(1) TFEU), collective agreements by European social partners can be used for almost anything and 'social policy' is remarkably wider than the fields mentioned in Article 153 TFEU. For example, Article 156 TFEU considers as 'social policy fields' matters relating to employment, labour law and working conditions, basic and advanced vocational training, social security, prevention of occupational accidents and diseases, occupational hygiene as well as collective rights.[92]

Agreements on such topics have to be implemented autonomously, i.e. via national procedures. Usually it is explicitly mentioned in the agreement that national parties have to implement the agreement in national law.[93]

Also, in respect of these agreements the question arises whether and how these agreements – not implemented by Council decision – can have a binding or even a legally binding effect based on the domestic law of the Member States. Since EU law has no explicit rules on the legal effects of such autonomously implemented agreements, it can be concluded that EU law does not grant them binding effect. Instead, domestic law has to provide for such an effect.

As indicated above, a crucial question is whether the provisions of the agreement contain 'normative' or 'obligatory' norms, to put it in labour law terms. If they have such norms, the binding effect of provisions of the agreement has to be derived from rules of international private law.[94] However, as said, most of the agreements specify the obligations for the parties to the agreement – the national employers' and employees' organisations. They use instruments other than conferring rights to individual employers or employees. The issues are, for example, related to work-related stress, workplace harassment and

[91] See on the issue of application of this type of agreements – which actually have a private law nature – Van Hoek & Hendrickx (2009).

[92] An example of the extensive range is ECJ 1985, C-281/85, C-283-285 and C-287/85 (*Germany and others v. Commission*), particularly §§21–24.

[93] See inter alia European agreement on the Implementation of the European Hairdressing Certificates §8. The agreement is signed by the European parties as well as by the national social parties.

[94] The EU regulations in this field (Regulation (EC) No 44/2001 and Regulation (EC) No 593/2008) are guiding here. For more on these questions see Section 2.4.

violence, labour market access, training facilities, certification etc.[95] Although these agreements contain few rights and duties for individuals, it is still possible that they do.[96]

5.2.3. TRANSNATIONAL COMPANY AGREEMENTS

5.2.3.1. Introduction

Transnational bargaining on company level has been developed in the wake of the growing internationalisation of companies in the 1970s in reaction to the globalisation of industrial relations that followed from the internationalisation of the economy. Working and employment conditions have been challenged by that development. The OECD as well as the ILO took the initiative to explore possible regulation of Multinational Enterprises (MNEs).[97] In this period the European Commission, in the context of company law, put forward proposals on the internal structure and decision-making in companies, including workers' participation.[98] In the mid-1980s the first Transnational Company Agreement (TCAs) in Europe was concluded between the French Danone group and an international union.[99] German companies followed this path. Along with the trade union the works council took part in the negotiations. These agreements served as models for the directive on European Works Councils of 1994.

Since then, transnational collective bargaining on company level has become a feature that is spreading over Europe and beyond. Although a legal framework for the negotiation process including the parties taking part in the bargaining, and its results (transnational collective agreements) did not exist, that did not hinder the making of these kinds of transnational arrangements.

In the second half of the 1990s, the European Commission[100] drew the attention to the social dialogue in transnational companies at the European level starting with cross-border regions. In 2004 it launched the debate on the need for a framework for transnational collective bargaining.[101]

---

95 Cf. European Social Dialogue Committee (2006), *Report on the implementation of the European Framework Agreement on Telework by the European Social Partners*, pp. 15–28.

96 That might be connected to the nature of the duties imposed on the employer. A possibility could be the Framework Agreement on Work-related Stress of 2004 where it refers to obligations based on Framework Directive 89/391.

97 See Schömann (2012), pp. 198/199. And further elaborated Da Costa and Rehfeldt (2008), p. 45 ff.

98 See Chapter 7. It did not result in any regulation on this matter.

99 International Union of Food, Agricultural, Hotel, Restaurant, Catering, Tobacco and Allied Workers' Association (IUF).

100 European Commission (1996), *Communication concerning the Development of the Social Dialogue at Community level*, COM(1996)448 final, p.16.

101 European Commission launched a study on this subject; See Communication from the Commission, *Partnership for change in an enlarged Europe – Enhancing the contribution of*

The importance of European Works Councils for creating a European culture of trade unionism and cooperation of employee representatives can hardly be underestimated.[102]

What has to be understood by the term 'Transnational Company Agreement' has been subject to international debate. It can include all kinds of transnational texts negotiated between workers' organisations or representatives at enterprise level, including European trade unions and European works councils on the one hand, and specific Multinational Enterprises on the other. In the EU framework a Transnational Company Agreement is defined as:

> an agreement comprising reciprocal commitments, the scope of which extends to the territory of several States and which has been concluded by one or more representatives of a company or a group of companies on the one hand, and one or more workers' organisations on the other hand, and which covers working and employment conditions and/or relations between employers and workers or their representatives.[103]

In the literature a more precise definition has been proposed, a Transnational Company Agreement is:

> an agreement comprising reciprocal commitments the scope of which extends to the territory of several States and which has been concluded by one or more representatives of a company or a group of companies on the one hand, and one or more workers' organisations on the other hand, and which covers working and employment conditions and/or relations between employers and workers or their representatives.[104]

Though the last definition is more concise than that of the Commission, it still is a wide definition and can contain all kinds of arrangements between the parties on both sides, ranging from 'joint declarations' and codes of conduct to (framework) agreements. One of the main issues that has been discussed is the legal character. However, a lack of legal effects in the strict sense does not mean that they do not have any meaning. This can be seen as forms of 'soft law' or, in other words, 'best practices'.

European social dialogue, COM(2004)557 final, p. 11. The study of Ales (2006) is part of these initiatives.

102 See for more details about European Works Councils, Chapter 7 of this book. See also Hürtgen (2011); Schömann et al. (2012).

103 European Commission (2012), *Transnational company agreements: realising the potential of social dialogue*, SWD(2012)0264.

104 Van Hoek and Hendrickx (2009), p. 2. In 2008 the European Commission added the last part to its previous definition; see European Commission (2008), *Commission staff working document – The role of transnational company agreements in the context of increasing international integration*, SEC(2008) 2155, p. 3, footnote 2.

By early 2012, 224 Transnational Company Agreements had been recorded in 144 companies, mostly with headquarters in Europe, covering over 10 million employees.[105] By 2015 the number had increased to more than 280.[106] In 2008, the Commission drew up a 'Mapping of transnational texts negotiated at corporate level'[107] and currently there is a Database on transnational company agreements.[108]

This section will deal with the following subjects:

- the level of concluding of Transnational Company Agreements (Section 5.2.3.2);
- the parties involved in and concluding Transnational Company Agreements (Section 5.2.3.3);
- content of the Transnational Company Agreements (Section 5.2.3.4); and
- nature and (legal) effect of Transnational Company Agreements (Section 5.2.3.5).

5.2.3.2. Levels

Transnational bargaining on company level can and does take place at a 'global' or at European level. The majority of the current Transnational Company Agreements have a European scope or are focused on the European Union. Although 'globally' concluded agreements have a worldwide scope and focus, they may also address specific European issues, in which case European Works Councils are usually heavily involved.[109] The global agreements addressing specific European issues are called 'mixed' Transnational Company Agreements.[110] However, the differences between these types of agreements are not very significant. The vast majority of global agreements have been concluded by multinationals with headquarters in Europe and are thus linked to a European Social Model.[111] Global Union Federations and European Works Councils usually cooperate closely in negotiation and monitoring.

---

105 Commission staff working document of 10 September 2012, *Transnational company agreements: realising the potential of social dialogue*, SWD(2012)0264.

106 See for a historical overview: Papadakis (2009), pp. 15–62; see also Telljohann (2009), pp. 510–513; and Commission staff working document of 10 September 2012, *Transnational company agreements: realising the potential of social dialogue*, SWD(2012)0264.

107 European Commission (2008), *Mapping of transnational texts negotiated at corporate level*, EMPL F2 EP/bp 2008 (D) 14511.

108 <http://ec.europa.eu/social/main.jsp?catId=978> accessed 05.06.2019.

109 Cf. Database TCAs: <http://ec.europa.eu/social/main.jsp?catId=978&langId=en> accessed 05.06.2019

110 European Commission, 2 July 2008, EMPL F2 EP/bp 2008 (D) 14511.

111 Cf. Greven (2006), p. 12; Blanke & Hoffmann (2006); Kocher (2008a).

5.2.3.3. *Negotiating and Signatory Parties*

The parties to the negotiations are usually European and/or international workers' trade unions, federations, and, in most cases, European Works Councils (EWCs) or World Works Councils (WWCs) on the one side, and central management of the multinational companies (hereafter MNC) on the other. National trade unions can be co-signing parties, which may contribute to a more (legally) 'easy' application and enforcement of the Transnational Company Agreement.[112] On the management side, national and local management can be involved in the negotiating process, together with corporate management. That can vary from one company to another. As to the 'global' arrangements, it should be noted that they usually have a trilateral (or mixed in the Commission's terms) nature, which means that they are concluded between (the management of) multinational companies, global unions and European Works Council.

The most disputed question is that of the involvement of European Works Councils. European Works Councils generally play a key role, often taking the initiative to start transnational negotiations.[113] Although they have no specific negotiating powers, in many cases they act as co-signatories.[114] It is argued that without an explicit provision in the European Works Councils Directive (neither Directive 94/45/EC nor Directive 2008/38/EU) the European Works Councils lack the power to negotiate and conclude agreements. That could be remedied by the explicit recognition of this power by the other negotiating parties, at least the party on the employer's side.[115] Other obstacles could be whether they have a mandate (from whom?) and whether they meet the representativity requirements. Apart from lacking negotiating powers they do not have the possibility or powers to initiate and organise collective actions such as strikes. It is argued that, therefore, they are less effective than trade unions usually are.

In practice, Transnational Company Agreements exist and play a role in shaping industrial relations. In almost all cases Transnational Company Agreements have been are concluded with the combination of European or international trade unions and European Works Councils. The participation of European Works Councils has not been an obstacle to conclude these agreements or putting it in a more positive way: they have contributed to the establishing

112 In Section 5.2.3.5 the effect of Transnational Company Agreements will be dealt with.
113 E.g. Müller (2013), p. 51 ff.
114 See Laulom (2005), p. 46. Müller (2013). See also the EU database <http://ec.europa.eu/social/main.jsp?catId=978&langId=en&company=&hdCountryId=&companySize=&sectorId=&year=&esp=62&geoScope=&refStandard=&keyword=&mode=advancedSearchSubmit> accessed June 2018.
115 See Jagodzinski (2012), pp. 173–75.

of Transnational Company Agreements. The experiences vary across the parties in the various sectors.[116]

5.2.3.4. *Content and Issues*

The content and the issues covered in a Transnational Company Agreement may differ between a European Transnational Company Agreement and an international company agreement, usually called an International Framework Agreement (IFA). That is mainly the result of the way the agreements have been established and the form they are given. When International Framework Agreements are established as unilateral 'Codes of conduct' or other legally non-binding forms they define social rights for their own employees as well as for those of their subcontractors.

Generally speaking, International Framework Agreements can be divided into two broad categories: (a) fundamental principles and rights at work, such as freedom of association, collective bargaining, non-discrimination, abolition of forced labour and elimination of child labour;[117] and (b) minimum terms and conditions of employment in particular working time, occupational safety and health. In some of them, more specific issues can also be found, such as mobility, training, job security, subcontracting and even accidently issues related to restructuring, however usually in very general terms.[118] It has to be kept in mind that they can rather be seen as a commitment by the company 'to respect a number of principles of labour relations and conditions of work' than as a legal obligation.[119] They provide almost no concrete, enforceable rights, neither to the workers' organisations nor to individual workers employed in an international company and its subsidiaries.

Overall, fundamental social rights or core labour standards nowadays seem to constitute the lowest common denominator.[120]

European Company Agreements[121] with a more regional scope of application are more diverse, both in terms of content and issues covered. From the beginning – as the Danone agreement shows – issues are identified that go beyond professional equality of men and women and the right of association. Two other areas are frequently covered: professional training and

---

116 Schömann (2012), p. 200.

117 Next to the ILO core conventions also referring to OECD Guidelines for Multinational Enterprises (2011). Cf. Papadakis (2008), p. 71.

118 See extensively the study of Papadakis (2008), particularly chap. 4, p. 89 ff; and Daugareilh (2006).

119 Papadakis (2008), p. 71.

120 Kocher (2004), pp. 27–31; Schömann (2008), p. 1; Kocher (2008a), pp. 67–86.

121 In literature they are usually called European Framework Agreements (EFAs) referring to their nature: framework agreements. They have to be distinguished from the framework agreements on European level concluded between social partners within the ambit of TFEU concluded on cross-industry or sectoral level.

information/consultation of employee representatives.[122] In particular the last one is an issue typical for European agreements as well as European 'in substance', as it refers to the core aspiration of European social policy. In its overview of 2012 the Commission listed the subjects frequently appearing in these European Company Agreements: restructuring, training, qualification and mobility, health and safety,[123] equal opportunities,[124] financial participation, data protection, and use of internet and social dialogue.[125]

The General Motors case in 2003/2004 can serve to illustrate the 'effectiveness' of a coordinated action of the (European) trade union and the European Works Council.[126] After management had announced that 12,000 jobs were to be cut in Europe, the European Metalworkers' Federation (EMF) together with the GM European Employees Forum (the European Works Council at GM Europe) succeeded in organising a European day of industrial action, i.e. coordinated manifestations and stand-stills in several European plants. As a result of these actions, a European Company Agreement[127] concerning restructuring was concluded in December 2004, according to which GM management agreed to refrain from closing plants, avoid forced redundancies and instead use early retirement schemes, outsourcing and various national schemes of labour market policies to cut jobs.

5.2.3.5. *Nature and Legal Effects of Transnational Company Agreements*

The effectiveness of a Transnational Company Agreement is directly connected to its nature and subsequently to its actual application. To be effective as a Transnational Company Agreement the agreement has to be applied and implemented in the multinational company itself as well as in its subsidiaries – of course only in so far as they are substantively covered by the agreement. Transnational Company Agreements belong to the category of autonomous agreements, which means that they are negotiated and concluded by the management and labour on multinational company level. The effect of a Transnational Company Agreement is furthermore dependent on the form of the arrangement reached by the parties. All forms of non-binding arrangements, such as codes of conduct or guidelines and the like, cannot be granted direct legal effect, what does not imply that they are ineffective.[128] If they have a legal nature, that does not ensure its actual effect.

---

122 Schömann (2012), p. 199.

123 See Section 7.4.3.

124 Kocher (2008b), pp. 371–78.

125 See European Commission (2012), *Commission staff working document, Transnational company agreements: realising the potential of social dialogue* pp. 4 and 13.

126 See on this case the Ales report (2006), pp. 28/29.

127 Actually it was called a European Framework Agreement; see about it in previous footnote.

128 That might have an effect as soft law or serve as best practice.

Since it is an agreement according to civil law its effect is dependent on the international private law rules. However, neither the Rome I Regulation nor the Brussels I Regulation, as regards to jurisdiction, give final answers on their legal effect in the Member States and which law is applicable.[129] Although the principle of freedom of choice as provided by Article 3 Rome I Regulation offers the parties the possibility to agree on which national law applies, even then the actual application in the subsidiaries in the Member States where they are located is not guaranteed.[130] If a choice of applicable law is not made, the second rule (Article 4 of the Rome I Regulation) does not give a definite answer either to the question which law is actually applicable. The terms used in Article 4(2, 3 and 4) are not clear enough for a decisive answer. In case of a multinational company it is hard to decide whether the 'characteristic performance of the contract' is taking place at the 'habitual residence' of the party that claims application of the Transnational Company Agreement.[131] When that is not sure, the next rule might give the solution by stating that 'the contract shall be governed by the law of the country with which it is most closely connected', for which several circumstances have to be taken into account.[132] The incorporation of a Transnational Company Agreement into national (labour) law – which mainly means the national law on collective agreements – is subject to the fulfilment of the domestic rules and procedures for collective agreements. have been fulfilled. If that is the case, a Transnational Company Agreement qualifies as a national collective labour agreement, and thus allows recourse to national enforcement rules and mechanisms. However, the large differences in Member States' laws as to the qualifying requirements for concluding a collective agreement and for a general application of the collective agreement appear to be real obstacles for this solution.[133]

In addition, it can happen that one and the same agreement will be treated differently according to a variety of applicable laws, depending on the conflict that is subject to litigation.[134] And, finally, the significant differences between Member States in respect of the legal capacity of workers' organisations to lodge claims at a national court for application of the agreement may lead to legal uncertainty and unpredictability.[135]

As it stands now, an effective application of Transnational Company Agreements in the multinational company as well as in its subsidiaries is

129 Cf. Van Hoek & Hendrickx (2009), p. 14.

130 Elaborated by Van Hoek & Hendrickx (2009), pp. 22–24.

131 The country of the 'leading' company (the parent company most likely) seems the most obvious outcome.

132 See Van Hoek & Hendrickx (2009), pp. 24–27.

133 The study of Rodriguez et al. (2011) pictures these differences and the problems to be overcome due to these differences.

134 See on this Van Hoek & Hendrickx (2009).

135 See on this also Even (2008), pp. 743–770.

at least doubtful.[136] A solution may be found in creating a European legal framework, as has been proposed in the literature[137] and by the European Commission and the European Parliament. It is felt necessary in order to guarantee an effective implementation and application of Transnational Company Agreements.

In 2012, the Commission was convinced that an impetus had to be given to the promotion of Transnational Company Agreements. At the same time, it was also fully aware that for providing legal effect to transnational texts, numerous obstacles have to be overcome. The main obstacles were identified as: (1) the absence of procedural rules, which hinders the start of content-related negotiations; (2) the absence of clear capacity and/or legitimacy of the signatories; (3) the big differences between countries hindering the consistent implementation of Transnational Company Agreements; (4) uncertainties as to the legal effects of Transnational Company Agreements and to the application of private international law rules; and (5) resentment among managers and workers' representatives at lower levels about the top down imposition of measures agreed at an upper level.[138]

The support at EU level for the Transnational Company Agreements has to be flexible, which means meeting the needs of the companies and the workers, designed in close cooperation with social partners. It must also be optional, meaning that parties should be free to negotiate and conclude agreements that are custom-built to their needs and to a specific situation.[139]

At the time of writing (in 2019), it is not very clear what will be the outcome. Employers and their organisations are not really in favour of having a legal framework, even when it has an optional nature. The ETUC is in favour of an optional legal framework for TCAs.[140] An issue raised by the ETUC is the effective exercise of the right to collective action in case of disputes related to the bargaining of Transnational Company Agreements with the aim of putting the employers' side, i.e. the management of the multinational company, under pressure. The workers' associations as well as doctrine have pointed to the case law of the Court of Justice in the *Viking* and *Laval* cases that might have a restricting effect on the right to take collective action also in cases of disputes at multinational company.[141]

---

136 Cf. Schömann (2012), pp. 227–228.

137 Cf. Ales report (2006), Jaspers (2012b), p. 233 ff. and Schömann (2012), p. 219 ff.

138 European Commission (2012), *Commission staff working document, Transnational company agreements: realising the potential of social dialogue*, p. 6; See also Sciarra (2012), p. 10. National trade unions were fearing an erosion of the freedom of trade unions and the correlated freedom of bargaining.

139 European Commission (2012), *Commission staff working document, Transnational company agreements: realising the potential of social dialogue*, p. 7.

140 ETUC (2016).

141 See Section 5.3.1.5.

A final issue debated among workers' organisations is the relationship between the European Works Councils and trade unions and the role of European Works Councils in transnational company bargaining. This relationship is ambiguous, since European Works Councils and trade unions often act successfully together. However, unions sometimes fear that an explicit acknowledgement of a mandate for European Works Councils to negotiate and conclude agreements may weaken the position of trade unions as bargaining parties.[142] Another argument is that European Works Councils might be not as independent from the employer, and do not have the power of collective action, which means that their bargaining position depends exclusively on the cooperation of employers.

5.3. TRADE UNION RIGHTS IN EU LAW

5.3.1. INTRODUCTION

Regulation of trade union rights is not a subject that falls within the competence of EU legislation. Article 155(5) TFEU excludes from regulation the right to association and the right to strike, as its predecessor did,[143] although the EU Charter on Fundamental Rights recognises the freedom of association (Article 12 EU Charter), the right to negotiation and conclusion of collective agreements, and the right to take collective action (Article 28 EU Charter) as fundamental rights. Therefore, the European Union has abstained from regulating on this matter. The regulating systems of the various Member States differ substantially and that was one of the main reasons for not giving legislative powers to the European Union.[144] Besides that, the European Union has deliberately refrained from interfering in the autonomous competences of the Member States on this issue.

That does not mean that EU law does not influence trade union rights, since these can collide with primary European law. In particular, competition law may affect the conclusion of collective agreements between employers and trade unions.[145] Also the right to strike and its exercise is restricted substantially by EU law, in particular when it interferes with the economic freedoms.[146] Both aspects will be dealt with hereafter.

---

142 Jagodzinski (2012), p. 180.

143 Article 137(5) TEC.

144 Studies have shown how big the differences are. See Valdés Dal-Ré (2006); and Rodriguez (2011), chap. 2.

145 By the decisions of the Court in the series of cases starting with ECJ 1999, C-67/96 (*Albany*); ECJ 1999, C-115/97-117/97 (*Brentjes*); ECJ 1999, C-219/97 (*Drijvende Bokken*); ECJ 2000, C-222/98 (*Van der Woude*). See Section 5.3.1.4.

146 By the decisions of the Court in the *Laval* and *Viking* cases, see Section 5.3.1.5.

The recognition of the fundamental rights of employers' and workers' associations by the European Union implies that EU law has to take into consideration the way these rights are worded by other international fundamental rights instruments and by supervisory institutions of other international organisations interpreting these rights and their exercise. For that reason, this aspect will dealt with in the next section.

5.3.1.1. Historical Development: The Route to Recognition of Trade Union Rights

Until the Treaty of Lisbon, which entered into force on 1 December 2009, trade union rights were not recognised and guaranteed by the European Community. The Treaties did not provide any competence in the field of collective labour rights, apart from the possibility for the (European) social partners to conclude agreements on European level dealing with issues mentioned by the Treaties.[147] In 1989, as part of the Social Agenda, the EEC adopted the Community Charter of the Fundamental Social Rights of Workers, which included a provision in which the fundamental right of association, including the right to take collective action, was recognised (Article 11). However, this provision did not have direct effect, because the Community Charter was not primary European legislation.

The Treaties did not grant the European Council legislative competence with regard to this matter. It was the exclusive competence of the Member States.[148] One may wonder whether this approach is tenable since the case law of the Court of Justice actually affects trade union rights, in particular when they might collide with European 'hard' law, such as competition law and the fundamental (economic) freedoms. Trade union rights may even collide with European procurement law.

In this respect a question arises: what effect do the fundamental rights of the EU Charter have in relation to trade union rights? This question has to be answered by the Court of Justice. An important issue is whether fundamental rights of the EU Charter can have direct effect, meaning that individuals and private parties can appeal to it directly in a law-suit (see Chapter 1, Section 1.4.4.2).

Impact of European law on the national law on collective bargaining and collective agreements is traceable in the situation of free movement of workers. According to Article 8 of Regulation (EC) 492/2011, workers who are nationals of a Member State who are employed in another Member State can make use of the whole repertoire of trade union rights in the same way as the workers who

---

147 See Section 5.2.2.3.

148 Cf. Article 137(5) EC Treaty.

are nationals of that Member State. This includes joining a trade union, forming a trade union, and exercising all the rights connected to union membership.[149]

5.3.1.2. Impact of International Regulations on Trade Union Rights in the EU

Although, just like its 'predecessors' (the EEC and EC), the EU is not directly bound by international treaties in which fundamental social rights are recognised,[150] these treaties are not without influence or even effect. However, the effect is not very strong, because EU law does not explicitly refer (or barely refers) to these international sources. Reference to international sources is only made in policy documents of the European Council.

In the 1990s, the Council adopted conclusions on (trade and) labour standards in which it supported strongly the protection of core labour rights as laid down in ILO conventions.[151] The ILO standards are considered to complement the *acquis communautaire* in areas which are not covered or that are only partly covered by EU legislation and policies, which includes trade union freedom and collective bargaining.[152] Apart from references in Commission documents the EU legislator is silent on ILO conventions. In the Community Charter of the fundamental social rights of workers and in the EU Charter of fundamental rights, ILO conventions are not even mentioned as a source of inspiration, whereas other international, in particular European, fundamental rights sources are quoted.[153]

That is contrary to the position of the Commission, which has declared that the EU's aim is to promote and fully integrate fundamental rights – including core labour standards – in all its policies and actions referring to adoption of the EU Charter.[154] The policy of the European Union on this issue is to promote and encourage Member States to apply the fundamental trade union rights in domestic law and practice.[155]

---

149 Regulation 492/2011 mentions the exercise of trade union rights, 'including the right to vote and to be eligible for the administration and management posts of a trade union, as well as the right of eligibility for workers' representative bodies in the undertaking'. Discrimination on trade union membership and activities is prohibited in Directive 2000/78/EC as well (Article 3(1)(d)).

150 Apart from ILO Conventions (ILO 87 and 98) one can think of UN Treaties/Covenants such as ICCPR and ICESCR.

151 Council conclusions in October 1999, Annex 1 in COM(2001)416. In 2006 the Commission issued a Communication on *Promoting Decent Work for All*, COM(2006)249.

152 See Herzfeld Olsson (2011), p. 33.

153 Not even the explanatory reports to the documents mention international conventions. See also Herzfeld Olsson (2011), pp. 37–39. The treaties of the Council of Europe (ECHR and ESC) are mentioned in the Preamble of the EU Charter.

154 In 2001 the Commission referred to the EU Charter of Fundamental Rights of the European Union (proclaimed in Nice in 2000), COM(2001)416, p. 10. See also Herzfeld Olsson (2011), pp. 38–39.

155 For some Member States that does not seem necessary because they have adopted these rights in their national constitutions. For those that have not done so, this can be worthwhile.

The EU institutions refer more explicitly and often to the instruments of the Council of Europe. Article 151 TFEU, for instance, explicitly refers to the (Revised) European Social Charter ((R)ESC),[156] leaving open what the effect of this reference may be, or has to be, on its interpretation and application. For the time being it seems to be considered as a mere point of reference, even in cases in which the Court of Justice deals with these internationally recognised rights. In the *Viking* and *Laval* decisions the Court referred to ILO Convention 87 as well as to the ESC, although the influence of these sources was very limited.[157] In other cases the Court also used the reference as 'inspirational' source.[158]

An explanation for this approach of the EU legislator could be that many Member States, if not all, are parties to these treaties. Moreover, joint constitutional traditions of the Member States as referred to in the preamble of the EU Charter, may be seen as enhancing the importance of fundamental rights including fundamental social rights.[159] And the majority of the Member States recognise in their Constitutions the core trade union rights.

Since EU law has an impact on collective bargaining and the results of the bargaining and since the Court of Justice has been involved in questions directly related to these issues, it is necessary to highlight the main issues. EU law itself is more or less silent about the content of the rights. To find an (internationally) common denominator of the substance of these rights other international sources have to be consulted. In relation to EU law and the way it deals with collective bargaining, special attention has to be given to the possibilities which law – either international or European or even national law – provides to restrict the exercise of these rights.

5.3.1.3. *Content of Trade Union Rights*

The main trade union rights can be divided in three categories. The first is the right to organise, which includes the right to establish a trade union, to freely join or not join a trade union; freedom of the internal management of a trade union; and protection of exercising trade union rights, in particular by trade union officials and trade union members. The protective rules are important because they should protect trade union officials and members against all kinds of disciplinary measures by the employer or measures that may be harmful for them because they limit the officials and members carrying out activities as trade unionists or may have a negative impact on their employment.[160]

---

156 It refers also to the Community Charter of the Fundamental Social Rights of Workers.

157 Herzfeld Olsson (2011), p. 39

158 ECJ 2010, C-271/08 (*Commission v. Germany*), §37. See Hertzfeld Olsson (2011), p. 40.

159 Cf. EU Charter, §5 preamble. See also Article 6 TEU.

160 ECSR Conclusions 2010 (*Albania*). ECtHR 2015, Appl. No. 36807/07 (*Ismail Sezer v. Turkey*), §§55–57 and ECtHR, 2015 Appl. No. 7152/08 (*Dogan Altun v. Turkey*), §§49–52.

The second and third category are the right to collective bargaining resulting in the conclusion of collective labour agreements and the right to take collective action. These are also considered to be fundamental rights and they are closely linked to each other. Hereafter the possible restrictions that could be imposed on the exercise of these rights will be discussed (Sections 5.3.1.4 and 5.3.1.6).

According to all international labour law sources, these rights and freedoms are not absolute. They can be restricted on pre-established grounds, as is the case for all fundamental rights. Violations can be challenged before courts or other supervisory institutions. The sources to rely on in the context of European (labour) law, are ECHR, (R)ESC and, partly, ILO Conventions 87, 98 and 151. In this respect the ECtHR plays an important role, since the articles of the ECHR related to the issues here at stake, have a strong, if not binding effect. The opinions of other supervisory institutions, including the European Committee on Social Rights and the ILO Committees, have – from a legal point of view – less impact.[161]

(a) The Right to Organise

The freedom of association is recognised in the ECHR (Article 11), (R)ESC (Article 5) and in both the Community Charter (Article 11) and the EU Charter (Article 12(1)).[162] This freedom contains two components: the right to establish an association and the right to join or not to join a union.

The freedom to establish a union – for both employers and employees – implies that trade unions and employer organisations must be free to organise themselves without prior authorisation by the State.[163] It also imposes on the State the negative obligation to refrain from placing any restrictions on that right and the exercise thereof in any other way than what is permitted by the Treaty provisions concerned.[164] It also contains the (positive) obligation for States to take adequate legislative or other measures to guarantee the exercise of the right to organise and, in particular, to protect workers' organisations from any

161 Since the opinions of both ILO Committees (CEARC and CFA) and the ECSR are not legally binding, they can and should give guidance to the Court of Justice and to national courts to interpret the rights. See the study of Niklas Bruun (2017), p. 220 ff.; Samuel (2002).

162 Inspired and guided by ILO conventions 87 and 98.

163 A kind of registration is allowed if the rules regarding this do not restrict the possibility to establish an organisation. Registration can be used in an administrative manor, e.g. to make it publicly clear which unions exist and are acting as such. In EU Member States various regulations exist dealing with this kind of registration.

164 In conformity with Article 11(2) ECHR and Article G (R)ESC. They contain a fairly standard formulation, also used in EU law and by the Court of Justice of the EU in rather similar words.

interference on the part of employers.[165] It implies that neither the State nor employers must impose restrictions on employees who want to become or are trade union members. The State is under the obligation to take the necessary measures to prevent this from happening.[166] It also entails an obligation to protect workers who face discrimination on ground of union membership or because of carrying out activities as union member.[167]

The 'freedom to establish' contains also the freedom to issue its own rules for the organisation and functioning of the trade union.[168] The State and international institutions such as the EU are not allowed to impose restrictions on this, except under the rules that allow restrictions laid down in the treaties. This means that a trade union is free to adopt rules for membership as well as for election or appointment of representatives unless these discriminate on forbidden grounds. A trade union is also free to adopt rules with regard to disciplinary measures, once again unless forbidden discrimination is involved. This freedom also means that union leaders have access to the workplace and that union members can have meetings 'in so far as employers' interests and company requirements permit this'.[169]

Applying for legal personality must be free. It is up to the organisation itself whether to adopt legal personality. Specific requirements can be set, provided they are reasonable.[170]

The right to organise has to be guaranteed in the private sector as well in the public sector. That means that an 'absolute' prohibition on forming trade unions imposed on civil servants is not permitted, as the ECtHR decided in the Turkish *Demir* case.[171] Any restriction must be tested against the provisions of Article 11(2) ECHR. Although the Court grants the States a rather large margin of appreciation, this appreciation is strictly scrutinised by the criteria of appropriateness and necessity.[172]

---

165 ECSR Conclusions I 31. See Harris and Darcy (2001), pp. 93–94; Jacobs (2016), p. 220 ff.; and Samuel (2002), pp. 104–12. The State has to prevent it from happening. See on this Dorssemont (2006a), p.10 et seq; Van Hiel (2013), p. 287 et seq.

166 See e.g. ECSR complaint No. 12/2002, Decision on the merits of 15 May 2003 (*Confederation of Swedish Enterprise v. Sweden*), §29.

167 ECtHR 2009, Appl. No. 67336/01, (*Danilenkov*) §135. The Court referred explicitly to an opinion of the Freedom of Association Committee on the same issue; see Digest (2006) §769, 818, 820 and 835.

168 ECtHR 1985, Appl. No. 10550/83 (*Cheall*).

169 See ECSR Conclusions XIII-5, *Portugal*, p. 172; Conclusions XV-1, *France*, p. 240; Conclusions 2010, *Georgia*, p. 286. Protection of trade union officials and members in the exercise of their rights is usually guaranteed in the national laws of States.

170 In the majority of the EU Member States, trade unions have legal personality. Belgium is an exception.

171 ECtHR 2008, Appl. No. 34503/97 (*Demir and Baykara*). See on this case and the consequences for the fundamental right to organise Ewing and Hendy (2010).

172 See e.g. the *Demir* case, §§119–126. See Ewing and Hendy (2010), p. 20.

A particular aspect of the freedom to organise is the right not to join, the so-called negative trade union freedom.[173] In practice, this 'negative' right is less relevant for the employers' side, although it is a right for an employer not to be forced in one way or another to join an employer organisation.

This negative freedom for workers is in practice linked to the issue of 'closed shop' practices. These practices imply that workers are more or less forced to become member of a trade union on penalty of losing their job or not being hired. This 'obligation' or strong coercion is usually laid down in collective agreements as specific clauses.[174] In general, closed shop practices are contrary to the negative freedom of association, although the treaties concerned (ECHR, ESC and ILO Conventions 87 and 98) do not explicitly recognise the choice or even the right not to become a member. Study of the case law of international courts and supervisory bodies shows that although a provision in the Treaties recognising the negative freedom was deliberately omitted, this does not imply that the negative aspect of a person's freedom of association falls completely outside the ambit of Article 11 ECHR.[175] A certain pressure to join a trade union is not prohibited; however, it is necessary to balance the interests of the employee who wants to stay outside, and the interests of the trade union. This interpretation refers to a theory of freedom to organise which has two sides: the individualistic and the collectivistic. The individualistic emphasises the individual freedom, to stay outside, not to be forced or coerced; the collectivistic approach promotes the power of the group – the trade union – that has to be strong in order to attain the main goal: defending the interests of the workers.[176] While the employee has the freedom to stay outside a union or not to be forced to become a trade union member, this freedom may be exploited in a negative way, as an instrument to detach a worker from a trade union. An attempt by an employer to use this 'negative' right as to induce employees not to become or to end their union membership by giving financial incentives to surrender important union rights is considered as an infringement of the right to organise.[177] Another example is the restriction of unemployment benefit to trade union members or to arrange a higher benefit for them. This can also amount to an interference with the right not to join an association and consequently is considered an infringement.[178]

---

173 See on this Dorssemont (2006a), p. 10 et seq.; and ECtHR 1985 Appl. No. 10550/83 (*Cheall*). Van Hiel (2013), p. 287 et seq.

174 That means based on an agreement of both parties: employer(s) and trade union(s).

175 ECtHR 1981, Appl. No. 7601/76; 7806/77 (*Young, James and Webster*) §52. See Dorssemont (2010b), p. 195 ff.

176 See Barnard (2012a), pp. 702–703; and Ewing (2003), p. 1 ff.

177 ECtHR 2002, Appl. No. 30668/96, 30671/96 and 30678/96 (*Wilson and Palmer*), §48.

178 ECtHR 1993, Series A No. 264 (*Sigurjónnson*); N 31. See ECSR Conclusions 2014 (*Iceland*). Similarly, ECtHR 2010, Appl. No. 20161/06 (*Vörður Ólafsson v. Iceland*).

(b) The Right to Collective Bargaining

Collective bargaining is a common feature in the EU, since 1989 when the Single Act introduced the system of collective bargaining between organisations of employers and of workers as a means of co-legislation.[179] At that time EU law did not provide a legal system for collective bargaining and even the question of which parties were to be involved in the negotiations was not addressed. As shown above (Section 5.2.2.1) the Commission has developed guidelines and the Court of Justice has developed rules to determine which organisations could be recognised as bargaining parties. The exclusion of regulating collective bargaining on Member State level from the legislative competences (according to Article 153(5) TFEU (previously Article 135(5) TEC) implies that the EU did not want to, and could not, act on this issue.

The benefits of collective bargaining between employers and workers' organisations have been 'praised' by Advocate-General Jacobs in the *Albany* case, in which a possible collision between competition law and collective agreements as the result of bargaining was at stake. Benefits listed by Jacobs were: prevention of labour costs conflicts, reduction of transactions costs, promotion of predictability and transparency. It 'helps to ensure a balanced outcome for both sides and for society as a whole'.[180]

The right to collective bargaining has been recognised in EU law and policy by the Community Charter of 1989. Article 12(1) speaks of the right to negotiate and conclude collective agreements under the conditions laid down in national law and practice. The reference to 'national law and practice' shows the modest role of EU law. This was in conformity with the legal practice of other European legislation. Up until 2008 the ECtHR, applying Article 11 ECHR, took the stand that 'although collective bargaining may be one of the ways by which trade unions may be enabled to protect their members' interests, it is not indispensable for the effective enjoyment of trade union freedom'. An obligation to recognise a trade union or conclude collective agreements did not exist.[181] In his Opinion in the *Albany* case, AG Jacobs supported that opinion: there is no fundamental right to bargain collectively.[182]

A radical change took place in 2008 when the European Court of Human Rights (ECtHR) decided that 'the right to bargain collectively with the employer has, in principle, become one of the essential elements of the right to form and to join trade unions for the protection of [one's] interests'.[183] The ECtHR stated that it had to adapt its case law 'so as to take account of the perceptible evolution

179 See Barnard (2012a), pp. 709–717.

180 Opinion AG Jacobs in C-67/96, §181.

181 ECtHR 2002, Appl. Nos. 30668/96, 30671/96 and 30678/96 (*Wilson and Palmer*), §44.

182 Opinion AG Jacobs in C-67/96, §160.

183 ECtHR 2008, Appl. No. 34503/97 (*Demir and Baykara*), §154.

in such matters, in both international law and domestic legal systems'.[184] A similar approach can be noted in decisions of the Court of Justice. In its decision of 2010 the Court indirectly recognised the fundamental nature of the right to collective bargaining, to which it added that that right must be exercised in accordance with European Union law.[185] A year later the Court confirmed this approach.[186] However, it put also a limit to the exercise of this fundamental right, in accordance with its interpretation in the *Viking* and *Laval* cases: a balance has to be struck between the right to collective bargaining resulting in collective agreements on the one hand and the economic right of freedom of establishment and to provide services.[187]

5.3.1.4. *Collective Agreements and Single Market Requirements (Competition Law)*

The single market, which has been created as a means to contribute to the economic welfare of the European Union as well as of the Member States and of the citizens, constitutes, together with the economic freedoms, the main pillar of the European Union.[188] It was also assumed that the single market is good for the workers as it grants them free movement within the EU, equal treatment with national workers and rights of residence. It also guarantees free and fair competition. As a consequence (national) labour law may collide with the rules on the freedom of movement, in particular freedom of establishment and freedom of providing services, as well as with EU competition law. In various cases the Court of Justice has had to decide on the outcome of potential collisions. The cases on the posted workers issue are well-known.[189]

In the field of collective labour law another question of potential collision was raised: a conflict between competition law and collective bargaining and collective agreement law. Competition law aims at prohibiting agreements between undertakings which may affect trade on the market and which have as their object or effect the prevention, restriction or distortion of competition within the market.[190] Price fixing is therefore prohibited by the rules on free and

---

184 The ECtHR refers to ILO conventions, the ESC and also to the EU Charter, in particular Article 28 as well as the domestic law systems of the Member States. §§147–54.

185 The Court referred to the *Viking* and *Laval* judgments.

186 ECJ 2011, C-297/10 and C-298/10 (*Sabine Hennigs*) and ECJ 2011, C-447/09 (*Prigge v. Deutsche Lufthansa*).

187 See Section 5.3.1.5.

188 In 2017 a 'social pillar' was added. Its aim is formulated in §13 of the Preamble. See about the social pillar and its meaning for European labour law, see Chapter 1, Section 1.2.5.

189 See Chapter 2. In a series of cases the Court of Justice has had to decide on potential collisions, of which the *Laval* and *Viking* judgments are most relevant when it comes to trade union rights.

190 E.g. Article 101 TFEU. In national laws similar provisions exist.

fair competition.[191] Collective bargaining resulting in collective agreements has – explicitly and deliberately – the effect of setting the price of labour, with the aim of creating stability and certainty for employers and workers and to avoid unfair competition on employment conditions. However, from the perspective of free competition, the conclusion of collective agreements by employers and workers' associations can be considered as agreements between undertakings prohibited according to Article 101 TFEU. Therefore, competition law can easily collide with the right to bargain collectively and to conclude collective agreements on employment conditions. If collective agreements can be considered as falling under the cartel prohibition of Article 101 TFEU, that might imply that collective (labour) agreements lose their effect unless they are exempted from competition law.

Since the right to collective bargaining aiming at concluding collective labour agreements in which the results of the negotiations are laid down is considered as a corollary to the right to organise, the question rises whether the (exercise of the) fundamental right can be restricted by competition law rules.[192] If the possibility of safeguarding workers' interests by means of collective agreements were to be restricted, this could be seen as 'substantial' restriction to the right of association. That might be an infringement of the fundamental right as laid down in Article 28 EU Charter.

The collision between collective agreements and competition law has been challenged in a couple of cases, starting by the *Albany* case in 1999. The outcome of these procedures is crucial for the continued existence of the system of regulating employment conditions by collective agreements.

For more than a century it was accepted that regulation was an essential objective of socio-economic policy. The collective agreements system, which was regarded as a fundamental means for achieving that policy, was said to entail a certain degree of adjustment of the market, including the labour market. It inevitably implied a certain restriction of competition. In the USA this is embedded in and developed in the *anti-trust law* that dates from the end of the nineteenth century. The first Federal act on this subject was issued in 1890. Applying the new act the US Supreme Court restricted the trade unions substantially. That led to an interference by the US government, which introduced an exemption for trade unions in the Clayton Act of 1914, further extended by the Norris-LaGuardia Act of 1942.[193] The law introduces 'immunity for the cartel prohibition' by stating (in Section 6) that 'nothing contained in the antitrust laws shall be construed to forbid the existence and operation of labor … organizations, … nor shall such organizations, or the members thereof, be held or construed to be illegal combinations or conspiracies in restraint of

191 E.g. Graig & De Burca (2008), p. 950 ff.
192 E.g. Barnard (2012a), p. 193 ff.; Roth & Rose, Bellamy & Child (2013). See also Wirtz (2006).
193 Meltzer (1965).

trade, under the antitrust laws'.[194] This immunity of trade unions is not meant to be absolute. Section 20 puts some conditions on an appeal to immunity: (1) It has to be a labour dispute involving a 'labor group'; (2) the trade union must act in its self-interest; (3) The union must not combine with non-labour groups, pointing at employers in particular.[195] The US Supreme Court decided in the 1970s that collective agreements[196] were exempted provided they regulate employment conditions.[197]

The Court of Justice of the EU followed the way that the US courts have chosen in a series of cases in 1999 and 2000 by granting – in general – collective agreements immunity.[198]

Since collective labour agreements are price-setting agreements, there was no doubt that the cartel prohibition of Article 101 TFEU was infringed. Nor is there any doubt that they interfere with the market because, to a large extent, they fix the labour costs in a sector of the economy. In the formula developed in *Albany, Brentjes, Drijvende Bolkken* and *van der Woude*, also known as the *immunity rule*, the Court subjected the exemption to the cartel prohibition to a number of conditions:

> agreements *concluded in the context of collective negotiations* between management and labour *in pursuit of social policy objectives* such as the improvement of conditions of work and employment must, *by virtue of their nature and purpose*, be regarded as falling outside the scope of Article 85(1) of the Treaty [now: Article 101 TFEU].[199]

Collective agreements do not infringe the cartel prohibition of Article 101 TFEU if they meet the following conditions:

- they are the result of collective bargaining between management and labour;
- they pursue social policy objectives, in particular improvement of conditions of work or employment;
- by virtue of (a) their nature, (b) their purpose.

---

194 This exemption is called the statutory exemption.

195 US Supreme Court *United States v. Hutcheson;* 312 US 219. AG Jacobs refers to it in his conclusion to the *Albany* case, C-67/96 (*Albany*), §97.

196 US Supreme Court 2 June 1975, No. 73-1256, 421 US 616, (*Connell Construction v. Plumbers and Steamfitters Local Union*). See, about the labour exemptions in US law, Steven D. Wheeless (2011). Collective agreements have not been mentioned explicitly in the Act.

197 In their conclusions AG Jacobs and AG Wahl explicitly have referred to this and other US Supreme Court decisions. Jacobs in his conclusion in *Albany* case (C-67/96), §97–107 and Wahl in his conclusion in the *FNV KIEM* case (C-413/13), §97/98.

198 ECJ 1999, C-67/96 (*Albany*); ECJ 1999, C-115/97-117/97 (*Brentjes*); ECJ 1999, C-219/97 (*Drijvende Bokken*); ECJ 2000, C-180/98–184/98 (*Pavlov*); ECJ 2000, C-222/98 (*Van der Woude*).

199 See ECJ 1999, C-67/96 (*Albany*), §60 (emphasis added).

In the case law of the Court the assessment of whether these conditions are fulfilled is focused on the two major requirements: (1) by its nature and (2) by its purpose. The other conditions are part of the assessment of the two main ones.

(a) The Result of Collective Bargaining and 'by its Nature'

As shown before, EU law neither defines what is considered as collective bargaining nor provide a definition of which organisations can be identified as bargaining parties. It can be assumed that it is left to the law of the Member States to establish which organisations of employers and workers can operate as bargaining parties. That is in conformity with the absence of competence to regulate this matter. EU law does not provide a definition of collective agreement; this is also left to the domestic law of Member States. That might imply that who is qualifies as a bargaining party and what is considered as collective agreement resulting in immunity for infringing the cartel prohibition can differ from Member State to Member State.

The issue of the limits of the results of collective bargaining, as relevant for the immunity from competition law, has been tackled by the Court of Justice in the *FNV KIEM* case.[200] The issue was raised by the Dutch competition authority alleging that the agreement concluded between the employers' association and the trade union FNV KIEM did not meet the condition of 'by virtue of its nature'.[201] The collective labour agreement laid down, along with the wages for the employees, minimum fees for the self-employed persons who substitute for 'ordinary' members of the orchestra (i.e. the musicians who are regularly employed by the orchestra) and who are hired as and when the orchestra needs them. On the trade union side, the agreement was negotiated by a workers' organisation (FNV KIEM) claiming that it represented these persons as members of the trade union. The Dutch government claimed that the trade union had not acted as an employees' association, but as an association for self-employed workers. Therefore, it was not covered by the immunity clause. A collective labour agreement also including provisions on contracts for professional services is altered in its legal *nature* and acquires the characteristics of an inter-professional agreement and the trade union acts as an association for self-employed workers. The Court of Justice decided that *if* this argument is correct, the collective agreement 'cannot be the result of a collective negotiation between employers and employees, and therefore cannot be excluded, by reason of *its nature*, from the scope of Article 101(1) TFEU'.[202]

---

200 ECJ 2014, C-413/13 (*FNV KIEM*), §30.

201 The government based this proposition on a DCA/NMA (2007), p. 13 ff. In his conclusion AG Wahl took the same position; see C-413/13 (*FNV KIEM*) §25–32. See also Jaspers (2015), p. 41 ff.

202 ECJ 2014, C-413/13 (*FNV KIEM*) §§30 (emphasis added).

However, the Court added that the situation will be judged differently if the self-employed persons have to be classified as false (or quasi) self-employed persons, provided the other requirements are fulfilled that has to be decided by the national court.[203] In conclusion, if these persons qualify as quasi self-employed, the collective agreement containing also minimum fees for these 'workers' can be covered by the immunity clause. Since it is an issue under Article 101 (competition law) the Court states that the worker has to be understood and classified as an employee within the meaning of EU law provided his independence is merely notional, thereby disguising an employment relationship.[204] 'False self-employment' refers to cases where a person has been hired as a self-employed person, although, according to European law, that person would have to be classified as 'employee'. The FNV KIEM decision is interesting insofar as it uses a definition of employee which differs from the *Lawrie Blum* definition[205] by extending it. If such a 'worker' does not share in the employer's commercial risks and, for the duration of the relationship, actually forms an integral part of employer's undertaking, so forming an economic unit with that undertaking,[206] he is a worker within the meaning of EU law. In some EU countries, in particular Germany, it is argued that it therefore also covers all workers who are economically dependent[207] or work in the employer's organisational unit.[208] These questions are particularly relevant for new forms of employment relationships.[209]

(b) The Requirement of 'by Purpose'

The 'purpose' requirement contains three elements. First, *social policy objectives*, which can be divided in two: (a) *conditions of work* and (b) *employment* and, second, *improvement of conditions of work or employment.*

Pursuing social policy objectives is self-evident in the EU policy context. Social policy is one of the main objectives of the European Union, laid down in

---

203 ECJ 2014. C-413/13 (*FNV KIEM)* §42.

204 ECJ 2004, C-256/01 *(Allonby)*, §71–72. Confirmed in ECJ 2014, C-270/13 (*Haralambidis*), §28.

205 ECJ 1986 Case 66/85 (*Lawrie Blum*), §17. See Chapter 1, Section 1.5.

206 ECJ 1989, C-3/87 (*Agegate*), §36; ECJ 1999, C-22/98 (*Becu*), §26; ECJ 2014, C-413/13 (*FNV KIEM*), §36.

207 Junker (2016), p. 184; Temming, (2015), p. 509.

208 Kocher (2019), pp. 173–214.

209 See Section 1.2.5; Risak & Dullinger (2018). In a proposal for a directive, the Council and European Parliament proposed a definition of 'worker' which is closer to *Lawrie-Blum* and therefore less wide: 'worker' means a natural person who for a certain period of time performs services for and under the direction of another person in return for remuneration; Article 2(1)(a) COM(2017)797 final. The proposal is not undisputed: see position paper of UEAPME (2018).

the European Treaties as well as in the case law of the Court of Justice.[210] What has to be understood by 'social policy objectives' has been subject to a series of decisions of the Court regarding the potential collision between competition law and collective bargaining. Improvement of conditions of work and employment, as appears in almost all decisions, is recognised as meeting this criterium, without doubt,[211] but has been criticised as rather vague.[212] The concept of *the conditions of work* does not seem uncertain, although that has been disputed inter alia by AG Jacobs in his conclusion in the *Albany* case. He suggested 'as a possible criterion that the collective agreement must be one which deals with *core* subjects of collective bargaining such as wages and working conditions and which does not directly affect third parties or markets'.[213] From the case law of the Court of Justice as well as of the EFTA Court[214] it can be seen that the Courts use a broad definition of 'conditions of work'. Next to wages or working hours it also entails pension schemes and contributions to social security schemes as well as health insurance schemes.[215] The EFTA Court even goes further by stating that matters as safety, the workplace environment, holidays, training and continuing education, and even consultation and co-determination between workers and management are included.[216] It can be concluded that, in the view of the Courts, all elements in a collective agreement from which an employee may benefit will qualify for meeting the 'purpose' requirement.[217]

In his opinion to the *FNV KIEM* case AG Wahl suggested that the inclusion of a minimum fees scheme – for the false self-employed people – in the collective agreement can be accepted as a legitimate purpose. He argued that those provisions improve directly the employment and working conditions of the false self-employed, who are employees, because the provisions contribute genuinely and effectively to the prevention of social dumping and do not go beyond what is necessary to achieve that objective.[218] He refers 'directly' to the fundamental right to collective bargaining: 'If workers were deprived of the possibility to negotiate those matters freely, the essence of their right to collective bargaining

210 E.g. Article 4(2) TFEU (originally Article 1 of the Agreement on Social policy). The social policy objective has been recognised by the Court of Justice since the decision in the Defrenne case: ECJ 1976, 43–75 (*Defrenne II*), §§62 and 63.

211 ECJ 1999, C-67/96 (*Albany*), §59. ECJ 2000, C-222/98 (*Van der Woude*), §25.

212 E.g. Evju (2001), p. 176 seq.

213 AG Jacobs C-67/96 (*Albany*), §§193 and 194 (emphasis added).

214 The EFTA Court is competent to decide this kind of cases for countries belonging to the EFTA states ('European Free Trade Association') applicable to Iceland, Liechtenstein, Norway and Switzerland.

215 ECJ 1999, C-67/96 (*Albany*); ECJ 1999, C-115/97–117/97 (*Brentjes*); ECJ 1999, C-219/97 (*Drijvende Bokken*).

216 EFTA 2002, E-8/00 (*Norwegian Federation of Trade Unions*), §53. See in more detail Wirtz (2006), p. 202 ff.

217 See AG Fenelly in his opinion to case C-222/98 (*Van der Woude*), §44.

218 AG Wahl in his opinion to case C-413/13 (*FNV KIEM*), §100.

would be frustrated.'[219] The Court shared the view of AG Wahl, stating that 'the minimum fees scheme put in place by the provision in the collective labour agreement *directly contributes* to the improvement of the employment and working conditions of those substitutes'.[220]

The *notion of employment* is even more vague than improvement of employment conditions. What has to be understood by that notion? So far, the Court of Justice has not filled in the term more precisely. However, the *FNV KIEM* case shows the importance of the prevention of 'social dumping'; i.e. employment by regular employees – meaning employees employed by the employer on a contract of employment – can be jeopardised by other persons who are willing to perform the work for the employer on a lower cost basis than the employees bound by the collective agreement. Thus, employees may be replaced by the 'cheaper' workers. In these circumstances, collective agreements may cover all the people who perform the work for the employer, regardless of whether they act as employees or as false-employees. Advocate General Wahl has raised just that issue in his conclusion to the *FNV KIEM* case, concluding that this way of preventing social dumping has to be considered as a social policy objective.[221] The Court did not go into this argument, either deliberately or because it did not find it necessary for its decision.

A third issue is the use of the term *improvement*. What has to be understood by improvement and how can it be measured? Does it have to be assessed on basis of the conditions of work and employment separately, or as part of the package deal between employers and trade unions that is laid down in the collective agreement? The main characteristic of collective bargaining on conditions of work and employment for the employees is to reach a compromise and exchange of interests. Moreover, it may be difficult to judge on the basis of a collective agreement as a whole or on the basis of each separate provision whether a provision is an 'improvement' or not. This suggests that a broad definition can be used and that another point of view could be problematic. The social partners' freedom to negotiate could be at issue and thus the autonomy of trade unions and employers and their organisations could be affected. Here, too, the rule is that a balance between the various interests must be sought.[222] The case law of Court of Justice does not make it clear what exactly the Court had in mind. The EFTA Court has shed some light on this issue. It states that the national judge in

219 See AG Wahl, case C-413/13 (*FNV KIEM*), §72. He referred, a contrario, to ECJ 2010, C-271/08 (*Commission v. Germany*), §49.

220 ECJ 2014, C-413/13 (*FNV KIEM*), §39 (emphasis added). In its final paragraph the Court decided in that way: it is to the national courts to decide on that. Legislations of Member States are using a broad definition, such as the Dutch competition law. National competition authorities also use a broad definition. E.g. Wirtz (2006), pp. 223/224.

221 AG Wahl, case C-413/13 (*FNV KIEM*), §§75–83.

222 See inter alia ECJ 2010, C-271/08 (*Commission v. Germany*), §52. In her opinion to the case AG Trstenjak took the same position: §188–195.

the concrete case also has to consider the cumulative effects of the provisions.[223] In his opinion in the *Van der Woude* case A-G Fennely proposed applying the proportionality test.[224] This test implies an assessment whether trade unions could have reached the objective of improvement with less far-reaching means. The Court expressly did not follow the A-G in this respect.[225] It 'would constitute an unwarranted restriction on the freedom of both sides of industry'. The parties must be able to determine the content of their collective agreement themselves. Another approach would damage the freedom to negotiate too much.

5.3.1.5. *The Right to Take Collective Action*

(a) Introduction

The right to take collective action as a corollary of collective bargaining is widely accepted in Europe.[226] It has been recognised explicitly in the European Social Charter since 1961. In the European Community it was inserted in the Community Charter of the Fundamental Social Rights of Workers of 1989 in §13. At the time it lacked legally binding effect, but since the adoption in 2000 of the EU Charter on fundamental rights, the European Union has explicitly recognised the right to take collective action. Article 28 of the EU Charter states: in cases of conflicts of interest employees *and* employers have the right 'to take collective action to defend their interests, including strike action'. Another source is the ECHR, in which the right to collective action is not explicitly recognised. Rather recently the ECtHR decided that this right is a right that is closely connected to the right to form and join trade unions, which has as its objectives the protection of the interests of the trade union and its members.[227] In all EU Member States the right is recognised either in the constitution of the State or in practice by judge-made law. In some countries the right has been elaborated in national legislation,[228] in others there exists either regulation in more general terms or no legislation specifically covering collective action at all.[229]

---

223 Court EFTA 2002, E-8/00 (*Norwegian Federation of Trade Unions*), §77.

224 AG Fennely, case C-222/98, (*Van der Woude*), §32. In his opinion to the *Albany* case, AG Jacobs went even further, but was not followed by the Court, C-67/96 (*Albany*), §193.

225 ECJ 2000, C-222/98 (*Van der Woude*), §26. See about this issue Evju (2001), in particular pp. 178 and 182.

226 See Novitz (2003), and Barnard (2012a), p. 717 ff.

227 Explicitly ECtHR 6 November 2009 (Appl./Requête No. 68959/01) (*Enerji Yapı-Yol Sen c. Turquie*); and ECtHR 8 September 2014 (Appl. No. 31045/10) (*RMT v. UK*). The case was about a so-called secondary action, in other words a sympathy strike. In a dissenting opinion three members of the Court had a differing opinion on this point.

228 The content of these laws can vary. Common is the way collective actions have to be called and organised. In some countries the consequences of organising a strike of participating in a collective action is also regulated, sometimes in detail.

229 The elaboration of the right is completely left to courts. A striking example is the Netherlands.

In the TFEU it is explicitly confirmed that the EU legislator has no competence to make legislation on the right to strike. This is laid down in Article 153(5) TFEU, from which it follows that the EU legislator cannot interfere by its own regulations in the national rulings or practices of industrial dispute resolution of the Member States.[230] The EU Charter can potentially change this situation, when a direct appeal to Article 28 EU Charter is recognised and permitted. However, until now the issue has not been brought before the Court of Justice.

EU law has only in an indirect way interfered with the right to collective action, i.e. in the *Laval* and *Viking* cases. In this section, first the legal system will be dealt with, in which the right to collective action is embedded. It is generally accepted that this right is not absolute. Second, the development of a formal recognition to the imposing of restrictions on the exercise of the right will be pictured. Finally, the focus will be on whether the case law of the Court has or can have an impact on Member States.

(b) The Legal System

Although according to Article 153(5) TFEU the EU itself does not have the competence to rule on the right to collective action, Article 28 of the EU Charter provides a legal ground for claiming the right to the collective action in general. It is a general recognition which means that it could be subject to legislative measures by the Member States or to decisions of national courts. That is based on two grounds. First Article 28 EU Charter itself adds a limitation to the exercise of the right. The use of the right cannot infringe EU law. The *Laval* and *Viking* cases[231] have made clear what that might mean. Article 28 EU Charter provides a second restriction by stating that the exercise of this fundamental right has to be 'in accordance with … national laws and practices', which means that is to the Member States to put restrictions either by law, meaning legislation or case law. That is in line with limitation of competence of the EU legislator on these matters, in accordance with Article 153(5) TFEU, as already mentioned. However, it has to be taken into account that the Court of Justice has stated that the right to collective action may not be *substantially impaired*.[232] Article 52 of the EU Charter contains a similar restricting clause: 'respect the essence of those rights'.

Article 52 EU Charter allows reasons to limit the exercise of fundamental rights, including the right to strike, that are in essence similar to other international law sources. They must be provided by law and limitations may be

---

230 See also Fuchs & Marhold (2014), p. 457.

231 ECJ 2007, C-438/05 (*Viking*) and ECJ 2007, C-341/5 (*Laval*). See Section 5.3.1.5(c).

232 As the Court has explicitly stated in ECJ 2003, C-112/00 (*Schmidberger*), §§74–80. Article 52 EU Charter also contains a similar clause: 'respect the essence of those rights'.

made only if they are necessary and genuinely meet objectives of general interest recognised by the Union or the need to protect the rights and freedoms of others, hereby adopting the principle of proportionality as a tool of assessment. Article 52(3) EU Charter adds an important reference to the ECHR. The 'meaning and scope of those rights shall be the same as those laid down by the said Convention'. An extensive protection can be provided by EU law. This can be interpreted as meaning that the EU has to take into account the case law of the European Court of Human Rights on the meaning of similar provisions in the ECHR.[233] It can be noted that in the preamble of the EU Charter reference is made also to the European Social Charter. The impact of this source, in which the right to strike is also recognised (Article 6(4)), might be less, due to the fact that the ESC has a different, lower, legal status and it is not explicitly mentioned in Article 52 EU Charter. Actually, the impact of the ESC appears to be less, because the Court of Justice does not refer in its decisions related to this matter to the extensive case law of the European Committee of Social Rights.[234]

The two other European law sources (ECHR and ESC) have been subject to a more extensive interpretation of the fundamental right to take collective action. Article 6(4) ESC explicitly grants to employees and their organisations as well as to employers and their associations the right to collective action. The ECHR does not mention the right to collective action, but a recognition of this right can be derived from Article 11 ECHR, which recognises the right to 'freedom of peaceful assembly and to freedom of association with others, including the right to form and to join trade unions for the protection of his interests'. The European Court of Human Rights has for a long time refused to give a wider interpretation to Article 11, including the right to take collective action. It therefore did not want to interfere with national laws that impose limitations to the right to strike.[235] More recently, however, the ECtHR has changed its position. In 2002, it was still rather cautious: although the right to strike was not explicitly included in Article 11, the ECtHR found that a strike had to be regarded 'as one of the most important means for a trade union to defend its members' interests'. For that reason, strike action has to be considered 'as concerning the occupational interests of the applicant's members in the sense covered by Article 11 of the Convention'.[236] In 2009 the Court went a bit further. In the *Enerji* case, the Court – more in line with the view of the supervisory bodies of the ILO – recognised the right to strike as 'le corollaire indissociable du droit d'association syndicale' (an indissociable corollary of the right to association). The ECtHR saw the right to take collective action as a means to guarantee the effective exercise of the right

233 In the preamble to the EU Charter this is explicitly stated, §5.

234 This is the body of experts that is supervising the application of the ESC by the countries bound by it. See about this, Committee Bruun a.o. (2016) and it particular on this specific issue, Dorrsemont (2016), p. 265 ff.

235 ECtHR 1976, Appl. No. 5589/72 (*Schmidt and Dahlström*).

236 ECtHR 2002, Appl. No. 53574/99 (*Unison*).

to collective bargaining,[237] which did not, however, mean that no restrictions could be imposed on the exercise of the right.

Looking at the developments on this matter in the last decades, the right to take collective action or more precisely the exercise of that right is focused on possible restrictions. That is the case for the case law of both European courts as well as for the case law of national courts. In the view of the ECtHR and the ECSR, public servants have in principle the same right to collective actions as workers in the private sector have.[238] The ECSR has been more explicit about this.[239]

A crucial issue that has been, and still is, the subject of debate is whether the right to take collective action is explicitly linked to the process of collective bargaining or whether it could have a broader material scope. The issue is discussed also in relation to the case law of the Court of Justice in the *Laval* and *Viking* cases.

In the doctrine, the right to collective action is put in the context of collective bargaining: to ensure the effective exercise of the right to bargain collectively workers have the right to collective action in cases of conflicts of interest. Does it include all of the kinds of subjects that could be an issue for collective bargaining? The ECSR answers this in the affirmative and argues that collective action must *to be able to represent and defend the interests of the workers*.[240]

Article 28 EU Charter follows the same path. It grants the workers and employers, or their respective organisations, in cases of conflicts of interest the right to defend their interests. Does this include being used to influence economic decisions of the employer, such as relocation of the firm or other restructuring measures? Is the decisive point whether the issue at stake can be the subject of collective bargaining between employer(s) and trade unions? Even, when it does result in a collective agreement? The Court of Justice has never been asked to take a stand. In the case law of Member States this question is assessed differently.[241]

---

237 ECtHR 2009, Appl. No. 68959/01 (*Enerji Yapi-Yol Sen*), §24.

238 ECtHR 2009, Appl. No. 22943/04 (*Saime Ozcan v. Turkey*); ECtHR 2009, Appl. No. 30946/04 (*Kaya and Seyhan v. Turkey*). In a 2010 case on disciplinary measures against Russian dockworkers, the Court ruled in the same vein: ECtHR 2010, Appl. No. 67336/01 (*Danilenkov and others*). See on this Ewing and Hendy (2010), p. 2 ff.

239 See recently ECSR Conclusions 2014 (*Estonia – Article 6-4*). E.g. Harris & Darcy (2001), pp. 111–12; and Samuel (2002), pp. 155–59. Germany is a striking example of precluding civil servants from the right to strike; contrary to BVerwG 27 February 2014 – 2 C 1/13, the Constitutional Tribunal (BVerfG, 12 June 2018 – 2 BvR 1738/12 held this principle not to be in conflict with Art. 11 ECHR.

240 See among other references ECSR Conclusions XX-3 (*United Kingdom – Article 6-4*). E.g. Jaspers (2007), p. 39; and Novitz (2003), p. 287 ff. See also *The Committee of Freedom of Association* (2006), §§526–31.

241 See e.g. BAG 24 April 2007, AZR 252/06. E.g. Deinert (2010), pp. 62–65, and Warneck (2007), pp. 32, 33.

(c) From Recognition to Restrictions

Currently, the right to take collective action is not under discussion. It is generally accepted as a fundamental right of workers and their organisations. However, the discussions are concentrated on the restrictions that can be imposed on the exercise of the right. Restrictions are allowed if, according to the general wording of Article G (R)ESC, they are 'prescribed by law and be necessary in a democratic society for the protection of the rights and freedoms of others and for the protection of public order, national safety, public health or morals'.[242] The EU Charter takes a similar approach. However, it adds explicitly that the essence of those rights and freedoms has to be respected. The other European sources do not use this wording, but the case law substantively points to the same result. The EU Charter, being focused on the EU, points to objectives of general interest *recognised by the EU* that have to be 'genuinely' met. That seems to be a narrower approach than that of the ESC. Thus according to the EU Charter, the *interests of the EU* have to be taken into account. For the interpretation of these terms it is crucial what is understood by *interests recognised by the EU* and what is meant by *genuinely met*. An indication of how these terms can be interpreted can be found in some EU legislative measures. In Regulation 2679/98/EC as well as in Regulation 1176/2011/EU and also in Directive 2006/123/EC, all dealing with hard core political objectives of the EU (internal market and related subjects), it is stated that by applying these regulations, and also the directive, Article 28 of the EU Charter has to be taken into account and accordingly does not affect in any way 'the (exercise of the) right to … take collective action in accordance with national law and practices'.[243] In his conclusion in the *Albany* case, Advocate General Jacobs uses the same approach: 'the right to take collective action in order to protect occupational interests in so far as it is indispensable for the enjoyment of freedom of association is also protected by Community law'.[244]

The impact of primary European law, in particular of the four freedoms, being the pillars of the EU, on the exercise of fundamental rights among which is the right to take collective action, can be traced when analysing the case law of the Court of Justice in cases in which a potential collision might occur between a fundamental right and a fundamental (economic) freedom. That was the case in the *Viking* and *Laval* cases,[245] but also in the cases *Spanish Strawberries*

242 Article 11(2) ECHR and Article G RESC.

243 Article 2 Regulation 2679/98/EC; Article 1(3) Regulation 1176/2011/EU; and Article 1(7) Directive 2006/123/EC on services in the internal market.

244 AG Jacobs in his opinion C-67/96 (*Albany*), §159.

245 ECJ 2007, C-438/05 (*Viking*) and ECJ 2007, C-341/05 (*Laval*).

and *Schmidberger*.[246] The last two cases concerned a blockade of the border hindering the free movement of goods.[247] In these cases the fundamental rights of *freedom of expression* and of *freedom of (peaceful) assembly* collided with the free movement of goods that has to be guaranteed by the EU and the Member States.[248] In accordance with previous case law[249] the Court started by stating that both the European Union and the Member States are obliged to respect the fundamental rights. The protection of these rights is a legitimate interest, which in principle justifies a restriction of a fundamental freedom guaranteed by the Treaty, such as free movement of goods. However, this does not mean that they have absolute validity. They have to be considered 'in relation to their function in society'.[250] The exercise of these rights can be subjected to restrictions 'provided that the restrictions in fact correspond to objectives of general interest and do not, taking account of the aim of the restrictions, constitute disproportionate and unacceptable interference, impairing the very substance of the rights guaranteed'.[251] Thus the Court requested that a balancing of interests has to be struck, which is the approach the Court also followed in the 'strike' cases, *Viking* and *Laval*.

The ECtHR does allow some margin of appreciation because it gives the national authorities a certain degree of discretionary power with regard to the concrete interpretation of the restrictions that can be imposed by national rules within the conditions laid down in Article 11(2) ECHR.[252] Below, the issue of the margin of appreciation will be discussed in further detail (Section 5.3.1.6). This also plays a part in the case law of the CJEU where collisions between economic freedoms and fundamental social rights are concerned. The supervisory body of the Council of Europe (the ECSR) assessing the application of the RESC, has developed a detailed system of restrictions to the exercise of the right.[253]

---

246 ECJ 1997, C-265/95 (*Spanish Strawberries*) and ECJ 2003, C-112/00 (*Schmidberger*).

247 In the *Spanish Strawberries* case the question at stake was whether France had taken sufficient action against the protesting farmers so as to keep the border open. ECJ 1997, Case C-265/95 (*Spanish Strawberries*).

248 See on this Dorssemont & Jaspers (2007).

249 See the case law with regard to, inter alia, equal treatment. See e.g. ECJ 2002, Case C-442/00, (Rodríguez Caballero), §30. See also Chapter 2, Section 2.2.2.

250 ECJ 2003, Case C-112/00 (*Schmidberger*), §80.

251 ECJ 2003, Case C-112/00 (*Schmidberger*), §§74–80. This is in line with the case law of the ECtHR, see footnote 256. Article 52 EU Charter also contains this clause.

252 See for instance ECtHR 1996, Appl. No. 15573/89 (*Gustafsson*), §45; and ECtHR 2008, Appl. No. 34503/97 (*Demir and Baykara/Turkey*), §§119 ff. ECtHR 2006, Appl. Nos. 52562/99 and 52620/99 (*Sørensen and Rrasmussen v. Denmark*), §58; and lately ECtHR 2014, Appl. No. 31045/10 (*RMT v. UK*), §§86–91.

253 Eg. Dorssemont (2017), p. 272 ff.

5.3.1.6. *Criteria for Balancing: The* Laval *and* Viking *Cases*

The *Viking* case[254] concerns collective action by Finnish trade unions of transport workers supported by the International Transport Workers' Federation (the ITF) against the Finnish shipping company Viking, which provides ferry lines between Finland and Estonia run by a Estonia subsidiary founded for that purpose.[255] The actions of 2003 against Viking (a boycott of the ships) were intended to pressurise Viking to comply with the Finnish collective agreement and not to apply the much cheaper Estonian collective agreement it had concluded with an Estonian trade union. Another goal of Viking was to replace the chiefly (expensive) Finnish crew by an Estonian crew and subject them to the cheaper Estonian collective agreement. In reply to the collective actions the Finnish company started legal proceedings to have the actions banned.[256]

In more or less the same period there was a similar case in Sweden: *Laval*.[257] The Swedish municipality of Vaxholm called for tenders for the construction of a school. The Latvian construction company Laval and Partners Baltic were awarded the contract. The company did not use local Swedish construction workers, but recruited its employees in Latvia, who were temporarily posted to Sweden to build the school. Contrary to what the Latvian company, Laval, had originally promised in its tender, namely to conclude a collective agreement with a Swedish union or at least to enter into an existing Swedish collective agreement, it refused to pay the prevailing Swedish wages. It wanted to apply the – cheaper – Latvian collective agreement, concluded with a Latvian trade union. After months of negotiations, neither a collective agreement according to the Swedish standard was reached, nor did the Latvian firm enter into a Swedish construction industry collective agreement. The Swedish union called for a boycott of the work deployed by the Latvian company in Sweden.[258] After a few weeks, as a result of a hardening of the conflict, the boycott was complete and all construction activities came to a complete standstill. After some time Laval went into trouble and in March 2005 it was declared bankrupt. The case was submitted to a Swedish court, asking the European Court of Justice whether actions of this kind are compatible with the fundamental freedoms guaranteed by the European Union.

254 ECJ 2007, C-438/05 (*Viking*).

255 This process is called 're-flagging or flagging-out'.

256 An interesting point to mention is that Viking choose to lodge its claim before an English court because the ITF, established in London, was involved in this case. The English judge took the case to the European Court of Justice.

257 ECJ 2007, C-341/05 (*Laval*).

258 Initially only affecting the project in Vaxholm. This was later extended to a refusal of Swedish workers to supply the construction site with the necessary building materials and blocking the access of Latvian employees to the site in Vaxholm.

After confirming the right to take collective action as a fundamental right, being an integral part of the general principles of Community law, the Court reconfirmed that it is subject to restrictions under Community law and national laws and practices, such as the rules on free movement (Articles 49 and 56 TFEU).[259]

In analogy to the decisions on collision of collective labour law, in particular the right to conclude collective agreements, and competition law, it was advocated in literature and by governments[260] that the 'immunity' rule should be applied equally to this element of collective labour law. However, the Court did not follow this reasoning and did not accept the idea of immunity for the rules and regulations on free movement.

In comments to this decision it was argued that the approach of the Court is inconsistent. In *Albany* and similar cases,[261] the Court assigned immunity in order to avoid depriving collective bargaining of its effectiveness. In *Laval* and *Viking* the Court did not assign such immunity and by consequence collective bargaining was separated from the possibility to use collective action to put pressure on the employers' side in order to bring the bargaining to the outcome trade unions wanted to achieve. These two elements are so closely linked,[262] that restrictions to the means of putting pressure on the bargaining process by using the strike action would jeopardise the collective bargaining.[263]

Even though the Court did not deny the link, it did not want to accept the consequences and refused to exclude the right to collective action from the scope of Article 49 (and Article 56) TFEU.[264]

Stating that no kind of hierarchy exists between the fundamental right of taking collective action and the fundamental freedom to provide services, the Court of Justice, referring to its case law in similar situations (collision of fundamental rights and fundamental freedoms), decided that the collision had to be assessed by the application of the proportionality principle, which consists of three steps: (1) Does the action that hinders free movement of service (or establishment) have a legitimate objective and does it constitute an overriding

---

259 ECJ 2007, C-438/05 (*Viking*), §44 and ECJ 2007, C-341/05 (*Laval*), §91.

260 The Danish and Swedish governments had taken this position (ECJ 2007, C-341/05 (*Laval*), §89). The exception of immunity was submitted for a preliminary ruling to the Court of Justice by the English Court (see ECJ 2007, C-341/05 (*Laval*), §40). See about this Dorssemont & Jaspers (2007), p. 11; and Bercusson (2007).

261 ECJ 1999, C-67/96 (*Albany*).

262 The ECtHR has accepted this approach in its more recent decisions: ECtHR 2008, Appl. No. 34503/97 (*Demir and Baykara/Turkey*) §140. It also generally accepted the expert committees of the ILO and the Council of Europe (the ECSR). E.g. Jaspers (2007) pp. 32–74; Novitz (2008), pp. 541–62.

263 See inter alia Dorssemont & Jaspers (2007), p. 11; Barnard (2008), p. 469.

264 ECJ 2007, C-438/05 (*Viking*) §36 and pp. 42–55.

reason of general interest? If that is indeed the case, it is necessary to examine whether the action is (2) appropriate and (3) required to achieve the objective of the action?[265]

(a) Legitimate Aim

In its decisions, in both *Viking* and *Laval*, the Court was rather reticent in its assessment of the legitimacy of the objective pursued with the action in accordance with comparable cases.[266] However, the wide margin of appreciation the Court grants to public authorities to abstain from restrictive measures against those who make use of their fundamental rights[267] seems to be reduced for trade unions when they decide how to make use of their right to call strike actions.[268] That is not in accordance with the practice in many Member States, where judges grant trade unions wide discretionary power to initiate collective actions.[269] In *Viking* (§81) the Court started by stating that taking collective action with a view to protecting employees against possible social dumping practices[270] can be considered as a legitimate aim.[271] In *Laval* (§107) the Court confirmed this reasoning, but in a more conditional way. Protection of the workers of the host State (Sweden) against possible social dumping (by applying lower Estonian employment conditions to posted Estonian workers) could be an *overriding reason of public interest* and therefore a legitimate aim justifying a restriction to the fundamental freedom of services.[272]

Since the Court does not decide individual cases, which is up to the national courts to do so, it can only mention some elements to be used by the national judge when deciding the case. First, the Court, referring to Article 154 TFEU, stated that the Treaty not only has an economic objective, but also a social

---

265 E.g. Weatherill (2014), pp. 35–36; and Bogg (2014), pp. 57–58 and 69–72.

266 In the *Schmidberger* case: protection of the environment and public health; ECJ C-112/00 (*Schmidberger*), §66. In the *Omega* case: protection of human dignity; ECJ 2004 C-36/02 (*Omega*), §35.

267 ECJ 2003, C-112/00 (*Schmidberger*), §79–82.

268 Cf. Davies (2008), p. 142.

269 See Waas (2014), p. 235 ff. for Germany.

270 A situation which would occur if the Finnish workers should also have to work under the less favourable Estonian terms of employment or if the cheaper Estonian employees 'were to oust their Finnish colleagues from the market'. The fight against social dumping has been accepted as an overriding reason of public interest by the Court in ECJ C-244/04 (*Commission v. Germany*), §61.

271 Also AG Mengozzi in his Opinion to ECJ 2007, C-341/05 (*Laval*), §§249 ff. See also Prechal & De Vries (2008), p. 433; Syrpis & Novitz (2008), p. 425; Dorssemont & Jaspers, (2007), pp. 12–13.

272 It qualifies as such under the condition that the rules to be applied to all employees are sufficiently precise and accessible for the 'foreign' employer and, equally, generally to be applied to all employers and employees without any exception; public interest is failing. ECJ 2007, C-341/05 (*Laval*), §§110 and 118–20.

one.[273] The next step was how to assess whether the social objective can weigh out the economic objective. The Court stated that protection of employees, including protection of employment of the workers, as such. One element of this assessment is whether jobs or terms of employment are *effectively at stake* or *seriously jeopardised*. And even when that is the case, the Court of Justice added another requirement: the national judge has to ascertain whether the collective action is suitable for ensuring the achievement of the objective pursued and does not go beyond what is necessary to attain that objective (the second element; see below).

This element might open the door for the national judge to go into the content of terms of employment and/or (personnel) organisation of the enterprise, and such investigation might be contrary to the autonomy of trade unions being part of the fundamental freedom of association.[274] Moreover, the law and practices of the Member States tend to keep judges away from assessing the legitimacy or even the appropriateness of the demands of trade unions in the negotiation process. It is the core competence and power of the negotiating parties. The suggested inquiry can also raise questions such as: what should be understood by '*serious* impairment'? Or, when does a 'serious threat to the jobs' occur? Apart from being not in compliance with the case law of the international supervising bodies, another possible consequence of this approach could be (rather) large differences between decisions of national courts.[275] Therefore this approach has been heavily criticised in the literature.[276]

(b) Proportionality Principle: Necessary and Appropriate

Provided that the requirement of legitimate aim is met, the collective action has to be justified by complying with the proportionality principle: is it necessary and appropriate to attain the goals with the action? It must be assessed whether the restriction of the fundamental freedoms of the EU that are directly related to the single market can be justified in terms of necessity and appropriateness of the collective action for attaining its goals. This is a matter of weighing the economic interests against the social interests. With reference to social policy objectives of the European Union, the Court – in line with the opinions of the Advocates-General – underlined that the Union serves social as well as

273 ECJ 2007, C-438/05 (*Viking*), §79.

274 The ILO Committees and the ECSR consistently express this opinion.

275 See about differences in a number of Member States, Ales & Novitz (2010); Warneck (2007); and Freedland & Prassl (2014).

276 Jaspers (2008b), p. 60; Davies (2008), p. 142 ff; Dorssemont (2009); Novitz (2010b); Veldman (2013).

economic purposes. Therefore, the rights regarding the free movement of services and the freedom of establishment must be weighed against the social policy purposes. From this it can be argued that social interests are not, or may not be, subordinated to economic interests, but must be put more or less on a par with these.[277]

Similarly to the requirement of the legitimate aim, the Court of Justice cannot fill in the proportionality criterion. That has to be done by the national courts deciding the concrete cases. What the Court did, and was allowed to do, was to give some guidelines to the national judges by identifying the elements to be taken into consideration. So, whether the collective action does not go beyond what is necessary to attain the objective aimed at has to be judged by the national courts for which the European Court may *provide guidance* to the national courts.[278] The handles the Court mentioned are: first, did the trade union(s) have other means at its/their disposal that would not hinder or at least less restrict the freedom of establishment or freedom to provide services and by which they could attain the objectives pursued as well? And, second, has/have the trade union(s) exhausted these – less restricting – means before starting the actions? Collective action must be the 'last resort'.[279] The literature and case law of international supervising bodies point to means such as conciliation or mediation, or a cooling down period.[280]

The freedom of assessment by courts, including the Court of Justice in setting guidelines, is limited. The right to take collective action and the exercise of that right have to be respected when weighing against the fundamental economic principle of freedom of movement, so that *the very substance of the right guaranteed* is not harmed[281] or in the wording of Article 52 EU Charter: as long as the right to collective action is not *substantially impaired*.

The guidance offered by the Court includes whether the means used (i.e. strike action) is proportionate to the objective (i.e. improving the terms of employment for all employees including the posted workers). The Court

---

277 Mention is made of a social market economy. See Barnard (2012a), p. 27; and Barnard (2008), p. 483.

278 ECJ 2007, C-438/05 (*Viking*), §85.

279 ECJ 2007, C-438/05 (*Viking*), §87.

280 This 'last resort' criterion is used in a lot of legal systems. Mandatory arbitration without the consent of both parties in the dispute goes too far in the view of these bodies. See ECSR Conclusions X-1, P. 130 (Norway). See Nowitz (2003), p. 278 ff; Jaspers (2007), p. 54 ff.; Dorssemont (2017), p. 274 ff.

281 ECJ 2003, C-112/00, (Schmidberger), §§74–80. The ECSR stated that 'the substance of the right to strike may not be affected so as to render it ineffective', ECSR Conclusions I (1969), Statement of Interpretation on Article 6-4; repeated in Conclusions 2014, (Netherlands), Article 6-4.

doubted that in this case.[282] The specific situation in Sweden made this reasoning understandable.[283]

Another criterion that can be derived from the *Laval* decision, is whether the situation for the employees has been improved in reality or substantially. The first question will be: how to assess this criterion? Should it be left to trade unions to decide what is substantial? If not, a judge has to go into this question and in that case the judge cannot avoid interfering in what is usually seen as the prerogative of the bargaining parties.[284] The question may rise of whether judges are competent to assess the merits of the industrial dispute.[285] Apart from that, this assessment goes beyond what is the legal practice in most countries and it is not in conformity with the case law of the European and international supervisory bodies.[286] One may wonder whether by this approach the *very substance of the right* is jeopardised, because trade union(s) have to ask themselves whether no other suitable means were/are available that are less restrictive towards the freedom of establishment or providing services or whether the means were exhausted before initiating a collective action.[287]

The Court added some other criteria such as the nature and the duration of the action, both rather common in Member States. The *Schmidberger* judgment showed that the duration of the actions could be a decisive factor.[288] This approach of the Court of Justice is heavily disputed among lawyers, in particular labour law experts.[289]

A related question can be how wide the margin of appreciation is for trade unions when deciding to initiate a collective action. In the *Schmidberger* case, as well in the *Omega* case, this issue came up in respect of the response of the government of the country in which an action takes place that hampers the freedom of movement. In this case the activists and their organisation were not made responsible for their blockade of the border. The Court granted a wide margin of appreciation to the government to take the measures necessary to end the blockade. The Austrian government weighed the free movement rule against the right to demonstrate and the right of assembly. The criteria mentioned

---

282 By claiming that the Swedish collective agreement had to be applied to all employees and by consequence Laval Parteri had to join the Swedish collective agreement. The Court decided that this was not proportionate. ECJ 2007, C-341/05 (*Laval*), §§112–20.

283 It was not certain that the posted – Latvian – workers were better off when taking the whole situation of these workers into account. Another reason could be that not all Swedish construction enterprises were covered by the collective agreement. See ECJ 2007, C-341/05 (*Laval*), §110 ff.; see Rönnmar (2008a), p. 515 ff.

284 See Weatherill, (2014), pp. 36–39.

285 See Novitz (2010b), p. 258.

286 E.g. Novitz (2003); Dorssemont (2017), p. 272 ff.; and Iossa (2011), p. 276 ff.

287 In this sense the Adoptive Parents (2014), p. 103.

288 ECJ 2003, C-112/00 (*Schmidberger*), §90.

289 See recently Freedland and Prassl (2014).

by the Court were related to the fact that the action did not create serious and repeated disruption to public order. An isolated incident does not generate a climate of insecurity and therefore did not have a dissuasive effect on intra-Community trade flows as a whole.[290] It was the competent national authorities that were 'entitled to consider that an outright ban on the demonstration would have constituted unacceptable interference with the fundamental rights of the demonstrators to gather and express peacefully their opinion in public, protected by Article ECHR'.[291] The duration of the collective actions (in this case, the blockade) is an important, if not decisive factor. The blockade of the premises of the constructors in the *Laval* case was not time-limited, which has explicitly taken into consideration by the Court.[292] From this a general rule can be derived: the more that a collective action limits free movement – which is exactly what increases the effectiveness of the action – the harder it is to justify it.[293] By linking the acceptability of actions to the gravity of the restriction of free movement there is a risk of taking the sting out of the right to strike.[294]

By conclusion it can be stated that the way the Court filled in the proportionality test for trade union actions is more restrictive than it did for governments as in the *Schmidberger* case.[295] In consequence, trade unions may be deprived from their autonomy in a substantial way to opt for an effective way of defending the interests of the workers, restricted as they are by the interpretation of the Posting of Workers Directive (see also Chapter 9).

5.3.1.7. Post Laval *and* Viking

The *Laval* and *Viking* judgments of the Court of Justice have given rise to heavy discussions among European (labour) law experts, as well lawyers in the various Member States that mainly cantered on the impact the decisions could have in national case law.[296] in Sweden the impact has been substantial where the law on collective bargaining has been adapted affecting also the right to collective action.[297] In the UK, the *BALPA* case showed the influence of the decisions.[298] In other countries, the decisions did not have much effect on the case law in practice.[299]

---

290 As on the contrary did the blockade of the French/Spanish border as in the *Spanish strawberries* case.
291 ECJ 2003, C-112/00 (*Schmidberger*), §§89 and 90.
292 ECJ 2007, C-341/05 (*Laval*), §100.
293 See Davies (2008), pp. 141–42.
294 See inter alia Davies (2008).
295 See on the difference, Leczykiewicz (2014), pp. 312–13.
296 See inter alia the comparative studies Ales & Novitz (2010); Bücker & Warneck (2011); Freedland and Prassl (2014). See also Davies (2008) and Dorssemont (2009).
297 Rönnmar (2014), pp. 241–60.
298 See Ewing (2012), p. 5 ff.; Killpatrick (2014), p. 313 ff.; and Novitz (2010a), p. 200 ff.
299 Freedland, M. & J. Prassl (2014), pp. 113–276.

The decisions were also heavily criticised by the European trade unions. They fear erosion of their fundamental right to take collective action.[300] International supervisory bodies criticised the decisions as well. The ILO CEACR expressed as its opinion that 'it has never included the need to assess the proportionality of interests bearing in mind a notion of freedom of establishment or freedom to provide services. ... The Committee thus considers that the doctrine that is being articulated in these Court of Justice judgements is likely to have a significant restrictive effect on the exercise of the right to strike in practice in a manner contrary to the Convention'.[301] The ECSR, assessing the application of Article 6(4) ESC, was even more critical. The Committee felt that the principle of free movement of services 'cannot be treated, from the point of view of the system of values, principles and fundamental rights embodied in the Charter, as having a greater a priori value than core labour rights, including the right to collective action'. Restrictions imposed on the enjoyment of this right should not prevent trade unions from engaging in collective action to improve the employment conditions.[302]

In response to the criticism from many sides, the European Commission took the initiative to make a proposal for an EU regulation. Inspired by another regulation on free movement principles and the functioning of the internal market, the Monti I Regulation,[303] the Commission clarified the relationship between the freedom of establishment and the freedom to provide services on the one hand and the fundamental right to take collective action on the other. The free movement of goods or of services have to guaranteed by the State. Proper functioning of the internal market may not be gravely obstructed by actions of private persons or entities, but it may not be interpreted as affecting in any way the exercise of fundamental rights such as the right or freedom to take collective actions. Economic freedoms have to respect fundamental rights and vice versa. The Monti II Regulation was therefore intended to create clarity with regard to the role of the national courts when assessing collective action which could possibly turn out to be contrary to fundamental (economic) freedoms. Although the relevant Articles 1(2) and 2 of the proposal did neither mention nor refer to the principle of proportionality, the Explanatory Memorandum as well as the preamble of the proposal were clear by presenting the proportionality principle as the methodological instrument to reconcile both rights. In fact it confirmed the approach of the Court of Justice in the *Viking* and *Laval* cases.[304]

---

300 The ETUC discussed the issue and issued a resolution and an Explanatory Memorandum on 4 and 5 March 2008.

301 CEARC (2010), p. 109. See on this case Ewing and Hendy (2010), p. 44.

302 ECSR 3 July 2013, CC No. 85/2012 (*Swedish Trade Union Confederation*).

303 Regulation 2679/98/EC. See Dorssemont & Jaspers (2007); Dorssemont (2012), p. 3 ff.

304 See Section 5.3.1.6.

The Monti II proposal did not have a clarifying effect.[305] Due to fierce criticism to this Monti II proposal from different angles,[306] it died a quiet death and was withdrawn in 2012. It is therefore still not clear what the proportionality test entails or should entail. The discussion is about the nature of the test: should it be a substantively assessed test that might imply a more substantive assessment of the collective actions by trade unions with the possibility of putting the economic interests of the internal market against the social interests of the workers. The other route can be that it will be left to a more procedural test. The national courts have to assess whether trade unions can show 'proof' that they have acted according to the rule that they had engaged effectively in negotiations before they went on strike and have considered alternatives to strike action. A restriction to the exercise of the right to collective action will be assessed as to whether the application of the proportionality principle could result in undermining the essence of the right being protected.[307] Recently the rule as proposed in the – withdrawn – Monti II Regulation was inserted in the revision of the Posting of Workers Directive (Article).[308] In the revised Posting of Workers Directive the question of the application of the proportionality principle is not clarified, neither in the text of the provision nor in the explanatory part of the directive (§10 of the preamble). This may imply that the criticism on the application of the proportionality principle is still valid. In the first place, the order of reasoning still is that restrictions to the freedom to provide services are 'permissible only if they are justified by overriding reasons in the public interest and if they are proportionate and necessary'. Restrictions to the freedom to provide services have to be justified and not the other way round. Both 'freedoms' still seem not to be on a par. And, second, the national judges have to assess whether according to their national law and practices a strike action that infringes the economic freedom, is justified.

A last question to be raised is whether the accession of the EU to the ECHR will have a substantial impact on the assessment of collective actions. The relevance of a possible accession has increased since the ECtHR, in its more recent decisions, has taken a clearer stand as to the scope of Article 11. In the *Enerji* case,[309] the Court argued that the right to strike is essential, as being an indissociable corollary of the right to collective bargaining. In later decisions the Court confirmed this statement and confirmed also that restrictions to the right has to fall within the boundaries of Article 11(2) ECHR.[310] In 2014

---

305 The Monti II proposal was withdrawn in September 2012.

306 Bruun, Bücker & Dorssemont (2012), p. 279 ff.; and the Adoptive Parents (2014), p. 95 ff.

307 See about this Barnard (2012b), pp. 131–35.

308 Directive 2018/957/EU, preamble §10.

309 ECtHR 2009, Appl. No. 68959/01, §24.

310 See inter alia ECtHR 2009, Appl. No. 67336/01 (*Danilenkov v. Russia*), §123; ECtHR 2009, Appl. No. 22943/04 (*Saime Özcan v. Turkey*); ECtHR 2009, Appl. No. 30946/04 (*Kaya*

the Court reconfirmed the principle.[311] What the relationship between the ECtHR and the Court of Justice would look like is still under discussion in the European Union and the Council of Europe. But even when the accession will take place the question will not be solved fully. By claiming that EU law preserves its autonomy in regard to the interpretation and application of the rights guaranteed in the ECHR and sticking to guaranteeing the fundamental freedoms – the free movement principles as the 'backbones' of the EU – the Court of Justice can still apply its *Viking* and *Laval* rulings and impose restrictions beyond the realm of the ECHR as interpreted by ECtHR.[312]

and Seyhan v. Turkey), §30; and ECtHR 2010, Appl. No. 4241/03 (*Trofimchuk v. Ukraine*). E.g. Novitz (2014), p. 366 ff.

311 ECtHR 2014, Appl. No. 31045/10 (*RMT v. UK*).

312 Velyvyte (2015), pp. 86–87; and Veldman (2013b), p. 104 ff. Veldman and De Vries (2015).

CHAPTER 6
RESTRUCTURING OF COMPANIES

Niklas BRUUN and Sylvaine LAULOM

6.1. INTRODUCTION

The three 'restructuring' directives – the Transfers of Undertakings Directive, the Collective Redundancies Directive and the Insolvency Directive[1] – are among the oldest European directives adopted in the field of labour law. Their origins can be traced back to the Social Action Programme adopted in 1974,[2] after the Paris Summit of 1972, where the Heads of States declared that the Member States 'attached as much importance to vigorous action in the social field as the achievement of economic union … [and considered] it essential to ensure increasing involvement of labour and management in the economic and social decisions of the Community'. As its name suggests, the Social Action Programme defined an agenda to be followed by the Commission involving more than 30 measures to be adopted over an initial period of three to four years. The three main objectives were: the attainment of full and better employment in the Community; the improvement of living and working conditions; and the increased involvement of management and labour in the economic and social decisions of the Community and of workers in companies. The programme was ambitious, but the political consensus to fully accomplish it was missing. However, some directives were adopted, among which were the three 'restructuring' directives. The choice of these three areas can be explained by the economic situation of that time, i.e. large restructurings of enterprises as reaction to inter alia the economic crisis of the 1970s and also the growing impact of the common market.

The three directives provide a degree of employment protection in the restructuring of companies. They address social consequences of restructuring and economic change, and aim to promote industrial democracy and worker participation.[3] The adoption of the 1975 Directive (collective redundancies) was also a response to a case of mass redundancies in a multinational company, AKZO, that drew a lot attention in the media. Akzo announced that it would make circa 5000 workers redundant in those Member States where the costs of redundancies were the lowest.

At that time, there was no specific Treaty basis on which the Commission could propose legislation on employment and labour matters. Under Article 117 EEC, Member States 'agree upon the need to promote improved working conditions and an improved standard of living for workers, so as to

1 Directive 75/129/EEC, amended by Directive 92/56/EEC and codified by Directive 98/59/EC (Collective Redundancies); Directive 77/187/EEC, amended by Directive 98/59/EC and codified by Directive 2001/23/EC (Transfers of Undertakings); Directive 80/987/EEC, amended by Directive 2002/74/EC and codified by Directive 2008/94/EC (Insolvency of the Employer).

2 Council Resolution of 21 January 1974 (Social Action Programme).

3 Rönnmar (2008), p. 30; Jaspers (2005).

make possible their harmonisation while the improvement is being maintained'. However, the Treaty provided no more than that such harmonisation could flow from the functioning of the common market and the Commission should promote close co-operation between Member States (Article 118 EEC); there was no competence to adopt legislation on social issues. As a consequence, unanimity was necessary within the Council of Ministers to base the proposal on a more general Treaty article, i.e. Article 100 EEC, which enabled the approximation of national provisions which directly affect the establishment of functioning of the Common Market.

As stated in the preamble of the directives, their main objective is to afford greater protection to workers in the event of restructuring. However, the preambles of the Transfers of Undertakings Directive and the Collective Redundancies Directive also refer to the existing differences among the Member States, which could 'have a direct effect on the functioning of the internal market'. This reference is not without consequence on the recent interpretation of the Collective Redundancies Directive by the Court of Justice. Until recently, the principle of protection of workers was the leading principle for the Court when interpreting the directives. However, since 2015 the Court has taken into consideration the double objectives of the Collective Redundancy Directive and considers that by harmonising the rules applicable to collective redundancies, the EU legislature intended both to ensure comparable protection for workers' rights in the different Member States and to harmonise the costs which such protective rules entail for EU undertakings.[4] There is little doubt that, if this interpretation of the directive were to be confirmed without taking into account the basic feature of this instrument as a minimum directive, it would lose its ability to afford greater protection to workers effectively.

The main objectives of the three directives are to protect employees' rights in the three restructuring situations defined by them. However, although their aim, as defined in their preamble, is the same, the three directives are very different in nature. The Transfers of Undertakings Directive, which has led to many Court of Justice cases, has the ambition of a comprehensive regulation of the situations when a transfer of a business takes place; the Collective Redundancies Directive only regulates some aspects of the procedure (information and consultation) in situations where the workforce has to be reduced for economic reasons. The Insolvency Directive also has only limited ambitions: it introduces certain obligations on the Member States to take a limited economic responsibility for unpaid wages when a business can no longer pay its debts or wages.

---

4 See ECJ 2015, C-229/14 (*Balkaya*); ECJ 2015, C-80/14 (*USDAW*); ECJ 2015, C-182/13 (*Lyttle*); ECJ 2016, C-201/15 (*AGET Iraklis*).

Since the 1970s, the three directives have been amended and codified, mainly to clarify and harmonise some of the definitions. In the preamble of the directives a reference is included to the Community Charter of the Fundamental Social Rights of Workers, adopted in 1989.

More than 40 years after their adoption, the restructuring directives are still, and unfortunately, at the heart of today's social preoccupations. The crisis affecting Europe since 2008 has increased, among other things, the level of company restructuring and as a result the number of redundancies. Even if it is not possible to establish a direct link between the European economic situation and the Court's case law, the number of the latter's judgments on the interpretation of the Collective Redundancies Directive has increased, and the Transfers of Undertakings Directive continues to generate European case law. In this case law it can, generally speaking, be seen that the more comprehensive directives are, the more they lead to difficulties and national divergences.

6.2. THE COLLECTIVE REDUNDANCIES DIRECTIVE

The aim of this directive is to improve protection for workers in the event of a collective redundancy through the involvement of workers' representatives. The directive does not provide individual rights to workers. It does, however, define its scope and it lays down the procedure for a collective redundancy. This is a dual procedure, comprising, on the one hand, consultation with workers' representatives with a view to reaching an agreement, and on the other hand an administrative procedure for allocating public funds and resources to seek ways of alleviating the social consequences of collective redundancies. For many years, there have been very few cases dealing with the interpretation of the Collective Redundancies Directive. This has recently changed, possibly as a consequence of the 2008 crisis and the evolution of national legislations.

6.2.1. THE DEFINITION OF COLLECTIVE REDUNDANCIES

With the exceptions of public administrative bodies or establishments governed by public law, the crews of seagoing vessels and redundancies effected under fixed-term contracts (except if such redundancies take place prior to the date of the expiry of the contract),[5] all employers employing at least 20 workers in an establishment are concerned by the directive. The directive determines the scope of collective redundancies. It is based on two cumulative elements: an objective or quantitative element, concerning the scale of the redundancies

5 Article 1(2) Collective Redundancies Directive.

(number or percentage of workers to be made redundant over a given period) and a subjective or qualitative element concerning the reasons for the redundancies. Regarding the quantitative element, the directive requires that the number of workers to be dismissed as redundant reach a minimum limit, set according to one or two alternative methods to be selected by each Member State. As a general rule the reasons of the dismissals cannot be based on or related to personal aspects of the individual workers, for instance their poor performance.

As regards the criteria for when dismissals qualify as collective redundancies, the directive gives the Member States the choice between two reference periods within which dismissals count for reaching the threshold for collective dismissals. If a Member State has opted for a 30-day period whether the number of dismissals qualifies as collective redundancies depends on the size of the establishment:

- at least 10 dismissals in establishments normally employing more than 20 and less than 100 workers;
- at least 10% of the number of workers in establishments normally employing at least 100 but less than 300 workers;
- at least 30 workers in establishments normally employing 300 workers or more.

If a Member State has opted for a 90-day period, the number of dismissals that qualifies as collective redundancies is at least 20.[6]

In applying this European definition of collective redundancy, three main issues arise:

- How should 'worker' be defined for the calculation of the thresholds specified in the directive?;
- What types of terminations of contract of employment are to be taken into account for calculating the number of redundancies?; and
- What is an establishment within the meaning of the directive? What perimeters should be taken into account when calculating the number of redundancies?

6.2.1.1. *The European Definition of 'Worker' in the Collective Redundancies Directive*

Whereas the concept of worker is defined by the Court of Justice in the areas of freedom of movement of workers and equal treatment in employment (see Chapters 2 and 3), the situation is different for the directives dealing with

6 According to Article 1(1)(a) of the directive.

working conditions, such as the restructuring directives; most of the latter provide that it is for national laws to define the concept of worker.[7]

Until recently, the definition of worker under the Collective Redundancies Directive did not lead to many debates or discussions. It could be argued that, as in case of the Transfers of Undertakings Directive, the concept had to be defined by reference to national laws. However, contrary to most of the working conditions directives, the Collective Redundancies Directive does not contain any reference to the concept of worker to be included in the calculation of the thresholds specified in the directive. In the *Balkaya* case,[8] the Court of Justice had to rule for the first time on this issue with regard to this directive and, in a somewhat unexpected judgment, decided that this concept has to be defined at European level.

The case concerned a German company terminating the contracts of employment of 19 of its employees without notifying the competent public authority of the projected collective redundancies. For the company the number of dismissals was lower than the required threshold. One of the dismissed workers, Mr. Balkaya, claimed that two other persons who were also employed by the company must be counted in that category to determine whether the threshold of 20 persons had been reached. One person was M.L., the director of the company, who did not hold any shares in the company and who was entitled to act on behalf of the company with another director. The other person was Ms. S., who was undergoing training within the company and received a public training grant and did not receive remuneration from the employer. Could these two persons be qualified as workers for the purpose of the directive, and more specifically for the meaning of Article 1(1)(a) of the Collective Redundancies Directive?

For the Court – and this is certainly the most important statement in the decision – the concept of 'worker' referred to in Article 1(1)(a) of the directive has to be given an autonomous and independent meaning in the EU legal order. Otherwise, the methods for calculation of the thresholds laid down in that provision, and therefore the thresholds themselves, would be within the discretion of the Member States, which would allow the latter to alter the scope of that directive and thus to deprive it of its full effect (§33). The Court justified its interpretation by referring to the goal of the directive: 'by harmonising the rules applicable to collective redundancies, the EU legislature intended both to ensure comparable protection for workers' rights in the different Member States and to harmonise the costs which such protective rules entail for European Union undertakings'. To justify a broad concept of worker, the Court referred to the other objective of the directive, which is to protect workers. In accordance with that objective, a narrow definition cannot be given to the concepts that

7 See further Section 6.3.4.

8 See ECJ 2015, C-229/14 (*Balkaya*).

define the scope of the directive, including the concept of 'worker'. Following this statement, in order to define the concept of 'worker' the Court referred to its settled case law in the area of equality and free movement of workers. For the Court, that concept must be defined in accordance with objective criteria, which distinguish the employment relationship by reference to the rights and duties of the persons concerned. In that regard, the essential feature of employment relationship is that, for a certain period of time, a person performs services for and under the direction of another person, in return for which that person receives remuneration. In its earlier case law, the Court had determined that a relationship of subordination could be established with regard to a member of the board of directors of a capital company.[9] It was necessary to consider the circumstances in which the board member was recruited; the nature of the duties entrusted to the board member; the context in which those duties were performed; the scope of the board member's powers and the extent to which the board member was supervised within the company; and the circumstances under which the board member could be removed. In this case, the director in question was appointed by the general meeting of shareholders of the company, which also had the power to revoke his appointment. Furthermore, the director was subject to the direction and supervision of that body, and he did not hold any shares in the company for which he carried out his functions. The Court concluded that subordination could be established.

With regard to Ms. S., the Court held that its well-established case law indicates that the concept of worker in EU law extends to a person who serves a traineeship or periods of apprenticeship in an occupation that may be regarded as practical preparation related to the actual pursuit of the occupation in question, provided that the periods are served while performing a genuine and effective activity as an employed person, for and under the direction of an employer. The Court stated that that conclusion cannot be invalidated by the fact that the productivity of the person concerned is low, that the person does not carry out full duties and that, accordingly, the person works only a small number of hours per week and thus receives limited remuneration.[10]

The *Balkaya* case should not be ignored by the Member States. They should check that their national concept of 'worker' used to calculate the thresholds of employee laid down in the directive meets the broad European concept, which is far from obvious. With the *Balkaya* case, a new issue arises regarding the discrepancy between the Transfers of Undertakings Directive on the one hand,

9 ECJ 2010, C-232/09 (*Danosa*) in particular §§39 and 56. This case was related to Directive 92/85/EEC (regarding pregnant workers and workers who have recently given birth or are breastfeeding).

10 ECJ 2015, C-229/14 (*Balkaya*), §50. Cf. also ECJ 1986, 66/85 (*Lawrie-Blum*), §§19–21.

where Member States can determine who is protected as an employee under national law, and the Collective Redundancies Directive on the other, which does not include such a freedom for the Member States.

6.2.1.2. *Redundancies and Other Forms of Termination of Employment Contracts*

The Collective Redundancies Directive applies to dismissals effected by an employer for one or more reasons not related to the individual workers. In order to calculate the number of redundancies relevant to the directive, terminations of employment contracts other than dismissals on the initiative of the employer should be equated to redundancies, provided that there are at least five redundancies. In other words, the directive applies to economic dismissal and to other types of terminations of contract of employment such as, for example, early retirement, contractual termination of the contract of employment or resignation. However, these other types of termination of employment can only be taken into account if there are at least five redundancies (Article 1(1)). This restriction is difficult to understand; it can only be explained by the political consensus to reach agreement on a final text.

In a preliminary ruling, the Court of Justice was asked if 'in order to establish whether there is a "collective redundancy", the condition laid down in the directive, according to which "there (are) at least five redundancies" must be interpreted as relating solely to redundancies or as covering terminations of employment contracts that may be assimilated to redundancies'.[11] For the Court, the wording of the directive was clear and the condition laid down in the directive that there be at least five redundancies had to be interpreted as relating not to terminations of employment contracts that may be assimilated to redundancies, but only to redundancies *sensu stricto*. However, the Court defined the concept of redundancy very broadly. With impeccable logic, the Court stated that the directive does not give an express definition of the concept of 'redundancy' and it must be regarded as a concept of EU law which cannot be defined by reference to the laws of the Member States. For the Court, redundancies are characterised by the lack of consent by the employee, which means that a significant and unilateral change to an essential element of the employment contract, operating to the employee's detriment, falls within the directive's definition of a 'redundancy'. Therefore, the Court decided that, in the case it had to deal with, the termination of the employment contract by common consent with an employee whose wages had been decreased significantly constituted a redundancy within the scope of the directive. The Court considered, that given that it was 'the worker who sought the termination of her employment contract, she might, prima facie, be regarded

[11] ECJ 2015, C-422/14 (*Pujante Rivera*).

as having consented to the termination. However, the fact nonetheless remains that the termination of that employment relationship arises from the change made unilaterally by her employer to an essential element of the employment contract for reasons not related to that individual worker. Therefore the termination of her contract of employment could be defined as a redundancy'.[12] One could wonder whether this broad definition of redundancy renders the inclusion of the other forms of termination of employment contracts within the scope of the directive unnecessary. It also may indicate that the protection of workers has to be given priority in further development of the case law.

6.2.1.3. *The European Definition of 'Establishment'*

The concept of establishment is a phenomenon that appears in several EU labour law instruments. Among others, it can be found in directives that are related to workers' involvement as well as in equal treatment law.[13] Whether it has a European law meaning or it is for the Member States to determine what its meaning is depends on the wording of the directives concerned and on the context of the concept concerned.

The concept of establishment is not defined in the Collective Redundancies Directive. It is, however, an essential concept for the purpose of defining what is a collective redundancy under this directive. How is the reference unit for calculating relevant redundancies to be defined if an undertaking is divided into various establishments? The problem is that Member States, as described above, can choose between two options and, as some recent cases highlight, the way the concept establishment has been interpreted by the Court has resulted in a weakening of the level of protection of workers.[14]

In the *Rockfon* case[15] of 1995 the Court laid down the guidelines to be followed. It is important to recall the context of the case to better understand the meaning of the ruling. Rockfon was a company employing 165 workers and belonged to a much larger group of companies, employing more than 1000 workers in Denmark only.[16] Rockfon decided to dismiss 24 workers without any consultation. In implementing the directive, the Danish legislator chose the first option for determining the relevant number of redundancies (Article 1(1)(a)(part 1), Collective Redundancy Directive 1975/129). As a result, if Rockfon by itself constituted an 'establishment', the employer had to inform and consult workers' representatives when 16 workers were dismissed

12 ECJ 2015, C-422/14 (*Pujante Rivera*), §50.

13 See Chapters 3, 5 and 6 of this book.

14 See also the analysis of Butler (2018).

15 ECJ 1995, C-449/93 (*Rockfon*).

16 Rockfon belonged to the multinational Rockwool Group. The multinational employed at that time more than 5,000 employees.

(i.e. at least 10% of the number of workers in establishments normally employing at least 100 but less than 300 workers). However, Rockfon claimed that the company was part of a larger undertaking, the Rockwool group, and that Rockfon itself did not constitute an 'establishment' within the meaning of the directive, since the power to recruit and dismiss staff lay with another company in the group. Therefore, the dismissals carried out by Rockfon had to be regarded as having been made by an undertaking having more than 300 employees. In this case, the information and consultation procedure had to be observed only if at least 30 employees were made redundant over a period of 30 days. The competent body at first instance confirmed this reasoning. The Danish High Court referred the matter to the Court of Justice.

The Court did not follow the interpretation of the court of first instance. According to the Court of Justice: 'the term "establishment" appearing in Article 1(1)(a) of Directive 75/129 on the approximation of the laws of the Member States relating to collective redundancies must be understood as meaning, *depending on the circumstances*, the unit to which the workers made redundant are assigned to carry out their duties. It is not essential, in order for there to be an establishment, for the unit in question to be endowed with a management which can independently effect collective redundancies'.[17] The Court stated at first that 'establishment' is a concept of Community law and cannot be defined by reference to the laws of the Member States. To make the definition of 'establishment' dependent on the existence of such a management within the unit would be incompatible with the aim of the directive. That would allow companies, belonging to the same group, to try to make it more difficult for the directive to apply to them by conferring on a separate decision-making body the power to take decisions concerning redundancies. This means they would be able to escape the obligation to follow certain procedures for the protection of workers, such as their right to be informed and consulted. 'Such an interpretation therefore appears to be incompatible with the aim of the Directive'.[18]

It follows from this judgment, first, that the concept of 'establishment' must be given a uniform European definition and, second, that, *depending on the circumstances*, it could be defined as the unit to which the workers are assigned to carry out their duties, even if the unit has no power to decide on collective redundancies. It is also clear from the judgment that the principle of protection of workers, recognised as the main objective of the directive, was the principle guiding the interpretation of the Court.[19]

---

17 ECJ 1995, C-449/93 (*Rockfon*), §32 (emphasis added).

18 ECJ 1995, C-449/93 (*Rockfon*), §30.

19 See Butler (2018), p. 304 ff.

The Court gave a further clarification in the case *Athinaiki Chartopoiïa AE.*[20] An establishment may consist of a distinct entity, having a certain degree of permanence and stability, which is assigned to perform one or more given tasks and which has a workforce, technical means and a certain organisational structure allowing for the accomplishment of those tasks. Like in *Rockfon*, the definition of the establishment takes into account the main purpose of the directive, which is to promote greater protection of workers in the event of collective redundancies. In the specific context of the case, this interpretation ensures the right of workers' representatives to be informed and consulted.

However, the interpretation given in the *Rockfon* and *Athinaiki Chartopoiïa* cases can also lead to a result that might be not quite in conformity with the (social) objective of the directive: to provide workers' representatives information and consultation rights in case of collective redundancies.[21] The decisions in *USDAW* and *Lyttle* cases of 2015[22] show that the interpretation in the *Rockfon* and *Athinaiki Chartopoiïa* cases could limit these rights. In these cases the situation was the opposite of the *Rockfon* and *Athinaiki Chartopoiïa* situations, since in the new cases the UK had chosen the second option of Article 1(1)(a)(ii).[23] The issues raised in the *USDAW* and *Lyttle* cases were very similar. Both cases concerned two very large clothing retailing companies, which decided to dismiss thousands of workers: more than 4,500 workers in the *USDAW* case and 1,100 workers in the *Lyttle* case. The British legislation implementing the directive had imposed only the duty to consult if 20 or more employees were made redundant in 'one establishment' over a period of 90 days. According to the UK law no information and consultation took place because the big majority of these employees worked in stores with fewer than 20 employees. The referring courts in *USDAW* and *Lyttle*[24] considered that it is possible to construe Article 1(1)(a)(ii) as meaning that the number of 20 refers to the number of employees within a particular establishment, but that it is also possible to consider that that number refers to persons dismissed across the employer's entire undertaking or several 'establishments' within a certain area. The UK courts stated that a purposive interpretation is appropriate in the circumstances and that, referring to the judgment in *Rockfon*, the provision concerned had to be given an interpretation that would cover the largest possible number of redundancy-related dismissals.[25] In order to obtain clarification

20 ECJ 2007, C-270/05 (*Athinaiki Chartopoiïa AE*).

21 See also Butler (2018) in his analysis of this topic and the cases ECJ 2015, C-80/14 (*USDAW*) and ECJ 2015, C-182/13 (*Lyttle*).

22 ECJ 2015, C-80/14 (*USDAW*) and ECJ 2015, C-182/13 (*Lyttle*).

23 Redundancy of at least 20 workers in a period of 90 days employed in an establishment regardless the size of the establishment.

24 Employment Appeal Tribunal 30 May 2013, UKEAT/0547/548/12/KN (*USDAW*).

25 Industrial Tribunal Northern Ireland, 7 February 2013, Case Refs: 555/12, §101.

the courts referred preliminary questions to the Court of Justice as to how to understand the meaning of establishment in Article 1(1)(a)(i) and (ii). Does this term have the same meaning as established in *Rockfon*, or can the concept in Article 1(1)(a)(ii) refer to all of the employer's establishments in which dismissals are effected and not only to a particular establishment, i.e. one local employment unit?[26] The question was raised because under (a)(i) the number of (collective) dismissals is related to the size of the establishment whereas in (a)(ii) no relation is made between the number of (projected) dismissed workers and the size: 20 dismissals in 90 days. It is left the Member States to choose.

The Court first recalled that the concept of 'establishment' is a term of EU law that must be given a uniform and autonomous interpretation in the EU legal order. Furthermore the Court referred to the interpretation adopted in *Rockfon* and argued that the same concept cannot be given a different meaning in the same Article of the directive. It stated that where an 'undertaking' comprises several entities, it is the entity to which the workers made redundant are assigned to carry out their duties that constitutes the 'establishment' for the purposes of Article 1(1)(a) of Directive 98/59, regardless of the choice for (a)(i) or (a)(ii).

The Court noted that an interpretation of the directive that requires that account to be taken of the total number of redundancies across all of the establishments of an undertaking would significantly increase the number of workers eligible for protection, which would correspond to one of the objectives of the directive. The Court, however, preferred a formalistic approach which could be justified by the need for a consistent interpretation of the concept of 'establishment', but departed from the important objective of protection of workers.

The decisions of the Court in *USDAW* and *Lyttle* clearly fail to meet the main objective of the directive. In addition to the main argument regarding the need for a consistent interpretation the Court came up with a number of more or less superfluous arguments for its position.[27] It argued that one of the objectives with the directive is to ensure comparable protection of workers on the internal market and to harmonise the costs. Since the directive however, establishes a minimum protection and Member States and social partners can apply more favourable provisions this argument is not convincing, especially since the directive in its preamble states that the harmonisation must be promoted while the social improvement is being maintained within the meaning of Article 117 (1998) of the Treaty.

---

26 ECJ 2015, C-80/14 (*USDAW*), §42; and ECJ 2015, C-182/13 (*Lyttle*), §23.

27 See also Advocate General Wahl's opinion in cases C-182/13 (*Lyttle*) and C-80/14 (*USDAW*) where such arguments are listed.

Maybe what is at stake in the *USDAW* and *Lyttle* decisions is a misunderstanding of the collective rights of workers and of the information and consultation procedure. It is clear from the decisions that the Court of Justice considers that another interpretation will lead to an absurd solution: 'It should be added that that interpretation would bring within the scope of Directive 98/59 not only a group of workers affected by collective redundancy but also, in some circumstances, a single worker of an establishment – possibly of an establishment located in a town separate and distant from the other establishments of the same undertaking – which would be contrary to the ordinary meaning of the term 'collective redundancy'. In addition, the dismissal of that single worker could 'trigger the information and consultation procedures referred to in the provisions of Directive 98/59, provisions that are not appropriate in such an individual case'.[28] For the Court, the directive only concerns 'the socio-economic effects that collective redundancies may have in a given local context and social environment'.[29] This is a very limited conception of the role of workers' representatives, which contradicts the content of the directive itself. First, because it is the employer who is responsible for informing and consulting workers' representatives. Second, because these consultations shall 'at least cover ways and means of avoiding collective redundancies or reducing the number of workers affected, and of mitigating the consequences by recourse to accompanying social measures'. Therefore, the information and consultation procedure is not only about the consequences of the decision to dismiss workers for economic grounds, but also on the decision itself. Another consequence of the Court's decision is that it allows the employer to organise its company over several establishments in order to make it more difficult for the directive to apply. This was considered as contrary to the directive in the *Rockfon* case.

However in a later case,[30] the Court returned to a more traditional way of interpreting the Collective Redundancies Directive. Spanish legislation mentioned the undertaking, and not the establishment, as the sole reference unit for calculating the threshold. In this case, the effect of applying the criterion of 'the undertaking' to establish whether the number of collective redundancies was enough to impose the information and consultation procedure provided for in Articles 2 to 4 of the directive was that the number was too low. For the Court, 'Article 1(1)(a) of Directive 98/59/EC must be interpreted as precluding national legislation that introduces the undertaking and not the establishment as the sole reference unit, where the effect of the application of that criterion is to preclude the information and consultation

---

28 ECJ 2015, C-80/14 (*USDAW*), §64.

29 See ECJ 2007, C-270/05 (*Athinaiki Chartopoiïa AE*), §28.

30 ECJ 2015, C-392/13 (*Cañas*).

procedure provided for in Articles 2 to 4 of that directive, when the dismissals in question would have been considered "collective redundancies", under the definition in Article 1(1)(a) of that directive, had the establishment been used as the reference unit'.

The Court seems to be confronted by its earlier case law that may give unintended effects in other situations: 'it has fallen on its own sword'. The Court has given room to Member States to adopt a definition that best suits their domestic system. The UK makes as much as possible use of this room, and one of the effects is that the information and consultation duty/obligations can be evaded. It appears, however, taking into account the way the Court has decided other issues relating to this directive and the Transfer of Enterprises Directive, the Court is opposed to a practice that deprives effectively employees from fundamental rights such as information and consultation on managerial decisions (redundancies and transfer). The effective exercise of these rights may not be hampered or deprived by a domestic law instrument/choice when that implies that the right is effectively circumvented by national law measures.[31] It is very surprising that the Court did not even address the fact that the right to information and consultation is codified as a fundamental right in the EU Charter of Fundamental Rights (Article 27). A (fundamental) right as the information and consultation right has to be recognised and may not be infringed in its essence. This has been consistent in the case law of the Court of Justice. Where the Court considers that its decisions must be consistent with its earlier interpretation of one of the options, and it will have difficulties unravelling that tangle, it may be a task for the legislature to ensure the social protection envisaged by the directive.

6.2.2. THE INFORMATION AND CONSULTATION PROCEDURE

The sole purpose of the Collective Redundancies Directive is to require the employer to inform and consult workers' representatives with a 'view to reaching an agreement'. The directive clarifies some aspects of this procedure. First, the directive recognises a very general right of workers' representatives to information on the redundancy. This general right is complemented by a list of topics on which the employer must give information in writing to workers' representatives, in good time during the course of the consultation: the reasons for the projected redundancies; the number of categories of workers to be made redundant; the number and categories of workers normally employed; the period over which the projected redundancies are to be effected; the criteria

[31] See e.g. ECJ 2007, C-385/05 (*CGT*); ECJ 2015, C-229/14 (*Balkaya*); ECJ 2009, C-466/07 (*Klarenberg*); ECJ 1994, C-383/92 (*Commission v. United Kingdom*).

proposed for the selection of the workers to be made redundant in so far as national legislation and/or practice confers this power on the employer, and the method for calculating any redundancy payments other than those arising out of national legislation and/or practice.[32]

The right to information is further strengthened by the possibility for Member States to allow workers' representatives to call upon expert assistance in accordance with the measures in force at the national level.[33] The recourse to an expert was not foreseen by the first Collective Redundancies Directive in 1975. However, it is up to the Member States to decide whether this is a right for workers' representatives.

The Collective Redundancies Directive was the first directive recognising information and consultation rights to workers' representatives and it does not define, like the subsequent directives, the meaning of consultation or the precise timing of the collective redundancy consultation, both questions being closely related. The question of when does the duty to begin the consultation arise is critical as it is essential for employee representatives to have an early access to the decision-making process in order for them to influence the employer's decision.[34]

The directive states that an employer contemplating collective redundancies must consult with workers' representatives with a view to reaching an agreement. These consultations must, at the least, cover ways and means of minimising the impact, in particular by recourse to accompanying social measures aimed at redeploying or retraining workers who are made redundant (Article 2(2)). On the basis of these indications, the Court has clarified the meaning and the timing of the information and consultation procedure. The Court specified that 'consultation' and 'consultation with a view to reaching an agreement' are two different procedures and that Article 2 of the directive imposes an obligation to negotiate.[35] The Court also provided important guidance on when this negotiation shall take place. For the Court,

> the case in which the employer 'is contemplating' collective redundancies and has drawn up a 'project' to that end corresponds to a situation in which no decision has yet been taken. By contrast, the notification to a worker that his or her contract of employment has been terminated is the expression of a decision to sever the employment relationship. The actual cessation of that relationship on the expiry of the period of notice is no more than the effect of that decision.

---

32 The 1992 directive expanded the information to be given to the categories of workers normally employed and to be made redundant, the criteria to be employed in selecting workers for redundancy, and the method for calculating a redundancy payment.

33 Article 2(2) of the directive.

34 See on this issue Chapter 7.

35 ECJ 1994, C-383/92 (*Commission v. United Kingdom*) and, explicitly, ECJ 2005, C-188/03 (*Junk*), §43.

> Thus, the terms used by the Community legislature indicate that the obligations to consult and to notify arise prior to any decision by the employer to terminate contracts of employment.
>
> Finally, this interpretation is confirmed, in regard to the procedure for consultation of workers' representatives, by the purpose of the directive, as set out in Article 2(2), which is to avoid terminations of contracts of employment or to reduce the number of such terminations. The achievement of that purpose would be jeopardised if the consultation of workers' representatives were to be subsequent to the employer's decision.[36]

In the *Fujitsu Siemens* decision,[37] the Court applied this principle in a case where redundancies were contemplated within a group of companies. One of the main contributions of the new amended directive adopted in 1992 was precisely to address the transnational dimension of decision-making on collective dismissals. In groups of companies, the decision can be taken by the central management located outside the country where the dismissals occur, and employees are affected by key decisions taken at a level higher than their immediate employer. The new Article 2(4) provides that the requirements of the directive apply irrespective of whether the decision regarding the redundancies is taken by the employer or by a controlling undertaking and that in considering alleged breaches of these requirements, it will be no defence for an employer to show that the necessary information was not supplied by the undertaking which took the decision leading to the redundancies.

The solution given by the directive is pragmatic and avoids the problem of extraterritoriality. The employer remains the subject of the obligation. But it is acknowledged that the legal structure of the employer may be articulated with other undertakings nationally and transnationally, so that dismissals in the employer's undertaking may be decided by, or be the consequence of, decisions by other undertakings.

The legal obligations are placed upon the local employer as confirmed by the *Fujitsu Siemens* decision. The employer is responsible for compliance with the information and consultation requirements, even if the decision on collective redundancies is made not by the employer itself, but by the undertaking controlling the employer. The obligation rests on the employer, even though the employer may not have been immediately and properly informed of the decision by the controlling undertaking. The consultation procedure must be started by the employer, once a strategic or commercial decision has been taken compelling the employer to contemplate or to plan for collective redundancies.[38]

---

36 ECJ 2005, C-188/03 (*Junk*), §§36–38.

37 ECJ 2009, C-44/08 (*Fujitsu Siemens*), §§67–72.

38 ECJ 2009, C-44/08 (*Fujitsu Siemens*), §43.

This implies that the employer has to start consulting workers' representatives even if it is not possible to supply at that time all the information required to the workers' representatives. The information can be provided during the consultations and not necessarily at the time when they start.

The *Fujitsu Siemens* case highlights some of the limits of the directive. In a group of companies, especially in transnational groups, when the local company is not the one deciding on the restructuring of the company, the consultation will de facto be limited to the consequences of the decision to dismiss. If the local company has the obligation to provide the information, how can it discuss a decision when it was not part of the decision-making process? In this regard, it also highlights the importance of another directive: the European Works Councils Directive, which regulates the European procedure of information and consultation and the national procedure.[39]

The implementation of the information and consultation procedure has raised a final issue regarding the definition of workers' representatives. This was considered by the Court in two landmark cases brought forward by the Commission against the United Kingdom in the 1990s.[40] According to Article 1(1)(b) of the directive, the term 'workers' representatives' means the 'workers' representatives provided for by the laws or practices of the Member States. The competence here given to the Member States is perfectly understandable, as it will be very difficult, or even impossible, to directly interfere with the national systems of workers' representation. The two directives leave it to the Member States to decide whether information and consultation rights are granted to elected or recognised trade unions or to elected works councils. There is no explicit preference in the directives between a single channel of representation or multi channels representation (i.e. trade unions, respectively trade unions and works councils). The issue what is meant by workers' representatives, has been raised in a procedure before the Court of Justice in 1994 where a typical UK practice was challenged by the Commission. At that time, in the United Kingdom, employers' recognition of trade unions was traditionally voluntary. Only recognised trade unions were given rights of information, consultation and negotiation and if an employer did not recognise any trade unions, the employer would not be subject to the obligations laid down in the directives. The British government argued that this was not contrary to the directive, which left to the Member States the freedom to designate who will be the workers' representatives to be informed and consulted. The Court did not agree with this interpretation: Article 1(1)(b) of the Collective Redundancies Directive leaves to Member States only the

39 Directive 2009/38/EC (European Works Council) (recast).

40 ECJ 1994, Case C-382/92 and ECJ 1994, C-383/92 (*Commission v. UK*); one case was about the implementation of the Collective Redundancies Directive and the other about the Transfers of Undertakings Directive.

task of determining the arrangements for designating workers' representatives. However, adopting the interpretation proposed by the United Kingdom would allow Member States to determine the cases in which workers' representatives may be informed and consulted and may intervene. As a consequence in the British system as interpreted by the UK government, information and consultation including notification of and intervention with public authorities could be restricted to undertakings where national law provided for the designation of workers' representatives. Such an interpretation would permit Member States to deprive Articles 2 and 3(2) of the directive of their full effect'.[41]

Here, again, the case highlights one of the limits of the directive. How can the information and consultation procedure be effective if there are no workers' representatives in the undertaking? As a result, the UK introduced a reform requiring companies to organise the designation of workers' representatives in companies where no trade unions were recognised and, in 1999, a new statutory right of trade union recognition was adopted. The case also contributed to the adoption of the 2002 Directive on information and consultation, which established general principles on the minimum information and consultation rights for employees.[42]

This case highlights one of the limits of the Collective Redundancies Directive and also the Transfers of Undertakings Directive: the competences given in these directives to Member States have important consequences. The effectiveness of the rights granted by the directives depends on the strength of the national system of workers' representation; it depends on their capacity to exercise at the appropriate time their social and economic prerogatives. For example, in countries like France, Germany and the Netherlands the implementation of these information and consultation rights was easy since works councils have become a normal feature in these countries alongside to trade unions as organisations representing workers. In a dual channel context of representation,[43] these rights were largely similar to the one already granted to works councils. However, a problem may rise because in nearly all Member States works councils do not have any prerogative to negotiate. Germany is an exception.[44] Usually only trade unions can negotiate and conclude collective agreements. From a formal point of view it can be stated that a works council cannot act in the way formulated in the directive: to be informed and consulted 'with a view to reaching an agreement'. In countries where the works council plays a

41 This is another example of application of the *effet utile* principle in order to provide effective application of EU law. See about this principle Chapter 1.

42 Directive 2002/14/EC (General framework for informing and consulting employees). See further Chapter 7.

43 See Chapter 7.

44 By way of *Betriebsvereinbarungen*. See Däubler, Kittner, Klebe & Webbe (2018), §77.

significant role it is not a real obstacle to being involved in these negotiations. However, this divergence has never been rectified or challenged in court.

6.2.3. NOTIFICATION OF THE COLLECTIVE REDUNDANCIES TO PUBLIC AUTHORITIES

Section III of the Collective Redundancies Directive provides the content and scope of the procedure for collective redundancies, which involves public authorities. The purpose of the directive is to encourage governmental intervention regarding ways of alleviating the social consequences of collective redundancies, such as measures for retraining and redeployment.

According to the directive, employers shall notify the competent public authority in writing of any projected collective redundancy. This notification shall contain all relevant information concerning the projected collective redundancies and the consultations with workers' representatives. The workers' representatives are to be given a copy of this notification and they may send comments on it to the public authority. The projected collective redundancies notified to the public authority shall take effect not earlier than 30 days after the notification, but this is without prejudice to individual rights to longer periods of notice of dismissal.[45] Member States may grant the competent public authority the power to reduce this period or to extend it. Where the initial period of notification is shorter than 60 days, Member States may grant the public authority the power to extend the initial period to 60 days following notification of the proposed collective redundancy where the problems relating to the redundancy are unlikely to be solved within the initial period. In addition, Member States may grant the public authority wider powers of extension. The employer must be informed of the extension and the grounds for it before the expiry of the initial 30-day period.

Although the directive requires the competent public authority to be informed about dismissal, its role in the process of restructuring is not well defined by the directive. This is certainly a problem, because the role of public authorities varies considerably from one State to the other. The directive does not specify the scope or nature of the public authorities' intervention. It does not require the administration to control the consultation procedure or to check if the social measures are strong enough. Nor does the directive say anything about the precise obligations on the administration to seek solutions to redundancies. In this way, it can be seen as a compromise between

[45] Member States can decide not to apply this article to collective redundancies arising from termination of the establishment's activities where this is the result of a judicial decision (Article 4(4)).

an industrial relations model of enforcement (social measures are defined by the employer and workers' representatives) and an administrative model (public authorities playing a central role in the definition of the social measures). The result is a soft conception of administrative intervention, which leaves considerable freedom to Member States.

This very soft European obligation in the Collective Redundancies Directive could explain why this part of the directive did not give rise to any European case law until 2016, when the directive was used to challenge a national administrative authorisation for dismissals.[46] Is an administrative authorisation to dismiss compatible with the directive? If so, could the authorisation be restricted in order to upheld the employers' prerogative to conduct the business as they found it necessary? The question referred by the Greek Council of State was twofold. The first question was whether the system of prior ministerial authorisation for the implementation of a collective redundancies scheme provided for under Greek legislation is compatible with Directive 98/59. Second, if the answer on that question is positive, does the Greek rule infringe the freedom of movement principle and rules of EU law, in particular the freedom of establishment under Article 49 TFEU?[47] As the ground for an administrative authorisation the Greek government put forward socio-economic policy considerations, pointing to an acute economic crisis and very high unemployment.

As to the first question, the Court considered that the situation did not fall within the scope of the directive, even if the authorisation was needed exactly when the employer and the trade unions could not reach an agreement. According to Article 1(1) and Article 5 of Directive 98/59, the directive is intended to provide *minimum* protection with regard to informing and consulting workers in the event of collective redundancies. That implies that Member States remain free to adopt national measures that are more favourable to those workers.[48] However, for the Court, this position would, exceptionally, be different if a national regime were to result in depriving Articles 2 to 4 of Directive 98/59 'of their practical effect'.[49] The limited character of the harmonisation that the directive is aiming to achieve cannot have the consequence of depriving provisions of the directive of practical effect.[50] Therefore, the employer should

46 ECJ 2016, C-201/15 (*AGET Iraklis*).

47 The question was raised whether it could violate the free movement of capital under Article 63 TFEU. That question was on the table because it was about investment by the parent company to the Greek subsidiary. The Court stated that in a case like this, restrictive effects on the free movement of capital are so closely linked to the freedom of establishment that a separate examination was not necessary. ECJ 2016, C-201/15 (*AGET Iraklis*), §5.

48 ECJ 2016, C-201/15 (*AGET Iraklis*), §§32 and 34.

49 ECJ 2016, C-201/15 (*AGET Iraklis*), §35.

50 This approach by the court fits with the theory of partial harmonisation. Similarly in ECJ 2009, C-12/08 (*Mono Car Styling*), §35.

not be denied the right to dismiss. It is left to national judges to decide whether this is actually the case.[51]

Next, the Court examined whether the Greek legislation was compatible with Article 49 TFEU on freedom of establishment, interpreted in the light of Article 16 of the Charter of Fundamental Rights of the European Union, laying down the freedom to conduct a business. That entails the whole variety of choices employers can make for conducting their businesses, such as the nature and extent of the economic activity, scaling down that activity, or even the freedom to give up the business activity and establishment. So employers for their own reasons can opt to bring the activity of the establishment to an end, or to decide whether and when they should formulate plans for collective redundancies due to a cessation or reduction of the activity of the undertaking or a decline in demand for the product which they manufacture, or as a result of new working arrangements within an undertaking unconnected with its level of activity.[52]

The Court held in this regard that the Greek legislation was liable to constitute a serious obstacle to the exercise of freedom of establishment in Greece. That legislation was such as to render access to the Greek market less attractive and to reduce considerably, or even eliminate, the ability of any economic operator from another Member State – if it proposes to adapt its activity or give it up – to part, where appropriate, with the workers previously taken on. The Court concluded from this that there was a restriction on freedom of establishment.[53] It recalled that such a restriction may be justified by overriding reasons in the public interest, such as the protection of workers or the encouragement of employment and recruitment. In this regard it stated that the mere fact that a Member State provides that projected collective redundancies must first be notified to a national authority endowed with powers of review enabling it, in certain circumstances, to oppose the projected redundancies on grounds relating to the protection of workers and of employment, cannot be considered contrary either to freedom of establishment or to the freedom to conduct a business enshrined in the Charter of Fundamental Rights. Such a regime does not have the consequence of excluding entirely, by its very nature, the ability to effect collective redundancies, but is designed solely to impose a framework on that ability, in such a way as to strike a fair balance between the interests connected with the protection of workers and of employment (in particular protection against unjustified dismissal) and those relating to freedom of establishment or conduct a business. Such a regime is capable of satisfying the requirement of proportionality and, furthermore,

---

51 Taking into account the criteria in the national law with which the authority has to apply (§43).

52 ECJ 2016, C-201/15 (*AGET Iraklis*), §§53–55, referring to previous case law.

53 Ibid., §59.

does not affect *the essence* of the freedom to conduct a business. The Court then examined the three criteria in the light of which the Greek authorities had to examine projected collective redundancies. The Court held that the first criterion (interests of the national economy) could not be accepted, since economic aims cannot constitute a reason in the public interest that justifies a restriction on a freedom such as freedom of establishment. The other two criteria (the situation of the undertaking and the conditions in the labour market) did appear *prima facie* to be capable of relating to the legitimate objectives in the public interest that are constituted by the protection of workers and of employment. The Court found, however, that those two criteria were formulated in very general and imprecise terms. The employers concerned did not know in what specific objective circumstances the Greek authorities might oppose projected collective redundancies: the situations were potentially numerous, undetermined and indeterminable and the criteria left the Greek authorities a broad discretion that was difficult to review. Imprecise criteria of that kind, which are not founded on objective, verifiable conditions, go beyond what is necessary in order to attain the objectives stated and therefore cannot satisfy the requirements of the principle of proportionality. Finally, in answer to the second question asked by the Greek court, the Court of Justice stated that the fact that the context in a Member State may be one of acute economic crisis and a particularly high unemployment rate is not such as to affect the outcome reached by it. Neither the directive nor the TFEU provides for a derogation based on such a national context.

Is this balancing exercise between social rights and freedoms of the internal market undertaken by the Court really balanced? One might doubt it. Like the *Laval* and *Alemo-Herron* cases, at the end of the day, the balancing exercise between social rights and freedoms of internal market led to a restriction of social rights. Here again, a national provision of labour law has to be justified and its proportionality investigated with respect to the freedom of establishment and the freedom of undertaking of Article 16 of the European Charter of Social Rights. Also, here it can be stated that this test has never been done the other way round.

6.3. THE TRANSFERS OF UNDERTAKINGS DIRECTIVE

6.3.1. INTRODUCTION

Compared with the Collective Redundancies Directive and the Insolvency Directive, the Transfers of Undertakings Directive is the most complicated directive, and the one which deserves the main part of this chapter. It regulates:

- issues related to the pre-transfer employment relationship;

- the legal effects of the transfer on the employment relationship;
- issues related to the post-transfer employment relationship and its terms; and
- issues relating the procedure during all stages of the transfer.

During the first 20 years after its adoption the scope of the application of the directive gave raise to many disputes. The Court has quite successfully harmonised the definition of transfer of undertakings, we know more or less when the directive becomes applicable and which characteristics have to be taken into account when assessing whether a transfer has taken place. These criteria were partly codified when the directive was amended by Council Directive 98/50/EC, although some problems have still not been solved.

The main difficulties at present seem to be related to public-private transfers and private-public transfers, as well as to post-transfer situations in case of outsourcing and transfers within groups of undertakings. In particular, rights arising from collective agreements and situations where different collective agreements apply with the transferor and the transferee may cause complications.

6.3.2. OBJECTIVE OF THE DIRECTIVE

The explicit objective of the directive is to safeguard the rights of employees in the context of business restructurings, which have been regarded as an inevitable consequence of the functioning of the European internal market. According to the objective of the directive, the safeguarding of the rights of employees is not limited to the individual rights of the employees affected by the transfer of an undertaking, but also applies to the collective level, as the preamble recognised. Information, consultation and participation for workers is the other element of safeguarding rights as elaborated in Article 7 of the directive. Since the directive aims for partial harmonisation, as does the Collective Redundancies Directive,[54] it sets out a minimum standard; more favourable terms for employees can be adopted on a national level (Article 8). The mandatory protection of employees under the directive is mainly restricted to the effects of the transfer on the conditions of employment and to the required information and consultation procedure. The Court has underlined the partial harmonisation objective in 1985 in the *Danmols* case.[55] The protective function is basically fulfilled by the stipulation in Article 3(1), according to

54 Paragraph 5 of the preamble explicitly states that account has to be taken of the practice in force in the various Member States.

55 See ECJ 1985, 105/84 (*Danmols Inventar*), §26.

which the rights and obligations arising from a contract of employment or from an employment relationship existing on the date of a transfer shall, by reason of such transfer, be transferred to the transferee.

This rule not only protects the employees from being dismissed by the transferor, it is also rational from a business perspective. The transferor is the appropriate person to make future business and employment decisions regarding the acquired undertaking. The directive protects the employee during the transfer, but as will be explored below, only to a limited extent in the situation where the transfer has taken place and new business decisions are made.[56]

Although not explicitly mentioned in the directive itself, that does not imply automatically that the interests of the transferee (and the transferor) in terms of being bound to apply the employment conditions of the transferor to the transferred employees – generally based on the collective agreement the transferor is bound to – do not play a role at all. The directive itself adopted economic, technical or organisational reasons (ETO reasons) for a dismissal, provided the transfer in itself is not the reason for the dismissal. It does not exclude totally a downgrading of working conditions, including remuneration.[57] It has to be kept in mind that the Transfers of Undertakings Directive as well as the Collective Redundancy Directive are adopted in the realm of the social policy of the EEC in the 1970s and 1980s. The process of restructuring of enterprises at a large and transnational scale caused a two-pronged approach: protection of employees affected by transfers, on national as well as if not predominantly on cross-border level, on the one hand, and preserving the competitiveness of enterprises, on the other.[58] The issue of balancing the interests of the employer and the employees' rights can be seen as inserted as objectives in the directive, be it implicitly. This balancing approach, which has been debated in the literature,[59] has come to the surface in the more recent cases before the Court of Justice.[60] Against the employees' rights were placed freedom of establishment (Article 49 TFEU) and the fundamental right, recognised in the EU Charter, to conduct a business (Article 16), and the judge has to balance these.[61]

---

56 In several Member States this kind of regulation has been introduced long ago and is supported by employers′ organisations, in France even since 1928. See Barnard (2012a), p. 578.

57 Article 4(2) Directive 2001//23 states that if the reductions are substantial the termination of the contract to the detriment of the employee, the termination is considered as an employer's action facing a sanction according to the national law. Cf. ECJ 20, C-425/02 (*Delahaye*), §35.

58 See Barnard (2012a), p. 577; and Fuchs & Marhold (2014), p. 298. In the context of the functioning of the internal market.

59 Cf. Prassl (2013); Brameshuber (2016).

60 See ECJ 2013, C-426/11 (*Alemo Herron*); ECJ 2014, C-328/13 (*Österreichischer Gewerkschaftsbund*); ECJ 2016, C-201/15 (*AGET Iraklis*); and ECJ 2017, C-680/15 and C-681/15 (*Asklepios*).

61 See more extensive hereafter Section 6.3.7.

6.3.3. SCOPE AND DEFINITIONS

According to Article 1(a) of the directive it shall apply to any transfer of an undertaking, business, or part of an undertaking or business to another employer as a result of a legal transfer or merger. According to Article 1(b) there is a transfer within the meaning of this directive where there is a transfer of an economic entity which retains its identity, meaning an organised grouping of resources which has the objective of pursuing an economic activity, whether or not that activity is central or ancillary. Furthermore the directive shall apply to public and private undertakings engaged in economic activities, whether or not they are operating for gain (Article 1(c)). An administrative reorganisation of administrative authorities or functions is, however, not a transfer under the directive (Article 1(c)).

The change of employer is the key condition for the application of the directive. Changes of employer can take different forms. The main question therefore is what changes qualify for a transfer of employership in the sense of the directive. It is generally accepted that when the majority of shares are acquired by a new owner in a joint stock company, there is (legally) no change of employer and consequently no transfer. However, on several occasions the Court of Justice has held that the directive applies where there is a change in the legal or natural person who is responsible for carrying on the business, regardless of whether or not ownership of the undertaking is transferred.[62] In fact, the directive's requirement of change of employer could be criticised, as very often the consequences for workers are the same even if there is legally no change of employer. Even if formally the employer remains the same, the restructuring could lead to a reorganisation and changes in working conditions of workers. Since the adoption of Directive 2002/14 (on information and consultation), however, such restructurings of companies have been covered and workers' representatives shall be informed and consulted on any decisions that could lead to substantial changes in the way work is organised or in contractual relations (Article 4(2)).

The Transfers of Undertakings Directive shall apply to cross-border transfers as far as the transferee is situated within the European Union (Article 1(2)).

The approach to the question of whether a transfer of economic identity has taken place was set out by the Court in the mid-1980s. In the famous *Spijkers* case, the Court pointed out that there are a number of single factors that should be taken into account; however these cannot be considered in isolation, but must be part of an overall assessment. It stated that the decisive

---

62 See for instance ECJ 1988, 324/86 (*Daddy's Dance Hall*) or ECJ 2018, C-472/16 (*Colino Sigüenza*).

criterion is whether the business has retained its identity after the transfer. For this purpose, according to the Court it is necessary to consider whether the business was disposed of as a going concern with the same or similar activities after the transfer as before. The Court set out some criteria for this consideration:

> It is necessary to consider all the facts characterising the transaction in question, including the type of undertaking or business, whether or not the business's tangible assets, such as buildings and movable property, are transferred, the value of its intangible assets at the time of the transfer, whether or not the majority of its employees are taken over by the new employer, whether or not its customers are transferred and the degree of similarity between the activities carried on before and after the transfer and the period, if any, for which those activities were suspended.[63]

In its judgments the Court has consistently based its conclusions on a factual assessment of the situation. Therefore, several formal criteria which are applied in the Member States have been regarded as irrelevant by the Court. For instance, the date of the transfer was not assessed in accordance with contractual arrangements, but the date on which responsibility as employer for carrying on the business of the unit transferred moved from the transferor to the transferee.[64] The lack of direct contractual relationship or even a legal link between the transferor and transferee was not regarded as an obstacle for application of the directive.[65] Instead, in situations where an entrepreneur replaces another entrepreneur or leases out equipment and property the criteria of a transfer may be fulfilled;[66] this may also be in situations of insolvency of the transferor combined with continuation of the business or part of the business by the transferee.[67] Public procurement procedures where a bidder may take over a business earlier conducted by another party have consistently been regarded as a transfer, if the general criteria are met.[68] A transfer of an undertaking was also accepted when a public sector undertaking providing services to another public sector undertaking under a service operating agreement decided to terminate that agreement without taking over the employees of the latter undertaking, on the ground that it would henceforth perform that activity itself with its own staff.[69]

---

63 See ECJ 1986, 24/85 (*Spijkers*), §13.

64 ECJ 2005, C-478/03 (*Celtec*).

65 ECJ 1987, 287/86 (*Mølle Kro*).

66 Cf. ECJ 1987, 287/86 (*Mølle Kro*); ECJ 1988, 324/86 (*Daddy's Dance Hall*) and ECJ 1988, 144/87 and 145/87 (*Berg*).

67 Note, however, that bankruptcy procedures are not covered by the directive, unless the Member State has decided otherwise.

68 See ECJ 2001, C-172/99 (*Liikenne*) and ECJ 2017, C-200/16 (*Securitas*).

69 See ECJ 2015, C-509/14 (*ADIF*).

When the Transfers of Undertakings Directive was adopted in 1977, the common forms of transfers were direct transactions between buyer and seller. Since that time, public-private transactions, complex leasing and similar arrangements as well as public procurement procedures have become common.[70] The Court has consistently held that the directive and the concept of a transfer apply to these new forms of business restructuring as long as some 'economic identity is retained'.

National courts have been less willing to follow this approach; this explains the many requests for preliminary rulings and the fact that several national courts had to reconsider their earlier case law. For instance, in 1990 the Cour de Cassation in France abandoned its earlier requirement for a direct contractual link between the successive employers and also its view that the directive does not apply to a situation where the employer loses a contract in a competitive tender.[71]

As shown by the various and regular preliminary rulings, the definition and the general method adopted by the Court of Justice for assessing the existence of a transfer of an entity which retains its identity still give rise to numerous problems. National judges keep asking if a particular case is a transfer of undertaking or not. These difficulties have been recognised by the Court of Justice itself in a case where it stressed the obligation for the national judges to refer cases:

> [T]he question as to how the concept of a 'transfer of a business' should be interpreted has given rise to a great deal of uncertainty on the part of many national courts and tribunals which, as a consequence, have found it necessary to make a reference to the Court of Justice. That uncertainty shows not only that there are difficulties of interpretation, but also that there is a risk of divergences in judicial decisions within the European Union. It follows that, in circumstances such as those of the case before the referring court, which are characterised both by conflicting lines of case law at national level regarding the concept of a 'transfer of a business' within the meaning of Directive 2001/23 and by the fact that that concept frequently gives rise to difficulties of interpretation in the various Member States, a national court or tribunal against whose decisions there is no judicial remedy under national law must comply with its obligation to make a reference to the Court, in order to avert the risk of an incorrect interpretation of EU law.[72]

As far as the scope and definition are concerned, the case law of the Court has led to difficulties in interpreting the concept at national level, in particular in relation to issues such as outsourcing, transfers within groups of undertakings and transfers involving public services.

---

70 See Davies (2001), p. 134.

71 See further Laulom (2001), p. 157.

72 ECJ 2015, C-160/14 (*Ferreira da Silva e Brito*).

In the *Schmidt* case,[73] the Court distinguished between activities based essentially on manpower, such as cleaning and surveillance, and activities based essentially on assets, such as public transport or catering. Therefore, in case of providers of services whose activities are based essentially on manpower, the taking over by the new employer of a major part, in terms of their numbers and skills, of the employees specially assigned by its predecessor to the provision of the services in point can result in the maintenance of the identity of the entity.[74] Similarly, in the case of providers of services whose activities are based essentially on assets, the taking over by a new operator of the assets indispensable for the provision of the services can result in the maintenance of the identity of the entity, even when the essential part of the staff has not been taken over. However, the identity is not maintained when the new operator does not take over the assets indispensable for the provision of the services.[75] There is, however, no need for the ownership of the tangible assets to be transferred.

When activities are based essentially on manpower, there is no need of a transfer of assets. A consequence revealed in the *CLECE* decision[76] is that if the transferee decides not to take over the employees, there is no transfer of undertaking. Here, the application of the directive has become dependent on the transferee's will. In fact, contrary to what the Court stated, in activities based mainly on manpower, the fact that the activities before and after the transfer are identical can be characterised as a transfer of undertakings. Otherwise, a consequence of the transfer (the take-over of the employees) becomes a condition used to characterise the mere existence of a transfer of undertakings. However, until now, the *CLECE* case has remained an isolated one.

Much less debated is the recognition of transfer of undertakings in groups of companies. The Court held that the directive applies to a situation in which a company belonging to a group decides to subcontract to another company in the same group contracts in so far as the transaction involves the transfer of an economic entity between the two companies.[77] The Court also adopted a broad purposive interpretation of the notion of transfer of undertakings in *Albron*, where it acknowledged a dual employer.[78] For the Court, Article 3(1) requires either an employment contract or an employment 'relationship' from the date of transfer. The directive does therefore not prevent the non-contractual employer from being regarded as a 'transferor' within the meaning of the directive.

73 In this case, the Court held that one employee who cleans a bank can be an undertaking within the meaning of the directive, ECJ 1994, C-392/92 (*Schmidt*).

74 ECJ 1998, C-173/96 and C-247/96 (*Sánchez Hidalgo*).

75 ECJ 2001, C-172/99 (*Liikenne*).

76 ECJ 2011, C-463/09 (*CLECE*).

77 ECJ 1999, C-234/98 (*Allen*).

78 ECJ 2010, C-242/09 (*Albron*).

The Court concluded therefore that, if there are two employers within a group of companies (one which has contractual relations with the employees, and the other which does not), the transferor can be the employer responsible for the economic activity of the entity transferred, although it had no contractual relationship with the affected employees. This is the only case where the Court acknowledged a dual employer.

Finally, the Court of Justice acknowledged several times that the directive applies to transfer of public services.[79] The directive has therefore played an important role in cases of privatisation of public services. These cases exist when some public sector activity is out-sourced to the private sector, or when an undertaking responsible for providing a public service resumes the direct management of that service. The directive applies to public undertakings engaged in economic activities whether or not they are operating for gain. The Court has therefore held that the mere fact that the transferee is a public-law body cannot be a ground for excluding the existence of a transfer from the scope of the directive. The only exclusion explicitly accepted by the directive is an administrative reorganisation of public administrative authorities, or the transfer of administrative functions between public administrative authorities.[80]

In these situations, the problem is not so much the existence of the transfer of undertakings but the change of working conditions which can occur because of the changing nature of the employer from a public employer to a private one, and vice versa. According to the Court,

> an obligation, prescribed by national law, to terminate contracts of employment governed by private law in the case of transfer of an activity to a legal person governed by public law, constitutes a substantial change in working conditions to the detriment of the employee resulting directly from the transfer, with the result that termination of such contracts of employment must, in such circumstances, be regarded as resulting from the action of the employer.[81]

To a certain extent, the Court takes into account the fact that the new (public) employer will not necessarily have the same powers as the previous (private) employer. In *Delahaye*,[82] the Court stated that, in the event of a transfer of an undertaking from a legal person governed by private law to the State, the latter, as new employer, was not precluded from reducing the amount of the remuneration of the employees concerned for the purpose of complying with the national rules in force for public employees. However, those rules had to

79 ECJ 2000, C-343/98 (*Collino*); ECJ 2000, C-175/99 (*Mayeur*); and ECJ 2011, C-463/09 (*CLECE*).
80 Article 1(1)(c).
81 ECJ 2000, C-175/99 (*Mayeur*).
82 ECJ 2004, C-425/02 (*Delahaye*).

be interpreted so as far as possible in the light of the purpose of that directive, taking into account in particular the employee's length of service. A substantial reduction in the employee's remuneration would therefore constitute a substantial change in working conditions to the detriment of the worker, which must be regarded as a termination of his contract of employment, in accordance with Article 4 of the directive.

6.3.4. THE CONCEPT OF EMPLOYEES UNDER THE DIRECTIVE

As in several other working conditions directives, but different from the Collective Redundancies Directive, the Transfers of Undertakings Directive also refers to a national definition of employee. Article 2(1)(d) defines employee as 'any person who, in the Member State concerned, is protected as an employee under national employment law'.[83] The directive leaves it to the national law of the Member States to determine who is an employee covered by the directive. Covered by the directive is the worker who falls under personal scope of national employment law of the country. As a consequence, civil servants are not covered when they do not qualify as employees under national labour law.[84]

By leaving it to Member States to determine the personal coverage there may be differences from country to country, although the directive makes certain restrictions to the discretion of Member States. Article 2(2) places contracts of employment on a par with employment relationships, by which provision the personal scope is wider than that of employee. Next to this it is not allowed to exclude some contracts of employment or employment relationships from coverage, based solely on the number of working hours, fixed term contracts or relationships and temporary agency workers.[85]

In recent case law, the Court of Justice has in some cases defined the term 'worker' independently of the national legal system concerned in order to ensure uniform interpretation of this concept. Thus it limits the freedom of Member States to define the term in such way that certain categories of persons are excluded from the protection that the directive is envisaged to give.[86]

As seen in Chapters 1 and 2, the term worker in the freedom of movement for workers instruments have a community meaning, as otherwise the freedom of movement rules would be frustrated, as Member States would

83 This is different from primary European law (and the secondary law on free movement) where a community definition is used; see ECJ 1982 case 53/81 (*Levin*), §§11–13 and see Chapter 1.

84 ECJ 2000, C-343/98 (*Collino*), §§39–40. In some countries public servants are or will be brought under the general labour law and consequently the difference will disappear. In the Netherlands such transition will take place in 2020.

85 Article 2(2) under (a), (b) and (c). Article 2(2) (b) and (c) refer to Article 1(1) and 1(2) Directive 91/383/EEC (fixed-duration or temporary employment relationship).

86 Cf. Risak and Dullinger (2018), pp. 40, 41.

be able to exclude at will certain categories of persons from the benefit of the Treaty.[87] For the Court, the situation is different when interpreting the Transfers of Undertakings Directive. This directive is intended to achieve partial harmonisation by extending the protection guaranteed to workers independently by the laws of the individual Member States to cover the case where an undertaking is transferred. Although the directive does not intend to establish a uniform level of protection throughout the Community on the basis of common criteria, it aims to ensure that the contract of employment or the employment relationship continues unchanged with the transferee. The employees affected by the transfer of undertaking may not be placed in a less favourable position solely as a result of the transfer.[88]

This approach is also visible from several options offered to Member States. They may, for instance, provide that, after the date of transfer, the transferor and transferee shall be jointly and severally liable in respect of obligations which arose before the date of transfer from an employment relationship existing on the date of the transfer (Article 3(1, 2)).

Within this strict system of national concepts of 'employee', the Court has set rather narrow limits for the Member States to exclude categories of employees from the scope of the application of the Transfers of Undertakings Directive. In the *Albron* case,[89] the Court decided that employees do not have to be formally employed by the transferor in order to be covered by the directive. In this case, two companies ('employers'), within a group of companies, had relations with the employees of that group. One had contractual relations and the other had non-contractual relations with them. The employer responsible for the economic activity of the entity transferred an entity which, in that capacity, established working relations with the staff of that entity, despite the absence of contractual relations with those workers.

In the *Ricardo* case,[90] the employment contract had been suspended for four years. Contrary to the prevailing Spanish legislation, the Court held that a person whose employment contract is suspended and who does not actually perform his duties is covered by the directive as far as that person is an employee under national law.

6.3.5. THE LEGAL POSITION OF THE EMPLOYEES

The main idea behind the Transfers of Undertakings Directive is to guarantee the continuation of the employee relationship in the transfer process. The directive

---

[87] ECJ 1982, 53/81 (*Levin*), §11 and, similarly, ECJ 1985, 105/84 (*Danmols*), §24.

[88] ECJ 1985, 105/84 (*Danmols*), §§25 and 26.

[89] ECJ 2010, C-242/09 (*Albron*).

[90] ECJ 2017, C-416/16 (*Ricardo*).

states that the transfer shall not in itself constitute grounds for dismissal by the transferor or the transferee (Article 4(1)). In order to avoid misinterpretations, the provision clarifies that this shall not stand in the way of dismissals that may take place for economic, technical or organisational reasons entailing changes in the workforce.

The directive also stipulates that the transfer as such must not have any negative impact on transferred rights and obligations of the employee. The 'transferred' employees retain the rights (and obligations) they had in their employment relationship with the transferor, including the working conditions. That is also the case as to the terms and conditions laid down in the collective agreement applicable to the transferor but limited to the date of termination of expiry of the collective agreement or the entry into force or application of another collective agreement (Article 3(3)). However, that does not guarantee that the conditions of employment will not change as a consequence of the transfer for reasons other than those directly related to the transfer as such. This stipulation in fact means that if the applicable collective agreement expires soon after the transfer, employees might face significant losses in benefits, wages and other working conditions.[91]

The transfer is an automatic consequence of the transfer, it requires an information and consultation procedure, but it does not require any specific legal act, either from the part of the employee or the transferee. Although the protection against dismissal directly related to the transfer guarantees that the employee can stay in the job, that does not mean that the directive obliges employees to continue their employment relationship with the new employer. Although, in practice the great majority of employees see the continuation of the employment relationship with the transferee as the best option, there can be several reasons for not wishing to be transferred. Employee might see better opportunities if they continue to work for the transferor, the change of employer might – at least in the long term – lead to decreased benefits and wages, or the new employer might have a 'bad reputation'.

The question whether the employee has a right to object to the transfer (regarding him or herself) has been raised in several cases.[92] The Court consistently stated that the employee can object to his or her transfer to the transferee if the employee wishes to do so. The consequences for the employee depends on the reason for the objection. Objection as such does not imply that the employee will remain in the service of the transferee. In the *Katsikas* case this issue was at stake.[93] Katsikas was an employee in a restaurant run by his employer Konstantinidis. The employer had sub-let the restaurant to

91 ECJ 2008, C-396/07 (*Juuri*). Apart from a loss of wages it also can be a change of the place of work (*Juuri*), §13 and ECJ 1996, C-171/94 and C-172/94 (*Merckx and Neuhuys*), §9.

92 See ECJ 1988, 144 and 145/87 (*Berg*), §12.

93 ECJ 1992, C-132/91 (*Katsikas*).

another person, Mitosis. Katsikas refused to work for Mitosis and was for that reason dismissed by Konstantinidis, who also argued that he had ceased to be the employer of Katsikas on the date when he transferred his undertaking to Mitosis.

The case was referred to the Court of Justice by a German Labour Court (Arbeitsgericht Bamberg), which asked as its main question whether it is possible under Article 3(1) of the directive for an employee of the transferor at the date of transfer to object to the transfer of rights and obligations from the transferor to the transferee, with the result that the transferor's rights and obligations are not transferred to the transferee? The background for the question was the German legislation, BGB para 613a, which had been interpreted to give a right to employees to object to a transfer of their employment relationships. This right was in Germany seen as a fundamental right for employees, in the spirit that 'labour is not a commodity'.

The Court of Justice took the position that the directive cannot be interpreted as obliging employees to continue their employment relationship with the *transferee*. On the contrary, such an obligation would jeopardise the fundamental rights of the employees, who must be free to choose their employer and cannot be obliged to work for an employer they have not freely chosen.[94]

The Court further noted that the purpose of the directive is neither to ensure that the contract of employment or employment relationship with the *transferor* is continued in a situation where employees refuse to change employer.[95] From this reasoning the Court drew the conclusion that this question was not harmonised by the directive and consequently that in the event of the employees deciding of their own accord not to continue with the contract of employment or employment relationship with the transferee, the directive does not require the Member States to provide that the contract or relationship is to be maintained with the transferor.

It is left to the Member States to determine what the fate of the contract of employment or employment relationship should be. The Member States may, in particular, provide that in such a case the contract of employment or employment relationship must be regarded as terminated either by the employee or by the employer. They may also provide that the contract or relationship should be maintained with the transferor. The consequences of an objection depends on how Member States have regulated this issue. In Austria and Germany the employee is still employed by the transferor and the transferor has normal duties against this employee, who, of course, often will risk dismissal.[96]

---

94 ECJ 1992, C-132/91 (*Katsikas*), §32.

95 ECJ 1985, 105/84 (*Danmols*), §16; and ECJ 1988, 144/87 and 145/87 (*Berg*), §12.

96 See Laulom (2001), p. 172.

Germany further strengthened the right not to be transferred by introducing a new subparagraph 6 to BGB §613a in 2002.[97] This article gives the employee one month of reflection time within which the employee can object to the transfer. This reflection time only starts when the employer has given the employee full and detailed information regarding the effects of the transfer. This obligation to provide information is independent of the collective procedure of information and consultation and it exists regardless of the size of the undertaking.[98] The information must cover the legal, economic and social consequences of the transfer. In practice, it is difficult to fulfil the requirements regarding this information, and as a result the start of the reflection period is often postponed. By consequence the employee stays employed by the transferor.[99]

In Sweden employees have a similar right to object to a transfer, but there is no individual right to information. The collective information and consultation procedure is expected to produce enough information and the employee must inform the transferor about the objection within a reasonable time after receiving information about the transfer. The effect is that the employment relationship with the transferor remains in force unless terminated separately by a regular procedure and regular grounds for a dismissal.

In most Member States it is possible for the employee to terminate the employment relationship when the employee refuses to be transferred. The termination of the employment relationship will be in accordance with the national law on dismissal by the employee.[100] So the employee has the choice between two 'bad' options: the employee can either choose to change employer and give up the objection, or the employee must terminate the employment relationship him or herself. In some countries some specific requirements have to be fulfilled. For instance in Finland the employees shall be entitled to terminate the employment contract as from the date of assignment, regardless of the period of notice otherwise applied to the employment relationship or of its duration, provided they have been informed of the assignment by the employer or the transferee of the undertaking no less than one month before the date of assignment.

Article 4(2) limits the risks for employees where they terminate the employment relationship because they refuse the transfer to the new entrepeneur. The provision stipulates that if the contract of employment or

[97] It reads: 'Der Arbeitnehmer kann dem Übergang des Arbeitsverhältnisses innerhalb eines Monats nach Zugang der Unterrichtung nach Abs. 5 schriftlich widersprechen'.

[98] Gotthardt (2010), p. 258 ff.

[99] According to German law it is in that case not impossible for the contract to be terminated by the transferor (after the transfer) but only if the ground for termination is not related to the transfer as such. The law on dismissal has to be taken into account fully. For instance, if the undertaking is liquidated, dismissal is possible.

[100] Usually by taking into account the notice period.

the employment relationship is terminated because the transfer involves a substantial change in working conditions to the detriment of the employee, the employer shall be regarded as having been responsible for termination of the contract of employment or of the employment relationship. The situation is restricted to a transfer that involves a *substantial* change in working conditions to the detriment of the employee. The first question that can arise is what is meant by 'a substantial change in working conditions to the detriment of the employee'. In the *Merckx and Neuhuys* decision,[101] the Court decided, assessing the facts of the case by itself, that the refusal of the transferee to guarantee the previous pay that was higher than the transferee would pay is a substantial change in working conditions within the meaning of that provision.[102] In a later case the Court took a step back, in the sense that the Court itself did not take a decision on whether the change of the remuneration was substantially detrimental to the employee. That had to be assessed and decided by the national judges, who were obliged to interpret and apply the (national) law 'as far as possible in the light of the purpose of the directive'.[103] From the case law it can be deducted that the national courts have to evaluate the legal and factual circumstances surrounding the employee at the time of the termination of the contract.

A second question to be answered is what is meant by 'the employer shall be regarded as having been responsible for termination of the contract of employment'. Does it mean that the situation equals a lawful dismissal by the employer, an unlawful dismissal by the employer or something else? This issue was raised in the *Juuri* case,[104] referred to the Court of Justice by the Finnish Supreme Court. Ms Juuri worked for Rautaruukki Oyj ('Rautaruukki') from 5 April 1994 as an employee in the staff canteen in Hämeenlinna. The metal industry collective agreement applied to her employment relationship. On 31 January 2003 – the last day of validity of that metal industry collective agreement – the canteen undertaking in Hämeenlinna was transferred from Rautaruukki to Amica, a catering company. Amica informed Ms Juuri that as from 1 February 2003 the collective agreement for the accommodation and catering sector, binding on Amica, would apply to her employment. Ms Juuri insisted, however, that the metal industry collective agreement should continue to apply to her. When Amica did not agree to that, Ms Juuri terminated her contract of employment on 19 February 2003 with immediate effect.

---

101 ECJ 1996, C-171/94 and C-172/94 (*Merckx*), §38.

102 The transferee had calculated the pay by reference to turnover. As a result it was lower than the amount paid previously.

103 In this case the Court stated that it would be contrary to the spirit of the directive if the specific way of calculating the remuneration – seniority – was not taken into account. The difference was 37% less. ECJ 2004, C-425/02 (*Delahaye*), §§33 and 34.

104 ECJ 2008, C-396/07 (*Juuri*).

Ms Juuri then brought an action before the Helsinki District Court, claiming that Amica – being the employer who qualified as 'responsible' in the sense of Article 4(2) – should pay compensation in lieu of notice in an amount corresponding to four months' pay; compensation for holiday leave in respect of the notice period; and compensation for unlawful termination of the employment contract in an amount corresponding to 14 months' pay.

Ms Juuri lost her case in lower courts and it went up to the Finnish Supreme Court. The latter referred preliminary questions to the European Court of Justice, asking whether an employee who has terminated the contract of employment due to a substantial worsening of the employment conditions following the transfer, has the right to obtain financial compensation from the employer in the same way as in the case where the employer has unlawfully terminated the employment contract. And if the interpretation of the responsibility of the employer is not so extensive, what kind of compensation has to be provided by the national law implementing the directive, for example, for pay and other benefits for the notice period to be observed by the employer.

As AG Ruiz-Jarabo Colomer[105] pointed out in his opinion, Directive 2001/23 like its predecessor 77/187 has a double objective and has openly sought a balance between the two: protecting employees, on the one hand, and, on the other hand, promoting the organisational flexibility of undertakings. As a consequence the directive allows the transferee considerable freedom of action when it comes to making changes to the working conditions of staff, but it balances this flexibility with a series of measures in favour of the employee, including the option of unilateral termination. So the directive is aiming at a reconciliation of the protection of the employee and the support of reorganisation of businesses. As part of the reconciliation the directive adds that the employer is to be regarded as responsible for the termination if, by reason of the transfer, the worker's employment conditions deteriorate. The compromise between protection for the employee and flexibility for the employer is struck by leaving the system of compensation to national law. The directive offers the employee the certainty that any deterioration in working conditions will be compensated by the transferee but it allocates the task of specifying the detail of the financial content of the compensation to national law.

The Court of Justice decided in a rather similar way. It found that the situation in *Juuri* could not be regarded as similar to an unlawful dismissal. Member States are not required to guarantee the employee a right to financial compensation, for which the transferee employer is liable, in accordance with the same conditions as the right upon which an employee can rely where the contract of employment or the employment relationship is unlawfully terminated

[105] Conclusion A-G Ruiz-Jarabo Colomer in C-396/07 (*Juuri*), §§50 and 51.

by the employer. On the other hand, the national court is required to ensure that, at the very least, the transferee in such a case bears the consequences that the applicable national law attaches to termination by an employer of the contract of employment, such as the payment of the salary and other benefits relating to the notice period.[106]

6.3.6. EXCEPTIONS REGARDING PENSIONS AND INSOLVENCY PROCEDURES

6.3.6.1. Pensions

The Transfers of Undertakings Directive provides for certain exceptions to the main rule that all terms and conditions of employment are transferred to the new employer. These exceptions relate primarily to old age pension schemes and insolvency procedures. The directive, however, also explicitly allows for the Member States to stipulate that these terms and conditions are covered by the national legislation. According to Article 3(4), unless Member States provide otherwise, the main rules of the directive shall not apply in relation to employees' rights to old-age, invalidity or survivors' benefits under supplementary company or intercompany pension schemes outside the statutory social security schemes in Member States. The directive, however, also provides that where these groups are excluded, alternative measures should be adopted to protect the interests of persons no longer employed in the transferor's business at the time of the transfer in respect of rights under such schemes.

Although the directive has this limitation, it is clear from the case law of the Court of Justice that this and other exceptions under the directive must be given a strict interpretation. In the *Beckmann* case,[107] the Court decided that early retirement benefits and benefits intended to enhance the conditions of such retirement, paid in the event of dismissal to employees who have reached a certain age, are not to be regarded as old-age, invalidity or survivors' benefits under supplementary company or inter-company pension schemes within the meaning of the directive.

The issue of retirement benefits and their transferability can have a significant economic impact for individual employees. In several Member States the legislation prior to the directive covered pension benefits agreed upon in the employment contract. Also, after the national implementation of the directive many Member States choose to apply the rules of transfer to supplementary

---

106 In this case another issue was at stake connected to the rule of Article 3(3) of the directive related to a collective agreement. See Section 6.3.7.

107 ECJ 2002, C-164/00 (*Beckmann*).

pension benefits. According to Hepple and Mumgaard, in 1998 Belgium, Denmark, France, Germany, Luxembourg, the Netherlands, Portugal and Spain had such rules.[108]

In Finland, the Supreme Court ruled in 1991 with reference to the Transfers of Undertakings Directive that the Finnish legislation regarding transfers did not cover supplementary pension benefits.[109] This decision was heavily criticised, because there had been no documented intention to change the law when the directive was implemented in Finland in 1993.[110] The legislator reacted and the law was revised in 2002 to cover supplementary pension benefits,[111] and as a result the Supreme Court changed its case law.[112]

6.3.6.2. *Insolvency Procedures*

The original directive was silent about transfers and situations of insolvency. The Court of Justice filled that gap by deciding in 1985 that the directive does not apply to transfers effected in bankruptcy proceedings designed to liquidate the transferor's assets under the supervision of the competent judicial authority.[113] The Member States by themselves may apply the principles of the directive wholly or in part.[114] The 1998 Directive (Directive 98/50) inserted, based on the case law of the Court and the discussions about that case law, the possibility for Member States 'not to apply Articles 3 and 4 of Directive 77/187/EEC to transfers effected in the framework of liquidation proceedings, and certain derogations from that Directive's general provisions should be permitted in the case of transfers effected in the context of insolvency proceedings'.[115] The 2001 Directive rules in Article 5, that unless Member States provide otherwise, Articles 3 and 4 shall not apply to any transfer of an undertaking, business or part of an undertaking or business where the transferor is the subject of bankruptcy proceedings, or any analogous insolvency proceedings which have been instituted with a view to the liquidation of the assets of the transferor, and are under the supervision of a competent public authority.

---

108 Hepple & Mumgaard (1998), p. 310.
109 Finnish Supreme Court 2001:72.
110 See Bruun (2001), pp. 543–562.
111 See the Finnish Employment Contract Act 1:10,2 as amended by Act 943/2002.
112 See the Finnish Supreme Court 2009:83.
113 ECJ 1985, Case 135/83 (*Abels*), §23. One of the grounds was that the Court feared that if in such liquidation proceedings the directive is to apply, a serious risk of a general deterioration in working and living conditions could exist, which is contrary to the social objectives of the Treaty.
114 On the contrary the directive has to be applied, the Court decided in the *Abels* case, if an undertaking is transferred to another employer in the course of a procedure such as a '*surseance van betaling*' (judicial leave to suspend payment of debts); cf. Barnard (2012a), p. 620.
115 Recitals 7 and 8 directive 98/50/EEC.

However in para 2 it has been added that if a Member State has chosen that Article 3 and 4 are to apply to a transfer during insolvency proceedings which have been opened in relation to a transferor and provided that such proceedings are under the supervision of a competent public authority, there are two options:

- notwithstanding Article 3(1), the transferor's debts arising from any contracts of employment or employment relationships and payable before the transfer or before the opening of the insolvency proceedings shall not be transferred to the transferee, provided that such proceedings give rise, under the law of that Member States to protection at least equivalent to that provided for in situations covered the Insolvency Directive;[116] or
- the transferee or transferor, on the one hand, and the representatives of the employees, on the other hand, may agree alterations, in so far as current law or practice permits, to the employees' terms and conditions of employment designed to safeguard employment opportunities by ensuring the survival of the undertaking, business or part of the undertaking and business (in terms of an economic entity).

Article 5(3) allows Member States to apply the second provision to any transfers where the transferor is in a situation of serious economic crisis, as defined by national law, provided that the situation is declared by a competent public authority and open to judicial supervision, on the condition that such a provision already existed in national law on 17 July 1998. This provision was primarily adopted to satisfy strong concerns raised by Italy.[117] As a consequence that provision accepts that by collective agreement with the workers' representatives derogations from the legislative minima are permitted, even if these are less generous than before. The final responsibility rests on the Member State to prevent misuse of insolvency proceedings in such a way as to deprive employees of their rights in the event of a transfer.

A problem has come up when a distinction has to be made between insolvency proceedings, to which the directive usually not applies, and pre-insolvency proceedings, including the decision by the court to suspend the obligation to pay the debts. In several procedures by various national courts,[118] the Court of Justice has been asked to take a stand to this. The outcome of the procedures were not always the same. The Court looked very carefully at the requirement

116 See Section 6.4.

117 See also Mulder (2004), p. 239.

118 Italian courts: see ECJ 1991, C-362/89 (*d'Urso*) and ECJ 1995, C-472/93 (*Spano*). Belgium courts: ECJ 1998, C-319/94 (*Dethier*) and ECJ 1998, C-399/96 (*Europièces*). See on these cases Barnard (2012a), pp. 622–24. And more recently a Dutch case: ECJ 2017, C-126/16 (*Smallsteps*).

that the proceedings must be supervised by a competent public authority and at the purpose of the proceedings. In the *Spano* case the Court was clear. When an undertaking is in an economically critical situation, the purpose (of getting the declaration by the competent insolvency authority) is to promote the continuation of its business with a view to its subsequent recovery rather than being subject to a procedure aiming at its liquidation. Moreover, the procedure whereby an undertaking is declared to be in critical difficulties does not involve any judicial supervision or any measure whereby the assets of the undertaking are put under administration, and does not provide for any suspension of payments. In this situation, the directive is to be applied to the transfer.[119] The Court added that the economic and social objective pursued by that procedure cannot explain or justify the result that, when all or part of the undertaking concerned is transferred, its employees lose the rights which the directive confers on them (§30).

In conclusion, it can be stated that the Court is weighing the interests of the transferee and transferor and the creditors, on the one hand, and those of the employees affected by a transfer in that situation, on the other. It has to be taken into account that employees could be better off when an undertaking is in an economically critical situation if, as a result of the insolvency proceedings, the undertaking or parts of it are sold and the activities of the undertaking are continued after the insolvency proceedings (under the terms and conditions required by the directive) and a number of employees who had been made redundant are then employed by the undertaking to which the activities are transferred as part of the insolvency proceedings.

The crucial question is: should the exceptions under Article 5 be interpreted narrowly in favour of the rights of the employees? In the recent *Pre-pack* case, also called *Smallsteps* case, the Court of Justice has been asked to clarify how to decide.[120] The case was related to Estro Groep BV, the largest childcare company in the Netherlands, with almost 380 childcare centres throughout the country and 3,600 employees. The company had economic difficulties and a plan for restructuring was made. A new company, Smallsteps, was created in order to relaunch 243 of the childcare centres, retaining almost 2,500 employees. On 5 June 2014, Estro Groep submitted a court application for the appointment of a prospective insolvency administrator. On 20 June, Smallsteps was created. On 3 July, all staff were informed that declaration of insolvency was to be submitted on 4 July; on 5 July, an application for a declaration of insolvency was submitted and this was granted on the same day. On 5 July, a pre-pack sale agreement was signed between the insolvency administrator and Smallsteps, by which Smallsteps purchased 250 childcare centres and undertook to employ

119 ECJ 1995, C-472/93 (*Spano*), §§28 and 29.
120 ECJ 2017, C-126/16 (*Smallsteps*).

2,600 Estro Groep employees. On 7 July, the insolvency administrator dismissed all the Estro Groep employees, while Smallsteps offered new contracts to almost 2,600 staff. Four former Estro Groep employees who were dismissed but not offered new contracts took legal action and argued that they must be regarded as having been transferred to Smallsteps under the Transfers of Undertakings Directive.

The Court of Justice acknowledged that the pre-pack procedure had been undertaken in order to safeguard the value of the undertaking and also the employment of the employees (§49). The Court did, however, also point out that the procedure did not take place 'under the supervision of a public authority' as required under Article 5(1). On the contrary, it was the undertaking's management which conducted the negotiations and adopted the decisions concerning the sale of the insolvent undertaking. Therefore, there could not be any derogation from the protection of Articles 3 and 4 of the directive.

The Court concluded that Article 5(1) must be interpreted as meaning that the protection of workers guaranteed by Articles 3 and 4 applies in a situation in which the transfer of an undertaking takes place following a declaration of insolvency and in the context of a 'pre-pack', where that 'pre-pack' is prepared before the declaration of insolvency and put into effect immediately after that declaration, and, in particular, a court-appointed prospective insolvency administrator investigates the possibilities for continuation of the activities of that undertaking by a third party and prepares for acts which must be carried out shortly after the insolvency to enable such continuation. It is irrelevant in that regard that the 'pre-pack' is also aimed at maximising the proceeds of the transfer for all the creditors of the undertaking in question.

6.3.7. RIGHTS ARISING FROM A COLLECTIVE AGREEMENT

6.3.7.1. Introduction

The basics of the Transfers of Undertakings Directive have been clarified by many cases decided by the Court of Justice, as illustrated above. That is also the case with Article 3(3) of the directive.[121] Article 3(3) states straightforwardly that following the transfer the transferee shall continue to observe the terms and conditions agreed in any collective agreement on the same terms applicable to the transferor under that agreement, until the date of termination or expiry of the collective agreement or the entry into force or application of another

[121] The wording of Article 3(3) has not been changed in the 2001 directive compared to its predecessor, Directive 77/189.

collective agreement. Furthermore, Article 3(3) stipulates that Member States may limit the period for observing such terms and conditions, with the proviso that this shall not be less than one year.

Several factors complicate the application of Article 3(3). The systems and coverage of collective bargaining differ considerably between Member States as does the relationship between terms and conditions of collective agreements and of individual employment contracts. In many Member States conditions of employment established by collective agreements are automatically incorporated in individual contracts by domestic law.[122] Furthermore, another way of extending the application of a collective agreement to all employees, which has become quite common in Member States, is the inclusion of an *incorporation clause* in individual employment contracts resulting in a general application of the terms and conditions of the collective agreement to all employees of the undertaking covered by it.[123] The use of this clause has yielded some far-reaching decisions of the Court of Justice. Article 3(3) of the directive has not, however, caused other problems. Since 1985 it has been clear that following the transfer the transferee has to apply the collective agreement of the transferor to all employees, provided they were employed by the undertaking – the transferor – at the date of the transfer and not as regards persons who were engaged after that date.[124]

In an Austrian case (*Österreichischer Gewerkschaftsbund*),[125] a question related to the effect of a collective agreement in terms of time was submitted to the Court of Justice: could terms and conditions of a collective agreement be binding to the transferee (and to the transferred workers) after the expiry date of the collective agreement: the so-called 'aftereffect', which means that terms and conditions under the agreement remain in force during the interim period between the termination of an old agreement and the entering into force of a new one. The issue was regulated in the Austrian law in 13 ArbVG. In other Member States the application of this rule is based on case law.[126] The Court had no difficulty in answering this question positively,

122 It could be explicitly in the labour law, or by actual application of the collective agreement provisions concerning employment conditions or by declaring the collective agreement generally binding to all employees covered by the collective agreement. Barnard (2012a), p. 608. Commission report SEC (92) 857 final 1992, p. 29.

123 For Member States that do not rule by law that the collective agreement has a binding effect, such as the UK, incorporation by a clause in the contract is the 'easiest' way ensuring the application of the collective agreement to individual employees. In Member States in which a general binding effect does not exist – usually the binding is restricted to the members of the trade union party to the collective agreement – the incorporation clause is a common instrument.

124 ECJ 1987, Case 287/86 (*Ny Mølle Kro*).

125 ECJ 2014, C-328/13 (*Österreichischer Gewerkschaftsbund*).

126 Such as in the Netherlands by decision of Hof van Justitie Nederlandse Antillen, 5 July 1977, NJ 1978, 134. The aftereffect of collective agreements has also been established by case law in Sweden (Supreme Court NJA 1959 p. 562) and Finland (Supreme Court 1981 II 55).

Article 3(3) covers all 'terms and conditions agreed in any collective agreement'. It fits in the interpretation given in the *Scattolon* case. With reference to the objective pursued by Directive 2001/23: preventing workers subject to a transfer from being placed in a less favourable position solely as a result of the transfer, the Court decided that if the terms and conditions subject to that rule were excluded from the scope of Article 3(3) of Directive 2001/23, the transfer alone would have the effect which that rule seeks to avoid. According to the basic principle of partial harmonisation aimed at by this directive, a rule of domestic law covering the aftereffect of terms and conditions of a collective agreement as Article 13 ArbVG does, is applicable. A fair balance between the interests of the employees, on the one hand, and those of the transferee, on the other, as the directive requires, is not jeopardised because and provided that it does not appear that such a rule hinders the transferee's ability to make the adjustments and changes necessary to carry on its operations.[127] So, during such an interim period, the terms and conditions which were applicable under Article 13 ArbVG were binding on the transferee.

Another issue subject to Court decisions is the substantive scope of the rights of the transferred employees established in the collective agreement of the transferee in case of a transfer. The Court was asked to decide whether length of service as laid down in the collective agreement of the transferor has to be taken into account by the transferee for the calculation of the employee's remuneration[128] or of employee's termination payment based on an extended period of notice.[129] The Court started by stating that Article 3(2) of the Directive leaves a margin for manoeuvre allowing the transferee to arrange salary integration of the transferred workers in such a way that the latter is duly adapted to the circumstances of the transfer in question.[130] However, that does not imply that the arrangements chosen are in conformity with the aim of that directive being that workers subject to a transfer are placed in a less favourable position solely as a result of the transfer. So, the length of service with the transferor has to be taken into account when the collective agreement is applied, because otherwise the transferred employees would face a substantial loss of wages. It is to national court to verify that is the case.[131]

In the other case, *Unionen*,[132] the Swedish Labour Court asked whether it was compatible with the directive, after a year has elapsed following the transfer of an undertaking, to apply a specific provision in the transferee's

---

[127] ECJ 2013, C-426/11 (*Alemo Herron*), §25.

[128] ECJ 2011, C-108/10 (*Scattolon*).

[129] ECJ 2017, C-336/15 (*Unionen*). In ECJ 2000 (*Collino and Chiappero*) the Court has decided similarly.

[130] ECJ 2011, C-108/10 (*Scattolon*), §75.

[131] ECJ 2011, C-108/10 (*Scattolon*), §82.

[132] ECJ 2017, C-336/15 (*Unionen*).

collective agreement. This provision stipulated that a certain continuous length of service with a single employer was the condition for an extended period of notice to be granted, that would increase the termination payment. The Court repeated that the directive does not reject that the employment relationship may be altered with regard to the transferee to the same extent as it could have been with regard to the transferor, provided that the transfer of the undertaking itself may never constitute the reason for that amendment. Referring to its case law on Article 3, the Court emphasised that the directive has a double objective: protection of the employees as to their rights in case of transfer, on the one hand, and the interest of the transferee to be able of making the adjustments and changes necessary to carry on its operations, on the other.[133] From that the Court derived that a fair balance should be struck between the interests of the employees, on the one hand, and those of the transferee, on the other.[134] Given the way that the directive had been implemented in Swedish law it was clear that only the collective agreement of the transferee was to apply. By result, the disputed benefit was the extended period of notice of six months.[135] The Court did not really discuss the issue of the principles of Transfers of Undertakings Directive in this case, but reformulated the question to fit into its earlier practice and decided it in favour of the employees, in accordance with the principles set out in the case *Scattolon*.[136]

6.3.7.2. *The Incorporation Clause*

The incorporation clause has given rise both to Court decisions and discussions about its decisions. The issue at stake is the character of the incorporation clause. In particular, the so-called 'dynamic clause' is posing problems, as the case law of the Court shows. In a series of cases, starting in 2006 up to 2017,[137] the Court struck a rather coherent line of reasoning.

The first case in which the problem of the dynamic incorporation clause came up was the German case *Werhof*.[138] The *Landarbeitsgericht* in Düsseldorf

---

[133] ECJ 2006, C-499/04 (*Werhof*), §31. Similarly ECJ 2014, C-328/13 (*Österreichischer Gewerkschaftsbund*), §29. See, on this issue, Section 6.3.7.2.

[134] ECJ 2017, C-336/15 (*Unionen*), §27.

[135] The Court went further by stating (§31) that the extended period of notice has to be taken into account even after the one-year period (of Article 3(3) second subparagraph) if the transferee has not carried out an adjustment to the terms and conditions and the terms of the collective agreement by which the transferor was bound are worded identically to the collective agreement by which the transferee is bound. In that case the employees cannot be made subject to less favourable working conditions than those which were applicable prior to the transfer.

[136] ECJ 2011, C-108/10 (*Scattolon*).

[137] ECJ 2006, C-499/04 (*Werhof*); ECJ 2013, C-426/11 (*Alemo Herron*); ECJ 2014, C-328/13 (*Österreichischer Gewerkschaftsbund*); and ECJ 2017, C-680/15 and C-681/15 (*Asklepios*).

[138] ECJ 2006, C-499/04 (*Werhof*).

put preliminary questions to the Court. It concerned a transfer between Siemens DUEWAG and Freeway Traffic Systems (FTS). DUEWAG was a member of the employers association AGV and bound by the collective agreement for the iron and steel, metal and electrical industry. Mr. Werhof had been employed by DUEWAG since 1 April 1985. His individual employment contract contained a clause according to which his contract of employment was to be governed by the framework collective agreement and the wage agreement in force in the mentioned sector. He started to work for FTS after the transfer, which took place on 1 April 1999. On 23 May 2002, AGV and IG Metall concluded a new collective agreement for the iron and steel, metal and electrical industry. It provided for an increase of the wage rates by 2.6% and an additional payment.

Werhof brought action in a national German court, referring to the clause in his individual employment contract referring to the collective agreement and claimed a right to receive benefits in accordance with the 2002 collective agreement.

The question raised for the German court concerned a transfer of an undertaking where the transferee, was not subject to a collective agreement, but, was confronted by an incorporation clause in the individual employment agreement of a transferred worker, that bound the worker and transferor to a collective agreement. Did this incorporation clause only bind the transferee to the collective agreement in force at the time of the transfer or also to the collective agreements entering into force subsequently? Or putting it in terms of a dynamic or static incorporation clause: is the transferee bound by a static incorporation clause or also by a dynamic clause? A static interpretation means that the transferee of the business is bound by the collective agreement in force at the date of transfer, and is not bound by subsequent collective agreements. A dynamic interpretation would apply to the employment contract in accordance with its wording, implying that the transferee would be bound by future collective agreements if the employment contract remained unchanged.

The Court opted for a static interpretation. It argued that the main rule under Article 3(1) is that the transferee is only bound by the terms and conditions of a collective agreement until it expires or alternatively during a one-year time limit. According to the objective of the Directive, which is merely to safeguard the rights and obligations of employees in force on the day of the transfer, the Court stated that it does not go further to protect also hypothetical advantages flowing from future changes to collective agreements. Besides the main objective of the directive to protect the interest of the employees concerned, the interests of the transferees to make adjustments and changes necessary to carry on their operations cannot be disregarded.[139]

[139] ECJ 2006, C-499/04 (*Werhof*), §§29 and 31.

In that respect, the Court took into account the fundamental right of freedom of association as enshrined in Article 11 ECHR being one of the fundamental rights which, in accordance with the Court's settled case law, are protected in the Community legal order to be guaranteed to the employer: the right not to join. In view of respecting this fundamental right it found that a dynamic interpretation would mean that 'future collective agreements apply to a transferee who is not party to a collective agreement and that his fundamental right not to join an association could be affected'. In case of a static interpretation, the right of association is fully respected. Therefore it concluded that Article 3(1) does not necessarily require a dynamic interpretation.

It can be noted that the judgment in the *Werhof* case did not exclude a dynamic interpretation altogether. Based on Article 8 of the directive, which allows for more favourable (to employees) arrangements, it seemed that Member States could introduce different solutions in this regard.

The issue was again on the table of the Court in the *Alemo-Herron* case.[140] The case concerned a contracting-out situation where a public authority privatised its leisure services to a private undertaking, CCL, which was later transferred to another private sector undertaking, Parkwood, in May 2004. According to the UK system in which the economic activity was the responsibility of the public authority: negotiations on the terms and conditions of employment take place in a local government collective bargaining body. The agreements negotiated were binding as a result of an incorporation clause in the individual contracts of employment.[141] In June 2004 – after the transfer to Parkwood – a new relevant collective agreement was reached in the public sector. Parkwood did not find that it was bound by the new agreement and did not grant the employees the pay increase agreed upon in the agreement. Different British courts reached various outcomes and the Supreme Court finally submitted the case to the Court of Justice, asking in essence whether Article 3 of the directive precludes Member States from providing that dynamic clauses referring to collective agreements negotiated and agreed after the date of the transfer are enforceable against the transferee.

Again the Court referred to the approach that the directive is not only aiming to safeguard the interests of employees in the event of a transfer, but it seeks to ensure a fair balance between the interests of the employees and the transferee. The Court repeated what it has said in Werhof: 'the transferee must be in a position to make adjustments and changes necessary to carry on

---

140 ECJ 2013, C-426/11 (*Alemo Herron*).

141 It reads: 'During your employment ..., your terms and conditions of employment will be in accordance with collective agreements negotiated from time to time .... supplemented by agreements reached locally through negotiating committees' (ECJ 2013, C-426/11 (*Alemo Herron*) §10).

its operations'.[142] It also presented the view that it was obvious that inevitable differences in working conditions exist between those two sectors. Therefore, significant changes and adjustments had to be made.[143]

The Court again was pointing to fundamental rights of the employer. It did not refer to the ECHR but directly to the Charter of Fundamental Rights of the EU.[144] Although the right not to join an association (Article 12 EU Charter) was not at stake in the present case, the Court was pointing to Article 16 of the Charter, laying down the freedom to conduct a business. The Court of Justice recalled that this right covers the freedom of contract and argued that in the light of Article 3 of the directive, it is apparent that, by reason of the freedom to conduct a business, the transferee must be able to assert its interest effectively in a contractual process to which it is party and to negotiate the aspects determining changes in the working conditions for its employees with a view to its future economic activity. Since these preconditions were not fulfilled, the Court concluded that the transferee's contractual freedom is seriously reduced to the point that such limitation is liable to adversely affect the very essence of its freedom to conduct a business.

In conclusion, the Court decided that Member States do not have to provide that dynamic clauses referring to collective agreements negotiated and adopted after the date of a transfer are enforceable against the transferee, by reason that and if the transferee does not have the possibility of participating in the negotiating process of such collective agreements concluded after the date of the transfer.[145]

In *Asklepios*,[146] the Court had, once again, to consider the issue of the legal effect of dynamic referral clauses. The case was about a twofold transfer of a hospital. The first transfer was from a (public) local authority to a limited liability company, and a few years later the part of the hospital business where the workers were employed was transferred to another undertaking, KLS FM. Ten years later, KLS was transferred to another company in the group (to which KLS belonged), Asklepios. KLS and Asklepios were not bound to any collective agreement nor member of any employers' association. The contracts of employment concluded between KLS FM and the workers contained a 'dynamic' incorporation clause providing that their employment relationship would be governed, as was the case before the transfer, by the Federal framework collective agreement for employees of municipal authorities and businesses, 'BMT-G II', and also, in the future, by the collective agreements supplementing, amending and replacing it.

---

142 ECJ 2006, C-499/04 (*Werhof*), §31; and more explicitly in ECJ 2013, C-426/11 (*Alemo Herron*), §25.

143 ECJ 2013, C-426/11 (*Alemo Herron*), §27.

144 See about the impact of the EU Charter on labour law, Chapter 1.

145 ECJ 2013, C-426/11 (*Alemo Herron*), §37.

146 ECJ 2017, C-680/15 and C-681/15 (*Asklepios*).

The employees started legal proceedings, seeking a declaration that the 'dynamic' incorporation clause to the BMT-G II in their respective contracts of employment remained in force after the transfer to Asklepios.

Asklepios contended that the directive and Article 16 of the Charter (freedom to conduct a business) preclude the legal consequence, provided for in national law, whereby the rules of the public service collective agreements to which the contract of employment refers apply dynamically. It argued that after the transfer those agreements should be applied as they originally stood (*statically*), meaning that only the terms of employment agreed in the contract of employment concluded with the transferor-employer, based on the collective agreements referred to by that contract, may be relied on against the transferee-employer.

The case ended up in the Federal Labour Court, Germany, which submitted a request for a preliminary ruling to the Court of Justice. The crucial question was whether this dynamic clause fitting in the German legal rulings on this point has to be respected and applied by the transferee if national law provides for the possibility for the transferee to make both consensual and unilateral adjustments.

The Court of Justice started by noting the importance of the contractual freedom for the parties to arrange their own affairs. It argued that nothing in the wording of the directive and, in particular, Article 3 thereof, indicated that the EU legislature intended to derogate from that principle. It follows that the directive and, in particular Article 3 thereof, should not be read as intended to prevent a 'dynamic' clause from producing its effects under all circumstances. The Court continued that if the transferor and the employees have freely consented to a 'dynamic' contractual clause and if it is in force on the date of transfer, transfers must be interpreted as providing, in principle, that that obligation arising from an employment contract is transferred to the transferee.[147]

The Court, however, recalled that the directive seeks, in the case of a dynamic contractual clause, 'to ensure a fair balance between the interests of those employees, on the one hand, and those of the transferee, on the other'. As the Court has decided before,[148] this means in practice that the transferee must be in a position to make the adjustments and changes necessary to carry on its operations. That also implies that, seen in view of the freedom to conduct a business, the transferee must be able to assert its interests effectively in a contractual process to which it is party and able to negotiate the aspects determining changes in the working conditions of its employees with a view to its future economic activity.[149] So, if the national legislation provides for

---

147 ECJ 2017, C-680/15 and C-681/15 (*Asklepios*), §§19–21.

148 ECJ 2013, C-426/11 (*Alemo Herron*), §25; and ECJ 2014, C-328/13 (*Österreichischer Gewerkschaftsbund*), §29.

149 ECJ 2013, C-426/11 (*Alemo Herron*), §33.

the possibility, after the transfer, for the transferee to adjust the working conditions existing at the date of the transfer, either consensually or unilaterally, as in this German case, a dynamic incorporation clause is not precluded by the directive.

The decisions of the Court on this matter have given rise to extensive discussion in the literature. It illustrates some of the problems with the partial harmonisation of the regulation of transfers. The legal position of the transferee or the rights and obligations of the transferred employees after 'the date of termination or the expiry of the collective agreement' or the expiry of the one-year optional time limit can differ substantially depending on the national regulation. First, it must be noted that only terms in a collective agreement that create rights and obligations for the individual employee are and can be transferred to the transferee.[150] Second, given the fact that in many Member States these rights and obligations become part of the individual employment contract, it differs from Member State to Member State whether and how such contract can be changed by mutual agreement between the employer and employee, be it by collective and/or individual procedures or even by unilateral changes to the individual employment contracts.[151] For instance, in Finland the change of significant terms and conditions in the employment contract requires that the employer has the right to dismiss the employee on economic, technical or organisational grounds. In such a situation, unilateral changes to the individual contract terms are possible. A similar approach is applied in the UK.[152] There may also be different traditions regarding how dynamic clauses are interpreted. In some cases, they are given only a declaratory meaning of what applies in a certain employment relationship and as such they do not create contractual commitments. There is also reason to observe that several important benefits for employees can be based on a unilateral commitment from the employer: bonuses, daycare services, right to recreation activities etc. Such benefits can be changed or withdrawn by the transferee in the same manner as could be done by the transferor and to a large extent unilaterally.

The complexity regarding the highly decentralised Nordic collective agreements and transfers has to date yet not reached the Court of Justice. This complexity might include situations where both the transferor and the transferee are bound by the same collective agreement, but the local agreements based on these may differ significantly. In such a situation the wording of Article 3(3) seems to indicate that the terms and conditions under the local agreement will be transferred to the transferee, but only for the statutory one-year period.[153] In Sweden the implementation of the directive has led to an

150 See ECJ 2000, C-343/98 (*Collino*), §37.

151 It is rather usual for mutual agreement to exist for unilateral changes.

152 Collins, Ewing & McColgan (2012), p. 897.

153 See the Swedish Labour Court Judgment AD 2013 No. 6.

interesting consequence: if the transferor is bound by a collective agreement, but the transferee is not, the transferee has an obligation after the transfer to apply the collective agreement to all the employees. If a company with 400 employees buys a business with 20 employees, the company has to apply the collective agreement of the transferor to all 420 employees.[154]

Another aspect of the case law that is subject to discussion is the introduction of the freedom of (conducting a) business as a counterweight to the acquired rights of employees; this has to be balanced with the interests of the employee which are explicitly worded in the directive. Since the freedom to conduct a business is relative, it must be balanced against other rights.[155] It has to be noted that the preamble explicitly says that in the event of a change of employer related to changes in the structure of undertakings, in particular through transfers of undertakings, employees need to be protected in order to ensure that their rights are safeguarded.[156] The question that rises is what elements have to be taken into account when weighing the freedom of conducting a business and the interests of employees, and what will, or has to be, decisive. In *Werhof*, the Court referred to a fundamental right of freedom of association, including the right to not join a bargaining party and therefore not being bound to a collective agreement to its solution he has not participated. As a result he could not have any influence on the setting of terms and conditions of employment in the collective agreement (and its successors) to which he was bound in relation to the transferred employees. In *Alemo*, the reference was made to the fundamental right of the freedom of conducting a business. In both cases, the Court gave greater weight to the safeguarding of the rights of employees to a violation of the employer's freedom or at least a substantial reduction of it, preventing the employer from being able 'to make the adjustments and changes necessary to carry on its operations'. When assessing this way of reasoning, which affects the right to collective bargaining on employees' side substantially, it should be remembered that the Court has never made any assessment of whether such adjustments are endangered in a specific case. On the contrary, it has made only a general statement about the 'significant differences between private and public sector working conditions', referring to a difference in hourly wages. As Prassl deducts from this reasoning: 'the higher the disparity in working conditions is in a given business transfer, the less protection workers will enjoy'.[157] These factors seem to indicate that the Court's outcome in the *Alemo Herron*-case is not in conformity with

154 Källström & Malmberg (2013), p. 290.
155 Prassl (2013), p. 442.
156 Preamble to Directive 1977/187 and Directive 2001/23, §§2 and 3.
157 Prassl (2013), p. 440.

earlier and later judgments on Article 16 of the Charter.[158] The Court also seemed to presume that the application of the collective agreement based on the referral clauses would go on for ever, which is not the case, looking at the national labour laws. The *Alemo-Herron*-judgment is exceptionally categorical, because it precludes certain types of dynamic clauses, without taking into account that these kind of clauses might have to be applied in different national contexts. When looking at the decision in the *Asklepios* case, can it be seen as a recognition of the fact that the Court went too far in *Alemo-Herron*?

6.3.8. INFORMATION AND CONSULTATION OF WORKERS' REPRESENTATIVES

The Transfers of Undertakings Directive gives similar obligations as the Collective Redundancies Directive for employers to inform and consult workers' representatives. On this aspect both directives have significantly the same content, and the amendments made in 1998 reproduced the amendments made in 1992 to the Collective Redundancies Directive. The difference between the two texts lies in the subject-matter of information and consultation: collective redundancies on the one hand, transfer of undertakings on the other.

Since both employers are involved in the transfer, both the transferor and the transferee, are required to inform the representatives of their respective employees affected by the transfer. The directive defines the content of the information, which has to be given in good time, before the transfer is carried out, by the transferor, and before the employees are directly affected by the transfer as regards their conditions of work and employment, for the transferee. The information concerns the date or proposed date of the transfer; the reasons for the transfer; the legal, economic and social implications of the transfer for the employees; and any measures envisaged in relation to the employees (Article 7 Directive 2001/23).

The obligation to provide information is more general, whereas the consultation obligation is focused on measures the transferor or transferee envisages taking in relation to the employees. One can assume that this will happen in most cases of transfer. The consultations must take place in good time before the change in the business is affected. As in the Collective Redundancies Directive, the consultation is to take place with a view to reaching an agreement. Similarly, since 1998, the obligations to inform and negotiate shall apply irrespective of whether the decision resulting in the transfer is taken by the employer or an undertaking controlling the employer.

---

158 See e.g. earlier judgment ECJ 2013, C-281/11 (*Sky Österreich*) and, more recently, alongside ECJ 2017, C-680/15 and C-681/15 (*Asklepios*), e.g. ECJ 2017, C-322/16 (*Starnet*) and ECJ 2017, C-277/16 (*Polkomtel*).

The directive itself adds that in considering alleged breaches of the information and consultation requirements laid down by this directive, the argument that such a breach occurred because the information was not provided by an undertaking controlling the employer shall not be accepted as an excuse. Consequently, the employer, whether the transferor or transferee, cannot hide behind the controlling employer.

As the aim of the directive is partial, not full, harmonisation, Member States may limit the obligations to inform and consult workers' representatives to undertakings or businesses, which in respect of the number of employees fulfil the conditions for the election or nomination of a collegial body representing the employees. One can guess that the ground for not laying down this possibility in the Collective Redundancies Directive is based on the definition of a collective redundancy: establishments employing fewer than 20 workers do not come within the scope of the directive.

The right to be informed and the obligation to inform is not limited to the situation where a workers' representation is present in the undertaking. If there are no representatives of the employees in an undertaking or business, through no fault of their own, the employees concerned must be directly informed in advance on the transfer in the same way as the representatives should be informed. It is remarkable that in the Transfers of Undertakings Directive, in contrast to the Collective Redundancies Directive, the workers' representatives are not explicitly provided with the right to be assisted by an expert. In Member States where a regulation on this matter exists, it is part of the regulation on information and consultation of employees and their representatives.[159]

A problem related to the right to information and consultation of employees' representatives that could occur, is how the rights of the workers' representatives are preserved following the transfer. Article 6 of the Directive states that the status and function of the representatives or of the representation of the employees affected by the transfer shall be preserved on the same terms and subject to the same conditions as existed before the date of the transfer. An important element of the regulation of Article 6 is the retention of the identity of the entity that is transferred. It is only in that situation where the transfer classifies as a transaction within the meaning of the directive. If the entity – being an undertaking, business or part of it – preserves its autonomy, the rights of representation remain. In a Spanish case the question was raised as to what the situation will be when after a transfer the transferee is faced with double representation. According to the directive the status and function of the representatives or of the representation of the transferor will be preserved by the transferee. A Spanish municipality decided to take over certain

159 In several Member States, such as Germany, Austria, France, and the Netherlands, the Works Council Act regulates this issue.

in-house (public) services[160] that were outsourced to private undertakings. The employees were taken on by the municipal authority and integrated into its staff. They remained in the same posts and carried out the same duties as before the takeover, in the same places of work and under the orders of the same immediate managers (line managers), without any significant changes in their working conditions. The representatives of the employees of the transferor requested that they should be entitled to time off in which to carry out their duties as before. The municipal authority rejected their requests on the ground that the employees concerned were no longer, because of their integration into the municipal workforce, carrying out their functions as lawfully appointed representatives. The Court decided that if the entity even after full integration of the employees in transferee's organisation continues to exist as an entity, the transferee has to respect the rights of the representatives and to accept that the employees' representation and representatives carry out its/their function as lawfully appointed or elected representatives provided, as long as the employees stay in the same posts and carry out the same duties as before the takeover, in the same places of work and under the same hierarchical structure. If the organisational powers have been reduced and can no longer be described as autonomous, the interests of those employees are therefore no longer the same and, consequently, the terms and conditions of their representation must be adapted to the changes which have occurred. In such circumstances, the term of office of the representatives of the employees affected by the transfer must be restricted to merely the period required for the reconstitution or reappointment of the representation of employees.[161]

6.4. THE INSOLVENCY DIRECTIVE

6.4.1. BACKGROUND

The Insolvency Directive is the third of the restructuring directives presented by the European Commission in the 1970s; its first version was adopted in 1980.[162] In 2008 the directive was adapted to take account of the case law since 1980. The basic structure has not been altered, but adaptation to the changes in insolvency law in Member States felt to be necessary.[163] The aim of the directive is to provide for the protection of the employees in the event of the

160 It concerns services such as caretaking and cleaning in public schools, street cleaning and maintenance of parks, see ECJ 2010 C-151/09 (*UGT-FSP*).

161 ECJ 2010 C-151/09 (*UGT-FSP*), §§44–46.

162 Directive 80/987/EEC. This section on the Insolvency Directive has highly benefitted from the analysis in Sädevirta (2015), pp. 416–32.

163 Cf. Barnard (2012a), p. 643.

insolvency of their employer and to ensure a minimum degree of protection in order to guarantee payment of outstanding claims. To this end, the Member States should establish a body which guarantees payment of the outstanding claims of the employees concerned.[164] The Directive applies to employees' claims arising from contracts of employment or employment relationships against employers who are in a state of insolvency. The Insolvency Directive raises some specific problems due to the fact that the Member States are directly involved in these procedures. In fact, in some situations the employees and the employer may have a common interest in claiming guarantee payments in order to reduce the employer's responsibilities towards the employee.

In comparison, the Transfers of Undertakings Directive seems to create the most complications and problems, while the Collective Redundancies Directive and the Insolvency Directive have been easier to implement and apply. The Insolvency Directive has raised questions of its scope of application and how different exceptions should be interpreted. On the other hand, the legal environment in which these directives have been implemented have differed considerably in Member States, which will give them different impact in the national context.[165]

Insolvency is defined in the following way:

> [A]n employer shall be deemed to be in a state of insolvency where a request has been made for the opening of collective proceedings based on insolvency of the employer, as provided for under the laws, regulations and administrative provisions of a Member State, and involving the partial or total divestment of the employer's assets and the appointment of a liquidator or a person performing a similar task, and the authority which is competent pursuant to the said provisions has: (a) either decided to open the proceedings; or (b) established that the employer's undertaking or business has been definitively closed down and that the available assets are insufficient to warrant the opening of the proceedings.[166]

Under the Insolvency Directive, Member States are required to set up guarantee institutions and prescribe their liability for outstanding employee wage claims. Article 3(1) requires Member States to set up institutions to guarantee payment of outstanding employee pay claims resulting from employment contracts or employment relationships including, where provided by national law, severance pay on termination of employment relationships. Article 3(2) provides that the claims taken over by the guarantee institution are to be the outstanding pay

164 Preamble of Directive 2008/94/EC, §3.

165 E.g. what position outstanding wage claims have in an insolvency procedure and how redundancies generally are regulated: can a breach of procedural obligation make a dismissal null and void?

166 Article 2 Directive 80/987/EEC.

claims relating to a period prior to, and/or as applicable, after a given date determined by the Member States. According to Article 4(1–2) Member States have the option of limiting the liability of guarantee institutions. If a Member State exercises this option, it must specify the length of the period for which outstanding claims are to be met, which may not be shorter than a period covering the remuneration for the last three months of the employment relationship. Article 4(2) allows Member States to include this minimum three-month period in a reference period of not less than six months. Member States with a reference period of not less than 18 months may limit the period for which the guarantee institutions meet outstanding claims to eight weeks, whereupon the periods most favourable to the employee will be used for calculating the minimum period.

Article 4(3) allows Member States to impose ceilings on the payments made by the guarantee institutions. Member States exercising this option must inform the Commission of the methods used to impose such a ceiling.

According to Article 12, Member States can take the measures that are necessary to avoid abuses of guarantee institutions by refusing or reducing the liability of the guarantee institution referred to in Article 3. This will be possible, in the first place, if it appears that fulfilment of the obligation is unjustifiable because of special links between the employee and the employer, and of common interests resulting in collusion between them. Limitation of liability is also possible in cases where the employee, either alone or together with close relatives, owns an essential part of the employer's undertaking or business and had considerable influence on its operations.

These limitations on the responsibility of the guarantee institutions should, however, be compatible with the social objective of the Insolvency Directive and allow for various levels of claims. Thus, the interpretation of limitations is subordinate to the main objective of the Insolvency Directive, which is to provide a minimum degree of protection for employees in order to guarantee payment of their outstanding claims, while taking into account the need for a balanced economic and social development in the Union. On the other hand, the limitations are justified by the need for Member States to allow for their financial capacity and to preserve the financial stability of their guarantee institutions.

The main aim of the Insolvency Directive is to give a certain minimum protection to employees as creditors. In this regard the directive seeks not only to protect the subsistence level of employees, but its aim is also to ensure that they are fully paid, even in the event of employer insolvency.

6.4.2. KEY CONCEPTS

The concept of insolvency is explicitly defined in Article 2 of the 2008 directive. It covers apart from bankruptcy proceedings other collective insolvency proceedings. Member States may extend the protection of employees to other situations of insolvency (Article 2(4)), and many have actually done so.[167]

Since the aim of the directive is partial harmonisation, defining of the other concepts is left to the Member States as Article 2(2) explicitly states: the directive is without prejudice to national law as regards the definition of the terms 'employee', 'employer', 'pay' and 'right conferring to immediate or prospective entitlement'.

6.4.2.1. *Employee*

Although the definition of employee was left to the legislators of the Member States, the Court has limited to some extent the discretion of Member States to determine, in their national laws, the concept of an employee within the meaning of the directive. In *Wagner-Miret*, the Court clarified to what extent Member States are free to define the personal scope. According to the objective of the directive to provide protection to all categories of employees, higher staff members may not be excluded, as the Spanish law did.[168] In the *Gharehveran* case, the Court stated since the directive aims to ensure a minimum degree of protection for all employees, exclusions must be exceptional and must be interpreted strictly.[169] In a case a few years earlier the Court had decided that the possibility of excluding certain categories of worker from the scope of the directive, by reason of the particular nature of their contract of employment, their employment relationship, or the existence of guarantees of other kinds providing them with equivalent protection, is a possibility provided for by way of exception by Article 1(2) of the directive and is limited by that provision itself to the categories expressly mentioned in the list annexed to the directive.[170] Managers, apprentices and out-workers could not be excluded from the guarantee system provided by the Italian 'Cassa integrazione guadagni': all fell within the scope of the directive. The more recent *Tümer* case[171] examined a Dutch law withholding the right to an insolvency benefit in the event of insolvency of his employer from a third-country national, who was illegally resident in the Member State concerned. The Court referred to its case law and argued that the first subparagraph of Article 2(2) must be interpreted in the light of the social objective of that directive, which is to guarantee

167 They may differ from country to country. The method of protecting the employees depends on the specific regulations regarding the various insolvency situations in the country concerned. Examples can be found in Belgium, France, the Netherlands and the UK. Cf. Bouwens, Roozendaal & Bij de Vaate (2015).

168 ECJ 1992, C-334/92 (*Wagner-Miret*).

169 ECJ 2001, C441/99 (*Gharehveran*), §26.

170 ECJ 1989, 22/87 (*Commission v. Italy*), §23.

171 ECJ 2014, C-311/13 (*Tümer*).

employees a minimum of protection at EU level in the event of the employer's insolvency through payment of outstanding claims resulting from contracts of employment or employment relationships and relating to pay for a specific period. Member States therefore cannot define at will the term 'employee' in such a way as to undermine the social objective of that directive. The discretion enjoyed by Member States to define the term 'employee' is thus circumscribed by the social objective of the directive.

The Court found that it was contrary to the social objective of directive to deny the protection provided for under that directive in the event of the employer's insolvency to individuals to whom national legislation generally attributes the status of employees and who, by virtue of that legislation, have wage claims *vis-à-vis* their employer arising from contracts of employment or employment relationships. The directive therefore precludes national legislation under which a third-country national has no right to an insolvency benefit because that individual is not lawfully resident, even though that third-country national is recognised under the civil law of that Member State as having the status of an 'employee' with an entitlement to pay.[172]

By Directive 2002/74 amending the previous directive in order to adapt certain provisions of the regulation on protection of employees in situations of insolvency to changes in the insolvency laws in the Member States and to the development of the internal market, the European legislator has prohibited Member States from excluding some categories from their national definition such as part-time workers, workers with a fixed-term contract and temporary agency workers, as was the case in the Transfers of Undertakings Directive of 2001. It also prohibits setting a minimum duration for the contract of employment or the employment relationship in order for employees to qualify for claims under this Directive.[173]

6.4.2.2. *Pay and Payment*

The fact that the definition of the term 'pay' has been left to be determined in national legislation has led to differences between Member States with regard to the coverage of the guarantee. The Court of Justice has, however, emphasised that national law must respect the general principle of non-discrimination when determining the benefits payable by a guarantee institution.

In the *Rodriguez Caballero* case,[174] the question concerned the interpretation of national law and its conformity with Insolvency Directive in circumstances where all employees who were unlawfully dismissed were in the same situation,

172 ECJ 2014, C-311/13 (*Tümer*), §§45–46.
173 Article 2(2) and (3) Directive 2008/23.
174 ECJ 2002, C-442/00 (*Rodríguez Caballero*).

in the sense that they were all entitled to a certain payment from a national wage guarantee. However, in the event of the employer's insolvency, Article 33(1) of the Spanish Workers' Statute treated dismissed workers differently to the extent that the right to payment by the State Guarantee Institution of claims relating to a conciliation procedure '*salarios de tramitación*' is acknowledged only in respect of those determined by judicial decision, but not for those confirmed in the conciliation procedure.

The Court ruled that national law excluding claims agreed in a conciliation procedure from the concept of pay within the meaning of Article 2(2) of the directive infringed the principle of non-discrimination included in EU law. Therefore, the Court considered that claims concerning compensation for unlawful dismissal awarded by a judgment or administrative decision, and claims of the same type established in a conciliation procedure, must be equally regarded as claims for the purposes of Article 3 of the directive. Consequently, the Court found that the national court must set aside domestic legislation which, in breach of the principle of equality, excludes the latter claims from the definition of 'pay' under the Spanish legislation.

On the other hand, the right to compensation for unlawful dismissal awarded in an extra-judicial settlement may be treated differently when referred for guarantee payment within the meaning of the Insolvency Directive. According to the Court of Justice, these claims may be excluded from the scope of guarantee payments, as such extra-judicial conciliation procedures do not offer the same safeguards as judicial procedures against abusive claims. This may then be deemed a measure seeking to avoid abuse that falls under Article 12.

In the case *Eva Soraya Checa Honrado*, Ms Checa Honrado was a cleaner in a theme park in Alicante, Spain employed on an indefinite employment contract.[175] After she had been informed that her place of work was going to change to the theme park San Martin de la Vega situated 450 km away from Alicante she opted to terminate her employment contract. She was therefore entitled to severance payment which her employer did not pay in full before becoming insolvent.

According to Spanish law (Workers Statute Art 40) she was not entitled to payments from the guarantee fund in this situation, since she had not been dismissed by her employer as required by the Workers Statute Articles 50–52. Checa Honrado had requested compensation for outstanding severance pay from the national guarantee institution, and the High Court of Justice in Valencia asked the Court of Justice for a preliminary ruling of whether Article 3 of the directive covered such severance pay, as Checa Honrado requested. The Court argued that workers who opt to terminate the employment relationship pursuant

175 ECJ 2018, C-57/17 (*Soraya Checa Honrado*).

to Article 40 of the Workers' Statute are in a situation comparable to that of workers who are made redundant pursuant to Article 50 of the Workers' Statute, in so far as they chose that termination as because the employer has made substantial changes to their working conditions. Therefore basically the forms of statutory compensation payable on termination of a contract of employment at the worker's request and those payable in the case of dismissals on objective grounds, such as those envisaged by the referring court, fell within the concept of 'severance pay on termination of employment relationships'. Consequently, Checa Honrado was eligible to receive guarantee payments for outstanding severance pay.

In the case *Hampshire*, Mr Hampshire had been employed between 1971 and 1998 with the company T&N.[176] He had taken early retirement 1998 at the age of 51. Due to legislative changes in the UK and after the evaluation that the T&N scheme's assets exceeded its protected liabilities so that the Pension Protection Fund (PPF) did not assume responsibility for the scheme, Hampshire's pension benefits fell to approximately 25% of his accrued pension entitlements. Mr Hampshire, along with 15 other former employees of T&N who were affected by similar reductions, referred the matter to the Pension Protection Fund Ombudsman, challenging the valuation of the T&N scheme, as approved by the Board of the PPF. After that challenge was rejected Mr Hampshire brought an appeal before the High Court of Justice (England & Wales) and further to the Court of Appeal. He claimed, in essence, that the provisions of the 2004 Act on which the decision of 19 September 2011 was based did not comply with Article 8 of Directive 2008/94, as interpreted by the Court of Justice, since those provisions meant that some employees received less than 50% of the value of their acquired entitlement to old-age benefits.

The Court of Justice referred to its earlier practice and answered that Article 8 of Directive 2008/94 must be interpreted as meaning that every individual employee must receive old-age benefits corresponding to at least 50% of the value of the employee's accrued entitlement under a supplementary occupational pension scheme in the event of the employer's insolvency. The Court also explicitly answered that the Board of the Pension Protection Fund is a State body and therefore Mr Hampshire could invoke the direct vertical legal effect of Article 8. He could therefore invoke it directly before a national court in order to challenge a decision of a body such as the Board.

These cases clearly illustrate the difference between the directives on collective redundancies and transfer of undertakings, on the one hand, and the Insolvency Directive, on the other. Due to the fact that the Insolvency Directive regulates

---

[176] ECJ 2018, C-17/17 (*Grenville Hampshire*).

State obligations, it can be enforced by individuals in national courts even in cases where national law has deprived an individual of rights under the directive.

6.4.3. MEASURES AGAINST ABUSE OF THE STATE GUARANTEE

The Insolvency Directive gives Member States the option of taking measures against abuses of the right to compensation payments from guarantee institutions. Abuse under the directive refers to practices that adversely affect the guarantee institutions by giving rise to an artificial claim for pay, and thereby illegally creating a payment obligation. The regulation against abuse may also impose restrictions on employee protection. Such situations have been examined by the Court. In the case *Walcher*,[177] it considered the right of Member States to restrict the protection of employees on grounds of abuse. The Supreme Court in Austria asked whether it is contrary to the objectives of the Insolvency Directive if, by operation of the principles relating to loans in lieu of capital contributions applied by the Austrian courts, a shareholder (25%) who has no dominant influence on the company loses the entitlement to the guarantee in respect of certain claims. These regarded outstanding wages resulting from insolvency, where, the shareholder in his or her capacity as an employee of the company, fails, within 60 days from the time the shareholder is first in a position to know that the company is no longer creditworthy, to make any genuine demand for payment of salary in arrears and/or does not resign early on the ground of non-payment of salary. The Court started its answer by stressing that the application of a national rule intended to prevent abuse must not prejudice the full effect and uniform application of law in the Member States. Because Article 12 establishes an exception to a general rule, it must be interpreted narrowly and in a way that is compatible with the social objective of the directive.

The Court recognised that continuing an employment relationship beyond the time when an employee could have become aware of the employer's critical financial situation can constitute an abusive practice within the meaning of the directive. It also considered that the fact that a shareholder-employee remains in the employment relationship beyond the date on which an employee who is not a shareholder would, under the same circumstances, have resigned on the grounds of non-payment of salary, constitutes evidence, but not proof, of an abusive intention of the employee concerned. The Court found it to be clear from Article 4(2) that the Union legislature considered it not unusual for an employee to continue to perform duties where unpaid wages relate to a period of less than three months. It would therefore not be compatible with the

[177] ECJ 2003, C-201/01 (*Walcher*).

purpose of the directive to assume that, as a general rule, an employee who is not a shareholder would have resigned on the grounds of non-payment of salary before the end of a three-month period.

The Court concluded that a national rule denying entitlement to the guarantee payment for claims covered by Article 4(2) of the directive to an employee with a significant shareholding in a private limited company – but who does not exercise a dominant influence over that company – who fails to submit any genuine demand for payment of outstanding wages within 60 days of the time when the employee could first have become aware of the lack of credit worthiness of the company, is contrary to the directive.

In line with its narrow interpretation concerning the measures permitted to Member States seeking to prevent abuse of guarantee payments, in the *Gharehveran* case,[178] the Court again interpreted Article 1(2), and determined the scope of the directive narrowly. The Supreme Court of Sweden asked the Court whether the annex to the directive that included exceptions to the guarantee payment could be interpreted to allow Sweden to exclude, from the group of persons entitled to a wage payment provided under the directive, an employee who did not personally own any share in the undertaking, but whose close relative (spouse) owned at least 20% of the shares in the company less than six months before the petition for insolvency. Such an interpretation would have implied a broader interpretation of the provision governing the exception than the strict wording of the provision would have allowed. The Court did not accept such an interpretation. It referred to the wording of the annex, which provides the exclusion only in respect of employees who owned, themselves or together with their close relatives, an essential part of the undertaking employing them. According to the Court, the exclusion in the Insolvency Directive cannot be broadened without misconstruing the clear wording of the provision to include employees whose relatives alone were owners of an essential part of the company. The Court also recalled that the aim of the Insolvency Directive and the exceptional character of the possibility of exclusion provided in Article 1(2) required a strict interpretation of the exclusions provided in the annex to the directive. It concluded that the annex to the directive could not be interpreted in a manner that allowed Sweden to exclude groups from the protection of the Insolvency Directive other than those expressly referred to in the wording of the provision.

6.4.4. CROSS-BORDER INSOLVENCIES

If an undertaking with activities in the territories of at least two Member States is in a state of insolvency within the meaning of Article 2(1), the institution

178 ECJ 2001, C-441/99 (*Gharehveran*).

responsible for meeting employees' outstanding claims shall according to Article 9 of the Insolvency Directive be the one in the Member States in whose territory they work or habitually work. The extent of employees' rights shall be determined by the law governing the competent guarantee institution (Article 9(2)).

Member States shall take the measures necessary to ensure that in these situations of cross-border insolvency, decisions taken in the context of insolvency proceedings referred to in Article 2(1), which have been requested in another Member State, are taken into account when determining the employer´s state of insolvency within the meaning of the Insolvency Directive (Article 9(3)).

Article 10 stipulates that for the purpose of implementing Article 9, Member States shall make provisions for sharing of relevant information between their competent administrative authorities and/or guarantee institutions, making it possible in particular to give the guarantee institution responsible for meeting the employees' outstanding claims the relevant information.

Articles 9 and 10 were adopted only in 2008, when the Insolvency Directive was consolidated. The amendments codified a development that had taken place in the case law of the Court of Justice, where cross-border or transnational insolvencies had been examined in two important cases.

In the case *Mosbaek*,[179] Mrs Mosbaek, who lived in Denmark, was employed by the English company Colorgen Ltd as commercial manager for Denmark, Norway, Sweden, Finland and Germany. In July 1994 Colorgen was declared insolvent and its employees, including Mrs Mosbaek, were dismissed. She declared an outstanding claim of DKR 471996 representing her salary, commissions and expenses and required payment from the Danish Guarantee Fund. The Fund refused to settle the claim on the ground that responsibility lay with the guarantee institution of the State where the employer was established, in this case the UK National Insurance Fund. Mrs. Mosbaek brought proceedings against the Danish Guarantee Fund in a Danish court. The Court of Justice was asked to respond to the question whether either the English or the Danish guarantee institution had to grant the guarantee Mrs Mosbaek was claiming, in her situation where the employer was not established in the Member State in which the employee was resident and the employee was representing the employer's business and carried out the work in office premises rented by the employer for the employee's use.

The Court replied that where the employer is established in a Member State other than that in which the employee resides and is employed, the guarantee institution responsible for the payment of that employee's claims in the event of the employer's insolvency is the institution of the State in which, in

179 ECJ 1997, C-117/96 (*Mosbaek*).

accordance with Article 2(1) of the Insolvency Directive, it is decided to open the proceedings for the collective satisfaction of creditors' claims or it where has been established that the employer's undertaking or business has been closed down. Therefore the UK guarantee institution was responsible for covering the employee's outstanding claims.

The factual situation in the *Everson* case[180] was different from that in *Mosbaek*. In *Everson*, the employer was established in more than one Member State. In this case the question concerned an Irish company with establishments in several Member States that was also registered in the UK. Everson and other employees were employed in the UK and brought proceedings for outstanding claims against the guarantee institution in the UK. The Court found that the fact that the employer had its registered office in the UK and that the employees (among them Everson) had their place of work in the UK meant that the guarantee institution in the UK had to settle the outstanding claims in this case.

In a more recent case the Court has been asked to take a stand in another transnational situation. This situation is closely connected to the free market of the EU cross-border traffic of goods, which is a growing industry. Again, the question was at stake which guarantee institution has to grant the protection to an employee in case of insolvency of the employer established in one Member State when an employee travels across different Member States. The Swedish Insolvency Authority referred the question to the Court whether the protection of the Swedish insolvency law has to be granted to a lorry driver employed by a Swedish haulier and travelling around Europe.[181] The Swedish law states that an employee is entitled to the payment of an employee's claim against an employer only if the employee performs or performed the work for the employer primarily in Sweden. Because the driver performed his work for that employer primarily in another European Union country, the payment was not granted under the guarantee of the Swedish law.[182] Directive 80/987 does not require an undertaking to have a place of business or a branch in another Member State in order to be regarded as carrying out activities there,[183] and since the haulier carried out activities principally in Germany, Austria and Italy, therefore, the lorry driver, Mr. Holmqvist, should not be covered by the wage guarantee provided for by Swedish law.

The Court of Justice did not follow this reasoning. Having activities in the territory of another Member State does not exclude the possibility that the State

---

180 ECJ 1999, C-198/98 (*Everson*).

181 ECJ 2008, C-310/07 (*Holmqvist*).

182 The Law on wage guarantees (Lönegarantilagen) of 4 June 1992 (SFS 1992 No. 497).

183 Article 8a (1 and 3) Directive 80/987 (similar, Article 9 Directive 2008/94) regulates this and requires Member States to take measures to ensure that the protection is guaranteed. In this case Swedish law was not in compliance.

in which the employer has its seat will be liable to grant the protection. The Court stated that it is, however, untenable to require an undertaking necessarily to have a physical infrastructure in order for it to have a stable economic presence in a Member State other than that in which it has its seat. Given the fact of cross-border economic activities, as in the transport sector, various aspects of an employment relationship, inter alia communication of instructions to the employee, reporting back to the employer, and payment of remuneration, can now be, and often are, performed remotely. In the case of a transport undertaking established in a Member State, the mere fact that a worker employed by the undertaking in that State delivers goods between that State and another Member State cannot demonstrate that the undertaking has a stable economic presence in another Member State. The conclusion was that the travelling lorry driver was entitled to the guarantee of his outstanding claims in Sweden.

CHAPTER 7

WORKERS' PARTICIPATION IN BUSINESS MATTERS

Teun Jaspers and Pascale Lorber

7.1. INTRODUCTION

In the European Union, participation of workers in decision-making at enterprise level is considered as a core right of employees ever since it has been accepted as a fundamental right in the Community Charter of Fundamental Social Rights of Workers adopted in 1989 and in the EU Charter on Fundamental Rights of 2000. Participation of workers is a comprehensive concept. It includes the right to information and consultation of employees in decisions taken by the central management. It can also refer to the right to participation of employees' representatives, which usually is understood as participation in the management itself, for example on the board of companies or on the supervisory board.[1] Finally, it can also mean financial participation of workers which, obviously, is related to a form of shareholdership. The right of workers' participation is elaborated in various directives. This chapter will focus on information and consultation rights of workers in undertakings or a group of undertakings.

The first regulations on these subjects were drafted and accepted for cross-border issues in accordance with the legislative competence of the European Community. Cross-border restructuring of multinationals in the 1970s and 1980s leading to mass redundancies in multinationals in which employees had no say, prompted the European Commission to start proposing legislation on

1 In the majority of the Member States this form of participation exists either on the board (Germany and Austria) or on the supervisory board.

social issues. The directive on collective redundancies of 1975 was the first piece of legislation.[2] Transfer of undertakings is usually part of restructuring strategies of large companies, and in 1977 the Commission took the initiative to propose a directive on the safeguarding of employees' rights in the event of transfers of undertakings, businesses or parts of undertakings or businesses.[3] In quite another field the need to regulate was also felt: health and safety at the workplace. In a directive of 1989,[4] employees were granted the right to information and consultation on measures on health and safety in undertakings.

It took some years before multinationals that operated in several Member States became the object of rules on information and information for decisions that affected the position of workers. In 1994 the Directive on the European Works Council was adopted.[5] In the first decade of the 21st century similar regulations were adopted for European companies and Cooperative Societies.[6]

The range of regulations in this field was completed by the adoption of the 2002 Framework Directive on the information and consultation of employees in the European Community.[7]

In the following sections the general aspects of employees' participation in the decision-making within undertakings, including groups of undertakings, will be discussed. After a historical overview, the foundations of European employee participation law will be outlined. The general aspects of the right to participation common to all regulations in this field will be dealt with. Subsequently, the European Works Council will be the subject of a more profound analysis, in particular regarding cross-border issues of the Community-scale undertakings or group of undertakings and the European Company. The 2002 Framework Directive will not be discussed separately, but it will be included in the sections where the relevant topics are dealt with.

7.2. INFORMATION AND CONSULTATION OF EMPLOYEES

7.2.1. HISTORICAL BACKGROUND

Participation of employees in the undertaking where they work has been a known phenomenon within Europe since the 1970s. Four Member States

2 Directive 75/129/EEC.

3 Directive 77/187/EEC.

4 Directive 89/391/EC.

5 Directive 95/45/EC, in 2009 replaced by the Recast European Works Council Directive 2009/38/EC.

6 Directive 2001/86/EC (European Company); Directive 2003/72/EC (European Cooperative Society).

7 Directive 2002/14/EC.

of the European (Economic) Community already had legal regulations on employee participation within the undertaking as early as the 1950s, albeit with some differences.[8] However, in all four of these Member States this amounted to a right to information and consultation in the social sphere.[9] In the 1970s workers participation was made part of the social policy agenda of the European Economic Community. The Social Action Programme of 1974 stated that 'increased involvement of workers in the life of undertakings' should be a priority of the Community. It suggested to 'progressively involve workers or their representatives in the life of undertakings'.[10] Well over 20 years later, the idea of employee participation in the affairs of their undertaking was also greeted in the European Social Charter of the Council of Europe.[11] By a protocol of 1988 – effective since 1992 – a newly introduced article recognises the right to information and consultation as a fundamental social right. This provision refers to the promotion of information and consultation 'with a view to ensuring the effective exercise of the right of workers to be informed and consulted within the undertaking'. Workers are not only entitled to regular, timely and comprehensible information about the economic and financial situation of the undertaking, they must also be consulted in good time about proposed decisions that could have a considerable impact on their interests and, in particular, about decisions that could have significant consequences for the employment situation within the undertaking.[12]

When considering how to give a say to employees and their representatives in business matters, four models have been circulated in Europe. They correspond with models of employee participation already found in European countries. This is illustrated in Figure 7.1.

Two of the models were related to the composition of the management board and/or the supervisory board, aiming to achieve substantial influence of employees or employees' representatives on management decisions. Two others start from another angle. Whereas the first two models imply not only a certain influence on business matters, but also could include responsibility of employees' representatives for decisions taken, the other two reject this responsibility of employees and do not go further than an independent role of

8 Countries like Germany, the Netherlands, Belgium and France.

9 During the 1970s and 1980s in Germany, Austria and the Netherlands the competences of the Works Council have been extended and strengthened on social issues, for instance the right to consent in matters such as working time and health and safety.

10 Council Resolution of 21 January 1974 (Social Action Programme).

11 The scope of countries covered by the ESC was much larger.

12 Article 2 of the Additional Protocol of 1988. The text of this article was transposed in Article 21 revised European Social Charter (rESC). It does not mention the establishment of works councils, thus the right to information and consultation can also be assigned to trade unions, or even to other forms of workers representing bodies.

Figure 7.1. Models of employee participation

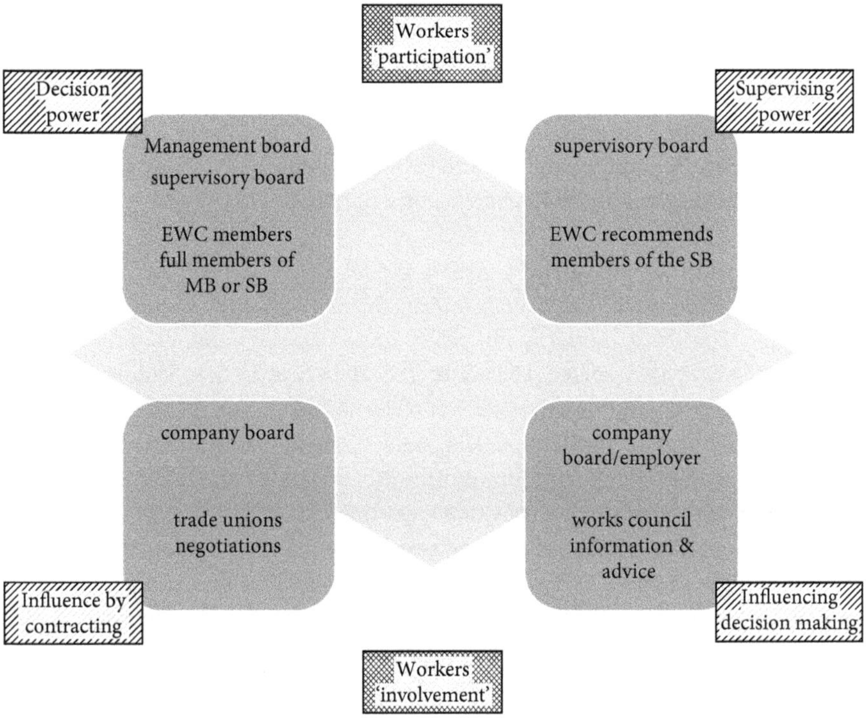

EWC – European Works Council
MB – Management Board
SB – Supervisory Board

workers' representatives. One of these two models is directly related to existing collective bargaining systems in which trade unions have negotiating power resulting in binding arrangements. The fourth model confers an advisory role on employees' representatives (the works council) by providing them a right to information and consultation about business matters.

The four models are:

1. The employees appoint a part (at least one third and maximum half) of the management board or the supervisory board.[13]
2. The employees obtain the right to recommend members of the supervisory board. The appointment itself is done by the supervisory body. Attached to

[13] This depends on whether there is a one-tier board (management and supervisors in one board) or a two-tier structure (a management board and a supervisory body with separate powers).

this is the right to oppose the appointment of members of the body who are proposed by the supervisory board. In that case appointment is only possible after an independent body has disallowed the objection.
3. The employees have a say through a separate body in the undertaking entitled to information and consultation on important decisions (for example works councils).
4. Participation is regulated in and through collective labour agreements. Here the trade unions will exercise this right.

The first model resembles the German model to a large extent. The second model is in line with the Dutch model in the case of statutory two-tier companies. The third model is not really linked to a specific country: France has the *Comité d'entreprise*, Germany the *Betriebsrat*, the Netherlands the *ondernemingsraad*. The fourth model is to be found in the northern countries and is also typical of the United Kingdom.[14] These patterns were subject to discussions in the European Community. According to the basic subsidiarity principle, in the various proposals that were made over time the choice was left to the Member States themselves. The result was that for most of the Member States nothing changed, in accordance with their explicit demand and strongly supported by employers' organisations. It would take decades before the idea of a more independent right for workers and their representatives to gain actual influence on business decisions would be accepted, and in this light the adoption of the European Works Council Directive in 1994 can be considered as a milestone.[15]

7.2.1.1. The Gradual Introduction of Employees' Participation

Before the European Works Council Directive was adopted, in the EU law the right to information and consultation had already been laid down in a number of directives. The first related to collective redundancies.[16] The next followed a few years later and concerned workers' rights in the event of a transfer of undertaking.[17] These European rules and regulations were made against the background of the cross-border restructuring operations of international undertakings that took place in those years and of which the Dutch AKZO Group was a well-known example.[18] The idea was that employee organisations should be involved in decision-making in the sense that when the employer is contemplating restructuring resulting in collective redundancies, there should

14 In these countries works councils did not play a role.
15 Directive 94/45/EC.
16 Directive 75/129/EEC.
17 Directive 77/187/EEC.
18 This example concerned a cross-border restructuring of the Dutch multinational enterprise leading to mass dismissals in some European countries. See Blanpain (1991), p. 153.

be a dialogue with the workers' representatives on the intended decision to make workers redundant. Although the final decision rests with the employer, the employee organisations were to be given some say where the workers' livelihood was concerned.[19] The concept of employees' participation that was introduced in social policy and in the legislation was wider in the sense that it did not make a choice as to the form participation could take. In other words, dialogue between employer and employees' representatives was felt necessary but the form it could take was left to the national practice. On the employees' side, this could be either trade unions or elected works councils.

Ten years later, the Framework Directive in the field of health and safety at the workplace was adopted, as a result of which the employees were given the power to influence the health and safety policy of the undertaking.[20] Pursuant to Article 11(1) of the Framework Directive workers are entitled to being consulted and to 'balanced participation' with regard to the handling of issues related to safety and health in the workplace. In the same subsection the employees (and/or their representatives) are also given the right to make proposals in the matters in question (the so-called right of initiative). According to subsection 2, the employees' representatives have to be consulted in advance and in good time by the employer about, inter alia, all measures that could substantially affect safety and health. They must also be given all the necessary information on the safety and health risks as well as on the protective and preventive activities, both in general and for every type of workstation and/or job.

Another line of development in the European legislation on employee participation can be found in company law. In 1972, in a draft directive on the internal structure and decision-making in companies, the outlines of a participation regime appeared for the first time.[21] The birth of such European regulations was protracted because of the variety of participatory systems that existed and still exist in the Member States. It was not until the 21st century that some form of coordination and regulations at the European level were realised.

The attempts made by the European Commission in the 1970s to set up general rules and regulations failed due to the opposition of, in particular, employer organisations, while at the same time there was also a lack of unanimity within the European trade unions on the matter. The name of European commissioner Henk Vredeling is inextricably linked with the attempts to introduce information and consultation rights for employees in Community-scale enterprises. The suggestion was to create legal information and consultation rights for employees' representatives in groups of undertakings

---

19 E.g. Jaspers (2004), p. 47 ff. See also Chapter 6. A well-known example of massive restructuring was, apart from AKZO in the 1970s, Renault in the 1990s.

20 Directive 89/391/EEC, see Chapter 8.

21 COM(1972)887 def, [1972] OJ C 131, p. 49. Cf. Jaspers (1999), p. 15 ff.

about decisions of the management with a cross-border impact. It took 10 years before such a mechanism was established. In 1994 the European Works Council was introduced.[22] Later, similar regulations followed for the European Company[23] and the European Cooperative Society.[24] In 2002, there was a new Framework Directive in which employees were granted the right to information and consultation in the undertaking all over the Community.[25] In 2009, the European Works Council Directive underwent a major recast with its most important objective being to increase the effectiveness of the involvement of the European Works Council.

For a long time, the discussion on the European employee participation rules was mostly a succession of well-meant attempts, but mostly weak compromises. The plans were faced with ample opposition from some Member States, notably Member States unfamiliar with structures like these, as well as from employer organisations.[26] Numerous proposals were shelved. This is unsurprising, given that the proposals regarding employee (co)participation directly affect the existing power relations within the company, thus impairing the prerogatives of the employer. Furthermore, this kind of European legislation is seen by its opponents as an obstacle to the unrestricted functioning of undertakings in a free European market. Moreover, it could cause serious damage to the international competitive position of European undertakings.[27] A third explanation is the existence of significant differences between the Member States in terms of their historical, political, economic and cultural background at the socio-economic level. These translate into major differences between the Member States in terms of labour relations – and as a result employee participation.[28]

If one takes a look at the developments since the 1970s, one cannot but find that, not counting the first two directives which came about relatively fast and 'easy',[29] the 'real' participation directives had a far harder time becoming established. Meanwhile, within the European Union the value of information and consultation procedures for employees at the level of the undertaking was increasingly recognised. The directives on collective redundancies and transfer of undertaking already included provisions granting employees' representatives a right to information and consultation, but in context this usually meant trade unions. The more recent directives, the recast European Works Council

---

22 Directive 94/45/EC.

23 Directive 2001/86/EC.

24 Directive 2003/72/EC.

25 Directive 2002/14/EC.

26 The UK was heavily opposed to this approach, cf. Barnard (2012a), pp. 664–65.

27 See previous note.

28 Fuchs & Marhold (2014), p. 345 ff. points to the great differences among Member States; see also Nebe & Ritschel (2009), p. 160 ff.

29 These directives came about during a period of an economic crisis; the so-called oil crisis in the mid-1970s led to mass reorganisations and mass redundancies.

Directive, the sister directives for the European Company and the European Cooperative Society as well as Framework Directive 2002/14, emphasise the advisability of effective information and consultation procedures at enterprise level by establishing works councils. In the documents accompanying the European Cooperative Society Directive it is stated 'that it is desirable to coordinate information and consultation arrangements at Community level in order to develop dialogue between the executive committees of the European Association and employees'.[30] In the recast European Works Council Directive, this is underlined in paragraph 14 of the preamble:

> The arrangements for informing and consulting employees need to be defined and implemented in such a way as to ensure their effectiveness with regard to the provisions of the Directive. To that end, informing and consulting the European Works Council should make it possible for it to give an opinion to the undertaking in a timely fashion, without calling into question the ability of undertakings to adapt. Only dialogue at the level where directions are prepared and effective involvement of employees' representatives make it possible to anticipate and manage change.

The directive emphasises the need to have employee participation at the transnational level, where decisions on cross-border mergers, takeovers and joint ventures occur. This is in response to the functioning of the internal market. The involvement of employees or their representatives must benefit the development of 'economic activities in a harmonious fashion'.[31] The Framework Directive of 2002 uses similar terms. Information and consultation are referred to as means to promote the flexibility of the organisation of work, the willingness of employees to participate in measures and actions to improve their employability and to promote the workers' involvement in the undertaking's plans for the future, as a result of which the competitiveness will be boosted. Special attention is paid to the importance of information and consultation of employees on

> the situation and likely development of employment within the undertaking and, where the employer's evaluation suggests that employment within the undertaking may be under threat, the possible anticipatory measures envisaged, in particular in terms of employee training and skill development, with a view to offsetting the negative developments or their consequences and increasing the employability and adaptability of the employees likely to be affected.

Finally, the directive considers timely information and consultation as 'a prerequisite for the success of the restructuring and adaptation of undertakings

---

30 Amended proposal for a Council Directive supplementing the Statute for a European association with regard to the involvement of employees, COM(93)252 final, p. 31.

31 Cf. Preamble Directive 2009/38/EC, §10.

to the new conditions created by globalisation of the economy, particularly through the development of new forms of organisation of work'.[32]

7.2.1.2. *From the Draft Directive on the Structure of Public Limited Companies to the Recent Directives*

In September 1994, after a long journey,[33] the directive 'on the establishment of a European Works Council or a procedure in Community-scale undertakings and Community-scale groups of undertakings for the purposes of informing and consulting employees' was adopted. The title explains the purpose of the directive: improving the employees' right to information and consultation in Community-scale undertakings and Community-scale groups of undertakings (Article 1(1) Directive 94/45/EC). Its history was long and hard-fought. It was preceded by a proposed directive in 1980 'on procedures for informing and consulting the employees of undertakings with complex structures, in particular transnational undertakings', the so-called 'Vredeling Directive'.[34] The aim was to grant employees a right to information and consultation in matters pertaining to business economics and organisation as well as regarding decisions of the employer that affect the undertaking's structure and the employees' situation. It was assumed that important decisions taken by the general management of a multinational usually have consequences for the employees in the branches in other EEC countries, whereas the rules related to the employees' influence on decisions of employers have a purely national character and, therefore, are only effective to a limited extent.[35] In fact, the concept of transnationality was introduced. This issue has caused debate and remains controversial today as the discussions on the recast of the European Works Council directive show. This will be discussed in Section 7.3.1.5.

The proposal did not reach the directive stage because the support of the European Trade Union Confederation was no match for the considerable opposition of the employers.[36] Some Member States were also in the opposition camp.[37] The political deadlock regarding the drafts shows that in the field of

---

32 Similarly, Preamble Directive 2002/14/EC, §§7, 8 and 9.

33 See Jaspers (2004), p. 15 ff.

34 Proposal for a Council Directive on procedures for informing and consulting the employees of undertakings with complex structures, in particular transnational undertakings [1980] OJ C 297/3. See W.L.D. II (1984), p. 1482.

35 The *AKZO* and *Ford* cases in the 1970s were mentioned above.

36 After the proposal was sent to the European Parliament in 1983, the opposition against it increases rapidly. The opposition did not only arise from within the EEC, but also from multinational companies and employers' associations including American multinationals and their lobbyists such as Mars Inc., International Harvester, Union Carbide, General Motors, Ford, Kodak and IBM. Even the U.S. Chamber of Commerce and the US National Foreign Trade Council joined in at a certain moment; see Kilimnik (1983) and Barnard (2012a), pp. 664–65.

37 In particular the Governments of the United Kingdom, Ireland and Denmark. See footnote 26.

company law there are fundamental differences between the national traditions. The attempt to harmonise using detailed and compulsory rules in order to remove distortions between Member States was deemed to have led to the failure of the project. This induced the legislator to have more consideration for the powers of the national legislators and the contractual freedom of the economic actors. In 1986 this finally led to the withdrawal of the draft directive.[38]

However, the introduction of a European social policy in 1986 and the adoption of the Single European Act as well as the establishment of the European Charter on fundamental social rights of workers in 1989 gave a new impulse to the idea of employee participation. An explicit reference in the European Works Council Directive to Articles 17 and 18 of the 1989 Charter, in which the right to information and consultation was recognised as a fundamental social right, shows the acceptance of the idea of giving a say to workers in business matters.

Although the European Works Council Directive had a long history with deep and sometimes heavy discussions, the adoption of the directive did not end the discussions. The content and value of the EWC Directive continued to be the subject of discussions, with particular emphasis placed on the experience of the stakeholders. It took until 2009 before a new version of the European Works Council Directive was laid down. As the preamble of the recast European Works Council Directive of 2009[39] (point 7) shows, the European legislator was especially concerned about four matters. First, modernisation was considered to be necessary to guarantee the effectiveness of the workers' rights to transnational information and consultation. The second reason was the increase of the number of companies with a European works council. Furthermore, something had to be done about the problems with the practical application of the existing directive of 1994. To increase legal certainty a number of provisions needed clarification and better wording and some deficiencies had to be rectified. Besides the introduction of the term 'in good time', the definitions of the crucial notions (eg consultation) were also given a makeover. Moreover, in the subsidiary requirements a distinction was made between the subjects about which the European works council had to be informed and the subjects about which it had to be consulted. The undertakings' obligation of information was specified in the preliminary stages of the establishment of a European works council, with a view to increasing the number of undertakings with a European works council. Although there was not abundant case law by the Court of Justice, the Court shed some light in its decisions on the issues raised in practice, which included attempts to

38 Conclusion of the Council of 21 July 1986, [1986] OJ C 203.

39 This was the name of the amended and revised directive. By the term recast words as 'revision' or 'new' could be avoided; they were seen as contaminated.

circumvent the obligations stemming from the directive.[40] The Recast Directive was intended to codify the case law of the Court.

7.2.2. FOUNDATIONS OF EUROPEAN PARTICIPATION LAW

Within the European context – and outside – information and consultation of employees is regarded as a fundamental (social) right. In the Community Charter of 1989, in the (revised) European Social Charter of the Council of Europe of 1996 and in the EU Charter of 2000 this right to information and consultation is named and regarded as such. These catalogues of fundamental rights play an important part, not only for the recognition of the right to employee participation but also for the realisation of that right. In its Article 21 the European Social Charter provides that the employees or their representatives have to 'be informed regularly or at the appropriate time and in a comprehensible way about the economic and financial situation of the undertaking' and furthermore that they have to be consulted in good time 'on proposed decisions which could substantially affect the interests of workers, particularly on those decisions which could have an important impact on the employment situation in the undertaking'. A similar right is granted to employees and their representatives in the case of collective dismissals.[41] Article 27 EU Charter formulates this in a similar way, albeit in more general terms: 'Workers or their representatives must, at the appropriate levels, be guaranteed information and consultation in good time …'. Both sources make it clear that this should be a matter of effective participation. This is expressed in terms such as 'in good time' and 'at appropriate levels' with a view to enabling the employees and/or their representatives to influence the decisions of the employer. In accordance with the character of the legislative competence of both European organisations, the obligation for the Member States to implement this fundamental right is rather limited. The European Social Charter uses in this respect the terms 'in accordance with national legislation and practice', which is understandable given the powers of the Council of Europe and the nature of the European Social Charter. It goes without saying that the – contracting – States have the freedom and the competence to do it their own way and in keeping with their existing legal framework. The EU Charter emphatically refers to 'the cases and the conditions provided for by Union law and national laws and practices'. Neither of the fundamental rights rules requires a (complete)

40 See ECJ, C-62/99 (*Bofrost*); ECJ 2004, C-440/00 (*Kühne & Nagel*); ECJ 2004, C-349/01 (*Anker*).

41 Article 29 of the (revised) European Social Charter. The (revised) European Social Charter does not provide a provision regarding safeguarding of employees' rights in case of transfer of undertaking.

harmonisation of national laws. They only oblige employers to inform and consult their employees.[42] The way in which the national legislators do this, is to a large extent, up to them. In the Council of Europe this is monitored by the European Committee of Social Rights.[43] The various directives in the EU include the requirements which the national legislations implementing the directives must meet. The legal basis for this has been laid down in the EU Treaty itself.[44]

Whereas employees' rights to information and consultation of employees laid down in the older directives were based on the articles on the common and internal market,[45] with the adoption of the Treaty of Amsterdam,[46] Article 137 (now Article 153 TFEU) assigned a legal basis for further rules with regard to employees' rights to information and consultation in matters concerning the undertaking. The directive with regard to the European Works Council (94/45/EEC) was based on that provision.[47] The same goes for the Framework Directive of 2002. It is not the case for the directives with regard to the role of employees in the European Company and the European Cooperative Society.[48] For the participation of employees in the Societas Europaea (European Company), use was made of Regulation (EC) No 2157/2001 in which the statute for the European Company is laid down and in which it is expressly provided that the role of employees in a Societas Europaea has been established more precisely in Directive 2001/86/EC. The same generally applies for the European Cooperative Society. Article 1(6) Regulation (EC) 1435/2003 stipulates that Directive 2003/72/EC regulates the role of employees in a Societas Europaea.[49]

7.2.3. MAIN FEATURES OF THE RIGHT TO INFORMATION AND CONSULTATION

7.2.3.1. Spirit of Cooperation

A characteristic of the European rules and regulations in this domain is the emphasis on the idea of cooperation.[50] In Framework Directive 2002/38, both

42 Cf. Blanke (2006), p. 287 ff.
43 Supervising the application of the (r)ESC. Its Conclusions can be found in <http://hudoc.esc.coe.int/eng#> accessed 05.06.2019.
44 Previously (since 1997) Article 118 EC, currently Article 153 TFEU.
45 Articles 114 and 115 TFEU (previously Articles 94 and 95 EC).
46 It entered into force on 1 May 1999.
47 More precisely, it was based on Article 2(2) Social Agreement of 1992.
48 For the European Company (Societas Europaea, SE) as well as for the European Cooperative Society (Societas Cooperativa Europaea SCE), a works council must be established.
49 It has been argued that, since the European Company is a new supra-national entity, a regulation for its statute cannot be a measure for the approximation of national law. Therefore, the regular legal ground of the TFEU could not be used. See Edwards (2003), pp. 443, 447.
50 Cf. Dorssemont (2010a), p. 55 seq.

sides are asked to shape and implement participation in a spirit of cooperation. This bilateralism is underlined by the explicit addition that the mutual rights and duties must be observed and that the interests of both the undertaking and the employees must be taken account of.[51] The European Works Council and the Societas Europaea Directives also refer expressly to that spirit of cooperation.[52] From the preparation of the directives it can be inferred that the European legislator does not assume that the interests of employer and employees run parallel. In the European Commission's view it is a matter of 'close cooperation in mutual trust'.[53] Although the Court of Justice has not defined in clear terms what cooperation should entail,[54] from the objectives behind the directives one may infer that what the European legislator has in mind is a prohibition of obstruction on the part of both the employers and the employees. The directive must be implemented 'in good faith'. That good faith is a requirement not only for the European works council's functioning in practice, but also for the preliminary stages of the European works council. The various directives dictate that the members of the Special Negotiating Body (SNB) must come to an agreement in a 'spirit of cooperation'.[55] This implies that there is an obligation to set up and organise a European works council. In the same vein, Advocate General Saggio emphasised in the *Bofrost* case of 2001 that 'the management of the undertaking must collaborate fairly with the employees' representatives'.[56] In the view of the Court of Justice, cooperation implies the obligation of the central management to provide the employees' representatives (in the Special Negotiating Body) with the information necessary to enable them to determine if, and how, a European works council should be established. That is an obligation on a group of undertakings to supply information about, for example, the legal form of the various subsidiary companies, the structures of representation, the average number of employees of the group, as well as their distribution among the various Member States as a start of the negotiations. It even may include the names of the employee organisations and their representatives, as well as the means necessary to start

---

51 Article 1 Directive 2002/14/EC.

52 Articles 6(1) and 9 Directive 2009/38/EC. Its predecessor (Directive 95/45/EEC) contained a similar provision. See also Article 4(1) Directive 2001/86/EC (SE); and Article 4(1) Directive 2003/72/EC (ECS).

53 Cf. European Communities, *Bulletin of the European* Communities 3, no. 8 (1970). The ILO also referred to this in Recommendation no. 129 (25 June 1969) on the Convention concerning Labour Inspection in Agriculture.

54 In ECJ 2004, C-440/00 (*Kühne & Nagel*), §44 and in ECJ 2004, C-349/01 (*Anker*), §49 the Court explicitly required that the parties have to negotiate in a 'spirit of cooperation' with a view to reaching an agreement on the establishment of a European works council.

55 Article 6(1) Directive 2009/38/EC. Similarly, in Directive 2001/86/EC (SE) and Directive 2003/72/EC (ECS), both Article 4(1).

56 AG Saggio in C-62/99 (*Bofrost*), p. 7.

the negotiation process with the employees' representatives.[57] The management of a group of undertakings cannot and may not hide behind a reluctant attitude of the management of a subsidiary.

Of vital importance is respect for the mutual rights and duties. The employer has to take account of the interests of the undertaking's employees while the works council, for its part, must keep an eye on the interests of the undertaking, national or European, when exercising its rights. Both sides have joint responsibilities, but also their separate ones. This may lead to the conclusion that employee participation does not harm the employer's prerogatives. The directives do not deny the fact that there can be a difference between the employer's interests and those of the employees, but they do embrace the idea that in both parties' interest, the employer and employees should solve problems 'in close cooperation and mutual trust'.[58] This approach fits in with the ideas in the Netherlands, Germany and Austria.

7.2.3.2. Contractual Character

A second feature of the rules and regulations on employee participation in European undertakings is their contractual character. This is apparent from a number of rules in the directives concerned. The European Works Council Directive, as well as the Directives for a European Company Works Council and the European Cooperative Society Works Council, stipulate that the establishment of those participation bodies must be negotiated on by the general management of the undertaking or group with the employees' representatives in the Special Negotiation Body. From Article 4 of the European Works Council Directive it can be inferred that the employees' representatives have the right to start negotiations with the central management with a view to setting up a European works council. Next, the employer must negotiate the content of the mutual rights and duties. The undertaking, i.e. the central management, has the duty to cooperate in such a way that the result, as far as content is concerned, has a contractual basis.[59] This duty to cooperate – which is, as mentioned above, a key principle – already applies in the (pre-contractual) stage of establishment. The Court of Justice decided in the *Kühne & Nagel* and *Anker* judgments[60] that 'it is essential that the employees concerned be guaranteed access to information enabling them to determine whether they have

57 ECJ 2001, C-62/99 (*Bofrost*); ECJ 2004, C-440/00 (*Kühne & Nagel*); ECJ 2004, C-349/01 (*Anker*).

58 In this sense in the commentary on draft Regulation of the European Company of 1970, in European Communities, *Bulletin* of the *European Communities* 3, no. 8 (1970).

59 In literature it is called 'double subsidiarity'. Cf. Heerma van Voss (1995), and Dorssemont (2004), pp. 1701–16.

60 ECJ 2004, C-440/00 (*Kühne & Nagel*), §46 and ECJ 2004, C-349/01 (*Anker*), §50.

the right to demand the opening of negotiations between central management and the employees' representatives'. The Special Negotiating Body and the central management of the undertaking are the ones which, after negotiations, conclude agreements about the establishment, the elements and the content of the rights to information and consultation. They also lay down these arrangements in an agreement. If – in certain circumstances – no European works council (or European company works council or European cooperative society works council) is set up, the directives in the so-called 'subsidiary requirements' lay a number of rules with regard to the minimum levels that information and consultation procedures have to amount to. These requirements will be dealt with separately below. However, it should be noted that the subsidiary requirements have a significant influence, in the sense that they streamline the content of the agreements between the parties, as a result of which the negotiating position of the employees' representatives is reinforced (see Section 7.3.2). They establish a kind of a minimum standard and this is the positive effect of the reflexive nature of the law.

In addition, Article 14 Recast European Works Council Directive provides that European works councils which were established prior to the implementation of the European Works Council Directive by agreement between the management and employee representatives, continue to exist.[61] Therefore, it could be and is actually the case that existing participation bodies in a European undertaking[62] keep functioning as such with a level of participation below the level laid down in the directive. The European legislator did clearly not want to hamper these multinationals. With the prolongation of these agreements, the existing regime with a low level of participation could (also) be maintained. According to the existing EU rules on workers' participation, the prolongation of such a European participation body needs the approval of both parties. So, if the undertaking or the employees' representation (the European works council on the basis of Article 14 European Works Council Directive)[63] refuses such approval, the regular procedure to set up a European Works Council has to be started, i.e. negotiations between central management and a Special Negotiating Body.

The contractual character can also be found in the Framework Directive, in which Article 5 stipulates that 'Member States may entrust management and labour at the appropriate level, including at undertaking or establishment level, with defining freely and at any time through negotiated agreement the practical arrangements for informing and consulting employees'. This provision

61 Based on the so-called 'pre-existing agreements'. See Section 7.3.1.6.

62 Examples are, among others, the French company Danone and the Italian company ENI. Cf. Papadakis (2008), p. 26 ff. and p. 35 ff.

63 See Section 7.3.1.6.

has a supplementary character because the directive first lays down the provision that Member States are obliged to include further arrangements in their national laws ensuring that the right to information and consultation is exercised in a certain way at the appropriate level.[64] This can be seen as a fall-back option which once again underlines the contractual nature of the EU arrangement. Parties are free to interpret the obligation of information and consultation, provided that they observe the principle of information and consultation and thus guarantee a minimal substance. This will be discussed further in Section 7.3.4.1.

7.2.3.3. Confidentiality

All directives on employee participation contain rules on the confidentiality of the information supplied. That is not the case for the two older directives relating to collective redundancies and transfers of undertakings.[65] From this it could be inferred that, in the context of collective redundancies or transfer of undertaking, the information which must be supplied according to the directives cannot be refused on the basis of such a reservation. This does not mean that the employer cannot ask the employees' representatives for secrecy because of important business interests. In the case of transfer of undertaking this is understandable, because certain information could jeopardise a transfer. However, it is not possible to make this request for secrecy without giving sound reasons. The confidentiality obligation must relate to crucial data with regard to the transfer. It can be argued that, in cases concerning collective redundancies, the same approach has to be followed as laid down in the information and consultation directives.

The four directives specifically aimed at employee information and participation allow the right to information to be linked with the requirement of confidentiality for the members of the Special Negotiating Body, the European works council, the works council and the experts assisting them, with the objective of guaranteeing that confidential information will not be transmitted to third parties. It is not quite clear what is meant by 'third parties'. Commonly, persons who do not work in the undertaking or one of its establishments are considered to qualify as third parties. It is disputed in the literature,[66] however, whether employees can be considered as a third party. If they are not a third party that may imply that the confidentiality obligation of the persons referred to in the directives (i.e. members of the Special Negotiating Body, the European works council, the works council and the

64 See recital 23 Preamble and Articles 4 and 5 Framework Directive (2002/14/EC).

65 These Directives are silent on that matter.

66 E.g. Dorssemont (2010a), p. 78 ff.

experts assisting them) does not apply to employees working in the undertaking, although the employees themselves can be subjected to the confidentiality clause. Confidentiality clauses are quite common; they are usually laid down in the arrangements between employer and works council, and this type of clause is also not unknown in individual employment contracts.

The directives leave it to the Member States themselves to regulate this in their national laws. Some Member States have done so, with considerable differences.[67] The directives make a distinction between general arrangements of confidentiality of information laid down in the first subsection of the articles concerned: information explicitly given to them as being confidential may not be revealed to third parties. In this respect the question arises as to whether the undertaking itself determines which information is confidential. Framework Directive 2002/14 contains an important addition: only the information 'which in the legitimate interest of the undertaking or establishment, has expressly been provided to them in confidence'. The (Recast) European Works Council Directive also takes this as a basis as Article 8(1) shows. An example of the way this obligation can be understood is Article 19(6) of the Dutch law on the European Works Council, which states: 'which would plausibly cause serious harm to or be prejudicial to the functioning of the (European) undertaking or group of undertakings'.[68] This addition limits the freedom of the entrepreneur or, in other words, gives the (E)works council members more room for disclosure. Although, (so far) there is no case law of the Court of Justice on this matter, a judgment of the Court on a matter that is similar can be taken as a reference. The Court indicates that a criterion could be whether the information supplied might increase the risk that the information can be used for a purpose contrary to the interest of the undertaking with regard to its functioning.[69]

Another argument in favour of not too strict an interpretation of this arrangement could be that in the European Works Council Directive a so-called 'report back' clause has been included in Article 12: members of the European works council may inform the representatives of the establishments or of the undertakings of a European group of undertakings – or, in the absence of representatives, the workforce as a whole – of the content and outcome of the information and consultation procedure. The article, however, contains

---

[67] See Laulom & Dorssemont (2015), p 45 ff., in particular table 4, pp. 48–55. The provisions in the European Company Directive and the European Cooperative Society Directive are similar.

[68] In Belgian law it is similarly worded: confidential information is information that when disclosed outside can cause serious damage to the undertaking.

[69] See ECJ 2005, C-384/02 (*Knud Grongaard*), §36. This case concerns insider dealing and the prohibition of disclosure of inside information to third parties (here information on a merger by an employee-member of the board to the trade union he belonged to).

the proviso that this is 'without prejudice to Article 8'. The meaning of this addition is not entirely clear. The possibility of exchange of information is not without significance for the employees when this concerns a merger, takeover or liquidation of a division of a European undertaking. A limited interpretation of the restriction to reveal information to employees would be obvious if the works councils' right to involvement is to be effective. This will support the conclusion given above, that a restriction of the disclosure of information is not justified with regard to any of the European participation bodies as well as to employees employed in the undertaking – at least on subjects directly affecting the employees unless the general restriction clause is applicable: 'the nature of the information is such that, according to objective criteria, it would seriously harm the functioning of the undertaking(s) concerned or would be prejudicial to them'. So a limitation can only be justified with regard to 'third parties' which means persons from outside the undertaking and its establishments; i.e. the public, the media, friends and acquaintances.[70] It should be noted here that the European Works Council Directive provides the possibility of regulating confidentiality in more detail in an agreement concluded on the basis of Article 6 European Works Council Directive. The parties are free in this respect.[71] In conclusion, if no special limitations have been laid down in an agreement, a restriction with regard to the 'report back' cannot be imposed.

Besides the possibility of (expressly) imposing an obligation of secrecy as provided for in Article 8(1) European Works Council Directive, there is also the provision in subsection 2 of this article that Member States can determine that the (requested) information will not be transmitted if that information would seriously harm the functioning of the undertaking or would be prejudicial to it.[72] This requires objective criteria and is only allowed in specific cases. The conditions and restriction must be laid down in national legislation. Logically, the reason for exemption from this obligation has to be an exceptionally serious interest in order to avoid rendering the obligation of information meaningless.[73] It does have to concern a serious business interest which the undertaking will have to prove.

70 The Framework Directive seems to clarify this. Confidential information cannot be revealed to third parties unless they are bound by an obligation of confidentiality (Article 6 (1)).

71 The other workers participation directives offer the same possibility to regulate this issue in more detail in agreements between the employer and the participation bodies. That is the case not only for the European undertakings (European Company and European Cooperative Society included). The Framework Directive 2002/14/EC offers the same possibility in Article 5.

72 In the European Company and European Cooperative Society Directives a similar provision has been inserted: Article 8 (SE) and Article 10 (SCE).

73 See Lamers (1995), p. 316. In similar terms Dorssemont (2010a), pp. 78 ff; and Laulom & Dorssemont (2015), p. 46.

Finally, the directives stipulate that the national laws must provide for administrative or judicial procedures with a view to keeping the discretionary power of the employer under control.[74] In other words, it must be possible to subject the power of the employer to judicial control. This aspect is very important for the effectiveness of employee participation. Therefore, the ability to bring an employer's refusal to supply information – for whatever reasons – before an independent body is essential and crucial. Access to a similar procedure in a situation where an employer makes use of the confidentiality clause that might not be justified must be guaranteed as well. It is therefore crucial that an independent body – a court preferably – can objectively and impartially assess the criteria applied by the employer to withhold the information. It is essential to ensure that companies' interests are not put above the right of employees without check and balance. This possibility to appeal to an independent body directly affects the effectiveness of the directive itself. Additionally, in case of breach of the confidentiality obligation by any of the parties (either employees representatives, experts assisting them, employees or employer) the sanctions have to be effective (as discussed in 7.2.5 and 7.3.1.7) Research has shown that the way of sanctioning can differ substantially in the various Member States. They vary from financial penalties and civil damages for potential harm inflicted on the company to penal sanctions, including imprisonment.[75]

7.2.4. THE CONCEPTS OF INFORMATION AND CONSULTATION

All directives dealing with employees' rights to participation contain two basic concepts: information and consultation. These must be read in the light of the objective of the directives: giving employees and their representatives influence on the decision-making within the undertaking with regard to matters that affect the employees. Though this objective is explicitly worded neither in the directives nor in their preambles, it is their intended purpose.[76] However, the details and, in particular, the extent to which this influence may or must weigh on the decision-making differs, although over the years there has been a development towards more concordance. In the first European Works Council Directive (1994/45/EEC) the concepts of information and consultation were formulated rather rudimentarily: supplying information, so that the works council can take cognisance thereof and examine it, and leading to 'exchange of views and establishment of dialogue'. In the Recast European Works Council

74 Article 11(3) Directive 2009/38/EC (European Works Council); Article 12(2) Directive 2001/86/EC (SE); Article 14(2) Directive 2003/72/EC (ECS); and Article 6(3) Directive 2002/14/EC (Framework Directive).

75 Cf. Laulom & Dorssemont (2015), pp. 46, 47 and Table 4, pp. 48–55.

76 It can clearly be derived from §7 and §8 Preamble of the Framework Directive 2002/14/EC.

Directive an explicit choice is made for an increase of the effectiveness of the participation arrangements by specifying the definition of the concepts of information and consultation. In its comment on a Proposal in this respect in 2008, the European Commission pointed out that 'the European works council is not sufficiently informed and consulted in the case of restructuring'.[77]

Furthermore, the works councils must be up to the 'task of playing their full role in anticipating and managing change and building up a genuine transnational dialogue between management and labour. The objective of this proposal is thus 'to ensure that employees' transnational information and consultation rights are effective'.[78] The descriptions of both concepts are synchronised with those in the directives for a European company works council and a European cooperative society works council. The revision of the European Works Council Directive has been used to bring more coherence with definitions in all directives concerning information and consultation.[79]

7.2.4.1. Concept of Information

The more recent directives describe what must be understood by information: 'transmission of data by the employer to the employees' representatives in order to enable them to acquaint themselves with the subject matter and to examine it; information shall be given at such time, in such fashion and with such content, as are appropriate to enable employees' representatives to undertake an in-depth assessment of the possible impact and, where appropriate, prepare for consultations with the competent organ of the undertaking'.[80] The Recast European Works Council Directive clarifies that the goal of providing information is 'allowing employees representatives to carry out an appropriate examination, which implies that the information be provided at such time, in such fashion and with such content as are appropriate without slowing down the decision-making process in undertakings'.[81]

As observed before, the Framework Directive of 2002 is more general and not as clear as the more recent Recast European Works Council Directive: 'transmission by the employer to the employees' representatives of data to enable them to acquaint themselves with the subject matter and to examine it'.[82]

---

77 European Commission (2008), *Commission staff working document accompanying the proposal on the establishment of a European Works Council – Impact assessment*, COM(2008)419 final and SEC(2008) 2167, p. 17.

78 *Explanatory memorandum to a proposal on the establishment of a European Works Council*, COM(2008) 419 final, Nos. 4 and 5.

79 Cf. Laulom & Dorssemont (2015), p. 34.

80 Article 2(1)(f) Directive 2009/38/EC (European Works Council Recast); Article 2(I) Directive 2001/86/EC (European Company).

81 Directive 2009/38/EC, Recital 22.

82 Article 2(f) Directive 2002/14/EC (Framework Directive).

In the concept of information two aspects can be distinguished which from the point of view of effective influence are the most important: (1) content and quality of the information; and (2) timing of the supply of the information.

(a) Content and Quality

Let us first take a closer look at the two older directives on collective redundancies and transfer of undertaking. These give a clear indication as to what the employees and their representatives have to be informed about. This is prompted by the purpose and the subject matter of the respective directives. Besides the general element 'all useful data', the directive on collective redundancies refers to specific aspects: reasons for dismissal, numbers and categories of employees, selection criteria for dismissal, and the manner of calculating redundancy pay. The directive on transfers of undertakings does something similar. A general indication is lacking, but the directive lists a number of essential elements, such as the date or the planned date of the transfer, the reason for the transfer, the legal, economic and social consequences of the transfer for the employees, and the measures envisaged vis-à-vis the employees.[83]

The first European Works Council Directive (1994/45) does not give a definition of information as a central concept and therefore not of the subject matters to which that obligation applies either. In accordance with the contract principle this was left to the parties setting up the European works council. They themselves could lay down, if they so wished, on which subjects the general management would give information. An indication as to the ideas of the European legislator could be found in the subsidiary requirements.[84] These points return in a nearly identical form in the subsidiary requirements in the annex of the Recast Directive; these (can) play a role if the employers and employees' representatives cannot reach an agreement on the content of the contract.[85]

Besides the general description the recast directive adds a couple of elements which should increase the effectiveness of the involvement. The information must have an appropriate content so as to enable the employees to make an in-depth assessment of the possible consequences, with a view to the preparation of the consultation.[86] The directives regarding the European company and the European cooperative society use the same phrasing.[87] The text also requires

83 Article 2 Directive 98/59/EC (Collective redundancies); Article 7 Directive 2001/23/EC (Transfer of undertaking).

84 See Paragraphs 2 and 3 of the Subsidiary Requirements.

85 See on the subsidiary requirements, Section 7.3.1.6.

86 Article 2(f and g) Directive 2009/38/EC (recast European Works Council).

87 Article 2(i and j) Directive 2001/86/EC (European Company) and Article 2(i and j) Directive 2003/72/EC (European Cooperative Society).

that the information supplied by the employer has to specify the possible effects of the measures. This implies that the information must be based on transparent, accurate and complete data. It is for the employees' representatives to check whether these conditions are met.[88] Incidentally, such concepts are also used in other international sources, such as the Council of Europe (Revised European Social Charter)[89] and the OECD. For instance, the OECD Guidelines dictate that for matters of mutual interest 'consultation and co-operation between employers and employees and their representatives' must take place. The information to be supplied must enable them 'to obtain a true and fair view of the performance of the entity or, where appropriate, the enterprise as a whole'.[90]

Given the autonomy of the contracting parties conferred by Article 6 of the European Works Council Directive, there is a great deal of discretion when it comes to the content of the information. Looking at the practice of Article 6 agreements, one cannot but find that there is a considerable diversity with regard to the subject matters on which the employer has to supply information.[91] However, case law of the Court, on the one hand, and the subsidiary requirements annexed to the European Works Council, European Company Works Council and European Cooperative Society Works Council Directives – by way of guidance – on the other, provide more clarity not only about the content of the information but also in terms of the quality of the information to be supplied.[92] The Court of Justice, for instance, ruled in three judgments that the central management is obliged to give the information which the employees' representatives ask for and which they need in order to be able to exercise their rights effectively. In the *Bofrost* case,[93] the Court decided that the right to information goes further than that which has been expressly mentioned in the directive. The group of undertakings must also supply information about the structure or the organisation of the group if this information is necessary to enable the employees to exercise their rights. According to the Court, 'communication of documents clarifying and explaining the information which is indispensable for that purpose may also be required, in so far as that communication is necessary'.[94]

---

88 Enforcement will be dealt with in Section 7.2.5.

89 In Articles 21, 22 and 29 (r)ESC. See Kollonay Lehoczky (2010), p. 10 ff.; also Bruun, Lörcher, Schömann, Clauwaert (2017), pp. 381–411 and 477–492.

90 OECD (2008), Part 1, 4, p. 17.

91 See ETUI, European Works Council database, 11/2013 <https://www.worker-participation.eu/European-Works-Councils/EWC-Database> accessed 24 June 2019.

92 The case law is based on the European Works Council Directive (Directive 94/45/EC). The content of the case law has been codified in the Recast Directive 2009/38/EC.

93 ECJ 2001, C-62/99 (*Bofrost*).

94 Strictly speaking the case was not about the content and quality of the information provided. The claim was about the application of Article 2(1) (a–c) of Directive 94/45/EC (requirements for qualifying as European undertaking covered by the directive).

In both other cases the Court continued in the same vein.[95] In these cases too, the central management's obligation to provide information was said to go further than the strict requirements of the directive.[96]

Another source is national case law, even though there are hardly any judgments of national courts on this matter.[97] In this respect, French judges have set a good example. In the *Alcatel-Lucent* case,[98] the French judge decided that the parent company had to provide the European works council with the exact data which it needed in order to start conferring with the central management about the plans for reorganisation. Not only the nature of these plans, but also the number of jobs that were at stake, as well as the distribution thereof in the various subsidiary companies, including the motivation for that distribution and the categories of employees that would be affected, had to be specified.[99] In a previous case, concerning a merger between two large energy companies, the French judge had reached similar conclusions. The judge not only found that the information had come too late and was incomplete, but also decided which information should have been supplied.[100]

The subsidiary requirements in the directives constitute another source. They give a picture of the subject matters which the European legislator had in mind. The list found in the annex to the directive includes: the structure; the economic and financial situation; the production and sales of the undertaking as well as the situation and the probable trend of employment; investments; essential changes in the organisation; the introduction of new work methods or production processes; transfer of production; mergers, reduction or closure of undertakings; establishments or important divisions thereof; and collective redundancies (point 1a).

The Framework Directive also gives a list of subject matters for the participation rights at enterprise level:

- the recent and probable development of the undertaking's activities and economic situation;
- the situation, structure and probable development of employment within the undertaking and any anticipatory measures envisaged, in particular where there is a threat to employment;

95 ECJ 2004, C-440/00 (*Kühne & Nagel*) and ECJ 2004, C-349/01 (*Anker*).

96 The Court decided that the employer has to provide even the numbers and names of the employee representation bodies and their representatives ('names and players' numbers').

97 Cf. Dorssemont (2010a), p. 260 ff.

98 Tribunal de Grande Instance de Paris 27 April 2007, nr. 07/52509.

99 See about these cases Verburg (2007), p. 84 ff.; Dorssemont (2010a), pp. 145, 260 and 324.

100 Tribunal de Grande Instance de Paris 21 November 2006 (RG No 06/59279) and in appeal Cour d'Appel de Paris 21 November 2006 (RG No 06/20033). The Cour de Cassation

- decisions likely to lead to substantial changes in work organisation or in contractual relations, including those mentioned in the directives on collective redundancies and transfers of undertakings.[101]

This list is not exhaustive. Based on one of the core elements of the European law of workers' involvement – its contractual character (see Section 7.2.3.3)[102] – the list of subjects can be extended by agreement.[103] The question may arise as to whether it could also be shortened. The starting point of contractual freedom, including in this directive, is not contrary to this, as illustrated by the terms of Article 5 of the directive,[104] although there may be some doubt as to whether the 'effectiveness' of the principle of information and consultation underpinning these arrangements is still fulfilled in that case. In actual practice the list of Article 4(2) is certain to have a significant influential effect, due to the reflexive nature of the law.[105]

Neither the directives nor the case law tell us much about the quality of the information to be supplied. However, they do give us a clue how to determine whether the quality is sufficient. The nature of the information must be such that the employees' representatives can assess the possible effect of the (planned) decisions and measures thoroughly. They must be given the opportunity to prepare properly for the consultative stage in order to be able to express an opinion that could be useful to the decision-making and be taken into account by the undertaking. It is up to the European works council to see to it that this is achieved. In this respect the enforcement mechanism is of great, if not overriding, importance (see Section 7.2.5).

The directives say nothing about the form in which the information has to be supplied. This aspect played no part in the discussions about the review of the European Works Council Directive. The only thing that has been

(Supreme Court) confirmed the decision of the Cour d'Appel de Paris in its decision of 16 January 2008 (No 07-10597).

101 Article 4(2) Directive 2002/14/EC.

102 Recital 23 of the preamble of Framework Directive states explicitly: 'management and labour have a leading role by allowing them to define freely, by agreement, the arrangements for informing and consulting employees which they consider to be best suited to their needs and wishes'.

103 See Article 5 Directive 2002/14/EC (Framework Directive), as well as Article 6 Directive 2009/38/EC and Article 4 Directive 2001/86. Extension of the number of subjects can be found in various Member States, see Ales (2007).

104 Article 5 Directive 2002/14/EC reads: 'Member States may entrust management and labour at the appropriate level, including at undertaking or establishment level, with defining freely and at any time through negotiated agreement the practical arrangements for informing and consulting employees'.

105 Procedures in European or in national case law claiming an infringement of the Framework Directive have not been reported yet.

laid down is that the data have to be supplied in a manner and a form that will enable the employees' representatives to acquaint themselves with these and found their opinion on them.[106] There is no requirement for a document as such. The subsidiary requirements in the European Works Council Directive – as well as in the European Company and the European Cooperative Society Directive – mention reports to be produced by the central management at regular intervals.[107] From this one could infer that supplying the requested and necessary data in writing has been considered, but nowhere this has been explicitly imposed. It can be assumed that the information has to be supplied in writing when the European Works Council asks for this. The French court decided in this vein in the *Otis* case.[108] Unlike certain national employee participation arrangements, such as the Dutch law on works councils in Article 31(1) Act on works councils, most national laws do not require written information,[109] not even when the European works council requests this. It seems justified to ask whether this does not detract from the 'effet utile', i.e. the effectiveness of the European rules, which in point 14 of the preamble of the Recast Directive is emphasised once again: the arrangements must be defined and implemented in such a way 'as to ensure their effectiveness with regard to the provisions of this Directive'. The effectivity requirement was applied in the first significant case related to workers' involvement in company decisions: the so-called *Renault* case. This case concerned a relocation of plants of the multinational Renault from Belgium to France in the 1990s. A French court appealed to the 'effet utile' of the information and consultation procedure. It acknowledged that *in casu* a posteriori information and consultation would deprive the dialogue between management and labour of its 'effet utile'.[110]

(b) Timing of the Information

A second crucial aspect of the employees' right to participation is the time at which the information is transmitted. It is generally recognised that the information has to be supplied at such a time that meaningful consultation

106 Article 2(1)(f) Directive 2009/38/EC.

107 Derived from paragraph 1(d) of the Subsidiary Requirements.

108 See Tribunal de Grande Instance de Nanterre 7 January 1998 (*Otis*). In the *Alcatel-Lucent* case, the Tribunal de Grande Instance de Paris, 27 April 2007 ordered even for a suspension of the consultation procedure, until the information was provided in a written way, both in English as well as in French. In both cases the European works council was involved, see Dorssemont (2010a), p. 260.

109 Cf. Laulom & Dorssemont (2015), p. 64.

110 Cour d'Appel de Versailles, 7 April 1997, *Revue de* Jurisprudence sociale 1997, nr. 829; *Droit social*, 1997, 506–508 (with observations by A. Lyon-Caen); cf. also Moreau (1997), pp. 493–503; Dorssemont & Jaspers (1999), p. 152 ff.; Dorssemont (2006b), p. 6.

is possible. The term 'in good time' can already be found in the very first directives on this matter. Although the directive on collective redundancies of 1975 does not explicitly prescribe that the information and consultation have to be provided 'in (good) time', domestic courts are of the opinion that information and consultation have to take place in time to ensure that the objective of the directive can be reached to enable the workers' representatives to exercise their rights.[111] The domestic courts deduct this requirement from the meaning of Article 2(3) of the 1975 Directive. In the 1992 Directive amending the previous one, the requirement of 'in good time' has been inserted explicitly in Article 2(1).[112] The Directive on transfers of undertakings (77/187) also states 'in good time, before the transfer is carried out'. This requirement is logical if the participation rights are to have any effect.

The arrangements in the ESC and in the OECD contain the same idea, although Article 21 European Social Charter only refers to 'regularly or at the appropriate time'. The Committee that monitors the correct application of the ESC interprets this as 'in good time'.[113] In the OECD Guidelines timeliness is emphasised in the case of reorganisation: if decisions on restructuring operations are concerned 'which would have major effects upon the livelihood of their employees, in particular in the case of the closure of an entity involving collective lay-offs or dismissals', then it would be 'appropriate if management were able to give such notice prior to the final decision being taken', so as to enable 'meaningful co-operation' with the aim 'to mitigate the effects of such decisions'.[114]

The EU Charter of Fundamental Rights also mentions information 'at the appropriate levels and in good time'.[115] In the first proposal for a Charter 'effective information and consultation' was mentioned and direct reference made to its timeliness so as to ensure that the information (and consultation) would have effect.

In this context it is remarkable that the original European Works Council Directive did not include the concept of timeliness. The subsidiary requirements[116] are also silent on this aspect and simply refer to the right of the employees and/or their representatives to a meeting with the general management at least once a year, to be informed and consulted, on the basis

---

111 Article 2(1)(f) Directive 2009/38/EC (European Works Council Recast), Article 2(I) Directive 2001/86/EC (European Company) and Article 2(f) Directive 2002/14/EC. See ECJ 2005, C-188/03 (*Junk*), §§35–39.

112 Directive 98/59/EC holds the same requirement in Article 2(1).

113 European Committee of Social Rights, Conclusions 2007 (Albania); Conclusions XVIII-2 (Slovak Republic); Conclusions XVIII-2 (Slovak Republic).

114 OECD Guidelines for multinational enterprises 2000, DAFFE/IME(2000)20, 97609, chapter IV.

115 Article 27.

116 See Section 7.3.1.6.

of a report of the general management, on the development of the activities and prospects of the undertaking.[117] In the literature the question has been raised whether the aspect of timeliness should be given a more prominent role when it comes to consultation (see Section 7.2.4.2).

7.2.4.2. Concept of Consultation

The European Works Council Directive of 1994 did not contain a definition or description of consultation. It simply speaks of 'exchange of views' and establishment of 'dialogue between employees' representatives and central management or any more appropriate level of management'. Here too, the more recent Directives brought more clarity. Article 2(1)(g) of the Recast European Works Council Directive of 2009 adds to the general notion of 'establishment of dialogue and exchange of views' at such time, in such fashion and with such content as enables employees' representatives to express an opinion on the basis of the information provided about the proposed measures to which the consultation is related, without prejudice to the responsibilities of the management and within a reasonable time, which may be taken into account by the undertaking or group of undertakings.[118] In the Subsidiary Requirements the meaning of the consultation is more explicitly expressed: it is not only a meeting with the management but also an opportunity to obtain a response, the reasons for the response and to express further opinions.[119] Once again, the Framework Directive in its Article 2(g) has a more concise definition: the exchange of views and establishment of dialogue between the employees' representatives and the employer. However, the specification in Article 4 of the Framework Directive shows that the European legislator had at least the same idea about what consultation within an undertaking should imply. On the basis of the information supplied, the employees' representatives:

1. are entitled to formulate an opinion to which;
2. they must obtain a response, and the reasons for that response.

The article adds a significant phrase:

3. with a view to reaching an agreement.[120]

---

117 Annex I Article 2 of the Subsidiary Requirements.

118 A similar wording is used in Article 2(j) Directive 2001/86/EC (European Company).

119 Article 1(a) Subsidiary Requirements Directive 2009/38/EC.

120 Article 4(4) Directive 2002/14/EC (Framework Directive). Article 1(2) Directive 98/59/EC (Collective Redundancies) and Article 7(1 and 2) Directive 2001/23/EC (Transfer of Undertaking) use the same phrase. It has to be born in mind that it is an obligation of effort rather than of result.

In the European Works Council and the European Company Works Council, this addition is lacking. The wording chosen in these directives could indicate that the directives do not demand this from the consulting parties, and, in particular, not from the employer. The outcome of the consultation, i.e. the opinion of the European works council, is just something the employer can take into account in its decision (Article 2(1)(g)). The Framework Directive does not mention any sanctions for not reaching or not wanting to reach an agreement.

With a view to ensuring the effectiveness of the arrangements, the preambles of the various Directives always emphasise that the consultation should be substantial. However, the European Works Council Directive adds 'without calling into question the ability of undertakings to adapt'. The European legislature was convinced that substantial consultation is also in the interest of the entrepreneurs themselves, as is shown by the statement that 'only dialogue at the level where directions are prepared and effective involvement of employees' representatives make it possible to anticipate and manage damage'.[121]

With regard to the effective exercise of this right to consultation a number of aspects can be distinguished.

(a) Material Scope: Subjects

The subjects on which the employees' representatives have to be consulted are referred to in the same way as in the case of the right to information and, therefore, are dependent on the nature and objectives of the participation arrangement. For the special directives (collective redundancies and transfers of undertakings) this is obvious. The directives themselves lay down the minimum requirements. In actual practice, when they are not established in an agreement, this list can be extended, something which indeed happens frequently.

For the directives on employee participation (European Works Council Directive, European Company employee involvement Directive and the Framework Directive) this is not so clear. As information and consultation are usually bracketed together, it is clear that the material scope is the same as for the obligation of information (see above).[122]

(b) In Good Time

All directives regarding this matter use the term 'in good time' or an equivalent. It is generally accepted that in good time means: 'prior to the final decision of

121 See Recital 14 of the preamble of Directive 2009/38/EC (European Works Council). The other Directives do not mention this aspect.

122 See Article 4(2) Framework Directive 2002/14/EC; and §1(a) Subsidiary Requirements Directive 2009/38/EC.

the management'. Only then the opinion of the employees' representatives can be respected and their observations involved in the decision-making of the undertaking's management.[123] The European Works Council Directive of 2009, the European Company employee involvement Directive and the European Cooperative Society Works Council Directive mention a certain chronology: consultation must take place at such time as to enable employees' representatives to give their opinion within a reasonable time for the undertaking to take account thereof.

What exactly does 'in good time' mean in the various possible circumstances? Although the directives do not explicitly refer to the chronology of the information and consultation procedures, one can infer from the structure of the directives and the logic of the procedures themselves that a certain chronology of the various stages of these procedures must be observed if there is to be effective involvement of workers as intended by the directives.[124] The Directives on collective redundancies (Directive 75/129/EEC, Directive 92/129/EEC and Directive 98/59/EC) are more specific in terms of chronology. Article 2 of the 1975 Directive does not explicitly refer to the chronological order of the information and consultation procedure. However, by implication it requires that the information has to be provided and the consultation on the intended collective dismissals has to take place prior to the dismissal decision by the employer. The revised Collective redundancies directives of 1992 and 1998 have made it clear: they not only require the consultation to take place in good time, but also more specifically demand that an employer who wants to carry out a large-scale restructuring which will lead to collective lay-offs must inform and consult the employees' representatives when considering taking such a decision. So, this is a clear reference to anteriority and chronology. In the *Junk* judgment the Court expressly confirmed this.[125]

The Directives for the European Works Council, the European Company employee involvement and the European Cooperative Society Works Council seem to start from the same chronology. In its definition of consultation, the European Works Council Directive uses the term 'proposed' measures. The European Company Works Council Directive and the European Cooperative Society Works Council Directive refer to the measures 'envisaged'. These different wordings could amount to more than a semantic difference. Chronologically speaking, an envisaged measure comes before a proposed measure, especially when assessed in view of the possibility to influence the

123 See inter alia Blanke (2006), p. 263.

124 Based on the 'general principle of EU law the observance of which the Court of Justice ensures', as the Court stated, ECJ 1974, Case 4/73 (*Nold*). Cf. Jaspers (2008a), pp. 7–18.

125 ECJ 2005, C-188/03 (*Junk*), §§35–38. Confirmed by ECJ 2009, C-44/08 (*Fujitsu Siemens*), §51. See also Chapter 6, Section 6.2.2.

measure that will be taken. To avoid this potential difference in meaning, the European Economic and Social Committee proposed, in the context of the review of the European Works Council Directive of 1994, to streamline the terminology and to have both directives use the word 'envisaged' because this is more in line with the objective of the participation arrangements.[126]

Although neither of the texts lay down the chronology explicitly, one can infer from them that (information and) consultation have to take place before the undertaking has made a decision. In both national and European case law this principle has meanwhile been fully accepted. As early as in the *Renault* case of 1997, French judges had decided that information and consultation have to take place in good time, even though the appeals judge did not go as far as the court of first instance which ordered prior information and consultation of the European works council. The higher court did not go so far partly because in that case a so-called pre-existing agreement (in accordance to Article 13 European Works Council Directive 1994) was involved, in which such an arrangement had not been included. However, invoking the idea behind the right to involvement as already laid down in the Community Charter of the Fundamental Social Rights of Workers of 1989 in which the European Works Council Directive of 1994 was referred to as a source of inspiration, the French judge held the view that the European works council had been wronged. Article 18 of the Community Charter stated that 'this information, consultation must be implemented in due time, particularly in connection with restructuring operations in undertakings having an impact on the employment of workers and in cases of collective redundancy procedures'.[127]

In two more recent French cases this aspect resurfaced.[128] In both cases the European works council complained about the nature of and the lack of timeliness of the information and consultation. In both cases the judge ruled that decisions could only be taken after consultation with the European works council.[129] In the *GDF* case, the highest French court decided that the consultation had to take place prior to the decision being taken and not just before the decision would be implemented. In both cases, as in the *Renault* case, the judge sustained the claim for suspension of the decision process which had been started by the undertaking and which was considered to be contrary to

126 CES(2009)175.

127 Cf. Jenkins (2002), pp. 147–148, pp. 152 ff.; Dorssemont & Jaspers (1999); Dorssemont (2006b), pp. 8–9.

128 Tribunal de Grande Instance de Paris, 21 November 2006 and in appeal Cour d'Appel de Paris, 21 November 2006, confirmed by the Cour de Cassation, 16 January 2008 (*Gaz de France/GDF*). Tribunal de Grande Instance de Paris 27 April 2007, nr. 07/52509 (*Alcatel-Lucent*).

129 This decision was in line with the decision in the *Renault* case. See Dorssemont & Jaspers (1999).

the participation rules. In the *Fujitsu/Siemens* case of 2009, the Court of Justice took a similar stance.[130] This case was dealt with in Chapter 6 (Section 6.2.2.)

This interpretation corresponds with the goal-oriented idea in several directives. The two special Directives (collective redundancies and transfer of undertaking) as well as the 2002 Framework Directive have a component covering intention, in that they instruct that when it comes to decisions which are important for the workers and which could lead to drastic changes in the work organisation or employment contracts, the consultation must be aimed at achieving an agreement.[131] This goal-oriented idea can also be found in the European Company Directive, although not in the main text, but in the subsidiary requirements. If the management of the European Company does not wish to follow the advice of the representative body, a new meeting with the management is required to try to reach an agreement.[132] Obviously, this directive considers this to be an important objective of the participation arrangements within the Union which should also be included in the national rules. It should be noted here that the (recast) European Works Council Directive of 2009 does not contain such a provision. It does not go further than granting the possibility to advise.

From the various arrangements it can be inferred that the first objective of reaching an agreement is to ensure that the consultation with the employees' representatives has to be genuine so that they have effective influence in matters affecting the employees' interests. This does not mean that an agreement has to be reached in a legal sense, i.e. a binding agreement, as is apparent from the additions in the various directives that all of this leaves the responsibilities of the undertaking's management intact. The employer's prerogatives are restricted by the participation arrangements, but not cancelled.[133] This is confirmed once more in the preamble of the Recast European Works Council Directive, which as regards the principle of timeliness also states that this may not lead to 'calling into question the ability of undertakings to adapt'.[134] So in European participation law too, in the end it is the employer who will decide after 'constructive' consultations with the employees' representatives.[135]

---

130 ECJ 2009, C-44/08 (*Fujitsu Siemens*), §51. Cf. Verburg (2010), p. 65.

131 Article 2(1) Directive 98/59/EC (Collective Redundancies); Article 7(2) Directive 2001/23/EC (Transfer of Undertaking); Article 4(4)(e) Directive 2002/14/EC (Framework Directive). This principle has not been transposed in all Member States, but it was transposed in Austria, Germany, Finland, the Netherlands and Sweden and also in some 'new' Member States, as Slovakia and Slovenia. Cf. Ales (2007), p. 20.

132 Annex Part 2c Directive 2001/86/EC.

133 Cf. Dorssemont (2010a), pp. 42–43.

134 Recital 14 Preamble Directive 2009/38/EC (European Works Council).

135 In its case law the Court of Justice referred to the term of 'freedom of undertaking'; see ECJ 1995, C-449/93 (*Rockfon*), §21. Confirmed in ECJ 2009, C-44/08 (*Fujitsu Siemens*), §59: 'how the management of a group of undertakings is organised is an internal matter and, secondly, it is not the purpose of Directive 98/59, any more than it was of Directive 75/129, to restrict

A special issue in this respect is the concordance of information and consultation by a transnational works council with the information and consultation rights of national works councils or other workers' representing bodies. This subject will be dealt with separately (see Section 7.3.1.5).

7.2.5. ENFORCEMENT AND SANCTIONS

In all the directives considered, it is acknowledged that infringement of the obligations must be subject to sanctions. Member States are also instructed to have procedures in place to guarantee the compliance with the information and consultation obligations. The wording and the content of the various directive provisions differ in this respect. In the Collective Redundancies and Transfer of Undertaking Directives, national laws must provide for administrative and/or judicial procedures which offer the employees and their representatives the possibility to demand compliance with those obligations. On the basis of settled case law of the Court of Justice,[136] this means that these should be effective procedures and effective sanctions. It is left to the Member States to regulate this in their national laws in their own way, provided that the aim is achieved. The sanction provisions in both of these directives are worded in a general way.

A different approach was adopted in the four participation directives. The European Works Council, the European Company Works Council and the European Cooperative Society Works Council Directives require all Member States to make sure that the management of the undertakings established on their territory and their employees and/or their representatives observe the obligations defined in the directives, whether or not the central management has its headquarters in their territory.[137] In recital 36 of the Preamble this was stressed once again: 'In accordance with the general principles of Community law, administrative or judicial procedures, as well as sanctions that are effective, dissuasive and proportionate in relation to the seriousness of the offence, should be applicable in cases of infringement of the obligations arising from this Directive.' Thus, the case law of the Court of Justice[138] was, once again, summarised and confirmed concisely. It also concurs with an explicit

the freedom of such a group to organise their activities in the way which they think best suits their needs'.

136 The Court has set a clear line in a continuous series of decisions starting with ECJ 1984, C-14/83 (*Von Colson and Kamann*).

137 Article 11 Directive 2009/38/EC (European Works Council); Article 12 Directive 2001/86/EC (European Company); and Article 14 Directive 2003/72/EC. Article 8 Directive 2002/14/EC (Framework Directive) entails a similar obligation obviously without the last part of the sentence.

138 See note 136.

provision in the Framework Directive (Article 8) where it is stated in so many words that the Member States must 'provide for appropriate measures in the event of non-compliance with this Directive by the employer or the employees' representatives. These sanctions must be effective, proportionate and dissuasive.'

The Directives (Framework and European Works Council Directive) include a separate arrangement with regard to supplying (confidential) information. Administrative or judicial procedures must be available to employees' representatives when the central management demands confidentiality or withholds information. These procedures may also include procedures designed to protect the confidentiality of the information in question.[139] Member States must provide these procedures and guarantee effective compliance with that obligation.[140]

To assess whether or not the Member States really provides for and apply these effective sanctions, national case law must be looked at. Studies reveal that sanctions laid down in the national laws meeting the criteria of effectiveness are very scarce and not heavy.[141] The Recast of European Works Council Directive (2009/38/EC) presented the opportunity to review sanctions, but this was not acted upon.[142] The Recast Directive reiterates the provision of the 1994 Directive: Member States have to provide for 'appropriate measures in the event of failure to comply with this Directive', more specifically, to ensure that 'adequate administrative or judicial procedures are available to enable the obligations deriving from this Directive to be enforced' (Article 11). The provision itself specifies no further details. It does not even lay down a uniform process or any criteria concerning the enforcement procedures. Only the Preamble, being not legally binding, states, as a compromise, that sanctions must be effective, dissuasive and proportionate in relation to the seriousness of the offence.[143]

However, there are a few examples of sanctioning of offences that meet the criteria laid down in the preamble. Especially, the French courts and, in one or two cases, the Belgian courts stand out. In France there were a few cases in which this issue was raised more or less explicitly. In all of these cases the

139 Article 6(3) Framework Directive and Article 11 European Works Council Directive 2009.

140 As decided by ECJ 2001, C-62/99 (*Bofrost*). Similarly, the other cases ECJ 2004, C-440/00 (*Kühne & Nagel*) and ECJ 2004, C-349/01 (*Anker*). See above Section 7.2.3.3.

141 As the study of Jagodzinski, R. & P Lorber, (2015) shows.

142 Ibid.

143 Directive 2009/38, recital 36. The proposal to insert requirements of effectiveness has been rejected. The proposal was heavily debated between Council, Commission and Parliament. Cf. European Commission, *Informal Trialogue, December 2008*, reported in European Commission (2010) *Expert Group Report on Implementation of Recast Directive 2009/38/EC on European Works Councils* p. 65. See also Jagodzinski & Lorber (2015), pp. 151–154.

point was the effectiveness of the information and consultation procedures in multinational undertakings with their head office and central management in the EU.[144] The question was always whether in the context of a reorganisation, the European Works Council's rights to information and consultation, sometimes in connection with the same rights of the local works councils, had been observed and if not – which was always the point at issue – whether there were effective sanctions to guarantee this. Although the rulings were not sufficiently clear in all of these rulings, one may infer from them that the French court imposes measures to stop strategies and actions on the part of the undertaking to evade these obligations, even if this is not always expressed in so many words. The French judge in the *Renault* case, and also the Belgian judge in the *BA* case, ruled explicitly that the decision-making and the implementation of the decision had to be suspended until the European works council had been informed and had had the opportunity to assess the situation and to transmit this to the undertaking's management. In the *Alcatel-Lucent* case the French judge was very clear about the scope of the management's obligation of information,[145] but refused to allow the request for suspension of the restructuring plans until the completion of the consultation of the European works council. The court has been quite explicit about the content of the information to be provided by the employer in order to guarantee a real exchange of views. That should imply precise and concrete figures that supported the decision to close down or relocate activities as well as giving the number of redundant jobs. The reason for this was not that the sanction would be too severe, but because this consultation did not have to be formalised in an opinion.[146] In the *Alston and Beiersdorf* cases the French court ruled in a similar vein.[147] In the *Marks & Spencer* case, which concerned the question whether the information and consultation of the European works council took precedence over those of the local works councils, the decision for the European works council went a somewhat different way. Marks & Spencer had asked for preferential consultation by the European works council over the consultation by the local works councils. The French judge decided in the opposite way by suggesting that a chronological order does not exist. Marks & Spencer had to grant participation

---

144 This was at stake in the following cases: Renault in 1997 (see above), Marks & Spencer in 2001 (TGI Paris, 9.4.2001), Alston in 2003 (TGI Nanterre, 1.8.2003), Beiersdorf in 2006 (TGI Melun, Ordonnance du 13 octobre 2006 n° 06/00327) and *Alcatel-Lucent* in 2007 (see above), see Dorssemont & Blanke (2010a), pp. 260–66.

145 Cf. Tribunal de Grande Instance de Paris 27 April 2007, nr. 07/52509 (*Alcatel-Lucent*).

146 Cf. Verburg (2010), p. 96 ff.

147 TGI Nanterre, 1 August 2003 (*Alston*); TGI Melun, Ordonnance du 13 octobre 2006 no 06/00327 (*Beiersdorf*).

rights not only to the European works council, but also to the local works councils. However, it had to be genuine participation.[148]

The explicit suspension of decision when information and consultation were not complied with was envisaged in the 2002 Framework Directive. Proposals were made to make such sanction applicable in the directive, but opposition from employers and Member States prevented the provision from reaching the final text.[149]

Research shows that a variety of sanctions exist where European works council agreements are not complied with.[150] The breach of national legislation is classified as either administrative, civil or even criminal law depending on the Member States' systems. By reference in the directives concerned to the national systems of sanctioning, different sanctions may therefore be applied among Member States.[151] Judicial orders and even imprisonment is possible in some Member States, but a fine or financial penalty is the usual remedy across Member States. The level of fines paid is, however, greatly different from country to country. Quite a number of Member States do not have a minimum fine.[152] In some countries, suspension of the decision by the management – for instance continuing a restructuring without proper information of consultation of the European Works Council – is possible.[153] In conclusion, a lack of effective sanctions may potentially undermine the effectiveness of the right of information and consultation for employees and their representatives.

---

148 TGI Paris 9 April 2001 (*Marks & Spencer*). The relation between the European Works Council and the notional workers' representing bodies (mainly works councils) will be dealt with in Section 7.3.1.5(b).

149 Lorber (2003), p. 303.

150 Jagodzinski & Lorber (2015), p. 150 ff.

151 Jagodzinski & Lorber have classified the different sanctions. See Jagodzinski & Lorber (2015), pp. 156–58.

152 If they have fines, they vary from €4 (Poland) to €2,000 (Slovenia). A maximum to the fines is common; it varies from €890 (Romania) to €187,000 (Spain); See Jagodzinski (2014), figures 1 and 2, p. 3. Also Jagodzinski & Lorber (2015), pp. 169–71, table 20. In a few countries (France and UK) nullity and invalidity of managerial decisions, or for the decisions to be put on hold, are possible.

153 See the *Renault* case in 1997: both French courts: TGI Nanterre 4 April 1997 and Cour de Versailles 7 May 1997; the case of Gaz de France: TGI Paris 21 November 2006, Cour d'Appel Paris 21 November 2006 and Cour de Cassation 16 January 2008. Cf. Jagodzinski & Lorber (2015), p 173; Dorssemont & Blanke (2010a), pp. 261–62. In the UK, the Central Arbitration Committee (CAC) can give orders; for example it can order the company to disclose information to employees or their representatives when they request information to ascertain whether the company falls within the remit of a Community-scale undertaking or Community-scale group of undertakings (regulation 8 TICER 1999). However, the CAC is expressly prohibited by statute from suspending a decision of the company ('No order of the CAC under this regulation shall have the effect of suspending or altering the effect of any act done or of any agreement made by the central management or the local management.' Regulation 21A(9) TICER 1999).

7.3. INFORMATION AND CONSULTATION IN CROSS-BORDER ENTERPRISES

The following section considers more specifically two instruments which deal with transnational information and consultation. The European Works Council Directive and the Directive on worker involvement in the European company were created to allow collective voice and participation in firms that operate across borders. Given free movement of capital and services in the EU, but also general globalisation, decision making is often remote from the workforce; European law therefore created transnational channels that should make multinationals' decisions that affect their workforce more accountable and transparent and subject to influence by employee representatives.

The European Works Council Directive and worker involvement in the European Company will therefore be scrutinised below in terms of aim and origin, scope, content and procedures as well as implementation. The themes already explored above will not be revisited, but simply referred to where appropriate. Other directives promoting cross border employee participation, such as the European Cooperative Society and its accompanying Directive on worker involvement (Directive 2003/72/EC), as well as the Directive on Cross Border Mergers (Directive 2005/56/EC) will not be considered here.

7.3.1. EUROPEAN WORKS COUNCILS

7.3.1.1. Introduction

While the genesis and aim of the 1994 European Works Council Directive are briefly mentioned in Section 7.2.1, this European instrument responded to two imperatives: first, the increased internationalisation of undertakings facilitated by the development of the internal market (through 'concentration of undertakings, cross border mergers, take-overs, joint ventures')[154] and, second, the unequal availability of rules geared towards transnational information and consultation, leading to unequal treatment of workers throughout the European Community.[155] The changing economic and corporate context and lack of uniformity in employment law across Member States legitimised EU intervention. Cross-border management required a form of cross-border worker voice. While the European Community had attempted to establish transnational worker voice through the Vredeling Proposal (mentioned in Section 7.2.1.1),

[154] Directive 94/45/EC, Preamble.
[155] Ibid.

a decision by a multinational company (Hoover) to move its workforce from France to Scotland catalysed the impetus to find agreement among Member States on transnational information and consultation as national processes of information and consultation were frustrated by the American multinational management.

The process to facilitate transnational dialogue of EU workers was to be achieved by the establishment of a body (the European works council) composed of workers' representatives where the undertaking operates. As indicated in the previous section, the method adopted was not the imposition of a single model, but the choice to entrust social partners or management and employee representatives to negotiate an agreement on information and consultation (see Section 7.2.1 on the contractual character of the rules) that suited their circumstances (in terms of identifying workers' representatives, content of information and consultation and timing, frequency of meetings, etc.). The Directive also allowed companies that had established transnational fora to retain them provided they fulfilled some minimum criteria (Article 13 Pre-existing agreements), thus also recognising and avoiding disrupting well-established communication systems.

While the directive promoted cross-border dialogue and participation and encouraged the creation of European works councils, the Commission led reviews and other independent research demonstrated a number of drawbacks that needed addressing.[156] As a result, the 2009 Directive aimed to 'ensure the effectiveness of employees' transnational information and consultation rights …, to increase the proportion of European Works Councils [in the total number of transnational companies]. That should resolve the problems encountered in the practical application of the (former) Directive 94/45 and remedy the lack of legal certainty resulting from some of its provisions ….'[157] In this endeavour, the directive included a definition of information and improved the definition of consultation (see Sections 7.2.4.1 and 7.2.4.2), while it further defined 'transnational' to increase clarity. European social partners were recognised as useful and expert channels to assist in creating more European works councils, for example by allowing trade union officials to attend negotiating meetings as experts. Finally, effectiveness of the right was also increased by requiring management to provide the European works council with the means necessary to perform its functions. In 2018 another review of the European Works Council Directive was published in order to assess whether the changes from 2009 have had the expected impact.[158] The Commission concluded that the number

156 European Commission (2008), *Proposal for a Directive on the establishment of a European Works Council*, COM(2008)419 final; Lorber (2009) p. 125; Jagodzinski (2011), p. 229.

157 Directive 2009/38/EC preamble (7).

158 European Commission, COM(2018)292 final.

of European works councils has increased, but not significantly, consultation remains limited, and enforcement is varied across Member States. It therefore recommends soft initiatives, such as the creation of a handbook that will contain practical advice and good practice, coupled with financial support to projects that will advertise and disseminate the handbook. Assistance is also offered to Member States to improve enforcement and sanctions, notably by exchanges between Member States on what constitute effective, proportionate and dissuasive sanctions.[159]

In 2000, the European Commission established that all Member States had transposed the original 1994 Directive,[160] and the 2009 Recast Directive had also been implemented across Europe.[161]

7.3.1.2. *Establishing a European Works Council*

As indicated above, the intention of the drafters of the European Works Council Directive was to allow flexibility for stakeholders when establishing the new European bodies: maximum freedom should be given to management and employee representatives. A model would only be imposed if negotiations failed or management failed to respond to a request from employees. Multinationals were therefore given three options to set up the European Works Council. The first possibility was time limited and aimed to either recognise best practice already in place or encourage creation of a European Works Council. If by September 1996, companies had a European Works Council in place, they would not be subject to the directive. Companies were therefore enticed to embrace the objective of the directive (transnational worker participation), but with little interference from the legislator, provided that three criteria were fulfilled: an agreement on information and consultation, covering the entire workforce, by the date of implementation of the directive.[162] This option proved particularly popular and by September 1996, a third of the multinationals potentially caught by the directive already had a European works council or equivalent procedure.[163] This option is sometimes referred as the opt-out option or Article 13 Agreement European Works Councils.

The second option is referred to as the Article 6 Agreement option or the Negotiated agreement option. If companies missed the September 1996 deadline, they could still negotiate an agreement which is suitable to their circumstances

---

159 Ibid, p 9.

160 European Commission, COM(2000)188 final, 2–3.

161 Jagodzinski (2015), p. 12 and table 1, pp. 13–15.

162 Directive 94/45/EC, Article 13.

163 In 1996, 400 European Works Councils were created, a number never matched since, the highest number of European Works Councils created was 84 in 1999 and 2000, Cf. ETUI, European Works Council database, 11/2013 <https://www.worker-participation.eu/European-Works-Councils/European Works Council-Database> accessed 05.06.2019.

by following the procedure found in Article 6 (which is discussed in more detail below). The content of the agreement remains largely at the discretion of the parties. The trigger for such option either comes from management or employees or their representatives, provided they represent at least 100 workers across at least two undertakings situated in two different Member States.[164] The numerical and geographical requirements may constitute barriers to the establishment of European works councils if workers are not unionised or organised, in particular if they cannot access workforce across borders. This requirement also renders the transnational dialogue optional, since if neither parties act, there is no sanction or automatic application of the European Works Council Directive. The latter was recognised as a potential obstacle for the creation of new European works councils: according to the European Commission, 'the absence of an obligation to set up European works councils' is one of the factors explaining why the number of European works councils is not increasing significantly.[165]

Finally, if parties fail to negotiate or management does not respond to a request for negotiations from the workforce, a model European Works Council will apply, as described in the subsidiary requirements (and explained further below).[166]

Following the extinction of first option, the take up for European works councils has been slower. In 2018, there were 1,133 active European works councils compared to 533 in 1996.[167] The 2009 Directive sought to increase the number of European works councils as one of its main aims, but since then only an additional 118 European works councils have been added to the list of active European works councils.[168] In 2015, 39% of the European works councils are pre-directive and 49% are Article 6.[169] It has therefore been argued that additional reforms may be needed, such as the review of the trigger mechanisms to significantly increase the number of European works councils. This is currently not envisaged by the Commission in light of the 2018 review.

7.3.1.3. Scope of the Directive (Personal)

The Directive applies to Community-scale undertaking or Community-scale group of undertakings, which are defined as entities with at least a 1,000 employees within the Member States and at least 150 employees in

164 Directive 2009/35/EC, Article 5.
165 COM(2018)292, p 7.
166 Directive 2009/35/EC, Article 7.
167 ETUI, European works councils database, stats and graphs <http://www.ewcdb.eu/stats-and-graphs> accessed 05.06.2019.
168 European Commission, COM(2018)292 final.
169 Spiegelaere & Jagodzinski (2015), p. 13.

each of at least two Member States.[170] The cross-border requirement of the personal scope evidences the aim of adding a transnational dimension to national processes of worker participation. This is not limited to companies which are solely EU based. This definition encompasses global companies that may not be headquartered in the European Union, but meet the threshold of Article 2. In this case, the directive foresees that the entity responsible for setting up the European Works Council is the one in the country designated as the representative of the company, and if this appointment has not been made, the country where the multinational employs most people.[171] As a result, an American multinational company with enough undertakings and employees in the EU, including the UK, may, for example, decide to appoint the UK firm as responsible for the establishment of the European Works Council. If it fails to do so and employees wish to trigger negotiations, they would need to address their request to the largest subsidiary of that company in the EU (which may not be the UK). ETUI estimates that 23% of European Works Councils are in companies headquartered outside the UK and most non-EU companies will chose the UK, Denmark, Belgium or France as their as their EU headquarters for the purpose of choosing which national law applies when establishing EWCs. The UK is also the country with the third largest number of European works councils, after Germany and France.[172] The withdrawal of the UK from the EU ('Brexit') may soon have an impact on the national law applicable to numerous European works councils, as well as potentially affecting the scope of the directive, especially if no withdrawal agreement is agreed between with the UK and the EU.[173]

7.3.1.4. Procedure of Negotiations

Given the flexibility left to parties in establishing a European works council, the directive does stipulate in more detail what the negotiations process should entail. This is in contrast with the 2002 Framework Directive, which leaves to national settings the choice to conduct negotiations as parties see fit. The difference may be explained by the supranational nature of the instrument and the need to ensure true cross-border involvement and negotiations.

Once either central management or the required number of employees or their representatives has triggered the negotiations, a Special Negotiating Body must be appointed. The Directive indicates how the body should be composed and what its mission is. In terms of composition, some discretion is

---

170 Directive 2009/35/EC, Article 2.

171 Directive 2009/35/EC, Article 3(6).

172 Spiegelaere & Jagodzinski (2015), p. 16.

173 Lorber (2018) <http://regulatingforglobalization.com/2018/09/07/brexit-workers-rights-meaning-no-deal-transnational-consultation/> accessed 17 June 2019.

left to Member States to facilitate national traditions associated with workers' representation. National law determines how employee representatives from their own countries are elected or appointed. For example, in some countries trade unions representatives will be appointed (e.g. Italy), while in other national systems persons sitting in national works councils will be selected to sit on the Special Negotiating Body (e.g. Germany).[174] The number of members of the Special Negotiating Body is determined by a formula in the directive: one member per country where the company operates, with one member representing 10% of the workforce.[175]

The main task of the Special Negotiating Body is to negotiate with management the 'scope, composition, function and terms of office of the European Works Council'.[176] The content of the agreement is discussed in the next section. The negotiations must take place in a spirit of cooperation (a special feature of worker participation as considered in Section 7.2.3.1). The Special Negotiating Body and management may decide not to negotiate by a two-third majority and chose, de facto, the option to apply the subsidiary requirements (discussed further below).[177] The function of the Special Negotiating Body is time-limited, as once the agreement is reached and the negotiations are over, the Special Negotiating Body is dissolved.

Two additional points are significant to the procedure for the effectiveness of the negotiations and the establishment of a European works council. First, employee representatives members of the Special Negotiating Body are entitled to hold pre and post meetings without central management.[178] This is essential in a context where workers will come from different countries with different experience in national settings. Second, the recast Directive explicitly entitles representatives to seek the assistance of experts for their negotiations, including European trade unions officials who will have experience in transnational negotiations. Central management is responsible for the cost of such experts, but national law may limit the cost to be borne by management to one expert.[179]

7.3.1.5. Content of the Agreement

Article 6 of the directive simply lists the items that will need to be part of the agreement negotiated between the Special Negotiating Body and central

174 Comparing national procedures for appointing Special Negotiating Body and European Works Council members, ETUI database <https://www.worker-participation.eu/European-Works-Councils/Legal-Matters/Comparing-national-procedures-for-appointing-SNB-and-EWC-members> accessed 02.06.2019.

175 Article 5(2)(b).

176 Article 5(3).

177 Article 5(5).

178 Article 5(4).

179 Article 5(6).

management. The details of the composition and operation of the European Works Council is left to the negotiating parties. The agreement will first stipulate which Community undertaking or group of undertakings will be covered. The composition of the new European works council is also to be negotiated and the agreement should indicate the number of representatives, the method of selection of the members and the length of their terms of office. The Recast Directive inserted a new requirement that a balanced representation should seek to be achieved, in particular in relation to gender.[180] While it is indicated that the agreement should refer to the method and content of information and consultation, stakeholders are left to decide topics for discussions, frequency of meetings, process and method. There is no minimum requirement. The main theme is that the information and consultation is transnational in nature, covering cross-border topics, and the agreement should consider how the European works council will liaise with national structures of information and consultation (as discussed below). Despite this freedom of negotiations, research has shown that parties have been influenced by the content of the subsidiary requirements which lay out what is considered as the model European Works Council, i.e. the system to refer back to if negotiations fail. The subsidiary requirements act therefore as a benchmark.[181]

The Recast Directive added a couple of requirements which were also seen as essential for the effectiveness of European works councils. First, an agreement can specify that a select committee should be appointed. This specific body was originally found in the subsidiary requirements as an essential component of the worker participation machinery. Its role is to manage and coordinate the European works council activities and meetings. Its addition to the items that could be negotiated between the Special Negotiating Body and management is testimony of its usefulness for the process of worker involvement. Second, the agreement should indicate what the financial and material resources are allocated to the European Works Councils. Research had shown that often, there was uncertainty as to the means that could be used by the European Works Council to enforce its rights.[182]

7.3.1.6. Cross-Border Issues

The objectives of the Recast Directive include the willingness to clarify certain concepts, to increase legal certainty, to ensure the effectiveness of the right to information and consultation, and to have a better link or relationship between the different obligations to participate in decision making. In this context, the cross-border aspect of consultation needed to be refined in two ways.

---

180 Article 6(2)(b).

181 Marginson et al. (1998), p. 73. Carley & Marginson (2000).

182 See Section 7.3.1.7.

First, stakeholders had sought better understanding of what was meant by 'transnational'. Second, legal comprehension of the link between European Works Council and national structures of information and consultation was required. As stated in Article 1(3) of the Recast Directive:

> Information and consultation of employees must occur at the relevant level of management and representation, according to the subject under discussion. To achieve that, the competence of the European Works Council and the scope of the information and consultation procedure for employees governed by this Directive shall be limited to transnational issues.

It is obvious that the European works council deals with transnational issues. Issues of a purely national nature belong to the national bodies in the enterprises in the Member State concerned. The division of competence between the transnational and the national employees' representative bodies seems clear. However, a problem may rise and has been risen when an issue of a clearly cross-border nature affects a particular enterprise in a Member State. Two questions arise: first, are both bodies competent for the process of information and consultation or only the transnational body; and, second, if both are involved, should one body be consulted first or should they both be consulted simultaneously? These questions will be explored in the next subsections.

(a) The Concept of Transnational

In the 1994 European Works Council Directive, the word transnational was not defined as such, even if the measure aimed to counteract the transnationalisation of businesses (through cross-border merger and acquisitions, for example) with the addition of transnational dialogue with the workforce. The subsidiary requirements did make reference to the competence of the European works council in a way which suggests what is understood by transnational:

> The competence of the European Works Council shall be limited to information and consultation on the matters which concern the Community-scale undertaking or Community-scale group of undertakings as a whole or at least two of its establishments or group undertakings situated in different Member States.[183]

The Recast Directive clarified this notion by inserting the definition in the directive itself and stating that the term transnational refers to matters that affect the entire workforce or at least two undertakings located in two different

[183] Directive 94/45/EC, Annex 1(a).

Member States.[184] For stakeholders, therefore, the European works council would be engaged if geographical and quantitative criteria are met.[185] The scope of the potential effect of the decision is therefore of importance (for example, if changes are proposed across the multinational) as well as the type of decision if it involves activities between Member States (for example, the closure of a factory in one country and the opening of another entity in another Member State). This definition is enriched by a number of recitals in the Preamble that suggest that the transnational nature of the dialogue is also engaged when the decision is taken outside the country where the employee is located (Recital 12) and the level of management responsible for making the decision (Recital 16). Most Member States have copied the definition found in the directive without the subtleties of the Preambles,[186] which suggests that deciding what is transnational should not necessarily be a mechanical decision.

This definition does not seem to have necessarily alleviated difficulties, but some good practice has been developed in stating in agreement what transnational means, even if it goes beyond the directive's definition.[187]

The Recast Directive also re-emphasised that the nature of the information and consultation is transnational. For example, when negotiating the content of the agreements, the parties are asked to consider, in particular, information in relation to transnational questions.[188]

(b) Relationship between European Works Council and Local Information and Consultation Mechanisms

One of the difficulties that had occurred when implementing the European Works Council Directive of 1994 was the absence of regulation over the relationship between the European works council and the national works councils or equivalent body when a transnational issue had a national impact. Two issues need to be examined as mentioned above.

First, the question arises as to whether both bodies are competent or does the competence of one body prevails over the other one. In other words, is the national works council tied to the opinion the European works council has expressed to the central management on the subject that affects the competence of the national works council on the issue at stake?[189]

---

184 Directive 2009/38/EC, Article 1(4).

185 Ales et al. (2018), p. 1610.

186 Laulom & Dorssemont (2015), pp. 56–59.

187 European Commission, COM(2018)292.

188 Directive 2009/38/EC, Article 6(3).

189 A striking example is restructuring of the transnational company by which plants in different Member States are affected. The *Renault* case of 1997 is such an example; see Section 7.2.4.2(b); see also Dorssemont & Jaspers (1999); Dorssemont (2006b), pp. 8–9.

Second, the question of which body is consulted first when a measure of the transnational company has a cross-border and a national impact for workers is also essential. In the European Works Council Directive of 1994 the issue was not regulated – the need to do so was simply not felt.

The principle of the two-level system (national and international) was made clearer by the legislator in 2009:

> Workers and their representatives must be guaranteed information and consultation at the relevant level of management and representation, according to the subject under discussion. To achieve this, the competence and scope of action of a European Works Council must be distinct from that of national representative bodies and must be limited to transnational matters.[190]

For the principle to be enshrined, the directive leaves it to negotiating parties to include a clause in their agreement on how the European works council will liaise with the national structure.[191] In the absence of such a clause, national law must provide that the information and consultation should take place both at the national and transnational level.[192]

As for the timing, the directive itself is silent but as an indication of how to regulate it, the preamble suggests the linking of information within each undertaking or group of undertakings must be regulated in a way the parties agree, in accordance with the contractual nature of the involvement of workers and their representatives. However, if there are no agreements on this subject and where decisions likely to lead to substantial changes in work organisation or contractual relations are envisaged, the process must be conducted at both national and European level in such a way that it respects the competences and areas of action of the employee representation bodies. A hierarchy is not proposed, either as to the timing or as to the substance. It is up to the parties to the European work council agreements or, if they fail to do, the Member States to regulate this. But, it has to be ensured – if national regulation is needed because agreements lack suitable provisions are lacking – that the European works council can, where applicable, receive information earlier or at the same time as the national employee representation bodies. The Directive cannot be used to reduce the general level of protection for employees.[193]

The legal solution has, however, not alleviated practical questions of timing and substance unless either in the national law implementing the directive

190 Directive 2009/38, Preamble (15).

191 Directive 2009/38, Articles 6(2)(c) and 12(2) and Preamble (21).

192 Directive 2009/38, Article 12(3).

193 Directive 2009/38, Preamble (37).

or in the European works council agreements a chronological order has been established.[194] Looking at the variety of national regulations in Member States, some patterns can be identified:[195]

- information and consultation are linked at both levels, without any indication about how or when (France);
- information and consultation linked at both levels, within a reasonable time (UK) or in a coordinated way (Italy); the indication about how and when the processes should be linked is imprecise;
- the process should be simultaneous (Belgium) or 'as far as possible' simultaneous (the Netherlands);
- if not before, then simultaneously (suggesting that, ideally, one should happen before the other) (Germany).

A further recent analysis of the Member States' implementation in law suggests that the regimes are varied. When considering what body has priority, legislation in some Member States is silent on the issue, in States simultaneous participation is recommended and in others the European works council is put first.[196]

In national case law the question of timing has been addressed in different ways and differs from country to country.[197] A common approach is that in situations where a decision in headquarters of the multinational is likely to affect the whole workforce, the European works council has to be *informed* first, but this does not mean that the information to the local works councils is suspended – it is for the sake of the effectiveness of the involvement of workers in these business matters with a cross-border effect.[198] The line of the case law in different Member States can even vary as the case of *Renault* shows. The Belgian courts took the stand that the local management had to start the information and consultation procedures immediately whereas the French judges decided to inform the European works council first and to suspend the local procedures until the opinion of the European works council had been issued.[199] As to the *consultation*, the approach is a little different. Priority for the European works council in such cases is never recognised in the case law of Member States. There might be good reasons: a willingness to ensure effectiveness of the involvement

194 The study by Laulom & Dorssemont (2015), p. 56 ff. has shown that the question has not been solved in the national legislation.

195 Dorssemont & Kerckhofs (2015), pp. 11–13. The study has been focused on Member States where the most headquarters are located.

196 European Commission, COM(2018)292, SWD(2018)187 final, p. 29.

197 Cf. Laulom & Dorssemont (2015), p. 56 ff.

198 Tribunal de Grande Instance de Nanterre, 1 August 2003 (*Alstöm*); Cour de Cassation 16 January 2008 (*GDF-Suez*).

199 It has to be kept in mind that in Belgium the focus was on collective redundancies in a Belgian plant (Vilvoorde), whereas in France the restructuring as such was at stake.

procedures on all levels by involving the European works council from the start, but that does not imply that local information and consultation has to be suspended in favour of the outcome of the procedure at transnational level.[200]

Questions about the type of information to be supplied and the content of the consultation may have different answers, depending on whether the process takes place in the European works council or in the national works council. It is still not clear what type of information should be disclosed to the European works council and what to the national works council, and whether that can or may differ.[201] The relevant criteria should be what constitutes effective information and consultation for the relevant level. What seems clear – for the moment – is that in some cases the local works council(s) can be and has been bound by the opinion of the higher level works council as to issues with cross-border or transnational impact.[202]

Some of these issues can be circumvented by the newer obligations imposed on European works council representatives to report back to their national counterparts. Article 10(2) European Works Council Directive states that members of the European works council have to inform the workers' representatives in the multinational companies and its plants on the content and outcome of the information and consultation procedure, although without defining a time order.[203] The Directive therefore suggests a chronology whereby the European works council is first informed and consulted. The relevant information on the outcome of the process is subsequently trickled down to the local structures for more detailed and local discussions on the national or undertaking implementation.

A solution to the problem of chronology and substance between the levels could be based on article 12(3) European Works Council Directive: in essence, the European works council agreement or best practice could be that the European works council has to trickle down the relevant information on the outcome of the information and consultation process at its level to the local levels for more detailed discussions on the implementation of the measures envisaged and affecting the employees of local plants.[204]

The lack of clarity between the provisions in the directive, the choice left to Member States and the variety of regimes applied shows that whilst the issue of interplay was acknowledged in the Recast Directive, it has not been fully addressed.

---

200 See Tribunal de Grande Instance de Nanterre, 1 August 2003 (*Alstöm*); Cour de Cassation 16 January 2008 (*GDF-Suez*).

201 European Commission, COM(2018)292, SWD(2018)187 final, pp. 24–25.

202 See Dorssemont (2010a), p. 264 ff; and Laulom & Dorssemont (2015), p. 59 ff.

203 Many Member States have not implemented this article in their national laws, Laulom & Dorssemont (2015), p. 63.

204 Also the other way round: from 'the bottom to the top'.

7.3.1.7. Subsidiary Requirements

The subsidiary requirements found in the Annex to the directive have had a double role. They are engaged when management has not responded to employees' request to start negotiations, when negotiations have failed and when the Special Negotiating Body and management have decided to apply this model by a qualified majority (two-third). They constitute the fall-back position and dictate to the undertaking how the European works council will be populated and how it will operate. As such, their second role has been to act as benchmark for negotiations, as parties understand that if they cannot reach agreement, this is the system they would need to operate with. This gives power to employee representatives who would not wish to go below a certain level (in terms of type of information to be disclosed for example) and leverage to employers who do not wish to go beyond the directive's requirements (for example co-determination on some topics).

The subsidiary requirements are divided into sections that consider composition and function of the European works council. In terms of function, the Annex dictates the content of the information and consultation. A list of topics that relate to the financial, economic and social health of the undertaking must be provided by the central management to disclose to the European works council: the structure, economic and financial situation, probable development and production and sales of the Community-scale undertaking or group of undertakings. In addition, information and consultation should take place on another set of topics: situation and probable trend of employment, investments, and substantial changes concerning organisation, introduction of new working methods or production processes, transfers of production, mergers, cut-backs or closures of undertakings, establishments or important parts thereof, and collective redundancies.[205]

While the form of the information is not specified, the process of consultation is defined as entailing written responses from management following opinions expressed by workers' representatives. Additionally, the subsidiary requirements foresee a specific process in cases of crisis, i.e. where special circumstances affect the workforce significantly or restructuring is envisaged. In this case, the select committee, which is a compulsory element of the worker participation machinery under the subsidiary requirement, is consulted, together with representatives of the affected workforce. This permits a swift response in exceptional circumstances.

In relation to composition of the European works council, the members are selected according to national legislation for the country they represent, proportionally according to the workforce found in each country (with the same formula found in Article 6).

---

[205] Annex, para 1(a).

The European works council is additionally given the means to operate by obtaining the relevant resources from management, both financially and materially. This includes the payment of experts if they are required to assist with analysis of information and input for consultation. As for the Special Negotiating Body, national legislation may limit the expenses to be paid to one expert.

7.3.1.8. Enforcement

As mentioned in Section 7.2.5, procedures to enforce the rights and obligations found in information and consultation directives as well as accompanying sanctions are usually left to the Member States. The European Works Council Directive is no exception, in relation to processes.[206] The Recast Directive however added requirements to ensure that the transnational right of information and consultation was effective (in compliance with the objectives stated in Article 1). It has been established by research, in particular when considering the case law on the European works council at national level, that there was legal uncertainty about the possibility for European works councils, as bodies, to challenge managerial decisions under the European Works Council Directive before a court or adjudicating body.[207] Their legal status and financial means were not addressed either in the directive and seldom in national laws. The Recast Directive therefore addressed this issue by stating in Article 10(1) that:

> Without prejudice to the competence of other bodies or organisations in this respect, the members of the European Works Council shall have the means required to apply the rights arising from this Directive, to represent collectively the interests of the employees of the Community-scale undertaking or Community-scale group of undertakings.

Questions still remain, however, on how this provision can be applied in practice, in particular as Member States have either simply copied and pasted this article without additional explanations or did not transpose this part of the directive.[208] In this regard, the European Commission in its 2018 Report still acknowledges 'weaknesses in the means in place allowing European Works Councils to enforce their rights'.[209]

In relation to sanctions, the Recast Directive added in its Preamble (Recital 37) that sanctions are determined at national level, but that, in conformity with well-established case law, they must be effective, proportionate and dissuasive. Research has shown that a variety of sanctions exist where European Works

206 Directive 2009/38, Article 11.
207 See e.g. Lorber (2010), p. 216
208 Jagodzinski & Lorber (2015).
209 European Commission, COM(2018)292, pp. 6–7.

Council agreements are not complied with.[210] The breach of national legislation is classified as either administrative, civil or even criminal law depending on the Member States' sanctioning approach to which the directive itself refers to. Different sanctions may therefore be applied (orders or imprisonment), but a fine or financial penalty is a usual remedy across all Member States. The level of fine paid is, however, greatly different from country to country. Quite a number of Member States do not have a minimum fine. If they do, they range from less than €10 (Poland) to €2,000 (Slovenia).[211] A maximum fine is very common, ranging from almost €1,000 (Romania), €110,000 (UK), and even more (for example €187,000, Spain). By conclusion, a lack of effective sanctions may potentially undermine the effectiveness of the right of information and consultation as different laws punish the breach of the same transnational right in various ways. Suspension or putting on hold the decision by the management – for instance continuing a restructuring without proper information of consultation of the European works council – can be considered as a more effective remedy. As mentioned above (Section 7.2.5) this option is provided in only very few Member States.[212] In the literature the lack of effective sanctions is often criticised, but without any result.[213] In its 2018 assessment, the Commission acknowledges shortcomings in relation to sanctions, but does not offer strong remedies.[214] It does state that it will encourage cooperation between Member States to determine what constitute 'effective, proportionate and dissuasive sanctions'.[215]

7.3.2. THE EUROPEAN COMPANY (SOCIETAS EUROPAEA – SE) AND WORKER PARTICIPATION

7.3.2.1. Introduction

Since early in the history of the European Community, there has been a drive to allow companies to operate across borders in a more fluid and regulation-free way.

210 Jagodzinski & Lorber (2015), pp. 150 ff.

211 See Jagodzinski (2014), figures 1 and 2, p. 3. Also Jagodzinski (2015), pp. 169–71, table 20.

212 France and Belgium, see Section 7.2.5. The example of the Netherlands is interesting. In the national situation, this sanction can be imposed on companies in this kind of cases, whereas the law on European works councils has deliberately not inserted this sanction.

213 Cf. Kilpatrick (2000); Malmberg (2003) and Bercusson (2009).

214 European Commission, *Evaluation study on the implementation of Directive 2009/38/EC on the establishment of the European Works Council, Final report*, 2016. Discussions in the past, also in the European Parliament, show the great differences between Member States but they also reveal the strong opposition of the employers' associations.

215 European Commission, *Evaluation study on the implementation of Directive 2009/38/EC on the establishment of a European Works Council. Final report*, 2016, in particular p. 49; and European Commission COM(2018)292 final.

The idea of a common market where free movement of capital, services and people operate should be accompanied by the opportunity for companies to be created under EU law, without having to register in one country or dissolve in another to continue producing goods or providing services. Such economic idea was coupled with the social aim of the European Union. Any new EU company (*Societas Europaea*, European Company) regulated by EU law should promote and apply worker participation. This facet of a socially aware and democratic undertaking constituted a stumbling block for many years. While there was a large consensus for the creation of a European Company Statute that would regulate the operation of newly created transborder companies, the variety of national regimes on worker participation prevented Member States from reaching an agreement on this topic. Worker participation was understood as appointing workers' representatives on board of companies. On one end of the spectrum, some Member States had elaborate systems of industrial democracy, where up to half of supervisory boards were assigned to employees representatives (in Germany for example). At the other end of the spectrum, representation of workers on company boards was non-existent (in the UK or Ireland for example). As a result, opposition to a European system of worker involvement was either prompted by a fear of dilution of national systems or of imposition of a new model, totally alien to national industrial relations and company law.

After a number of attempts in the 1970s and 1980s, the deadlock was resolved at the start of the millennium following the Davignon group of experts' report. Its recommendations focused on flexibility of worker involvement, with the proviso that existing system of worker participation should not be jeopardised by the transformation into a European Company. The adoption of the European Works Councils Directive in 1994 had provided a model to build upon: giving stakeholders the power to negotiate worker involvement with a set of fall back rules if an agreement was not reached.

The Statute of a European Company was therefore adopted in 2001[216] and accompanied by a specific directive supplementing the regulation with regard to employee involvement.[217] The latter re-emphasises the need to have a social facet to the new European company in the form of worker involvement: 'In order to promote the social objectives of the Community, special provisions have to be set, notably in the field of employee involvement'.[218] The directive was also clear that the new EU law should not be a means to avoid national systems of worker participation. Article 11 states to that effect: 'Member States shall take appropriate measures in conformity with Community Law with a view to preventing the misuse of an SE for the purpose of depriving employees of

216 Regulation 2157/2001.
217 Directive 2001/86.
218 Recital (3).

rights to employee involvement or withholding such rights.' The preservation of existing models is equally paramount and the principle is coined in the Preamble of the directive as the 'before and after' principle. Recital 18 states:

> It is a fundamental principle and stated aim of this Directive to secure employees' acquired rights as regards involvement in company decisions Employee rights in force before the establishment of SEs should provide the basis for employee rights of involvement in the SE (the 'before and after' principle). Consequently, that approach should apply not only to the initial establishment of an SE but also to structural changes in an existing SE and to the companies affected by structural change processes.[219]

Those aims are also found in the text of the directive as explained below.

The operation of worker involvement in the European Company are complex, as they vary depending on how the European Company is established. The 2001 Regulation envisages four scenarios: creation from existing companies by merger, transformation, formation of a subsidiary or of a holding company.[220] The main premise is that the management of the European Company must negotiate with a Special Negotiating Body how worker involvement will operate and a fall-back position will apply if negotiations fail, as is the case in the European Works Council Directive. One significant difference with the European works council is the lack of an optional trigger mechanism for the negotiation on worker involvement. While in the European Works Council Directive, the management or employees (or their representatives) have to act to engage the negotiations, permitting the transnational obligation to inform and consult to be optional, the employees' involvement Directive requires management to start negotiations as soon as the European Company is formed.[221]

Worker involvement is defined as 'any mechanism, including information, consultation and participation, through which employees' representatives may exercise an influence on decisions to be taken within the company'.[222] Participation is understood as worker representation on boards of companies and one of the essential requirements is that it must continue if it was already present in the previous companies. The Directive supplementing the Statute for a European Company with regard to the involvement of employees goes therefore further than the European Works Council Directive, as it adds another layer to the dialogue on decisions that affect the workforce: it requires the establishment of an information and consultation body and allows workers to be at the heart of the decision making process by being on the board of companies.

The next section will examine how worker involvement can be negotiated and what the standard rules require, in particular by comparison with the European

[219] Directive 2001/86/EC, Preamble (18).
[220] Regulation 2157/2001, Article 2.
[221] Directive 2001/86, Article 3(1).
[222] Directive 2001/86, Article 2(h).

Works Council Directive. The last section gives some contextual analysis of the implementation of the directive in Member States and the difficulties encountered by stakeholders and policy makers.

7.3.2.2. *Information, Consultation and Participation in the European Company*

(a) Definitions

In terms of definition, the content and processes are found in Article 2 of the directive. They were more substantial than what had been found in the original 1994 European Works Council Directive, but the Recast Directive of 2009 copied and pasted some of the definitional elements of the 2001 European Company Directive for clarity and coherence.

Information must relate to issues relating to the European Company or more than one of its subsidiaries or establishments in different Member States. It must be disclosed in a timely manner to allow for 'an in depth assessment of the impact' and to prepare for consultation.[223] Consultation resembles the European Works Council Directive definition of exchange of dialogue, but requires that the information and consultation body has time to express an opinion which may influence decision making.[224] Finally, participation means 'the influence of the body representatives of the employees … in the affairs of a company by way of a right to elect or appoint some of the members of the supervisory or administrative organ' or the right to recommend or oppose such appointments.[225]

(b) The Special Negotiating Body (SNB)

The Special Negotiating Body effectively operates and is populated mainly according to the same rules found in the European Works Council Directive. The composition must reflect the location of the establishments making up the European Company, in proportion to the number of employees found in each Member States (one member per 10%), with some exception for more members if the European Company is created by merger.[226] Selection of members is left to national law, but trade unions are explicitly mentioned as potential members of the Special Negotiating Body and not only in an expert capacity.[227] The provision is a positive feature, given the expertise of such representatives. Its main role is to negotiate an agreement for worker involvement. The timeline

223 Directive 2001/86, Article 2(i).
224 Directive 2001/86, Article 2(j).
225 Directive 2001/86, Article 2(k).
226 Directive 2001/86, Article 3(2)(a).
227 Directive 2001/86, Article 3(2)(b).

for negotiations is six months, which can be extended to 12.[228] The outcome of negotiations between the Special Negotiating Body and management can be threefold: first, an agreement is reached and the content of such agreement is discussed in the next subsection; second, negotiations fail and standard rules apply (considered below); finally, the Special Negotiating Body may decide by a qualified majority that negotiations should not start or be ended and national rules on information and consultation will therefore apply, notably on European works councils. This latter option is prohibited where the European Company is created by transformation and worker participation was in place, applying the principle that the European rules cannot be used to undermine existing worker participation systems.[229]

(c) Agreement on Worker Involvement

As with the European Works Council Directive, the emphasis on negotiations and flexibility given to the stakeholders means that the content of the agreement is lightly regulated. The directive simply lists the items that must be found in the agreement, but leaves the details to Special Negotiating Body and central management. The negotiations should cover the scope of the agreement, the composition of the representative body, its function in terms of information and consultation, the frequency of meetings, the resources allocated and the duration of the agreement as well as the procedure for renegotiations.[230] The difference with the European Works Council Directive is the possibility to negotiate on the presence of workers' representatives on the board of the company. The agreement should cater for the number of members, their selection and rights.

(d) Standard Rules

The standard rules stipulate the composition of the representative body (which would be the equivalent of a European works council), its function and operation, but also add rules on participation of workers representatives. In relation to composition, the rules ensure proportionality of representation to reflect number of employees and location. As with the European Works Council Directive, a select committee should be formed from the membership of the representative body. The function of the transnational body is to be informed and consulted on the situation of the company and its plans, at least once a year. There is also the obligation to call a meeting in case of exceptional circumstances. While this is in line with what happens under the European Works Council Directive, the European Company standard rules allow the representatives to

228 Directive 2001/86, Article 5.
229 Directive 2001/86, Article 3(6).
230 Directive 2001/86, Article 4(2).

ask for additional meetings if their opinions are not taken into consideration,[231] giving the consultation process a more substantial meaning. The participation standard rules apply the 'before and after' principles. Employee representatives must be appointed to the board of the company by members of the representative body (reflecting location and employee numbers in each country where the European Company operates). The number of employee representatives will be the same as the number appointed in the country where there is the highest number (for example, if there is a German subsidiary, it may be half of the supervisory board). There is a different regime for European Companies formed by transformation: the participation system that was in place before the European Company should apply to the European Company as in this case the company simply 'transforms' itself into a European Company without new additions of other companies.[232]

7.3.2.3. Implementation and Impact

All EU Member States have transposed the directive.[233] As of March 2018, there were 3,000 established European Companies.[234] This represents a significant increase in number since the six established in 2004, the deadline for the implementation of the directive in national law. This number is, however, misleading as the great majority of the European Companies (2,057) are described as 'UFO' European Companies by the SE Europe Network (Unidentified Flying Objects) because information on these European Companies is lacking.[235] The European Companies are otherwise categorised as 'Normal European Companies', i.e. European Companies with operations and employees, of which it is estimated that there are about 534 at the time of writing.[236] The final category is 'micro/empty European Company' which has no or very few employees (less than five). This category represents 409 European Companies. The overall majority of European Companies are found in the Czech Republic (principally UFO and micro/empty European Companies), but some are also found in Germany. Most of the normal European companies are formed by subsidiary (41%) and conversion or transformation (35%).[237] While one of the

---

231 Directive 2001/86, Annex part 2(c).

232 Directive 2001/86, Article 4(4).

233 Valdes Dal-Re (2006).

234 ETUI, *Societas Europaea: Facts and Figures*, March 2018 <http://www.worker-participation.eu/About-WP/What-s-new/Societas-Europaea-latest-developments-update-by-Anders-Carlson-Workers-Participation-Europe-Network> accessed 02.06.2019.

235 Stollt & Wolters (2011). See ETUI, *Societas Europaea*, Facts and Figures March 2018, p. 20, where the 'UFO' European Company is defined as a European Company 'on which insufficient information is available for categorisation (the number of employees) .... This group also contains so-called shelf SEs which were set up without any operations or employees'.

236 ETUI, *SEs Facts and Figures*, March 2018.

237 Ibid.

aims of the directive was to promote worker involvement, research suggests that this is limited (only present in 144 of European Companies out of the overall total of 3,000),[238] even in the 'normal European Companies' where only 74 European Companies have negotiated board level representation.[239] These participation mechanisms are primarily prevalent in European Companies registered in Germany.[240] However, while those European Companies will have had prior experience of board level participation, empirical research establishes that 'board-level employee representation in European Companies should be regarded as specific, as it is not a mere international extension of the German codetermination, but is rather at the "intersection of country-specific and transnational influences"'.[241] The same study reveals that the boards are active, meeting four times a year, and that employee representatives feel that they have say in the decision-making process.[242]

238 Ibid.
239 ETUI, *Benchmarking Working Europe 2018*, p. 79.
240 ETUI, *SEs Facts and Figures*, March 2018.
241 Waddington & Conchon (2017), p. 49.
242 Waddington & Conchon (2017), pp. 47–48.

CHAPTER 8

OCCUPATIONAL HEALTH AND SAFETY AND WORKING TIME

Edoardo Ales and Jan Popma

8.1. INTRODUCTION

The right to life and the right to human dignity are two of the most fundamental human rights.[1] These rights also apply to workers while at work:[2] every worker has a 'right to working conditions which respect his or her health, safety and dignity'.[3] However, these rights in themselves do not automatically guarantee

1 Articles 1 and 3 Universal Declaration of Human Rights; Articles 1 and 2(1) EU Charter of Fundamental Rights.

2 Articles 23 and 24 Universal Declaration of Human Rights; Article 7 ICESCR, Article 3 Part I ESC.

3 Article 31 EU Charter of Fundamental Rights. The ESC (1961) also states that workers have a right to safe and healthy working conditions (Part I, Article 3) and a right to just conditions of work (including reasonable daily and weekly working hours – Part II, Article 2(1)). See also Popma (2008).

safety and health at work. Every year, hundreds of thousands of workers die as a result of occupational accidents or occupational diseases. According to the World Health Organisation, world-wide over 350,000 workers die during occupational accidents, whereas the number of workers dying prematurely due to occupational diseases is estimated to be over two million, of whom 900,000 die as a result of exposure to dangerous substances.[4]

This premature death as a result of unsafe or unhealthy work does not limit itself to the sweatshops in Asia or 'third world' countries. European workers too fall prey to the dangers at work. Some 167,000 European workers annually die prematurely as a result of poor working conditions.[5] Next to premature death, the loss of quality of life due to (sometimes very lengthy periods of) occupational diseases also has to be taken into account. It is estimated that one out of 12 workers within the Member States of the European Union (EU-28) is experiencing work related health problems.[6] Nearly one out of four workers fear that their health is at risk due to their working conditions.[7]

So, the mere fact that fundamental rights are part of declarations or charters in itself does not guarantee adequate protection of health and safety. The more so, as these fundamental rights are not always directly enforceable in an individual employment relation – let alone in contractual relations between companies and self-employed workers. Still, the aforementioned fundamental rights are not without meaning in the context of individual employment relations, as they may be useful for the interpretation of private labour law in the national as well as international context.

Moreover, EU Member States, being signatories of various charters, are obliged to take fundamental rights into account when devising national law or, in the case of the EU Charter of Fundamental Rights, when they implement EU law.[8] They are also instructed to ensure that the various obligations are upheld in practice or, in the wording of the European Social Charter 'to (ensure) the effective exercise' of the fundamental rights. Article 3(2) of Part II of the European Social Charter, for example, places an obligation upon its signatories to issue health and safety regulations, whereas Article 3(3) instructs them to 'provide for the enforcement of such regulations by measures of supervision'. Article A(4) of Part III ESC obliges the signatories to 'maintain a system of labour inspection'.

---

4 Nemonen et al. (2014), p. 17.

5 Takala et al. (2009), p. 17; Jongeneel et al. (2016).

6 Eurostat (2010), p. 41 ff. Also, it is estimated that over 350 million working days are lost as a result of poor working conditions (ibid., p. 53).

7 Eurofound (2015), p. 6.

8 Next to the aforementioned charters, the Member States have to implement the various Conventions of the International Labour Organisation – provided that they have ratified the Conventions.

Even though the European Union is not (yet)[9] a signatory of the European Social Charter or other international charters, the Court of Justice has held in its consistent case law that fundamental rights in such charters are general principles of the Community legal order, and as such they are an integral part of the general legal principles that the Union as well as its Member States have to respect.[10] Moreover, the EU Charter of Fundamental Rights is relevant for all Member States when implementing Union law (Article 51 EU Charter) including – most importantly in the context of this chapter – European directives.

This chapter will deal with the central pieces of European legislation in the field of health and safety: Council Directive 89/391/EEC on the introduction of measures to encourage improvements in the safety and health of workers at work (also called the Framework Directive) and Directive 2003/88/EC (Working Time Directive).

This chapter will give an overview of the general principles of the Framework Directive (Section 8.3), as well as of some of the main 'daughter' directives issued on the basis of Article 16 Framework Directive (Section 8.4). This section will also touch upon the instrument of Framework Agreements, that have been concluded by the social partners on the basis of Article 155 TFEU. In Section 8.5, the European legislation regarding working time will be introduced. Both bodies of legislation are to be enforced by the Labour Inspectorate, even if civil procedures may play a part. Enforcement is the subject of Section 8.6. But before a more detailed picture of the legislation is painted, Section 8.2 will describe the historical background of the legislation.

8.2. OCCUPATIONAL HEALTH AND SAFETY IN THE TREATIES AND EU CHARTER OF FUNDAMENTAL RIGHTS

Occupational health and safety (hereinafter Occupational Health and Safety) can be seen as the oldest social commitment of the Community Institutions,[11] as confirmed by the establishment of the Mines Safety Commission in September 1956,[12] already under the aegis of the European Coal and Steel Community (ECSC).

---

9 See Article 6(2) TEU.

10 Ferraro & Carmona (2015).

11 See, on EU occupational health and safety law, Ales (2017); Bercusson (1995); Neal (1990) and (1998); Valdés de la Vega (2013); Weiss (2010); and Wright (1992).

12 The Mines Safety Commission has been merged into the Advisory Committee on Safety and Health at Work in 2003 (Council Decision 2003), which, at its turn has substituted the Advisory Committee on Safety, Hygiene and Health Protection at work established in 1974 (Council Decision 1974).

Notwithstanding the lack of regulatory competences, in the early 1970s Member States and Community Institutions decided to become active in the social domain. In hindsight, the year 1974 appears to have been one of the most significant turning points in the history of the social commitment of the EEC. The Social Action Programme, adopted in that year, indicated various objectives to be achieved in order to increase that commitment.[13] Among these objectives, the promotion of employment, improved living and working conditions, so as to make possible their harmonisation while the improvement is being maintained, which was and is still one of the main drives of Community/Union action according to Article 117 TEC (now Article 151 TFEU), is most crucial.

The Action Programme on Safety and Health at Work 1978,[14] was based on the Social Action Programme and mentioned actions including: (a) research on accident and disease aetiology connected with work; (b) protection against dangerous substances; (c) prevention of the dangers and harmful effects of machines; and (d) monitoring and inspection – improvement of human attitudes.

The main product of the 1978 Occupational Health and Safety Action Programme was the adoption of Directive 80/1107/EEC on the protection of workers from the risks related to exposure to chemical, physical and biological agents at work. From a legal point of view, it is interesting that, in order to overcome the lack of a specific Treaty provision allowing the Council to act, it was decided to go back to Article 100 TEC (now Article 115 TFEU), which provides that the Council shall issue directives for the approximation of such laws, regulations or administrative provisions of the Member States as directly affect the establishment or functioning of the common market. This gives the powers to harmonise national legislations if their differences are likely to hamper the functioning of the common market.[15] Consequently, occupational health and safety has been at the very centre stage of the turning point in the history of the social commitment of the EEC.

This also appeared from Article 118a(1) TEC, introduced by the Single European Act (1986),[16] which provides that Member States shall pay particular attention to encouraging improvements, especially in the working environment, as regards occupational health and safety and shall set as their objective the harmonisation of conditions in this field, while improvement is being maintained. In order to help to achieve that objective, the Council, acting by a qualified majority, shall adopt, by means of directives, minimum

---

13 Council Resolution 1974 (Social Action Programme 1974).

14 Council Resolution 1978 (Action Programme on Safety and Health at Work 1978).

15 See also Section 1.4.3.2.

16 On the Single European Act, the first aborted attempt to create something very close to a political union, see Bermann (1989); Fuchs (2004a); Lodge (1986); Majone (1993).

requirements to be gradually implemented, having regard to the conditions and technical rules present in each Member State. Such directives shall avoid imposing administrative, financial and legal constraints in a way that would hamper the creation and development of small and medium-sized undertakings (Article 118a(2)). And Article 118a(3) reads that the provisions adopted pursuant to Article 118a shall not prevent Member States from maintaining or introducing more stringent measures for the protection of working conditions whether compatible with the Treaty. (Article 118a TEC is now Article 153 TFEU.)

Since it is relevant to the worker as a human being, occupational health and safety is not only one of the most important issues of labour law,[17] but also one of the most comprehensively regulated areas of EU Law.[18] This statement is not contradicted by the fact that Community institutions have recently focused more strongly on political strategies than on new legislative instruments;[19] that these strategies are less precise than before;[20] and that occupational health and safety, too, has become the domain of a non-regulatory agency.[21] On the contrary, the centrality of occupational health and safety is now confirmed by Article 31 EU Charter of Fundamental Rights,[22] which, under the headline of 'Fair and just working conditions', focuses on health, safety and dignity at work, on the one hand, and to working time, rests and paid holiday, on the other.

8.3. THE FRAMEWORK DIRECTIVE

Directive 89/391/EEC (the Framework Directive) is the major instrument of EU occupational health and safety law. It has had a large impact on the occupational health and safety law of the Member States.[23] The Framework Directive provides a comprehensive regulation of the subject matter, although leaving to the Member States the task to identify the nature of the employer's liability and to define sanctions to be applied in the case of violation of the rules.[24]

---

17 See Ales (2013), p. 411.

18 See Valdés de la Vega (2013), p. 1.

19 Smismans (2003).

20 Compare, for instance, European Commission, COM(2002)118 final and COM(2007)62 final with COM(2014)332 final.

21 Chiti (2013).

22 On which, extensively, Bogg (2014).

23 For an overview, see Ales (2013); Biagi (2003); and Howes (2003).

24 On the importance of deterrence and sanction in occupational health and safety, see Purse & Dorrian (2011).

8.3.1. OBJECTIVES AND INSTRUMENTS

The objective of the directive is 'to introduce measures to encourage improvements in the safety and health of workers at work'. It sets general principles concerning the prevention of occupational risks, the protection of occupational health and safety, the elimination of risks and accident factors, the information, consultation and balanced participation in matters relating to health and safety[25] (in accordance with national laws and/or practices) and training on occupational health and safety of workers and their representatives. It also provides general guidelines for the implementation of these principles.[26]

Both the objective (measures to encourage improvements) and the way in which it will be pursued (general principles) do not mirror the real aim and the very content of the directive, which is laid down in its Preamble, i.e. setting minimum requirements in the field of occupational health and safety. The directive is not (only) an instrument for encouraging improvement and a generic instrument, but it is a quite precise legislative tool, setting duties for employers, employees and their representatives.

Consequently, the Framework Directive gives a good description of the instruments through which employers, above all, have to guarantee occupational health and safety:[27]

- the prevention of risks and accident factors, as well as their elimination and the protection of workers' occupational health and safety if prevention and elimination of risks and accident factors is not reasonably possible;
- consultation and balanced participation, in accordance with national laws and/or practices of workers and their representatives;
- information and training of workers and their representatives in the field of occupational health and safety.

The directive defines 'prevention' as 'all the steps or measures taken or planned at all stages of work in the undertaking to prevent or reduce occupational risks'.[28] In this way, it refers to both prevention and reduction of risks.

The directive does not define the word 'information'. However, it regulates, in a detailed way, the reciprocal information duties and rights of employers and employees.[29] A distinction has to be made between information on occupational health and safety prevention and protection measures on the one side and on

[25] ECJ 2003, C-441/01 (*Commission v. Netherlands*), confirmed by ECJ 2006, C-428/04 (*Commission v. Austria*), §49 ff.
[26] Article 1.
[27] Article 1.
[28] Article 3(d).
[29] Articles 6(1), 7(4), 10, 11(2)(c), 12(1) and 13(2)(d).

the organisation and management of the occupational health and safety system in the undertaking on the other. Both have to be provided by the employer to workers and their representatives for their protection and/or the consultation rights.

The word 'consultation' is not defined in the directive either. However, it mentions the duty of the employer to 'consult workers and/or their representatives and allow them to take part in discussions'[30] on all questions relating to occupational health and safety. This presupposes the consultation of workers, the right of workers and/or their representatives to make proposals and the 'balanced participation' 'in accordance with national laws and/or practices'. 'Balanced participation', not defined by the directive, seems to refer to the participation of workers and/or their representatives in discussions on health and safety, as it is not logical that it refers to their consultation.

No definition is found of the term 'training' in the directive either. It is an elaboration of the duty of the employer to ensure that each worker receives adequate occupational health and safety training (Article 12), in particular in the form of information (Article 6(1)) and instructions specific to that person's workstation or job. This must happen on recruitment; in the event of a transfer or a change of job; in the case of the introduction of new work equipment or change of equipment; and in case of the introduction of any new technology.

The provisions of the Framework Directive are without prejudice to existing or future national and EU Law provisions that are more favourable in the field of occupational health and safety, as is provided by Article 1(3). This statement, on the one hand, directly recalls Article 118a(3) TEC (now Article 153(4) TFEU), according to which EU measures 'shall not prevent any Member State from maintaining or introducing more stringent protective measures compatible with the Treaties';[31] on the other hand, it refers to EU Law instruments already existing at the time of the adoption of the directive, such as Directive 80/1107/EC. On top of that, as a framework instrument, the directive shall be without prejudice to future EU Law provisions including those adopted according to Article 16 of the directive, the so-called individual or 'daughter directives'[32] or to Article 15, which aims to protect particularly vulnerable risk groups. (See Section 8.3.8)

---

30 Article 11.

31 As confirmed, in the field of occupational health and safety, by ECJ 1998, C-2/97 (*Borsana*). On the contrary, directives adopted on the basis of Article 100a TEC, such as Directive 89/686/EEC, aiming to attain the objective of ensuring the free movement of personal protection equipment between the Member States, preclude them from prohibiting, restraining or interfering with the putting on the market of such equipment, which satisfies its provisions and which bears the EC marking, by evoking the more stringent protection argument: ECJ 2003, C-103/01 (*Commission v. Germany*).

32 ECJ 2003, C-65/01 (*Commission v. Italy*), §48: 'The Italian Government cannot justify the infringement with which it is charged by invoking the argument that it has put into operation

8.3.2. SCOPE AND DEFINITIONS

The Framework Directive is very wide in scope, since it covers all sectors of activity and all employees, both public and private, except certain specific public service activities, such as the armed forces, the police, or certain specific activities in the civil protection services.[33] However, in those domains, too, occupational health and safety must be ensured as far as possible, in the light of the objectives of the directive (Article 2).

It has to be emphasised that, notwithstanding Article 153(2)(b) TFEU, according to which 'directives shall avoid imposing administrative, financial and legal constraints in a way which would hold back the creation and development of small and medium-sized undertakings', that the directive applies to all undertakings whatever their size. It thus imposes the same occupational health and safety costs for micro-, small-, medium-sized or big companies.

The Framework Directive clarifies the meaning of some important terms or expressions. First, it defines the term 'worker' as any person employed by an employer, therefore any employee, plus trainees and apprentices. Since no case law of the Court of Justice has developed with reference to this directive, one may wonder whether the so-called new forms of employment[34] also fall under the scope of application of the directive. A decisive criterion for the answer to this question could be whether the tasks are performed on the premises of the employer or undertaking, even if, of course, this leaves unsolved the problem of work performed in 'virtual factories', i.e. on platforms.[35] In any case, also temporary agency workers are covered by the directive.

The directive does not refer to self-employed workers, who therefore do not fall within its scope of application. However, one has to recall that Article 2(1)(d) of Directive 92/57/EEC[36] defines a self-employed person as

---

legislation based on the necessary adaptation of the safety regulations to progress. Such an approach, which, moreover, itself arises from Council Directive 89/391/EEC …, does not relieve a Member State of the obligation to bring into force the minimum requirements of Directive 89/655 of 30 November 1989 concerning the minimum safety and health requirements for the use of work equipment by workers at work (second individual Directive within the meaning of Article 16(1) of Directive 89/391/EEC) ([1989] OJ L 393, p. 13), as amended by Council Directive 95/63/EC of 5 December 1995 ([1995] OJ L 335, p. 28)'.

33 This is not the case of 'the activity of primary care teams' and of 'activities of emergency workers in attendance in an ambulance or emergency medical vehicle in the framework of an emergency service for the injured or sick', to which the Framework Directive applies: ECJ 2000, C-303/98 (*SIMAP*); ECJ 2004, C-3971/01 – C 403/01 (*Pfeiffer*), respectively. This is because, in order to define its own scope of application, the Working Time Directive refers to the meaning of Article 2 Framework Directive.

34 See e.g. Waas (2016).

35 See Ales (2018).

36 Council Directive 92/57 (Minimum safety and health requirements at temporary or mobile construction sites) (eighth individual directive).

any person other than those falling within the scope of the Framework Directive 'whose professional activity contributes to the completion of a project'.

With reference to temporary or mobile working sites, Directive 92/57/EEC foresees relevant obligations for the self-employed, both in view of their own occupational health and safety and of the risk of effects of their activities on employees.[37] Within the limits of the liability of the client and the project supervisor, the self-employed have to respect individual preventive and protective provisions laid down in that directive.

The Framework Directive defines the term 'employer' as 'any natural or legal person who has an employment relationship with the worker'; it refers therefore to any employer in the technical meaning of the expression, i.e. the entrepreneur or his or her delegate.

The directive defines a 'workers' representative with specific responsibility for the safety and health of workers' as any person representing workers in case occupational health and safety problems arise at work (from now one: occupational health and safety workers' representatives). Member States are free to choose whether occupational health and safety workers' representatives are elected, chosen or designated in accordance with national laws and/or practices. 'However, where a Member State provides that workers' representatives with such responsibility must be elected, it is for that Member State to ensure that workers can elect their representatives in accordance with national legislation and/or practices.'[38]

The directive does not provide any definition of the term 'health'. However, the Court of Justice defined this term in its landmark decision of 1996,[39] dismissing the British Government's arguments against the interpretation of Directive 93/104/EEC (Working Time Directive). By providing an answer to the general question of the place of occupational health and safety in the EU legal and political discourse, the Court offered a clear definition of health. According to the Court, in fact,

> there is nothing in the wording of Article 118a (TEC) to indicate that the concepts of 'working environment', 'safety' and 'health' as used in that provision should, in the absence of other indications, be interpreted restrictively, and not as embracing all factors, physical or otherwise, capable of affecting the health and safety of the worker in his working environment, including in particular certain aspects of the organisation of working time. On the contrary, the words 'especially in the working

37 Articles 6(1)(b) and (d) and 8(1)(i); and above all Article 10. See Ales (2017a), p. 255 ff.

38 ECJ 2003, Case C-425/01 (*Commission v. Portugal*), §22.

39 ECJ 1996, C-84/94, (*UK v. Council*), §15. On this judgment and on the follow-up of the regulation also in a health and safety perspective, see Ellis (1997); Fitzpatrick (1997); Hardy (2006); Kenner (2004); Kenner (2005); Nowak (2008); Van Nuffel (1997); Waddington (1997).

> environment' militate in favour of a broad interpretation of the powers which Article 118a confers upon the Council for the protection of the health and safety of workers. Moreover, such an interpretation of the words 'safety' and 'health' derives support in particular from the preamble to the Constitution of the World Health Organization to which all the Member States belong. Health is there defined as a state of complete physical, mental and social well-being that does not consist only in the absence of illness or infirmity.

By adopting the notion of health as defined in the WHO Constitution, the Court of Justice broadened the concept of risk from mere physical to psychical and psychosocial risks,[40] thus emphasising the relevance of the workplace as 'environment' where the worker has the right to reach a state of complete physical, mental and social well-being.

Although one has to bear in mind that *physical* health (and safety) remains *the* focus of any occupational health and safety protection and management system, it has to be noted that interest in mental and social well-being at work has grown steadily in the last 50 years. This has been mainly due to the joint effort of the two UN agencies operating in this field, the International Labour Organization[41] and the World Health Organization, in doing research on the role psychosocial factors play at work.

This has materialised in the 1984 Report of the Joint ILO/WHO Committee on Occupational Health.[42] According to this report,

> The concept of psychosocial factors at work is difficult to grasp, since it represents worker perceptions and experience, and reflects many considerations. Some of these considerations relate to the individual worker, while others relate to the conditions of work and the work environment. Still others refer to social and economic influences, which are outside the workplace but which have repercussions within it. ... Fundamental individual factors include the worker's capacities and limitations relative to job demands, and the fulfilment of needs and expectations. Working conditions and the work environment include the task itself, physical conditions at the jobsite, worker/co-worker/supervisor relations, and management practices. Factors external to the workplace but relevant to psychosocial concerns at work include familial or private-life concerns, cultural elements, nutrition, ease of transport, and housing.

---

40 On psychosocial risks see Balandi et al (2012); Leka and Kortum (2008); Leka and Cox (ed) (2008); Leka et al (2011a); Leka et al (2011b); Leka et al (2011c); Lippel (2011); and Walters (2011).

41 Even though the ILO does not consider occupational health and safety as a core labour standard. On core labour standards and their controversial role see, with opposite views, Alston (2004) and Langille (2005). The right to healthy and safe working conditions is seen as a human right by Hilgertt (2013).

42 Joint ILO/WHO Committee on Occupational Health (1984).

The individual factors 'limitations relative to job demands' and 'the fulfilment of needs and expectations' may lead to stress at work. In fact, according to the European Social Partners, which signed an Autonomous Framework Agreement on 8 October 2004, *stress* can be described (not defined) as

> a state, which is accompanied by physical, psychological or social complaints or dysfunctions and which results from individuals feeling unable to bridge a gap with the requirements or expectations placed on them. The individual is well adapted to cope with short-term exposure to pressure, which can be considered as positive, but has greater difficulty in coping with prolonged exposure to intensive pressure. Moreover, different individuals can react differently to similar situations and the same individual can react differently to similar situations at different times of his/her life. Stress is not a disease, but prolonged exposure to it may reduce effectiveness at work and may cause ill-health.[43]

'Harassment' can be seen as referring to and deriving from 'bad worker/co-worker/supervisor relations, and bad management practices'.[44]

The latter concept confirms that the comprehensive notion of occupational health and safety, as developed by the Court of Justice, also encompasses dignity at workplace, thus guaranteeing fair working conditions as far as possible within the framework of EU law.

8.3.3. EMPLOYERS' OBLIGATIONS

One part of the Framework Directive refers to employers' obligations. Member States have to impose a comprehensive duty (responsibility or liability) on employers to ensure occupational health and safety of workers in every aspect related to work. This requires the adoption of a systematic occupational health and safety management,[45] which covers the work environment as a whole, going beyond individual protective measures and focusing on prevention of risks.[46] From this, it also follows that if employers make use of competent external services or persons[47] they are not discharged from their responsibilities as far as prevention and protection at work are concerned.[48]

Moreover, the fact that workers have obligations in the field of occupational health and safety does not discharge employers from their liability. Workers are

---

43 Ertel et al. (2011).

44 On sexual and moral harassment, see Friedman & Whitman (2003); Lerouge (2010); Lerouge & Hebert (2013); Quill (2005).

45 See Frick, Langaa Jensen, Quinlan & Wilthagen (2000).

46 Article 5(1).

47 Pursuant to Article 7(3).

48 Article 5(2).

only held responsible for the violations of their own obligations,[49] and this is meant to stimulate workers' responsibilisation.[50]

Article 5(4) states that Member States may 'provide for the exclusion or the limitation of employers' responsibility where occurrences are due to unusual and unforeseeable circumstances, beyond the employers' control, or to exceptional events, the consequences of which could not have been avoided despite the exercise of all due care'. Such exclusion, however, seems to be confined to cases of force majeure.

In this respect it is interesting that, in case C-127/05, the European Commission asked the Court of Justice whether, by restricting the duty on employers to ensure the safety and health of workers in all aspects related to work, to a duty to do this only 'in so far as is reasonably practicable', a Member State had failed to fulfil its obligations under the directive. This question is relevant for establishing what degree of liability Member States have to impose on the employer. In its judgment, a landmark and highly disputed decision,[51] the Court dismissed the interpretation of the Commission of Article 5(1) of the directive that the employer's liability 'extends to the consequences of any event detrimental to workers' health and safety, regardless of whether that event or those consequences can be attributed to any form of negligence on the part of the employer in adopting preventive measures.' In other words, Article 5(1) is interpreted as creating no-fault liability by the employer, whether civil or criminal'. On the contrary, according to the Court, 'it cannot be asserted that the employer should be subject to no-fault liability by reason merely of Article 5(1) of Directive 89/391. That provision simply embodies the general duty of safety to which the employer is subject, without specifying any form of liability'.

Therefore, as was already mentioned above, it is up to the Member States to define the *kind of liability* the employer faces. Comparative analysis shows that some Member States are more inclined to impose an employer's quasi-objective responsibility than others do.[52]

The Framework Directive further illustrates the general obligations of the employers within the context of their responsibilities (Article 6), as defined by each Member State. This means that the extent of the *necessary measures* for workers' occupational health and safety may vary from all those *technically available* to those *reasonably possible*, depending on how Member States approach employer's responsibility. In any case, these measures have to be prevention of occupational risks and the provision of information and

49 Article 5(3).

50 See Gray (2009); Rhebergen (2012).

51 ECJ 2007, Case C-127/05 (*Commission v. United Kingdom*). See Bell (2013).

52 See Ales (2013).

training to the workers and their representatives, as well as the necessary organisation and means for the occupational health and safety of workers. Within the framework of a dynamic approach to occupational health and safety, employers have to adjust the measures adopted in order to take account of changing circumstances, also due to technological progress, and with the aim of improving existing situations.

For this purpose, the directive enumerates some general *principles of prevention* the employer has to follow while implementing the above-mentioned measures. Some of the principles of prevention focus on risks that have to be avoided, combated at source or evaluated, if unavoidable.[53]

Despite the relevance of the notion of *risk*, the Framework Directive does not provide a definition of it. However, the Court of Justice having referred to the definition of health provided by the WHO as 'a state of complete physical, psychical and social well-being',[54] as already mentioned above, the scope of safety obligations in EU labour law is now wider than before. It departed from the narrow perspective of a tangible harmful event that produces physical ill health in the worker to a more comprehensive interpretation, in which psychical and psychosocial damages, which can derive from a tangible harmful event, or psychical and psychosocial risks that originate in a bad work organisation or in human misbehaviour are also taken into account.

Case law above all, but also national legislations and the doctrine have played a decisive role in modernising the legal discourse on health and safety by looking at already existing phenomena in terms of new factors of dangers (risks) and possible sources of harmful events.

As part of the non-physical risks, the concept of psychosocial risk has received considerable attention recently.[55] Indeed, as 'risk' can be regarded a super-concept that includes the concepts of 'danger' and 'risk', 'psychosocial risks' can also be looked at as a super-concept, that includes the concepts of 'psychophysical risk' and 'psychosocial risk'. As comparative analysis shows,[56] national legislations and case law differentiate between risks related to the work organisation, which are likely to produce negative consequences for the psychophysical sphere of the worker, and risks related to employer's or other workers' behaviours, which are likely to produce negative consequences on the emotional and relational sphere of the worker. The former risks should be defined as 'psychophysical' risks and the latter as 'psychosocial' risks. In many countries such organisational problems and individual or collective behaviour constitute a breach of the safety obligations and as such give rise to the right

53 Article 6(2)(a)(b) and (c).
54 ECJ 1996, C-84/94 (*UK v. Council*), §15.
55 Steinberg (2013).
56 Ales (2013).

to compensation in favour of the affected worker. This pragmatic approach to non-physical risks has made it possible to get around the problem of how to recognise work-related stress[57] as a psychophysical consequence of bad work organisation or of unlawful behaviour. Indeed, since no research has so far proven a link between the work organisation or the unlawful behaviour, on the one hand, and a worker's physical or psychical ill-health at the other, stress is mainly regarded (also within the European Social Dialogue)[58] as the result of the perception by the worker of the work organisation or of the behaviour of other workers. From this perspective, the employer cannot be held liable for the breach of the safety obligations, since the reasons for the ill health of the worker lie mainly in the worker himself or herself. Therefore, one can say that phenomena that already existed in the past are now considered as new risk factors (or sources of danger) and legislators have been obliged to define their very notion of risk in order to make this subject to sanctions and/or to compensation.

Some other *principles of prevention* focus on *adaptation* of the work to the individual[59] and to technical progress,[60] or to replace the dangerous by the non-dangerous or the less dangerous.[61]

The adaptation of the work to the individual refers, above all, to the design of workplaces, the choice of work equipment and the choice of working and production methods. According to the Framework Directive, the aim of adaptation is, in this case, mainly to alleviate monotonous work and work at a predetermined pace and to reduce their effects on health.

The *adaptation to technical progress* refers to any technological change that may produce a modification of the work organisation that has to be assessed within the perspective of the risk deriving from it for the worker. Robotisation and automatisation, for example, may be a means to replace dirty, dull and dangerous jobs to the benefit of the worker's health, but on the other hand could also lead to intensification of job demands due to increased job speed and loss of job autonomy, or to jobs where the worker is merely the slave of the machine.[62]

Adaptation may also occur by replacing the dangerous by the non-dangerous or the less dangerous, in sense of a permanent search of improving occupational health and safety, as required by the directive (Article 1(1)) and which is typical of the dynamic approach to occupational health and safety. The directive does not provide any definition of *danger*. In general, *danger*

57 Ibid.
58 Ibid.
59 Article 6(2)(d).
60 Article 6(2)(e).
61 Article 6(2)(f).
62 Geiskkovitch (2015).

can be defined as the capacity that a given entity has to cause a worker harm, whereas *risk* pinpoints the probability that a harmful event caused by that danger occurs to the worker.

One principle of prevention is related to the development of a coherent overall prevention policy, that covers technology, organisation of work, working conditions, social relationships and the influence of factors related to the working environment.[63] The relevance of the duty of the employer to adopt a prevention policy is twofold. On the one hand, it implies the elaboration of an occupational health and safety managerial strategy at the level of the undertaking, going beyond the mere sum of the measures mandatorily adopted under the law. On the other hand, the prevention policy has to cover technical, organisational, legal, social and 'environmental' aspects, in line with the broad perspective on health adopted by the Court of Justice.

It has to be stressed that the Framework Directive clearly favours collective protective measures instead of individual ones, thus recalling the idea of the occupational health and safety managerial strategy already mentioned above, which requires the adoption of a fully-fledged preventative approach. The *principle of appropriateness* of the instructions given to the workers by the employers or by their delegates is fully consistent with the preventative approach.[64] Clearly and precisely exercising managerial prerogatives in the field of occupational health and safety is likely to contribute, in a substantive way, to the prevention of harmful events.

8.3.4. THE DUTIES OF EMPLOYERS

The Framework Directive mentions a wide range of detailed duties employers have to fulfil, which does not seem to leave a substantive margin of manoeuvre to Member States. The directive starts with a non-exhaustive[65] list of *basic duties* ('general obligations')[66] that employers have to fulfil within the framework of the implementation of the principles of prevention mentioned in the previous section, taking into account the nature of the activities of the enterprise and/or establishment. The reference to the nature of the activities of the enterprise and/or establishment does not mean, however, that, in a deregulatory perspective, employers are free to decide whether they fulfil their basic duties according to the nature of their activities. On the contrary, the way in which basic duties have to be fulfilled has to be adapted to the nature of the activities performed in order to make them more effective.

---

63 Article 6(2)(g).

64 Article 6(2)(i).

65 'Without prejudice to the other provisions of this Directive'.

66 Article 6(3).

On top of the basic duties, the directive addresses 'first aid, fire-fighting and evacuation of workers'[67] as well as 'situations of serious and imminent danger, whatever the source of it'.[68] This is a highly specific domain that refers to very serious events and therefore deserves specific consideration.

Furthermore, the directive charges employers with some 'various obligations',[69] which have to be read in strict connection with the just mentioned 'general obligations' and basic duties.[70] The various obligations specify the general obligations, such as the assessment of risks,[71] or they integrate them, as is the case with protective measures[72] or, finally, they give new obligations.[73] These new ones consist, in particular, of the duty of the employer 'to keep a list of occupational accidents resulting in a worker being unfit for work for more than three working days'[74] and to 'draw up, for the responsible authorities and in accordance with national laws and/or practices, reports on occupational accidents suffered by his workers'.[75]

The directive also charges employers with three different duties regarding information.[76] The first information duty has to be fulfilled by every employer towards the workers and/or their representatives in the undertaking and/or establishment. The second information duty has to be fulfilled towards employers of workers from outside undertakings and/or establishments engaged in work within the undertaking and/or the establishment; the duty refers to and covers the issues in the previous paragraph. The third information duty has to be fulfilled towards workers with specific functions in protecting the safety and health of workers,[77] or workers' representatives with a specific responsibility for the safety and health of workers.[78]

The Framework Directive also specifies employers' duties where several undertakings share the same workplace.[79] In this case, employers have to cooperate in implementing the occupational health and safety provisions and, taking into account the nature of their activities, have to coordinate their actions for the protection and the prevention of occupational risks, and, where relevant, have to inform one another and their respective workers and/or

---

67 Article 8(1) and (2).
68 Article 8(3) to (5).
69 Article 9.
70 Article 6.
71 Article 9(1)(a) as for Article 6(2)(a).
72 Article 9(1)(b) as for Article 6(2)(h).
73 Article 9(1)(c) and (d).
74 Article 9(1)(c).
75 Article 9(1)(d).
76 Article 10.
77 *Ex* Article 7(1).
78 *Ex* Article 3(c).
79 Article 6(4).

workers' representatives of these risks. All this will help avoiding or reducing the so-called interference risk, i.e. the risk following from the interaction of workers managed by different employers, who operate in an alien working environment. Countervailing interference risks is crucial, among other sectors, in the construction sector, as shown by the adoption of Directive 92/57/EEC on occupational health and safety at temporary or mobile construction sites.

As a general and last principle, the adoption of measures related to occupational health and safety 'may in no circumstances involve the workers in financial costs', i.e. the costs have to be entirely at charged to the employer.[80]

8.3.4.1. The Basic Duties of Employers

(a) Risk Assessment

As for their basic duties, employers have, first, to assess all risks to the occupational health and safety for workers that can exist within the undertaking and/or establishment (the so-called risk assessment). For this purpose 'the choice of the work equipment, the chemical substances or preparations used, and the fitting-out of work places' are relevant aspects, but it is not an exhaustive list ('inter alia').[81] Depending on the result of the assessment, the employer can be called to implement preventive measures and production methods aimed to 'assure an improvement in the level of protection afforded to workers' with regard to occupational health and safety. If necessary, these measures and methods 'shall be integrated into all the activities of the undertaking and/or establishment and at all hierarchical levels'.

For the risk assessment the employer has to make a document which refers also to risks relevant for specific workers only. According to the Court of Justice *all* employers or the undertakings must have such document.[82]

Employers cannot rely on Article 9(2) in order to be exempted from the obligation to keep the risks assessment document. Indeed, this article provides that Member States 'shall define, in the light of the nature of the activities and size of the undertakings, the obligations to be met by the different categories of undertakings in respect of the drawing-up' of the document, thus confirming the need to have it.

Where employers entrust tasks to a worker, they have to take into consideration the worker's capabilities as regards occupational health and safety and take appropriate steps to ensure that only workers who have received adequate instructions may have access to areas where there is serious and specific danger.

---

80 Article 6(5).

81 Confirmed by ECJ 2003, C-49/00 (*Commission v. Italy*), §§10–18.

82 ECJ 2002, C-5/00 (*Commission v. Germany*), §35.

Employers have to ensure that workers and/or their representatives are consulted on the planning and introduction of new technologies and the effects of the choice of equipment, the working conditions and the working environment on their health and safety. It is up to the Member States to decide whether the employer has to consult workers directly or through their representatives or both.[83] Even though the directive does not make explicitly such link, consultation presupposes information of workers and/or their representatives.[84]

(b) The Establishment of the Preventive and Protective Services

Among the basic duties of employer, the establishment of a preventive and protective service within the undertaking and/or the establishment plays a central role (Article 7). The creation of a preventive and protective service does not exonerate employers from the just mentioned obligations; they remain the sole physical or juridical person responsible for the fulfilment of the obligations and liable for their infringement (Article 7(1)). However, 'the protection from, and prevention of the health and safety risks ... shall be the responsibility of one or more workers, of one service or of separate services whether from inside or outside the undertaking and/or establishment' (Article 7(6)). This should not be seen as contradictory, but only means that the responsible persons of preventive and protective service has to be clearly identified by the employer in order to be responsive.

In order to create a preventive and protective service the employer has to designate one or more workers who carry out activities related to the protection and prevention of occupational risks within the undertaking and/or establishment (Article 7(1)).

If a preventive and protective service cannot be organised for lack of competent personnel in the undertaking and/or establishment, the employer has to enlist competent external services or persons (Article 7(3)).

In this view, 'worker(s) and/or agency(ies) must work together whenever necessary' (Article 7(6)). The meaning of this provision is not clear. The fact that it refers to worker or workers might lead to presume a link with Article 7(1) ('the employer shall designate one or more workers'), thus opening the possibility of a mixed system, in which internal and external preventive and protective services interact and cooperate whenever necessary. By way of interpretation no decisive answer can be given on whether this possibility is allowed.

83 As confirmed by Article 11.

84 In the form specified by Article 10.

Member States may define, in the light of the nature of the activities and the size of the undertaking, the categories of undertakings in which employers, provided they are competent, may themselves take responsibility for the activities related to the protection and prevention of occupational risks. The implementation of these apparently clear provisions has proved to be controversial; the Commission started infringement procedures before the Court of Justice against Member States that allegedly failed to comply with the directive. The Court decided that Article 7(1) and (3) has to be interpreted as requiring employers, *in all circumstances*, to engage staff with the requisite capabilities or to enlist persons or services outside the undertaking if the capabilities within it are insufficient.[85] Second, Article 7(1) imposes on employers a principal obligation to designate one or more workers to carry out activities related to protection against and prevention of occupational risks, while Article 7(3) provides for an obligation to enlist competent external persons or services. However, that obligation is merely subsidiary to that laid down in Article 7(1). In the view of the Court of Justice this obligation arises only 'if such protective and preventive measures cannot be organised for lack of competent personnel in the undertaking and/or establishment'.[86] Therefore, 'Article 7 ... places the obligations imposed on employers in an order of precedence' (§21). Therefore Article 7(8) obliges Member States 'to define the necessary capabilities and aptitudes that the workers must have and it is open to those States to lay down further objective criteria to guide employers in their assessment of the competence within their undertaking' (§24). In the view of the Court, 'the decision, to favour, where there is sufficient competent personnel within the undertaking, (the) participation of the workers in the activities related to protection against and prevention of occupational risks over the enlistment of external competent persons or services is an organisational measure consistent with the aim of participation of workers in their own safety' (§40).

The Court considered that designated workers may not be placed at any disadvantage because of their activities related to the managing of a preventive and protective service, and adequate time to enable them to fulfil their obligations arising from the directive has to be allowed (Article 7(2)).

The designated workers and the external services and persons consulted must be sufficient in number to perform effectively their tasks (Article 7(5)). Member States may determine the sufficient number or leave it to the employer (Article 7(8)). This is a controversial point, since it leaves to Member States a wide margin of manoeuvre. However, Member States have to define, by laws and regulations, the necessary capabilities and aptitudes of workers designated

85 ECJ 2001, C-49/00 (*Commission v. Italy*), §28.

86 ECJ 2003, C-441/01 (*Commission v. the Netherlands*), §20. On the Dutch situation, see Jaspers & Pennings (2013).

and of the external services or persons consulted. According to the Court of Justice, this task cannot be entrusted to employers.[87]

(c) First Aid, Fire-Fighting and Evacuation of Workers Plus Situations of Serious and Imminent Danger

The directive addresses 'first aid, fire-fighting and evacuation of workers' (Article 8(1) and (2)) as well as 'situations of serious and imminent danger, whatever the source of it' (Article 8(3) to (5)). As for the first issue, the employer has to take the necessary measures for first aid, firefighting and evacuation of workers, appropriate to the nature of the activities and the size of the undertaking and/or establishment, taking also into account the presence of other persons. The employer must, inter alia, designate the workers required to implement such measures.[88] According to the Court of Justice 'the reference in the first subparagraph of Article 8(2) of the Directive to Article 8(1) thereof does not mean that the employer's obligation of designation is subject to the nature of the activities and the size of the undertaking and/or establishment'.[89] The number of workers required to implement the measures, their training and the equipment available to them must be adequate, taking into account the size and/or specific hazards of the undertaking and/or establishment (Article 2). Since the directive does not refer to Member States in this case, one may argue that the employer is directly responsible for respecting that the measures are adequate.

As for 'situations of serious, imminent and unavoidable danger (of risk), whatever the source of it', the directive does not provide any definition of the expressions 'serious', 'imminent' and 'unavoidable'. Therefore, it is up to the workers and to the employer to estimate whether there are such dangers. In order to ensure that workers are able to cope with such situations, the employer must (Article 8(3)):

- as soon as possible, inform all workers (not their representative) who are, or may be, exposed to serious and imminent danger of the risk involved and of the steps taken or to be taken as regards their protection;
- take action and give instructions to enable workers in the event of serious, imminent and unavoidable danger to stop work and/or to leave

87 ECJ 2001, C-49/00 (*Commission v. Italy*), §37.

88 From the use of the expressions *particularly* and *inter alia*, one can derive that the references provided by the directive are, in both cases, not exhaustive. As for the first, this means that the employer shall seek for interaction with all the external entities able to contribute to the fulfilment of the safety obligation. 'Inter alia' means that workers also have to be designated for other tasks.

89 ECJ 2006, C-428/04 (*Commission v. Austria*), §60.

immediately the workplace and proceed to a safe place (no definition is provided of the latter);
- save in exceptional cases for duly substantiated reasons, refrain from asking workers to resume work in a working situation where there is still a serious and imminent danger.

Workers who, in the event of serious, imminent and unavoidable danger, leave their workstation and/or a dangerous area may not be placed at any disadvantage because of their action and must be protected against any harmful and unjustified consequences (victimisation), in accordance with national laws and/or practices (Article 8(4)).

The employer has to ensure, through information and training, that all workers are able, in the event of serious and imminent (unavoidable is not mentioned here) danger to their own safety and/or that of other persons, and where the immediate superior responsible cannot be contacted, to take the appropriate steps in the light of their knowledge and the technical means at their disposal, to avoid the consequences of such danger. In such cases, their actions must not place them at any disadvantage (victimisation), unless they have acted carelessly or there was negligence on their part (Article 8(5)). It is questionable whether the consequences of careless actions or negligence can be qualified as disadvantages for the worker, since they can be considered as penalties or damage compensation requests for a misconduct.

8.3.5. THE OBLIGATIONS OF EMPLOYERS

8.3.5.1. 'Various Obligations'

The directive also imposes 'various obligations' on employers (Article 9), which provision has to be read in strict connection with the general obligations which have already been illustrated (Article 6). The various obligations specify the general obligations, such as for the assessment of risks,[90] or integrate them, such as for protective measures[91] or they provide for additional obligations (Article 9(1)(c) and (d)).

As for protective measures, the employer has to decide which measures have to be taken and, if necessary, what protective equipment has to be used. Both the protective measures that have to be taken and the protective equipment that has to be used have to be registered in a written document, as follows from Article 9(2), which refers to the document provided for in Article 9(1)(b).

---

90 Article 9(1)(a) as for Article 6(2)(a). See above.

91 Article 9(1)(b) as for Article 6(2)(h).

The additional obligations (Articles 9 and 6) consist of the duty of the employer 'to keep a list of occupational accidents resulting in a worker being unfit for work for more than three working days' (Article 9(1)(c)). Employers have also to 'draw up, for the responsible authorities and in accordance with national laws and/or practices, reports on occupational accidents suffered by his workers' (Article 9(1)(d)). One may argue that the occupational accidents referred to by Article 9(1)(d) are only those 'resulting in a worker being unfit for work for more than three working days' according to Article 9(1)(c). In this case too, Member States have to define, in the light of the nature of the activities and size of the undertakings, the obligations to be met by the different categories of undertakings when preparing the documents provided for in paragraph 1(c) and (d) (Article 9(2)).

Quite understandably, Article 9(1)(c) and (d) do not refer to occupational diseases. Occupational diseases need a (long-term) medical assessment that cannot be carried out by employers, since they are usually not allowed by national legislation to investigate workers' health themselves and have to rely on independent medical doctors within or outside the company. The latter will report to the competent authorities.

8.3.5.2. Obligations to Provide Information and Training

The directive also imposes three different information obligations on employers (Article 10). The first obligation has to be fulfilled by every employer towards the workers and/or their representatives in the undertaking and/or establishment. Information has to be provided in accordance with national laws and/or practices that, in defining the ways in which it will be delivered, may take into account, among the other things, the size of the undertaking and/or establishment.

This obligation covers all the necessary information concerning safety and health risks and protective and preventive measures and activities in respect of both the undertaking and/or establishment in general and each type of workstation and/or job. It also concerns the measures for first aid, fire-fighting and evacuation of workers according to Article 8(2) (Article 10(1)).

The second information obligation has to be fulfilled towards employers[92] of workers from outside undertakings and/or establishments engaged in work within the undertaking and/or the establishment the information refers to, and has to cover the issues mentioned in the previous paragraph. The information has to be provided in accordance with national laws and/or practices, and in a way that allows the relevant workers to be reached.

The third information obligation has to be fulfilled towards workers with specific functions in protecting the safety and health of workers (Article 7(1)), or

[92] Not directly to their workers: ECJ 2006, C-428/04 (*Commission v. Austria*), §81.

workers' representatives with specific responsibility for the safety and health of workers (Article 3(c)), in order to enable them to carry out their functions and in accordance with national laws and/or practices.

This obligation consists of guaranteeing them access, in accordance with national laws and/or practices, to:

- the risk assessment and the list of protective measures;[93]
- the list of occupational accidents resulting in a worker being unfit for work for more than three working days (Article 9(1)(c)), and the reports for the responsible authorities on occupational accidents suffered by workers in the undertaking (Article 9 (1)(c) and (d));
- the information yielded by protective and preventive measures, inspection agencies and bodies responsible for safety and health.

The directive also mentions the duty of the employer to ensure that each worker receives adequate occupational health and safety training, in particular in the form of information (Article 6(1)) and instructions specific to that employee's workstation or job:

- at the time of recruitment;
- in the event of a transfer or a change of job;
- in the event of the introduction of new work equipment or a change in equipment;
- in the event of the introduction of any new technology.

Training has to be adapted to take account of new or changed risks, and has to be repeated periodically if necessary. It may not be at workers' or the workers' representatives expense and must take place during working hours.

Workers' representatives with a specific role in protecting occupational health and safety are entitled to appropriate training that must take place during working hours or in accordance with national practice, either within or outside the undertaking and/or the establishment.

The employer has to ensure that workers from outside the undertaking and/or the establishment engaged in work in the undertaking and/or establishment have received appropriate instructions regarding occupational health and safety risks during their activities in the undertaking and/or establishment.

8.3.5.3. *Consultation and Balanced Participation*

A second fundamental point of the directive is the regulation of consultation and participation of individual workers, which is crucial for the functioning

93 As referred to in Article 9(1)(a) and (b).

of the occupational health and safety management system. This is a very complicated topic, since Article 11 makes a distinction between the following categories of worker.

- The workers of the undertaking and/or the establishment (Article 11(1)), who have to be consulted by the employer and have to be allowed 'to take part in discussions on all questions relating to safety and health at work'. They are entitled to appeal, in accordance with national law and/or practice, to the authority responsible for occupational health and safety if they consider that the measures taken and the means employed by the employer are inadequate for that purpose (Article 11(6)).
- Workers' representatives within the undertaking and/or the establishment, who have to be consulted by the employer, where they exist, in addition or in alternative to workers, and have to be allowed to take part in discussions on all questions relating to safety and health at work (Article 11(1)). They are also entitled to appeal to the occupational health and safety authority, under the conditions mentioned above (Article 11(6)). They must also be given the opportunity to submit their observations during inspection visits by the competent authority (Article 11(6)).
- Workers with specific responsibility for occupational health and safety (Article 11(6)), who cannot be substituted by the works council as a general representative body of the workers,[94] and who have to take part in a balanced way, in accordance with national laws and/or practices, or have to be consulted in advance and in good time by the employer with regard to: (a) any measure which may substantially affect occupational health and safety; (b) the designation of workers who carry out activities related to the protection and prevention of occupational risks for the undertaking and/or establishment (*ex* Article 7(1)) and who implement the measures on first aid, fire-fighting and the evacuation of workers (*ex* Article 8(2)); (c) the activities related to the protection and prevention of occupational risks for the undertaking and/or establishment (*ex* Article 7(1)); (d) the information referred to in Articles 9(1)[95] and 10;[96] (d) the enlistment,

---

94 ECJ 2006, C-428/04 (*Commission v. Austria*), §77. On the situation in Austria, see Kohlbacher & Marhold (2013).

95 I.e. on (a) the assessment of the risks to occupational health and safety, including those facing groups of workers exposed to particular risks; (b) the protective measures to be taken and, if necessary, the protective equipment to be used; (c) the list of occupational accidents resulting in a worker being unfit for work for more than three working days; (d) the reports for the responsible authorities and reports on occupational accidents suffered by the workers.

96 I.e. that which must be provided to workers and/or their representatives concerning the safety and health risks and protective and preventive measures and activities in respect of both the undertaking and/or establishment in general and each type of workstation and/or job (Article 10(1)(a)); that which must be provided by the employer to employers of workers

where appropriate, of the competent services or persons outside the undertaking and/or establishment;[97] (e) the planning and organisation of the training, as for Article 12.

- Workers' representatives with specific responsibility for occupational health and safety, who shall take part, in alternative to workers mentioned under the previous indent, in a balanced way, in accordance with national laws and/or practices, or shall be consulted in advance and in good time by the employer with regard to: (a) any measure which may substantially affect occupational health and safety; (b) the designation of workers who carry out activities related to the protection and prevention of occupational risks for the undertaking and/or establishment[98] and who implement the measures on first aid, fire-fighting and the evacuation of workers;[99] (c) the activities related to the protection and prevention of occupational risks for the undertaking and/or establishment;[100] (d) the information referred to in Articles 9(1) and 10; (d) the enlistment, where appropriate, of the competent services or persons outside the undertaking and/or establishment;[101] (e) the planning and organisation of the training.[102]
- Workers' representatives with specific responsibility for occupational health and safety have the right to ask the employer to take appropriate measures and to submit proposals to the employer to that end to mitigate hazards for workers and/or to remove sources of danger.[103] They must also be provided with adequate time off work, without loss of pay, and provided with the necessary means to enable them to exercise rights and functions deriving from the directive.[104] Furthermore, they must not be placed at a disadvantage because of their activities.[105] The consultation of workers and/or their representatives and their participation to the discussions on all questions relating to occupational health and safety presupposes the consultation of workers (*sic*), the right of the workers

from any outside undertakings and/or establishments engaged in work in the undertaking and/or establishment of the employer (Article 10(2)), and that to which workers or workers' representatives with specific functions in protecting the safety and health of workers must have access to carry out their functions, including the information yielded by protective and preventive measures, inspection agencies and bodies responsible for safety and health (Article 10(3)(c)).

97 *Ex* Article 7(3).
98 Articles 7(1).
99 Article 8(2).
100 Articles 7(1).
101 *Ex* Article 7(3).
102 *Ex* Article 12.
103 Article 11(3).
104 Article 11(5).
105 Article 11(4).

and/or their representatives to make proposals to be understood as *balanced participation* in accordance with national laws and/or practices.[106]

This is the most controversial provision of Article 11 and probably of the whole Directive.[107] Consultation of the workers, the right of the workers and/or their representatives to make proposals and for balanced participation are, of course, different ways in which the participation of the workers and/or their representatives can occur. For this reason, one may wonder whether they can be seen as alternatives to be chosen by each Member State, in accordance with its national laws and/or practices. Such approach finds confirmation in Article 11(2), which regards consultation as alternative to balanced participation for workers and workers with specific responsibility for occupational health and safety.[108]

8.3.6. OBLIGATIONS OF WORKERS

The directive also regulates obligations of workers.[109] For many Member States, this has been a relevant innovation, sitting within the perspective of a more dynamic approach to subordination in which the employee can no longer be seen as a passive recipient of the orders of the employer.

As a general principle, each worker has to take care, as far as possible, of the worker's own occupational health and safety and that of other persons affected by the worker's acts or omissions at work in accordance with the training and the instructions given by the employer.[110]

At least four elements of reflection may be derived from this general provision.

- The responsibility of workers may be derived directly from the directive, since it is clear and precise enough to be applied to the worker also in absence of a national legislation implementing it.
- Workers have to take care of their own occupational health and safety not only in order to avoid negative consequences for themselves, but also for other persons who might be affected by their acts or omissions at work.
- There is no no-fault liability of workers, since the directive[111] uses the expression as far as possible, to be understood as 'as far as reasonably possible'.

106 Article 11(1).
107 In the same vein, see Biagi (1991).
108 Article 11(2).
109 Article 13.
110 Article 13(1).
111 Article 13(1).

Therefore, the worker may prove that the negative consequences occurred could not have been reasonably avoided.

- The responsibility of workers has to be measured taking into account whether they have received the necessary training and has respected the instructions given by the employer. This is a crucial point, since it corresponds to the obligation of the employers to train their workers and to exercise in a precise and effective manner their managerial prerogatives.[112] In any case, workers' obligations in the field of occupational health and safety must not affect the principle of the responsibility of the employer.[113] This means that without prejudice to the responsibility of workers for the violation of occupational health and safety rules, the employer is liable for damages that could have been avoided by the fulfilment of the obligations of the worker and employer.

After having stated this general principle, Article 13 enumerates a wide range of worker's obligations. First, the duty to make correct use of machinery, apparatus, tools, dangerous substances,[114] transport equipment, other means of production;[115] to make use of the personal protective equipment supplied to the workers and, after use, to return it to its proper place;[116] and to make use of safety devices.[117] Second, the obligation to refrain from disconnecting, changing or removing arbitrarily safety devices fitted, e.g. to machinery, apparatus, tools, plant and buildings.[118] Third, an obligation to inform immediately the employer and/or the workers with specific responsibility for occupational health and safety of any work situation they have reasonable grounds for considering represents a serious and immediate danger to occupational health and safety and of any shortcomings in the protection arrangements.[119]

---

112 Articles 4, 5 and 6.

113 Article 4(3).

114 'The fact that Article 13(2)(a) of the Directive lists dangerous substances amongst other means of production does not preclude a distinction being made at national level between those different causes of occupational risk, in so far as the objective stated in Article 13(1) is attained. That provision states that each worker is to take care of his own safety and health and that of other persons affected by his acts or omissions at work', ECJ 2006, C-428/04 (*Commission v. Austria*), §100.

115 Article 13(2)(a).

116 'Article 13(2)(b) of the Directive makes a clear distinction between the obligation to make correct use of the equipment in question and the obligation to return it to its proper place after use. Although the choice made in [a] national legislation, for reasons of hygiene, of providing that equipment is for the personal use of each worker may facilitate compliance with the second obligation referred to in that provision, it does not, however, ensure that that equipment is returned correctly', ECJ 2006, C-428/04 (*Commission v. Austria*), §105.

117 Article 13(2)(c).

118 Article 13(2)(c).

119 Article 13(2)(d).

Fourth, an obligation to cooperate with the employer and/or workers with specific responsibility for occupational health and safety, for as long as may be necessary to enable them to carry out any tasks or requirements imposed by the competent authority to protect occupational health and safety[120] and to ensure that the working environment and working conditions are safe and pose no risk to occupational health and safety within the workers' field of activity.[121] It is up to the employer ('in accordance with national practice') to define the way in which workers have to cooperate.

Summing up, one can say that on top of the principle of (self)responsibility, which is limited to the sphere of the employment relationship, Article 13 creates a broad obligation on employees to cooperate for the fulfilment of the safety obligations; however, the employer remains responsible, as far as damages are concerned. It is up to each Member State to decide how the consequences of the employers' responsibility will be regulated, in view also of its industrial accident and occupational diseases insurance scheme.

8.3.7. HEALTH SURVEILLANCE

Health surveillance is another crucial point of the directive. The directive does not provide a definition of health surveillance, but Member States have to introduce, in accordance with national law and/or practices, measures aimed to ensure that workers receive health surveillance appropriate to the occupational health and safety risks they can incur at work.[122] Health surveillance has to be such that each worker, if he or she so wishes, may receive it at regular intervals.[123] Nothing is said on the qualification and the independence of the practitioners providing it. More specific rules on health surveillance can be found in the individual directives adopted on the ground of Article 16 of the directive.

8.3.8. PARTICULARLY SENSITIVE RISK GROUPS

The directive also introduced protection for 'particularly sensitive risk groups', which must be protected against dangers that specifically affect them.[124] From the early 1990s, the European Community adopted several directives,

[120] Article 13(2)(e).
[121] Article 13(2)(f).
[122] Article 14(1).
[123] Article 14(1).
[124] See Ales (2017a).

also under the form of individual directives, with the view to introducing or supplementing the measures to encourage improvements in occupational health and safety of particularly sensitive risk groups. In this way, the legislature has indirectly defined these groups and the personal conditions that fall under this category.

According to EU Law, these groups are:

- workers with a fixed-duration employment relationship or a temporary employment relationship;[125]
- pregnant workers and workers who have recently given birth or are breastfeeding;[126]
- young people at work;[127]
- workers working at temporary or mobile construction sites.[128]

To these categories disabled persons may be added; disability is defined by the Court of Justice as 'a limitation which results in particular forms of physical, mental or psychological impairments which in interaction with various barriers may hinder the full and effective participation of the person concerned in professional life on an equal basis with other workers'.[129] According to Article 5 of Directive 2000/78/EC,[130] employers shall take appropriate measures, where needed in a particular case, to enable a person with a disability to have access to, participate in, or advance in employment, or to undergo training, unless such measures would impose a disproportionate burden on the employer. There is no reason to assume that appropriate measures do not include occupational health and safety measures.[131] One can conclude, therefore, that people with disabilities also belong to particularly sensitive risk groups.

8.4. DAUGHTER DIRECTIVES, FRAMEWORK AGREEMENTS AND ADJACENT LEGISLATION

8.4.1. THE FRAMEWORK NATURE OF THE DIRECTIVE

Directive 89/391/EEC may be considered a *Framework* Directive in two respects. First of all, it sets a general framework for the interplay between

[125] Directive 91/383, amended by Directive 2007/30/EC.
[126] Directive 92/85/EEC.
[127] Directive 94/33/EC.
[128] Directive 92/57/EEC.
[129] ECJ 2013, C-335/11 and C-337/11 (*HK Danmark*).
[130] Directive 2000/78/EC (Equal Treatment).
[131] Ales (2015).

the three parties involved in devising an effective occupational health and safety policy at the company level – employer, workers (representatives) and occupational health and safety specialists or designated workers. This core of the Framework Directive has been described in the previous sections.

The Framework Directive, however, also serves as a framework, on the ground of Article 153(2) TFEU, for setting more specific provisions or technical standards for, inter alia, workplace requirements,[132] work equipment,[133] personal protective equipment,[134] working with dangerous substances,[135] and various physical risks such as vibrations,[136] noise[137] and electromagnetic fields.[138] These specific provisions have been laid down in over 20 individual directives (so-called Daughter Directives), adopted under the provision of Article 16(1) of the Framework Directive. One of the main reasons to provide for individual directives is that these, in some cases, may be amended more rapidly via delegation or Comitology[139] (under the provision of Article 17 Framework Directive), thereby keeping pace with rapid technological developments (see below, Section 8.4.2) as well as changes in international regulations or specifications, and taking account of the adoption of a directive in the field of technical harmonisation and standardisation.

Article 17 also allows the European Commission to make purely technical adjustments to the individual directives. According to Article 17(1), in adopting those measures, the Commission shall be assisted by a Committee. For this purpose, Articles 5a(1) to (4) and 7 of Council Decision 1999/468/EC[140] shall apply, having regard of the provisions of Article 8 thereof. More precisely, the development of individual directives belongs to the competence of the Council and Parliament, on the initiative of the Commission and after consultation of the tri-partite Advisory Committee on Health and Safety at Work, on the basis of (now) Article 153 TFEU.

132 Directive 89/654/EEC.

133 Directive 89/655/EEC, amended by Directive 2009/104/EC. As concerns work equipment, health and safety requirements are also laid down on the basis of the Machinery Directive 2006/42/EC and its Daughter Directives, see below.

134 Council Directive 89/686/EEC, amended by Directive 93/68/EEC and Directive 96/58/EC.

135 Directive 98/24/EC; Commission Directive 2000/39/EC.

136 Directive 2002/44/EC.

137 Directive 2003/10/EC.

138 Directive 2013/35/EU.

139 The term 'comitology' refers to the set of procedures through which the European Commission exercises the implementing powers conferred on it by the EU legislator, with the assistance of committees of representatives from EU countries. Such comitology committees are chaired by a Commission official and give an opinion on implementing acts proposed by the Commission. Regulation (EU) No 182/2011 lays down the general principles concerning mechanisms for control by EU countries of the Commission's exercise of implementing powers. It puts into practice Article 291 TFEU.

140 Council Decision of 28 June 1999 as amended by Council Decision 2006/512/EC.

Apart from paving the way for directives dealing with more or less technical issues, Article 16(1) of the directive also provides for some individual directives meant to safeguard the position of particularly vulnerable groups such as young workers,[141] as well as pregnant workers and workers who have recently given birth or are breastfeeding[142] (see Section 8.3.8). Also, there are specific directives concerning construction sites,[143] mining[144] and fishery.[145]

Next to the aforementioned daughter directives, there are more or less 'adjacent' bodies of legislation, that are not directly aimed at worker protection (on the basis of Article 153(2) TFEU), but at the proper functioning of the internal market (on the basis of Article 95 TFEU). However, even if the health and safety of workers is not directly envisaged, these legislations, such as the Machinery Directive[146] or Regulation 1907/2006 on the Registration, Evaluation, Authorisation and Restriction of Chemicals (REACH), have an indirect impact on health and safety of workers. For this reason they will be addressed briefly in Section 8.4.4.

8.4.2. DAUGHTER DIRECTIVES

As noted earlier, there are over 20 individual or daughter directives based on Article 16 of the directive. Clearly, it would be beyond the reach of this chapter to describe these directives in full here. The discussion will be confined to some general characteristics that may add to the understanding of the philosophy as well as legislative technique behind this occupational health and safety legislation.

8.4.2.1. Daughter Directives: Common Features

A first feature that is common to all individual directives, is that the provisions of the Framework Directive remain applicable to specific sectors or issues covered by the individual directive without prejudice to more stringent and/or specific provisions contained in the individual directive(s). Individual directives, in other words, complement the Framework Directive. While implementation of the directives is obligatory to all Member States, this does not prevent the Member States from maintaining or introducing more stringent protective measures compatible with the Treaties (Article 154(4) TFEU).

141 OJ L 216, 20 August 1994.
142 Directive 92/85/EEC.
143 Directive 92/57/EEC.
144 Directives 92/91/EEC and 92/104/EEC.
145 Directive 93/103/EEC.
146 Directive 89/392/EEC, currently 2006/42/EC.

A second common feature is that the daughter directives are moulded in the same fashion as the Framework Directive. Almost all daughter directives contain:

- a specific duty of care, notably a duty to replace dangerous activities by less dangerous ones and to prevent harm being done;
- an obligation to perform a risk assessment, geared to the specific risks addressed by the directive;
- an obligation to draft a preventive policy and take specific preventive measures, in consultation with the workers (or workers' representatives); and
- an obligation to inform and train all workers with respect to the specific risk and risk management measures.

In some cases, the individual directives contain provisions on occupational exposure limits (see below), as well as on health surveillance (see Section 8.3.7), and an obligation to keep an up-to-date list of workers that are likely to be exposed to the risk at hand. To illustrate, see Table 8.1 listing the relevant articles in four individual directives.

Table 8.1. Core Elements of Daughter Directives

	Chemical Agents Directive (98/24/EC)	**Carcinogens and Mutagens Directive (2004/37/EC)**	**Biological Agents Directive (2000/54/EC)**	**Electromagnetic fields (2013/35/EU)**
Definition	2	2	2	2
Occupational Exposure Limits	3	5(4)/16		3
Risk Assessment	4	3	3	4
Duty to replace dangerous sources by less dangerous ones	6 (2)	4/5	5	5 (1)
Control measures	5/6	5	4/6/8	5
Measurements	6	5(5 sub e)		4 (1)
Information and training	8	12	9/10	6
Records of workers engaged in dangerous activities		12 (c)	11	8
Health surveillance	10	14	14	8

A third feature of the directives is that neither of them makes reference to a notion that is quite common in national occupational health and safety legislation, i.e. that preventive measures should be taken 'so far as is reasonably practicable'. This 'practicability clause' implies that, excluding some specific cases (see below), the employer may balance the need to take effective preventive measures with the notion of technical and organisational feasibility as well as, more importantly, economic considerations on the side of the employer (such as cost/benefit analyses). The fact that none of the directives explicitly refers to the notion of 'reasonably practicable' – most importantly not the Framework Directive – does not, however, mean that the employer's duty of care is unconditional. This was established by the Court of Justice in *Commission v. United Kingdom* in 2007; see also Section 8.3.3 where it has already been seen that the Court ruled that the notion of 'reasonably practicable' was not at odds with the directive.[147]

Some room for considering the costs of preventive measures is, henceforth, granted. This may also (albeit a contrario) be derived from the wordings in some of the daughter directives, notably the Carcinogens Directive, that technical measures are to be taken 'in so far as is *technically* possible' (e.g. Article 4 of the Carcinogens and Mutagens Directive 2004/37/EC). This means that in such cases measures are to be taken irrespective of costs. But in other directives, there is no specific mention of technical feasibility.

It may also be recalled that Article 153(2)(b) TFEU states that the requirements in the directive 'shall avoid imposing administrative, financial and legal constraints in a way which would hold back the creation and development of small and medium-sized undertakings'. However, as has been illustrated earlier (Section 8.3.4), this in no way means that small and medium-sized enterprises may be exempted from the obligations imposed by the Framework Directive or the individual directives. It is also clear that the employer should at least achieve compliance to the level of the so-called 'occupational exposure limit' – which will be dealt with below (Section 8.4.2.2).

A fourth common feature is that most of the individual directives are geared to technical or 'tangible' risks. There is no directive that pertains to 'intangible' risks, such as work-stress, work-related aggression and so on. This is attributable to the fact that in the late 1980s and early 1990s, when the corpus of daughter directives was established, emphasis was on *safety* and physical health rather than on mental health. Moreover, psycho-social risks were often considered to be an *individual* rather than a structural problem. There are, however, some initiatives in the field of the social dialogue that have resulted in (framework) agreements on these subjects (see Section 8.4.3). Also, it was established earlier (Section 8.3.2) that, even if the concept of psychosocial factors may be difficult to grasp, it is quite clear that psychophysical and psychosocial risks do fall under the comprehensive notion of occupational health. Even if there are no specific directives in this field, it is clear that the employer should avoid these risks or assess the risks which cannot be avoided (Article 6(2) of the Framework Directive) and take appropriate preventive measures.

---

[147] ECJ 2007, C-127/05 (*Commission v. United Kingdom*), §45.

8.4.2.2. *Occupational Exposure Limits*

As indicated above, some of the individual directives contain occupational exposure limits.[148] These are laid down in the Annexes to the respective directives, which allow for relatively rapid revision according to the latest scientific knowledge. The occupational exposure limits relating to dangerous substances and electromagnetic fields respectively are established on the basis of Article 3 of the Chemical Agents Directive (CAD),[149] Article 6 of the Carcinogens and Mutagens Directive (CMD)[150] and Article 3 of the Electromagnetic Fields Directive, according to the procedure established in Directive 2000/39/EC.[151]

The aim of the occupational exposure limits is to establish levels of workplace exposure that even after frequent exposure over a longer period of time will not harm the health of the worker (or his offspring). These are called *health-based* occupational exposure limits, that are considered to be sufficiently low to prevent adverse effects to health.[152] If it is impossible to define safe thresholds (as is the case in various carcinogenic, mutagenic or sensitising substances), a 'risk-based' occupational exposure limit will be set, intended as guidance to minimise exposure. In Germany and the Netherlands, for example, this 'risk based' approach, defines the occupational exposure limit on the basis of the notion that no more than one out of 10,000 (or 1 million) workers may develop cancer or an allergy to specific substances.

The occupational exposure limits are to be implemented in national legislation within a given transition period. Still, only a very limited number of these occupational exposure limits are binding in character (meaning that all Member States have to implement them directly and without derogation). The overwhelming majority of occupational exposure limits are 'indicative' in nature, meaning that the national legislator *must* develop an occupational exposure limit, but the EU occupational exposure limits should only be taken 'into consideration'. The national limit values will be set 'in accordance with national legislation and practice'.[153] If a Member State fails to (timely) issue the

148 Even though occupational exposure limits have been developed already some 50 years ago, the first legally based occupational exposure limits for chemicals date from 1991. Directive 91/322/EEC established indicative occupational exposure limits for 27 substances. These were the first results from a scientific and policy practice that was started in 1980 (Directive 80/1107/EEC, which addressed not only chemical agents, but also biological and physical agents).

149 Directive 98/24/EC.

150 Directive 2004/37/EC.

151 Commission Directive 2000/39/EC; most recently amended by Commission Directive (EU) 2017/164.

152 SCOEL (2013), p. 8.

153 Directive 2000/39/EC, Recital 3.

required occupational exposure limit, the Member State can be taken to the European Court of Justice.[154]

The occupational exposure limits are based on a case-by-case scientific opinion, issued by, for example, the Scientific Committee on Occupational Exposure Limits (SCOEL)[155], or recommendations by the International Commission on Non-Ionizing Radiation Protection (ICNIRP). The first stage in setting the occupational exposure limit is the development of draft recommendations on the basis of the best available scientific knowledge. The recommendations are sent to all Member States for scientific consultation. The result of this procedure forms the scientific basis for policy discussion at EU level over the actual setting of the occupational exposure limit.

The occupational exposure limits are, in the end, established by the Commission, after consultation of the European Parliament following an ordinary legislative procedure (formerly co-decision procedure) on the basis of Article 153(2) TFEU. This procedure starts with the Commission issuing a proposal, which is then submitted to national parliaments' opinion as well as the opinion of the EESC and the Committee of the Regions. This consultation results in a draft report, which is then submitted to trilogue and voted on in plenary. The most recent proposals entail the introduction of new occupational exposure limits covering 13 and 7 carcinogens respectively,[156] as well as an expansion of the scope of the Carcinogens and Mutagens Directive.

Interestingly, occupational exposure limits are also set in a different arena, on the basis of Article 114 TFEU, which seeks to regulate competition. This arena is the setting of Derived No Effect Levels (DNELs) for dangerous substances under the so-called REACH Regulation.[157] REACH, an acronym for Registration, Evaluation and Authorisation of Chemicals, requires producers of chemicals to assess the risks of these chemicals for consumers, the environment and workers. The findings of these assessments should lead to guidance for so-called 'downstream users' who are working with these chemicals, on how to work safely. This information should be shared via so-called 'exposure scenarios' and, in an abridged form, safety data sheets (SDS). In this light, REACH and the occupational health and safety legislation are complementary, in that the risk assessment demanded by the Chemical Agents Directive and Carcinogens and Mutagens Directive respectively, should partly be based on information provided in the safety data sheets. This is but one example of how legislation meant to harmonise

[154] ECJ 2003, C-67/03 (*Commission v. Italy*); ECJ 2005, C-360/03 (*Commission v. Austria*); ECJ 2005, C-66/03 (*Commission v. France*).

[155] The SCOEL was established in 1995, via Commission Decision 95/320/EEC, and consists of 21 national experts.

[156] COM (2016)248 and COM(2017)11 respectively.

[157] Regulation 1907/2206/EU.

the internal market also spills over in health and safety legislation (another example being the 'essential health and safety requirements' emanating from the aforementioned Machinery Directive, see Section 8.4.4.1). Even if it is the producers themselves who are obliged to develop the guidance for safely working with dangerous chemicals (which could lead to underestimating the risks) or conformity with safety standards on the basis of the Machinery Directive, it may be surmised that the producers will not be too lenient on themselves, given the risks of possible product liability.[158]

Still, this system of self-regulation is flawed in several ways, most importantly as concerns the setting of clear-cut safety standards. As has been said just now, it is the producer of the chemical himself who is responsible for an adequate chemical safety assessment, albeit on the basis of various 'Guidance Documents' developed by the European Chemicals Agency (ECHA).[159] Most importantly, this chemical safety assessment should lead to the establishment of the aforementioned Derived No Effect Levels or, for chemicals without a safe threshold,[160] so-called 'derived minimal effect levels'. Even if these derived no effect levels have to be established by the producers of the chemicals themselves, the quality of the derived no effect level is to be evaluated by the European Chemicals Agency.

This system of deriving derived no effect levels poses several fundamental questions for the legislative system. First of all, even if the risk assessment is evaluated by the European Chemicals Agency, this is done on the basis of a rather small sample (5%) of all submitted safety assessments. Critical analysis by independent researchers has shown that the quality of the chemical safety assessments and of the derived no effect levels is rather poor.

A second problem is that, even if supported by the same 'Guidance documents' prepared by the European Chemicals Agency, different producers may come up with widely diverging derived no effect levels or hazard classifications concerning the exact same chemical,[161] which may leave both workers and employers empty-handed when they want to find information on exactly how to work safely and comply with the 'exposure limit' – which may lead to legal uncertainty. Third, if it is not quite clear whether or not all workers are covered by the same derived no effect levels; this may lead to legal

158 See European Group on Tort Law (2005).

159 Most importantly ECHA (2012).

160 Notably carcinogenic, mutagenic and reprotoxic substances.

161 Hazard classifications are not based on the REACH Regulation, but rather on Regulation 1272/2008. The main idea of the Regulation is that producers of chemical substances should 'classify' the risk according to an intricate system of 'hazard identification'. Some of the classifications are 'toxic', 'explosive' and 'carcinogenic'. For the most dangerous substances, the classification is performed by ECHA on the initiative of either a Member State or a (group of) producer(s). But in the overwhelming majority of cases, classification is done by the various producers, which results in widely diverging classifications.

inequality in general and unequal protection of workers in particular. These last two problems also apply, mutatis mutandis, to the fact that the derived no effect levels are in many cases quite different from the occupational exposure limits that are established on the basis of occupational health and safety legislation.

The relation of occupational health and safety legislation to the REACH Regulation and the Machinery Directive will be dealt with in more detail in Section 8.4.4.

8.4.3. THE SOCIAL DIALOGUE

Next to being the basis for issuing directives relating to the policy areas listed in Article 153 TFEU, the Treaty also provides for another way of regulating occupational health and safety: the promotion of social dialogue between European trade unions and employers' organisations (Article 152 TFEU). As mentioned in Chapter 1, Article 155(1) TFEU provides that, should the social partners so desire, the dialogue between them at Union level may lead to contractual relations, including agreements, which may, in matters covered by Article 153 TFEU, at the joint request of the signatory partners, result in a Council decision to implement the agreement – i.e. to give it the status of a directive. Occupational health and safety clearly falls under the scope of Article 153 TFEU.

The social partners may also decide to bypass the Commission and conclude an 'autonomous agreement'. In the field of health and safety, there are five such agreements, one of which has been nominated for a Council implementing decision, namely the Agreement on the protection of the health and safety of hairdressers (2012). However, the Council refused to implement the agreement, because within the framework of the ongoing operation to simplify the regulatory environment ('Regulatory Fitness', or REFIT), the Council was opposed to implementing any further European directives.[162] Other examples of autonomous agreements are the agreements on teleworking, including the ergonomics of the workspace (2002), agreements on reducing work-related stress (2004), and bullying and violence at work (2007).

The fact that these are 'autonomous' agreements implies that they are not legally binding on the basis of implementation on EU level (via Article 155(2) TFEU). However, they are binding on the basis of contractual obligations accepted by the signatories. Enforcement of the agreement is left to the signatory parties – not only the EU partners, but also their members (national employers' organisations and trade unions). The fact that enforcement

[162] European Commission (2005).

is left to the parties at the national level, also entails that national practices vary widely, as will be shown below.

The most interesting example of autonomous agreements in the field of occupational health and safety is the Framework Agreement on work-related stress (2004), signed by, inter alia, the European Trade Union Confederation, the Union of Industrial and Employers' Confederations of Europe, and the European Association of Craft Small and Medium-sized Enterprises. The agreement applies to all companies, regardless of size. In the agreement 'work-related stress' is defined as a state which is accompanied by physical, psychological or social complaints or dysfunctions and which results from individuals feeling unable to bridge a gap with the requirements or expectations placed on them. The agreement is limited to factors having to do with job content and workload, and explicitly does not relate to violence, bullying or post-traumatic stress.

The aim of the agreement is, according to Article 2, 'to increase awareness and understanding of employers, workers and their representatives of work-related stress [.. and] to provide employers and workers with a framework to identify and prevent or manage problems of work-related stress'.

The agreement identifies the following factors that may contribute to work-related stress:

- work content;
- work organisation and processes (such as working time arrangement, degree of autonomy);
- working conditions and environment;
- poor communication (uncertainty what is expected at work); and
- subjective factors.

The agreement mentions several measures to prevent, eliminate or reduce work-related stress. This involves both collective and individual measures. Measures that are listed in the agreement are, inter alia management and communication, training of managers and employees, and information. But as the agreement circumvents the topic of 'job demands'[163] or, even more importantly, 'work load', it is clear that, as concerns preventive measures, these are not really geared to the primary causes of work-related stress. Communication, training and provision of information seem more focused on *dealing* with stress than *prevention* of stress. In this sense, the agreement is clearly at odds with the preventative approach engrained in the Framework Directive and the daughter directives.

The agreement stipulated that it was to be implemented within three years after it was signed, i.e. no later than 8 October 2007. In most European

163 Karasek (1979).

countries, this was actually achieved;[164] however, there were wide divergences among Member States. This may be attributed to the way the agreement was implemented. Since the social partners did not ask the Commission to implement the agreement in a directive on the basis of Article 155(2) TFEU, implementation was a matter to be dealt with on the national level, leaving the national partners a large degree of freedom. For example, social partners may try to convince the national authorities to implement the agreement in national legislation. This was done in seven Member States.[165] Another strategy could be to convince all organisations that are member of the signatory parties to include the subject in collective labour agreements. In that case, the specific provisions in the agreement are binding for individual employers and workers. This strategy of collective labour agreements was followed in five Member States.[166] In most cases, however, the national organisations limited themselves to merely drafting recommendations and codes of conduct.

Still, in practice the agreement has resulted in new policies, e.g. the development of practical tools to help companies deal with stress at work.[167] Furthermore, it is clear that the agreement raised awareness of the need of joint action of the social partners, which purportedly led to a shared commitment to tackle stress at work on a more structural basis.[168] As a result in many EU countries social dialogue on psycho-social issues at work was boosted, according to an evaluation conducted by the European Commission.[169] However, the Commission also found that 'there are persistent discrepancies in the levels of protection available across Member States, and that it is not possible to conclude that a minimum level of protection has been established throughout the EU'.[170]

This critical remark may be relevant to autonomous agreements in general. Even if they undoubtedly contribute to the social dialogue in the field of occupational health and safety and may help to raise awareness of and offer guidance to prevent occupational health and safety risks, most of the stipulations in the agreement are non-binding in a strict sense and there are little if any means of enforcement if the social partners are unwilling or unable to use these. As a result, (legal) inequalities may arise, which is at odds with one of the basic tenets of the Framework Directive as well as the Daughter Directives – equal protection of all workers via gradual harmonisation of national systems of occupational health and safety legislation.

---

164 ETUC (2008).

165 European Commission (2011), *Report on the implementation of the European social partners 'Framework Agreement on Work-related Stress'*, SEC(2011)241 final, p. 2.

166 Ibid.

167 Ibid.

168 Broughton (2010), p. 7.

169 SEC(2011)241 final, p. 2.

170 SEC(2011)241 final, p. 3.

8.4.4. OTHER RELEVANT EU LEGISLATION

Health and safety is not only addressed by the occupational health and safety legislation described so far, but is envisaged directly or indirectly by various other bodies of legislation as well. Machinery Directive 2006/42/EC,[171] for example, not only seeks to promote the free movement of machinery within the Single Market, but also aims for a 'high level of health and safety of persons', in particular of workers (recital (3)). Regulation 1907/2006 on the Registration, Evaluation and Authorisation of Chemicals (REACH), to mention another example, explicitly aims to 'ensure a high level of protection of human health and the environment as well as the free movement of substances, on their own, in mixtures and in articles, while enhancing competitiveness and innovation' (Recital 1 Regulation 1907/2006 on the Registration, Evaluation and Authorisation of Chemicals).

Both of these bodies of legislation are based on Article 95 TEC (currently Article 114 TFEU), aimed at ensuring the functioning of the internal market, which allows for less leeway on the national level than EU legislation, does based on Article 153. Still, Article 15 of the Machinery Directive, for example, states that this Directive

> shall not affect Member States' entitlement to lay down, in due observance of Community law, such requirements as they may deem necessary to ensure that persons, and in particular workers, are protected when using machinery, provided that this does not mean that such machinery is modified in a way not specified in this directive.

Both the Machinery Directive and the Regulation 1907/2006 on the Registration, Evaluation and Authorisation of Chemicals explicitly aim at worker protection, even if they are not directly addressed to the employer.

8.4.4.1. The Machinery Directive

The Machinery Directive 2006/42/EC is geared to the harmonisation of the internal market,[172] as well as to the protection of the users of machinery and other equipment. One of its considerations is that 'the social cost of the large number of accidents caused directly by the use of machinery can be reduced by inherently safe design and construction of machinery and by proper

---

171 Directive 2006/42/EC (machinery), amended by various specific Directives and Regulations.

172 Since the objective of this directive, namely to lay down the essential health and safety requirements in relation to design and manufacture in order to improve the safety of machinery placed on the market, cannot be sufficiently achieved by the Member States and can be better achieved at Community level (Recital 28).

installation and maintenance' (Recital 2). The directive therefore aims, albeit indirectly, to protect workers handling machinery. Indirectly, because the directive does not address the employer, but rather the producers of machinery, equipment and so on (Article 1). Producers may only put machinery on the European market if it conforms to the essential health and safety requirements listed in the Annexes to the directive – this means that 'enforcing' health and safety is partly left to market mechanisms rather than surveillance by government inspectorates.

The essential health and safety requirements have to be satisfied in order to ensure that machinery is safe; these requirements have to be applied with discernment to take account of the state of the art at the time of construction and of technical and economic requirements. The directive defines only the essential health and safety requirements of general application, supplemented by a number of more specific requirements for certain categories of machinery. The manufacturer also has to ensure that a risk assessment is carried out for the machinery which it wishes to place on the market. For this purpose, the manufacturer should determine the essential health and safety requirements applicable to the machinery in respect of which the manufacturer must take measures. A high level of protection of the health and safety of persons (Article 9(3)) is to be ensured.[173]

If a machine is produced according to the technical standards laid down by the Standardisation Bodies, the machine is thought to comply with the 'essential health and safety requirements' (Article 7(2) Machinery Directive), as well as the individual directives on the basis of the Framework Directive.[174] In short, the employer may only purchase, or deploy, machinery that has been labelled with a CE-mark, which indicates conformity with health, safety and environmental protection standards.[175] For specifically dangerous machinery, the employer is required to be in possession of an independent test report. In some cases, more stringent requirements apply on the basis of occupational health and safety legislation.

This short introduction of the Machinery Directive is also interesting, because it is one of the first examples of the 'New Approach' to EU legislation. This 'New Approach' was introduced in 1985,[176] its fundamental point of view being that harmonisation of legislation should be limited to the most essential

---

173 A similar structure can be distinguished with regard to personal protective equipment referred to in the third Daughter Directive (Directive 89/656/EEC). The third individual directive stipulates the cases in which personal protective equipment is to be used, whereas the personal protective equipment must comply with the annex to the directive.

174 See e.g. Article 4 of Work Equipment Directive 2009/104/EC.

175 Valdés (2013), p. 11.

176 Council Resolution 85/C 136/01, see European Commission 2000 and European Commission 2016a.

safety requirements (or other requirements of public interest), whereas these general requirements are to be fleshed out by the market parties themselves. This is done via technical standardisation, notably in technical committees of the European Standardisation Bodies[177] (and indirectly the International Standardisation Organisation (ISO)). As stated in the recital to the directive:

> In order to help manufacturers to prove conformity to these essential requirements, and to allow inspection of conformity to the essential requirements, it is desirable to have standards that are harmonised at Community level for the prevention of risks arising out of the design and construction of machinery. These standards are drawn up by private-law bodies and should retain their non-binding status.

One major advantage of this approach is that it is easier to react to the changing state of the art in technological development – not only because standardisation procedures are thought to be shorter than legislative procedures, but also because the parties that are involved in standardisation are for a large part active in the forefront of technological development and therefore are more apt to assess whether or not an update of technical requirements may be necessary.

This 'New approach' is particularly interesting in the field of occupational health and safety, because it contains a mix of private standardisation within a public law framework, notably the fundamental right of workers to safe and decent working conditions as formalised in the Occupational Health and Safety Directives. This means that the private-law process of standardisation should be consistent with the fundamental legislative principles of public law, such as transparency, equal protection of all interests involved, and legal certainty.[178] For this reason, it has been laid down in Regulation 1025/2012 that the representation of societal interests and societal stakeholders in European standardisation activities has to refer to the organisations and parties representing interests of greater societal relevance.[179] The representation of social interests and social stakeholders in European standardisation activities refers particularly to the activities of organisations and parties representing employees and workers' basic rights, for instance trade unions (Recital 17). The regulation is meant to regulate the cooperation between European Standardisation Bodies, i.e. national Standardisation Bodies, the Member States and the European Commission, but also offers a framework for financial support of European stakeholders (such as the trade unions). Also, a working party on 'standardisation' has been set up by the tripartite Advisory Committee

---

177 In particular the European Committee for Standardization (CEN), European Committee European Committee for Electrotechnical Standardization (CENELEC) and the European Telecommunications Standards Institute (ETSI).

178 See Popma (1999), pp.149–189.

179 Regulation (EU) No. 1025/2012.

on Safety and Health at Work, which must warrant balanced participation of all parties involved.

Whether or not this regulation is actually a firm guarantee to reach a high level of protection is a matter that is disputed. Not all technical standards conform to the essential requirements in the Occupational Health and Safety Directives and enforcement by means of 'market surveillance' alone is in many cases insufficient.[180] One of the explanations is that, despite the aforementioned Regulation, in most standardisation processes societal stakeholders are clearly outnumbered by industry representatives.[181] Moreover, there are considerable differences between workers' involvement in standardisation processes on the national level. For example, the German trade unions are well represented in the tripartite *Kommission Arbeitsschutz und Normung* (Committee on Occupational Health and Safety and standardisation), whereas in the Netherlands the Dutch trade unions have rather in vain been calling for better facilities for worker involvement in standardisation since the mid-1990s of the last century. There are also concerns regarding the transparency of standardisation processes.[182]

So even if the system of New Approach Directives, along with stakeholder involvement in standardisation, promises a balanced approach to regulating the internal market, taking into account societal values such as health and safety of workers (as well as environmental and consumer protection), the European Trade Union Conference deemed it necessary to publish a resolution on the rationale for trade union participation in standardisation.[183] This resolution called for workers to participate in standardisation in order to 'prevent standards to encroach upon national labour laws, collective agreements and collective bargaining, and impede any attempt to use standards for a parallel recodification of labour laws (and) promote a high level of health and safety at work and quality working conditions above the level of existing public regulations', but also called on the Commission, EU Member States and private European standardisation organisations to 'make the standardisation system at European and national level more transparent and democratic by implementing the recommendations on inclusiveness identified by the "Independent review on the European Standardisation System", ensuring trade unions' free access to formal standardisation procedures and standards, and providing financial support at national level for trade unions effective participation

180 Fraser (2012), pp. 9–10: 'In some Member States and for some products, there is still next to no enforcement activity. Even in the Member States with a serious market surveillance system, the public services concerned are all suffering in cuts in budgets and staff' (this is also true for supervision and enforcement of public law).

181 Vogel (2013).

182 Vogel (2013), p. 15.

183 Resolution adopted on 16–17 December 2015.

in standardisation'. This was later formalised in the 2016 Joint Initiative on Standardisation, signed by, inter alia the ETUC itself.[184]

8.4.4.2. *Regulation on the Registration, Evaluation and Authorisation of Chemicals and Regulation on Classification, Labelling and Packaging of Substances and Mixtures (1272/2008)*

Another important area of worker protection where occupational health and safety guidelines are influenced by related regulations is the protection of workers who may be exposed to hazardous chemicals. In this area lie the Regulation 1907/2006 on the Registration, Evaluation and Authorisation of Chemicals[185] and the Regulation 1272/2008 on classification, labelling and packaging of substances and mixtures, which are highly relevant to the protection of workers. Both regulations have their basis in Article 114 TFEU and, like the Machinery Directive, these two regulations do not address the employer directly, but are aimed at producers (in this case producers of chemicals). However, the regulations do have an influence on the interpretation of the duty of care of the employer that is the essence of both the Framework Directive and, implicitly, the Chemical Agents Directive (Directive 98/24/EC) as well as the Carcinogens and Mutagens Directive (Directive 2004/37/EC).

Next to the performance of risk assessment and setting of the already mentioned 'no-effect level', these two regulations are intended to inform workers about hazardous substances: first, by means of the obligation for producers who place chemicals on the market to label clearly any hazardous chemicals (Titles III and IV Classification and Labelling Regulation) and, second, by the obligation for producers to draw up Safety Data Sheets describing possible risks and safe working procedures (Article 31 Registration, Evaluation and Authorisation of Chemicals directive). Although both obligations focus primarily on the producer (or parties that place the chemicals on the market), they are integrated into the health and safety guidelines by means of providing the employer with information that the employer has to convey to the workers on the basis of Article 8 Chemical Agents Directive and Article 11 Carcinogens and Mutagens Directive respectively.

However, information about risks is only one of the elements of the occupational hygiene strategy. More importantly, the two regulations are also relevant to determining which *preventive* measures are deemed to be adequate. For example, the required level of protection as referred to in the Chemical Agents Directive (CAD) and Carcinogens and Mutagens Directive (CMD)

---

184 Also see Joint Initiative on Standardisation, signed by various stakeholders (inter alia, the European Trade Union Conference (ETUC)) on 12 July 2016.

185 See Section 8.4.4.

must be adapted to the level of the risks emanating from working with chemicals. This is to be established by means of the risk assessment (Article 4 Chemical Agents Directive and Article 3 Carcinogens and Mutagens Directive respectively), whereby the employer should 'take into consideration information on safety and health that shall be provided by the supplier (e.g. the relevant safety data sheet in accordance with Regulation (EC) No 1907/2006 of the European Parliament and of the Council' (Article 4 Chemical Agents Directive)). Also, the employer is obliged to take into account the classification of substances on the basis of the Regulation (Article 2 Carcinogens and Mutagens Directive), whereas substances which meet the criteria for classification as a category 1A or 1B carcinogen are subject to more specific demands concerning the risk assessment as well as more stringent risk management obligations. In the development of control measures, the employer must also focus on the 'risk management measures' described in the Safety Data Sheet. Which requirements are set for the Safety Data Sheet once again depends on the classification based on the Classification and Labelling Regulation (Article 31 Registration, Evaluation and Authorisation of Chemicals Regulation). The most far-reaching consequence of the Registration, Evaluation and Authorisation of Chemicals Regulation and the Classification and Labelling Regulation is that for some substances of very high concern 'authorisation' to place them on the market must be granted by the Commission, or that the Commission may impose 'restrictions' on the use of such substances, including stipulations for safe use.

It is important to note, however, that the information about chemicals primarily comes from the producers themselves. This concerns both the classification based on the Classification and Labelling Regulation and the substance information and risk management measures under the Registration, Evaluation and Authorisation of Chemicals Regulation. Direct involvement of the legislature or interested NGOs such as trade unions is not warranted – with the effect that in many cases the quality of the risk information leaves much to be desired, or that the classification by different producers of the same substance may vary considerably. This may create legal uncertainty, in the sense that the employer will not always know what level of protection is required, or what risk management measures the employer should abide to.

So even if the Registration, Evaluation and Authorisation of Chemicals Directive and Classification and Labelling system provides information on the risks of chemical agents, which is also supposed to be regularly updated to conform to the current state of knowledge, it is clear that not all substances and/or uses of these substances are properly assessed, leading to significant 'data gaps'.

Also, it may be noted that both the Chemical Agents Directive and the Carcinogens and Mutagens Directive are fundamentally more stringent than the Registration, Evaluation and Authorisation of Chemicals Regulation. Whereas both directives prescribe that risks to the health and safety of workers at work involving hazardous chemical agents shall be eliminated or reduced *to a minimum* (Article 5 Chemical Agents Directive) or exposure should be either prevented of reduced to as low a level as is technically possible (Article 5 Carcinogens and Mutagens Directive), the Registration, Evaluation and Authorisation of Chemicals Regulation only requires '*adequate*' control to ensure that exposure is below the threshold level (recital 70 Registration, Evaluation and Authorisation of Chemicals Regulation.). Furthermore, it appears that in the risk management measures described in the Safety Data Sheets, emphasis is on the use of personal protective equipment rather than on the preventive strategies (notably substitution of dangerous by less dangerous chemical) that are required by both directives. These differences in wording or even the implicit differences in stringency may also lead to differences in interpretation as concerns the legal duties of the employer.[186]

8.5. WORKING TIME

8.5.1. INTRODUCTION

Reduction and regulation of working times is one of the oldest spearheads of the labour movement. The fight for the introduction of the eight-hour working day dates back to the nineteenth century, in Europe as well as in the United States. The regulation of working time came about under massive pressure by the international trade union movement. In the United States, in 1884 the American Confederation of Labor adopted a resolution calling for an eight-hour working day, resulting in a massive demonstration on 4 May 1886 that ended in violent rioting. Three years later, the Second International decided that 1 May should be a day to commemorate the bloody crackdown on the demonstration, thereby initiating Labour Day – one of the main symbolic cornerstones of the international labour movement. Also, internationally, the regulation of the working hours was high on the agenda. In 1919 the International Labour Organization adopted a Convention on working time.[187] In Europe, many countries had already adopted national legislation concerning the eight-hour working day even before 1919,[188] aiming to put a stop to the ruthless

[186] Also see Senior Labour Inspectorate Committee (2013).

[187] ILO Hours of Work (Industry) Convention, 1919 (No. 1) Limiting the Hours of Work in Industrial Undertakings to Eight in the Day and Forty-eight in the Week (Entry into force: 13.06.1921). It was the first convention adopted by the ILO. Due to the composition of the ILO – employers' associations, trade unions and governments – the results are called 'conventions'. E.g. Servais (2009).

[188] France, Germany, Austria, Finland, Spain, Portugal and Czechoslovakia. In most of the other European countries, national legislation was issued in 1919 or shortly afterwards.

exploitation of the labour force in the nineteenth and the beginning of the twentieth century, as well as responding to the wish and necessity of improving human conditions of labour and enablement of self-fulfilment and well-being. Social justice was the main driver. As later stated by the ILO, all human beings 'have the right to pursue both their material well-being and their spiritual development in conditions of freedom and dignity, of economic security and equal opportunity'.[189] Regulation of working time was more than limiting the number of daily or weekly working hours and guaranteeing rest periods; it also includes reduction of overtime and (paid) leaves. Protection of special groups, such as pregnant women and young people, was another objective.

Protection of the health and safety of workers has always been a major goal of labour law. The European Union has focused its legislation on that objective. The first Working Time Directive (93/104/EC) on 'certain aspects of the organisation of working time' explicitly refers to Article 118a EC, providing that the Council shall adopt the directive 'to ensure a better level of protection of the safety and health of workers'. The fact that the Working Time Directive also makes explicit reference to Directive 89/391/EEC indicates that it is set within the realm of health and safety.

Two of the more specific risks in the field of occupational health and safety are working at non-standard working time (especially night shifts) and working excessive hours. Various studies indicate that night work (or rather work that involves disruption of the day/night rhythm) is associated with various types of medical conditions, ranging from a higher incidence of coronary disease to various types of cancer.[190] Studies show that the number of accidents during night work is significantly higher than during dayshifts. Structural overtime work is also associated with all kinds of health problems and leads to an increase of accidents.[191] Work related stress is the more recent health risk at work and is often connected with actual working hours and time constraints.[192]

However, despite the fact that it was intended to safeguard fundamental rights of workers, the regulatory process leading to the Working Time Directive was loaded with fierce debate,[193] which in many respects echoed the contentious nature of the earlier calls for an eight-hour working day, or more generally for

---

189 ILO Declaration of Philadelphia of 1944, p. II(a).

190 In 2007 the IARC (International Agency for the Research on Cancer) classified 'shiftwork that involves circadian disruption' to be 'probably carcinogenic to humans', IARC (2010), p. 764.

191 Dembe (2008), pp. 1185–94; Salminen (2010), pp. 14–18; Geurts (2014).

192 It is called the new work-related disease. E.g. Eurofound, Work-related stress, report of 18 November 2010. The Fourth European Working Conditions Survey, carried out in 2005, reports that 22% of European workers reported suffering from stress, lower back ache, muscular pain and fatigue. See also the study commissioned by the European Parliament, *Occupational health concerns: stress-related and psychological problems associated with work*, European Union 2013.

193 In particular the United Kingdom was strongly opposed, see Bercusson (1993).

decent working hours. Fierce debates also surrounded the proposed revision of the later version of the Working Time Directive (2003/88/EC). The resistance against legislation such as the working time directives of the EU did not only come from the UK, although the UK had taken the lead. Recently, under the influence of the need felt in several Member States for more flexibility on the labour market that contributes to the competitiveness of the economies of the EU and its Member States, the pressure on deregulation or seeking the edges of the rules is increasing. A proposal of the European Commission in 2004[194] is still in stalemate. In 2010, the Commission attempted to launch a second round of consultation of social partners on possible amendments to the directive.[195] Social partners participated in these consultation rounds, but did not succeed in putting forward shared proposals for changes – quite the contrary. Both partners held (and hold) diametrically opposed views on the way working time should be regulated by means of European directives. The economic crisis in 2008 and the years after did not contribute to an impetus for making new legislation. On the contrary, experiments with all kinds of employment and work patterns have pushed developments on this matter into the background.[196]

8.5.2. INTERNATIONAL LAW ADDRESSING THE RIGHT TO DECENT WORKING HOURS

Still, given the importance of health and safety, being a fundamental right, and its connection with working time, it is not surprising to find the issue of decent working hours addressed in a range of fundamental legal sources. Article 2 of the European Social Charter (1961, revised in 1996)[197] lists under the 'just conditions of work' a right to reasonable daily and weekly working hours, adding that 'the working week [should] be progressively reduced'. Also, the Charter calls upon the signatory partners to provide for paid holidays and to ensure a weekly rest period which shall, as far as possible, coincide with the day recognised by tradition or custom in the country or region concerned as a day of rest. These provisions are echoed in Article 31(2) of the Charter of fundamental rights of the European Union, stating that 'every worker has the right to limitation of maximum working hours, to daily and weekly rest periods and to an annual period of paid leave'. Founded in these Charters, it is evident that decent working times are a fundamental right of workers.

194 COM (2004) 607, amended by COM (2005) 246.

195 European Commission, *Public consultation on the review of the working time directive background of 1 December 2014.*

196 E.g. Barnard (2012a), pp. 557–58.

197 The revised Charter has left this provision unchanged.

Even more so, they are fundamental *human* rights as stipulated by the United Nations. Article 24 Universal Declaration of Human Rights (1948), as well as Article 7 of the Covenant on Economic, Social and Cultural Rights (CESCR 1966), acknowledge a right to 'Rest, leisure and reasonable limitation of working hours and periodic holidays with pay, as well as remuneration for public holidays'.

Furthermore, it is worth noting that workers' rights must also be interpreted in the light of a wider human right, namely the right to family life (Article 10 CESCR). More specifically, Article 10(2) CESCR awards 'special protection [to] be accorded to mothers during a reasonable period before and after childbirth. During such period working mothers should be accorded paid leave or leave with adequate social security benefits.' Even if it is clear that the right to paid leave is both fundamental to the right to family life and instrumental to the recuperation of the worker (and hence the protection of the worker's health), and therefore entails questions of fair remuneration, this chapter will not dwell on the extensive case law concerning remuneration and other preconditions to assert workers' rights to vacation or maternity leave.[198] Still, it is clear that European legislation on working times envisages more than merely the protection of health and safety, which has led to fierce contestation of the legal basis of the Working Time Directive.[199]

8.5.3. THE WORKING TIME DIRECTIVE: CORE PROVISIONS

The objective of the successive Working Time Directives, i.e. improvement of workers' safety and health at work, is clearly stated in their preambles.[200] Explicit reference is made to the Framework Directive 89/391/EEC on safety and health of workers at work, the provisions of which are fully applicable to the areas covered by the Working Time Directive.[201] The expressed purpose of the directive (Article 1) is to lay down minimum *safety and health requirements* for the organisation of working time. The notion of 'minimum requirements' leaves room for the Member States 'to apply or introduce laws, regulations or administrative provisions more favourable to the protection of the safety and health of workers' (Article 15). Since 2004, when the amended directive (2003/88/EC) came into force, the directive applies to all sectors of activity, both public and private, within the meaning of Article 2 of the Framework Directive 89/391/EEC. Finally, it can be noted that the objective of the directive has been repeatedly affirmed by the Court of Justice: 'Harmonisation at Community level

198 The rights to parental leave and the right to part-time work will be dealt with in Chapter 4.
199 ECJ 1996, C-84/94 (*UK v. Council*). See also Section 1.3.3.2.
200 Directive 93/104/EC, recitals 5 and 8; and Directive 2003/88/EC, recitals 1–4.
201 Directive 2003/88/EC, recital 3.

in relation to the organisation of working time is intended to guarantee better protection of the safety and health of workers'.[202]

The 'minimum safety and health requirements for the organisation of working time', include:

- minimum daily rest of 11 consecutive hours per 24-hour period; and
- a rest break where the working day is more than six hours (the duration and the conditions for granting are to be determined by collective agreement or, if an agreement is lacked, by national legislation);
- weekly rest amounting to a minimum uninterrupted period of 35 hours (a reduction to a period of 24 hours can be justified by objective technical or organisational reasons)[203] (this will normally be calculated over a 14-day reference period);
- maximum average weekly working time, including overtime, not exceeding 48 hours (this will normally be calculated over a four-month reference period);
- paid annual leave of at least four weeks in accordance with the conditions for entitlement to, and granting of, such leave laid down by national legislation and/or practice; and
- night work not exceeding an average of eight hours in any 24-hour period[204] (national law, collective or other industry agreements will determine the reference period).

The core of the requirements, listed in Chapter 2 of the directive, are quite straightforward. Articles 3 to 6 set rather unequivocal standards for daily rest, daily breaks, weekly rest periods and maximum working time. Article 8 lays down more stringent standards pertaining to night work, whereas Article 7 bestows upon the Member States a more general obligation to take the measures necessary to ensure that every worker is entitled to paid annual leave of at least four weeks' and leaves it to the Member States to fill in the further conditions.

It is interesting to note that the stipulations concerning rest time precede Article 6 on the maximum working time. That may be interpreted as that *rest* (and recuperation) is the main focus of the regulation. Adequate resting time is seen as the key to health protection. It has to be noted as well that the stipulations are primarily directed to the employer according to the general

202 ECJ 2000, C-303/98 (*SIMAP*); ECJ 2003, C-151/02 (*Jaeger*); ECJ 2004, C-3971/01-C 403/01 (*Pfeiffer*); ECJ 2015, C-266/14 (*Tyco*).

203 Kenner (2005).

204 Night workers whose work involves special hazards or heavy physical or mental strain do not work more than eight hours in any period of 24 hours during which they perform night work. More specific rights are connected to night work in Articles 8 and 9 Directive 2003/88/EC.

principle that the obligation of taking care of the health and safety of the workers rests primarily on the employer. This responsibility is closely related to the employer's position to set the conditions of work – more specifically the power to give directions. But at the same time it means that the workers are bound by the measures taken. It also implies that the employer has to supervise that the worker actually takes his rest. The Court of Justice has affirmed this in its decision on a British case by requiring that the employer has to *ensure that the workers actually exercise such rights*. If the employer does not do so and the national law does not provide measures that the exercise of the right is actually guaranteed, the state has failed to fulfil its obligations under Articles 17(1), 3 and 5 of the directive.[205]

Even if the above provisions *may* appear to be rather straightforward, they rest on two intertwined pillars: personal scope of application and the definition of *rest* and *working time*. Those questions have been approached by the CJEU in several decisions, which can, nevertheless, all be traced back to two ground-breaking cases: *SIMAP* and *Kiel Jaeger*.[206]

As to the personal scope of the directive, the Court of Justice ruled in the SIMAP judgment that it is clear from both the objective of the directive – encouraging improvement of the safety and health of workers at work – and from the wording of Article 2(1), that the scope must be necessarily broad. By implication the exceptions to the scope must be interpreted restrictively. Consequently, doctors in primary health care cannot be excluded from the directive since they do not fall under the explicit exceptions referred to in Articles 1(3) and 17.[207]

On the issue of what is 'rest' and what has to be understood by 'working time', there has been a lot of confusion, in which debate the Court has shed some light without solving the problem fully. The debate centres on the wording in Article 2 of the directive. A key provision is the guarantee of *adequate rest* periods in Article 2(9), which is further elaborated in Articles 3–5 by minimum requirements. However, 'rest' is not clearly defined. A rest period is 'any period which is not working time' (Article 2(2)). This implies that the notion of 'working time' is crucial, but at the same time very contested. Article 2(1) defines working time as 'any period during which the worker is working, at the employer's disposal and carrying out his activity or duties, in accordance with national laws and/or practice'. The Court has been asked to clarify this notion,

---

205 ECJ 2006, C-484/04 (*Commission v. UK*), §§42–44.

206 ECJ 2000, C-303/98 (*SIMAP*) and ECJ 2003, C-151/02 (*Jaeger*), followed by many others, among which are ECJ 2001, C-241/99 (*Confederación Intersindical Galega*); ECJ 2004, C-3971/01-C 403/01 (*Pfeiffer*); ECJ 2005, C-14/04 (*Dellas*); ECJ 2010, C-227/09 (*Accardo*).

207 ECJ 2000, C-303/98 (*SIMAP*), §§34–38; and ECJ 2001, C-241/99 (*Confederación Intersindical Galega*). In the Directive (2003/88) it is made even clearer in what situations workers are excluded; see Articles 1(3) and 17.

which it did in a series of decisions that have had far-reaching consequences for the law and practice in Member States. The questions concerned situations in which workers had exceptional working time conditions, such as working in an on-call service or on stand-by times. In *Simap*, the Court held that time spent on call by doctors in health centres must be regarded in its entirety as working time if they are required to be present at the health centre. Mandatory and actual presence is decisive if they are obliged to be present and available at the workplace with a view to providing their professional services when required;[208] for in these circumstances they are not free to spend their time outside the centre as they wish. That situation has to be distinguished from the situation that they are contactable at all times, but without having to be at the centre/workplace. In that situation, even if they are at the disposal of their employer, they can manage their time with fewer constraints and pursue their own interests.[209] In *Jaeger*,[210] the Court reiterated its *SIMAP* decision. Also, in case of on-call duty ('*Bereitschaftsdienst*', '*service de garde*') doctors who are required to keep themselves available to their employer at the place determined by the employer for the whole duration of periods of on-call duty, are subject to appreciably greater constraints since they have to remain apart from their family and social environment and have less freedom to manage the time during which their professional services are not required. Decisive is whether the worker is required to be physically present at the place determined by the employer and to be available to the employer in order to be able to provide the appropriate services immediately in case of need.[211] These criteria also have to be applied to emergency workers in attendance in ambulances in the framework of an emergency service, even when this necessarily entails periods of inactivity of varying length in between calls.[212] In a recent case, the Court further clarified the material scope of the notion 'working time'. The case concerned the work of a volunteer firefighter (Mr. Matzak) in a Belgian town, which work he performed next to his regular job. Volunteer firefighters are involved in the operations of a public service and they must, inter alia, be on stand-by and on duty at the fire station, for which a roster is established at the beginning of the year. Matzak, claimed the payment of a provisional sum of one euro for his services as a volunteer firefighter during his years of service, particularly for his stand-by services. He has a double obligation: to be contactable during his stand-by time under the condition to respond to

208 ECJ 2000, C-303/98 (*SIMAP*), §§49–52.

209 So also AG Saggio in his opinion in ECJ 2000, C-303/98, §37. E.g. Kenner (2004), p. 593 ff.

210 ECJ 2003, C-151/02 (*Jaeger*). This case was also about doctors in hospitals and other health centres. See also ECJ 2005, C-14/04 (*Dellas*), §46, which concerns a special needs teacher in residential establishments for disabled young people.

211 ECJ 2005, C-14/04 (*Dellas*) §48.

212 ECJ 2004, C-3971/01–C 403/01 (*Pfeiffer*), §§93 and 94.

calls from his employer within eight minutes and to be physically present at the place determined by the employer, which was in this case Matzak's own home. The Court felt considered the requirement to reach the place of work within eight minutes objectively limited the opportunities of a worker – in Matzak's circumstances – to devote himself to his personal and social interests. That leads to the conclusion that these standby periods were to be regarded as working time.[213]

It can be concluded that all these forms of time related to work were classified as working time and not as rest period.[214] The explicit reference of the Court to the preamble of the directive can be seen as a 'proof' that social considerations, i.e. the improvement of workers' safety, hygiene and health at work, should not be subordinated to purely economic considerations.[215]

A remaining question is whether 'travel time' is or can be considered as working time. In many countries this issue is regulated mostly in collective agreements. According to Article 15 of the directive it is allowed because it is in favour of the worker. However, if it is not regulated, the question is whether the answer can be derived from the directive. In the *Tyco* decision the Court was asked to answer this question. In this case, the worker was a technician employed by a firm maintaining security systems in Madrid. He had to travel every day from his home to the places where he carried out his tasks. The distance from the worker's home to those places varied a great deal and was sometimes more than 100 kilometres. The Court argued that the decisive factor was that the worker was required to be physically present at the place determined by the employer and to be available to the employer in order to be able to provide the appropriate services. Although the worker had a certain freedom to manage the way that he did the work and how he travelled to the place of work, the Court found that during the journeys.

The workers acted on the instructions of the employer, who might change the order of the customers or cancel or add an appointment. It is apparent that, during the necessary travelling time, which generally could not be shortened, the worker was not able to use his time freely and pursue his own interests. Consequently, during the travelling time he was at his employer's disposal. In conclusion the travelling time had, in the given circumstances, to be considered as working time.

It has to be noted that the above-mentioned decisions of the Court, in which the notion of working was interpreted quite broadly, do not imply that the hours spent to these forms of work have to be remunerated either as belonging to the normal working hours or as overtime. The directive covers only some aspects

---

213 ECJ 2018, C-518/15 (*Ville de Nivelles v. Rudy Matzak*).

214 ECJ 2003, C-151/02 (*Jaeger*), §§56 and 71.

215 ECJ 2003, C-151/02 (*Jaeger*), §§67.

of the organisation of the working time and anyhow it does not regulate the remuneration. Remuneration is part of the national regulations, be it the law or collective agreements.[216] However, the decisions of the Court on this matter can certainly have a large impact on the practice of the Member States in respect of the health care institutions, ambulances' and firefighters' services.[217] By consequence, national laws have to be adapted to the content of the Court decisions in so far as they fully or partly deviate from them.

In its key decisions *SIMAP* and *Jaeger*, the Court ruled that the concepts of 'working time' and 'rest period' within the meaning of Directive 93/104 are concepts of Community law. Therefore, they must be interpreted in accordance with objective characteristics by reference to the scheme and purpose of the directive[218] and it is the competence of the Court to establish the meaning of these concepts. In the view of the Court only an autonomous interpretation is capable of securing full efficacy and uniform application of the directive in all Member States. Although the definition of the concept of working time refers to 'national law and/or practice', this does not mean that the Member States may unilaterally determine its scope. The right of employees to have working periods and corresponding rest periods stems directly from the provisions of the directive. Any other interpretation would frustrate the objective of the directive of harmonising the protection of the safety and health of workers by means of minimum requirements.

8.5.4. SCOPE, DEROGATIONS AND OPT-OUT

8.5.4.1. Personal Scope

While the directive does not contain a specific article setting its personal scope, its operative provisions refer to a 'worker'. This concept of 'worker' is not defined in the directive itself. Since Directive 2003/88/EC refers to Framework Directive 89/391/EEC the personal scope can be derived from that directive. Also this provision is not absolutely clear since it reads that any person employed by an employer is a worker. It adds that this includes trainees and apprentices but excludes domestic servants. The only sector excluded (by Directive 1999/63/EC) is seafarers.

---

216 Explicitly in ECJ 2015, C-266/14 (*Tyco*), §48. Similarly, in ECJ 2005, C-14/04 (*Dellas*), §38–39. It has to be kept in mind that this different from the regulation of paid holidays that is guaranteed by Article 7 of the directive.

217 See COM(2003)843 final/2, p. 20. Figures based on the monitoring of Directive 104/93/EEC. A more recent report on the implementation of Directive 2003/88/EC gives an update without providing figures (COM(2017)254 final).

218 ECJ 2000, C-303/98 (SIMAP), §§48–50 and ECJ 2003, C-151/02 (*Jaeger*), §§58–59. See also Kenner (2004), p. 596.

The notion of 'worker' is interpreted as a European Union concept.[219] As to the personal scope of the directive 2003/88 in the *SIMAP* case,[220] the Court has taken a general stand by deciding that it is clear both from the objective of the directive – encouraging improvement in the safety and health of workers at work – and from the wording of Article 2(1), that the scope must necessarily be broad. By implication, the exceptions to the scope must be interpreted restrictively. One important remaining issue is whether self-employed people could also be covered by the Working time directive. In general, it can be said that self-employed persons are not covered by the directive since they are not workers in the meaning of the case law of the Court. However, the decision in the *FNV KIEM* case might also be relevant here. In *FNV KIEM*, the Court makes a distinction between the self-employed and the 'bogus' self-employed. The Court held that 'the classification of a 'self-employed person' under national law does not prevent that person being classified as an employee within the meaning of EU law if the independence is merely notional, thereby disguising an employment relationship'.[221]

If the scope of working times regulation were to be extended to the bogus self-employed, this would clearly limit the possibilities of employers to use 'flexible' work at the expense of workers' health.

8.5.4.2. Derogation

On the other hand, the directive itself leaves ample room to fit working times regimes to the employers' needs of flexibility. Most notably, Article 17 of the directive contains various possibilities to derogate from some of its core stipulations to a certain extent and Member States can make use of this at the implementation of the directive. One of the reasons for opening up possibilities to derogate is to accommodate the wish of the employers to introduce more flexibility in order to be more competitive. Or as the preamble states: 'In view of the question likely to be raised by the organisation of working time within an undertaking, it appears desirable to provide for flexibility in the application of certain provisions of this Directive'. In order to keep the objective of the directive intact, it is added that compliance has to be ensured in line with the principles of protecting the safety and health of workers, implying that derogation may only

219 ECJ 2010, C-428/09 (*Isère*) and ECJ 2011, C-519/09 (*May*). E.g. Barnard (2012a), p. 537.

220 ECJ 2000, C-303/98 (*SIMAP*), §§34–38; and ECJ 2001, C-241/99 (*Confederación Intersindical Galega*).

221 ECJ 2014, C-413/13 (*FNV Kiem*), §§35–37. See, on this case, Chapter 5. One might wonder whether this interpretation can be used in the context of regulating working time of quasi-self-employed people. There is no case law on this question so far.

be acceptable under the condition that the workers concerned must be given equivalent compensatory rest periods.[222]

Derogation may either be made by the government or invoked via collective arrangements.

8.5.4.3. *National Law*

In order to be able to rely on a derogation in the national law a Member State has to make an explicit choice for a certain normative/legislative technique, be it a collective agreement or an agreement by both sides of industry. If it opts for such a technique, the general principles of EU law have to be respected fully, including the principle of legal certainty. The (from the directive) derogating provisions must be formulated with the requisite precision and clarity necessary to satisfy the requirements flowing from that principle.[223] In line with the case law of the Court, derogations must be interpreted in such a way that their scope is limited to what is strictly necessary in order to safeguard the interests that those derogations seek to be protected.[224] Although not being an explicit possibility for derogation, Article 16 of Directive 2003/88/EC gives Member States the possibility to extend the period to be taken into account when calculating the maximum weekly working time to 16 weeks (the so-called reference period).

A more general ground for derogating from the directive is laid down in Article 17(1), which permits derogation in cases where on account of the specific characteristics of the activity concerned, the duration of the working time is not measured and/or predetermined or can be determined by the workers themselves, and particularly in the case of managing executives or other persons with autonomous decision-taking powers. They have to be given more freedom to organise their own working times. The term 'autonomous decision-taking powers' has to be interpreted very strictly, meaning that the derogation applies only to workers who are *entirely* free to organise their own working time, and not to workers who are only partially free to do so.[225]

8.5.4.4. *Collective Agreement*

For an important part, derogations are connected to the nature of the activities in certain sectors and branches of industry, such as offshore work, seagoing fishing

222 Directive 2003/88/EC, preamble recitals 15 and 16.
223 ECJ 2010, C-227/09 (*Accardo*), §§51–55.
224 ECJ 2003, C-151/02 (*Jaeger*), §89.
225 ECJ 2006, C-484/04 (*Commission v. UK*), §47.

vessels or enterprises in which work cannot be interrupted because of technical or organisational reasons. One can think of health care centres in so far as they concern primary care for emergency treatment, ambulance services, fire and civil protection services subject to emergency of acting provided the principles of protecting the safety and health of workers are ensured. Therefore it may be desirable to conclude sector-specific derogations, which may be based not only on national legislation but also, and more particularly, on (collective) agreements by both sides of industry. This form of derogation may be based on Article 18, which allows workers and employers to derogate from the stipulations on *rest* time, thereby allowing for more flexibility in organising rest time or the number of night shifts, be it 'on condition that equivalent compensating rest periods are granted to the workers concerned'. Article 18 does not allow derogation from Article 6 (working time).

8.5.4.5. Opt-Out

The most contentious form of derogation is the *individual opt-out* provided for in Article 22 of the directive 2003/88/EC. This opt-out clause was inserted in Article 18 of the first Directive (93/104/EC), and left open, to every Member State, the option not to apply Article 6, 'while respecting the general principles of the protection of the safety and health of workers' (Article 18(1)(b)). Individual opt-outs are now possible in more than half of the Member States,[226] five of which pose no limitations at all to the possibility to opt-out.

However, this does not imply that every employer may one-sidedly demand that workers agree to more than 48 hours a week. This may only be demanded from the worker after if the worker has agreed to perform such work, and no worker may be 'subjected to any detriment by his employer because he is not willing to give his agreement to perform such work'.[227] The consent has to be given by the workers themselves, and the consent of a trade union representative cannot be given in place of the worker's consent.[228]Also the employer is required to provide the competent authorities at their request with information on cases in which workers have consented to opt-out.

This individual right to opt-out was (in 1993) meant to be a temporary option, to keep the UK on board. It is not removed in the 2003 directive, again under pressure from the UK.[229]

226 SEC(2010)1611 final, p. 96.

227 Empirical evidence has shown, however, that many workers are indeed put under pressure to work long hours. Barnard (2003), pp. 223–52.

228 ECJ 2004, C-3971/01-C 403/01 (*Pfeiffer*) §81; already in ECJ 2000, C-303/98 (*SIMAP*), §74.

229 The UK was not the only country that used it, many other countries did in response to the *SIMAP* and *Jaeger* decisions. E.g. Barnard (2012a), p. 550.

8.6. SUPERVISION AND ENFORCEMENT

It is clear, both from the structure and the content of the various occupational health and safety directives, that is primarily the responsibility of the employer to protect the health and safety of the worker. This responsibility is closely related to the employer's position to set the conditions of work – more specifically the power to give directions, which may include ordering the worker to perform (possibly) dangerous tasks. However, it is not a matter of course that all employers wholeheartedly assume this responsibility and fully comply with the requirements of the occupational health and safety legislation. For that reason, the Member States, in the wording of Article 4 of the Framework Directive, have to ensure adequate control and supervision.[230]

Even if it may be obvious to directly interpret 'control and supervision' to mean control by public authority (notably the Labour Inspectorate), this by no means is the only form of control provided for by the Framework Directive (or national legislations).

The first line of supervision is to be found within the companies themselves. The Framework Directive contains various provisions on this topic. For example, it is the express obligation of any worker to immediately inform the employer of any work situation that represents a serious and immediate danger to safety and health (Article 13(2) Framework Directive). Furthermore, the directive bestows upon the individual worker a right to stop work in the event of serious, imminent and unavoidable danger and to immediately leave the workplace (Article 8). In some European countries, workers' representatives have specific powers to stop work in the case of imminent danger – notably Spain, Sweden and the Netherlands.

Most importantly, workers and/or their representatives are entitled to appeal to the authority responsible for safety and health protection at work if they consider that the measures taken and the means employed by the employer are inadequate for the purposes of ensuring safety and health at work. This responsible authority is, primarily, the Labour Inspectorate, which is usually part of the Ministry of employment and social affairs. The Labour Inspectorate may be considered a cornerstone of the occupational health and safety legislation.[231]

The directive does not give binding rules on how to set up Labour Inspectorates and to a large extent this is based on national legislation. This does not mean, however, that each Member State can organise its Labour Inspection at its sole discretion. First, when designing national supervision,

---

230 Working Time Directive 2003/88/EC does not address the issue of enforcement, but it is clear from ILO Convention 81, Article 3 (see below), that the enforcement of working time legislation does fall within the realm of the Labour Inspectorate.

231 DG Employment (2015).

Member States must regard the provisions of ILO Labour Inspection Convention 81.[232] This ILO Convention has been ratified by all EU Member States. Second, at EU level, coordination is sought between the national inspection services, through periodic consultation in the so-called Senior Labour Inspectors' Committee (SLIC). One of the guiding documents released by the SLIC, is the *Common principles for labour inspection in relation to health and safety in the workplace* (2015).[233]

8.6.1. ILO CONVENTION 81

The ILO Convention on Labour Inspection obliges all countries that have ratified this convention to establish a national Labour Inspectorate for industrial companies (Article 1) and other commercial companies (Article 22). In 1995, the scope was extended to companies in the non-commercial sector (Article 1(3) Protocol 81).[234] In some Member States, the inspection services do not carry the name Labour Inspection, which is permitted on the basis of Article 2 of Convention 81.

The task of the Labour Inspectorate consists, according to Article 3(1)(a) of the Convention, primarily in the enforcement of national regulations in the field of health and safety and working hours (as well as in the field of wages[235]). In addition, the Inspectorate has a supporting role towards employers and employees in the form of providing technical advice and information.

The Labour Inspectorate must have a 'sufficient' number of inspectors (Article 10), 'duly qualified' experts (Article 9), and must be able to operate independently of political influence (Article 6). The Convention also implies that the Member States must ensure that provisions concerning the general

---

232 Labour Inspection Convention, 1947 (No. 81), Convention concerning Labour Inspection in Industry and Commerce. Also see Labour Inspection (Agricultural) Convention, 1969 (No. 129) and Labour Inspection (Seafarers) Convention, 1996 (No. 178).

233 Very recently, the European Commission also adopted a proposal for a regulation establishing a European Labour Authority (COM(2018)131 final). However, as enforcement of health and safety legislation falls outside of the scope of the proposal, this regulation shall not be dealt with here.

234 Protocol P81 of 1995 to the Labour Inspection Convention 1947.The Protocol has come into force in 1998, and has by now been ratified by 11 ILO Member States. Of the EU Member States, only Cyprus, Finland, Ireland and Luxembourg have signed the Protocol. Still, in various EU countries the scope of ILO Convention 81 is much wider in practice than for just industrial companies. In some Member States, certain sectors are exempted from the provisions in the Treaty.

235 The specific interpretation of this provision differs per country. In the Netherlands, for example, the role of the Labour Inspectorate in this field is limited to enforcement of the Minimum Wage Act only, whereas in other Member States the Inspectorate also plays a role in supervising collective labour agreements.

powers of the inspectors are laid down in national legislation. In particular, consideration should be given to: the right to 'enter freely and without previous notice at any hour of the day or night any workplace liable to inspection'; the right to carry out investigations and take samples of materials and substances (Article 12); and specific enforcement powers (direct intervention in dangerous situations (Article 13)). Workplaces may be inspected as often and as thoroughly as necessary to enforce proper compliance with the relevant regulations. Employers (or workers) who do not comply with legal provisions may be subject to sanctions according to the Convention without previous warning (Article 17). National legislation and regulations must also provide for a system of fines and other 'adequate penalties' (Article 18).

What constitutes a 'sufficient' number of inspectors or when they should be considered 'duly qualified' is not specified, but depends on a number of factors – such as the number of companies that need to be inspected, the nature of the regulations and the number of employees in individual Member States. With regard to the number of inspectors, the ILO uses a general guideline, from which it can be inferred that in 'industrial market economies' (such as the European Union) at least one inspector per 10,000 employees should be appointed.[236] However, this guideline is not binding. In 2011, the European Parliament called upon the European Commission to impose the standard of one inspector per 10,000 employees on the Member States.[237] The Commission, however, has not yielded to this request.

In various countries, the 1:10,000 ratio has been invoked by trade unions claiming that the number of inspectors in their country should be considered to be insufficient. This is done on the basis of Article 24 of the ILO Constitution – most recently by the Dutch Trade Union Federation (FNV), which filed a complaint against the Minister of Social Affairs and Employment about the alleged understaffing of the Dutch Labour Inspectorate.[238] Even if the ILO Committee indicated that

> the Convention does not contain any requirement for a specific number of labour inspectors (and that) the ratio of one inspector per 10,000 workers for industrial

---

236 International Labour Conference, 95th session, 2006, *Report III (part 1B)*, p. 66.

237 European Parliament Resolution of 15 December 2011 on the mid-term review of the European strategy 2007–2012 on Health and Safety at Work (2011/2147(INI)), 2013/ C 168 E/14.

238 Complaints may also be filed pertaining to other articles of the Convention, for example by the National Confederation of Trade Unions of Moldova (CNSM) concerning non-compliance with Article 12, upon which the ILO decided in favour of the complainant and 'invited the Government … to take such measures without delay as might be necessary to ensure the effective implementation of Articles 12 and 16 of the Labour Inspection Convention, 1947'. Article 16 contains a general obligation that 'Workplaces shall be inspected as often and as thoroughly as is necessary to ensure the effective application of the relevant legal provisions'.

> market economies is indicated as guidance and the main consideration to take into account by countries when determining the number of labour inspectors is whether they are sufficient to secure the effective discharge of the duties of the labour inspectorate

the Committee concluded in favour of the FNV. 'The Committee therefore requests the Government, in accordance with Articles 10 and 16 of the Convention, to ensure that the number and frequency of labour inspections is sufficient to ensure the effective discharge of inspection duties and compliance with the respective legal provisions in all workplaces.'[239] Partly as a result of the FNV action, and partly in response to a thorough analysis of the functioning of the labour inspection by the Dutch Senior Civil Service, in 2017 the Dutch government decided to increase the number of inspectors by over 50%.

8.6.2. EUROPEAN COORDINATION: THE SENIOR LABOR INSPECTORS COMMITTEE

Even, if ILO Convention 81 imposes general obligations on all Member States that have ratified the Convention, there are considerable differences between the national inspections of EU Member States (see below). In order to achieve more harmonised supervision in the Member States, an informal Senior Labor Inspectors Committee was set up in 1982, which has the task of supporting the Commission in monitoring enforcement of EU legislation at the national level. The Committee's importance increased after the implementation of the Framework Directive and the daughter Directives after 1989. The already ongoing processes of coordination between National Labour Inspectorates were formally ratified in 1995 in Commission Decision 95/319/EC establishing a Senior Labor Inspectors Committee. The establishment of the Senior Labor Inspectors Committee was, according to the recitals of the Commission Decision, prompted, inter alia, by the need for effective implementation and enforcement of Community legislation in the field of social policy. The committee is primarily focused on the development of common principles for enforcement policy and on the exchange of knowledge on methodologies for effective enforcement. In addition, the Senior Labor Inspectors Committee has the task of monitoring the enforcement of occupational health and safety standards in Europe. Finally, the Senior Labor Inspectors Committee advises on the possible impact of various policy proposals by the Commission relating to health and safety legislation.

---

[239] ILO Governing Body, November 2014, GB.322/INS/3/7, p. 27.

8.6.3. THE RIGHTS OF WORKERS (AND THEIR REPRESENTATIVES)

In the Framework Directive, it is not only stipulated that Member States must ensure adequate inspection, but a number of implicit requirements are also set for their performance, one of them being cooperation with workers (or workers' representatives) while inspecting the premises of a company. In particular, Article 11 of the Framework Directive stipulates that employees' representatives must be given the opportunity to submit their observations and opinions during inspection visits. In addition, workers may take the initiative to contact inspectors, according to the provision that 'workers and/or their representatives are entitled to appeal, in accordance with national law and/or practice, to the authority responsible for safety and health protection at work if they consider that the measures taken and the means employed by the employer are inadequate' (Article 11(6)). Finally, employees' representatives are entitled to a copy of any accident reports filed by the Labour Inspectorate (Article 9(1)(d), Article 11(2)(c)).

8.6.4. NATIONAL DIFFERENCES

As repeatedly stated in the Framework Directive, the specific implementation of occupational health and safety legislation has to be done in accordance with national laws and/or practices. Even if this notion of national practices is not expressly included in Article 4 of the Framework Directive, and despite the coordination initiatives discussed above (notably the Senior Labor Inspectors Committee), there clearly are quite fundamental differences between national Inspectorates. Even though health and safety legislation is the core business of the Inspectorates, in various countries the Inspectorate also enforces compliance with public law concerning non-domestic workers and (minimum) wage (e.g. in the Netherlands) or even supervises compliance with collective labour agreements (e.g. in France). Roughly speaking, general inspectorates are typical of Latin European countries, like France, Spain and Portugal, as well as the Baltic States, whereas in Sweden and the UK they mainly (albeit not exclusively) focus on health and safety at work.[240]

There are also differences in the position vis-à-vis the national legislature. As occupational health and safety legislation is, for an important part at least, public law, in most countries the Inspectorate is managed by and accountable to central government (notably the Ministry of Labour or Social Affairs). In some counties, however, there are also other forms of organising the

240 Walters (2016).

labour inspection. In Italy, for example, there are also labour inspectorates, or rather bilateral bodies, established by collective agreement that may play an active role in the compliance and control system. Hence, a fundamental role in occupational health and safety management is assigned to Joint Committees set up on the initiative of one or more of the entrepreneurs/workers' comparatively most representative organisations at national level. This is done on the basis of Article 2(ee) of Legislative Decree no. 81/2008. Another peculiarity is that the Italian Labour Inspectorate is only marginally competent in the domain of health and safety, which is covered by Local Health Authorities inspectors.

Finally, in some countries supervision on health and safety is also shared with social insurance institutions. A paramount example comes from Germany, where a dual system of safeguarding and promoting occupational health and safety is in place, including tasks for public authorities as well as for the autonomous bodies (*Berufsgenossenschaften*) of the Occupational Accident Insurance.[241] In Belgium, a pivotal role is assigned to the Fund for occupational accidents and the Fund for occupational diseases (recently merged into the Federal Agency for occupational risks), which play an important role both in the administration of workers' benefits in case of occupational accidents or an occupational disease.

8.6.5. ADMINISTRATIVE AND CRIMINAL CONSEQUENCES OF VIOLATION OF OCCUPATIONAL HEALTH AND SAFETY PROVISIONS

In case of violation of occupational health and safety provisions, both the employer and the worker may have to bear the consequences. However, as a result of the employer's right to instruct the worker, it is most often the employer who is subject to sanctions. The legal status as well as the use of administrative means of enforcement differ among the Member States, but the main instruments are: issuing an order to comply or rectify infringement, imposing pecuniary sanctions (fines); or ordering suspension of dangerous activities; or shutting down work. Finally, the employer (as well as the worker) may face criminal charges. Note that the violation of occupational health and safety provisions may be sanctioned by administrative law even if it has not resulted in a harmful event.

In some Member States, punitive sanctions may be used to 'convince' the employer to restore a situation which complies with the law. In Sweden, for example, compliance may be 'stimulated' by contingent fines, which have to be paid by the entrepreneur only in if the entrepreneur does not respect the specific

241 Deinert (2013).

orders issued by the Inspector. A similar method may be deployed by means of a 'non-compliance penalty' (cease and desist order). In specific cases, notably pertaining to high-risk companies falling under the Seveso Directive, the Dutch Labour Inspectorate has a right to issue an operating ban.

Criminal law applies in case of violations which lead to the death or serious ill health of the worker or even, in the Netherlands, for example, in situations where the employer has put workers *at risk* of serious health effects or injury. As far as the applicable criminal law provisions are concerned, further to the norms provided by general penal codes for death, injuries or procured disease, national legislators (the Austrian excluded) either: (a) provide for specific norms related to the health and safety domain within general penal codes (like in France, Hungary, Italy and Spain); (b) have issued a criminal social code (like in Belgium); or (c) integrate criminal law provisions directly into health and safety regulations (as in Germany, Sweden, the Netherlands and the UK).

CHAPTER 9

EUROPEAN LABOUR LAW AS THE RESULT OF CONFLICTING NORMS AND INTERESTS

Frans PENNINGS

9.1. INTRODUCTION

In the preceding chapters the main areas of European labour law were discussed. We have seen that in some of these areas strong legal standards were developed, e.g. requiring equal treatment of men and women and free movement of workers. There are also domains in which the Treaty gives no powers to make instruments and these are affected by EU law to a much lower extent. An example is dismissal law. On some topics, however, the impact of EU instruments other than labour law has been considerable, such on strikes and wages. European labour law certainly has a varied character.

Recent publications on European labour law often have a pessimistic tone. One reason is that in the past decade few new labour law instruments have been adopted. In the meantime, judgments of the Court of Justice have led to intensive debates because of their presumed negative impact on labour law. Some authors have even gone so far as to declare European labour law dead.[1]

Syrpis mentions the following reasons for being pessimistic regarding European labour law: there is only a limited amount of social legislation; the ways social legislation has been interpreted in recent years by the Court of Justice; much of the potential of European human rights law has not been realised; EU internal market law imposes important restrictions on the power of States and trade unions to apply labour law standards to mobile workers; and the Eurozone and crisis management measures taken to maintain the euro have led to sharp downward pressures on social standards in all Member States.[2]

This chapter will discuss this diagnosis and the prospects of European labour law. It will show that European labour law is a product of the interaction of various actors: the EU legislature; the European Commission; the Member States; private organisations, including employers' and employees' organisations; and the Court of Justice. These actors may have different interests; frequently rules and interests in the economic and social domains, respectively, conflict with each other. European labour law is the result of this battle.

In this cross-cutting analysis the topics that were also dealt with in the preceding chapters will be discussed. Here this is done from the perspective of asking what powers have been granted to the EU legislature, what conflicts exist between economic and social rights, and how do the various actors deal with these tensions. As a result, this chapter is not a summary of the preceding chapters, but instead it will approach the topics from this overall perspective. This analysis is not the common view of the authors of the preceding chapters – in some aspects they may even have different views. Thus this chapter is not a summary, but it is meant to provide food for discussion.

The following topics will be addressed: the free movement of workers (Section 9.2), the free movement of services (Section 9.3), equal treatment (Section 9.4) and social policy issues, including collective redundancies, consultation of employees, transfer of undertakings, health and safety and working time (Section 9.5). After this, in Section 9.6, the interaction of labour law and economic rights is discussed. This order is not the same as that of the preceding chapters, but corresponds with the differences which can be

---

1 For instance Ewing (2015), p. 9; Ter Haar et al. (2016), p. 293.

2 Syrpis (2016), p. 21.

observed in the European labour law landscape – strong standards in some areas (Sections 9.3–9.4); areas with specific instruments of EU social policy (Section 9.5); areas where EU labour law rules are absent but which may be strongly impacted by other EU law (Section 9.6).

9.2. FREE MOVEMENT OF WORKERS AND PERSONS

Free movement of workers belongs to the fundamental economic freedoms and has been ensured by the Treaties since the very establishment of the EEC. It not only prohibits impediments to free movement, but also, unlike the other economic freedoms (services, capital and establishment), prohibits discrimination on ground of nationality, to which there are only few exceptions. These exceptions have been interpreted narrowly by the Court of Justice.[3]

The free movement of workers is nowadays under pressure, mainly because it allows movement of persons who have very little prospect of finding work in the host State. Some Member States are concerned that this leads to burdens on their welfare systems, since these persons can, even if they have only a very low paid job or work very few hours, claim benefits to top up their low income. For the British government the perceived influx of foreign workers threatening the welfare state was an important issue in the negotiations with the European Union (Autumn 2015) before the 'Brexit' referendum and, even after the decision to leave the European Union, migration is still a major issue in the UK.[4] Some other Member States also see the issue of immigration of EU citizens with small resources as a problem.[5]

Although this presumed 'welfare tourism' should be put into perspective – there is much less migration of EU citizens between Member States than one might expect – the fear of this is a political reality.[6] A possible response to meet these fears will not lie in revising Article 45 TFEU, for instance by introducing a minimum period of work in the host country before this Article could be invoked. In order to revise the Treaty, the consent of all Member States would

3 See also Section 2.2.5.

4 See the agreement of the Council and the UK, EUCO 1/16. One element, meant to discourage exit from the EU, was a proposal to amend Regulation 492/2011, which would have allowed Member States to respond to situations of inflow of workers from other Member States of an exceptional magnitude over an extended period of time. The Council could authorise the Member State concerned to limit the ability of newly arriving EU workers to access non-contributory in-work benefits for a total period of up to four years from the commencement of employment. After the decision of the UK to leave the EU, this agreement was declared void.

5 See e.g. Section 2.1.

6 See Seeleib-Kaiser and Pennings (2018), p. 4.

be required and that would be extremely difficult to obtain. Moreover, the right to free movement is one of the pillars of the Treaty, and changes to this pillar entail the danger of a collapse of the whole framework.[7] After all, Treaty requires non-discrimination not only in relation to social advantages (benefits), but also regarding access to work and employment conditions. Therefore, if measures are necessary to regulate any possible negative effects of migration, they will have to be sought elsewhere.

One actor that could take action is the European Commission. As discussed in Chapter 2, Article 45 TFEU is elaborated in Regulation 492/2011, of which, in particular, Article 7 is relevant. This article ensures equal treatment of migrant workers with national workers in respect of social advantages. Therefore, for instance, income support and other social benefits provided to those with low wages cannot be refused on the ground of nationality. The Court of Justice has developed a broad interpretation of the term *worker*: any person performing, in exchange for remuneration, effective and genuine activities under supervision of another person or body, with the exclusion of activities on such a small scale as to be regarded as purely marginal and ancillary.[8] However, in order to restrict access to their welfare system, some Member States have set higher thresholds for considering a person as a 'worker'. For example, the UK has laid down in its regulations that only a person who works at least 40% of the regular number of full-time working hours is a worker for the purpose of Article 45 TFEU. For some benefits, an individual has to be *habitually resident*, meaning that the person must have lived already for some time legally in the country. Other countries have also introduced qualifying requirements for access to social rights, e.g. Sweden, whose legislation provides that a person only has access to health care if that person is registered in the Population Register; one condition for registration is that the person can show that he or she has the prospect of work for at least one year in Sweden.[9] In the Netherlands, the Dutch Policy rules on study grants require that a person must work at least 56 hours a month in order to be considered as a worker and thus have access to study loans. Until 2014 the condition was 32 hours a month, but the government wished to restrict access to the study grants. In contrast, in order to claim income supplementing benefits in the Netherlands a person has to earn at least 50% of the applicable public assistance rate or work at least 16 hours per week.[10] So even within one

7 For this reason the deviation from the right to free movement mentioned in note 4 was restricted to an emergency situation and on a temporary basis, as mentioned in the agreement. To those arguing for withdrawal from the EU, the agreement did not constitute a convincing response to their concerns.

8 ECJ 1982, 53/82 (*Levin*).

9 Hyltén-Cavallius (2018).

10 Pennings (2018).

and the same country different criteria are used to define 'worker'. Moreover, not all Member States have made or published the criteria they use to consider a person as a worker; in some Member States decisions solely depend on (discretional) individual assessments of the situation. These situations are at variance with the case law of the Court of Justice on the term worker, which, as previously mentioned, considers a person as a worker even if that person has a job with very low pay or low hours, or has worked for a short period only.[11]

These variations in the interpretation of the term worker impede free movement and lead to legal uncertainty. There are very good reasons for the broad interpretation by the Court of Justice of the term *worker*. In the words of the Court: 'it must be stressed that these concepts define the field of application of one of the fundamental freedoms guaranteed by the Treaty, and, as such, may not be interpreted restrictively'.[12]

However, in view of the need to reduce legal uncertainty and in order to avoid situations in which the difference between worker and economically inactive person becomes too small and therefore leads to unjustified differences in treatment, the European Commission could make a proposal for introducing a threshold for being considered a worker, e.g. in Regulation 492/2011. Of course, this must not reduce the freedom of movement, enshrined in Article 45 TFEU too much. However, a new article could provide, for instance, that one must have worked 56 hours a month in order to be considered as a worker. The disadvantage of this proposal is that it would deprive some persons from some social advantages; however, legal certainty and a more uniform regulation throughout the Union would be the benefit. Whether such a proposal would be accepted depends on the Member States, which have very different interests. Some Member States are not unhappy with the 'export' of their unemployed workers by making use of their access to other labour markets. These countries have no interest in setting higher thresholds. Other countries may prefer an even higher threshold in order to protect their labour market. Generally applicable rules, even if they were more restrictive than the present case law, would be preferable to ad hoc and discretionary policies.

Not only do Member States have different views on possible revisions of EU law, their contributions to the development of EU labour law also differ. Some countries criticise EU law and/or the case law of the Court of Justice, but are unwilling or unable to change their national law in order to try to solve the problems they perceive. Other countries follow a different approach: they adjust their national labour law, if necessary, to remain in line with or to respond to developments of EU law. Sometimes they undertake initiatives to influence EU law if they deem this necessary.

---

11 ECJ 2009, C-22/08 and C 23/08 (*Vatsouras and Koupatantze*).

12 ECJ 1982, 53/82 (*Levin*), §13.

Some national courts appear to request few or even no preliminary rulings from the Court of Justice on issues of free movement of workers. As a result, possible inconsistencies between national and EU law can remain undiscovered or unresolved for a long time.[13] Other courts undertake prompt action to have case law developed and clarity obtained on particular issues.

Next to trying to influence the development of EU law, Member States can also consider whether they wish to adjust their system to developments following from changes in EU legislation, new case law or developments resulting from the common market. This is also true regarding how they react to free movement. As has been pointed out in several chapters, including Chapter 1, Member States are exclusively competent to organise their own labour market and social system, and thus pass legislation on inter alia professional education, dismissal protection, minimum wages and social benefits. Such legislation can highly influence the organisation of the labour market. Does the labour market have a relatively large share of low paid work? Is there a particular need for low skilled workers, or is there a highly developed service industry? Migration responds to such characteristics of the market; low skilled workers seek markets which offer jobs they can do and where they can find a way of living. Of course, other factors also play a role – such as the state of the economy, the language and the climate – but availability of work and income are of decisive importance. Member States can thus consider whether the organisation of their labour markets is sustainable in view of migration. Migration itself has large beneficial effects and is in any case unavoidable in present day economies, so it makes more sense to investigate how to deal with it, rather than simply to seek to raise barriers against migrants.

This is, of course, a general remark and it is not always easy to operate in this way. However, the example of the Directive on cross-border healthcare (Directive 2011/24) may be useful to illustrate the statement that the characteristics of a national system are very important for the national response to a European instrument or development. Countries with a contributory health care system, e.g. Germany and the Netherlands, welcomed this directive, since in their systems, only those persons who are insured can receive care. The insurance company of these persons has to reimburse the costs, and taking on new clients can even be advantageous for the health care providers, since their turnover increases. For health care systems that are free at the point of access, such as in the UK or Denmark, however, in which it is difficult to produce invoices for delivered care and thus to ensure that costs are costs reimbursed, the directive may be perceived as a threat to their system.[14] In this way, exchange

13 A particular example is Denmark, see Jacqueson (2016), p. 183.
14 Pennings (2018).

of experiences between Member States and, where appropriate, technical help by the European Commission to enable national law to be adjusted to work more smoothly with EU law can be useful to reduce some of the tensions between national and EU law.

9.3. FREE MOVEMENT OF SERVICES AND LABOUR LAW

9.3.1. THE LIMITS TO RESTRICTING FREEDOM OF SERVICES BY LABOUR LAW

The legal framework for posting of workers is very different from that for free movement of workers. Whereas from the establishment of the European Economic Community the fear of unfair competition and *social dumping* was the justification for requiring equal treatment of migrant workers with the national workers of the state of employment, this approach was not followed in respect of employees who are posted by their employer.

That the equal treatment principle of workers does not apply to posted workers does not automatically follow from the posting construction itself: equal treatment is, from a legal point of view, perfectly possible. In the *Rush Portuguesa* judgment, however, the Court of Justice applied the Treaty provision on free movement of services, which does not require equal treatment of workers, since in this case the Court could not follow the free movement of workers path.[15] The workers in the latter judgment did not have at that time have the right to free movement and a fine was imposed on the employer which had posted Portuguese workers without a work permit to France. As a result, the facts of the case meant that the Court had to rely on free movement of services. The facts of the case were atypical, but had an enormous impact on the further development of the posting rules, although it has to be admitted that it is not possibly, of course, to know how these would have developed had this case never been presented to the Court of Justice. In *Rush Portuguesa*, the Court was not asked questions on the position of the workers concerned; however, in response to remarks by Member States, it considered that Community law does not preclude Member States from extending their legislation or collective labour agreements to any person who is employed, even temporarily, within their territory, no matter in what country the employer is established; nor does Community law prohibit Member States from enforcing those rules by appropriate means.

In later case law, however, the Court set restrictions to the imposition of the national labour law rules of the host State, since these can infringe the free

15 ECJ 1990, C-113/89 (*Rush Portuguesa*).

movement of services.[16] Indeed, some countries went quite far in subjecting foreign employers to their own labour law. Moreover, the playing field changed radically when in 2004 a number of Middle and Eastern European countries accessed the EU. For these countries 'export' of cheap labour was an important means to further the growth of their economy. This was understandable from their point of view. Cheap labour constituted their major, or even only, way to compete, since these countries had to build up their market economies from scratch.

There appeared to be considerable legal uncertainty as to which restrictions to free movement were allowed and which were not. Since in this competitive market some social thresholds were necessary, a compromise was reached in the Posted Workers Directive. This provides that protection by labour law of the host State is restricted to the areas mentioned in Article 3 of the Directive. Thus the Posted Workers Directive defines precisely which parts of the host State's labour law can *and* have to be imposed (the core labour law) on employers established in another Member State who post workers to the host State.

The minimum wage is the most important part of the core labour law that can be imposed. The Posted Workers Directive leaves intact the principle that Member States remain free to design their own system. However, it only allows imposition of a minimum wage on foreign employers if that is regulated in law, regulation or administrative provision, or by collective agreements if it is certain that they have general applicability, since the foreign companies must not be discriminated against. Although a declaration that a collective labour agreement is universally applicable is the clearest way to give it the function granted by the directive, the Posted Workers Directive is also attuned to systems that do not have a system for declaring agreements universally applicable. Collective agreements which have been concluded by the most representative employers' and labour organisations at national level and which are applied throughout national territory, provided equality of treatment on the core provisions of Article 3 is guaranteed, can thus also be the source of minimum wage provisions (Article 3(8)).

In the *Laval* judgment,[17] the Court decided that the host country cannot impose more of its labour law on foreign companies than the core provisions mentioned in the Directive. It made clear that Article 3(7) of the Posted Workers Directive, providing that paragraphs 1 to 6 shall not prevent application of terms and conditions of employment which are more favourable to workers, applies only to more favourable provisions in the law or collective agreements of the Member State of origin (§81). An interpretation that would allow host Member States to impose more of its labour law than the core provisions would amount to depriving the directive of its effectiveness, the Court added.

---

16 See Section 2.4.1.

17 ECJ 2007, C-341/05 (*Laval*), see also ECJ 2008, C-346/06 (*Rüffert*).

This argument is not fully convincing, since an interpretation allowing the host State to impose more of its labour law would certainly also make sense. After all, Article 3 requires that Member States shall *ensure* that undertakings guarantee workers posted to their territory the terms and conditions of employment according to Article 3(3). The wording as such does not give a limitation to the labour law rules that can be imposed. A reading of Article 3(7) which is broader than the Court's means that the Directive still imposes obligations on Member States to require the foreign companies to follow the hard core of labour law; without the Directive there is no such obligation. Thus, the alternative interpretation does not deprive the Directive from its meaning. However, that interpretation would give Member States more room to make it less attractive for foreign companies to operate in their country and it would be more difficult to define when a host State had gone too far in impeding free movement.

The dilemma was thus whether Member States should have the freedom to decide to impose more than the core labour law on foreign employers, which may have the effect that the free movement of services is further restricted, or should this not be allowed, which may result in wage competition, and even social dumping. The Court chose for the second approach, i.e. to strictly limit the restrictions on free movement of services.

The Court has been seriously criticised for this interpretation. However, it has to be acknowledged that Member States and/or trade unions can be tempted to impose such extent of their labour law on foreign companies, so that the latter can effectively be kept out of the country. This seemed sometimes to happen before the Posting of Workers Directive came into force and it was difficult to develop clearly defined general criteria in the case law to prevent this.[18] Without the restrictions set by the Posting of Workers Directive, trade unions could, at least in theory, set higher wage demands for foreign than for national companies and effectively deter foreign companies from exercising their right to free movement. Workers' actions sometimes have the clear objective to exclude foreign workers see, for instance, the 'British Jobs for British Workers' slogan in the Lindsey Oil Refinery Disputes.[19] Therefore regulation of the relationship between labour law and free movement of services seems certainly necessary.

9.3.2. REACTIONS OF THE MEMBER STATES: ADJUST TO THE DIRECTIVE OR NOT?

The Posting of Workers Directive has also had some positive effects on the development of national labour law. Since countries without a statutory

18 ECJ 1999, C-369/96 (*Arblade*).

19 Barnard (2009b).

minimum wage (or minimum wages defined in collective agreements that are generally applicable in the sense of the Posting of Workers Directive) have no barrier against wage competition by service providers from abroad, some of countries, including the UK and Germany, have decided to introduce a statutory minimum wage. As a result the position of workers, including national workers, was indirectly (to some extent) improved by the Directive.

Other countries deliberately do not have a statutory minimum wage (or a system with universally applicable collective labour agreements), and have not introduced such a system in response to the Posting of workers directive, since they consider non-interference by the legislature in the process of collective bargaining essential to their system of labour relations. As discussed earlier *supra*, the Posting of workers directive has facilities for countries that do not have a system for declaring collective agreements universally applicable. Still, these cannot be easily used, as seen in the example of Sweden. As Bruun & Malmberg (2011) describe, collective bargaining in Sweden follows the so-called *autonomous collective agreements* model. In this system a collective agreement covers the branch of activity in question and there is no system for declaring such collective labour agreement generally binding. Instead, trade unions try to force domestic and foreign employers who do not belong to a signatory employers' organisation to conclude so-called *application* agreements to follow the agreement for the branch of activity in question.[20] If the employer refuses to sign such an agreement, collective action is undertaken. For Sweden this is an important element of its system, since collective bargaining at the workplace means that there is a direct contact between the trade union members and the trade unions. This system has traditionally stimulated employees to become members of the trade unions and has led to relatively high unionisation rates. Changing one part of such a system may therefore have huge effects on the overall labour relations.

After the *Laval* judgment, however, it was necessary to review the Swedish legislation, in order to take away its inconsistencies with this case law. The starting point for the government was that the system of autonomous collective agreements should be maintained. This led to the result that, according to the amended Swedish Posting of Workers Act, trade unions are allowed to take action with the aim of regulating the employment conditions of posted workers only if the employment conditions they demand correspond to the conditions in the nationwide collective agreement (the reference agreements); second, the demand can only concern the hard nucleus of the Posting of Workers Directive

20 Bruun & Malmberg (2011), p. 24.

and, third, the demands have to be compared with the employment conditions already applicable to the posted worker.[21]

This system follows the first indent of Article 3(8) of the Posting of Workers Directive, i.e. that Member States may base the minimum standards required on collective agreements or arbitration awards which are generally applicable to all similar undertakings in the geographical area and in the profession or industry concerned. The problem, however, was that, in the Swedish system, full coverage of the collective agreement could not be guaranteed. 'There might always be some employers at national level who for different reasons might fall outside the scope of application of these general agreements'.[22] Still, the Swedish legislature did not think that this made the use of the mentioned indent of Article 3(8) impossible.[23] A second problem was that in the last decade there has been a development, in which nationwide collective agreements often contain only a framework for workplace bargaining; the actual rates on pay are laid down locally. This makes it difficult to be in conformity with the Posting of Workers Directive's demands that these rates are laid down in national agreements.[24]

The case of Sweden has been discussed here extensively, as it shows clearly the tensions that can exist between implementation of EU law and domestic systems. Domestic systems are based on important traditional values and form a system that is not so easy to change. However, the impact of EU law may makes it unavoidable that the system has to be rethought, as otherwise the negative effects may undermine the system. Sweden did review its system but restricted the right to strike, instead of the system of autonomous collective bargaining.[25] The problem was therefore not solved and will remain to exist, even when equal pay is introduced by the revised Posting of Workers Directive. Also, under the revised Directive the labour law provisions that are imposed on posting companies have to be in line with the system of Article 3(8). This leaves it still to the Member State and the social partners to come to an agreement on how to make use of the possibilities of the Directive.

---

21 Bruun & Malmberg (2011), p. 26. This Act ('lex Laval') has been revised in 2010 so the extent of the restrictions on the right to strike have been reduced; however, it is still interesting to look at this reaction.

22 Bruun & Malmberg (2011), p. 28.

23 This seems to be correct; also in case of a system of generally binding collective labour agreements it may be possible, under some conditions, for collective labour agreements, to be exempted from the agreement which has been declared generally binding.

24 Bruun & Malmberg (2011), p. 30. Rönmar (2014), p. 242.

25 Rönnmar (2010b); European Parliament (2010) (*Impact of the ECJ judgments on Viking, Laval, Ruffert and Luxembourg on the practice of collective bargaining and the effectiveness of social action*), p. 9. The new Act was heavily criticised by the European Committee of Social Rights in a decision of 3 July 2013 (85/2012). In 2016/17 this Swedish law was revised again.

9.3.3. THE EU LEGISLATURE: EQUAL TREATMENT OR WAGE COMPETITION?

The fact that wage competition was possible under the Posting of Workers Directive has been a very sensitive issue. Wage competition is hard to reconcile with the important principles that traditionally underlie European labour law, i.e. that free movement must not lead to social competition and deterioration of the national social systems. The rules on posted workers are the more problematic since under the coordination rules for social security workers can be posted for a maximum of 24 months, and thus remain under the social security system of the country of origin. Countries with lower contributions than those of the host State have thus an additional advantage. In addition, tax law also has posting rules, although these apply for a maximum of 183 days only. This can mean an important cost advantage for the service providers.

For a long time it seemed impossible to change the rules and introduce equal treatment for posted workers. However, in 2016 the European Commission placed equal pay of posted and domestic workers on the agenda.[26] This proposal met heavy resistance from the Member States that had so far benefited from wage competition. Fourteen Parliaments issued reasoned opinions that the revised Directive would not satisfy the subsidiarity principle (the 'yellow card' procedure). From their comments it appeared that they were not really worried about the subsidiarity principle as such, but commented on the contents of the directive. These Member States considered the proposal to be protecting the labour markets of the richer Member States.[27]

It cannot be denied that in the short-term equal pay may negatively affect workers (and their employers) from the Eastern European States. However, the original argument underlying equal treatment of migrant workers, i.e. that economic integration must not lead to lowering of living conditions and of social protection in the State of employment, is still valid and has an important long-term meaning for social systems. This argument is also valid for pay for posted workers.

9.3.4. CONCLUSION

The actors discussed in this section can in various ways react to developments in European labour law. In order to promote the development of European labour

---

26 European Commission (2016) (Proposal for a Directive amending Directive 96/71/EC concerning the posting of workers in the framework of the provision of services), see also Section 2.4.3.

27 Fromage and Kreilinger (2017).

law and making clear its effects on domestic law, Member States should be more explicit and transparent in the choices they make in reaction to developments of EU labour law. For instance, what was the reaction of the country, and why, in response to the *Laval* judgment: to restrict the right to strike, to introduce a statutory minimum wage, to have a system in which collective labour agreements determine the minimum wage, or to do nothing? Social partners also have a role to play. They can bargain to determine the rates of pay in collective labour agreements and how these can be imposed in accordance with the framework of the Posting of Workers Directive.

Also for the European institutions it is important to react to tensions between national systems and EU law. One issue is to what extent persons in marginal jobs should have access to the welfare system in the first years of their stay. Thus it relates to the definition of 'worker'. Although proposals to change this definition may have negative effects, it is better to be transparent regarding possible options and to be in charge of the developments. Also, in relation to the Posting of Workers Directive, it is important that the European institutions are transparent on the options that exist to address the tensions that appear in this area.

9.4. EQUAL TREATMENT AND FUNDAMENTAL RIGHTS

For a long time equal pay and equal treatment of men and women were, apart from the (mainly economic) freedom of movement of workers, the only areas of EU social policy. Just as in the case of free movement of workers, the role of the Court of Justice has been very important. In its case law the Court 'promoted' the principle that men and women should receive equal pay for equal work (Article 119 EEC), which was originally meant to prevent unfair competition by those Member States not bound by the ILO Convention on equal pay, to a fundamental principle of European labour law.[28]

The Court's case law has had an important impact on many national systems, that were, until the 1980s, characterised by a low work participation rate of women and various forms of (direct or indirect) unequal treatment of men and women (e.g. certain advantages were paid to breadwinners only). EU legislation and the Court of Justice have had a dominant and fundamental role in enforcing equal treatment (see also Chapter 3). This has led, inter alia, to legislation on equal pay and equal employment conditions, individualisation of social security benefits, and adjustments of occupational pension schemes.

---

[28] ECJ 1976, C-43/75 (*Defrenne II*). See also Section 1.3.2.

Since the end of the 1990s, instruments on equal treatment on other grounds have been introduced: the Directive on race and ethnic origin and the Framework directive relevant to discrimination on grounds of, inter alia, disability and age (see also Chapter 3). These directives and, in particular, the case law of the Court of Justice, have led to significant developments in equal treatment law, including the application of equal treatment provisions also on facts existing before the implementation date of the directive (*Mangold* judgment)[29] and by giving horizontal effect to the provisions (*Kücükdeveci* judgment)[30]. The Court did so by referring to the general principles of Community law, which follow from the European Convention on Human Rights (ECHR) (see Chapter 1).

This application of general principles and the intended accession of the EU to the ECHR provide opportunities for further development of the area of equal treatment and other fundamental rights. Most of the fundamental rights mentioned in the Convention are also part of the EU Charter. The connection between the two documents may mean that the ECHR will reinforce the Charter. A condition for applying the general principles of the ECHR is, however, that the situation of the case in question lies within the field of application of EU law, as emphasised in the *Römer* judgment.[31] The impact of this restriction is yet fully clear. Take, for example, the issue of distinction on ground of sexual orientation in a statutory social security scheme. Since statutory social security is excluded from Directive 2000/78 (Article 3(3)) and the Directive on equal treatment in statutory social security (Directive 79/7) does not mention sexual orientation, it is uncertain whether a general principle prohibiting such a distinction can be invoked.

The equal treatment provision of the Framework Directive allows more exceptions and justifications in respect of the discrimination grounds of disability and age than for the other grounds. Therefore, distinctions on the basis of these grounds are still possible. It can be expected, however, that these equal treatment provisions will lead to discussions and initiatives in the Member States, and also by social partners, to see whether particular distinctions, such as dismissal at pension age, are still necessary or whether alternatives can be adopted. Member States also should investigate the possibilities in order to erase as quickly as possible barriers hindering disabled persons from participating in work and social life.

---

29 ECJ 2005, C-144/04 (*Mangold*).

30 ECJ 2010, C-555/07 (*Kücükdeveci*).

31 ECJ 2011, C-147/08 (*Römer*), §60.

9.5. LEGISLATION ON SPECIFIC SOCIAL POLICY ISSUES

In addition to the general topics discussed above there are also areas of labour law for which specific EU standards have been developed. These include consultation of workers, collective redundancies, transfer of undertakings, flexible working relations, health and safety and working times. These are not all traditional labour law areas; collective action and dismissal law are not included, even though they are mentioned in the Charter of Fundamental Rights.

Also social policy directives have required important changes in national systems, as seen in respect of, for instance, the interpretation of the term 'working time' (Chapter 8) and the transfer of undertakings (Chapter 6).

However, since the turn of the century there have been few or no new legislative activities on social policy. The absence of strong Treaty provisions like Article 45 TFEU or general principles such as the equal treatment ones explains the lack of new initiatives. Nor have existing directives been revised, even though it has been acknowledged that they should be clarified. Examples of issues that need clarification are, inter alia, the question when a transfer of undertaking takes place (Chapter 6); how to regulate working time and health and safety in case of teleworking (Chapter 8); and when and how workers' representatives have to be informed in order to be able to do their work effectively (Chapter 7).

The dynamics in these areas is different from those areas where Treaty provisions give clear standards, such as in the case of equal pay for men and women or prohibition of discrimination on ground of nationality. Article 3 TEU, further discussed in Section 9.6.1, does not give concrete standards that can be invoked in particular disputes; nor do the fundamental rights of the Charter as such create new rights.

A special element in the social policy title is that social partners have a role in the legislative process. Their position is special and unique, since they can, following the procedure of Article 154 TFEU, adopt agreements that can subsequently become EU law by means of implementing Directives. Other private actors, such as consumers' organisations, do not have such possibilities. Still, the social partners have made little use of these opportunities. The best known results are the agreements and subsequent directives on flexible working relations (see Chapter 4). However, as explained in Section 4.6, even though the results of these agreements are meagre in the sense that the agreements are to a large extent limited to equal treatment rules, they have led to interesting developments and case law, e.g. on reduction on the use of renewed contracts for a definite period (*Adeneler*).[32] It is therefore regrettable

[32] ECJ 2006, C-212/04 (*Adeneler*).

that after adoption of these directives in the 1990s no new agreements have been concluded that could be implemented by directives. Apparently, the differences in views and interests of the social partners are too large to come to new agreements.

Instead of agreements that are implemented by directives, in the past years some voluntary agreements have been made by the social partners, for example on combating stress. Although legal enforcement of such agreements may be complicated – such an agreement has to be elaborated in agreements at national level – they can contribute to further development of labour law, and they can be promoted by the European Commission in order to find solutions for problems in present legislation.

For the further development of European labour legislation, the existence of transnational agreements is an interesting phenomenon (Chapter 5, Section 5.2.3). These are agreements between multinational companies and international trade unions, which can, for instance, anticipate the restructuring of a company by making agreements on training and placing workers in other jobs, and on the role of the European works council and the management of the company. By such agreements European labour law can be developed in a 'bottom up' way. Another recently developed instrument provides the opportunity to realise objectives without hard rules. This is the open method of co-ordination, which has been applied already in various areas, such as employment policy and social exclusion (see Chapter 1, Sections 1.3.2 and 1.4.4). These new instruments are an important supplement to the older ones and provide interesting perspectives for further developments.

All in all, the social dialogue at EU level, in any case with a view to make binding agreements, does currently not have good prospects. Nor is it expected that the use of voluntary or transnational agreements, even though they can be useful, will have a large impact. The absence of a motor at EU level to develop social policy has had important effects on the (lack of) development of European labour law. For that reason the initiative of the European Commission to raise a European social pillar may create a highly needed new élan. Important principles mentioned in the Pillar are the following:

- Everyone has the right to quality and inclusive education, training and life-long learning in order to maintain and acquire skills that enable them to participate fully in society and manage successfully transitions in the labour market.
- Everyone has the right to timely and tailor-made assistance to improve employment or self-employment prospects. This includes the right to receive support for job search, training and re-qualification.
- Everyone has the right to transfer social protection and training entitlements during professional transitions.

- Young people have the right to continued education, apprenticeship, traineeship or a job offer of good standing within four months of becoming unemployed or leaving education.
- People who are unemployed have the right to personalised, continuous and consistent support. The long-term unemployed have the right to an in-depth individual assessment at the latest at 18 months of unemployment.
- Regardless of the type and duration of the employment relationship, workers have the right to fair and equal treatment regarding working conditions, access to social protection and training.
- The transition towards open-ended forms of employment shall be fostered.
- Employment relationships that lead to precarious working conditions shall be prevented, including by prohibiting abuse of atypical contracts. Any probation period should be of reasonable duration.
- Workers have the right to fair wages that provide for a decent standard of living.[33]

The staff of the European Commission have prepared a lengthy document to elaborate how the Commission is going to undertake to elaborate these principles and have them implemented. For this purpose it will inter alia propose revisions of directives, ask social partners whether they are interested in starting a social dialogue with the view to adopting agreements and ask Member States and NGOs to undertake initiatives.[34] Such a working programme may be a good way to stimulate dialogue of the various actors.

9.6. EUROPEAN LABOUR LAW: OVERRULED BY ECONOMIC RIGHTS?

In analyses of the tension between social and economic rights, scholars belonging to either the economic or social 'side' often approach the topics exclusively from their own viewpoint. One example is that in a chapter contributed to the book edited by Freedland and Prassl[35] on the *Viking*[36] and *Laval* judgments, the internal market lawyer Weatherill describes the framework of the Treaty and concludes that in principle the *Laval* and *Viking* judgments basically fit very well into this this framework. He solely criticises the Court

33 European Commission (2017) (*Proposal for an Interinstitutional Proclamation on the European Pillar of Social Rights*).

34 European Commission (2017) (*Staff Working Document Accompanying the document establishing a European Pillar of Social Rights*).

35 Freedland & Prassl (2014).

36 ECJ 2007, C-438/05.

for its ambiguity: it does not make clear whether (a) it is only in the specific circumstances of these cases that it does not give a margin of discretion to justify the restriction to free movement or (b) whether the Court follows a new, general approach, which would seriously undermine the right to collective action.[37] Another scholar who has contributed to this book is labour lawyer Bogg, who takes the ILO Conventions on collective action as a starting point, in which there is no room for justifications of restrictions of the right to strike on economic grounds and which affirm the autonomy of unions to determine their own objectives for the strikes. He is therefore in favour of the autonomy of labour law, in other terms, the exclusion model.[38]

It is therefore important to focus on the *intersection* of labour law and economic rights. In an analysis of the impact of the *Laval* and *Viking* judgments, Freedland and Prassl made an interesting typology of the different ways in which the interaction of EU internal market law, European labour law and national industrial relations can be conceived:

- The exclusion type, where EU internal market law does not have an impact on EU and domestic labour law.
- The reconciliation type, where EU internal market law functions in tandem with EU and/or domestic labour law.
- The supersession type, where EU internal market law is so extensively superimposed on labour law that it has to be regarded as having superseded European labour law, and consequently also domestic labour law.[39]

This categorisation may be useful for the following discussion.

9.6.1. COLLECTIVE LABOUR AGREEMENTS AND COMPETITION LAW

Economic rights can cause tensions with parts of labour law, and labour law can do the same with economic rights. Collective labour agreements, for instance, constitute a restriction on competition between employers, since if employers fall under the same collective labour agreement, they have to pay workers in comparable situations the same wage. In Chapter 5 we saw that in the judgments *Albany*, *Drijvende Bokken* and *Brentjes*,[40] the Court of Justice ruled that the social objectives laid down in the Treaty (now Article 3 TEU)

37 Weatherill (2014), pp. 35–37.
38 Bogg (2014), pp. 51 and 73.
39 Freedland and Prassl (2014), p. 15.
40 ECJ 1999, C-67/96 (*Albany*); ECJ 1999, C-115/97 and 117/97 (*Brentjens*); ECJ 1999, C-219/97 (*Drijvende Bokken*); see also Bruun & Hellsten (2001).

have to be taken into account when answering the question whether collective labour agreements are consistent with competition law. Article 3 provides that a particular task of the Community is 'to promote throughout the Community a harmonious and balanced development of economic activities' and 'a high level of employment and of social protection'. The Court further referred to (what are now) Articles 151 ff TFEU, which require that the Commission is to endeavour to develop the dialogue between management and labour at European level.[41] Therefore the Treaty provisions on competition are not applicable to collective labour agreements meant for the improvement of working conditions. In this way the Court created immunity of collective labour agreements from competition law.[42] Immunity also applies when collective labour agreements are declared universally binding.[43]

An essential condition for immunity is that the collective labour agreement is the result of collective bargaining and that its provisions have the objective to improve the working conditions of *workers*. In the *FNV-Kiem* judgment, the Court emphasised that the immunity of collective agreements from competition law does not extend to persons other than workers, such as the self-employed.[44] However, the Court gave a broad definition of *bogus* self-employed, thus allowing making rules on some types of workers in the collective agreements who are not considered as employees in some national systems; it is up to the social partners (on the national level) to make actually use of this possibility.[45]

Returning to the categorisation by Freedland and Prassl, mentioned in the introduction of this section, it is clear that the relationship between competition law and collective labour agreements belongs to the exclusion type, since EU internal market law is barred from having an impact on EU and domestic labour law. This immunity is sharply defined and does not include agreements other than those based on collective bargaining for improving the working conditions of workers.

9.6.2. THE RIGHT TO STRIKE AND FREE MOVEMENT OF SERVICES

9.6.2.1. The Argument of the Court

The *Laval* and *Viking* judgments have led to an enormous number of publications and other reactions. They are often analysed as being a threat to European labour

---

41 ECJ 1999, C-67/96 (*Albany*), §59.
42 See extensively Section 5.3.1.4.
43 Idem.
44 ECJ 2014, C-413/13 (*FNV Kiem*).
45 See also Jaspers (2015); Pennings (2015a).

law, since in these cases the Court gave priority to economic rights. For example, Syrpis wrote: '... the Court's internal market case law threatens the maintenance of high social standards'.[46] Because of this presumed effect on European labour law and its future, the discussion of these cases, and their reception in the labour-law world, this case law will be discussed in detail here.

In a publication with the ominous title 'The calm after the storm', Barnard analysed the various types of reactions to the judgments and the differences of methodology used. She made a list of the main criticisms of the case law: the structure of the Court's reasoning suggested that economic rights took priority over social rights; the Court of Justice failed to adopt a standard human rights approach, which starts from the premise that the right to strike is the rule and restrictions are the exception; the rulings had the effect of further restricting the right to strike since they subjected strike action to a strict proportionality review; and the Court's interpretation of the Posting of Workers Directive prevented the host State from applying its full labour law to posted workers.[47] In this publication Barnard emphasised that, despite the sometimes heard criticism on 'case law journalism', a precise analysis of the case is essential to carrying out good research and the possibility of developing reliable theories.

In the *Laval* judgment the core question was whether a strike that infringed the free movement of services was allowed. The trade unions involved in the case argued that, like in the *Albany* case, the right to strike has immunity from the application of economic rights. After all, the right to strike is essential to collective bargaining, and therefore these two areas are closely connected. Moreover, the right to strike is excluded from the powers of the Union legislature, so how could EU law impose restrictions on this?

The Court of Justice did not, however, follow this argument. It considered that a collective action meant to force a foreign undertaking which posts workers to Sweden to apply a Swedish collective agreement has to be assessed in the light of Article 56 TFEU (free movement of services). This is necessary, since even though the areas in which the Community does not have competence and the Member States remain, in principle, free to lay down the conditions for the existence and exercise of the rights at issue, they must nevertheless exercise that competence consistently with Community law. The fundamental nature of the right to take collective action is not such as to render Community law inapplicable to such action. So this area is not of an exclusionary type.

In the judgment the Court acknowledged that the right to take collective action is recognised both by various international instruments which the

---

46 Syrpis (2016), p. 35.

47 Barnard (2016), p. 342.

Member States have signed or cooperated in (e.g. the European Social Charter of the Council of Europe and ILO Convention 87 concerning Freedom of Association and Protection of the Right to Organise) and the Charter of Fundamental Rights of the European Union. It therefore considered the right to take collective action as a fundamental right which forms an integral part of the general principles of Community law. However, the exercise of this fundamental right must be reconciled with the requirements relating to rights protected under the Treaty and in accordance with the principle of proportionality. It continued to argue that a restriction on the freedom to provide services is warranted only if it pursues a legitimate objective compatible with the Treaty and is justified by overriding reasons of public interest. If that is the case, it must be suitable for securing the attainment of the objective which it pursues and not go beyond what is necessary in order to attain it. The right to take collective action for the protection of the workers of the host State against possible social dumping may constitute an overriding reason of public interest which, in principle, justifies a restriction of one of the fundamental freedoms guaranteed by the Treaty. Since the Community has not only an economic, but also a social purpose, the rights under the provisions of the Treaty on the free movement of goods, persons, services and capital must be balanced against the objectives pursued by social policy.

So the Court recognised the right to strike as a fundamental right, but it takes the right to freedom of services as the main right, and strike as an infringement of the right, which has to be justified.

Although the Court mentioned several criteria for the objective justification, at the end of its argument it made the assessment easy by deciding that the core labour law provisions mentioned in the Posted Workers Directive are the minimum, but also the maximum that can be imposed on foreign service providers. Since the trade unions required more favourable provisions, they wanted to have more than allowed by the Posted Workers Directive and therefore their strike was not a justified infringement of the right to provide services.

The trade unions argued, as discussed earlier, that the right to strike belonged to the exclusionary sphere, whereas the Court developed a conciliatory approach which should leave sufficient room for strikes in other situations.

The problem, however, is that in international conventions on the right to strike, mentioned earlier, economic reasons are not acceptable as a restriction of this right. Only very few restrictions are allowed under these conventions. Therefore, it can be said that in this conciliatory approach much more room is given to economic interests than is consistent with the fundamental character of this right. This is not so much the case in the final outcome of *Laval* – if unions wanted to strive for an aim which is not allowed under EU law, then the strike is against the law and prohibition is acceptable – but with the development of the criteria for the objective justification, this creates considerable room for economic interests to restrict this fundamental right.[48] The Court's approach fits in the EU framework, however, so only by revising this can a different approach be made possible.

Thus, there are two major problems with the *Laval* case: the decision that the minimum of labour law that can be imposed is also the maximum, and the argument that the freedom to provide services is the main right and that the objective of the strike has to justify certain conditions (mentioned supra) in order to allow it as an infringement on this economic right. The second problem is a fundamental one, now that the right to strike is considered as a subsidiary right to the economic right. However, it has to be kept in mind that the right to strike is not laid down in the Treaty itself, whereas the right to free movement of services is one of the economic freedoms in the Treaty. This is an unequal battle. Article 28 of the Charter of Fundamental Rights provides that '[w]orkers and employers, or their respective organisations, have, in accordance with Community law and national laws and practices, the right to negotiate and conclude collective agreements at the appropriate levels and, in cases of conflicts of interest, to take collective action to defend their interests, including strike action'. However, this provision did not persuade the Court in *Laval* not to take the economic right as the basis right, since according to Article 28 the right to strike is to be protected in accordance with Community law and national law and practices (§91 of the *Laval* judgment).

Also, in the *Viking* case,[49] the infringement of a collective action on an economic right was to be assessed by the Court. The Court again noted that the right to take collective action, including the right to strike, is recognised both by various international instruments and in the Community Charter of the Fundamental Social Rights of Workers. However, the exercise of that right may none the less be subject to certain restrictions. The Court referred to Article 28 of the Charter of Fundamental Rights of the European Union, which provides that the right is to be protected in accordance with Community law and national law and practices. The Court continued by saying that:

> In the present case, first, it cannot be disputed that (this) collective action … has the effect of making less attractive, or even pointless, as the national court has pointed out, Viking's exercise of its right to freedom of establishment, inasmuch as such action prevents both Viking and its subsidiary, Viking Eesti, from enjoying the same treatment in the host Member State as other economic operators established in that State.

A Treaty provision ensuring the right to strike in a more absolute sense would certainly lead to a different approach to the right to strike, since then it would

48 Barnard (2016), p. 342.
49 ECJ 2007, C-438/05 (*Viking*).

no longer be subject to an economic right. It is, however, not to be expected that such a proposal to revise the Treaty will be accepted by the Member States.

Another reason for not accepting an exclusionary domain for the right to strike should also be acknowledged. Immunity from competition provisions, relevant in the *Albany* case, means that certain agreements and behaviour are allowed, but it does not affect a fundamental freedom of a third party. Free movement of services is a fundamental right of one of the parties. This makes it much more difficult, if not impossible, to accept immunity for the right to strike. So here there is an example of the conciliatory type.

Another example where social and economic provisions clashed is the *AGET Iraklis* judgment,[50] which concerned the impact of the Greek system of dealing with collective dismissals on the freedom of establishment (Article 49 TFEU and Article 16 of the Charter). This company, of which a French company was a main shareholder, adopted a restructuring plan providing for the permanent closure of a plant, with mass redundancies as a result. It invited the trade union to meetings for the purpose of providing information on the restructuring and for consultation as to the possibilities for avoiding or reducing those redundancies and their harmful consequences. As the union did not take up either of those invitations, AGET Iraklis submitted to the minister a request for approval of the projected collective redundancies. The employment directorate of the Ministry of Labour drew up a report taking into account the conditions in the labour market, the situation of the undertaking, and the interests of the national economy, and recommending that that request be refused because there was no plan for relocating the workers concerned to other plants belonging to AGET Iraklis and because the statistics of the Greek Manpower Employment Organisation indicated an ever higher unemployment rate. The minister decided not to authorise the projected collective redundancies. The Greek court, to which AGET appealed, referred questions to the Court of Justice.

The Court first considered that a system that made it very difficult to dismiss employees infringes the right of establishment. This is a limitation on the exercise of the freedom to conduct a business enshrined in Article 16 of the Charter. Limitations, however, may be imposed on the exercise of rights enshrined by the Charter as long as the limitations are provided for by law, respect the essence of those rights and freedoms and, in accordance with the principle of proportionality, are necessary and genuinely meet objectives of general interest recognised by the EU or the need to protect the rights and freedoms of others. It was explained by the national court that the public interest objectives that are pursued by the disputed legislation relate both to protecting

50 ECJ 2017, C-201/15 (*AGET Iraklis*).

workers and combating unemployment and to safeguarding the interests of the national economy. The Court of Justice did not accept promotion of the national economy or its proper functioning as justification for obstacles prohibited by the Treaty. However, the protection of workers and encouragement of employment and recruitment which, being designed in particular to reduce unemployment, constitute a legitimate aim of social policy.[51]

Subsequently the appropriateness and proportionality tests had to be satisfied. The Court considered that Member States have a broad discretion when choosing the measures capable of achieving the aims of their social policy, but that discretion must not have the effect of undermining the rights granted to individuals by the Treaty provisions in which their fundamental freedoms are enshrined. The Court concluded that the fact that a Member State provides, in its national legislation, that projected collective redundancies must, prior to any implementation, be notified to a national authority, which has the power to oppose the projected redundancies on grounds relating to the protection of workers and of employment, cannot be considered contrary to freedom of establishment as guaranteed by Article 49 TFEU or the freedom to conduct a business enshrined in Article 16 of the Charter. The freedom to conduct a business is not absolute, but must be viewed in relation to its social function. The Greek system does not have, in any way, the consequence of entirely excluding, by its very nature, the ability of undertakings to effect collective redundancies, since it is designed solely to impose a framework on that ability. Therefore, such a regime cannot be considered to affect the essence of the freedom to conduct a business.

Finally, it must be established whether the particular detailed Greek rules – and especially the three criteria which the competent public authority is called upon to take into account for the purpose of deciding whether it opposes collective redundancies – are such as to ensure that the requirements are in fact complied with. The criterion of 'interests of the national economy' to which that legislation refers cannot be accepted. The other two assessment criteria, namely the 'situation of the undertaking' and the 'conditions in the labour market', are acceptable. However, such criteria are formulated in very general and imprecise terms. Where the powers of the minister are not qualified by any condition, save for very general ones and no indication of the specific objective circumstances in which those powers are to be exercised is given, this results in serious interference with the freedom concerned. This may have the effect of excluding that freedom altogether since the employers concerned do not know in what

51 The Court refers to *Viking* in order to support this argument.

specific objective circumstances that power may be applied. Such criteria go beyond what is necessary in order to attain the objectives stated and cannot therefore satisfy the requirements of the principle of proportionality.

So it can be seen that social policy systems that subject dismissals to authorisations are allowed, but the criteria that are used have to be precise, otherwise the freedom to exercise a business may disappear completely.

In this judgment the Directive on Collective Redundancies also had to be interpreted: the main objective of Directive 98/59 is to make collective redundancies subject to prior consultation with the workers' representatives and prior notification of the competent public authority to explore means of avoiding collective redundancies or reducing the number of workers affected, and of mitigating the consequences by recourse to accompanying social measures. The Court of Justice was asked whether the directive precludes national legislation, under which an employer can effect such redundancies only if the competent national public authority does not give a reasoned decision not to authorise some or all of the projected redundancies.

The Court considered that by harmonising the rules applicable to collective redundancies, the EU legislature sought both to ensure comparable protection for workers' rights in the various Member States and to harmonise the costs which such protective rules entail for EU undertakings. Member States remain, however, free to adopt national measures that are more favourable to those workers. Therefore the directive cannot, in principle, be interpreted as precluding a national regime which gives a public authority the power to prevent collective redundancies by a reasoned decision. However, the position would, exceptionally, be different, the Court added, if, in the light of its more detailed rules or of the particular way in which it is implemented by the competent public authority, such a national regime were to result in the Directive 98/59 being deprived of their practical effect. That could occur, for example, if, on account of the criteria in the light of which that authority is called upon to take a decision or of the specific way in which it interprets and applies those criteria, any actual possibility for the employer to effect such collective redundancies was, in practice, ruled out.

AGET Iraklis contended before the Court that the competent public authority had systematically opposed projected collective redundancies of which it has been notified. This has had the consequence that the workers' representatives generally refrain from taking part in consultations with a view to attempting to find an agreement on ways and means of avoiding the projected redundancies or reducing the number of workers affected, and of mitigating the consequences. The Court of Justice decided that the referring court has to determine whether any actual possibility for the employer to effect collective redundancies is, in practice, ruled out, with the result that the provisions of Directive 98/59 would be deprived of practical effect.

A fourth example is the *Alemo-Herron* judgment,[52] which concerned a situation where a public authority privatised its leisure services to a private undertaking. For the workers, collective labour agreements were applicable, and these were binding as a result of a reference clause included in the individual contracts of employment. After a second transfer of the undertaking, this time to Parkwood, some years later, a new collective agreement was adopted in the public sector. Parkwood argued that the new agreement did not bind it.

The Transfers of Undertakings Directive provides that '[t]he transferor's rights and obligations arising from a contract of employment or from an employment relationship existing on the date of a transfer shall, by reason of such transfer, be transferred to the transferee' (Article 3(1)). It is clear that this provision refers to the rights following from the collective labour agreement applicable at the moment of the transfer. However, does the provision in the individual labour contract only refer to that collective agreement (static interpretation) or also to its successors (dynamic interpretation)? Article 8 provides that this Directive shall not affect the right of Member States to apply or introduce laws, regulations or administrative provisions which are more favourable to employees or to promote or permit collective agreements or agreements between social partners more favourable to employees.

The Court of Justice considered that the aim of the Directive is not only to safeguard the interests of employees in the event of a transfer, but also to seeks to ensure a fair balance between the interests of the employees and the transferee. The directive must be interpreted in a manner consistent with the Charter of Fundamental Rights of the EU, in particular in this case, Article 16 of the Charter, laying down the freedom to conduct a business. The Court considered that by reason of the freedom to conduct a business, the transferee must be able to assert its interest effectively in a contractual process to which it is party and to negotiate the aspects determining changes in the working conditions for its employees with a view to its future economic activity. Since the transfer is of an undertaking from the public sector to the private sector, the continuation of the transferee's operations will require significant adjustments and changes, given the inevitable differences in working conditions that exist between those two sectors. A dynamic clause referring to collective agreements negotiated and agreed after the date of transfer of the undertaking concerned, which are intended to regulate changes in working conditions in the public sector, is liable to limit considerably the room for maneuver necessary for a private transferee to make such adjustments and changes. In this situation, such a clause is liable to undermine the fair balance between the interests of the transferee in its capacity as employer, on the one hand, and those of the employees, on the other.

52 ECJ 2013, C-426/11 (*Alemo-Herron*).

In the light of Article 3, it is apparent that, by reason of the freedom to conduct a business, the transferee must be able to assert its interests effectively in a contractual process to which it is party and to negotiate the aspects determining changes in the working conditions of its employees with a view to its future economic activity. However, Parkwood was unable to participate in the collective bargaining body on these agreements, since this collective agreement was made between public authorities and public union, and Parkwood was a private enterprise. In such circumstances, the transferee's contractual freedom is seriously reduced to the point that such a limitation is liable to adversely affect the very essence of its freedom to conduct a business. Whether the Court is right in the assessment of the facts is disputable, but if this assessment is taken as the starting point, then also here the economic right has prevalence, since otherwise it would have become void.

Whereas the judgment of the Court is understandable in this individual case – if a transfer is a form of privatisation, it is a bit odd to keep the enterprise subject to public collective agreements – it also had a broader scope as it did not recognise the dynamic character of the reference to collective agreements, and its reference, for this interpretation, to the freedom of enterprise. Indeed, in *Asklepios*,[53] where the transfer was not from the public to the private sector, the Court gave more room to the dynamic interpretation of clauses.

9.6.2.2. Assessment

Although in all these cases the social right 'lost' to the 'economic' aspect, the picture need not be considered so gloomy as is often argued. After all, in all the cases the Court acknowledged the legitimate interest of defending the interests of workers. In this argument it sometimes refers to the provision of the social market economy, or its predecessor in the Treaty, or to international treaties. However, the Court then construed a balance between the economic and social rights, and that suggests that fundamental rights also have to be weighed against economic rights. This makes the process and outcome uncertain.

However, in all the judgments the Court concluded that in these cases the disputed social legislation or activity excluded the exercise of the economic right fully or almost fully. Whether that is always absolutely true can be disputed – in some judgments the national court still had to investigate this, and in others the national court had claimed this in its questions – but, in these judgments, the Court did not really balance the rights, but limited itself to concluding that the economic right was superseded by the social right in this case. In other words, with adjusted criteria, the Greek system of authorising redundancies could be accepted. Unions are allowed to strike, if necessary, unless they

53 ECJ 2017, C-680/15 and C-681/15.

require conditions not allowed by the Posted Workers Directive. And also in *Alemo-Herron* the dynamic clause was not allowed, as this would result in the application of collective labour agreements for the public sector, that do not fit with private enterprise.

9.6.2.3. *The Impact of the* Laval *Case*

The reactions to the judgments have been quite different in the Member States, as appears from the contributions in Freedland & Prassl (2014). In some countries, like the UK, the right to strike has been seriously affected because the *Laval* judgment has been invoked in order to prohibit the strike and/or to claim damages from the trade unions involved. In other countries no impact at all has been seen, since in those countries imposing national wages on foreign companies was not something to strike for: 'There would be no practical reason to force a foreign company which posts workers to Poland to accept conditions negotiated by Polish social partners'.[54]

In some countries, the legal framework for trade unions and the right to strike was even reinforced. Whereas some readers could interpret the recognition of the right to strike as an EU fundamental right as merely being a form of lip service, this consideration was an important element in the context of national reforms in Estonia.[55] Moreover, in that country national courts have also reinforced the obligations of Estonian companies vis-à-vis workers posted in other Member States to actually pay the minimum wages due by the law or collective labour agreements of the host State where the posted workers were working. In addition, the cooperation between Estonian and Scandinavian trade unions has been intensified.[56] On the basis of these developments Evas, who described he impact on Estonia, did certainly not welcome the plea for autonomy of labour law, since national labour law received an important encouragement from EU law.[57] Thus, the national context and the types of reactions of the various actors are crucial for the actual developments in the various Member States.

The other actor in this area, the European Commission, issued a proposal for a regulation aiming to reduce the unrest after the *Laval* judgment. This so-called 'Monti II Regulation'[58] provided that the exercise of the freedom of establishment and the freedom to provide services enshrined in the Treaty shall respect the fundamental right to take collective action, including the right or freedom to strike, and conversely, the exercise of the fundamental right to take

[54] Mitrus (2014), p. 239.
[55] Evas (2014), p. 140 ff, at 148.
[56] Evas (2014), p. 140 ff, at 148.
[57] Evas (2014), p. 152.
[58] COM(2012)130 def.

collective action, including the right or freedom to strike, shall respect these economic freedoms. Article 3(4) read that national courts have to decide in labour disputes, in particular, to determine whether and to what extent collective action, under the national legislation and collective agreement law applicable to that action, does not go beyond what is necessary to attain the objective(s) pursued. The proposal was, however, withdrawn after some Member States drew the so-called yellow card, particularly since the proposal concerned the issue of the right to strike, an area on which the EU legislature is not competent. Scholars agree that the Regulation would have contributed little to clarifying the way in which the right to strike and free movement of services (should) relate to each other in the EU.[59]

The European Commission did not make a proposal to include the right to strike as a fundamental right in the Treaty. Currently, Article 28 of the Charter of Fundamental Rights provides that 'Workers and employers, or their respective organisations, have, in accordance with Community law and national laws and practices, the right to negotiate and conclude collective agreements at the appropriate levels and, in cases of conflicts of interest, to take collective action to defend their interests, including strike action'. However, this was not sufficient for the Court to come to a different outcome in *Laval*. Indeed the Court considered:

> Although the right to take collective action must therefore be recognised as a fundamental right which forms an integral part of the general principles of Community law the observance of which the Court ensures, the exercise of that right may none the less be subject to certain restrictions. As is reaffirmed by Article 28 of the Charter of Fundamental Rights of the European Union, it is to be protected in accordance with Community law and national law and practices (para. 91).

The reference to 'in accordance with Community law' offered the Court the possibility to decide that the right to strike has to respect the free movement to services and thus there was room to apply the objective justification test.

A Treaty provision ensuring the right to strike in a more absolute sense would certainly lead to a different approach to the right to strike, since then it would no longer be subject to an economic right. It is, however, not to be expected that such a proposal will be accepted by the Member States.[60]

---

59 For instance Bruun, Bücker & Dorssemont (2012).

60 An alternative is a proposal of the European trade unions to lay down in a protocol to the Treaty that economic rights have no priority over social rights, see ETUC, Proposal for a Social Progress Protocol, <https://www.etuc.org/proposal-social-progress-protocol> accessed 05.06.2019. A protocol meets the objections against legislation in this area. Whether such a protocol, were it to be accepted, would actually influence the case law of the Court of Justice remains, of course, to be seen.

The accession of the EU to the ECHR will probably influence the relationship between strike law and the economic freedoms.[61]

9.7. CONCLUSIONS

In this chapter several tensions were discussed. These mainly exist between EU law and national labour law and between labour law and economic rights. Tensions also exist between richer and poorer Member States and between employers' and employees' organisations. These tensions and how they are permanently or temporarily resolved explain the developments – and lack of developments – of European labour law.

A major area is that of tensions in the case of migrants (including posted workers) and these exist at several levels. For instance, there is a tension between EU standards on equal treatment (Articles 45 and 18 TFEU) and the characteristics of national systems. Some countries are more pragmatic than others in the adjustments of their systems to (developments in) EU law; for some countries the effects of EU law are greater than for others.

There is also a tension between the Member States, of which some have an interest in wage competition and thus unequal treatment of foreign and national workers, whereas other countries perceive the Posted Workers Directive as facilitating social dumping.

Finally, there is a tension between economic rights that are worded as economic freedoms and social rights that are formulated in weaker terms, such as the right to collective actions.

There are different interests between the social partners that, despite the innovative framework of Article 153 ff TFEU, make it difficult to make agreements on social policy issues. In addition, employers' or employees' organisations may want to use EU law to change the national situation. In the *Laval* case[62] it seemed that the Swedish employers' organisations wanted to reduce the power of the trade unions and give more room for proportionality tests in case of strikes, which would apply in domestic situations as well.

---

61 See extensively Veldman (2013). Since the ECHR requires a different treatment of strike law than so far applied by the EU, there will be various discussions on how to reconcile the different approaches. If the accession is realised, the European Court of Human Rights will have a say in the development of this case law, but the Court of Justice will also have a say in the case law of the European Court of Human Rights. This is a complicated issue. It is not excluded that more generally the right to strike may be watered down by including more room for economic rights. Thus, whether this will have only positive effects (from a labour law perspective) is uncertain.

62 ECJ 2007, C-341/05 (*Laval*).

Therefore they supported the Laval firm, including financially, in its case before the court.[63] The Swedish court could also have decided this case itself by ruling that the Lex Brittannia – which reserved social peace to (only) Swedish collective agreements – was contrary to EU law, so that social peace also had to be observed in relation to the collective agreement of Laval and Estonian unions. Instead, it asked a more fundamental question relating to the relationship between the right to strike and free movement of services before the Court of Justice, with the well-known results. In the Estonian situation, the trade unions used the same judgment in order to improve the institutional framework for the right to strike in their home country.

Thus European labour law is the result of a continuous struggle of interests and seeking ways to resolve tensions. Whereas in the *Laval* case it seemed that mainly the Court of Justice was criticised, the European Commission and Council, Member States and social partners were also important actors. Their reactions to the dilemmas have a predominant impact on the further development of European labour law.

The influence of EU labour law on national systems is particularly strong when equal treatment is required. This is not only true for equal pay and equal treatment of men and women, but also for equal working conditions of migrant workers, the prohibition of discrimination on the ground of age, equal treatment of part-time workers, etc. In the area of social policy it is more difficult for standards to be adopted, even though here important new doctrines have been developed, such as on the transfer of enterprises.

For other topics, such as collective dismissals, the scope of EU labour law rules is still modest. The directive on collective redundancies basically asks no more than timely consultation, and notification to the authorities on intended dismissals. Issues as compensation for dismissal, regulating a proportional distribution of the dismissals over categories of workers (so that, e.g. not only the younger workers are dismissed), support for placement into another job etc., are missing.

It is difficult to reach consensus on issues not regulated at the EU level, such as the right to *decent work*. The European Commission promotes ratification by Member States of ILO Conventions, hoping that the standards reached within the framework of this organisation will lead to a higher level of protection the national level. The question whether it is desirable to develop standards on, for instance, decent work in the EU Treaty can lead to a variety of responses. Also, proponents of a far-reaching level of protection of workers may adhere to the view that such protection can be better regulated

63 Rönnmar (2014), p. 257; Barnard (2016), p. 352.

at the national than the EU level. After all, a compromise at EU level may potentially lead to a lower level of protection than what is possible at the national level and there is a risk that Member States will then lower their level to that of the compromise. Moreover, at the EU level economic rights and interests may restrict social rights more than at the national level, and that affects fundamental rights in particular, such as the right to strike.

However, there are two areas EU labour where law should be further developed. The first is that where workers are confronted with cross-border effects of particular activities or rules. For instance, in view of the situation that employees receive (too) little information in case of an intended transfer of the enterprise or in case of collective redundancies since the body or person who has to provide this information resides in another Member State, it should be provided clearly that the information has to be given in time and the criteria for 'in time' and 'relevant information' have to be elaborated. Also in the case of health and safety a cross-border situation can have complicating elements, for instance if the employees do not understand the language in which the instructions are given, for example safety instructions, or if they cannot discover the exact composition of ingredients produced elsewhere. For such situations development of standards, possibly by means of agreements of social partners, are necessary.

The second area is that in which economic rights can infringe social (fundamental) rights, since the latter are not set out, or are not strongly worded, in the Treaty. Even if one accepts that economic rights may restrict social rights, this should not be the result of a lack of (specific) rules, but it should follow from a well-balanced regulation made by the EU legislature. For such regulation it is preferable – in line with the intended accession to the ECHR and the promotion of ratification of ILO conventions – that the EU's approach should be reconciled with that of the ILO and Council of Europe.

From the foregoing it follows that EU labour law is certainly not dead, but its future depends on various factors. European labour law has several sub-areas, that are designed in various ways. In the preceding sections it has been described, taking into account this design, which dynamics (could) exist, and which roles the various actors have or may play. These actors have different and possibly contrary interests, and therefore varying scenarios are possible for answering the question of whether and how they will further develop their role. It is essential to keep these differences in interests and interaction between actors into account in order to have a good understanding of European labour law.

BIBLIOGRAPHY

Adoptive Parents (2014), 'The Life of a Death Foretold: The Proposal for a Monti II Regulation', in: M. Freedland & J. Prassl (eds.), *Viking, Laval and Beyond*, Oxford and Portland: Hart, pp. 95–109.

Ahlberg, K. (2013), 'The Age of Innocence – and Beyond', in: Stein Evju (ed.), *Cross-Border Services, Posting of Workers, and Multilevel Governance*, Oslo: Institutt for privatrett Oslo universitet, pp. 297–28.

Aimo, M.P. (2016), 'In Search of a "European Model" for Fixed-Term Work in the Name of the Principle of Effectiveness', 7(2) *European Labour Law Journal*, pp. 232–60.

Albors-Llorens, A. (2017), 'Judicial Protection before the Court of Justice of the European Union', in: C. Barnard and S. Peers (eds.), *European Union Law*, Oxford: Oxford University Press, pp. 262–309.

Ales, E. (2007), *Directive 2002/14/EC establishing a general framework for informing and consulting employees in the European Community, Synthesis report*, Brussels: European Commission.

—— (2013), 'Occupational Health and Safety: A Comparative Perspective', in: E. Ales (ed.), *Health and Safety at Work: European and Comparative Perspective*, Alphen a/d Rijn: Wolters Kluwer, pp. 411–449.

—— (2015), 'Diritti sociali e discrezionalità del legislatore nell'ordinamento multilivello: una prospettazione giuslavoristica' 147 *GDLRI* pp. 457–497.

—— (2017a), 'The "Risk Approach" in Occupational Health and Safety (with an Eye to Italy): Alternative or Complement to the "Core/Contingent Approach"?,' in: E. Ales, O. Deinert & J. Kenner (eds.), *Core and Contingent Work in the European Union. A Comparative Analysis*, Oxford and Portland, Oregon: Hart 2017, pp. 255–277.

—— (2017b), 'Occupational Health and Safety', in A. den Exter (ed.) *European Health Law*, Antwerp: Maklu, pp. 53–87.

—— (2018), 'Protecting Work in the Digital Transformation: Rethinking the Typological Approach in the Intrinsically Triangular Relationship Perspective', in: E. Ales, Y. Curzi, T. Fabbri, O. Rymkevich, I. Senatori and G. Solinas (eds.) (2018), *Working in Digital and Smart Organizations. Legal, Economic and Organizational Perspectives on the Digitalization of Labour Relations*, Basingstoke, Palgrave MacMillan, pp. 11–28.

Ales, E. & T. Novitz (eds.) (2010), *Collective Action and Fundamental Freedoms in Europe*, Antwerp-Oxford-Portland: Intersentia.

Ales, E. et al. (2006), *Transnational Collective Bargaining: Past, Present and Future, report for the European Commission*, Brussels: European Commission.

—— (eds.) (2018), *International and European Labour Law*, Baden-Baden: Nomos and Beck.

Alidadi, K. (2017), *Religion, Equality and Employment in Europe*, Oxford: Hart.

Alston, Ph. (2004), '"Core Labour Standards" and the Transformation of the International Labour Rights Regime' 15 *EJIL* p. 457–521.

Amalfitano, C. (2018), General Principles of EU Law and the Protection of Fundamental Rights, Cheltenham: Edward Elgar.

Arrigo, G. & G. Casale (2010), *A comparative overview of terms and notions on employee participation*, Geneva: ILO.

Askenazy, P. (2013), 'Working time regulation in France from 1996 to 2012', 37(2) *Cambridge Journal of Economics*, pp. 327–347.

Atrey, S. (2017), 'Fifty Years on: The Curious Case of Intersectional Discrimination in the ICCPR', 35(3) *Nordic Journal of Human Rights*, pp. 220–239.

Bacchi, C. (2004), 'Policy and Discourse: Challenging the Construction of Affirmative Action as Preferential Treatment', 11(1) *Journal of European Public Policy*, pp. 128–46.

Balandi, G. et al. (2014), *Organisational and Psychosocial Risks in Labour Law. A Comparative Analysis* (2012) I Working Papers Di Olympus No. 14/2012 <http://ojs.uniurb.it/> (accessed 25.09.2014).

Barnard, C. (2008), '*Viking* and *Laval*: An Introduction', in: 8 *Cambridge Yearbook of European Legal Studies*, Cambridge: Cambridge University Press, pp. 463–492.

—— (2009a), 'Internal Market v. Labour Market: A Brief History', in: M. de Vos (ed.), *European Union Internal Market and Labour Law: Friends or Foes*, Antwerp: Intersentia, pp. 19–44.

—— (2009b), '"British jobs for British workers": The Lindsey Oil Refinery Dispute and the Future of Local Labour Clauses in an Integrated EU Market', 38(3) *Industrial Law Journal*, pp. 245–277.

—— (2011), 'EU "Social Policy": From Employment Law to Labour Market Reform', in P. Craig & G. de Búrca (eds.), *The Evolution of EU Law*, 2nd edn, Oxford: Oxford University Press, p. 641 ff.

—— (2012a), *EU Employment Law*, Oxford: Oxford University Press.

—— (2012b), 'A Proportionate Response to Proportionality in the Field of Collective Action', 37(2) *European Law Review*, pp. 117–35.

—— (2015), 'The Silence of the Charter: Social Rights and the Court of Justice', in: S. de Vries, U. Bernitz & S. Weatherill (eds.), *The EU Charter of Fundamental Rights as a Binding Instrument*, Oxford and Portland: Hart, pp. 173–188.

—— (2016), 'The Calm after the Storm: Time to Reflect on EU (Labour) Law Scholarship Following the Decisions in *Viking* and *Laval*', in: A. Bogg, C. Costello & A. Davies (eds.), *Research Handbook on EU Labour Law*, Cheltenham: Edward Elgar, pp. 337–362.

Barnard, C. & S. Deakin (2015), 'Age Discrimination and Labour Law in the UK: Managing Ageing', in: A. Numhauser-Henning & M. Rönnmar (eds.), *Age Discrimination and Labour Law. Comparative and Conceptual Perspectives in the EU and Beyond*, Alphen a/d Rijn: Wolters Kluwer, 297–317.

Barnard, C. & A. Ludlow (2016), 'Enforcement of Employment Rights by EU-8 Migrant Workers in Employment Tribunals', 45(1) *Industrial Law Journal*, pp. 1–28.

Barnard, C. et al. (2003), 'Opting out of the 48-Hour Week: employer Necessity or Individual Choice?', 32(4) *Industrial Law Journal*, pp. 223–252.

Barslund, M., M. Busse & J. Schwarzwälder (2015), *Labour Mobility in Europe: An Untapped Resource?, CEPS Policy Brief* 327, Brussels.

Beckers, T. (1983), *Planning voor vrijheid, een historisch-sociologische studie van de overheidsinterventie in rekreatie en vrije tijd*, Ph. Thesis, Wageningen: Landbouwhogeschool Wageningen.

Bell, M. (2002), *Anti-Discrimination Law and the European Union*, Oxford: Oxford University Press.
—— (2008), *Racism, Equality and the European Union*, Oxford: Oxford University Press.
—— (2011), 'Achieving the Objectives of the Part-time Work Directive? Revisiting the Part-time Workers Regulations', 40(3) *Industrial Law Journal*, pp. 254–279.
—— (2012), 'Gender Identity and Sexual Orientation: Alternative Pathways in EU Equality Law' (2012) 60 *American Journal of Comparative Law*, pp. 127–146.
—— (2013), 'Occupational Health and Safety in the UK: At a Crossroads?', in E. Ales (ed.), *Health and Safety at Work. European and Comparative Perspective*, Alphen a/d Rijn: Wolters Kluwer, pp. 375–410.
—— (2018), 'EU Equality Law and Precarious Work', in U. Belavusau and K. Henrard (eds.), *EU Anti-Discrimination Law Beyond Gender*, Oxford: Hart, pp. 75–94.
Benedi Lahuerta, S. (2016a), 'Ethnic Discrimination, Discrimination by Association and the Roma Community: CHEZ', 53(3) *Common Market Law Review*, pp. 797–818.
—— (2016b), 'Taking EU Equality Law to the Next Level: In Search of Coherence', 7(3) *European Labour Law Journal*, p. 348–367.
Bercusson, B. (1995), 'The Conceptualization of European Labour Law', 24 *Industrial Law Journal* pp. 3–48.
—— (1999), 'Democratic Legitimacy and European Labour Law', 28(2) *Industrial Law Journal*, pp. 153–170.
—— (2006) (ed.), *European Labour Law and the EU Charter of Fundamental Rights*, Baden-Baden: Nomos.
—— (2007), 'The Trade Union Movement and the European Union: Judgment Day', 13(3) *European Law Journal*, pp. 279–308.
—— (2009), *European Labour Law*, 2nd edn, Cambridge: Cambridge University Press.
Bercusson B. & N. Bruun (1999), 'The Agreement on Fixed-term Work: A First Analysis', in: C. Vigneau, K. Ahlberg, B. Bercusson & N. Bruun (eds.), *Fixed-term Work in the EU. A European Agreement against Discrimination and Abuse*, Stockholm: Arbetslivsinstitutet, pp. 51–131.
Bermann, G.A. (1989), 'The Single European Act: A New Constitution for the Community?', 27 *Colum. J. Transnat'l L.* pp. 529–587.
Berntsen, L.E. (2015), *Agency of labour in a flexible pan-European labour market: A qualitative study of migrant practices and trade union strategies in the Netherlands*, PhD Thesis, Groningen: University of Groningen.
Berntsen, L.E. & N. Lillie (2015), 'Breaking the Law? Varieties of Social Dumping in a Pan-European Labour Market', in: M. Bernaciak (ed.), *Market Expansion and Social Dumping in Europe*, Routledge, pp. 43–60.
Besselink, L. (2001), 'The Member States, the National Constitutions and the Scope of the Charter', 8(1) *Maastricht Journal*, pp. 68–80.
Betten, L. (1998), 'The Democratic Deficit of Participatory Democracy in Community Social Policy', 23(1) *European Law Review*, pp. 20–36.
Biagi, M. (1990), 'From Conflict to Participation in Safety: Industrial Relations and the Working Environment in Europe 1992', 6 *International Journal of Comparative Labour Law and Industrial Relations*, pp. 67–79.
—— (1997), 'The "Posted Workers" EU Directive', 32 *Bulletin of Comparative Labour Relations* pp. 173–180.

—— (ed.) (2001), 'Towards a European Model of Industrial Relations?', Alphen a/d Rijn: Kluwer Law International.

Blanke, T. (2006), 'Workers' Right to Information and Consultation within the Undertaking', in: B. Bercusson (ed.), *European Law and the EU Charter of Fundamental Rights*, Baden-Baden: Nomos Verlag, p. 263 ff.

Blanke, T and J. Hoffmann (2006), 'Auf dem Weg zu einem Europäischen Soizialmodell', *2006/2 Kritische Justiz*, pp. 134–150

Blanke, T., E. Rose, H. Voogsgeerd & W. Zondag (2009), *Recasting Worker Involvement?*, Alphen a/d Rijn: Kluwer.

Blanpain, R (2008), *European labour law*, Alphen a/d Rijn: Kluwer Law International.

Blanpain, R. & A. Numhauser-Henning (eds.) (2006), 'Women in Academia and Equality Law. Aiming High – Falling Short? Denmark, France, Germany, Hungary, Italy, The Netherlands, Sweden, United States', *Bulletin of Comparative Labour Relations* 57 Alphen a/d Rijn: Kluwer Law International.

Bobek, M. (2017), 'The Effects of EU Law in the National Legal Systems', in: C. Barnard & S. Peers (eds.), *European Union Law*, Oxford: Oxford University Press, pp. 143–176.

Bogg, A. (2014a), 'Article 31', in S. Peer and others (eds.) (2014), *The EU Charter of Fundamental Rights*, Cambridge: Hart.

—— (2014b), '*Viking* and *Laval*: The International Law Perspective', in: M. Freedland & J. Prassl (eds.), *Viking, Laval and Beyond*, Oxford and Portland: Hart, pp. 41–74.

—— (2016), 'EU Law and the Regulation of Working Time', in: A. Bogg, C. Costello & A.C.L. Davies (eds.), *Research Handbook on EU Labour Law*, Cheltenham: Edward Elgar, p. 267–298.

Bogg, A., C. Costello & A.C.L. Davies (2016), *Research Handbook on EU Labour Law*, Cheltenham: Edward Elgar.

Bouwens, W., W. Roozendaal & V. bij de Vaate (2015), *Werknemers en insolventie.* Amsterdam: Vrije Universiteit.

Brameshuber, E. (2016), 'Balancing vs Preservation of Rights under the Acquired Rights Directive', 45(3) *Industrial Law Journal*, pp. 443–54.

Broughton, A. (2010), *Work-related stress*, Dublin: European Foundation for the Improvement of Living and Working Conditions.

Brugmans, I.J. (1987), *De arbeidende klasse in Nederland in de 19e eeuw*, PhD thesis Utrecht (originally 1925), 10th edn, Utrecht/Antwerpen: Aula.

Bruun, N. (2001), 'EG-rätten, den tredje vågen och dyningarna I HD', *Juridiska föreningens tidskrift*, pp. 543–562.

Bruun, N. & J. Hellsten (eds.) (2001), *Collective Agreement and Competition in the EU*, Copenhagen.

Bruun, N. & J. Malmberg (2011), 'Lex Laval: Collective Actions and Posted Work in Sweden', in: R. Blanpain & F. Hendrickx (eds.), *Labour Law between Change and Tradition*, Alphen a/d Rijn: Wolters Kluwer, pp. 21–34.

Bruun, N., A. Bücker & F. Dorssemont (2012), 'Balancing Fundamental Social Rights and Economic Freedoms: Can the Monti II Initiative Solve the EU Dilemma?', 28(3) *International Journal of Comparative Labour Law and Industrial Relations*, pp. 279–306.

Bruun, N., A. Jacobs & M. Schmidt (2010), 'ILO Convention no. 94 in the Aftermath of the *Rüffert* Case', 16(4) *Transfer: European Review of Labour Law and Research*, pp. 473–88.

Bruun, N. et al. (eds.) (2017), *The European Social Charter and the Employment Relation*, Oxford: Hart.

Bruzelius, C., C. Jacqueson & M. Seeleib-Kaiser (2018), '(Dis)united in Diversity? Social Policy and Social Rights in the EU', in: F. Pennings & M. Seeleib-Kaiser (eds.), *European Citizenship and Social Rights: Entitlements and Impediments to Accessing Welfare*, Cheltenham: Edward Elgar, pp. 51–75.

Bücker, A. & W. Warneck (2011), *Reconciling Fundamental Social Rights and Economic Freedoms after Viking, Laval and Rüffert*, Baden Baden: Nomos.

Buelens, J. & J. Pearson (eds.) (2013), *Standard Work: An Anachronism?*, Antwerp-Cambridge: Intersentia.

Buelens, J. & M. Rigaux (eds.) (2016), *From Social Competition to Social Dumping*, Cambridge: Intersentia

Butler, M. (2018), 'A "Pick and Mix" Approach to Collective Redundancy: *USDAW*', 47(2) *Industrial Law Journal*, pp. 297–314.

Bustreel, A. et al. (2012), 'Concilier vie familiale et vie professionnelle en France: les disparites d'horaires de travail', 67(4) *Relations Industrielles*, pp. 681–702

Cabrita, J. (2015), *Opting Out of the European Working Time Directive*, Luxemburg: Publications Office of the European Union.

Caracciolo di Torella, E. & A. Masselot (2001), 'Pregnancy, Maternity and the Organisation of Family Life: An Attempt to Classify the Case-law of the Court of Justice', 26(3) *European Law Review*, pp. 239–60.

Carley, M. & P. Marginson (2000), *Negotiating European Works Councils. A Comparative Study of Article 6 and Article 13 Agreements*, Eurofound Brussels.

Carlson, L. (2007), *Searching for Equality, Sex Discrimination, Parental Leave and the Swedish Model with Comparisons to EU, UK and US Law*, Iustus Förlag.

Caruso, B. & S. Sciarra (eds.) (2007), *Flexibility and Security in Temporary Work: A Comparative and European Debate*, WP C.S.D.L.E. 'Massimo D'Antona', INT – 56/2007, <http://csdle.lex.unict.it/docs/workingpapers/Flexibility-and-Security-in-Temporary-Work-A-Comparative-and-European-Debate/1485.aspx> accessed 05.06.2019.

Chacartegui, C. (2013), 'Resocialising Temporary Agency Work through a Theory of "Reinforced" Employer's Liability', in: N. Contouris & M. Freedland (eds.), *Resocialising Social Europe in a Time of Crisis*, Cambridge: Cambridge University Press, pp. 213–229.

Chan, A. & K. Siu (2010), 'Analyzing exploitation: The Mechanisms Underpinning Low Wages and Excessive Overtime in Chinese Export Factories', 42/2. *Critical Asian Studies*, pp. 167–190

Chiti, E. (2013), 'European Agencies' Rulemaking: Powers, Procedures and Assessment', 19(1) *European Law Journal*, pp 93–110.

Chopin, I. & C. Germaine (2016), *A comparative analysis of non-discrimination law in Europe 2016. The 28 EU Member States, the Former Yugoslav Republic of Macedonia, Iceland, Liechtenstein, Montenegro, Norway, Serbia and Turkey compared*, The European network of legal experts in gender equality and non-discrimination, <http://www.equalitylaw.eu/downloads/3987-a-comparative-analyses-of-non-discrimination-law-in-europe-2016-pdf-1-2-mb> accessed 05.06.2019.

Clarke, L. (2007), 'Sexual Harassment Law in the United States, the United Kingdom and the European Union: Discriminatory Wrongs and Dignitary Harms', 79 *Comm. L. World Rev.*, pp. 79–105.

Clauwaert (2012) 'European Framework agreements: 'nomina nuda tenemus' or what's in a name? Experiences of the European social dialogue', in: I. Schömann et al. (eds.), *Transnational collective bargaining at company level. A new component of European industrial relations?*, Brussels: ETUI, pp. 117–155.

Cockburn, W. (2009), *Labour inspectorates' strategic planning on safety and health at work*, Bilbao: OSHA, 2009.

Collins, H., K.D. Ewing & A. McColgan (2012), *Labour Law*, Cambridge: Cambridge University Press.

Corazza, L. (2011), 'Hard Times for Hard Bans: Fixed-Term Work and So-Called Non-Regression Clauses in the Era of Flexicurity', 17(3) *European Law Journal*, pp. 385–402.

Cornelissen, R. (2008), 'Third-Country Nationals and the European Coordination of Social Security', 10(4) *European Journal of Social Security*, pp. 347–372.

—— (2016), 'Conflicting Rules of Conflict: Social Security and Labour Law', in: H. Verschueren (ed.), *Residence, Employment and Social Rights of Mobile Persons. On How EU Law Defines Where They Belong*, Antwerp: Intersentia, pp. 255–284.

Countouris, N. (2007), *The Changing Law of the Employment Relationship – Comparative Analyses in the European Context*, Abingdon: Ashgate Publishing.

Craig, P. & G. de Búrca (2015), *EU Law – Text, Cases and Materials*, 6th edn, Oxford: Oxford University Press.

Cremers, J. (2011), *In Search of Cheap Labour in Europe: Working and living conditions of posted workers*, Brussels: CLR/EFBWW/International Books.

Cremers, J., J.E. Dølvik & G. Bosch (2007), 'Posting of Workers in the Single Market: Attempts to Prevent Social Dumping and Regime Competition in the EU', 38(6) *Industrial Relations Journal*, pp. 524–541.

Cuypers, D. & H. Verschueren (2015), 'De aanpassing van het Vlaamse Taaldecreet na het arrest van het Hof van Justitie in de zaak-Las: een juridisch kaartenhuis', 23 *Rechtskundig Weekblad*, pp. 883–903.

Da Costa, I. & U. Rehfeldt (2008), 'Transnational Collective Bargaining at Company Level: Historical Developments', in: Konstantinos Papadakis (ed.), *Cross-border Social Dialogue and Agreements: An Emerging Global Industrial Relations Framework?*, Geneva: ILO, pp. 43–64.

Däubler, W., M. Kittner, T. Klebe & P. Webbe (2018), *Betriebsverfassungsgesetz*, Frankfurt am Main: Bund Verlag.

Daugareilh, I. (2006), 'Les accords-cadre internationaux: une réponse européenne à la mondialisation de l'économie ?', in: M. Descolonges & B. Saincy (eds.), *Les nouveaux enjeux de la négociation sociale internationale*, Paris: La Dé couverte, pp. 116–135.

Davidov, G. (2013), 'The Principle of Proportionality in Labor Law and Its Impact on Precarious Workers', 34 *Comparative Labor Law and Policy Journal*, pp. 63–80.

Davies, A.C.L. (2008), 'One Step Forward, Two Steps Back? The Viking and Laval Cases in the ECJ', 37(2) *Industrial Law Journal*, pp. 126–148.

—— (2012), *EU Labour Law*, Cheltenham: Edward Elgar.

Davies, P. (1993), 'Transfers Again: Contracting Out and the Employee's Option', 22(2) *Industrial Law Journal*, pp. 151–163.

—— (2001), 'Part I. Preliminary Remarks', in: Silvana Sciarra (ed.), *Labour Law in the Courts. National Judges and the European Court of Justice*, Oxford: Hart, pp. 131–144.

De Becker, E. & P. Schoukens (2017), 'De Europese Pijler van Sociale Rechten: een eerste evaluatie', *Tra* no. 86.
De Broeck, V. et al. (2008), *Onderzoek naar de omzetting van 4 arborichtlijnen in de regelgeving van 10 lidstaten*, Brussel: Prevent.
De Búrca, G. (2008), *The EU on the Road from the Constitutional Treaty to the Lisbon Treaty*, Jean Monnet Working Paper 03/08.
—— (2013), 'After the EU Charter of Fundamental Rights: the Court of Justice as a Human Rights Adjudicator', 20(2) *Maastricht Journal*, pp. 168–184.
De Gier, H.G. & C. Vos (1995), *Europese en Nederlandse arboregelgeving*, Utrecht: Lemma.
De la Mare, T. & C. Donnelly (2011), 'Preliminary Rulings and EU Legal Integration', in: P. Craig & G. de Búrca (eds.), *The Evolution of EU Law*, 2nd edn, Oxford: Oxford University Press, p. 363 ff.
De la Porte, C. & P. Emmenegger (2016), *The Court of Justice of the European Union and Fixed-term Workers: Still Fixed, but at Least Equal*, Brussels, European Trade Union Institute.
De Vos, M. (ed.) (2009), *European Union Internal Market and Labour Law: Friends or Foes?*, Antwerp-Oxford-Portland: Intersentia.
De Vries, S., U. Bernitz & S. Weatherill (eds.), *The EU Charter of Fundamental Rights as a Binding Instrument*, Oxford and Portland: Hart.
De Wispelaere, F. & J. Pacolet (2017), *The size and impact of intra-EU posting on the Belgian economy. With a special focus on the construction sector*, HIVA, KU Leuven.
De Witte, B. (2011), 'Direct Effect, Primacy, and the Nature of the Legal Order', in: P. Craig & G. de Búrca (eds.), *The Evolution of EU Law*, 2nd edn, Oxford: Oxford University Press, p. 323 ff.
—— (2012), 'New Institutions for Promoting Equality in Europe: Legal Transfers, National Bricolage and European Governance', 60 *American Journal of Comparative Law*, pp. 49–74.
De Zwart, B.C.H. (2011), *Onderzoek naar de positie van de bedrijfsarts, Eindrapport*, Leiden: AStri.
Degryse, C. & P. Tilly (2013), *1973–2013. 40 years of history of the European Trade Union Confederation*, Brussels: ETUI.
Dehousse, R. (1998), *The European Court of Justice: The Politics of Judicial Integration*, Bassingstoke: Macmillan.
Deinert, O. (2010), 'Collective Action in Germany', in: E. Ales & T. Novitz (eds.), *Collective Action and Fundamental Freedoms in Europe*, Antwerp: Intersentia, pp. 53–75.
—— (2013), 'Occupational Health and Safety in Germany: A Dual System in Change', in: E. Ales (ed.), *Health and Safety at Work: European and Comparative Perspective*, Alphen a/d Rijn: Wolters Kluwer, pp. 127–150.
—— (2013), *Internationales Arbeitsrecht*, Tübingen: Mohs Siebeck.
Dembe, A. et al. (2008), 'The Effect of Occupation and Industry on the Injury Risks From Demanding Work Schedules,' 50 *Journal of Occupational and Environmental Medicine*, pp. 1185–1194.
Dewhurst, E. (2018), 'Article 18 RESC. The right to engage in a gainful occupation in the territory of other parties; Article 19 RESC. The right of migrant workers and their families to protection and assistance', in: E. Ales et al. (eds.), *International and European Labour Law: A Commentary*, Baden-Baden: Nomos, pp. 310–316.

Dorssemont, F. (2004), 'Case C-440/00, Gesamtbetriebsrat der Kühne & Nagel v. Kühne & Nagel AG Co KG, judgment of the Court of Justice of 13 January 2004', 41(6) *CMLRev*, pp. 1701–1716.

—— (2006a), 'De vakverenigingsvrijheid ex artikel 11 EVRM, méér dan een sequeel van de vrijheid van vereniging?' 2 *Arbeidsrechtelijke Annotaties*, pp. 4–33.

—— (2006b), 'The Renault Saga (Revisited)', 3(1/2) *European Company Law*, pp. 5–10.

—— (2009), 'The Right to Take Collective Action *versus* Fundamental Economic Freedoms in the Aftermath of *Laval* and *Viking*', in: Marc de Vos (ed.), *European Union Internal Market and Labour Law: Friends or Foes?*, Antwerp-Oxford-Portland: Intersentia, pp. 45–101.

—— (2010a), 'Worker Involvement in Secondary EC Law Prior to the Recast Directive' in: F. Dorssemont & T. Blanke (eds.), *The Recast of the European Works Council Directive*, Antwerpen: Intersentia, pp. 31–90.

—— (2010b), 'The Right to Form and to Join Trade Unions for the Protection of his Interests under Article 11 ECHR', 1(2) *European Labour Law Journal*, pp. 185–235.

—— (2010c), 'The European Works Councils Directive and the Domestic Courts', in: F. Dorssemont & T. Blanke (eds.), *The Recast of the European Works Council Directive*, Antwerpen: Intersentia, pp. 225–270.

—— (2012), 'De ontwerp-Verordening Monti II, oude wijn (azijn) in nieuwe zakken?', 11(2) *Arbeidsrechtelijke Annotaties*, pp. 3–35.

—— (2017), 'Article 6. The Right to Bargain Collectively', in: Niklas Bruun et al. (eds.), *The European Social Charter and Employment Relations*, Oxford: Hart, pp. 249–88.

Dorssemont, F. & A.Ph.C.M. Jaspers (1996), 'De "Affaire Renault": Een les voor later of een storm in de Europese vijver!?', *Sociaal Recht*, pp. 152–62.

Dorssemont, F. & T. Jaspers (2007), 'Collectieve actie en vrij verkeer. Eindigen grondrechten waar 'fundamentele' vrijheden beginnen?', 154 *NjW*, pp. 2–11.

Dorssemont, F. & P. Kerckhofs (2015), *Linking Information and Consultation Procedures at Local and European Level*, Brussels: Eurofound.

Dorssemont, F., T. Jaspers & A. van Hoek (2007), *Cross-Border Collective Actions in Europe: A Legal Challenge*, Antwerp: Intersentia.

Dorssemont, F., K. Lorcher & I. Schomann (2013), *European Convention on Human Rights and the Employment Relation*, London: Bloomsbury.

Dougan, M. (2015), 'Judicial Review of Member State Action under the General Principles and the Charter: Defining the "Scope of Union Law"', 52(5) *Common Market Law Review*, pp. 1201–45.

Douglas-Scott, S. (2015), 'The Relationship between the EU and the ECHR Five Years on from the Treaty of Lisbon', in: S. de Vries, U. Bernitz & S. Weatherill, (eds.) *The EU Charter of Fundamental Rights as a Binding Instrument*, Oxford and Portland: Hart, pp. 21–45.

Edwards, V. (2003), 'The European Company – Essential Tool or Eviscerated Dream, 40(2) *Common Market Law Review*, pp. 443–47.

Ellis, E. (1997), 'Case C-84/94 *United Kingdom of Great Britain and Northern Ireland v. Council* [1996]', (1997) 34 *Common Market Law Review* pp. 1049.

Ellis, E. (ed.) (1999), *The Principle of Proportionality in the Laws of Europe*, Oxford: Hart.

Ellis, E. & P. Watson (2012), *EU Anti-Discrimination Law*, 2nd edn, Oxford: Oxford University Press.

Ertel, M. et al. (2010), 'European social dialogue on psychosocial risks at work: Benefits and challenges' 16 *EJIR* pp. 169.
ETUC, BUSINESSEUROPE, UEAPME, CEEP (2008), *Report on the implementation of the framework agreement on work-related stress, Adopted at the Social Dialogue Committee on 18 June 2008*, Brussels: ETUC.
Eurofound (2015), *First findings from the Sixth European Working Conditions Survey*, Dublin: European Foundation for the Improvement of Living and Working Conditions.
European Group on Tort Law (2005), *Principles of European Tort Law*, Wien: Springer Verlag.
European Parliament (2010), *The Impact of the ECJ judgments on Viking, Laval, Rüffert and Luxembourg on the practice of collective bargaining and the effectiveness of social action*, (author J Malmberg), Brussels: European Parliament.
Eurostat (2010), *Health and Safety at Work in Europe (1999–2007)*, Luxembourg: Publications Office of the European Union.
Evas, T. (2014), 'Estonia', in: M. Freedland & J. Prassl (eds.), '*Viking*, *Laval* and Beyond', Oxford and Portland: Hart, pp. 139–154.
Even, J.H. (2008), *Transnational collective bargaining in Europe*, Den Haag, Boom Juridische Uitgevers.
Everling, U. (1963), *Das Niederlassungsrecht im Gemeinsamen Markt*, Berlin: Verlag Franz Vahlen.
Evju, S. (2001), 'Collective Agreements and Competition Law. The Albany Puzzle, and van der Woude', 17(2) *International Journal of Comparative Labour Law and Industrial Relations*, pp. 165–84.
—— (2010), 'Revisiting the Posted Workers Directive: Conflict of Laws and Laws in Contrast', *Cambridge Yearbook of European Legal Studies*, pp. 151–82.
Ewing, K. (2003), 'The Implications of *Wilson and Palmer*', 32(1) *Industrial Law Journal*, pp. 1–22.
—— (2015), 'The Death of Social Europe', in: A. Swiatkowski (ed.), *Studia ad ius laboris et politicam socialem*, Krakow, pp. 9–15.
—— (2012), *The Draft Monti II Regulation: An Inadequate Response to Viking and Laval*, London: Institute of Employment Rights.
Ewing, K.D. & J. Hendy (2010), 'The Dramatic Implications of Demir and Baykara', 39(1) *Industrial Law Journal*, pp. 2–51.
Falkner, G. (1996), 'The Maastricht Protocol on Social Policy: Theory and Practice', 6(1) *Journal of European Social Policy*, pp. 1–16.
Farkas, L. (2017), *The Meaning of Racial or Ethnic Origin in EU Law: Between Stereotypes and Identities*, Luxembourg: Publications Office of the European Union.
Ferraro, F. & J. Carmona (2015), *Fundamental Rights in the European Union*, European Parliamentary Research Service.
Ferri, D. & A. Lawson (2016), *Reasonable Accommodation for Disabled People in Employment – a Legal Analysis of the Situation in EU Member States, Iceland, Liechtenstein and Norway*, Luxembourg: Publications Office of the European Union.
Fihel, A. et al. (2015), *Free Movement of Workers and Transitional Arrangements: Lessons from 2004 and 2007 Enlargements*, Warsaw: Centre of Migration Research, University of Warsaw.

Fitzpatrick, B. (1997), 'Straining the Definition of Health and Safety?', 26(2) *Industrial Law Journal* pp. 115–135.
Fontanelli, F. (2014), 'The Implementation of European Union Law by Member States under Article 51(1) of the Charter of Fundamental Rights', 20 *Columbia Journal of European Law*, pp. 193 ff.
Fornasier, M. & M. Torga (2013), 'The Posting of Workers: The Perspective of the Sending State – The Judgment of the Civil Chamber of the Estonian Supreme Court of 16 January 2013 No 3-2-1-179-12', *Europäische Zeitschrift für Arbeitsrecht (EuZA)* pp. 356–65.
Foubert, P., B. Susanne & A. Numhauser-Henning (2010), *The Gender Pay Gap in Europe from a Legal Perspective (including 33 country reports)*, Luxembourg: The European Commission.
FRA (2014), *Violence against Women: An EU-wide Survey. Main Results*, Luxembourg.
Franssen, E. & A.T.J.M. Jacobs (1998), 'The Question of Representativity in the European Social Dialogue', 35(6) *Common Market Law Review*, pp. 1295–1312.
Frantziou, E. (2019), *The Horizontal Effect of Fundamental Rights in the European Union*, Oxford: Oxford University Press.
Fraser, I. (2012), '"Social Europe" versus the "Internal Market": A False Dichotomy? The example of the Machinery Directive', *Observatoire Social Européen.*
Fredman, S. (2006), 'Transformation or Dilution: Fundamental Rights in the EU Social Space', 12(1) *European Law Journal*, pp. 41–60.
—— (2009), *Making equality effective: the role of proactive measures*, Brussels: European Commission.
—— (2011), *Discrimination Law*, 2nd edn, Oxford: Oxford University Press.
Freedland, M. & J. Prassl (2014), *Viking, Laval and Beyond*, Oxford and Portland: Hart.
Frick, K., P. Langaa Jensen, M. Quinlan, & T. Wilthagen (eds.) (2000), *Systematic Occupational Health and Safety Management*, Oxford: Elsevier Science.
Friedman, G.S. and J.Q. Whitman (2003), 'The European Transformation of Harassment Law: Discrimination versus Dignity', 9 *Colum.J.Eur.L.* pp. 241–274.
Fromage, D. & V. Kreilinger (2017), '"National Parliaments" Third Yellow Card and the Struggle over the Provision of the Posted Workers Directive', 10(1) *European Journal of Legal Studies*, pp. 125–60.
Fuchs, F. (2004), 'The Bottom Line of European Labour Law (Part II)', 20 *International Journal of Comparative Labour Law and Industrial Relations*, pp. 423–444.
Fuchs, M. (2004a), 'The Bottom Line of European Labour Law (Part I)', 20(2) *International Journal of Comparative Labour Law and Industrial Relations*, pp. 155–176.
—— (2004b), 'Germany: Part-time Work – A Bone of Contention' in: S. Sciarra, P. Davies & M. Freedland (eds.), *Employment Policy and the Regulation of Part-time Work in the European Union. A Comparative Analysis*, Cambridge University Press, pp. 121 ff.
Fuchs, M. & F. Marhold (2014), *Europäisches Arbeitsrecht*, 4th edn, Vienna.
Fuchs, M. & R. Cornelissen (eds.) (2015), *EU Social Security Law. A Commentary on EU Regulations 883/2004 and 987/2009*, München-Baden-Baden-Oxford: Beck-Hart-Nomos.
Fudge, J. (2015), 'Dignity, Disadvantage, and Age: Putting Constitutional and Fundamental Rights to Work for Older Workers', in: A. Numhauser-Henning (ed.), *Elder Law – Evolving European Perspectives*, Cheltenham: Edward Elgar, pp. 55–85.
García-Muñoz Alhambra, M.A. (2017), *La negociación colectiva europea de sector*, Marcial Pons.

Geiskkovitch, D. et al. (2015), 'Autonomy, Embodiment and Obedience to Robots', *Proceedings 10th ACM/IEEE conference on Human-Robot Interaction.*

Gerards, J. (2007), 'Discrimination Grounds', in: D. Schiek, L. Waddington & M. Bell (eds.), *Cases, Materials and Text on National, Supranational and International Non-Discrimination Law*, Oxford: Hart.

Geurts, S.A.E. (2014), 'Recovery from Work During Off-Job Time', in: G.F. Bauer and O. Hämmig, *Bridging Occupational, Organizational and Public Health: A Transdisciplinary Approach*, Dordrecht: Springer, pp. 193–208.

Giesing, R. (2003), 'Posting: Social Protection of Workers versus Fundamental Freedoms?', 40(1) *Common Market Law Review*, pp. 143–58.

Glassner, V. (2012), 'Transnational Collective Bargaining in National Systems of Industrial Relations', in: I. Schömann et al. (eds.), *Transnational Collective Bargaining at Company Level. A New Component of European Industrial Relations?*, Brussels: ETUI, pp. 77–115.

Gormley, L. (1992), 'Freedom of Establishment and Freedom to Provide Services: Workers and Services Distinguished', 17(1) *European Law Review*, pp. 63–67.

Gotthardt, M. (2010), 'Arbetstagares rätt att motsätta sig företagsövergång enligt tysk och svensk rätt. I Vänbok till Ronnie Eklund', *Iustus förlag*, pp. 255–66.

Graig, P. & G. De Búrca (2008), *EU Law*, 5th edn, Oxford: Oxford University Press.

—— (2015), *EU Law*, 6th edn, Oxford: Oxford University Press.

Gray, G.C. (2009), 'The Responsabilization Strategy of Health and Safety. Neo-liberalism and the Reconfiguration of Individual Responsibility for Risk', 49(3) *Brit.J.Criminol* pp. 326–342.

Greven T. (2006) 'Auf dem Prüfstand: Gewerkschaftsstrategien zur Regulierung globaler Konkurrenz', *WSI-Mitteilungen* pp. 10–15.

Group of Experts (2010), *Implementation of Recast Directive 2009/38/EC on European Works Councils*, Report December 2010, Brussels: European Commission.

Guðmundsdóttir, D. (2015), 'A Renewed Emphasis on the Charter's Distinction between Rights and Principles: Is a Doctrine of Judicial Restraint More Appropriate?', 52(3) *Common Market Law Review*, pp. 685–719.

Hämäläinen, R.M. (2008), *The Europeanisation of Occupational Health Services: A study of the impact of EU Policies*, Helsinki: Finnish Institute of Occupational Health.

Hammarberg, T. (2011), *Discrimination on Grounds of Sexual Orientation and Gender Identity in Europe*, 2nd edn, Strasbourg: Council of Europe Publishing.

Hardy, S. (2006), 'Harmonising European Working Time in an Enlarged EU: A Case of Failed "Humanisation"?', 22 *IJCCLIR* pp. 563–601.

Harris, D. & J. Darcy (2001), *The European Social Charter*, 2nd edn, New York: Ardsley.

Heerma van Voss, G. (2005), 'The Directive European Works Councils in Community-scale Undertakings. The Introduction of Double Subsidiarity in European Labour Law', 2(4) *Maastricht Journal of European and Comparative Law*, pp. 339–58.

Hendrickx, F. (2012), 'Age and European Employment Discrimination Law', in F. Hendrickx (ed.), *Active Ageing and Labour Law, Contributions in Honour of Professor Blanpain*, Antwerp: Intersentia, pp. 3–30.

Hepple, B. (1987), 'The Crisis in EEC Labour Law', 16 *Industrial Law Journal*, pp. 77–87.

Hepple, B. & K. Mumgaard (1998), 'Pension Rights in Business Transfers', 27(4) *Industrial Law Journal*, pp. 309–24.

Hervey, T. (2005), 'Thirty Years of EU Sex Equality Law: Looking Backwards, Looking Forwards' 12(4) *Maastricht Journal of European and Comparative Law*, pp. 307–25.

Herzfeld Olsson, P. (2011), 'The ILO Acquis and the EU Labour Law', in: M. Rönnmar (ed.), *Labour Law, Fundamental Rights and Social Europe*, Oxford and Portland: Hart, pp. 27–55.

Hilgertt, J. (2013), 'The Future of Workplace Health and Safety as a Fundamental Human Right' 34 *Comp.Lab.L.& Pol'y J.* pp. 715–736.

Hoet, L. (1995), 'Het sociaal protocol bij het Verdrag van Maastricht' 32(2) *Jura Falconis* pp. 233–256.

Holland, D. et al. (2011), *Labour mobility within the EU –The impact of enlargement and the functioning of the transitional arrangements*, London: National Institute of Economic and Social Research.

Hoskyns, C. (1996), *Integrating Gender – Women, Law and Politics in the European Union*, London: Verso.

Houwerzijl, M.S. (2005), *De detacheringsrichtlijn: over de achtergrond, inhoud en implementatie van Richtlijn 96/71/EG*, Deventer: Kluwer.

—— (2014), 'Regime Shopping across (blurring) Boundaries', in: S. Evju (ed.), *Regulating Transnational Labour in Europe: The Quandaries of Multilevel Governance*, Oslo: Skriftserie nr. 196, pp. 95–130.

Houwerzijl, M.S. & F. Pennings (1999), 'Double Charges in Case of Posting of Employees: The Guiot Judgment and its Effects in the Construction Sector', 1(1) *European Journal of Social Security*, pp. 91–112.

Houwerzijl, M.S. & A. Schrauwen (2018), 'From Competing to Aligned Narratives on Posted and Other Mobile Workers within the EU?', in: C. Rijken & T. de Lange (eds.), *Towards a Decent Labour Market for Low-waged Migrant Workers*. Amsterdam: AUP, pp. 81–108.

Howes, H. (2003), 'Health and Safety Regulatory Framework – A Comparative Perspective' 19 *IJCCLIR* pp. 85–107.

Hürtgen, S. (2011), 'Europäische Interessenvertretung – eine Frage der nationalen Kultur?', 18(4) *Industrielle Beziehungen*, pp. 315–335.

Hyltén-Cavallius, K. (2018), 'The Need of Residence Registration for Enjoyment of EU citizenship in Sweden', in: F. Pennings & M. Seeleib-Kaiser (eds.) (2018), *European Citizenship and Social Rights: Entitlements and Impediments to Accessing Welfare*, Cheltenham: Edward Elgar, pp. 127–148.

IARC (2010), *Painting, Firefighting, and Shiftwork*, Lyon: International Agency for Research on Cancer, Monographs on the Evaluation of Carcinogenic Risks to Humans, Vol. 98.

Ioannides, A., E. Oxouzi & S. Mavroudeas (2014), 'All work and no … pay? Unpaid overtime in Greece: determining factors and theoretical explanations', 45/1 *Industrial Relations Journal*, pp. 39–55.

Iossa, A. (2011), 'Protecting the Right to Collective Action and to Collective Bargaining: Developments and New Perspectives at European and International Levels', in: A. Bücker & W. Warneck (eds.), *Reconciling Fundamental Social Rights and Economic Freedoms after Viking, Laval and Rüffert*, Baden: Nomos, pp. 245–314.

Jacobs, A. (2005), *The European Constitution. How It Was Created. What It Will Change.* Nijmegen: Wolf.

—— (2016), 'The Right to Organise' in: Niklas Bruun et al. (eds.), *The European Social Charter and Employment Relations*, Oxford: Hart, pp. 220–248.

Jacqueson, C. (2016), 'From Negligence to Resistance: Danish Welfare in the Light of Free Movement Law', 18(2) *European Journal of Social Security*, pp. 183–206.

Jagodzinski, R. (2011), 'EWCs after 15 Years - Success or Failure', *Transfer* 2011/17.

—— (2012), 'Transnational collective bargaining: a literature review', in: I. Schömann et al. (eds.), *Transnational collective bargaining at company level. A new component of European industrial relations?*, Brussels: ETUI, pp. 19–76.

—— (2014), *Implementation and enforcement provisions of the European Works Councils Recast Directive: Are sanctions really 'effective, proportionate and dissuasive?* ETUI Policy Brief, European Economic, Employment and Social Policy, No. 7.

—— (2015) (ed.), *Variations on a theme? The implementation of the EWC Recast Directive*, Brussels: ETUI.

Jagodzinski R. & P. Lorber (2015), 'Enforcement frameworks and employees' rights of access to enforcement procedures' in: R. Jagodzinski (ed.), *Variations on a theme? The implementation of the EWC Recast Directive*, Brussels: ETUI p. 107–178.

Jaspers, A., 'The European Works Council Directive in its Community Context', M. Rigaux & F. Dorssemont (eds.), *European Works Councils*, Antwerpen: Intersentia, pp. 11–30.

—— (2004), 'Restructuring of Enterprises. The Legislative Initiatives of the European Community: Support of Workers' Interests', in: Corinne Sachs Durant, *La place des salariés dans les restructurations en Europe Communautaire/The situation of workers in restructuring in the European Union*, Strasbourg: Presses Universitaires de Strasbourg, pp. 47–72.

—— (2007), 'The right to collective action in European Law', in: F. Dorssemont et al. (ed.), *Cross-Border Collective Actions in Europe: A Legal Challenge*, Antwerp: Intersentia, pp. 23–74.

—— (2008a), 'Het Hof van Justitie EG en het Arbeidsrecht: Europeanisering van het nationale arbeidsrecht?', *SMA*, pp. 7–18.

—— (2008b), 'Collectieve acties door vakbonden beperkt wegens strijd vrijheid van diensten en vestiging', 12(2) *Sociaal Recht*, pp. 56–60.

—— (2009), 'Decentralisation and Proliferation of the Social Dialogue: a Crisis or a Challenge?', in: J. Schubert (ed.), *Sozialer Dialog in der Krise - Social Dialog in crisis?*, Baden-Baden: Nomos, pp. 175–193.

—— (2012a), 'Effective Transnational Collective Bargaining Binding Transnational Company Agreements: A Challenging Perspective', in: I. Schömann et al. (eds.), *Transnational collective bargaining at company level. A new component of European industrial relations?*, Brussels: ETUI, pp. 233–265.

—— (2012b), 'The future of the collective agreements system challenged', in: K. Malherbe and J. Slot-Nielsen (eds.), *Labour Law into the Future*, JUTA Claremont/Cape Town, p. 97–121.

—— (2015), 'Grenzen aan sociale concurrentie bij vrij verkeer van diensten en bij mededinging', *Arbeidsrechtelijke Annotaties*, pp. 36–71.

Jaspers, T. & F. Pennings (2013), 'Occupational Health and Safety in the Netherlands: A Shift of Responsibilities', in E. Ales (ed.) *Health and Safety at Work. European and Comparative Perspective*, Alphen a/d Rijn: Wolters Kluwer, pp. 329–374.

Jeffery, M. (1998), 'Not Really Going to Work? Of the Directive on Part-time Work, 'Atypical Work' and Attempts to Regulate It', 27(3) *Industrial Law Journal*, 193–213.

Jenkins, A. (2002), *Employment Relations in France. Evolution and Innovation*, New York: Kluwer Academic Publishers.

Joint ILO/WHO Committee on Occupational Health (1984), *Psychosocial factor at work. Recognition and control.* Report of the Ninth Session, Geneva.

Jones, C. (1996), 'Sexual Harassment', 3(90) *New York: Facts on File.*

Jongeneel, W.P. et al. (2016), *Work-related cancer in the European Union: Size, impact and options for further prevention*, Bilthoven: RIVM report 2016-10.

Junker, A. (2016), 'Die Einflüsse des europäischen Rechts auf die personelle Reichweite des Arbeitnehmerschutzes Der Arbeitnehmerbegriff in der Rechtsprechung des Europäischen Gerichtshofs', *Europäische Zeitschrift für Arbeitsrecht*, pp. 184.

Kall, K. & N. Lillie (2017), *Protection of posted workers in the European Union: Findings and policy recommendations based on existing research*, PROMO briefing paper, University of Jyväskylä, Finland.

Källström, K. & J. Malmberg (2013), *Anställningsförhållandet. Inledning till den individuella arbetsrätten*, 3rd edn, Uppsala: Iustus.

Karasek, R.A. (1979). '*Job demands, job decision latitude, and mental strain: Implications for job redesign*'. *Administrative science quarterly*, pp. 285–308.

Keller, B. & B. Sörries (1999), 'The new European social dialogue: old wine in new bottles?', 9 (2) *Journal of European Social Policy*, pp. 111–125.

Keller, B. & F. Werner (2011), 'News forms of employee involvement at European level – The case of the European Company (SE)', 50(4) *British Journal of Industrial Relations*, pp. 620–643.

Kenner, J. (2004), 'Re-evaluating the concept of working time: an analysis of recent case law', 35(6) *Industrial Relations Journal*, pp. 588–602.

—— (2005), 'Working Time, Jaeger and the Seven-Year Itch' 11 *Colum. J. Eur. L.* pp. 53–70.

—— (2017), 'Inverting the Flexicurity Paradigm: the United Kingdom and Zero Hours Contracts', in: E. Ales, O. Deinert & J. Kenner (eds.), *Core and Contingent Work in the European Union. A Comparative Analysis*, Oxford: Hart, pp. 153–183.

Kennett, A. & S. Nesbitt (2000), 'The Consequences of Employing a Mobile Workforce – a Patchwork of Protections', 11(12) *International Company and Commercial Law Review*, pp. 399–406.

Kilimnik, K. (1983), 'Landmark European Labor Law Nears Passage', 4(5/) *The Multinational Monitor*, <https://www.multinationalmonitor.org/hyper/issues/1983/05/kilimnik.html> accessed 05.06.2019.

Kilpatrick C. (2009), *British jobs for British workers? UK industrial action and free movement of services in EU law*, LSE Legal Studies Working Paper, No. 16.

—— (2011), 'The Court of Justice and Labour Law in 2010: A New EU Discrimination Law Architecture', 40(3) *Industrial Law Journal*, pp. 280–301.

—— (2014), 'Has Polycentric Strike Law Arrived in the UK? After *Laval*, After *Viking*, After *Demir*?', 30(3) *International Journal of Comparative Labour Law and Industrial Relations*, pp. 293–318.

Kilpatrick C. & M. Freedland (2004), 'The United Kingdom: How is EU Governance Transformative?', in: S. Sciarra, P. Davies & M. Freedland (eds.), *Employment Policy and the Regulation of Part-time Work in the European Union. A Comparative Analysis*, Cambridge: Cambridge University Press, pp. 299–357.

Kilpatrick, C., T. Novitz & P. Skidmore (eds.) (2000), *The Future of Remedies in Europe*, Oxford: Hart.

Kirton-Darling, J. & S. Clauwaert (2003), 'European social dialogue: an instrument in the Europeanisation of industrial relations', 2(03) *Transfer*, p 247–264

Knegt, R., J.R. Popma et al. (2011), *Het Nieuwe Werken en de arbeidsrechtelijke regelgeving*, Amsterdam: Hugo Sinzheimer Instituut.

Knook, A. (2005), 'The Court, the Charter, and the Vertical Division of Powers in the European Union', 42(2) *Common Market Law Review*, pp. 367–98.

Köbele, B. & J. Cremers (1994), *European Union: Posting of Workers in the Construction Industry*, Bonn/Witterschlick: Verlag Marg. Wehle.

Kocher, E. (2004), 'Selbstverpflichtungen von Unternehmen zur sozialen Verantwortung', *Recht der Arbeit*, pp. 27–31.

—— (2008a), 'Codes of Conduct and Framework Agreements and Social Minimum Standards - Private Regulation?', in: O. Dilling, M. Herberg & G. Winter (eds.), *Responsible Business: Self-Governance and Law in Transnational Economic Transactions*, Oxford: Hart, pp. 67–86.

—— (2008b), 'Equal Treatment and Gender Justice in Corporate Policies on Social Responsibility', in: F. Pennings, Y. Konijn & A. Veldman (eds.), *Social Responsibility in Labour Relations. European and Comparative Perspectives* - Liber Amicorum Teun Jaspers, Alphen a/d Rijn: Wolters Kluwer, pp. 371–378.

—— (2019), 'Crowdworking: Ein neuer Typus von Beschäftigungsverhältnissen? Eine Rekonstruktion der Grenzen des Arbeitsrechts zwischen Markt und Organisation', in: I. Hensel et al. (eds.), *Selbstständige Unselbstständigkeit. Crowdworking zwischen Autonomie und Kontrolle*, Nomos-Verlag: Baden-Baden, pp. 173–214.

Kommunal- og Arbeidsdepartementet (1987), *Internkontroll i en samlet strategi for arbeidsmiljø og sikkerhet*, Dokument NOU 1987: 10.

Konzen, H. et al. (eds.) (2008), *Festschrift für Rolf Birk zum siebzigsten Geburtstag*, Tübingen: Mohr Siebeck.

Kornezov, A. (2016), 'The New Format of the Acte Clair Doctrine and its Consequences', 53(5) *Common Market Law Review*, pp. 1317–1342.

Koukiadaki A. & I. Katsaroumpas (2017), *Temporary contracts, precarious employment, employees' fundamental rights and EU employment law*, <http://www.europarl.europa.eu/supporting-analyses> accessed 05.06.2019.

Kountouris, N. (2016), 'EU law and the Regulation of Atypical Work', in: A. Bogg, A. Costello & A.C.L. Davies (eds.), *Research Handbook on EU Labour Law*, Cheltenham: Edward Elgar, pp. 255–266.

Kullmann, M. (2015), *Enforcement of labour law in cross-border situations. A legal study of the EU's influence on the Dutch, German, and Swedish Enforcement systems*, PhD thesis, Deventer: Kluwer.

Kullmann, M. & M. Rocca (2017), 'Part-time Work with Part-time Retirement. Towards an Alliance between Labour Law and Pensions for the Healthy Ageing of the Workforce?', in: T. Addabbo et al. (eds.), *Well-being at and through Work*, Torino: Giappichelli, pp. 295–313.

Lamers, J.J.M. (1995), 'De Europese ondernemingsraden: een effectieve doorbraak?', *Nederlands Tijdschrift voor Sociaal Recht*, pp. 314–318.

Langille, B.A. (2005), 'Core Labour Rights – The True Story (Reply to Alston)' 16(3) European Journal of International Law, pp. 409–437.

Lapeyre, J. (2017), *The European Social Dialogue. The History of a Social Innovation (1985–2003)*, Brussels: ETUI.

Laulom, S. (2001), 'A Fallible Interlocutor?', in: S. Sciarra (ed.), *Labour Law in the Courts. National Judges and the European Court of Justice*. Oxford: Hart, pp. 145–178.

—— (2005a), 'Le Cadre communautaire de la représentation des travailleurs dans l'entreprise', in: S. Laulom (ed.), *Récomposition des systems de représentation des salariés en Europe*, Presses Universitaire de Saint-Étienne, pp. 21–112.

Laulom, S. & F. Dorssemont (2015), 'Fundamental principles of EWC Directive 2009/38/EG', in: R. Jagodzinski (ed.), *Variations on a Theme? The Implementation of the EWC Recast Directive*, Brussels: ETUI, pp. 33–67.

Lazear, E. (1979), 'Why is There Mandatory Retirement?', 87(6) *Journal of Political Economy*, pp. 1261–1264.

Leczykiewicz, D. (2015), 'Conceptualizing Conflict between the Economic and Social in EU law after Viking and Laval', in: M. Freedland & J. Prassl (eds.), *EU Law in the Member States: Viking, Laval and Beyond*, Oxford: Hart, pp. 307–322.

Lee, S., D. McCann & J.C. Messenger (2007), *Working Time around the World*, London: Routledge.

Lehoczky, K. (2010), 'The Fundamental Right of Workers to Information and Consultation under the European Social Charter', in: F. Dorssemont & T. Blanke (eds.), *The Recast of the European Works Council Directive*, Antwerp: Intersentia, pp. 1–30.

Leka, S. and E. Kortum (2008), 'A European framework to address psychosocial hazards' 50 *J Occ Health* pp. 294–296.

Leka, S. and T. Cox (ed.) (2008), *The European Framework for Psychosocial Risk Management: PRIMA-EF*, Nottingham: WHO Publications.

Leka, S. et al. (2011a), 'The development of the European Framework for Psychosocial Risk Management: PRIMA-EF', 53 *J Occ Health*, pp. 137–143.

—— (2011b), 'The role of policy for the management of psychosocial risks at the workplace in the European Union', 49 *Safety Sci*, pp. 558–564.

Leka, S. and others (2011c), 'Developing a standard for psychosocial risk management: PAS 1010', 49 *Safety Sci*, pp. 1047–1057.

Lenaerts, K., I. Maselis & K. Gutman (2014), *EU Procedural Law*, Oxford: Oxford University Press.

Lerouge, L. (2010), 'Moral Harassment in the Workplace: French Law and European Perspectives', 32 *Comp.Lab.L.& Pol'y J.*, pp. 109–152.

Lerouge, L. and L.C. Hebert, 'The Law of Workplace Harassment of the United States, France, and the European Union: Comparative Analysis After the Adoption of France's New Sexual Harassment Law', 35 *Comp.Lab.L.& Pol'y J.*, pp. 93–122.

Lester, G. (2015), 'Age Discrimination and Labour Law in the United States', in: A. Numhauser-Henning & M. Rönnmar (eds.), *Age Discrimination and Labour Law. Comparative and Conceptual Perspectives in the EU and Beyond*, Alphen a/d Rijn: Kluwer.

Lhernould, J.P. & B. Palli (2017), 'Posted Workers Remuneration: Comparative Study in Nine EU countries and Four Sectors', 24(1) *Maastricht Journal of European and Comparative Law*, pp. 108–26.

Lippel, K. (2010), 'Regulation of psychosocial risk factors at work: An international overview', 49 *Safety Sci*, pp., 543–546.

Lo Faro, A. (2004), 'Labour Market Reforms and new Part-time Legislation in Italy: Towards Unilateral Flexibility', in: B. Caruso & M. Fuchs (eds.), *Flexibility in Employment and Labour Market Legislation in Europe: Comparing Italy and Germany*, Baden Baden and Milan, Nomos-Giuffrè.

Lodge, J (1986), 'The Single European Act: Towards a New Euro-Dynamism?', 3 *JCMS* pp. 203–223.

Lorber, P. (2003), 'National Works Councils: Opening the Door on a Whole New Era in United Kingdom Employment Relations'. 19(3) *International Journal of Comparative Labour Law and Industrial Relations*, pp. 297–319.

—— (2009), 'Worker Participation and Industrial Democracy: Strengthening Information and Consultation' in: E. Ales et al. (eds.), *Fundamental Social Rights in Europe: Challenges and Opportunities*, Antwerp: Intersentia, pp. 125–40.

—— (2010), 'United Kingdom', in: F. Dorssemont & T. Blanke, *The Recast of the European Works Council Directive*, Antwerpen: Intersentia, pp. 213–223.

—— (2018), 'Brexit and workers' rights: the meaning of a No Deal for transnational consultation', *Regulating for Globalisation blog*, <http://regulatingforglobalization.com/2018/09/07/brexit-workers-rights-meaning-no-deal-transnational-consultation>, accessed 05.06.2019.

Lörcher, K. & I. Schömann (2016), *The European Pillar of Social Rights: Critical Legal Analysis and Proposals*, Brussels: ETUI.

Lyon-Caen, A. (1972), *A la recherche de la convention collective Européenne*, Brussels: European Commission.

MacGoris, S. (2012), *Changes over time – First findings from the fifth European Working Conditions Survey*, Dublin: European Foundation for the Improvement of Living and Working Conditions.

MacKinnon, C. (1979), *Sexual Harassment of Working Women*, Yale University Press.

Madsen, M.R. et al. (2017), 'Competing Supremacies and Clashing Institutional Rationalities: The Danish Supreme Court's Decision in the *Ajos* Case and the National Limits of Judicial Cooperation', 23(1/2) *European Law Journal*, pp. 140–150.

Majone, D (1993), 'The European Community between Social Policy and Social Regulation', 31 JCMS, pp. 153–170.

Malmberg, J. (2004), 'Effective Enforcement of EC Labour Law: A Comparative Analysis of Community Law Requirements', 10(2) *European Journal of Industrial Relations*, pp. 219–229.

Malmberg, J. & T. Sigeman (2008), 'Industrial Actions and EU Economic Freedoms: The Autonomous Collective Bargaining Model Curtailed by the European Court of Justice', 45(4) *Common Market Law Review*, pp. 1115–1146.

Malmberg, J. et al. (ed.) (2003), *Effective Enforcement of EC Labour Law*. The Hague: Kluwer.

Marginson, P., M. Gilman, O. Jacobi & H. Krieger (1998), *Negotiating European Works Councils – An analysis of agreements under article 13*, Dublin: European Foundation for the Improvement of Living and Working Conditions and European Commission DG V.

Masselot, A. & B. McLellan (2018), 'Directive 86/378/EEC: Equal Treatment in Occupational Social Security and Pension Schemes', in: E. Ales et al. (eds.), *International and European Labour Law: A Commentary*, Baden Baden: Nomos, pp. 481–494.

Masselot, A. et al. (2012), *Fighting discrimination on the grounds of pregnancy, maternity and parenthood. The application of EU and national law in practice in 33 European countries*, Report by the Network of Legal Experts in the Field of Gender Equality, Luxembourg.

Mazuyer, E. (2014), 'Critical Analysis of ECJ Case-law on Fixed-term Contracts in the Public Sector', 5(3/4) *European Labour Law Journal*, pp. 334–348.

McColgan, A. (2000), 'Missing the Point? The Part-Time Workers (Prevention of Less Favourable Treatment) Regulations 2000 (SI 2000, No 1551)', 29(3) *Industrial Law Journal*, pp. 260–267.

—— (2015), *Measures to address the challenges of work-life balance in the EU Member States, Iceland, Liechtenstein and Norway*, Report to the European network of Legal Experts in Gender Equality and Non-discrimination to the European Commission, Luxembourg.

Meenan, H. (2007), 'Age Discrimination – Of Cinderella and *The Golden Bow*', in: Helen Meenan (ed.), *Equality Law in an Enlarged European Union, Understanding the Article 13 Directives*, Cambridge: Cambridge University Press, 278–312.

Meltzer, B.D. (1965), 'Labor Unions, Collective Bargaining, and the Antitrust Laws', 32 *University of Chicago Law Review*, pp. 659–734.

Menendez, M., J. Benach & L. Vogel (2009), *The impact of safety representatives on occupational health – A European perspective*, Report 107, Brussels: European Trade Union Institute.

Mikkola, M. (2010), *Social Human Rights of Europe*, Helsinki: Karelactio.

Mitrus, L. (2014), 'Poland', in: M. Freedland & J. Prassl, *Viking, Laval and Beyond*, Oxford and Portland: Hart, p. 229–240.

Moreau, M.-A. (1997), 'A propos de l'affaire Renault', *Droit social*, pp. 493–503.

Mulder, J. (2004), *Anställningen vid verksamhetsövergång*, Lund.

Müller, T., H.-W. Platzer & S. Rüb (2013), *Transnational company agreements and the role of European Works Councils in negotiations*, ETUI Study 127, Brussels.

Murray J. (1999), 'Normalising Temporary Work. The Proposed Directive on Fixed-Term Work', 28(3) *Industrial Law Journal*, pp. 269–275.

Neal, A.C. (1990), 'The European Framework Directive on the Health and Safety of Workers: Challenges for the United Kingdom?', 6 *International Journal of Comparative Labour Law and Industrial Relations*, pp. 80–117.

—— (1998), '*Regulating Health and Safety at Work*: Developing European Union Policies for the Millennium', 14 *International Journal of Comparative Labour Law and Industrial Relations*, pp. 217–246.

Nebe, K. & A. Ritschel (2009), 'The Concept of Information and Consultation in European Directives', in: T. Blanke et al., *Recasting Worker Involvement?*, Deventer: Kluwer.

Nemonen, A. et al. (2014), Global estimates of occupational accidents and fatal work-related diseases in 2014, Singapore: Workplace Safety & Health Institute.

Nielsen, R. (2002), 'Implementation of EC Directives in Denmark', 18(3) *International Journal of Comparative Labour Law and Industrial Relations*, pp. 459–78.

Novitz, T. (2003), *International and European Protection of the Right to Strike*, Oxford: Oxford University Press.

—— (2008), 'A Human Rights Analysis of the Viking and Laval Judgments', *The Cambridge Yearbook of European Legal Studies*, Oxford and Portland: Hart, pp. 541–62.

—— (2010a), 'Collective Action in the United Kingdom', in: E. Ales & T. Novitz (eds.), *Collective Action and Fundamental Freedoms in Europe*, Antwerp: Intersentia, pp. 173–212.

—— (2010b), 'The Impact of Viking and Laval. Contesting the Social Function and Legal Regulation of the Right to Strike', in: E. Ales & T. Novitz (eds.), *Collective Action and Fundamental Freedoms in Europe*, Antwerp: Intersentia, pp. 251–273.

—— (2014), 'The Internationally Recognized Right to Strike: A Past, Present, and Future Basis upon Which to Evaluate Remedies for Unlawful Collective Action?', 30(3) *International Journal of Comparative Labour Law and Industrial Relations*, pp. 375–79.

—— (2018), 'Collective Bargaining and Social Dumping in Posting and Procurement: What Might Come from Recent Court of Justice Case Law and the Proposed Reform of the Posted Workers Directive?', in: A. Sanchez Graells (ed.), *Smart Public Procurement and Labour Standards Pushing the Discussion after RegioPost*, Bloomsbury, pp. 215–44.

Nowak, T. (2008), 'The Working Time Directive and the European Court of Justice', 15 *Maastricht J. Eur. & Comp. L.*, pp. 447–471.

Numhauser-Henning, A. (2002), 'Fixed-term Work in Nordic Labour Law', 18(4) *The International Journal of Comparative Labour Law and Industrial Relations*, pp. 429–458.

—— (2015), 'Labour Law, Pension Norms and the EU Ban on Age Discrimination: Towards Ultimate Flexibilization?' in: A. Numhauser-Henning & M. Rönnmar, *Age Discrimination and Labour Law. Comparative and Conceptual Perspectives in the EU and Beyond*, Alphen a/d Rijn: Wolters Kluwer, pp. 115–140.

Numhauser-Henning, A. & S. Laulom (2013), *Harassment related to Sex and Sexual Harassment Law in 33 European Countries, Discrimination versus Dignity*, European Network of Legal Experts in the Field of Gender Equality, Luxembourg: European Commission.

Numhauser-Henning, A. & M. Rönnmar (eds.) (2015), *Age Discrimination and Labour Law. Comparative and Conceptual Perspectives in the EU and Beyond*, Alphen a/d Rijn: Wolters Kluwer.

O'Brien, Ch. (2009), 'Social Blind Spots and Monocular Policy Making: The ECJ's Migrant Worker Model', 46(2) *Common Market Law Review*, pp. 1107–1141.

O'Cinneide, C. (2015), 'Constitutional and fundamental Rights Aspects of Age Discrimination', in: A. Numhauser-Henning & M. Rönnmar (eds.), *Age Discrimination and Labour Law. Comparative and Conceptual Perspectives in the EU and Beyond*, Alphen a/d Rijn: Wolters Kluwer, pp. 51–69.

O'Dempsey, D. & A. Beale (2011), *Age and employment*, European Network of Legal Experts in the Non-discrimination Field, Luxembourg: European Commission.

O'Leary, S. (2008), 'Developing an Ever Closer Union between the Peoples of Europe? A Reappraisal of the Case Law of the Court of Justice on the Free Movement of Persons and EU Citizenship', *Yearbook of European Law*, pp. 167–193.

Ojeda Aviles, A. & J. Garcia Viña (2009), 'Regulation of the Labour Market', in B. Hepple & B. Veneziani (eds.), *The Transformation of Labour Law in Europe. A Comparative Study of 15 Countries 1945–2004*. Oxford: Hart, pp. 59–98.

Overbeeke, F. van (2016), 'Do We Need a New Conflict-of-laws Rule in the European Road Transport Sector? Yes We Do!' in: J. Buelens (ed.), *From Social Competition to Social Dumping*, Antwerp: Intersentia, pp. 107–122.

—— (2017), 'The Commission's Proposal to Amend the Posting of Workers Directive and Private International Law Implications', *NIPR*, pp. 178–194.

Overmeiren, F. van, et al. (2014), *FreSsco analytical report 2014: The notions of obstacle and discrimination under EU law on free movement of workers*, Brussels: European Commission.

Palinkaš, I. (2018), *The Legal and Institutional Framing of Collective Bargaining in CEE Countries: Between Europeanisation and Decentralisation*, Alphen a/d Rijn: Wolters Kluwer.

Palma-Ramalho, M., P. Foubert & S. Burri (2015), *The implementation of Parental Leave Directive 2010/18 in 33 European countries*, Report to the European Commission by the Network of legal experts in gender equality and non-discrimination, Luxembourg: European Commission.

Papadakis, K. (2009), *Cross-border Social Dialogue and Agreements: An Emerging Global Industrial Relations Framework?* Geneva: ILO, International Institute for Labour Studies.

Parent-Thirion, A. et al. (2007), *Fourth European Working Conditions Survey*, Dublin: European Foundation for the Improvement of Living and Working Conditions.

—— (2012), *Fifth European Working Conditions Survey*, Dublin: European Foundation for the Improvement of Living and Working Conditions.

Pecinocsky, P. (2016), 'Evolutions in the Social Case Law of the Court of Justice. The Follow-up Cases of the Laval Quartet: ESA and Regiopost', 7(2) *European Labour Law Journal*, pp. 294–309.

Peers, S. (2010), 'Non-regression Clauses: The Fig Leaf Has Fallen', 39(4) *Industrial Law Journal*, p. 436–443.

Pennings, F. (2011), 'The Open Method of Coordination in the Area of Social Policy and the Legality Principle', in: L.F.M. Besselink, F.J.L. Pennings & A. Prechal (eds.), *The Eclipse of the Legality Principle in the European Union*, Alphen a/d Rijn: Kluwer Law International, pp. 153–68.

—— (2015a), 'Exceptie van de mededingingsbepalingen voor (schijn)zelfstandigen: de zaak FNV Kiem', 21(4) *Nederlands Tijdschrift voor Europees recht*, pp. 111–116.

—— (2015b), *European Social Security Law*, 6th edn, Cambridge-Antwerp-Portland: Intersentia.

—— (2018), 'Legal Barriers to Access of EU Citizens to Social Rights', in: F. Pennings & M. Seeleib-Kaiser (eds.), *European Citizenship and Social Rights: Entitlements and Impediments to Accessing Welfare*, Cheltenham: Edgar Elgar, p. 76–102.

Pennings, F. & M. Seeleib-Kaiser (eds.) (2018), *European Citizenship and Social Rights: Entitlements and Impediments to Accessing Welfare*, Cheltenham: Edward Elgar.

Pettersson, H. (2015), 'Discrimination against Part-Time and Fixed-Term Workers: A Critical Legal Positivist Analysis', 31(1) *International Journal of Comparative Labour Law and Industrial Relations*, pp. 47–67.

Plantenga, J. & C. Remery (2010), EU Expert Group on Gender and Employment (EGGE), *Flexible working time arrangements and gender equality: A comparative review of 30 European countries*, Luxembourg: Publications Office of the European Union.

Polychronakis, I. et al (2008), 'The legal context for Workplace Safety and Health Promotion: Thinking of Women', in: A. Linos & W. Kirch (eds.), *Promoting Health for Working Women*, Berlin: Springer Verlag.

Popma, J.R. (1999), 'Verprivaatrechtelijking van arbeidsomstandigheden?', in: P.F. van der Heijden, R.H. van het Kaar & A.C.J.M. Wilthagen (eds.), *Naar een nieuwe rechtsorde van de arbeid?*, Den Haag: SDU/HSI.

Popma, J.R. (2003), *Het arbo-effect van medezeggenschap*, Alphen a/d Rijn: Kluwer.

Prassl, J. (2013), 'Freedom of Contract as a General Principle of EU Law? Transfers of Undertakings and the Protection of Employer Rights in EU Labour Law: Case C-426/11 Alemo-Herron and others v Parkwood Leisure Ltd', 42(4) *Industrial Law Journal*, pp. 434–446.

Prechal, S. & S.A. de Vries (2008), 'Viking/Laval en de grondslagen van het internemarktrecht', *SEW*, pp. 426–427.

Prinssen, J.M. (2004), *Doorwerking van Europees recht*, PhD thesis, Amsterdam.

Purse, P & J Dorrian (2011), 'Deterrence and Enforcement of Occupational Health and Safety Law'. 27 *International Journal of Comparative Labour Law and Industrial Relations*, pp. 23–39.

Quinn, M. & N. McGowan, (1987), 'Could Article 30 Impose Obligations on Individuals?', 12 *European Law Review*, p. 163 ff.

Rasnača, Z. (2017), '(Any) relevance of the European Pillar of Social Rights for EU Law?', <http://europeanlawblog.eu/2017/11/17/any-relevance-of-the-european-pillar-of-social-rights-for-eu-law> accessed 05.06.2019.

Reich, N. (2008), 'Free Movement vs. Social Rights in an Enlarged Union – the Laval and Viking Cases before the ECJ', 9(2) *German Law Journal*, pp. 125–61.

Rhebergen, M et al. (2012), 'Can workers answer their questions about occupational safety and health: challenges and solutions', 50 *IndHealth*, pp. 239–249.

Risak, M. & T. Dullinger (2018), *The concept of 'worker' in EU law. Status quo and potential for change*, Brussels: ETUI.

Robin-Olivier, S. & P. Remy (2012), 'La protection des travailleurs atypiques est-elle en régression? Double réflexion sur l'arrêt *Kücük* de la Cour de Justice', *Revue de droit du travail*, p. 645 ff.

Robin-Olivier, S. (2016), *Les contrats de travail flexible. Une comparaison internationale*, Presses de Sciences Po.

Rocca, M. (2012), 'The Proposal for a (so-called) "Monti II" Regulation on the Exercise of the Right to Take Collective Action within the Context of the Freedom of Establishment and the Freedom to Provide Services', 1(1) *European Labour Law Journal*, pp. 19–28.

Rodríguez, R. et al. (2012), *Study on the characteristics and legal effects of agreements between companies and workers' representatives*, Brussels: European Commission.

Rogers, N., R. Scannell & J. Walsh (2012), *Free Movement of Persons in the Enlarged European Union*, London: Sweet & Maxwell.

Rönnmar, M. (2008a), *EU Industrial Relations v. National Industrial Relations*, Wolters Kluwer.

—— (2008b), 'Free Movement of services versus National Labour Law and Industrial Relations Systems: Understanding the Laval Case from a Swedish and Nordic Perspective', in: C. Barnard (ed.), *Cambridge Yearbook of European Legal Studies*, 10, Oxford and Portland: Hart.

—— (2010a), 'Labour Policy on Fixed-Term Employment Contracts in Sweden', in: H. Nakakubo & T. Araki (eds.), *Regulation of Fixed-Term Employment Contracts: A Comparative Overview, Bulletin of Comparative Labour Relations*, Alphen a/d Rijn: Wolters Kluwer, pp. 55–68.

—— (2010b), '*Laval* returns to Sweden: the final judgment of the Swedish labour court and Swedish legislative reforms', 39(3) *Industrial Law Journal*, pp. 280–287.

—— (2011a), 'Flexicurity, Labour Law and the Notion of Equal Treatment', in: M. Rönnmar (ed.), *Labour Law, Fundamental Rights and Social Europe*, Oxford: Hart, pp. 153–181.

—— (2011b), *Labour Law, Fundamental Rights and Social Europe*, Oxford: Hart.

—— (2014), 'Chapter 14. Sweden', in: M. Freedland & J. Prassl (eds.), *Viking, Laval and Beyond*, Oxford and Portland: Hart, pp. 241–260.

Rose, V., C. Bellamy & G.D. Child (2013), *European Union law of competition*, OUP Oxford.

Sachs-Durand, C. (2010), 'Information and Consultation in the Recast Directive', in: F. Dorssemont & T. Blanke (eds.), *The Recast of the European Works Council Directive*, Antwerpen: Intersentia, pp. 313–326.

Sädevirta, M. (2015), 'Limitations of Minimum Employee Protection through Guarantee Payment on Employer Insolvency – An Analysis of Minimum Rights and their Evolution under the Insolvency Directive', 4 *Europäische Zeitschrift für Arbeitsrecht*, pp. 416–432.

Samuel, L. (2002), *Fundamental social rights. Case law of the European social charter*, 2nd edn, Strasbourg: Council of Europe.

Sargeant, M. (2008), *Implementation report Directive 1999/70/EC concerning the Framework Agreement on fixed-term work concluded by UNICE, CEEP and ETUC*, Human European Consultancy and Middlesex University, <www.ec.europa.eu/social/BlobServlet?docId=2487&langId=en> accessed 05.06.2019.

Sartori, A. (2016), 'Temporary Agency Work in Europe. Degree of Convergence Following Directive 2008/104/EU', 7(1) *European Labour Law Journal*, pp. 109–125.

Schiek, D. (2010) 'Constitutional Principles and Horizontal Effect: Kücükdeveci Revisited', 1(3) *European Labour Law Journal*, pp. 368–379.

Schiek, D. & V. Chege (eds.) (2009), *European Union Non-discrimination Law: Comparative Perspectives on Multidimensional Equality Law*, Abingdon, Routledge-Cavendish.

Schiek, D., L. Waddington & M. Bell (2007), *Non-discrimination Law*, Oxford: Hart.

Schindlauer, D. (2016), *Country Report Non-discrimination: Austria*, Luxembourg: Publications Office of the European Union.

Schlachter, M. (2011), 'Mandatory Retirement and Age Discrimination under EU Law', 27(3) *International Journal of Comparative Labour Law and Industrial Relations*, pp. 287–299.

Schlachter, M. (ed.) (2014), *EU Labour Law – A Commentary*, Alphen a/d Rijn: Wolters Kluwer.

Schömann, I. et al. (2008), *Codes of conduct and international framework agreements: new forms of governance at company level*, Luxembourg: Office for Official Publications of the European Communities.

Schömann, I. et al. (2012), *Transnational collective bargaining at company level. A new component of European industrial relations?*, Brussels: ETUI.

Sciarra, S. (2004), 'New Discourses in Labour Law: Part-time Work and the Paradigm of Flexibility', in: S. Sciarra, P. Davies & M. Freedland (eds.), *Employment Policy and the Regulation of Part-time Work in the European Union*, pp. 3–34.

—— (2008), 'Fixed-term Work in the Recent Case Law of the ECJ', in: F. Pennings, I. Konijn & A. Veldman, *Social Responsibility in Labour Relations*, Wolters-Kluwer: Alphen aan den Rijn, pp. 299–310.

Sciarra, S., P. Davies & M. Freedland (eds.) (2004), *Employment Policy and the Regulation of Part-time Work in the European Union. A Comparative Analysis*, Cambridge: Cambridge University Press.

Sciarra, S. et al. (2012), *Towards a legal framework for Transnational Company Agreements*, Brussels: ETUC.

Seeleib-Kaiser, M. & F. Pennings (2018), 'Intra-EU Migration and Social Rights: An Introduction', in: F. Pennings & M. Seeleib-Kaiser (eds.), *European Citizenship and Social Rights: Entitlements and Impediments to Accessing Welfare*, Cheltenham: Edward Elgar, pp. 1–10.

Seikel, D. (2015), 'Class Struggle in the Shadow of Luxembourg. The Domestic Impact of the European Court of Justice's Case Law on the Regulation of Working Conditions', 22(8) *Journal of European Public Policy*, pp. 1166–1185.

Selanec, G. & L. Senden (2011), '*Positive Action Measures to Ensure Full Equality in Practice between Men and Women, including on Company Boards*', European Network of Legal Experts in the Field of Gender Equality.

Servais, J.-M. (2009), *International Labour Law*, The Hague: Kluwer Law International.

Shakespeare, T. (2014), *Disability Rights and Wrongs Revisited*, 2nd edn, Abingdon: Routledge.

Smismans, S (2003), 'Towards a New Community Strategy on Health and Safety at Work? Caught in the Institutional Web of Soft Procedures' 19 *International Journal of Comparative Labour Law and Industrial Relations*, pp. 55–83.

Spiegel, B. (2015), 'Persons Covered', in: M. Fuchs & R. Cornelissen (eds.), *EU Social Security Law. A Commentary on EU Regulations 883/2004 and 987/2009*, Munich-Baden-Baden-Oxford: Beck-Hart-Nomos, pp. 70 ff.

Spiegelaere, S. De & R. Jagodzinski (2015), *European Works Councils and SE Works Councils in 2015. Facts & Figures*. Brussels: ETUI.

Steinberg, M. (2012), 'Occupational Health and Safety in a Diverse, Post-Industrial Society: A Swedish Dilemma Responsibilities', in E. Ales (ed.) *Health and Safety at Work. European and Comparative Perspective*, Alphen a/d Rijn: Kluwer Law International, pp. 281–328.

Stollt, M. & E. Wolters (2011), *Worker involvement in the European Company (SE): A handbook for practitioners*, Brussels: ETUI.

Stone, K. & H. Arthurs (eds.) (2013), *Rethinking Workplace Regulation. Beyond the Standard Contract of Employment*, Russell Sage Foundation.

Strikwerda, L. (2012), *Inleiding tot het Nederlandse internationaal privaatrecht*, Kluwer: Deventer.

Syrpis, P. (2016), 'The EU's Role in Labour Law: An Overview of the Rationales for EU Involvement in the Field', in: A. Bogg, C. Costello & A. Davies (eds.), *Research Handbook on EU Labour Law*, Cheltenham and Northampton: Edward Elgar, pp. 21–41.

Syrpis, P. & Novitz, T. (2008), 'Economic and Social Rights in Conflict: Political and Judicial Approaches to their Reconciliation', 33(3) *European Law Review*, pp. 411–426.

Telljohann, V., Da Costa, I. da, Müller, T., Rehfeldt U. & R. Zimmer (2009), 'European and international framework agreements: new tools of transnational industrial relations', 3-4(09) *Transfer*, pp. 505–525.

Temming, F. (2015), 'Zum Anwendungsbereich der Vorschriften über die internationale Zuständigkeit für individuelle Arbeitsverträge', Praxis des Internationalen Privat- und Verfahrensrechts (IPrax), p. 509–555.

Ter Haar, B.P. (2012), *Open Method of Coordination. An analysis of its meaning for the development of a social Europe*, PhD thesis, Leiden: University of Leiden.

—— (2013), 'De onzichtbare hand van Europa. De invloed van de Europese open methode van coördinatie op het Nederlands werkgelegenheidsbeleid', *Tijdschrift Recht en Arbeid* 2013/13.

Ter Haar, B. et al. (2016), 'Europees en internationaal sociaal recht 1996–2016: over de top heen?', in: A. Houweling & L. Sprengers (eds.), *VVA jaar VVA: eind van het begin*, Deventer: Kluwer, pp. 293–350.

Thym, D. (2015), 'The Elusive Limits of Solidarity: Residence Rights of and Social Benefits for Economically Inactive Union Citizens', 52(1) *Common Market Law Review*, pp. 17–50.

Tobler, C. (2014), 'Equality and Non-Discrimination under the ECHR and EU Law. A Comparison Focusing on Discrimination against LGBTI Persons', 74 *ZaöRV*, pp. 521–561.

—— (2015), 'EU Age discrimination Law and Older and Younger Workers: Court of Justice of the European Union Case-law Developments', in: A. Numhauser-Henning & M. Rönnmar (eds.), *Age Discrimination and Labour Law. Comparative and Conceptual Perspectives in the EU and Beyond*, Alphen a/d Rijn: Wolters Kluwer, pp. 93–113.

Valdes Dal-Re, F. (2006), *Directive 2001/86/EC supplementing the European Company with regard to the involvement of employees*, Brussels: Labourasociados.

Valdés de la Vega, B (2013), 'Occupational Health and Safety: An EU Law Perspective', in: E Ales, (ed.), *Health and Safety at Work: European and Comparative Perspective*, Alphen a/d Rijn: Wolters Kluwer, pp. 1–28.

Van Hiel, I. (2013), 'The Right to Form and Join Unions Protected by Article 11 ECHR', in: F. Dorssemont et al., *European Convention on Human Rights and the Employment relation*, Oxford and Portland: Hart, 287–308.

Van Hoek, A. (2018), 'Re-Embedding the Transnational Employment Relationship: A Tale about the Limitations of (EU) Law?', 55(2) *Common Market Law Review*, pp. 449–487.

Van Hoek, A. & F. Hendrickx (2009), *International private law aspects and dispute settlement related to transnational company agreements*, Brussels: European Commission.

Van Hoek, A.A.H. & M.S. Houwerzijl (2011), *Comparative study on the legal aspects of the posting of workers in the framework of the provision of services in the European Union*, Radboud University Nijmegen.

—— (2012), *Complementary study on the legal aspects of the posting of workers in the framework of the provision of services in the European Union*, University of Amsterdam.

Van Nuffel, P (1997), 'Working Time Directive (UK v Council)', 3 *Colum.J.Eur.L.* pp. 298–309.

Veldman, A. & S. De Vries (2015), 'Regulation and Enforcement of Economic Freedoms and Social Rights: A Thorny Distribution of Sovereignty', in: T. van den Brink, M. Luchtman & M. Scholten (eds.), *Sovereignty in the Shared Legal Order of the EU*, Cambridge: Intersentia, pp. 65–92.

Veldman, A. & A. Timmer (2016), *Pay Transparency in the EU*, European Equality Law Network.

Veldman, A. (2011), 'Quasi-legislative Powers of the European Social Dialogue: Imperfect Delegation of Powers or Ambivalent Recognition of Contractual Autonomy?', in: L. Besseling, F. Pennings & S. Prechal (eds.), *The Eclipse of the Legality Principle in the European Union*, Alphen a/d Rijn: Kluwer Law International, pp. 187–210.

—— (2013), 'The Protection of the Fundamental Right to Strike within the Context of the European Internal Market: Implications of the Forthcoming Accession of the EU to the ECHR', 9(1) *Utrecht Law Review*, pp. 104–117.

Velyvyte, V. (2015), 'The Right to Strike in the European Union after Accession to the European Convention on Human Rights: Identifying Conflict and Achieving Coherence', 15(1) *Human Rights Law Review*, pp. 73–100.

Verburg, L. (2010), 'Het moment van de raadpleging van werknemersvertegenwoordigers op grond van de richtlijn collectief ontslag', 9(1) *Arbeidsrechtelijke Annotaties*, pp. 65–80.

Verburg, L.G. (2007), 'De Europese ondernemingsraad: driemaal in de rechtszaal gesignaleerd!', 7(2) *Arbeidsrechtelijke Annotaties*, pp. 84–101.

Verschueren, H. (2008), 'Cross-border Workers in the European Internal Market: Trojan Horses for Member States' Labour and Social Security Law?', 24(2) *International Journal of Comparative Labour Law and Industrial Relations*, pp. 176–199.

—— (2009), 'Special Non-Contributory Benefits in Regulation 1408/71, Regulation 883/2004 and the Case Law of the ECJ', 11(1–2), *European Journal of Social Security*', p. 217–234.

—— (2017), 'Economically Inactive Migrant Union Citizens: Only Entitled to Social Benefits if they Enjoy a Right to Reside in the Host State', 19(1) *European Journal of Social Security*, pp. 71–82.

Vickers, L. (2016), Religious Freedom, Religious Discrimination and the Workplace, 2nd edn, Oxford: Hart.

Vignes, D. (1961), 'Le droit d'établissement et les services dans la C.E.E.', *Annuaire Français de Droit International.*

Visser J. & A. Hemerijck (1997), *A Dutch Miracle: Job Growth, Welfare Reform and Corporatism in the Netherlands*, Amsterdam: Amsterdam University Press.

Visser J., T. Wilthagen, R. Beltzer & E. Koot-van der Putt (2004), 'The Netherlands: From Atypicality to Typicality', in: S. Sciarra, P. Davies & M. Freedland (eds.), *Employment Policy and the Regulation of Part-time Work in the European Union. A Comparative Analysis*, Cambridge: Cambridge University Press, p. 190–222.

W.L.D. II, 'The Proposed Vredeling Directive: A Modest Proposal or the Exportation of Industrial Democracy?', 70(7) *Virginia Law Review*, pp. 1469–1503.

Waas, B. (2016), *New Forms of Employment in Europe*, 94 Bulletin of Comparative Labour Relations.

Waas, B. (ed.) (2014), *The Right to Strike. A Comparative View*, Wolters Kluwer.

Waddington, J. & A. Conchon (2017), *Is Europeanised board-level employee representation specific? The case of European Companies (European Corporate Societies)*, ETUI Working Paper 2017-02.

Waddington, L. (2015), 'Saying All the Right Things and Still Getting It Wrong: The Court of Justice's Definition of Disability and Non-discrimination Law', 22(4) *Maastricht Journal of European and Comparative Law*, pp. 576–591.

Waddington, L. & M. Bell (2011), 'Exploring the Boundaries of Positive Action under EU Law: A Search for Conceptual Clarity', 48(5) *Common Market Law Review*, pp. 1503–1526.

Waddington, L. & A. Lawson (2009), *Disability and non-discrimination law in the European Union: An analysis of disability discrimination law within and beyond the employment field*, Luxembourg, Publications Office of the European Union.

Wagner, I. (2015), *Posted work and deteritorialization in the European Union: A study of the German Construction and Meat Industry*, PhD thesis, Groningen: University of Groningen.

Warneck, W. (2007), *Strike rules in the EU27 and beyond. A comparative overview*, Brussels: ETUI-REHS.

Watson, Philippa (2009), *EU Social and Employment Law. Policy and Practice in an Enlarged Europe*, Oxford: Oxford University Press.

Weatherill, S. (2014), '*Viking* and *Laval*: The EU Internal Market Perspective', in M. Freedland & J. Prassl, *Viking, Laval and Beyond*, Oxford: Hart, pp. 23–40

Weiler, J.H.H. (1981), 'The Community System: the Dual Character of Supranationalism', *Yearbook of European Law*, pp. 267–306.

Weiss, M (2008), 'Transnationale Kollektivvertragsstrukturen in der EG: Informalität oder Verrechtlichung?', in: H. Konzen et al. (eds.), *Festschrift für Rolf Birk zum siebzigsten Geburtstag*, Tübingen: Mohr Siebeck.

—— (2010), 'European Labour Law in Transition from 1985 to 2010' 26 *International Journal of Comparative Labour Law and Industrial Relations*, pp. 3–16.

Welz, C. (2008), *The European Social Dialogue under Articles 138 and 139 of the EC Treaty*, Deventer: Wolters Kluwer.

Wheeless, S.D. (2011), *Anti-trust Law Labor Exemptions: The LMRA's Distant Cousin*, Seattle: American Bar Association, Section of Labor and Employment Law, Seattle.

Williams, J. (2010), *Reshaping the Work Family Debate: Why Men and Class Matter*, Cambridge, MA: Harvard University Press.

Wirtz, M.S. (2006) *Collisie tussen CAO's en mededingingsrecht*, Deventer: Kluwer.

Woolfson, C., J. Fudge & C. Thörnqvist (2014), 'Migrant Precarity and Future Challenges to Labour Standards in Sweden', 35(4) *Economic and Industrial Democracy*, pp. 695–715.

Wright, F B (1992) 'The Development of Occupational Health and Safety Regulation in the European Communities' 8 *International Journal of Comparative Labour Law and Industrial Relations*, pp. 32–57.

Yogyakarta Principles (2006) on the Application of International Human Rights Law in relation to Sexual Orientation and Gender Identity.

Zahn, R. (2017), 'Revision of the Posted Workers Directive: a Europeanisation Perspective', *Cambridge Yearbook of European Legal Studies*, pp. 187–210.

INDEX

www.ingramcontent.com/pod-product-compliance
Ingram Content Group UK Ltd.
Pitfield, Milton Keynes, MK11 3LW, UK
UKHW051917100926
8556IPUK00021B/1234

9 781780 687049